Social
Purpose
for
Canada

Edited by

Michael Oliver

SOCIAL

FOR

Edited by

Michael Oliver

PURPOSE

CANADA

University of Toronto Press

University of Toronto Press

Diamond Anniversary 1961

Preface

This book, we hope, can speak for itself; it should require little introduction. But it cannot tell its own history, and parts of its story are worth relating.

The book began with an idea. An understanding of the sort of society which is evolving in Canada seemed to require something more than the descriptions which came from Royal Commissions and ordinary academic studies. Canadians were being lulled into accepting a glitter of prosperity which covered a reality of purposelessness, mediocrity and inequity and which, moreover, dulled their awareness both of the dangers of a post-Hiroshima world and of its potentialities. Since the 1930's, works of social criticism had been rare in Canada, and the time seemed ripe for a new venture. Preparation of this kind of volume was bound to be costly; but fortunately there existed a remarkable, indeed unique, source of funds. The marriage of the idea and the resources and imagination of the Boag Foundation and its trustees took place in the summer of 1957.

The Boag Foundation is a trust left by a British Columbian for "socialist education." Its funds have been devoted largely to university scholarships and to publishing ventures. The trustees were immediately interested in the plan for *Social Purpose for Canada*, and in January, 1958, a meeting was called in Ottawa to discover whether it could be undertaken. Those who attended, besides Mr. Harold Winch, M.P., who represented the Foundation, came from the faculties of Canadian universities, from trade union research offices, and from amongst individuals who shared a left-of-centre viewpoint. It rapidly became apparent that both the competence and the concern which were necessary to get the book written were available, and an editorial committee, made up of Professors F. R. Scott and George Grube, Dr. Eugene Forsey, M. Pierre-Elliott Trudeau, and Mr. David Lewis (Professor J. C. Weldon and Mr. T. Shoyama were added later) was appointed to assist Professor Stuart Jamieson of the University of British Columbia, the original editor, in its preparation.

Since that time there have been other meetings, during which the authors who were asked to contribute met each other, discussed the relation of one chapter to another and built up a common confidence in the worth of the project. There also emerged a continually wider range of shared opinions, and I doubt if anyone who has worked on the book has exactly the same ideas with which he began. But it was agreed from the outset that no attempt to achieve uniformity and complete consistency would be made. Each chapter or section, signed by its author, would be a single person's responsibility, and his responsibility would end there. The plan for the book, which had first taken shape at the Ottawa meeting, was changed gradually to fit the special interests and knowledge of the contributors.

Unforeseen developments inevitably overtook some of those who were closely involved with preparations. Professor Jamieson himself found that he could not continue his editorial duties and, to everyone's regret, he had to withdraw. Fortunately, he was able to write the section on labour he had planned. Dr. Eugene Forsey's appointment to the Board of Broadcast Governors, added to the pressure of his other duties, forced him to resign from the editorial board. Professor Irving Brecher, who had begun work on a chapter on Canada's external economic relations —on trade and aid—was named to an economic planning post in Pakistan, and as a result the book lacks a thorough treatment of this vital topic. Another disappointing and unexpected gap in the book resulted from the illness of M. Jean Le Moyne. He had already submitted a fascinating chapter outline on the future of Canada's, and especially French Canada's, culture, but he was unable to expand it as he had hoped. A great deal is owed to others too numerous to mention whose names do not appear in the list of authors, but who have contributed ideas, criticized manuscripts and added their encouragement and (equally valuable) their objections. They are, of course, in no way responsible for the book's shortcomings.

One comparison kept recurring to us as the book took shape. In 1935, the League for Social Reconstruction brought out *Social Planning for Canada*. Among its authors was Professor F. R. Scott who has been intimately connected with this book, both as a most active member of its editorial committee and as a contributor. The sense of continuity from the thirties to the present must have been strongest in him, but it was shared by all of us to some degree. We could not have escaped the influence of the democratic socialists who wrote *Social Planning for Canada* if we had wanted to, and in spite of striking differences sometimes between the remedies (and to a lesser extent the diagnoses) proposed in the two books, their common purpose is unmistakable.

Social Planning for Canada had an enormous influence on the thinking of the Co-operative Commonwealth Federation which had been founded shortly before the book appeared. J. S. Woodsworth wrote the Introduction and the LSR was widely recognized as a source of ideas for the CCF. The publishing of *Social Purpose for Canada* coincides with the founding of a new political party which will inherit the traditions of the CCF. But it would be incorrect to assume that there is a direct connection between the New Party and the book. Rather, both are products of a revival in social and political concern which will, I think, mark the 1960's as it did the 1930's. For a variety of reasons, the fifties were groping, hesitant years. As Canada, like the rest of the world, emerges from this atmosphere, it is not surprising that a sense of the urgency of social change should take both an intellectual and a political form. The ideas contained in this book will, we hope, influence not only the New Party but all political parties in Canada.

As editor, I would like to end this Preface with special thanks. First, to Mr. Harold Winch, M.P., Mr. W. W. Lefeaux, and their fellow trustees of the Boag Foundation, for their unfailing patience and understanding during the long months which preceded publication. This, of course, is in addition to the thanks which all those connected with the book owe to them for the generous sponsorship without which *Social Purpose for Canada* could not have been written. Second, to the University of Toronto Press. The manuscript had been completed before the Press read it and agreed to publish; it subsequently benefited enormously from the painstaking attention of Miss Francess Halpenny and her assistants.

MICHAEL OLIVER, *Editor*

Contents

POLITICS

Contributors

MICHAEL OLIVER is a political scientist at McGill University and a member of the editorial boards of *Cité Libre* and *Christian Outlook.*

GEORGE GRANT was formerly Head of the Department of Philosophy at Dalhousie University and has been serving as consultant to the Institute for Philosophical Research.

JOHN PORTER is a sociologist at Carleton University and co-editor of *Canadian Society: Sociological Perspectives.*

NEIL COMPTON is Chairman of the Department of English, Sir George Williams University, and formerly editor of *Anglican Outlook.*

ADAM GREENE is the pseudonym of a Canadian political scientist who has taught at both school and university. He is at present in Europe.

JOHN MORGAN is Professor of Social Work at the University of Toronto, Chairman of the Canadian Institute on Public Affairs and a member of the executive of the Canadian Welfare Council and the International Association of Schools of Social Work.

J. C. WELDON is an economist at McGill University and an editor of the *Canadian Journal of Economics and Political Science.*

GIDEON ROSENBLUTH is an economist at Queen's University and author of *Concentration in Canadian Manufacturing Industries.*

H. SCOTT GORDON, an economist at Carleton University, has recently published *The Economists versus the Bank of Canada.*

ALBERT BRETON is an economist at the Université de Montréal and director of the Groupe de Recherches Sociales.

MEYER BROWNSTONE, a Doctor in Economics and Public Administration from Harvard, is now Deputy Minister of Municipal Affairs in the province of Saskatchewan.

STUART JAMIESON is a specialist in labour relations and an economist at the University of British Columbia who has had wide experience in conciliation of labour disputes.

PIERRE-ELLIOTT TRUDEAU is a member of the Bar of the province of Quebec, co-founder and now joint publisher of *Cité Libre* and was formerly on the staff of the Privy Council Office, Ottawa.

F. R. SCOTT is Dean of Law at McGill University and a poet as well as a specialist in constitutional law. He was chairman of the National Council of the CCF from 1942–1950.

KEITH CALLARD is a political scientist at McGill University and author of *Pakistan: A Political Study*. He specializes in public administration as well as Islamic studies.

KENNETH MCNAUGHT is a historian at the University of Toronto and author of a biography of J. S. Woodsworth, *A Prophet in Politics*.

Moral
Issues

An Ethic of Community

GEORGE GRANT

In the last twenty years we Canadians have achieved the biggest economic expansion of our history. We have been able to impose our dominion over nature so that we can satisfy more human desires than ever before. We have moved from producing primarily raw materials to being an industrial society of mass production and mass consumption such as the United States. Every year a higher percentage of Canadians lives in the new environment of the mass society. This achievement has been due partially to special Canadian circumstances—the vigour and initiative of our people, the rewards from new resources on the northern frontier of this continent—but even more has it been due to the worldwide scientific and technological revolution of the twentieth century. The organizing genius of the American applied the scientific discoveries of the European with great vigour to the problems of production and so created the first mass consumption society in history. We now recognize that this form of society will spread to all parts of the world. Our growing knowledge of the economic achievements of other societies (particularly the Soviet Union) under other forms of organization and different historical circumstances, has made Canadians speak less piously in praise of our own achievements and made us recognize that North America was only first in a world-wide process.

It cannot be stressed too often what such control over nature can mean for mankind. In whatever other ways Marx's philosophy be inadequate, it stated unforgettably that the organization of pre-technological societies was founded above all on one necessity—the need to keep the mass of men at hard physical work for long hours so that life could be sustained. This necessitated the high degree of inequality and coercion that characterized all past societies. The application of intelligence to the mastery of nature means that the mass of men need not use most of their energies for physical work and that we can provide a comfortable standard of living without such labours. Obviously some physical work will continue to be necessary, but much more necessary will be organizational and technical skills. Nevertheless, this liberation of the mass of men from sustained labour and the economic and political consequences arising therefrom—indeed its effects in the most intimate corners of the individual soul—cannot be overemphasized in assessing our present situation.

Society is, of course, not only an expression of man's relation to nature, but also and more importantly of man's relation to man. We have attained dominance over nature by means of a particular structure of social organization in and by which some men are dominated by others. The best short description of this is "late state capitalism." It is "capitalist" because it places the leadership in economic affairs (and through it in all affairs) in the hands of privately owned and controlled corporations. The original principle of capitalism was that any society will best flourish when men are encouraged to make their own economic interest the ruling motive of their actions. That principle is still affirmed amongst us, even when our economic interest is now channelled and narrowly circumscribed by the ideas and practices imposed by massive corporations. The adjective "late" is used because the conditions under which men are able to exercise their economic self-interest have radically changed from the early days of market capitalism. Power is increasingly concentrated, so that most people have to pursue their individual gain within conditions set by the corporations, while the few who set the conditions operate the calculus of greed, ambition and self-interest to their own ends. Ours is also a "state" capitalism because our governments have taken an increasing role in the market, particularly because of the necessities of war (or as our euphemism puts it, defence).

Throughout the Western world the private corporations can properly be called private governments transcending the limits of national states. In a small country such as Canada they have even greater power than in the United States, because they are often continental institutions which are controlled beyond the range of our constituted government. The need of Canada for capital, the fact that the chief source of capital has been the United States, and the eagerness with which government leaders such as C. D. Howe accepted American capital on its own terms have meant that economically Canadians live more and more under the control of continental institutions whose books cannot even be scrutinized by our government.

It is often maintained that, because of the increasing role of the government, the pressure of the majority through the ballot, and the power of the unions, our society is not dominated by a capitalist élite. This is, however, a misrepresentation of the facts. The owners and managers of our powerful corporations still not only reap by far the largest benefits from our economy, but through their position in the structure decide in large measure what will be done and not done. It is indeed true that under state capitalism considerable power rests with government and is not held exclusively by the business élite as it was in the heyday of capitalism.[1] Nevertheless, it is foolish to believe that the power of government and business stand opposed to each other. Canadian governments, Liberal and Conservative alike, have in their major decisions identified their interests and the interests of Canada with those of the business élite. What else could be expected to happen? Inevitably, politicians are trained early to know in what alliances their possible power and political survival resides. Thus by the time they have served their apprenticeship they come to believe that acceptance of the interests of capitalism is the only patriotic course. For instance, anybody who has lived in a small Canadian town will know that ambitious young people are quite aware that they would not be likely to prosper in law or politics if they showed themselves opposed to the interests of the great corporations. The prosperous in small towns are more and more those who serve the continental institutions either directly or by doing them favours. They can less and less afford interests primarily identified with their own community and region. In the wider sphere of power in Ottawa the same process operates. A governor of the Bank of Canada moves to the board of a United States automobile firm; a minister of Public Works becomes the head of a large mining company.

The fact that the business community is the dominating and self-perpetuating élite must be insisted upon these days because of the recent prevalence of the idea that the power of organized labour constitutes the most present threat to our democracy. It is obviously true that labour in Canada is better organized to protect its interests than it was twenty years ago; it is also true that like all institutions the unions have not always exercised their power wisely (though this is less true in

[1]One should add the military to complete the modern triumvirate, but in Canada the power of the military is not on the same scale as in the United States.

Canada than in the United States). But when magazines such as *Life*
and *Time* are filled with stories about the abusive dictatorship of labour
leaders and yet write of the leaders of continental capitalism as "simple
guys" only interested in production and patriotism, one must begin to
question motives. Even if it may be disputable whether the control of
large-scale capitalism in our society is good or evil, it hardly seems
disputable that it is a fact.

In saying all this, however, it is necessary to disclaim any "cops and
robbers" or "conspiracy" view of history, which would imply that our
society is at the mercy of a few wealthy and powerful men with
Machiavellian intentions. To say our society is capitalist is simply to
point out a fact within which all Canadians live, including our ruling
élite. Though it is important to emphasize that a structure of power can
be changed by free acts, it is equally important to emphasize that this
particular structure has become a strait jacket, limiting the ways in
which all of us can act. With the large interlocking concentration of
power,[2] even the individuals at the top level of responsibility have little
freedom since the structure confines them in their decisions too. Capitalism then is not a conspiracy; it is a structure of institutions dedicated to
certain ends which it considers sacrosanct, and in the achievement of
which a society of certain virtues and vices arises.

What is even more fundamental about our society than its structure of
"state capitalist" power is that it is a "mass society." The term "mass
society" is inadequate shorthand for the radically new conditions under
which our highly organized technological society make us live. These
new conditions are experienced most profoundly in the growing urban
conglomerations such as Toronto and Los Angeles, but nearly all people
in North America now have a share of them. The farmer listens to
television and drives a car and may even organize his supply of rain;
he may not experience the mass society quite so directly as does a
resident of Toronto, but he still experiences it. What makes this aspect
of modern life more fundamental than the capitalist structure of power
is that this is the condition of life towards which all human beings are
moving, whether their institutions are capitalist or not. Certain problems
produced by these conditions are common to any mass society. Indeed,
even if our capitalist structure disappears in Canada we will still live in
a mass society. It seems imperative, therefore, to try to distinguish
between those problems which are directly a product of our capitalist
institutions and those which are indigenous to any mass society.

The term "mass society" is used to summarize a set of conditions
and experiences so new and so different from the past that nobody can
describe them adequately or fathom accurately what is coming to be in

[2] I refer the reader to fuller discussion of this question in the essays by
Professors Porter and Rosenbluth.

the world. Nevertheless, certain generalizations must be attempted. This is a society in which high individual acquisition and consumption of goods and services is increasingly open to most in return for comparatively short hours of work and in which an immense variety of commodities is ready to attract and to encourage a vast diversity of human desires. It is a society which requires a high technical competence from many to keep it operating efficiently and where therefore what is demanded of most poeple is to be skilled at one small part of the whole enterprise but not necessarily knowledgeable about the whole. It is a society in which most people live within and under the control of massive organizations (private and governmental), the purposes and direction of which are quite external to them. The population is more and more concentrated in the big cities, that is, in environments so complex that they must remain unfathomable to the individual and in which the individual's encounters with other persons cannot always or even frequently be with neighbours he knows, but are rather with strangers who are likely to appear as impersonal units to him. It is only necessary to compare shopping in a super-market and in a country store, or driving to work in a small town and on a metropolitan freeway to see the different human relations which arise in this new life.

The result of living in such a society is that individuals experience a new kind of freedom and independence, and also a new kind of control and dependence. The freedom is not only that in a high consumption economy a multitude of new choices and experiences is open to people, but also that in this environment the traditional standards of conduct become less operative. The high technical competence required and the kind of education necessary to produce it takes men to the point of technical reason where they see themselves as "wised up," and as not bound by the old ethical and religious standards. Authorities such as the family and the church become less powerful so that individuals are free to make their own standards. At the same time as the mass society produces this new sense of freedom, it also produces new impersonal authorities which bind the individual more than before, at the level both of action and of opinion. In large cities the maintenance of order in the vast tangle of conflicting egos requires a determined government and police force which must inevitably treat the individual arbitrarily and as a cipher. The individual is also coerced in what he desires and what he believes to be true by the instruments of mass communication which press on him from every side, presenting forcefully standards which suit the purposes of big organizations. Indeed this control of action and opinion has been intensified by the fact that the cold war has made North America something of a garrison state.

What is central to this new experience and what distinguishes it from living in the old small town and rural worlds is that the individual is at one and the same time more dependent on big institutions and yet less organically related to them. This has meant inevitably a dying away of the individual's effective participation in politics. The institutions which control us are so powerful and so impersonal that individuals come to believe that there is no point in trying to influence them; one must rather live with them as they are. The result is that more and more people think of the state as "they" rather than as "we." In great cities where so much of existence is public, individuals find their most real satisfaction in private life because here their freedom is operative, while in the public sphere they know their actions to have less and less significance. Thus the mass society calls into question the possibility of democratic government, founded as it was on the idea that each citizen could and should exert his influence on the course of public affairs.

In general it can be said that the mass society gives men a sense of their own personal freedom while destroying the old orders of life which mediated meaning to men in simpler environments. Indeed, as men sense their freedom to make themselves, unhampered by the old traditions, they may find it difficult to give content and meaning to that freedom, so that more easily than in the past their lives can reflect a surrender to passivity and the pursuit of pleasure as a commodity. When men have no easily apprehendable law of life given them by tradition, the danger is that their freedom will be governed by an arbitrary and external law of mediocrity and violence which will debase their humanity rather than fulfil it. This relation between increased freedom and the lack of well-defined meanings is the essential fact with which any politics of the mass age must come to grips. The capitalist structure of our institutions undoubtedly gives this problem its own peculiar tint, but basically the same probem will be present in all societies, whatever their economic structure once they have reached a mature stage of technological development.

What then should we think about this new society? What is good and bad about it now and what are the right ways to improve it? Those of a socialist persuasion would be wise to start from its indubitable achievements under state capitalism. North America has been the first society to organize mass production and distribution. Critics of capitalism are unwise if they deny its success in this field or if they claim that alternative economic arrangements could do a substantially better job at expanding such production. More people live with more consumer goods than at any time in history. The claim of the capitalist that this is the result of present institutions may not be as true as capitalists believe. Nevertheless, it must be acknowledged that the main reason why a vast majority of Canadians have continued to vote for two parties which accept capitalism is that by and large they do believe this claim.

To make this acknowledgment, however, is not to state that our capitalist society has been an unqualified economic success. For it is not true that the production of those goods and services which can be produced privately at a profit is the only goal of economic life. That there are other goals is evident as soon as one asks: "production of what? and at what sacrifices and rewards for whom? for doing what?" Indeed the central criticism of present-day capitalism must be that its very structure and mythology prevent the sufficient realization of economic goals (let alone supra-economic ones) other than the production of goods for the sake of private profit.

To take the first question, "production of what?" It is clear that in our society production is inevitably directed to those things which can be produced privately at a profit at the expense of those goods and services which cannot be.[3] Any sane person knows that efficient cars and detergents and household appliances are important to the good life, but he must know also that good hospitals and personnel to run them, good schools and teachers, good roads and adequate police forces, beautiful and efficient towns are equally necessary. These are as much part of a higher standard of living for individuals as are private goods and services. Yet under the present arrangements our productive capacity is of necessity primarily directed to what can be produced privately, even when there is a crying need for social goods. And this is caused by the very rationale of capitalism.

Indeed one of the strangest contradictions of today is the vast amount of energy used to persuade people to buy those goods which can be produced privately at a profit, while social needs have to fight for their right to expansion. We spend more money on advertising than we do on education. Much of our cleverest talent receives a high reward for devoting its energies to entrapping people into believing that they need a new kind of car or soap. It is a platitude these days to point out that the health of the North American economy depends on the ability of manipulators to persuade consumers to be dissatisfied with last year's luxuries, by appealing to all kinds of desires, particularly those associated with snobbery and sex. On the other hand governments at all levels are assailed for their prodigality if essential production of social goods is kept at even a minimum level.

Advertising originally justified itself on the grounds that it gave the consumer information on the basis of which he could make choices. Can it be said to do that now when it increasingly uses what are really

[3]To state this is to take over the main argument of Professor J. K. Galbraith's *The Affluent Society*. The closing words of that book should be engraved on the minds of North Americans. "To have failed to solve the problem of producing goods would have been to continue man in his oldest and most grievous misfortune. But to fail to see that we have solved it and to fail to proceed thence to the next task, would be fully as tragic."

vicious means to stimulate desires, not simply to present alternatives? In what sense can such artificial desires be called natural needs? Yet advertising is not now primarily dangerous because it appeals to fear and greed, snobbery and sexual inferiority in all who are exposed to it, but even more because it does so in the interests of the profit-making mechanisms of capitalism. It has become the most potent instrument whereby society is persuaded to direct production away from its most pressing social needs and to continue to concentrate on those goods which can be produced privately at a profit. Thus the starvation of those needs that can only be met collectively belongs to the economic and political logic of our present institutions.

The answer to the question, "at what sacrifices and rewards for whom and for doing what?", must also indict the state capitalism of the last twenty years. It has failed in distributing justly the wealth from the new technology. This injustice has often been hidden behind the "all-is-well" mythology of "people's capitalism" which puts out two fictions about our present situation. First, it is said that income has been radically redistributed in the last forty years to overcome inequalities; secondly, that poverty has largely been conquered amongst us. The first of these fictions has been able to maintain itself not only because of the capitalist associations with the public press but also because there has been a large growth in the national income. Nevertheless the proportion of that income going to various percentages of the total population has remained nearly the same. The wealthy top 10 per cent of the population continues to earn overy thirty times as much as the lowest 10 per cent.[4] The percentage going to the lowest three-tenths of those earning has declined over the last forty years. Although the real wages of organized labour have increased, the increase has never kept up proportionately with the growth of the national income. This puts into perspective attempts to persuade the public that unions are the chief cause of inflation. It takes but the smallest knowledge of every-day living in Canada to know that most families are under the shadow of mortgage and loan companies if they are to have even those things (enough room, a washing machine, adequate health services) which could be simply normal at our stage of technological development. At the same time other families live at the level of conspicuous consumption. It seems unlikely that for the vast majority of either of these kinds of family the situation can be explained (as it often is by capitalist propagandists) as the result of simple foresight, hard work and moral integrity on the part of the privileged.

Within this general picture of inequality, however, the greatest moral

[4]Unambiguous statistics for this comparison are not available in Canada. The figures are clearer for the United States. I have, therefore, used them assuming the situation is not likely to be radically different for us.

blots on our society are the particular geographic areas of poverty (both rural and urban) and particular groups (old people, unsupported women in charge of children, and others) where the level of inequality reaches degradation. Such groups account for at least one-fifth of our population. To be unconcerned about such degrading poverty (as our society has generally been) is particularly inexcusable where there is such affluence, and is particularly unpleasant alongside our rituals of self-righteousness. Yet any systematic attempt at the removal of deep poverty by social action is not a goal which logically can be pursued within the capitalist ethic.

In the expansion of the post-war era damage has especially been done to certain groups by economic changes (changes occurring sometimes to the general benefit of the community, but sometimes only to the private profit of the few) and these groups are often made up of members of the community least able to bear them. Through all parts of that expansion, working people have been instruments in the service of the market, to be used when needed, but left to fend for themselves when no longer required. There has been little recognition of what should surely be a part of a great egalitarian principle: that the community has an obligation to ease by compensation the insecurity of those sacrificed to economic progress. Unemployment insurance has done something in this direction but its inadequacy has been exposed in the recent recessions. The ethic of individual responsibility is often brought forward to maintain that the moral fibre of individuals will be weakened if they are cushioned against inevitable economic change. It is interesting, however, that the wealthy and their propagandists seem to apply this only to the employee families. The managers of economic power quietly cushion themselves and their families against insecurity in their own lives.

The questions of sacrifice consequent to economic progress are bound to grow in scope with the increase of automation. It is one of the saddest aspects of our present world that the development of automation, which makes possible that goal which men have longed for throughout the ages, should at the moment only produce anxiety in the minds both of capitalists and of the ordinary working population. This is surely because the results of automation are seen within the assumptions of our present economic system. The elimination of manual labour and constant human control which electronics increasingly allow will mean that sacrifices will fall on new groups. Are we to continue to allow the most painful sacrifices to fall on the individual worker and his family? Yet is not such an inequality part of the very structure of capitalism? Indeed the rise of automation illustrates more than anything else the crisis of our state capitalist institutions. To cope with this crisis will require more than compensationist policies; it will require policies which will allow a radical redistribution of income and a radical redistribution of rewards for the unpleasant toil of the world. Automation meets the centuries' long moral demand for equality by making it a practical necessity.

The failures of capitalism—underproduction of social goods and unfair distribution of the goods that are produced—can be seen together when one considers housing policy in Canada since the war. In 1945 the Liberal Government decided that housing development should be governed by the dictates of mortgage policy and that there should be little direct assistance by government for planned housing. This was done under the slogan of encouraging the individual Canadian to own his own home. The results have been unhappy. The poorest quarter of our population still lives in appalling housing in both town and country. The next two quarters are slaves to mortgage companies and in return live in ill-planned little boxes produced at great profit by speculative builders who are quite uninterested in planning attractive communities. A high percentage of our production has gone into the building of luxury apartments and houses for those who have profited from the boom and from whom the speculative builder in turn could derive his immense profits. The argument for housing regulated by mortgage policy was that it would safeguard freedom and individuality, but this has proved illusory. Our housing in big cities has the monotony of mass production; it lacks the efficiency and attractiveness of careful planning. In the ethos of capitalism, cities are considered encampments on the road to economic mastery, rather than worlds in which human beings attempt to lead the good life.

Despite the inadequacies of present economic arrangements a greater cause for criticism of our society can be found in areas which are not simply economic but extend over the whole range of human well-being. In these areas it is more difficult to judge what is good and bad in our society and thus more difficult for socialists to state clearly and realistically how their goals differ from those now served. This can be seen as soon as one compares the goals of socialism in a society of scarcity with its goals in a society of affluence. On what grounds does a socialist party ask people to vote for it under high consumption conditions? It is clear, for example, that if there were a major economic catastrophe in North America the power of a socialist party would be vastly increased. But no sane person desires such a catastrophe. Nor does it seem likely. What seems likely is that technology will continue to bring us growing prosperity and that our present institutions, though not dividing that prosperity fairly, will do a sufficiently adequate job of management to prevent any widespread or bitter discontent. In such a society there may not be the goads of hunger to provoke dissent. This being so, by what criteria of human well-being would the socialist criticize such a society?

It becomes more and more important for socialists to have a profound view of human good as society's most pressing problems become less simply quantitative and begin to involve qualitative distinctions. If a child is undernourished, if a family is living in one room, if a man has to do hard or boring physical work for twelve hours a day, it is easy to see what is needed for greater well-being: more food, more room, shorter hours. There is still a multitude of such direct quantitative problems in Canada and the old socialist ethic of egalitarian material prosperity is the principle under which they can be solved. Nevertheless, it is clear that as we move to greater technological mastery (a movement that can only be stopped by war) the most pressing social questions will call forth judgments as to which activities realize our full humanity and which inhibit it. What can be done to make our cities communities in which the human spirit can flourish? How far can we go in seeing that in all work, particularly in large factories, construction jobs and offices, the dull or even degrading element is cut to a minimum and the creative responsible part brought to a maximum? How far can we make the association of experts and power élite sufficiently open for large numbers of people to take part in those decisions which shape their lives? How can we stimulate education (in its broadest sense) so that the new leisure will be more than a new boredom of passive acquiescence in pleasures arranged by others? How can we see that in rightfully cultivating the fullest equality we do not produce a society of mediocrity and sameness rather than of quality and individuality? How can we produce an order and self-discipline in society which restrains the selfish and the greedy without becoming so authoritarian that individual initiative is crushed? How can we cultivate freedom for the individual without having it become identified (as it now is) with ruthless self-interest and the grasping of more than a fair share?

Any set of institutions is finally held together by a general conception of well-being which pervades them all. For example, in the last twenty years the chief Canadian ideal of manhood has become the ambitious young executive, aggressive in his own interests, yet loyal to his corporation, with a smart wife and two happy children. (He is sexually adjusted yet respectable, and never puts sex above the interests of the corporation.) He looks forward to a continually rising income and continually rising power and prestige. He will drive increasingly expensive cars and live in an increasingly expensive neighbourhood. He plays a part in respectable community activities (such as charities and art galleries), but sees that this does not interfere with the interests of his corporation or himself and keeps it clear that what really matters in life is business and ambition. He tries to make his opinions on all matters conform to what is considered "sound" in the higher échelons of his corporation and knows he can only take part in politics or other activities in so far as his superiors approve. That such a young man should be increasingly the ideal of our society is inevitable: this ideal best serves our corporations and they do everything in their power to encourage and even create it. The advertisements of conspicuous consumption are addressed to these young aspirants and their idealized image comes back to us from the advertisements.

Such concepts of well-being (let the cynical call them mythology) are the visions in response to which the individual models and fashions himself. In developing such an ideal capitalism has not been without sense. The people who take up this ideal are full of the energetic spirit which assists certain forms of economic growth. Yet at what price in human well-being has this image and reality been created? For it is an ideal which can be achieved by very few. As a wise man has written about Canada: "It needs only a simple exercise in arithmetic to show that at any given moment, all but a very small minority, even of employed adult men, have passed the age when they can expect any kind of promotion. Business ambition is available as motivation only for the few, even in Canada."[5]

The result of this is the frustration of many who attempt to pursue the ideal; but beyond this is the sad fact that its pervasiveness prevents any widespread expression of other ideals of human conduct which are more universally fulfilling. It thus persuades too much of our best talent to direct itself along one route. The immense rewards it offers (plus its public identification with true success) have led too large a percentage of our energetic young people into this one activity at the expense of other socially necessary and desirable activities, for example, school teaching, public service, pure science, social work, the ministry, and the arts. When we recognize how much better comparatively the Russians are doing in elementary education than ourselves, we must face the fact that the Russian communal idea encourages respect for school teaching in a way that our capitalist ethic cannot.

Since rewards in money and power are directed by state capitalism to those concerned with goods which can be produced privately at a profit, other activities tend to become pale shadows of business. The word "business" is now tacked on to all our professions and pursuits: "the medical business," "the legal business," "the entertainment business," "the education business," "the newspaper business." ("The religion business" is more advanced in the United States than it is as yet in Canada.) Health, entertainment, information, order, beauty and truth, are all commodities which individuals purvey at a profit and can only be socially justified if they can be "sold" at a profit. The economic self-seeking of the individual is the only instrument available for the produc-

[5]Sir Geoffrey Vickers, *University of Toronto Quarterly*, July, 1959, p. 315.

tion of excellence. Yet this must frustrate excellence arising in many fields where the profit motive is not sufficient for achievement. These fields, where capitalist incentives fail, are the very ones where we most need success in the age of affluence.

Questioning of this capitalist ideal may be raised at an even higher level of morality. The type of young executive described can easily pass over from healthy competitive energy to ruthlessness in his own interests within his corporation, and ruthlessness in the relations of his corporation to the rest of society. Indeed, the ideal tends to encourage ruthlessness as the very mark of the manly. But such ruthlessness is the mainspring of that division of person from person which is the cause of all social disruption. It is the very denial of our membership one with another: a more insidious type of sin than the personal weaknesses we often exclusively identify with that word. A society is not likely to be a place of healthy loyalties and ordered cohesion if its members are taught to pursue first and foremost their economic self-interest and if its leaders are chosen from those who pursue that self-interest more ruthlessly.

Indeed the most dangerous result of state capitalism is that our society recruits its chief leadership from the executives who have been most successful in living out the capitalist ideal. As later essays will show in more detail, the top executives of the corporations will not only control our economic life, but also decisively control other institutions of our society—our political parties, our universities, our churches, our charities. For example, the leaders of the great corporations are an overwhelming majority of the members of the governing boards of our universities. The higher education which they control must therefore be in the last analysis the kind which their vision of life dictates. Is it likely that men trained to manage corporations whose chief end is maximum profit will be people of wide social vision? Can it be hoped that they will fully understand the subtle problems that the mass society of high consumption now faces? Yet at every point where these new problems are arising the structure of our capitalism gives men with this limited view the deciding power in dealing with them. It produces a leadership impotent to take the obvious next step forward in our society. And this question of leaderships applies not only to domestic issues, but to the relation of our society to the rest of the world. In 1945 the business élite in North America had in their hands the unquestioned leadership of the world. Because of their restricted vision that leadership is now passing more and more away from North America and more and more into the hands of a tough communist élite. With all its initial advantages the capitalist leadership could not compete against the also limited communist ideal, because it could only put up against it the motives of corporate and personal greed and the impulses for personal publicity and prestige hunting. It is, of course, not only the business community in North America which will pay for this failure of leadership, but all free men who care about the traditions of the West.

Our state capitalism is indeed more than a practical system for producing and distributing goods; it is also a system of ideas and ideals which determines the character of leadership and inculcates a dominating ethic in our democracy. When socialists criticize it, therefore, they must recognize that they are not only concerned with alternative governmental techniques in economic affairs but with profound questions of what constitutes right and wrong for persons and for society. They are maintaining that not only capitalist arrangements but the very capitalist ethic is quite unable to come to grips with the problems of the mass technological world. Therefore, when socialists pass beyond criticism to their proposals for the future, these proposals must be put forward not only as a set of specific economic and political techniques but as a higher conception of well-being—that is as a morality. They must also be able to show that the social morality they propound comes to grips more cogently with our problems than does the present capitalist ethic. Socialist doctrine must be a morality and it must be a higher and more realistic morality than that which it is to replace.

Too often in the past socialists have been content to put up against the clearly defined capitalist account of human good a vague and innocent account of their own ethic. They often spoke as if the interests of mankind were simply identified with more commodities, and socialism was defined as the best technique for producing and distributing those commodities fairly. They often spoke as if the mass consumption society would bring with it automatically a unification of the people in equality in which the old evils of repressive power and stratified class would disappear. A mild-mannered utopia of reasonable men would take its place. In a society of more commodities, human ignorance and sin would no longer have to be contended with. Democratic socialists (rightly scorning revolution) believed that this would be accomplished eventually through the ballot box as in a prosperous world men would easily recognize the best interests of society. Belief in a simple doctrine of progress made socialists think that all this would inevitably come to be. There was an "obliging tendency" in history. Such naive doctrine stood in the way of socialists thinking profoundly about political or personal morality. It prompted woolliness about how human beings come to know their own true interests. By encouraging optimism about the potential sense and goodness of us all, it made questions of morality look easy since their solution depended on economic circumstances alone. By making progress an inevitable process rather than dependent on the free acts of free men, it dulled thought about the principles on which such free acts should be based.

In the light of what is coming to be in mass society such optimistic and unspecific theories do not suffice. Given the power of entrenched self-interest in individuals and institutions and the tendency to passive mediocrity among great numbers of persons, nobody can really believe that a just and creative society is emerging inevitably as our technological affluence increases. Neither can anyone believe that a new dawn will break after a great economic catastrophe, let alone after the absurdity of a violent revolution. Such ideas are the dreams of an innocent past. If we are to reach a better way of dealing with the problems of a mass society, this will only come about by the free choices of a multitude of Canadians who are highly conscious of true human good and determined on its wide social realization. In such a situation revitalized socialist theory is a necessary basis for effective socialist action. Only in terms of a consistent political and social morality will socialists be able to persuade Canadians that there is a better alternative to our present capitalist system and ethic. Such a morality can only be based on a profound vision of human well-being.

Such a moral view of socialism is contrary to a belief held by certain politicians and political theorists in Canada: that the art of politics is just the balancing and refereeing of the interests of various pressure groups. This is the Mackenzie King theory of politics and it has been taken over by his disciples who may be found in both the Liberal and Conservative parties. In such a view of politics there is no need to appeal to ultimate criteria of human good. A socialist edition of this doctrine is that the job of a socialist party consists in marshalling together the short-term self-interests of those opposed to capitalism and through the power of that marshalling to realize those self-interests. Such a doctrine is supposed to be "realistic" socialism. It is, however, not an alternative open to true socialists although it may be open to the slick and successful who were once Liberals and are now more likely to be Conservatives. The political technicians of the old parties are in a position to say that they are simply "honest brokers" and therefore need not think about issues of ultimate human good; actually their aim, of course, is to stay in power and work things out within the limits of the present capitalist structure. Indeed, they seriously delude themselves in thinking they are balancing in the name of democracy. What they are really doing is becoming servants of an ever more powerful corporate capitalism and what they call balancing is doling out minor concessions so that interests other than the capitalist will not make too great a fuss.

Socialists have not the alternative of this amoral theory of politics because what they are interested in is not simply power within the present system, but the art of using power to make men free. They cannot play the role of flatterers to a disappearing democracy, because they are the friends of a true and continuing democracy. A policy of drift in matters of theory about ultimate human good (which is the upshot of moral cynicism) has nothing to offer socialists because it simply serves to perpetuate the status quo.

There is a further and stronger reason why socialism must be a well-defined moral doctrine and not only an appeal to the limited self-interest of certain groups. In all mass consumption societies the number of persons who have been traditionally classified as "labour" is shrinking as a percentage of the total population. The maximum percentage that "labour" can reach in advanced societies does not comprise a majority of voters. The industrial machine has an increasing need of engineers who organize, maintain and repair that machine and of accountants who calculate and check its operations. Society has an increasing need of administrators, nurses, social workers, doctors, teachers, whose highly specialized functions keep the complex organization running efficiently. The percentage of skilled people must inevitably grow and the future quality of our society will more and more depend on the moral vision of these manifold specialists. No socialist party has any hope of success without large support among these groups and that support can only be gained by the reasonable persuasion of reasonable men.

The capitalist ethic can after all appeal to the short-term self-interest of such specialists by trying to persuade them that they can only defend the just interests of their skills under the present system and that a socialist party will put them at the beck and call of the less skilled majority. Most specialists now support the capitalist ethic for this reason — they see no chance of protecting their self-interest except by the competitive methods now employed. Yet while most specialists see no alternative to this present method, many of the best of them do not like it, for as sensible people they recognize that this warring of group against group must increasingly undermine any proper sense of community loyalty and cohesion. In such a situation socialists must offer specific reassurance that theirs is a doctrine of social order in which the principle of justice for all safeguards the just interests of a skill or profession. Only in terms of such a morality can the specialist be brought to see any alternative to the present ruthless methods of maintaining his proper self-interest.

Indeed it is possible to go further about this important group of highly skilled people. It is a tendency of modern industry no longer to need independent minds as it did in its early stages, but technical specialists of narrow training. The hope that such persons will have a high vision of human dignity will come not from their economic function but from their general education outside their technical training, that is, in their schools, their churches, their universities. The obvious point must therefore be made that since socialists depend very much on the support of such groups, they depend at the same time on the quality of these institutions. Conversely, socialist leaders can only appeal to these groups if they have an explicit doctrine of human good and an understanding of how this good is best to be realized in practice.

The cement which binds together the ethical system of socialism is the belief in equality. It is the principle which tells us whom we are talking about when we speak of human well-being. We are not speaking of some rather than others, or of some more than others — but of each person. This assumption of equality may seem so commonplace in Canada that it hardly needs discussing as a principle. Is not equality an assumed article of faith for all true Canadians? Every political orator must speak of it; even our capitalism must justify itself by calling itself "people's capitalism." At a deeper level, is not the central achievement of modern political theory the enunciation of the principle of equality, as against the principle of hierarchy which was central to the classical world? The chief driving force behind the social reforms of the last two hundred years has been this principle. Is not then a discussion of equality simply the rehashing of a platitude which every decent man accepts and to which the indecent have to pay lip service?

Yet is this so? As we move into the mass world, how much is the belief in equality sustained in our thought or practice? It is indubitable that theoretical criticisms of equality are increasingly prevalent. Is not equality the enemy of liberty? Will not the striving for equality produce a dead-level society? Is not the search for equality something we should eschew economically, as making us unproductive by holding back the energetic, the responsible, and the intelligent? Has it not produced mediocrity in our education? Wealthy men with no knowledge of moral or political philosophy will bring out as a triumphant discovery (what one might have considered an obvious fact) that men are not equal in talent, and rush on to deduce from this that equality is a ridiculous doctrine. Nor is such ridicule met with only in expected quarters. In his attempt to drive the Russians to work, Stalin maintained that equality was a petty bourgeois ideal.

More influential than these theoretical criticisms is the fact that equality is becoming more at variance with social reality. The tendency to stratification and non-participation which threatens equality is more than a product of capitalism, but is related to industrialism itself, as can be seen from the fact that a new class system is appearing in the Soviet Union as much as in North America. The very structure of mass society produces impersonal hierarchies of power in which equality can have no substance, particularly equality of participation in economic and political life. This tendency in any industrial society produces added difficulties with our capitalism in which vast accumulations of economic power in private hands and inequalities of possession are the very substance of the system. In such a situation double-think about equality becomes manifest. The popular leaders of governments orate about the glories of equality on the hustings while enacting economic policies which establish intractable inequalities as the very essence of our social life. In such circumstances, talk about equality becomes more and more ritual emptied of belief — part of the equipment of the "engineer of consent."

It must also be recognized, of course, that the principle of equality has been interpreted in a particular way within North American history. In our past, it meant a combination of political equality (with all its rich content of the ballot, equality before the law, and so on) with equality of opportunity for economic advancement. It was believed that political equality would safeguard equality of opportunity in economic and social life from attacks by sinister interests. This combination of political equality and open careers for the talented would prevent the unfair "conventional" inequalities, while leaving the "natural" inequalities to work themselves out. In the early days when our country was a frontier individualistic capitalism, this edition of the equality principle worked pretty well. The question is now, however, whether such a theory of equality is adequate for the conditions of the stratified mass society. Can formal political equality still safeguard equality of opportunity from the attacks of vested interests? Does not equality of opportunity become more and more to mean the necessity of the ambitious to serve the corporations? In a world where the very complexity of our society makes us increasingly dependent on one another, do we not have to move forward to a richer conception of economic equality than equality of opportunity? Is this not particularly pressing for our democracy, in which the problem of leisure is as urgent as the problem of work?

In such circumstances it is no longer possible to take equality as a platitudinous article of faith which all may be assumed to assume. To those who would attack the principle, openly or covertly, we must try to express why exactly we believe in it. We must elucidate how it is related to other necessary principles such as the recognition of the diversity of talent. No satisfactory or systematic answer to these problems is, of course, possible in a short essay. What follows is only intended as an introduction to the question.[6]

Equality should be the central principle of society since all persons, whatever their condition, must freely choose to live by what is right or wrong. This act of choosing is the ultimate human act and is open to all. In this sense all persons are equal, and differences of talent are of

[6]Our present social and political theory is in grave need of a systematic discussion of equality. It is lacking, however, because the political philosophers and scientists sadly mirror the impersonality of our age by concentrating their energies on technical matters and on serving the society as it is.

petty significance. Any man who is fair in his dealings, any woman who treats the interests of others as of the same importance as her own, may in so doing have achieved the essential human act of loving the good as much or more than the cleverest or most powerful person who ever lived. Because of this fact, no human being should be treated simply as a means, like a tree or a car, but as an end. Our moral choices matter absolutely in the scheme of things. Any social order must then try to constitute itself within the recognition of this basic fact of moral personality which all equally possess.

It is clear that the foregoing is an essentially religious foundation for equality. Such a foundation will seem to the unbeliever too limited a basis for social principle. It must be insisted, however, that the idea of equality arose in the West within a particular set of religious and philosophical ideas. I cannot see why men should go on believing in the principle without some sharing in those ideas. The religious tradition was the biblical, in which each individual was counted as of absolute significance before God. This belief united with the principle of rationality as found in the Stoic philosophers. Among the greatest Western thinkers the conception of rationality has been increasingly unified with the religious principle of respect. To state this historical fact is not to deny that many men have believed in equality outside this religious and philosophical tradition. The question is rather whether they have been thinking clearly when they have so believed. This religious basis for equality seems to me the only adequate one, because I cannot see why one should embark on the immensely difficult social practice of treating each person as important unless there is something intrinsically valuable about personality. And what is intrinsically valuable about all persons except their freedom as moral agents? At the level of efficiency it is surely more convenient to treat some persons as having no importance, and thus to build a society of inequality in which some people matter and some do not. If individuals are only accidental conglomerations of atoms, why should we respect their rights when it does not suit our interests or inclinations to do so?

It is clear that Marxism, as the dominant Western philosophy in the East, appeals to the sense of equality. The question is not whether this is good, but whether within Marxist materialism there is any consistent place for this belief; whether, indeed, one of the reasons why the Marxists in power have been so willing to sacrifice persons ruthlessly has not been that moral personality has no place in their theory. So also in the West ideas such as "the survival of the fittest," when taken over from biology and used about society, led to an undermining of respect for the individual. How often has one heard business people justify the results of the market by such an appeal to Darwin? What must be insisted upon is that in mass society the practice which sustains the rights of persons *qua* persons is very difficult to preserve. It will surely only be sustained by those who have thought clearly what it is about human beings which makes them worthy of being treated with respect.

To state this is, of course, in no way to imply that socialists who disagree as to the ultimate justification of equality cannot work together. Religious believers from various traditions will hold that in the hard pinches only such belief will make equality a possibility. The non-religious who are egalitarians may feel this is only superstition and have some other basis for their belief. But this need not prevent them working together. For, as the history of Canada manifests, common political ends can be sought without theoretical agreement.

It may still be argued (and has been) that although we should treat ourselves and others as of absolute worth, this does not imply equality in the day-to-day doings of life. A man is as free to save his soul in a slum as in a mansion, we are sometimes told, and therefore there can be no argument from this religious account to any particular worldly conditions. The truth of the first part of this statement may be admitted; the second part, however, must be categorically denied. The justification of equality must then make this denial. It is based on two facts about human personality which seem to the present writer indubitable. First, it is likely to be spiritually bad for any person to be in a position of permanent and inevitable inferiority in his relations with any one else. Secondly, it is likely to be spiritually bad for a person to be in a position of unchecked superiority in his relations with another. That is, relations of superiority-subordination tend to thwart the true good of the people on either side (whatever petty pleasures of sadism or masochism may result and whatever mechanical efficiency may be obtained). Because this thwarting tends to occur, social policy should be directed always to the elimination of such relations. And this policy should be applied in the factory, the office, the family, the general social and political order. For example, families require discipline, but if that discipline is not to degrade children and parents alike, it must be directed to its proper end of leading the children to a freedom equal to that of their parents. So in a factory or office there must be a proper ordering of work by somebody in authority, but that authority must not deny the equality of those ordered, or their creativity and responsibility for the work done. The end which any society should be working for, however slow and difficult its accomplishment, is the elimination of these relations of superiority and subordination in all aspects of life.

Nearly all in Canada will grant some degree of equality before the law or at the ballot box, but when it comes to equality of participation in wealth, responsibility and culture there is a violent anti-egalitarian reaction. Therefore, it must be insisted that a society which takes seriously its first principle that all its members are to be regarded as equal must give economic content to that regard. Men are living beings and if society does not allow them to sustain life it cannot be said to regard them. To have enough and to get it from reasonable hours of work is the condition not only of a comfortable and sensuously gratifying life (of which freedom from fatigue is not the least part) but of a life which can partake properly in love and play, art and thought, politics and religion. At the beginning of political theory Aristotle laid down that a free man must be a man with leisure — that is, a man who can get enough goods without working too hard. It is obvious that mothers with automatic washing machines are likely to have more energy to give to the cultivation of their children than those who must do the washing on boards, that a machinist who earns the same amount for forty as against sixty hours has more energy to go fishing, take responsibility in the union, or paint a picture.

It is now necessary to see how these arguments are related to the main argument against equality. This is based on an appeal to the fact of natural diversity of talent. It is said that men are unequal in talent and that therefore to base society on equality is to base it on an illusion which can only lead to social disaster in the form of stagnation and mediocrity. When society follows the facts of diversity of talent it naturally falls into a hierarchical structure. We so need the gifts of the talented that we must reward them greatly. It is obvious that this argument has cogency. Men do differ widely in talents. It is also obviously true that a wise social order will encourage certain talents for the sake of its continuing health and that any system of rewards must include the economic. Also, economic reward is not solely for the purpose of giving people things. Responsible officials, brain surgeons, and artists need a high standard of life to give them that peace necessary to their efficient performance.

Nevertheless this is not all the story: the principle of hierarchy which arises from diversity of talents must be balanced against the principle of equality which arises from the absolute worth of all men. That proper balancing must be based on the moral distinction between the valuing of qualities and the regarding of persons. This distinction is the following: to be with any set of people is to be aware of valuing disparate qualities of intellect and physique, responsibility and imagination. But this does not mean that we should regard the interests of one of those persons less highly than any of the others. That is, qualities are valued, persons are regarded. To make this distinction is to put two activities on different levels of moral importance. The regard which is due to persons is not dependent on the sum total of their qualities. We cannot score John 90 per cent in qualities and Richard 40 per cent and therefore say the regard due to Richard is limited by his low score. To do so is to deny the absolute regard which is due him. It is, of course, quite possible to give up the Judao-Christian truth. But if one holds it, then a hierarchy of talent and an equality of persons cannot be on the same level as principles for the ordering of society. How else have we learnt to scorn slavery? We scorn it because we do not find admirable a society whose leaders, thinkers, and artists bring forth their highest qualities in the freedom of being waited on by a slave class. We scorn it because the encouragement of these qualities cannot be measured in the same scale as the debasement of these other persons by slavery. The extreme case of slavery makes clear what is true in any circumstances. The value to be recognized in the highest artistic or scientific genius — in such men as Mozart or Einstein — gives me no reason to regard them more highly as persons than anybody else, or to fail to recognize that my duty to regard persons is a duty of a higher level than my valuing of the true, the noble or the beautiful. For this reason, the hierarchy of talents must always be subordinate as a social principle to the basic equality of persons.

To say this is not to deny that there is a grave difficulty in balancing properly the claims of equality and diversity of talent in any society. Differences in human talent are inevitably so great that the differences in ways of life and degrees of power must also be great. A corrupt belief in equality which stood in the way of people knowing what it is to do something well would obviously be pernicious. Society must offer incentives to encourage people to do things well and to do the difficult jobs well. It is clear that some persons give to society more than they take; while others use society simply for what they can get out of it. Social policy must obviously encourage the givers.

Once having granted the real substance in the argument about incentives, it must be repeated that most of the talk along that line now heard in Canada is mainly a justification of the belief that the most important thing in life is to make a lot of money. This becomes clear when one asks the question: what incentives and what social structure to produce these incentives? There are all kinds of varying systems to produce incentives towards differing social aims. And it must be insisted here that most people in our society who argue against equality in the name of incentives are arguing in the name of one particular structure of incentives — the structure which encourages men to assist profitable private production and distribution of goods. Moreover, the powerful instruments of opinion have tried to identify in the minds of the general public the capitalist model of incentive with all possible systems of incentive. They have tried (with some success) to convince people that only a capitalist society will maintain a proper care for incentive and that therefore an alternative form of organization will destroy initiative and energy. This is nonsense. What our present capitalism encourages is certain forms of activities at the expense of others.

It is often argued that by maintaining a wealthy and privileged class certain "finer things" are kept alive. It is not necessary to discuss this argument in general, because it is so patently absurd to apply it to the privileged groups which exist in Canada. What are these "finer things" that owe their survival to the rich, and which would not continue in a more egalitarian society? What valuable qualities of life do the very rich keep going in Canada with their pursuit of luxury (conspicuous or inconspicuous as their taste may be), their externalized culture and prestige seeking? Horse racing and collecting pictures are their greatest positive achievements. Among the moderately rich what noble culture is the product of Forest Hill and Westmount which might be threatened by greater equality? People who give their lives to the petty round of snobbery at home and relax playing cards in Florida in identical luxury hotels and mink stoles are hardly likely to be the vanguard of a Canadian renaissance.

Our capitalist system of incentives, then, can no longer be said to lead to that encouragement of diversity of talents which was its original justification. Equality of opportunity to serve General Motors or the Argus Corporation is not what earlier democrats meant by their doctrine. The incentives of capitalism no longer do what they are said they do. They no longer encourage that wide range of skilful activities which becomes increasingly our need in a mass society. In such a situation it is as much the function of a socialist morality to work out new and realistic schemes of incentive as it is to think out new means of sustaining and enlarging the equality of all persons against the threats of the mass age.

Two last points must be emphasized about the principle of equality in the technological society. First, it must be repeated that never before in history has it been open for the majority to have large amounts of goods with high degrees of leisure. This will be a growing possibility as techniques of automation increase, as the robots do more and more of the work in the factories and offices. Such equality to participate in leisure becomes moreover a pressing necessity of our economic health. Since 1939 a large percentage of the income of this continent has been devoted to defence. No sane man can want that to continue indefinitely. If the tension between the West and the communist world is reduced, however gradually, somehow the immense resources that have been put into the military effort will have to be used for peaceful purposes. This will only be possible if the old shibboleths of inequality are overcome. If our mastery of nature is to be used for peaceful purposes, a conscious policy of equality becomes a necessity. Such a policy within North America must, of course, be related to conditions in the rest of the world and our responsibility for and dependence on such conditions. How fast we should push for a realized society of leisure at home, and how far that should be restrained to help the Asians and Africans develop industrially, is a difficult question of balance and cannot be discussed in detail here. However it only suggests caution, it does not change the basic fact that the scientific economy of North America can only be healthy if it is set towards a basic policy of economic equality.

Secondly and more important, the very form of human existence created by the mass society makes imperative a struggle for equality of participation in mind; imperative, that is, if we are to escape the civilization of the ant-heap. If it be probable that in the future human beings grow up in conditions where physical survival does not take most of their time, what then will give life its meaning and purpose? What is worth doing when the robots are doing the work in the factories? In a society of widespread leisure, aimlessness and boredom will be much more likely than in the past when leisure was the privilege of the few.

To meet such a situation, our democracy must consciously stimulate the equality of participation in mind, in ways that it has never dreamed of in the past. When leisure is open to all, then education must be opened to all. To overcome the impersonality of the mass society, new relationships in work and leisure must be developed and lived out; indeed new relationships at every level of existence — in art, in sex, and in religion. It would be folly, of course, to think that these new experiences will come easily or inevitably. Human sin is a historical constant, however much the forms of it may vary from era to era. Under any conditions it is hard for us to make a success of living. Nevertheless one thing is certain. North America is the first continent called to bring human excellence to birth throughout the whole range of the technological society. At the moment, the survival of its capitalist ethic, more than anything else, stands in the way of realizing that opportunity. The only basis on which it could be realized is a clearly defined ethic of community which understands the dignity of every person and is determined on ways of fulfilling that dignity in our new conditions.

Power and Freedom in Canadian Democracy

JOHN PORTER

Power is the right that some people have to direct the affairs of others. It is a product of human society, and therefore appears wherever human beings associate. Most discussions of power are concerned with the power of the state because, at the national level, holders of power have effective means of enforcing their wills. It is wrong, however, to exclude from consideration the power which exists in all our institutions and associations, in small social groups as well as in large ones. Also, if we wish to understand the nature of power, we must look both geographically and historically beyond our own society. Even at the lowest levels of social development, where society is little more than a collection of related families, the power of some over others can be found. This ubiquity of power has its roots in human psychology, and power grows within social relationships. Even the commonly experienced social relationship of love has this quality of power. Tyrannical demands can be made in the name of love, and love can also lead to abject submissiveness.

Freedom is the very antithesis of power because in simplest terms it means the ability to direct one's own affairs. Throughout human society there is a struggle between freedom and power. Like power, this desire for freedom can also be traced to human psychology. It stems from needs which must be met if the human organism is to survive. The satisfaction of organic needs provides an elementary freedom; but it is of paramount concern only in societies near the border-lines of subsistence. At higher levels of social development a new order of needs appears which might be called cultural needs. An example is the need to acquire complex skills in order to realize one's potentialities. If these cultural needs are not fulfilled the individual's life is so restricted that he feels he is not free. As social development proceeds these cultural needs become much more varied and therefore the struggle for freedom is never won.

Thus, freedom is relative, depending on the level of social and cultural development. No discussion of freedom can be confined to its primitive aspects of satisfying material needs and removing despotic political restrictions. Rather, we must keep in mind that at higher levels of social development freedom must be assessed in terms of the quality of social life, and particularly in terms of the manner in which these derived cultural needs are satisfied.

Human beings are such complex organisms that it is not surprising that they have such contradictory psychological elements. Throughout history an explanation of these contradictions has been sought in the analysis of human nature. In the modern period explanations have been sought in the nature of human society. Even psychology, which has taken over from theology the task of understanding the individual soul, recognizes that social institutions mould human behaviour. An enormous range of consequences follows from the fact that human beings are social animals, and that their very existence and survival depend on relations with other human beings. Here we are concerned with only a narrow range of the consequences of man's need for society — the co-existence of power and freedom.

However simple the social structure, ordered relationships are essential. Among these ordered relations are those which grant the right to a few to make decisions on behalf of the group. At the primitive level the kinds of decisions which have to be made may seem to us elementary, but for the primitive group they may be crucial. Someone has to decide when the hunt should begin and the direction it should take, when planting should begin, whether or not the distribution of the catch or the harvest conforms to the customs of the community, whether or not a neighbouring tribe is to be attacked, and so forth. These decision-making rights, essential at any level of social development, inhere in the leaderships roles of particular social institutions — head of the kin group, tribal elder, magician, shaman, managing director, prime minister, arch-bishop, and so on.

It follows also from the nature of social organization that there can be no power or authority without obedience. There would be no point in assigning decision-making rights to individuals who hold particular institutional positions unless there was a high probability that their orders would be carried out. Men control or suppress their desire for freedom or, more likely, they are trained at an early age to accept par-ticular systems of authority as good. In return they get some security and a stable set of expectations about the behaviour of their fellows. Power and authority often bring personal gain as individuals appropriate rights beyond those granted for their institutional roles. A privileged ruling class based on a hereditary principle emerges when a number of power-holders transmit these appropriated rights to their children.

An individual's personal freedom can depend on the power that he has over other men. In the pre-industrial stage of social development the power that some men had to extract tribute from other men ensured their elementary freedom, and at the same time left them free to pursue other interests. Conversely the man who laboured so that he could deliver his tribute had a very restricted area of freedom. It is not pos-sible here to trace the long historical struggle between these contradic-tory qualities in social life nor the developments, particularly the personal appropriation of rights, that have strengthened personal and class power, hereditary ruling classes, and the development of ideologies such as the divine right of kings.

It is important, however, to remember that social organization cannot exist without power. Power cannot be shuffled out of the world by utopian philosophies; nor can the dangers associated with giving power rights to individuals — capitalists or planners — be completely removed. With a great deal of imaginative experimentation we could no doubt create an institutional order in which the risks were minimized. Such a goal requires a psychological transformation in our industrial masses, whose apathy perhaps constitutes the greatest impediment to the growth of a free society in which human creative potential can be released. There is, as Erich Fromm and others have pointed out, a widespread fear of freedom, because of the sense of isolation and impotence which individuals feel in the modern mass society. There is, moreover, a readi-ness to accept the standards of consumption provided through the super-market, the credit card, and the finance company, as the indices of free-dom. If a society is to be built in which human beings are free to develop and to experience the satisfaction of the higher order of needs which we have called cultural, it can only be done by the use of power. I shall return later to the problem of power in relation to democratic planning.

First we must look at some of the reasons why capitalism with its dominant theme of private appropriation is so widely accepted as the basis of the industrial order.

THE PLUTOCRATIC ETHOS

In Western industrial economies, the principle of power over other men through property rights became perpetuated, even though the legal binding of serf to master which had existed in the previous stage of development had been abandoned in favour of a common status of free citizens who could make their own contracts. Individual property rights meant that those who owned the instruments of production controlled their use and access to them. In many respects the new urban proletariat of the industrial revolution was less free than the feudal serf who had at least some legally defined claims against his master.

The statistics of misery, squalor and filth that describe the human cost of the nineteenth century's transition to industrialization are a part of every history student's notes. They were the evidence for the socialist condemnation of private ownership of productive instruments. Private ownership of property gave power to the privileged few over the many. There were various views about the condition of the new industrial masses, but the one which played such an important part in socialist thought was the Marxian doctrine of increasing misery, which held that at some point the intolerable conditions would explode into a class war in which private property, the source of all evil, would be abolished. While not all socialists agreed with the Marxian method of getting rid of private ownership, most of them agreed that private ownership of productive resources was an instrument of class oppression. Political institutions were thought, not without justification, to be mere agents of privately owned economic institutions. It followed that if the instruments of government were used to protect capitalist society, they could also become the means of destroying capitalism and thus enter into the service of the socialist principle of economic equality. Thus, to capture the state, either by bomb or ballot, became the goal of proletarian movements.

History never did follow the course predicted for it by nineteenth-century socialists. In the long run, rather than increasing misery, there has been a constant improvement in material standards, as measured by personal consumption, in societies where capitalism reached its highest development. Proletarian revolutions have taken place where capitalism has been retarded, or where there has been colonial rule. Moreover, in some capitalist countries with universal manhood suffrage, working class socialist parties have never come to power and in others they have been in power for only very short periods. It was not until 1945 in England that a working class party won a decisive victory at the polls. In Canada, although the socialist movement has had considerable strength in urban areas, it is in an agrarian province that it has acquired power. It is little wonder that socialist theorists, in the face of this widespread acceptance of the capitalist order, have begun to re-examine some of their fundamental ideas about social organization.

It is worth considering briefly some of the changes that have come about and confounded socialist doctrine. In the first place, within the economic system powerful trade unions have developed which, to some extent, have been able to counter the power of private ownership of productive instruments with the power of collective refusal to work them. Furthermore, the occupational structure of modern industry does not break the work world into two classes, one working in dirt and drudgery, and the other with more refined tasks and the power of command. Instead we find occupational gradations, involving increasing degrees of skill and supervising rights. The increasing complexity of industrial techniques has had its counterpart in the wide range of values we assign to the various occupations. Prestige attaches to the different kinds of skills that the industrial system requires. The recruiting ground for these skill groups has been the formerly unskilled labouring classes. While the Horatio Alger myth can be refuted by the facts of occupational inheritance at the very top levels of the industrial world, what cannot be refuted is the widespread movement upwards that is possible within the boundaries of the lower and middle levels. Along with an improved material standard of living has gone an increasing opportunity to improve one's status or to have one's children achieve higher status, however slight, than oneself.

Industrial societies have been upwardly mobile societies, at least sufficiently so to reduce resentment and frustration throughout the working classes. Along with this actual mobility has gone a very intense belief, particularly in North America, in unlimited opportunity to get ahead. While there is a great discrepancy between the image of a mobile society and the reality of the social impediments to getting ahead, the image is widely enough held to counteract most charges about the inequality of opportunity. Recent studies[1] would suggest that there is more mobility in some European societies than there is in North America, even though the latter continent is thought to provide greater opportunity. The image of opportunity in North America is to some extent a retention from an earlier period, when immigrants were escaping from political oppression or the misery of economic change. The fact is that some opportunity is inherent in the industrial growth which has been experienced in both capitalist Europe and America.

Another change in the twentieth century is the cumulative welfare

[1]See the review of these studies in S. M. Lipset and Reinhard Bendix, *Social Mobility in Industrial Society* (Berkeley, Calif., 1959).

measures which have created the "welfare state." While the associations of the corporate and some professional worlds still view these developments with horror, some basic welfare measures are a part of our social life. Most of these changes have been in response to popular demands expressed in the platforms of working class movements. Nowadays no political party of the right would think of removing them. In fact they have reached the status of electoral bribes. The development of social welfare can be seen as a series of concessions within the capitalist order, but these concessions are very important and have gone a long way towards destroying the doctrine of increasing misery. Along with welfare measures there has been some redistribution of income through transfer payments and the taxation of corporate wealth to bear the cost of heavy government expenditure on defence and other services. Capitalism, in other words has undergone sufficient transformation that it is difficult to relate present reality to the model built up in socialist theory.

While we have been talking about capitalist industrial society in general, what we have said applies also to Canadian experience. A strong labour movement, even though it is threatened from time to time, acts an an important check against economic exploitation. With the transition in Canada from agriculture to industry the occupational structure has become more complex, making for differentiation of occupational status and some mobility into skill classes. Although our welfare measures are not as extensive as in other countries, and anything but uniform from province to province, there is an improvement over earlier conditions. The doctrine of increasing misery is no more applicable to Canada than it is to other societies based on capitalism. These historical developments have meant that the power of economic exploitation of individuals through capitalist institutions has been curbed. Socialism's *raison d'être* therefore has to be reformulated. Particularly in need of examination is the idea that the solutions to the problems of power lie exclusively within the economic realm.

We must accept the fact that industrial capitalism has raised individual consumption standards, and provided in the process of its growth a new level of occupational opportunity. The words individual consumption standards have been used purposely to avoid the popular illusion that capitalism has brought the highest standard of living ever known. Such a notion implies the use of a measuring device or index which is rarely made more explicit than the per capita ownership of automobiles and refrigerators. International and historical comparisons using such indices are frequently pointless. In some countries with a different population distribution automobiles are not so important, and in others climate does not make refrigerators so essential for the preservation of food. A more important question is why are particular indices chosen rather than others? The answer in part is that in the capitalist ethos standards are erected in terms of individual ownership of things, but there are many other indices which could be used with equal or perhaps greater claims to validity. Canada, for example, ranks eighth in the world for its infantile mortality rate.[2] As I have tried to show in another paper in this volume it has nothing to be proud of in its educational systems. No one would argue that our cities are places where human beings can live a good life in an atmosphere free from pollution and traffic hazard. The condition of Lake Ontario prevents the inhabitants of the large urban mass in the vicinity of Toronto from swimming in it. None of our cities are likely to be held up as models of town planning. Of the billions of dollars spent in housing construction in the last decade it is safe to say that no more than a small fraction has been spent on projects that would conform to accepted standards of community planning. Statistics of owner-occupied dwellings are also used to demonstrate a high standard of living, but these figures ignore the fact that a large number of lower income families who do manage to find a down payment on a house can keep up their payments only by renting out a part of the house they have bought. Owners do not always have the exclusive use of their homes.

Within any measure of a standard of living there would have to be included that income which can only be derived from social investment: education, health and hospitalization, planned cities, roads, parks and so forth. In an index that did include these items capitalist Canada would probably do less favourably than some European countries in which capitalism has been modified by the presence, and in some cases a period in office, of powerful socialist parties.

Even if one accepted the argument that, measured by any index, capitalism has created the highest material standard of living ever known, it does not logically follow that it will continue to do so. We are only now beginning to see something of the enormous productive potential of the Soviet Union. It would simply be an extension of the error which I have pointed out if we tried to compare indices of production and consumption of capitalist North America and the Soviet Union. At higher levels of development social life cannot be compared in material terms, but if capitalism chooses to be compared on the criterion of material things it may well take fright at the challenge now presented to it by other systems.

The reformulation of socialist theory must start with the fact that, despite the material levels it has created, capitalism has not lost its exploitative character. There is no longer the exploitation by entrepreneurs of a disorganized proletariat, but what has emerged with the

[2]*Canada Year Book*, 1959 (Ottawa), 229.

new bureaucratic and corporate forms of capitalism is the monopolization of a society's creative potential. The new scale of corporate organization is such that our institutions become moulded to corporate needs.
What we might become as a society, judging by the manner in which we
welcome outside capital of corporations, is measured in terms of our
exploitability by corporations.

Social goals are now established by a much smaller number than in
the days of entrepreneurial capitalism. Because of the traditional rights
of private property, enshrined in the myth that corporations are individuals, the corporate élite hold the creative privileges available. Only a
few men have the creative privilege of building a new industry or destroying an old one, of establishing a new university, planning a new
hospital, or developing a new resource. Often it is the same men who do
all these things. From large industrial complexes to organized philanthropy, creative rights continue to be monopolized by the corporate
élite. So accustomed are we to seeing progress solely in terms of increased material welfare, the gross national product, or real wages, that
we ignore the fact that the vast majority in our mass democracies do
not participate in any kind of creative behaviour.

Freedom, as we have suggested, is relative to the level of social development. We recognize this relativity in material things when we include
in the cost of living index items which half a century ago would have
been considered luxuries, but we rarely think of creative experience
either in the individual sense or in the sense of group and social achievement as an item in the index of the good life. Such behaviour continues
to be a class privilege because those who engage in it are educated, or
have inherited a way of life which is essential to its realization, or they
occupy commanding positions in our institutional systems — economic,
religious, educational, and so forth. Since our institutional élites are
predominantly recruited from the higher segments of our class structure,
our social and cultural values tend to be defined in class terms. In
religious behaviour, for example, the enriched ritualism of the Anglican
Church is thought to be more refined and appropriate to high status
than evangelical forms of worship, and it is not unlikely that as a person
improves his status he will change his religion, if he is Protestant, and
start to read T. S. Eliot. Another cultural value which seems to be built
into our institutional structure is that an individual's status is related to
the number of men he controls in his work — which implies that power
itself is a value.

The pervasiveness of class values can be seen to some extent in the
modified goals of proletarian movements. Often their aims are no more
than to capture the items of bourgeois conventionality, or to achieve a
style of living as advertised in *Life*, a style that takes its cue in turn
from the bourgeois values of the *New Yorker* and *Harper's Bazaar*.

Recent studies in the United Kingdom would suggest[3] —that the reduced popularity of the Labour party can be accounted for by the improvement in the material standard of living among some of the working class. The name "Labour" party, it would seem, is regarded as not quite respectable. Why it is that the material items, often cheap and gaudy, of the bourgeois way of life should have such an appeal must ultimately be explained in terms of social psychology. Perhaps it is the result of the continuous assault on the mind by the advertisers. Instead of producing what it needs, a plutocratically controlled society must sell what it produces. Eventually we are convinced that the colour of a soap effects its cleansing qualities or that a triangularly shaped soda cracker is "dainty."

A further consequence of the creation of artificial demand through advertising is the standardization of taste and the obliteration of regional and ethnic cultures. Of all our ethnic groups the French Canadians are most aware of the possible loss of regional and ethnic identity. Frequently these fears can be exploited in the most Machiavellian fashion by our élites, but the French desire for cultural separation can be justified both psychologically and socially. A massive homogeneous national culture can only intensify that sense of isolation and powerlessness of which we have spoken. Democratic social planning must preserve and foster group differences, because it is through identification with small rather than massive social aggregates that the individual can avoid the feeling of isolation. The national mass is much more susceptible to the manipulative techniques of modern power and modern demagogues. A well-drilled uniformity ensures an uncritical predisposition to obedience.

If bourgeois values are to be transferred to the working classes why should capitalism not carry on, prodded from time to time by working class movements? The answer surely lies in the desirability of social participation in defining and achieving goals, in the release of the potential for a creative life shared with others, governed not through competitiveness and authoritarianism but through co-operation.

The use of words like creativity and spontaneity can be criticized on the grounds of their vagueness, and the difficulty of attaching them as labels to particular kinds of behaviour or to particular subjective states. In simplest terms what is meant by these words is the expression of the self. When a child is given the opportunity to paint or draw with his own choice of colours whatever he wishes, what results is a creative act. Similarly a group of children dancing will rarely be watching each other. Their movements are free and express feelings which are exclusively individual. Adults too experience this creative expression when they become amateur artists or join classes in writing or learn to play the flute. It is no doubt such a need for expression which is behind the do-it-

[3]See the comment of R. T. McKenzie, "Labour's Need for Surgery," *Observer*, London, Oct. 25, 1959.

yourself movement and the great zeal of suburban gardening. Whatever may be said of the architectural uniformity of suburban developments there is always some self-expression with house colour and landscaping or interior decorating. (One of the failures, incidentally, of public housing schemes is that tenants are frequently denied this freedom of expression.)

Bodily movements also permit the expression of the self. The heightened feelings which come from the skilful use of the limbs are akin to the satisfactions of creative activity. We recognize too that to be creative limbs must have freedom from clothing and therefore we make "appropriate" varying degrees of undress which in other situations would be considered immodest. Often the creativity of bodily movements is achieved in partnership with physical surroundings. The exhilaration of the skier comes as much from the sensory delight of sun and snow as it does from the control which he has over his movements. Creativity is not always self-expression. At the appropriate times we can be creative with others. Social organization requires us to work with others. What we must seek are the conditions under which working with others towards common goals produces the kinds of satisfaction and feelings which we associate with individual creativity.

The close and intimate atmosphere of the family affords the best conditions for individuals to work together to create bonds of affection and mutual support. It is in the primary social grouping that individuals can learn love and respect for others. The acquisition of these primary sentiments leads in turn to the establishment of social bonds outside the family, particularly within the community. It is doubtful that, except in unconscious perversions of them, such sentiments can be extended beyond community and region to encompass such large aggregates as modern nations, and for that reason, as I shall argue later, decentralization is essential in the democratically planned society. It is important to realize that creative expression cannot develop without policies to foster it. We place a great value on the family as a social institution and yet we require families to live in dismal surroundings which are scarcely conducive to the building of creative relationships. The vast conurbations which are beginning to sprawl out from our metropolitan areas are more likely to brutalize the senses than to spark that sensual element in creative behaviour. What a struggle it is to preserve parkland in our large cities from the subdividers and the developers!

Many will argue that continued socialist piety in an age of so-called affluence is a form of obsessive neurosis, but we can point to many indices of socially derived disorder — delinquency, mental illness, drug addiction, alcoholism, suicide and the like — which would suggest that we are not producing human happiness. It must be remembered too that these pathological conditions are not confined to a single class, although each class has its peculiar kind of deviant behaviour. The fate of a drunk or a mentally disturbed person will depend on his class position, so that statistics of any particular form of deviance will not reflect its true class incidence.

It was the great achievement of Emile Durkheim, the French sociologist, to show that the indices of deviant behaviour are as likely to be high in periods of prosperity as in periods of poverty. In periods of prosperity, when individual gain is the prevailing value there is an absence of an encompassing moral order which binds people together for common social ends. Even the rich comforts of *Crestwood Heights*, as the authors of that book have shown, do not make its members immune from anxieties and psychic strains.

In Canada we have seen recently many cases of corruption in public life and of the exploitation of responsible social roles for personal gain. Many of these instances lie in the financial and commercial worlds, whose institutions lend themselves so readily to this kind of behaviour. Business men do not really see restrictive trade practices as criminal behaviour, nor does their prestige fall when their firms appear in court. The stock manipulations of certain former Ontario cabinet ministers did not preclude them from running again for public office. Nor did they prevent their associates from continuing in office. This lack of conscience can only be explained in terms of habituation to the capitalist ethos and the complex of attitudes which legitimates predatory behaviour. Our élites do not endanger the public interest because the public so readily accepts their definition of its interest.

We tend to draw examples of the exploitative character of power roles from the economic realm, but they can be found in other institutions as well. The mass media, with their close ownership links with our local and national plutocracies, help to define the moral basis of capitalist institutions through their constant repetition of the stereotyped benevolence of these institutions. Among these images is the one that plutocratic power has the right to exploit the new medium of television for economic gain. Recent hearings before the Board of Broadcast Governors show how élites of Montreal, Toronto, Winnipeg and Vancouver seek to extend their power over the mass media by capturing a new set of rights. The unhappy problem is that public ownership of mass media is no guarantee of freedom of ideas, as long as so many other institutions are dominated by private interests. The controllers of the CBC frequently take on the role of guardian of our moral sensibilities when they prevent our contamination by an intellectual virtuoso like Simone de Beauvoir. No doubt they are responding to some extent to the élites of the church hierarchies, but the fact that they feel obliged to do so simply points out the ubiquitous quality of power. The organized pressure of religious groups in their complaints about the portrayal of the life of a woman who became a saint and the withdrawal by a large corporation of its sponsorship of a television drama show how the authoritative principle inevitably pervades the creative arts. The grotesque morality which underlies the brutality so typical of the mass media receives singularly little critical analysis. It is interesting also that in a 1959 television series in which members of the corporate élite were interviewed about big business not a single critical idea emerged.

The exploitive, predatory and restrictive character of capitalist institutions rests on a morality defined by those at the apex of our institutional hierarchies. This is not to suggest that they consciously propagate a morality which enhances their own worthiness — although the emergence of the modern advertising myth-makers would suggest that even this element of control is within their grasp — but rather that their view of the world is a product of institutional behaviour. Habitual behaviour within an institutional order provides its own justification by the psychological transformations, subtle and frequently beyond our grasp, which tell us that what we have done and continue to do is right and good simply because of the fact of doing it.

In turn this process of habituation permits class control of total social morality. By its control of philanthropic institutions, an élite with its own dubious morality watches over the morality of the under-privileged and the deviants of the lower class. It is no accident that professional social welfare has replaced social reform as the principal method of dealing with social problems. Reform suggests too much institutional change with a consequent erosion of privilege, but welfare permits the patching up of the casualties of a predatory economic system. As I have said, capitalism has been forced to accept a welfare state within its own institutions, but this it has done without giving up the creative privileges of its leaders.

THE REINS OF POWER

Socialist policy then must be directed towards releasing the spontaneous and creative forces within human society. Such a change can only be brought about through democratic planning and co-ordination. Planning, of course, means for some a restriction of freedom, but it is illusory to suppose that with our present institutions we live free of restriction. I have tried to argue that freedom is restricted by the monopolization of the creative role, but it is also restricted because we do not plan. We exercise little control over disordered social forces which because of their effects imprison us within an environment of accident. With almost primitive mentality we attribute these accidents to impersonal forces such as "the market," "public opinion," "temporary adjustment," and so forth. Social science has done something to reduce this animistic world of the social environment, and to provide us with some tools for the implementation of social policy, but at the most these tools are used as negative controls rather than as positive techniques for social planning.

It is wrong of course to argue that we are without planning, because as I shall try to show modern industrial society could not get along without it. The planning is done through the machinery of corporate bureaucracy countered from time to time by the bureaucracies of organized labour and government. The aims of corporate organization determine the shape of social development. This is the creative role. The countervailing role of government and organized labour is negative. As the Trans-Canada pipeline case indicates, at times the government gives positive aid to corporate power.

What is alarming on the contemporary scene are the erstwhile socialists who argue that all that is necessary is the extension of negative controls to keep the corporate world in order. As our society proceeds along the course of industrialization a greater degree of co-ordination and planning will be necessary if we are not to have a proliferation of the kind of dislocation that results from such things as the decision on the Avro Arrow, Nova Scotia coal mining, the uranium industry and so forth. The deficiencies in our educational systems and the crisis in our universities are no less examples of the absence of co-ordinated planning. As long as our institutes of higher learning must live by the corporate hand-outs and unplanned government grants the crisis in which they find themselves will continue, thus reducing the contribution they might make to social development. Similarly, our defence needs, agricultural policy, the rapid growth of our cities, immigration policy and aid to under-developed countries require planned co-ordination rather than unplanned plutocratically directed growth restricted only by negative government controls.

However, planning will fail to be democratic unless we devise new administrative techniques. Socialists have never given enough attention to how social participation in the definition and achievement of goals can be brought about. With the present bureaucratic machinery which governs most of our institutions the ends of the creative life can scarcely be served. The simple notion that a new age of socialist glory will be ushered in by changing the ownership of productive instruments overlooks the depressing quality of bureaucratic organization. Since bureaucracy can be a device equally of the corporate world or of a socialist world, for the masses there is little difference. Bureaucracy belongs to the industrial order, and while changes in the institutions of property and ownership may be necessary to solve the problems of power inherent in the bureaucratic structure of industry, it would be wrong to think that these problems are automatically solved by public ownership. Moreover, there seems little point in preparing for the first stage without some clear ideas about how the bureaucratic problem is to be solved.

In contemporary societies based on industry, most essential social activities are carried out through large-scale bureaucracies. If we want to understand modern forms of power we must first understand this organizational machine. The word bureaucracy has both a technical and pejorative meaning. In simplest terms it means rule by officials, but in the popular mind it is associated with cumbersome and irritating administrative machinery. Everyone at some time in his life has been enmeshed in the nets of private and public officialdom. The wrong order has come from the department store; the railways company has given the same berth to two people; the government department has lost the papers submitted to it. Quick to condemn the bumbling clerk and the pompous official, we ignore the fact that without large scale organization our social life would be chaotic. If they are to run smoothly, someone must organize and control the intricate schemes of social relations with their multifarious points of human contact.

Modern bureaucracy in its organizing of production and distribution has created an enormous range of middle level occupations between the factory bench and higher management, between the rank and file and the general staff. This white collar "salariat" keeps the accounts and records for corporations, governments, churches, trade unions, and many other organizations. Modern production of material goods, television programmes, engineers, missionaries and politicians requires knowledge — knowledge of consumers and incomes, congregations and collections, taxpayers and taxes, members and their dues, servicemen and their dependants. Someone, and in most cases more than one, records our birth, inoculations, school attendance, marriage, offspring, mortgage payments, hospitalization, car licences, monthly instalments, our sins if we transgress, and eventually our demise. We have all become facts in the filing cases of numerous offices, carefully accounted for, documented, and punched on to cards, ready to be sorted, resorted, cross-indexed, and catalogued in an infinite variety of ways. Somewhere in the organizational hierarchy we are the guardians of our statistical selves.

It is easy to condemn this unenchanting world of record and routine, but it is essential to the institutional planning without which our high standard of living would be impossible. There is, of course, a substantial tradition of criticism of the growth of bureaucracy, a process which has been called among other things "the new despotism," "the road to serfdom," the managerial revolution," and "Parkinson's Law." Most of these critiques are directed at government bureaucracy, and ignore completely the massive bureaucracies of privite industry, trade unions, churches and universities. Consider, for example, the huge army of officials required to operate corporate bodies such as the Canadian Pacific Railway, A. V. Roe, Eaton's, Canadian Breweries, Metropolitan Life, Bell Telephone, the University of Toronto, the Anglican Church, and the United Steel Workers of America.

It is frequently argued that these private bureaucracies are benevolent rather than despotic, because they have to contend with competitors and satisfy consumers. Nor are they, it is claimed, as pervasive as government bureaucracy. This view comes from a very distorted perspective of their behaviour, and the behaviour of the men who dominate them. Many of these organizations impinge on our lives in myriads of ways. It may be a uniform kind of beer from the breweries, a standard rate of interest from the banks, the transferable academic credit, the industry-wide contract, or the Christian view of divorce. Corporate "despotism" can be much more far-reaching, as, for example, when it holds the future of a community in its hands by deciding to move its operations from one city to another. Within the white collar mass, work procedures, personnel policies, and career lines are not dissimilar, whether the bureaucracy is private or public.

It is not here that I want to argue the relative despotic quality of public and private bureaucracy. I want simply to point out the principal feature of modern social structure based on industry. These battalions of officials must provide the productive system with a constant flow of information. They can do so only if they are organized into an orderly division of tasks, and governed by rules and regulations to cover all imaginable contingencies. The end of organizational activity, efficiency, is served by the new social sciences. No longer, as in the nineteenth century, is the role of social science to criticize, but rather its new function is to improve the techniques of bureaucratic control. Personnel psychology, industrial relations, rational accounting, linear programming, are all bureaucratic tools. Even the university, which should be the last resting place of the independent soul, has become absorbed, through the research contract, in the world of large organizations, to which by tradition and nature it has been opposed. The graduates of business and public administration are the direct descendants of the human engineers and the stop-watch holders.

Despite occasional blunders bureaucracy is efficient. Without its techniques masses of people could not be mobilized into the gigantic productive units that we have today. It is inconceivable that we could ever revert to more haphazard administrative devices and still support large populations at high standards of living.

The success of bureaucracy — its efficiency — is also its danger, because it becomes a power instrument *par excellence*. Hierarchically organized bureaucracies are systems of command and co-ordination. Those who work in them — and they are gradually absorbing us all — acquire the habits of obedience. Orders are followed and if orders cease to come the systems come to a halt. Whoever controls administrative machinery controls increasingly large segments of our institutions. There are psychological by-products of bureaucracy which deaden the critical faculties of men and, by narrowing their spheres of activity to the appropriate "office" or "position," leave them experiencing only a fragment of life. There is little opportunity for the worker, whether in overalls or white collar to relate his own activity to the productive aims of his society.

Bureaucracy provides socialist theory with a built-in contradiction. Socialism, which seeks to release men from productive drudgery, envisages larger productive units, more intricate co-ordination between these units, and more extensive planning of the total social effort, none of which can be achieved without a very great increase in administrative machinery. With the nationalization that took place in the United Kingdom during the first Labour government, large productive units, such as railways and coal mines, were brought under the centralized control of national boards. Neither workers nor consumers became conscious of increased freedom or dignity. The increase in the scale of operations can result in a greater alienation of the worker and consumer from the productive goals of the society.

Moreover, such large centralized units are easily transferable between public and private ownership. These changes in ownership and control resemble palace revolutions, in which élites change without a noticeable effect on the lives of the workers. In a system of political democracy, socialist gains under one government may be demolished under a subsequent government. The less that is done to change the quality of industrial bureaucracy, the easier it is to return to capitalist forms of organization.

Early socialist writers cannot be blamed for failing to see the bureaucratic explosion which has attended modern industrialization. They dreamt of a smaller world, based more on the community, where the harmonious relations between workers followed from common goals mutually understood and arrived at. Even in the early part of the twentieth century, the guild socialists visualized a society in which democratically organized functional groups would become associated in a co-operative productive system. It was easy to denounce private ownership, human greed, and profit-making as the barrier to this Eldorado of co-operation. Indeed it was a barrier at the time, and may still be today, but the world of large-scale organization makes a far more formidable barrier to socialist ideals. Socialists have not given enough thought to how this barrier might be removed.

It has been suggested that the last electoral defeat of the Labour party in the United Kingdom, was because the public, consumers and workers, had had enough of nationalization, and therefore public ownership, the core of socialist policy, should be removed from the party's platform. The fact that nothing was done, other than to replace private managers with public ones, probably more than anything else left the public susceptible to the massive corporate propaganda against nationalization.

If some of the time and talent spent on sharpening managerial tools could be spent on devising methods of democratic control of industry or eliciting consumer opinion, we would be much closer to the kind of industrial order which socialists desire. What, for example, should be the role of trade unions in that part of the economy which passes to public ownership and in which some form of worker participation in management is introduced? Trade unions themselves have used the organizational weapon of bureaucracy in their struggle against the capitalist order. In productive units where there is some semblance of industrial democracy, the role of unions must obviously be different.

Workers' representatives on boards of nationalized industries or crown corporations may simply be trade union leaders who have enhanced their own position. How many of them would be prepared to establish democratic work processes at the expense of the systems of power which they have built up in their struggle against capitalism? Some of the fruits of this struggle can be seen today with the appointment of workers' representatives to all kinds of boards, commissions and regulatory agencies. Because they are appointed by organized labour, these people are not so much workers' representatives as they are organizational watch-dogs. Trade union leaders and corporate officials share places on these boards because both groups command organizational machinery. Trade unions can suffer the same kind of bureaucratic ossification as any other organization if their only postures are those of consolidating gains or of winning more tournaments before labour relations boards. Unless they pass to their next creative stage and map out new territory of social development, they will find themselves economic fossils.

Account then must be taken of bureaucratic control, in any analysis of power and freedom in modern society. The picture which nineteenth-century theorists drew of society was of human beings living as a large collection of independent units. The problem of freedom was simply one of creating the physical conditions under which human atoms could attain their self-determination. The picture which twentieth-century theorists are drawing is of bureaucracy and counter-bureaucracy. The control of materials and men lies within these large administrative systems. The lines of control, like the reins of a thousand horses, come together in a relatively small number of hands. The drivers are few. It is they, the élites, at the top of our bureaucratic pyramids to whom are given the creative privileges, and to whom we entrust the job of directing us into our brave new worlds. If we can identify the main social institutions which have taken on this shape, we can, in turn identify the groups who are in effective control at the top. In a short essay it is impossible to analyse all the institutional hierarchies within which power coalesces. Economic institutions are selected because of their advanced stage of bureaucratization and the tendency for other institutions to be patterned after them.

Concentration of economic power and the separation of ownership from control are two of the most profound changes in twentieth-century capitalism. Capitalism is no longer a system of independent entrepreneurs making their profit according to the logic of classical economic theory. It is one of the greatest achievements of the contemporary myth-makers that the image of the business world is still that of the nineteenth century. Despite the enormous range of evidence which tells us otherwise we still see the economic system as being made up of men and their businesses. As long as this picture of the economic world is maintained all ambitious men can cherish the hope that they too can achieve the status of ultimate worth — that of the independent businessman. The public vocabulary of the corporate world as it finds its way into the Chamber of Commerce brief and institutional advertising is a collection of words from a dead language. "Free enterprise," "private enterprise," "competition," "the freedom of consumers," and the like are as outdated labels as "fief" and "benefice." It is significant that in their perennial attack on trade unions the corporate world draws a picture of giant trade unions crushing out the business man whose only concern is the public interest. In actual fact, the giant unions which we have are a direct response to the centralized control of the productive system.

The concentration of economic power means simply that a large proportion of the economic activity of the nation is in the hands of a very few large firms, and furthermore these very large firms become linked together and to the main financial institutions, the banks and insurance companies, through interlocking directorships. One only has to take the directors of the four largest banks in Canada — Bank of Montreal, Royal Bank of Canada, Canadian Bank of Commerce, Bank of Nova Scotia — to see the far-ranging economic power that lies in the hands of a few men. Professor Ashley has shown[4] that thirty directors of the Bank of Montreal held, at the time of his study, between them "220 or more" directorships in other companies. Similarly the twenty-five directors of the Royal Bank of Canada held 240 other directorships; the twenty-two directors of the Canadian Bank of Commerce held 225 directorships in other companies; the twenty directors of the Bank of Nova Scotia held 220 directorships. Altogether these ninety-seven men held between them 930 directorships in corporations operating in every sector of the economy. There are in Canada some very powerful holding companies which have within their portfolios the control of an enormous range of corporations. Outstanding among these is Argus Corporation. Twelve directors of Argus Corporation hold 150 directorships in banks,

[4]C. A. Ashley, "Concentration of Economic Power," *Canadian Journal of Economics and Political Science*, vol. XXIII, no. 1, Feb., 1957.

insurance companies, trust companies and in operating companies. The extensive economic power of Argus can be seen from the following list of firms which it controlled in 1960:[5]

1. Massey-Ferguson Ltd. (formerly Massey-Harris Ferguson Ltd.)
   Subsidiaries in Canada
   F. F. Barber Machinery Co. Ltd.
   Sunshine Waterloo Co. Ltd.

2. Dominion Tar and Chemical Co. Ltd.
   Principal Subsidiaries in Canada
   Gypsum, Lime and Alabastine Ltd.
   Siporex Ltd.
   Sifto Rock Salt Ltd.
   Goderich Salt Co. Ltd.
   Canada Creosoting Co. Ltd.
   Javex Co. Ltd.
   Chemical Developments of Canada Ltd.
        Irwin Dyestuff Corp. Ltd.
   Murray-Brantford Ltd.
   Inter-Provincial Brick Co. Ltd.
   Cooksville-Laprairie Brick Ltd.
   Howard Smith Paper Mills Ltd.
        The Arborite Co. Ltd.
        Donnaconna Paper Co. Ltd.
        Huron Forest Products Ltd.
        Canada Paper Co.
        Schofield Paper Co. Ltd.
        Kilgours Ltd.
        MacGregor Paper and Bag Co. Inc.
        Alliance Paper Mills Ltd.
        Don Valley Paper Co. Ltd.
        Federal Paper Co. Ltd.
        The Fred W. Halls Paper Co. Ltd.

3. St. Lawrence Corporation Ltd.
   Principal Subsidiaries
   Hinde and Dauch Paper Co. of Canada Ltd.
        The Corrugated Paper Box Co. Ltd.
   Price Bros. and Co. Ltd. (10 per cent of common shares)
   Angus Paper Products Ltd.

4. Dominion Stores Ltd.
   Principal Subsidiaries
   Thrift Stores Ltd.
   Town & Country Food Centre Ltd. (Alta.)
   Acadia Stores Ltd.

5. British Columbia Forest Products Ltd.

6. Canadian Breweries Ltd.
   Principal Subsidiaries in Canada
   The Carling Breweries Ltd.
   O'Keefe Brewing Co. Ltd.
   Dow Brewery Ltd.

[5]Compiled from *Financial Post Corporation Service*.

Western Canada Breweries Ltd.
Pelissier's Brewery Ltd.
Kiewel Brewing Co. Ltd.
Dominion Malting (Ontario) Ltd.
Dominion Malting Co. Ltd.
7. Canadian Equity and Development Co. Ltd.
Don Mills Development Ltd.
Greater Hamilton Shopping Centre Ltd.

At the apex of this enormous industrial empire are the four principal directors of Argus, who also hold dominating positions on the boards, and in many instances on the executive committees, of most of the parent companies listed.

The technique of control used by large holding companies, such as Argus, is simple: it is to buy up enough shares to outvote any other combination of shareholders and thus to elect their own directors to the board of the "captured" corporations. Usually the acquisition of between 10 and 20 per cent of the voting stock is sufficient with the aid of proxy votes, to gain control. Frequently too the capturing of corporations succeeds only after proxy battles which can be particularly vicious, as was the battle for the St. Lawrence Corporation.

Although Argus outclasses all others in its field, other groups of corporations have been brought under unified control in the post-war years. A. V. Roe, controlled by the Hawker-Siddeley interests in the United Kingdom, which holds a dominating position in the Canadian aircraft industry has absorbed the Dominion Steel and Coal Corporation, and Canadian Car and Foundry. Both of these firms have a variety of subsidiary companies. In British Columbia the recent merger of the Powell River Company and MacMillan and Bloedel Ltd. is another instance of the ever narrowing channels of control.

It is interesting that one director of MacMillan and Bloedel Ltd., is a member of the board of Argus Corporation. Four other directors are on the board of British Columbia Forest Products. In some instances individual men form the link between large industrial units, as is the case with George Weston Ltd. and Eddy Paper Company Ltd.[6] The former company controls (in Canada) William Neilson Ltd., McCormicks Ltd., Weston Bakeries Ltd., (a consolidation of numerous bakeries across the country), Dr. Jackson Foods Ltd., Paulin-Chambers Co. Ltd., Willards Chocolate Co. Ltd., Marven's Ltd., Somerville Ltd., Loblaw Companies Ltd. The Eddy Paper Company's principal subsidiaries are the E. B. Eddy Co., and Sidney Roofing and Paper Co.

Elsewhere I have tried to outline[7] the concentration of economic power in Canada that follows from the dominating position that a rela-

[6]*Ibid.*

[7]John Porter, "The Concentration of Economic Power and the Economic Elite in Canada," *Canadian Journal of Economics and Political Science*, vol. XXII, no. 2, May, 1956.

tively few large firms have in the economic system. A much more competent study of economic concentration is provided by Professor Rosenbluth in a paper in this volume. Each of these large corporations is bureaucratically organized into a careful division of tasks, hierarchy of offices, graduated careers, systems of promotion and so forth. At the apex of each pyramid, in effective command is a small group of senior officers and directors. The bureaucratic machines which they control produce for profit. They function too as channels of communication and supervision. In this sense there is power (the directing of the affairs of other people) downwards throughout the system. One salaried official carries out the directives from another salaried official above him and directs those below him.

The attitude of obedience is essential if the objectives of those at the top are to be reached, but it is also necessary for getting on in the bureaucratic system. The criteria of worthiness for promotion become related to the individual's efficiency in carrying out directives and showing good judgment, a bit of corporate sophistry meaning that his opinions are more or less the same as those of his seniors, or that time and luck proves his judgment to be good. He is a good "family" man, the family being the corporation to whose well-being he has committed himself. Historians have written of the devotion and servility of the domestic servant class of earlier periods. The modern counterpart of this group is the "organization man," devoted and servile to a bureaucratic order. I do not think I have been overdrawing this mentality of obedience. Even if the individual does not want to get on, he wants at least security, and since he has no property rights in his job, docility becomes the wise policy. Compensation for the loss of position is a right only at the very top where a chief executive who is ousted when his corporation has passed to the control of a new group is able to demand some kind of settlement. It is true that at the lower levels, workers' associations have been able to counter the arbitrariness of corporate officials with seniority clauses and the like. In the future, as the occupational structure shifts with accompanying undertones of white collar respectability and bourgeois identifications, more and more workers will become fully bureaucratized without the benefit of worker organizations.

The significance of all this for the problems of power is surely in the fact that a few control men and resources and therefore inevitably control the many who are prevented from full participtation in the creative life. The more the culture of bureaucracy develops — and economic concentration is an indication of how it has developed — the more the appropriate mental habits become those of servility. The case for public ownership to produce more material things may be weak, but the case for it as a means of allowing social participation and the humanizing of bureaucracy may be overwhelming.

The drift to centralized control of the economic processes is now well advanced. Centralized control means absentee control through a complex bureaucratic apparatus. More and more local industries become absorbed in these economic empires. When the dominant plant or mill in a small and remote community is brought into the network of a Toronto holding company and the former owners are replaced by corporate personnel, community responsibility and obligations change. This is not to suggest that privately owned local plants were operated with great beneficence or that absentee owners ignore community feelings. With absentee control economic forces become much more impersonal, and the responsibility for the social effects of economic change much more difficult to place.

As increasingly salaried officials implement remote decisions, the channels of control become more narrow. We have already spoken of the small group of men at the apex of industrial complexes like Argus and A. V. Roe, and there has been much talk in recent years of the yet remoter control which results from foreign investment. The small fraction of men who control the economic processes can be seen from the extensive interlocking directorships among large corporations. In a group of 170 large corporations in 1952 some 200 men held half of all the directorships in these companies as well as directorships in banks, insurance companies and trust companies.[8]

The corporate élite do not limit their activities to the direction of their economic empires. Their roles have the magnetic effect of drawing to them numerous other creative privileges, in the form of governorships of hospitals, universities, artistic associations and philanthropic organizations. There is scarcely a large city hospital or large university whose board is not graced by representatives of the corporate world. There are obvious reasons for their being there. They can raise money.

In her fascinating study of the control of philanthropy in a large Canadian city, Professor Ross has shown how the business world views fund raising as a means of legitimating its governing of the economic system. "Philanthropy rests squarely on the shoulders of big business," said one corporate executive; "we use that as a weapon to try to force business to give. We tell them if they want the system of free enterprise to continue they must continue to give."[9] The success too of any charitable campaign depends on the right people heading it up. Business men engage in reciprocal exchange of donations. Thus throughout the country, welfare agencies depend on the economic élite sponsoring them.

Other papers in this volume outline techniques to reduce the power that comes from economic concentration, but if these solutions involve

[8]*Ibid.*
[9]Aileen D. Ross, "Organized Philanthropy in an Urban Community," *Canadian Journal of Economics and Political Science*, vol. XVIII, no. 4, Nov., 1952.

little more than capitalism with controls, we will not be much farther ahead. Governmental control or all-out public ownership by itself will do little if anything to expand creativity, widen responsibility, or increase participation in the productive processes or solve the problems of bureaucracy.

VALUES AND ATTITUDES FOR A NEW SOCIETY

Democratic planning for freedom requires us to make advances on two levels: the psychological and the institutional. The creation of a democratic environment depends on rational inquiry guided by humanitarian values. The good society can never be achieved as long as we carry around in our minds our fictional accounts of social reality. Nor is it fostered in the current climate of anxiety: anxieties about economic stability, technological change, international relations, and personal status. Humanitarianism cannot come about without a shift in emphasis from the current social value of self-interest to the neglected value of common social interests.

We never cease to hear that in order to get essential social tasks performed we must reward men, particularly business men, with high incomes and opportunities to acquire great wealth, and to pass fortunes on to their families. The sense of social duty and the public good does not depend on such a grotesquely selfish account of human motives. The point is that we do so very little to develop the opposite motives. The opposite motives are demonstrated in those men who assume important social roles without high monetary rewards, and men who in their work are guided primarily by the desire for public service. Able and responsible men work in the federal public service, for example, for a fraction of what their talents could bring them in the corporate world. Teachers, clergymen, welfare workers, scientific researchers, and some doctors and lawyers do not see themselves primarily as serving selfish ends. Their reward comes often in the form of prestige, but prestige does not lead to the accumulation of fortune and excessive power. This type of person contradicts the theory that material rewards alone are the appropriate incentives to get social functions performed. It is, of course, necessary to pay people sufficient to induce them to undertake prolonged and rigorous training, but such differential rewards do not mean the huge incomes and capital accumulation that is alleged to be necessary to get business men to do their jobs properly.

We recognize the fact that public institutions are likely to contain some men whose prime motive is power *per se*. The very fact that decision-making roles are essential to social organization means that there is always a risk of personal appropriation. In a rational and humanitarian environment we would recognize the person motivated by power *per se* as deviant to our desired model. No one would suggest that there is a higher concentration of that type in our present public institutions than in our private ones. What is important here is that public institutions are much more open to inquiry than are private ones. It is the nation's business to know what is happening in the CBC, for example, but how often do we think it the nation's business to know what is happening in Argus Corporation? The public official accepts inquiry into his work and operations. If he resents it, his resentment is mainly because he is confronted every day with the kind of inquiry that seems to have as its aim political exploitation rather than genuine concern for the proper functioning of the public service. But his resentment is nothing compared to that of the business man's resentment of inquiries about restrictive trade practices.

This shift in emphasis on motives can only be achieved through educational systems and through some control of our ideological systems, particularly the mass media. We must plan to educate people to be democratic and humanitarian, a process which does not stop at the school- or college-leaving age. Perhaps, too, we should give some thought to social control of the mass media, particularly newspapers which increasingly become controlled by fewer and fewer people. We accept the idea of public trusteeship for some of our educational institutions, provincial universities for example, and we never suggest that they are not free. Freedom of the press from capitalist control would mean a liberation, and some of the greatest newspapers in the world, such as the London *Observer*, and in Montreal *Le Devoir*, have just this freedom to perform their proper social function. There is no reason why some of our large metropolitan dailies when they come up for sale could not be bought through public funds and operated under trusteeship. Such a publicly endowed paper may drop in circulation, but its educative value would be immense.

What we need in positions of power in a democratically planned society is a changed quality of leadership. Many writers have pointed out that men who desire power exhibit irrational elements in their behaviour, and that competitive institutions put a premium on pathological traits. It is the ruthless and the ambitious who get to the top. Actually such men are perceived with ambivalence. They conform to the model of determined competitiveness which capitalist institutions reward, yet their behaviour our humanitarian feelings deplore. Psycho-analytic writers have thrown much light on the importance of love and hate in all our social relationships, and how hate feelings enter into the power-seeking motives. To desire a social structure in which feelings of mutuality, co-operativeness, and love prevail is to desire an almost revolutionary transformation in our psychology of social relationships.

Such a change, however, must be the goal firmly in our minds as we move towards a new social order. In a democratically planned society the aims of leadership — that is the decision-making process which accounts for the ubiquity of power — must be the social good rather than personal gain. No doubt some differentiation of monetary rewards will always remain, but, as I have said, we do not need great fortunes and concentrated power. Men with a passion for such great rewards can only be satisfied at a cost to their fellows.

The role of leadership in a freely planned democracy is twofold: to aid in the searching out and articulation of social needs, and, secondly, to direct social operations to implement socially expressed choices. In our age of complex industrialization we must depend very heavily on men with expert skills and particularly on the social scientists, since it is the social order we seek to change. We cannot do without men of leadership quality, but in our training for leadership our emphasis must be on social obligation rather than personal ambition. In the economic realm, for example, contemporary leadership attitudes would be expressed as: "How can I persuade people to buy what I am producing, and how can I control the fellow who comes into the market I create?" The attitudes of democratic leadership should be: "How can I find out what is socially useful and desired, and enlist the support of others in producing it?" We have plenty of evidence too that power can lead to feelings of indispensability in the men to whom it has been given. This "Bonapartiste" psychology can only be inimical to the democratic way, and to combat it we must devise the necessary institutional checks.

Changes in the psychology of the masses are no less important than changes in the psychology of leadership. In both cases it must be remembered there is no such thing as a rigid psychological structure called human nature. There are rather social natures in the sense that the prevailing psychological dispositions are socially created. It is possible to create a society in which the prevailing personality is marked by humanitarianism and rationality, and while such a goal may be far-distant, it is the goal we must keep in mind. In all likelihood we need to discover the appropriate child-rearing techniques in the home and pedagogical methods in the schools. Where we do not know the appropriate methods we must look for them. If we spent less on such things as motivational research to discover how our unconscious feelings can be exploited in the interest of merchandising and allocated more to the discovery of the kind of training necessary for democratic living, we would be better off. Unfortunately much of the research in social psychology underwrites the value of conformity rather than the value of individual differences. The conformist belongs to the totalitarian industrial system, not to a democratic one, and it matters little from the point of view of individual freedom whether the conformity stems from political indoctrination or commercial beguilement. There are many ways to wash brains. The stereotyped minds of our modern mass societies may feel free, but their potentiality for growth becomes reduced by the standardizing effects of our current systems of education and communication.

Although educational methods are important instruments in the development of personalities more congenial to the democratic milieu, the fact remains that educational systems reflect the values of the dominant institutions within the society, and their influence in bringing about the desired psychological changes is thereby reduced. To achieve some measure of social change it may be necessary to find ways of changing the institutional structure before changing modes of thought. One obvious step which a government devoted to social planning could take through its investment policies is to reverse the influence which now flows from dominant economic institutions to other areas of social life. In the present phase of corporate capitalism such things as education, research in all fields, the social services, the arts and entertainment, the content of the mass media depend very largely on corporate support, and as a consequence of this dependence take on the shape and values and attract, in many instances, the same kind of leadership as the corporate world.

In education, from the business men who sit on local school boards to the corporate élite who sit on boards of universities, the incumbents derive prestige and status, but the inevitable feedback is the dominance of business and corporate mentality. How often is a great educator invited to the board of a large corporation? Why should such a practice be any less common than a corporate leader being on the board of a university?

In the many fields of research there is a similar waiting upon corporate initiative. Within industry the aims of research are overwhelmingly of the "building a better mouse-trap" variety or the application of science to the creation of marketable commodities. In a recent television advertisement we were told that after years of research the company concerned had now produced a spray shoe polish. Such a break-through in the field of personal grooming may serve us well, but it is the dominance of capitalist modes of thought that makes us value that kind of "scientific" advance rather than research in the fields of medicine, health and welfare, or basic work in physics.

These latter will at times be given a fillip as a by-product of our present economic institutions, but more often they proceed with what support governments have been prepared to give them. The élite of the corporate world will donate funds, set up a research institute, endow a chair at a university, or establish a foundation, but there is always the waiting upon corporate profits or the successful accumulation of personal fortunes. The Canadian élite are far behind those of other countries in the supporting of this kind of activity. In fact it is to American foundations and sometimes those of other countries that people in Canada interested in fostering research so often have to turn for funds. The economic élite in Canada complain that their accumulation took place after income tax had become a standard form of government revenue. While income tax has probably imposed some limit on personal accumulation, it is significant that the tax proceeds of the estates of two men were sufficient to establish the Canada Council.

The arts and what might be called without snobbish connotations the higher forms of entertainment have been in an even worse condition than research and education, no doubt because their value is almost entirely aesthetic and there is little probability of long term profitability. Metropolitan and community centres for the performing arts could be developed through social investment. It is typical of a capitalist society that in Toronto such a centre should have to wait upon corporate benefaction. The O'Keefe Centre came from Argus Corporation through its subsidiary Canadian Breweries Limited. As was revealed in the recent trial of the latter firm, the directors were convinced of the great advertising advantages that would follow from building it.

Living as we do in a milieu dominated by the corporate philosophy we have come to look upon various kinds of social investment as something which can be afforded only if it does not interfere with the stability of the corporate economy. This stability is threatened when avenues of profit are encroached upon by government, or when government has to tax in order to invest in what it considers desirable. We are frequently told the country cannot afford old age pensions, or other welfare measures because of their costs. Obviously there are costs to such measures, but principally the cost is a sacrifice of the prevailing economic order. The direction of the flow of institutional influence becomes clear when the corporate philosophy assumes the status of social doctrine for the entire community.

If this reciprocal relation between institutional behaviour and modes of thought is to be broken, the creation of new kinds of institutions through investment might be more effective than joining battle directly with present economic power, particularly if long-run goals are kept in mind. With the development of new institutions come new career systems creating in turn possibilities for new types of leadership which would not be modelled on that of the modern corporation. If this argument appears strange it should be remembered that within the last twenty years there has developed an entirely new type of career system within the federal public service. Although there is some interchange between corporate and public service careers, there are many men in public service who would not find the big business firm congenial to their personalities. New institutional development can be planned and in time be the source of new values and attitudes. Consider some of the possible lines of development beyond the generally accepted forms of social investment such as schools and hospitals. Why not establish a national university devoted to advanced study in all fields of intellectual inquiry; or a national medical research centre, or a national science foundation on a

larger scale than the present National Research Council, or a national
foundation for the arts which could greatly expand the work now being
done by the Canada Council? We also need a well endowed national
organization to develop physical fitness and to take athletics out of its
present commercial imprisonment.

In a democratically planned society there must be a desire for participation in the establishment of social goals. There is now a great deal
of literature which seeks to explain the widespread apathy in our Western industrial societies, and the common theme which these studies have
is that the apathy results from the sense of powerlessness and inability
to have any effect on the great social issues of the day. It is not only the
great social issues which seem beyond the grasp of men in the mass
society. Nowhere is apathy more marked than at the level of urban local
government, the level at which there is direct impingement on individuals
and their families. Yet we know there have been instances when large
segments of a community can be brought together to undertake particular community projects. The drama in Canada will be permanently
indebted to the public-spirited individuals in Stratford who worked so
hard for the Festival. It was a project furthermore which required the
kind of leadership we have been mentioning. It is often said that the
modern metropolitan mass cannot participate in governmental and social
processes of this kind. Why do we not search for the techniques of local
government more appropriate for democracy in metropolitan communities?

There is as much in our Western traditions which supports the principle of democratic social planning as there is that speaks out against
it. It is not a revolutionary doctrine. The values which are implied in
the democratic personality are as much a part of our inheritance as are
those values implied in the aggressive and personally ambitious model
of our contemporary folk heroes. We need to ensure that our next
epoch brings forward the desired type.

Equally important as these psychological changes are the changes
which must come at the institutional level. In particular we must search
out new techniques to deal with the problems of bureaucratic organization. In part we must move towards some system of industrial democracy, and since large productive units do not lend themselves well to
worker participation, planning must result in decentralization. There is
no reason to suppose that the breaking up of large industrial agglomerations into relatively autonomous units is incompatible with the idea of
centralized planning. Decentralization furthermore helps to strengthen
regional, cultural, and sometimes ethnic differences.

Within these decentralized economic units the machinery must be
found which permits and encourages worker association with management. Although at the moment we have only vague ideas of how this
goal can be achieved there are some possible lines of approach. Needless

to say an adequate system of worker participation can only be discovered by constant study and some experimentation. Creative social development must be experimental in its search for new techniques. The aim of worker identification with management decisions might be achieved through the election of direct representatives to the boards of the various regional levels of publicly owned industry. It is anomalous in Canada that the management of a publicly owned railway system behaves no differently in respect to its workers than a privately owned one. Rather the two managements behave as one. Another possible line of development is the creation of consultative bodies in industry corresponding to the various levels of the administrative hierarchy. Whatever the method the goal must be the replacing of the authoritarian character of bureaucratic structure by feelings of co-operation and common purpose.

In the future the pace of social development will depend to a great extent on the willingness and the ability of a society to experiment with its social machinery. We have lived now for a long time in a scientific age. This acquaintance with science and its achievements has given us the attitude that we can eventually master our physical environment, but as yet we are still bound by a built-in conservatism when it comes to mastering the social environment. Within the field of industrial relations there is tremendous scope for social experiment, but the capitalist corporation is limited in the extent to which it can experiment. One reason for this limitation is that experimentation would interfere with the structure of bureaucratic control and authority. This is why the so-called democratic work processes which have been tried in some corporations have as their aim the acceptance of management decisions rather than any democratic participation in policy-making. Workers are allowed to talk their way into accepting decisions from above. A further reason is, of course, that a corporation in competition with other corporations cannot afford to embark on experimentation in human relations except within narrow boundaries. Since efficiency is measured solely by profit, experiments concerned with the welfare of workers are always judged against the profitability of increased output or reduced absenteeism rather than against the criterion of welfare itself.

The possibility of experiment in industrial organizations free from the hazards of corporate enterprise is a strong argument for public ownership in some sectors of the economy. Social experiments, like any other kind, cost money and are subject to failure. There must therefore be flexibility in experimental policies. The belief that publicly owned economic enterprises should behave just as privately owned ones has been an important factor in the criticism of nationalization programmes. There seems to be an unwillingness to search for other criteria to judge the social as well as the strictly economic effects of public ownership.

Many people would view with alarm the setting aside of the economic criteria of technical efficiency and output. Their importance of course cannot be denied, but we must be prepared to accept some losses in the search for new social techniques. We do not hesitate to put a large proportion of our resources into experimenting on armaments that become obsolete within such a short time. Industrial nations blow up millions of dollars every year in rocket research and we accept these losses as a part of our scientific way of life. Could we not say of social experiments also that there may be temporary losses but in the long run we are going to find a better way for human beings to work in industrial organization?

Such government-undertaken social experiments could be viewed as an extension of other kinds of research and experimentation which the government already conducts through a variety of agencies such as the National Research Council, the Defence Research Board, Forest Products Laboratories, and the system of experimental farms. These agencies are necessary because the work they do would be neglected if we applied economic criteria to their operations. Why do we not go a step further into experimenting in the social field?

A central part of the argument in this essay has been that in its present form bureaucracy is inimical to the growth of the co-operative spirit. Yet an important fact to be remembered from the point of view of socialist theory is that people have become accustomed to working as salaried officials without personal property rights. At the level of management some form of teamwork in the planning and implementation of policy is now the accepted practice within industrial organization. It should not be impossible to create in industry the attitudes conducive to socialist goals rather than the maximizing of corporate profit.

As social planning proceeds there must be some change in the functioning of our political institutions. The fear is widespread that all social planning must be totalitarian and despotic. Often these fears can be exploited as an ideological weapon against social change. The fact remains, however, that social planning can lead to individual appropriation of power. We can, of course, devise institutional checks against such appropriation, but in the long run the safeguard depends on the democratic spirit which I have described as rational enquiry guided by humanitarian values. The psychological changes, which I have suggested are necessary for a democratically planned order, cannot take place over night. They can probably only emerge from the processes which they are intended to support in the same way that the current adaptation to a capitalist order is the result of a long period of habituation. What gives the present crisis its sense of urgency is that we stand at the point of choosing in the present industrial epoch between planning by concentrated private interests with continuing public indifference and acquiescence or democratic planning towards socially expressed goals.

Social
Problems

The Mass Media

NEIL COMPTON

A famous passage in the *Autobiography* of John Stuart Mill describes the faith of his father James Mill in the utopia which representative government, freedom of discussion and universal literacy would bring. "So complete was my father's reliance on the influence of reason over the mind of mankind," wrote Mill, "that he felt as if all would be gained if the whole population were taught to read, if all sorts of opinions were allowed to be addressed to them by word and in writing, and if by means of the suffrage they could nominate a legislature to give effect to the opinions they adopted." He thought that once the power of aristocracy and the church had been broken there would be no further obstacles to the free flow of ideas: working men would troop to the polls prepared to cast their ballots according to principles derived at first or second hand from the greatest thinkers of the ages, and each advance in literacy would bring further thousands of citizens in touch with the liveliest minds of their day.

Seldom can a confident expectation have been proved so wrong. One hundred and twenty-five years after James Mill's death we find the goal of literacy almost universally achieved in the Western world. More than that: the successive inventions of the telegraph, telephone, cinema, phonograph, radio, and television (not to mention improved techniques of printing and pictorial reproduction) have extended the range and means of human expression beyond anything Mill dreamed possible, certainly far beyond the range of mere literacy. Yet utopia seems as remote as it ever did. Perhaps it is even remoter than it once was, because we now possess the physical means of bringing it about, and are forced to admit that the failure to achieve it may be due not to external circumstances but to our own human limitations. In any event, we now find ourselves in the embarrassing position of achieving a millennial ambition to communicate with all men everywhere only to discover that we may have nothing very important to say.

The revolution in communications may not have brought about Mill's utopia, but it has radically transformed society. For better or for worse, most of the institutions of mass democracy depend upon the services offered by press, radio, and television for their healthy and efficient functioning. Nowhere is this more true than in Canada, where geographic, economic, and linguistic obstacles to nationhood have been overcome (so far as they have been) largely through the establishment of our own network of communications.

It follows that no vision of the good society can now be complete if it does not take into account the existence of the mass media and make provision for their creative use. This implies an understanding of why Mill's expectations for the future were founded upon incorrect assumptions, and (a more difficult requirement) a clear insight into the manifold role of the media in a modern community. Unfortunately this is a subject which is as yet imperfectly understood. The communications revolution has come upon us so swiftly and continues to bring about such bewildering cultural mutations that no one has evolved a fully satisfactory set of theoretical concepts to explain it. Moreover, the media are both social phenomena and a means of at least quasi-artistic expression: they occupy a territory which straddles the uneasy and uncertain boundary between the social sciences and the humanities. Only recently has there developed a school of critics and scholars with sufficient qualifications in both fields to do justice to the complex problem of interpretation and analysis. But agreement even on fundamentals has not yet been reached, and this essay, though polemic in tone, represents only one of a variety of approaches to the media.

THE BACKGROUND

The mass media are part of a series of social and cultural phenomena associated with the development of capitalism and technology in the Western world. Their crisis today is part of the larger crisis of free enterprise generally, and differences of opinion with regard to them are likely to be related to conflicting political and economic philosophies. In particular, argument rages over the question of whether publishing, broadcasting, and movie-making are businesses ("like any other" is the usual qualifying phrase) or arts. Should they give the public "what it wants," or what someone thinks it should want? Does the public get what it likes, or does it learn to like what it gets? This controversy is so characteristic of our age, and its terms are so remote from the considerations which governed creative expression in the pre-capitalistic era, that the whole phenomenon needs perhaps to be judged in a historical perspective.

The first potential medium of mass communication came to Europe in the fifteenth century, when Gutenberg developed the art of printing from movable type. This was not merely the first great technical advance of a series that was to create the modern world, and the one upon which virtually all subsequent achievements have been based. It also exhibited in miniature most of the classic features of modern industrialism: standardization, mass production, lowered unit costs, division of labour, and the assembly line. It made the written word what it had never quite been before — a secular commodity to be sold in the market-place.

Before the advent of printing there had been two almost completely separate traditions of formal culture in Europe — a popular or folk culture, oral in nature, preserved, enriched and transmitted entirely by word of mouth, and a high or learned culture sustained by a very few and depending for its preservation upon the manuscript. The esoteric, exclusive nature of this high culture is symbolized by the fact that for centuries its chief medium was Latin, an unknown tongue to the masses and one whose vitality was chiefly maintained in books. There was naturally some communication between high and low: the Church, for instance, was not merely the chief preserver of the high culture; she also gave birth to one of the most lively popular arts — the racy and vivid mediaeval sermon. The court poet Chaucer not only forsook Latin or French for the vernacular, but also made use of uproariously coarse folk material in the Miller's and the Reeve's Tales. But though folk culture could and did enrich high culture, movement the other way was limited not merely by illiteracy but also by a purely technical consideration — the scarcity and expensiveness of the manuscript books in which the high culture was preserved.

In neither culture was the economic motive an important incentive to creation. Artists, whether folk or learned, expressed themselves in response to a felt need or as a function of their membership in a community. Literary achievements may have led to social or political advancement, or to the protection of a patron; but almost never to profit derived from the sale of an individual work.

The availability of printed books served the interests of the high culture by both making its further dissemination a physical possibility and providing an incentive for mastering it. However, almost three centuries elapsed before the public demand for books began to press upon the ability of the machine to supply them. Perhaps the earliest publishing venture to experience this pressure was the *Spectator* (1711–12) of Addison and Steele. At the height of its success, this periodical achieved the astonishing daily circulation of three thousand in a nation of five and a half million (Addison estimated the actual readership, perhaps optimistically, at 60,000). But this remarkable accomplishment strained to the maximum the resources available to the publishers. It involved the use of four presses, two different printing houses (on alternate days), and two distinct hand settings of each issue. Nothing more ambitious could have been attempted without complicating intolerably the process of production.

So long as the press was operated by hand, printed matter remained expensive relative to the cost of other commodities, and the printers' and booksellers' costs accounted for most of the proceeds of sale. (Milton received only ten pounds for the manuscript of *Paradise Lost* (1667).) There was little temptation for the writer to seek his fortune by appealing to a large uncritical public. The hack writers satirized in *The Dunciad* (1728–41), Alexander Pope's prophetic attack on commercial literature, were mainly poor, whereas Pope himself became rich through his skill as an expositor of the high culture, a feat which he achieved by merchandizing expensive subscription editions of his work among the great and wealthy.

By the turn of the nineteenth century, however, many of the technical limitations which had hitherto restricted the dissemination of the printed word were overcome: improved presses, cheaper paper, and new methods of distribution such as instalment publication and the lending library all served to meet the demand for reading matter among the increasingly literate, increasingly urban population of England. The later introduction of steam power, newsprint, the rotary press, and the linotype completed the process.

With these developments, the true history of mass culture begins. Until the mid-eighteenth century, the chief functions of print had been to provide a medium for the transmission of the high culture (wherever *folk* culture made contact with the printed word it tended to atrophy: *Pilgrim's Progress* (1678) is the great exception). Success or failure was measured in terms not of sales, but of the approval of "the discerning few" whose judgment alone counted for something. Now, this oligarchy of taste was replaced by an impersonal and heterogeneous reading public. The artist was encouraged to write not to please his patron or his friends, but to exploit a market. Under the circumstances, there could no longer be any universally acknowledged standard of excellence:

in the most economically important sections of the publishing trade, profit and loss became the ultimate criterion of value.

It is significant that this age witnessed the first appearance of three literary types which are now so common that we sometimes forget that they are not characteristic of art generally but of art under capitalism: the lonely misunderstood genius (William Blake, 1757–1827), the best-seller with a formula (Sir Walter Scott, 1771–1832), and the posturing artist who exploits his public personality rather than his art (Lord Byron, 1788–1824). Each of these men possessed superlative talents, and each achieved a limited greatness, but the literary market-place, with its anonymous book-buyers and its lack of living contact between author and reader, was no substitute for the stimulating give and take of the old artistic community. Blake lapsed into angry obscurity (more rewarding, it is true, than the lucidity of lesser men), Scott wrote himself out of bankruptcy by reducing to a formula the feeling for tradition and the historical imagination which give life to his best works, and Byron was content for a while to do little more than exploit his own notoriety very profitably in meretricious verse, though he later proved, in his masterpiece *Don Juan*, that no one was better equipped than he to puncture his own romantic myth. Later on in this chapter, we shall have occasion to consider the similar difficulties and temptations with which the serious modern artist must cope.

One further development was necessary before the popular press could take the form in which we know it today. Late in the nineteenth century it was discovered by those simple-minded geniuses, the pioneer British press barons, that the modest rise in revenue that results from increasing the circulation of a popular magazine or newspaper may be greatly augmented by raising the advertising rates. Thus began the climb of the advertiser to dominance in the world of journalism: since, in the short run, it is he who now pays most of the bills, both writer and reader take second place to him in the publishers' frame of reference. In the *Spectator* of Addison and Steele, small factual and commercial announcements were occasionally inserted to fill up the bits of vacant space at the end of an essay, but a modern popular journal waxes and wanes with the seasonal volume of advertisements. Editorial matter is thus visibly subordinate to advertising — a conclusion that would probably be further confirmed by a comparison of the relative expenditure of time, imagination, and money upon each. (In many periodicals, for instance, colour is used far more lavishly among the advertisements than it is in the text.)

The rise of the advertiser has had a number of important effects upon the attitude of the editor or publisher to his readers. Addison and Steele aimed to reform the society for which they wrote: though they were not indifferent to profit, they measured their achievement mainly in terms of the change in manners and morals which they helped to bring about. Their main income, moreover, was derived from the direct sale of their work to readers. The modern journalist has to operate within a different framework of values. In order to survive today, a periodical must either have a huge general circulation or a smaller "quality" one among members of the executive and professional classes. In each case it is the advertiser who weights the balance between success or failure. In recent years a number of large-circulation periodicals have foundered through lack of advertisement income: among the more spectacular failures have been the American weekly *Collier's* (ceased publication 1952) whose two million subscribers were not enough to tempt advertising dollars away from its rivals the *Post, Life* and television; and the London daily *News Chronicle* which, in 1960, finally gave up the struggle to provide its million readers with a newspaper that was both popular and responsible. Not the readers but the advertisers precipitated these failures. It is difficult not to conclude that the whole profession of popular journalism is at the mercy of the advertising industry. Certainly the *Christian Science Monitor* and the *Daily Worker*s of London and New York are the only English-language exceptions which spring to mind. *PM*, the New York pictorial tabloid, lost millions in the attempt to survive without dependence upon advertising, and finally ceased publication.

This dominance can be detected even at the *New Yorker* where, we are told, the editorial staff regard the advertising department with such disdain that they refuse to share the same telephone number. Though the liberal humanism of the text is in apparent conflict with the plutocratic materialism of the advertisements, nevertheless the *New Yorker* undergoes a seasonal expansion and contraction even more spectacular than that of other journals, and, in the last two-thirds of each issue, the reader has to follow a thin trickle of civilized prose through a wasteland of whisky, jewellery, and undernourished models. What values, then, does the *New Yorker* communicate? Its schizophrenic make-up is an emblem of the paradoxes and dilemmas which confront the critic of the mass media.

Four hundred years after the invention of the first mass medium came the development of the second. The motion picture, even more than the printed book or periodical, is a characteristic artifact of modern technology; its production involves hundreds of complicated mechanical processes and the collaboration of dozens of specialists; the result is the work of no single individual (though a director may impose the stamp of his personality upon a picture) but a product of the interplay between author, producer, director, cameramen, cutter, and actors. It is also more obviously a mass medium than the book or periodical, because it speaks the universal language of pictures. Illiteracy is no bar to the enjoyment of movies, and differences of language can be compensated for by sub-titles or dubbed-in dialogue. The potential audience for the most popular movies makes the circulation of even the largest periodicals look insignificant.

Though the feature-length motion picture does not lend itself to exploitation by the advertiser as the periodical does, its production and distribution usually involve capital outlay on such a scale that only big business (or, more rarely, government) has the resources to back it. Thus, commercial values have always tended to be dominant in the movie world, a state of affairs which is reinforced by the publicity system: films are "plugged" by advertising on a large scale, "fan magazines" glamorize the Hollywood product in general and, in turn, the stars are used to provide a suitable aura for the soap, cars, and cosmetics of the big advertisers. Nevertheless, the cinema has come closer than any of the newer mass media to the production of works which rival the imagination and intelligence of the traditional high culture. Such actors as Chaplin, Garbo, and Jannings and such directors as Griffiths, Eisenstein, and von Stroheim rank among the greatest artists of our time — though it is significant that most of them flourished during the early years of the industry and eventually found themselves in conflict with the entrenched financial interests.

Recently, however, there have been signs of an artistic renaissance in the cinema — not only in the work of Bergman in Sweden or the producers of "La Nouvelle Vague" in France, but also in the quality of the average product of Hollywood or London. Can it be that the motion picture, like the book, has lost its mass audience to rival media, so that producers now find it profitable (especially when the film is made abroad, thousands of miles from the Hollywood trades unions) to cultivate a discriminating public who are willing to pay more for better movies?

Hardly a decade after the earliest movie classics had reached the screen, the first radio broadcasting stations began to experiment with regular programme schedules. Books, periodicals, and motion pictures make use of media (paper, film) which are theoretically unlimited: any man has the right (though seldom the means) to found a newspaper, publish a book, or produce a movie. In exercising this right he will not (in theory) impede the freedom of anyone else to enter into the same field of activity. But radio makes use of a medium that is inherently limited — the spectrum of radio waves. Only a few broadcast frequencies are available to would-be operators in any geographic region.

For this reason radio has always operated under the control of a government agency. The airwaves are conceived to belong to everyone, and the holder of a broadcasting licence enjoys a privilege under the public trust, one that can be suspended or revoked if he does not offer a satisfactory service.

"Freedom of the air" thus implies a different set of conventions from "freedom of the press." Tradition demands that a newspaper shall print a representative selection of the news without undue bias, but permits complete liberty of comment on editorial pages and in signed columns of opinion. Because the reader is theoretically free to read the paper of his choice, there is little effective pressure upon the editor to cater to all tastes, and any kind of governmental control of content is regarded with horror. But the monopoly position of a radio station implies an obligation to offer a "balanced" selection of opinions on controversial issues and a wide variety of programmes to meet the interests of a diversified audience.

The awareness of this obligation helped shape the policies of those who controlled the destiny of radio during the 1920's. In Britain the austere Sir John (later Lord) Reith deliberately conceived of the BBC as an institution which, while offering a wide variety of programmes, would gradually raise the level of taste and enhance the quality of public discussion. In the United States, though no public corporation such as the BBC was established, the manufacturers of radio equipment realized that the future of radio was dependent upon the kind and quality of programmes presented. In 1922, the Radio Corporation of America established the National Broadcasting Company for the sole purpose of producing network programmes of sufficient calibre to induce the public to purchase receiving sets. It is hard to recapture in 1961 the spirit of idealism in which the enterprise was undertaken. As David Sarnoff conceived it, NBC was to be financed by an annual percentage of the gross income of manufacturers of radio equipment. He hoped that it would "ultimately be regarded as a public institution of great value in the same sense that a library . . . is today." He wanted the company to be removed from "the atmosphere of being a commercial institution." This laudable sentiment helped to shape at least the overt policy of NBC and its competitors until the onset of the depression: as late as 1929, the "Standards of Commercial Practice" of the National Association of Broadcasters barred commercial announcements between the hours of seven and eleven in the evening.

There is no need to document the betrayal of these early principles. When the stock market crash siphoned off the high profits upon which such admirable intentions had been based, the commercial motive, hitherto suppressed, was allowed to develop without hindrance. Though the networks continued to pay lip-service to the idea of their role as a public trust (and implemented it in the maintenance of excellent news services, symphony orchestras and "sustaining" features), the control and production of their most popular programmes gradually shifted from their own hands into those of the advertising agencies. The level of what was considered to be tolerable or in good taste might range from the interminable succession of strident spot announcements on the independent local stations to the unctuously "soft sells" of the network sponsor, but commerce reigned supreme and unchallenged in all but a minority of American radio stations. "Public service," educational, and "cultural" programmes continued to be produced, but were scheduled at inconvenient hours on days when the listening audience was comparatively small. The logical consequence of such a mad pursuit of the mass audience was that those whose tastes were adjusted to the current fashions were fantastically over-provided for, while those who remained stubbornly deviant were virtually ignored. Thus, in many a large North American city one can hear news snippets as often as forty times a day and the top tunes on the hit parade seven or eight times each, but one will be lucky to get so much as an hour even of "light" classical music.

The rapid development of television after the end of the Second World War led to a situation which parodied or caricatured the pattern established in radio. Since production costs were so high and the competition for viewers was so great, the networks found themselves in a very weak position in relation to the commercial sponsors. As a result they were forced to cut down on such non-revenue-producing "prestige" symbols as symphony orchestras at the same time as they had to tolerate programmes of an insipidity and commercials of a vulgarity that radio even at its worst had not perpetrated. Nor was this development confined to the frankly commercial broadcasting system of the United States: in Britain, the BBC monopoly in television was broken to admit the "competition" of the profit-oriented ITV, and, in Canada, the CBC was apparently forced to lower drastically the standards of good taste which had hitherto been maintained in radio.

The final degradation of American radio and television was revealed in the great quiz programme scandals of 1959 and the ensuing investigations of "payola" among disc jockeys and popular recording artists. It is still too early to predict whether the commercial networks will be capable, without official pressure from outside, of eradicating such flagrant dishonesty; but it is safe to assume that such reforms as are affected will be chiefly negative in their implications. The pursuit of high Hooper and Trendex ratings is inconsistent with any real, positive standard of excellence.

The history of the mass media, thus briefly epitomized, has shown that they are, in essence, characteristic expressions of modern industrialism and, in the West, of the capitalistic system. When unhampered by regulation, they exhibit two complementary tendencies: an attempt to create the largest possible "market" (i.e., audience) for the products of press, microphone, or camera; and the progressive subordination of all motives for expression to the pursuit of profit, maximized by whatever means are possible. The great debate which rages about the media today resolves itself into the question of whether these characteristics are inherent — in which case we should have to regard the media as an almost unmitigated evil — or whether, through the exercise of wise public or private policy, it is possible to make them vehicles for genuinely intelligent and creative expression. This is still an open question, to which only history will provide the answer. (The anthology of articles *Mass Culture*, published in 1957 by the Free Press of Glencoe, Ill., contains a bewildering variety of opinions.) In the meantime, public policy must be based upon such incomplete evidence as we have. There is no time to wait and see. Complete laissez-faire in the field of communications would be as unthinkable as it now is in the realm of economic activity.

We can dismiss immediately any theory which condemns the media and their products as beyond hope of reform or improvement. Like any other technological phenomena, they are morally neutral until put to use. Nor would it be rational to deplore something which has brought so much simple pleasure to millions of people — something without which the institutions of the modern state could hardly function. Nevertheless, though the media are the indispensable means whereby information, ideas, and values may be transmitted in a mass society, there are problems inherent in their very nature which go beyond what can be accomplished by mere political or administrative reform.

To begin with, the mass culture fostered by the media tends to be both parasitic upon and destructive of the older cultures, high and folk. Artistic — and even intellectual — creativity flourishes best when there is a close and subtle communion between the creator and his public (however small it may be): in Arnold's famous formulation, the intellectual situation of which creative power can profitably avail itself is made up of two factors, the *power of the man* and the *power of the moment*. In other words, there must be a stimulating flow of ideas and energy in both directions before art can be precipitated.

It is precisely this kind of give and take that is difficult if not impossible to achieve in the media. The technical advances upon which mass communication is based have enormously extended the range of the creator's voice, but have done almost nothing to assist the reciprocal response of the listener. In consequence, the creation of mass art takes place in a partial vacuum: Trendex ratings, readership surveys, and ABC statistics are poor substitutes for the Elizabethan play house, the Athenian agora or the Parisian salon. Furthermore, the audience of the mass communicator is measured not in hundreds or thousands but in tens of millions of every degree of education or social class, perhaps scattered across five continents and even divided by differences of language. What image of his twelve million readers can the editor of the world-wide *Reader's Digest* have? What are the shared values of the enormous audience who will have to lay down the price of admission before *Ben Hur* shows a profit? No satisfactory answer to these questions can be given beyond the limited empirical evidence of sales and box office receipts. Thus, it is almost an adequate definition of mass culture to say that it is a form of culture in which a small, centralized cadre of active producers serves a larger and highly diversified body of consumers whose role in the process is almost entirely passive.

This one-sided relationship helps to account for the tendency of the mass media to exploit the material of other cultural traditions rather than to create vital new forms of their own. At best, in such straightforward transmutations as *Life's* reproductions of classic art, the Moyseyev Ballet on the Ed Sullivan Show, or the broadcasts of symphony concerts, the result is a much wider audience for an already achieved perfection. At their more usual worst, however, the media batten upon a living source of art and reduce its elements to a mechanical and repetitive sterility. A striking example of this is the sad history of jazz and the blues from the great early creative tradition centring on New Orleans and Chicago to the sorry stereotyped formula of Tin Pan Alley and the Hit Parade. The current craze for Rock 'n' Roll is based upon a vulgarization of real jazz, but its very popularity paradoxically adds to the professional difficulties of those whose creative achievement made the perversion possible.

In fact, the artist is the chief victim of the media. He is naturally anxious to communicate with as wide a public as is consistent with integrity and, like other men, he is not averse to maintaining a comfortable standard of living. Too often today, however, he is forced to choose between the obscurity and poverty of art, and the wealth and fame of *kitsch*. Ernst van den Haag contrasts the distractions which beset the modern artist with the comparative sureness of purpose of his ancestors. Dante, he observes, was not tempted to make *The Divine Comedy* a best-seller by calling it *Florence Confidential* (the poem circulated only in manuscript); no one tried to get him to condense it for *Reader's Digest* or offered him fat fees for a *Holiday* piece on the Guelphs and the Ghibbelines. So far as his art was concerned, Dante was miraculously free from the invidious and extraneous motives to creation which plague the modern writer. And even today, Dante continues to enjoy the advantage. His masterpiece, being a Classic and a Sure Thing, as well as in the public domain, can now be issued in large, cheap paper-bound editions, but the works of young contemporary writers are often not printed, because publishers in search of the mass market find it is too difficult and expensive to take a chance on a young and unknown writer.

(The mention of paper-bound books calls for an explanatory aside. Though the hard-cover book no longer qualifies as an instrument of mass communication, the paperback certainly does. The rise of the quality paper-back has been hailed as a major victory for intelligence and taste in the modern world. So it is for the consumer, and no regular book buyer would wish to return to the days before the revolution. Nevertheless, the reader's gain has been at the expense of the conventional bookseller — still an indispensable member of society — and the contemporary author. Paper-backs favour the dead or established writer, especially one of sound academic reputation; they are notoriously weak in current poetry except for anthologies or the collected works of a few fashionable poets; the combination of long runs and low royalties makes them an unsuitable medium for a young author, who must therefore compete in expensive hard covers with his elders and betters in inexpensive soft ones. Thus, the paper-back, like the other mass media, tends to capitalize on past achievements rather than to foster creative work in the present.)

Nevertheless, it would be wrong to end this survey on a negative note. Though excessive optimism about the future of the media would obviously be out of place in view of the problems we have been discussing, there has been achievement in the past and there is still room for creative action to improve upon their present level of performance. Nothing can equal the media as a means of disseminating information or conveying a sense of the surface texture of life. Though their value as a medium of education has perhaps been exaggerated in some quarters, few societies have even begun to exploit such potentialities as are manifestly within the realm of the possible. Finally, though the essence of true artistic expression may be ultimately beyond the range of the media, there are obvious distinctions to be made between the popular art which exploits violence and sex mostly as an escape from frustration and boredom, and that which, however crudely and journalistically, tries to give modern man a meaningful image of himself and his problems. Few human beings today are able to resist the manifold blandishments of the media; neither the most supercilious academic nor the most austere intellectual can easily ignore them. We owe it to ourselves not to allow the exploiters to debase the standards any further.

THE CANADIAN SCENE

As a nation, Canada represents the triumph of communications over geography. From coast to coast there are far fewer natural barriers between Canada and the United States to the south than there are between the regions of our own country, and the idea of a nation in which 90 per cent of the population live in a strip three thousand miles long by just over a hundred miles wide is, at first thought, absurd. When one adds to the geographical difficulties the further complications of racial tradition and language, then the absurdity comes almost to seem an impossibility.

Without the new media of communications, a united Canada would today be an impossibility. The country was first brought together by railroads, and now has airlines and the almost completed Trans-Canada Highway, but the most important links today are probably such institutions as the Canadian Press, the popular national periodicals, the Canadian Broadcasting Corporation, and the National Film Board. Canada is, perhaps, unique among modern states in this respect. Paradoxically she is also unique in her degree of exposure to the communications media of her powerful neighbour: most Canadians live within range of, and often prefer to watch, American television stations; more Canadians read American periodicals than read Canadian ones; American and (to a lesser extent) British feature-length films form virtually the only fare at most Canadian movie theatres; public opinion polls show that western Canadians often share more views with their neighbours to the immediate south than they do with their fellow-countrymen in the east. No Canadian government could be indifferent or complacent about these facts. It is communications, from the Last Spike to the micro-wave relay, that have fostered such unity as we have and it is the control and direction of communications that will prevent our geographical absurdity from becoming a gigantic relay station for the dissemination of American mass culture.

A survey of the institutions of mass communication in Canada should begin with the press, the earliest and still the most influential medium in the formation of intelligent opinion. The Canadian newspaper, in particular, tends to be an intransigently local institution (unlike its British counterparts) and enjoys a consequently close relationship with its readers and a comparative freedom from foreign economic or ideological entanglements.

Nevertheless the daily press of Canada presents an almost insoluble problem to the radical reformer. Newspapers in Canada as elsewhere are published first and foremost to make money, partly through receipts from newsstands, but chiefly through revenue derived from the sale of advertising space. When, after the Second World War, the Winnipeg *Citizen* was founded as a newspaper sympathetic to labour, it could not compete for advertising with the established papers and soon folded. *Le Devoir* alone survives as a newspaper devoted to principle rather than profit. But this has been accomplished only through the contributions of a small but devoted band of readers, the willingness of the staff to work for low salaries, and — ironic for a pro-labour newspaper — the payment of wages below the going scale. Even these measures have failed to avert periodic crises: as this chapter is being written the editor is warning his readers that *Le Devoir* cannot long continue to publish unless some new means of support is found.

The conclusion to be drawn from this evidence appears to be that the public for serious political discussion and solid information is severely limited, and newspapers which aim for a large enough readership to pay their way must compete with the popular press on its own terms. Even newspapers which are published by non-profit-making trusts have had to adjust their editorial policies to the prevailing idea of what a newspaper should be like. When ABC rating and readership surveys are of such influence in the apportionment of the advertising dollar no trust without unlimited funds can afford to ignore them.

If newspapers whose primary interest is not profit are nevertheless forced to sacrifice some of their objectives in order to succeed in the competition for advertising, it is hardly surprising that their commercially motivated rivals conform even more closely to the classic patterns of capitalistic development in our time. In particular, the Canadian newspaper industry shows strong tendencies towards monopoly, concentration of ownership, and standardization of content: about each of these trends the serious-minded reader may well have qualms.

During the past fifty years the total circulation of Canadian newspapers has risen sharply, but the number of individual dailies has dramatically declined. The *Star-Phoenix*es, *Globe and Mail*s, and *Chronicle-Telegraph*s of Canada are bizarre memorials of one-time competitors now joined in corporate togetherness. It is a lucky Canadian city (and, inevitably, a large one) which now offers its citizens the choice of more than one morning and one evening daily to read. Have they then a real opportunity to examine a variety of opinions on issues of the day?

A related tendency has been the formation of newspaper chains. Canada has not yet produced a press tycoon on the flamboyant scale of a Northcliffe or a Hearst, though she has exported Lord Beaverbrook and Mr. Roy Thompson, exotic specimens of the breed, to Great Britain where they have bloomed luxuriantly. Nevertheless, three chains — the Southam, Sifton, and Thompson interests — control between them two-thirds of the newspapers published in this country. This fact appears, in practice, to make little difference so far as quality or editorial policy is concerned. There is no clear evidence that the chains suppress or distort the news (which is not to suggest that this does not sometimes happen), the chain papers are not demonstrably inferior to the general run of Canadian dailies, and the Sifton and Thompson groups allow their editors freedom of comment — although one might complain that they do not seem to take any great creative advantage of this right.

A more immediately serious charge against the ownership of Canadian newspapers is that, chains or not, they all belong to and therefore ultimately reflect the values of very much the same kind of people. If variety of viewpoints, frank discussion, and balanced presentation of controversial news is desirable in a newspaper, then the business-oriented press of Canada does a poor job. Not all Canadian newspapers suppress the facts and withhold comment so unashamedly as the *Star* and *Gazette* of Montreal did during the Duplessis régime, but the complaints of union officials, radical politicians, and government anti-trust lawyers that the press seldom presents their cases so fully and clearly as it does those of their opponents are certainly justified. No conspiratorial theory is necessary to explain this state of affairs: when the whole world of journalism is dominated by businessman-proprietors, it is natural that many of those who make the profession their life-work will be men who share the same beliefs and prejudices or who are willing to conform to the implicit bias of their employers. Indeed, the business ethos is so ubiquitous that its assumptions pervade the sports section, the book and theatre reviews (when there are any), and even the Saturday religious page (see Norman Vincent Peale). Could one really gather from reading a typical Canadian newspaper that there is any rational alternative to the economic and political status quo? Radical criticisms of capitalist institutions are invariably ignored, parodied, or distorted to the point where serious discussion of them becomes impossible.

The modern newspaper is becoming increasingly standardized in form and content. This tendency manifests itself in many ways: the use by the chains of single correspondents in important centres to serve all member papers, the development of such news agencies as the Canadian Press and its foreign competitors and equivalents, the use of nationally stereotyped advertising material, and an ever greater reliance upon syndicated features. Most of these trends are inevitable, and some are desirable, though it cannot be denied that they detract from the newspaper's character as a local institution; nor can there ever be a real substitute for the reporter with a keen sense of the local issues important to his readers, whether his beat be another country, Ottawa, the provincial capital, or the municipal police headquarters.

The most obvious example of journalistic standardization in Canada is the service of the Canadian Press which supplies nearly a hundred co-operating member papers with most of their news. In addition to transmitting dispatches which originate in the news rooms of members (and are therefore subject to the selectivity and bias we have already noted), the Canadian Press maintains a corps of correspondents in the major Canadian news centres at home and abroad. For news without a specifically Canadian reference, however, most of our newspapers are almost totally dependent upon such foreign agencies as the Associated Press or United Press International of the United States or Reuter's of Great Britain. This is an unhealthy state of affairs. Though the news of the Canadian Press may impose a kind of uniformity upon papers from coast to coast, at least it is standardized to conform with some idea of the interests of the average Canadian. But the foreign agencies exist primarily to serve their own domestic clients; they may even be quasi-official instruments of the government. The principles upon which they select and interpret the news may be very different from those which would govern an organization serving the Canadian public. Obvious examples of situations where distortion might be feared are American reports on Formosa or British dispatches from Nyasaland or Cyprus. If Canada is to play a creative and independent role in world affairs, the public which ultimately determines foreign policy must surely cease to be dependent upon news sources which tend to assume, consciously or unconsciously, that American (or British, or French) interests are paramount when it comes to assessing significance. There is a clear case for greatly extending the international coverage of the Canadian Press, and no reason for believing the ad-rich Canadian newspapers would find the extra cost an intolerable burden.

A more spectacular but less defensible example of the trend towards standardization of newspaper content is the increasing use of syndicated features. It is tempting but would be unprofitable to dwell upon the bizarre variety of syndicated material available, from Walter Lippmann to "Li'l Orphan Annie," from Fulton J. Sheen to Old Doc Brady. With a very few exceptions — the better American columnists and a few comic strips are examples — such features serve to trivialize newspaper content, replacing solid information with gossip, half-baked "advice," and harmless amusement. Yet the popularity of most syndicated features is attested to by the cries of protest which arise from newspaper readers when, for any unexplained reason, their favourite column or strip does not appear. It is perhaps an additionally objectionable fact that most such features originate in the United States, but one is permitted to doubt whether mass-produced Canadian triviality would be inherently more desirable than the American product.

What can be done to improve the quality of our newspapers? The first answer to this question might well be that, granted the nature of the mass public, they are already better than one has any right to expect. Our newspapers probably print more straight news and serious political comment than all but a tiny minority of their readers require. But they are in business for profit, and what sells papers today is less news than features. An important sign of the times is the recent change in the format of Lord Beaverbrook's London *Daily Express* (circulation 4,175,000): the odd-numbered inside pages — always considered the most widely read parts of a newspaper, apart from the front page — are now entirely devoted to amusement, gossip, and personalities. The *Express* is now not so much a newspaper as a fun paper.

No Canadian daily has come even close to emulating the *Express,* but the recent history of a great Canadian newspaper (which shall remain nameless since its story is intended to be exemplary) may illustrate the pressures to which the publishers are gradually succumbing. Twenty years ago, this paper enjoyed a very modest circulation, but aspired (perhaps still does aspire) to fulfil the functions of a national quality newspaper, required reading for M.P.'s, senior civil servants and others concerned with the high-level management of Canadian affairs. Though not everyone took this claim seriously, the editors certainly did: the makeup was tasteful and chaste, the normal news agencies were supplemented by the service of a great American daily, and the text was almost entirely devoted to the traditional interests of a serious newspaper.

The circulation of this paper is now over three times its pre-war level, but it would be wrong to conclude that it is three times better than it used to be. The news coverage remains more or less what it always was, but is almost lost among the columns of local and syndicated feature material. There is a full page of comic strips, a fatuous gossip column, a malicious and faintly libellous New York column, a greatly expanded women's section (complete with advice on every conceivable kind of feminine disaster), a teen-age page and, periodically upsetting the queasy-stomached breakfaster, large, bilious coloured illustrations on the once austerely monochromatic front page. What remains of the original high purpose seems now to rest not upon the present basis of the paper's prosperity but upon a tradition inherited from the past. How long can a newspaper sustain two such divergent editorial aims?

There are some who believe that the solution to the problem of the press lies in government intervention either through the establishment of subsidized newspapers to be published by politically independent Crown corporations, or, as has been suggested, through the preparation by a publicly supported bureau of two or three pages daily of "straight" news which all Canadian newspapers would be compelled to carry. Both these measures would be violently opposed not only by the newspaper publishers but also by a significant majority of the politically conscious public, and it is doubtful whether the expected benefits of either plan would outweigh the ill-will and suspicion that it would certainly engender. The principle of freedom of the press is now so deeply established in our political tradition that not many of us are willing to sacrifice it even when the freedom is abused by plutocratic publishers and sensation-mongering editors.

Nevertheless, there is an obvious distinction between liberty of the press and licence, and the laws of libel are hardly sufficient to enforce it. The profession of journalism has no governing body to establish minimum standards of accuracy and objectivity or to promote higher standards of achievement. There would appear to be a need in Canada for a publicly chartered General Press Council with representation from education, labour, and all elements of the public at large, as well as from publishers and working journalists. Though a function of the Council would be to scrutinize the press and to investigate complaints about malpractice, its major task would be the positive one of raising standards, perhaps through the formulation of codes of ethics, the establishment of journalistic scholarships and fellowships, and the institution of a series of awards for outstanding achievement. Under the circumstances, the Council could hardly be vested with any specific power over the press, nor would it be realistic to expect that its rebukes would be either strongly expressed or greatly heeded by the offenders. In a modest way, however, it would exercise considerable moral authority of a negative kind, and would at least provide a forum for the airing of grievances and abuses for which at present there is no provision.

The daily press of Canada is relatively free from one threat, that of foreign competition: those Canadians at either end of the intellectual scale who regularly read the *New York Times* or the *Daily News* constitute an infinitesimal percentage of the public. By contrast, our magazine publishers are engaged in a desperate and losing battle for circulation against their American rivals. So far, no Canadian government has found an acceptable means to implement its desire to help them in their unequal struggle, though the Royal Commission on Publications (1960) may recommend some measures. There is clearly a case to be made for the contention that the Canadian editions of American magazines constitute unfair competition and are indeed a form of journalistic "dumping." Is there any other solution to this problem, though, than the discriminatory 20 per cent tax on the advertising revenues of such editions which was repealed by the Conservative government after the Liberals had imposed it in 1956?

In spite of one's sympathy with the Canadian publisher's plight, there appears to be no means of helping him that would not restrict the flow into Canada of many periodicals which have no Canadian equivalents and which are essential reading for alert and informed people all over the world. After all, competition is keenest at the level of the mass-circulation popular magazines, and few of us can feel the extreme urgency of defending *Liberty* or *Weekend* from their foreign rivals.

A much more urgent task is to revitalize the moribund intellectual and controversial press of Canada. A nation can tolerate a good deal of cheap and superficial journalism so long as there exist a few periodicals in which those who are interested may participate, directly or vicariously, in the intelligent and informed discussion of public affairs. To Canada's intellectual disgrace, we do not possess in the English language a single journal of this kind. Scholarly and literary quarterlies we now have in plenty, but the poor old *Canadian Forum* (once a mighty power in the land) is perhaps the only publication in existence which could conceivably fulfil this role. Unfortunately the *Forum* has for some years been deprived of the private subsidy which once took care of its deficit, and all the gallant efforts of its volunteer staff have been insufficient to compensate for the consequent loss in both size and editorial initiative. In 1960, the Canada Council turned down a request from the *Forum* for a grant to finance a subscription campaign, on the strange grounds that it was a journal of opinion. Yet surely one of the objects of the Canada Council is to raise the level of informed opinion in this country. Far from refusing their applications, the Council should welcome appeals from journals of the most diverse views. A healthy minority press of this kind would be the cheapest, surest, and most liberal remedy for the lack of real controversy in the journals of mass circulation. (It is good to see that the President of the Canada Council has recently announced that the Council would like to help a periodical which falls somewhere between the scholarly journals and the little magazines.)

Of all the media, the motion picture comes closest to rivalling the achievements of classic art. This is especially true when the circumstances of production make it possible for the director to cater to something less than the total mass audience. Thus a comparatively small percentage of the four hundred features which Hollywood used to turn out annually were worth serious critical consideration because the prospect of huge profits, the pressure of distributing chains, and the inflated salaries of stars made exploitation of the largest possible audience an economic necessity (the movie tycoons accepted Mencken's dictum: "Nobody ever lost money underestimating the intelligence of the American people"). Meanwhile, in Sweden, Italy, France and other countries where the same economic pressures did not exist, profitable films could be made for a world-wide minority audience. With far fewer resources than Hollywood the film industries of these countries have produced a much higher proportion of classic films; as recently as 1960, the movie critics of New York placed only two Hollywood productions among the ten best for the year. Now, however, that the motion picture industry has had to take second place to television, we have reason to hope that the new, smaller and more discriminating cinema audience will find North American producers willing to cater to it. That is where the opportunity for Canadian film makers may lie.

Canada's achievement in the production of feature films is inferior to that of almost any nation of comparable size and resources. This is, in part, owing to her proximity to the United States. But even when the rare full-length feature is produced in Canada, there is often difficulty in achieving distribution through the foreign-controlled theatre chains.

Fortunately, an enlightened government policy over some thirty years has ensured that our lack of distinction in this respect should be compensated for by an acknowledged pre-eminence in the field of documentary films. The achievements of the National Film Board and of the co-operating independent producers amount to the one completely satisfactory element in the whole complex of the mass media in Canada. One can only wish that it were possible to achieve a wider distribution of their films in those large eastern metropolises where the bulk of the population lives.

Nevertheless, documentaries are no substitute for feature films, any more than journalism is a substitute for art. In the context of modern society, Canadian culture will always be incomplete as long as we do not produce films which embody an imaginative vision of Canadian life and history on the largest scale. The technical skill and the facilities for this kind of production already exist, but capital and guaranteed theatre outlets are lacking. If we wish to establish a feature film industry in Canada, then the only answer is government backing in the form of guaranteed loans to producers, reinforced by a quota system whereby a set proportion of the films exhibited annually in each cinema must be of Canadian origin. The immediate result would not be the production of masterpieces — one remembers the "quota quickies" which plagued British audiences before the war — but there is no other way to build the foundation of experience upon which a successful industry would have to be based. Just as the execrable British films of the thirties led to the classic achievements of the forties and fifties, so the Canadian horrors of the sixties might be the forerunners of films which would make us pre-eminent not merely in the minor craft of documentary but in every branch of cinematic art.

The history of radio and television in Canada, and particularly of the Canadian Broadcasting Corporation, has already been adequately sketched in the reports of the three royal commissions which have concerned themselves with broadcasting policy. It is sufficient for us to note that up until the advent of television the almost unique Canadian combination of private and public, commercial and non-commercial broadcasting under the control of the CBC was, by general agreement, an extremely successful arrangement. Though the Tory press, the Canadian Association of Broadcasters (now the Canadian Association of Radio and Television Broadcasters), and the professional anti-intellectuals blew sour notes, the Massey Commission (1951) found that the great majority of the 170 organizations who discussed broadcasting in their briefs approved of the existing system. Such criticism as there was, was mainly devoted to means of raising intellectual and artistic standards and reducing the volume of commercially sponsored programming.

The recommendations of the Massey Commission with regard to broadcasting were designed to strengthen the CBC's position as a ruling body vis-à-vis the private operators, to provide adequate financial resources to maintain an expanded and improved radio service, and to lay the foundations for a national television network under the control of the CBC. There could hardly have been a more complete vindication of the CBC's conception of its role. Unfortunately, however, this was not to be the last investigation of the CBC is this decade: one of the recommendations of the Massey Report was that a new commission be appointed to inquire into broadcasting, three years after the inauguration of a television service.

The Fowler Commission Report (1957) was awaited with some trepidation by defenders of the status quo in Canadian broadcasting. The establishment of television had inevitably been attended by a good deal of carping criticism (some of it just), the cost of the service turned out to be even higher than had been expected, and, finally, the CBC, as a public corporation closely identified with the government in the common mind, came in for a major share of the resentment of an electorate growing restive after years of Liberal power. These fears were to a certain degree allayed when the Report appeared. Though the Commission yielded to CARTB pressure and recommended that the regulatory powers of the CBC Board be vested in a new body, the Board of Broadcast Governors, the Report as a whole was extremely favourable to the CBC and critical of both the tactics and the broadcasting performance of the private stations. For a moment, it looked as though the CBC had been vindicated once and for all, and that the corporation's role as the guarantor of the highest possible standards was now universally admitted.

But this was not to be. In a number of ways, the Fowler Report did undermine the CBC's position. The establishment of the BBG struck a psychological blow at the Corporation's sense of moral authority and purpose even though the Board's decisions have so far been unexceptionably favourable to CBC policy. Instead of being the one officially designated instrument of broadcasting policy, the CBC now finds itself merely the first among competing equals. That this was, in part, the intention of the Commission is suggested by the Report's injunction that the CBC ought to compete more aggressively for advertising revenue against her privately owned rivals. It did not seem to occur to the commissioners that competition of this kind among the mass media leads inevitably (as we have seen) to a deadening similarity of broadcast fare.

Almost simultaneously with the implementation of the Fowler recommendations, the CBC went through a triple crisis, the causes of which were not, of course, unrelated to the sense of uncertainty engendered by the Commission's activities: at CBC headquarters the resignation of the chairman and the illness of his successor, in Montreal a bitter and costly

strike of producers, and in Ottawa a wrangle about government interference with news commentaries which culminated in an inconclusive
and sterile but extremely acrid investigation by the House of Commons
Committee on Broadcasting (1959). As a result of all these circumstances morale at the CBC probably reached the lowest point in its
history, and the strong sense of purpose which had hitherto motivated
its planning and production staff seemed to be in danger of failing.
Though there are signs that the Corporation is regaining its nerve, it
might well be a major priority of any socialist government to restore
the CBC Board to its old role as arbiter of the national broadcasting
system, and certainly to encourage the Corporation to adopt the most
creative and adventurous policy possible. It will be convenient for us to
elaborate some of the details of this policy by considering in turn the
operations of radio and television.

The development of television has dramatically altered the role of
radio in the modern community. During the evening hours when the
biggest and most popular radio programmes used to be presented, the
eyes of the mass audience are now glued to their television sets. Radio
has responded to this situation by directing its appeal to specialized and
minority audiences and by concentrating on those daylight hours when
potential listeners are less likely to be free to succumb to the blandishments of TV.

On the private commercial stations, this means that the early morning
hours are devoted to hearty waker-uppers, mid-morning and early after-
noon to the wooing of housewives by silken-voiced agents of the super-
markets, mid-afternoon to teen-agers, the supper hour to commuting
suburban drivers, and the evening to lovers and other refugees from the
living-room TV. Throughout the broadcast day the schedule is spiced
with as many commercial announcements as sales and regulations make
possible, news every hour on the hour (delivered in a voice pregnant
with impending doom), competitions designed to bribe listeners into
remaining tuned in, and the idiot repetition of the top twenty record-
ings on the current hit parade. This description could probably be
applied without serious exception to 90 per cent of the private radio
stations in Canada.

It was with radio operated on these principles that the Fowler Commission advised CBC-owned stations to compete for advertising. The
results, in those instances where the advice has been partly put into effect,
have been unfortunate. Since the development of television, the obvious
function of CBC radio has been to cater to those large minorities who
are adequately served by neither television nor private radio — music
lovers, citizens seeking the intelligent discussion of public and international affairs, adults anxious to further their education, intellectuals,
lovers of the arts and sciences. It is precisely in this area that the CBC

has traditionally done a superlative job — and still does — but a return to sponsorship or even to spot commercials on any large scale would, in the present state of radio, seriously undermine that achievement. As it is, such locally sponsored programmes as have appeared on at least one major CBC station have rivalled the worst efforts of the private stations in bad taste and stupidity, and even broadcasts of classical music have been interspersed with singing commercials. There is surely no reason for the CBC to cater to tastes which are already sufficiently gratified on private radio, and a wise protection against this danger might be to outlaw commercials completely on CBC radio. The loss of income in relation to the CBC's budget would be negligible (less than 10 per cent of the total expenditure on CBC radio in 1959).

The CBC news and public affairs service probably constitutes the most objective and unbiased source of information and opinion in Canada. As was suggested earlier, it is the existence of alternatives such as this which makes the business orientation of the press less serious than it might otherwise be. There is thus every reason for building up the news-gathering services of the CBC. Since the demands of television make it necessary to maintain crews of cameramen and commentators, the Corporation is already less dependent than it used to be upon the dispatches of the Canadian Press and other agencies. It is time to turn this necessity into a virtue and to establish CBC News on a scale comparable to that of the BBC or the large American networks.

Few daily newspapers are genuinely interested in controversy; conflicting viewpoints are seldom given equal prominence, and "Letters to the Editor" columns infrequently rise above the level of the trivial or the eccentric. Radio, however, must be controversial: the principle of freedom of the air demands either that there shall be no expression of opinion (a virtual impossibility) or that all viewpoints shall be represented. The CBC has long recognized and accepted this responsibility, but the election of the Conservative government in 1957, coinciding as it did with resignations and reorganization at the highest management levels, led to a number of unpleasant incidents the cumulative effect of which seemed to have been to instil an unhealthy spirit of caution among the senior officials of the Corporation. Some producers offered to resign rather than emasculate their public affairs programmes, but the CBC as a whole seems at present to be possessed with a fear of offending those in high places, and too ready to apologize for performing its duty to the public.

A major concern of any government should therefore be to restore the confidence of CBC management in the Corporation's role as a medium of controversy and debate on every aspect of public affairs. On radio especially, now that the majority audience is catered for by both television and the private stations, there is no need to sugar the pill of knowledge or to talk down to listeners. A witty participant in a CBC panel show once remarked that in Canada one is permitted only to be serious about trivial matters or trivial about serious matters. There is some truth in this gibe. Apart from the comparatively "safe" topics debated on "Citizens' Forum" and "Farm Radio Forum," the chief vehicles for controversy on CBC are such panel shows as "Fighting Words" and "Court of Opinion" but the impromptu discussion, the limited time, the choice of "characters" rather than authorities as participants and the absence of agreed terms of reference often preclude the possibility of reaching dangerous conclusions.

Almost the opposite fault can be attributed to the party political broadcasts on both radio and television. Although, as is well known, the campaigns of the two largest parties rely heavily upon the assistance of two rival advertising agencies, there has been little evidence of this in the amateurish and often frankly boring broadcasts on such programmes as "The Nation's Business" or "Provincial Affairs." It is obviously undesirable that Canadian politics (unlike those of the United States) should acquire a reputation for dullness and mediocrity; it would be equally unfortunate if the agencies were to take over and to merchandise party programmes and personalities as they do soap and beer. The wise solution would be for the CBC to establish a production advisory staff to handle party broadcasts. This would ensure professional standards of presentation without a descent to slickness or banality. It would also mean that all parties would enjoy equally the kind of expert advice and assistance that is now within the means only of the wealthier parties. The need for this reform is urgent if the mass media are ever adequately to fill the gap left in our system of political communication by the decline of the old-time public meeting.

After every possible criticism has been made, CBC radio remains a remarkable institution, an indispensable agent in the formation of enlightened public opinion, a patron of the arts (about which, perhaps, there should be more in this chapter) and a stimulus to local creativity in a dozen cities from coast to coast. If it always stayed true to its own best traditions there would, in fact, be nothing for the critic to carp at.

The same, however, cannot be said of CBC television. In spite of some remarkable achievements, television in Canada is far less daring, exciting, and creative than radio has ever been. The reasons are complex, but not hard to grasp. The prime difficulty with Canadian television, as with Canadian cinema, is our proximity to the United States. Since so many Canadians had already become addicts of American television before a single station was in operation on this side of the border, the CBC was subject to an almost irresistible pressure to establish a service which incorporated many aspects of the American system. Of course, no Canadian television network could function without a high proportion of American programmes, but it was not necessary to imitate some practices which are irrelevant to the Canadian situation.

As we have seen, the high cost of television production has led, in the United States to the dominance of the sponsor over the networks, and the consequent subordination of all other motives for broadcasting to that of profit. Hence the frenzied competition for the largest possible audience at each hour of the day, the senseless reduplication of "successful" programme formulas such as the western or the police adventure series, the scheduling of rival "spectaculars" on different networks at the same time, the rigid packaging of minutes and hours in standardized programme lots, and a dozen other practices which serve, not the public interest, but that of the large corporations competing for the mass market.

Regardless of the merits or demerits of such a system, it is an inappropriate model for Canadian television. In this country, we lack an audience big enough to justify the expenditures of lavish sums in the hope of commercial return. It is unlikely that any national television network in French or English will ever become economically self-sufficient. Even now when the new competing private stations authorized by the BBG have begun operating, millions of Canadians continue to be dependent upon a single television outlet. There is thus every reason why CBC-TV should not be simply one more North American network with slightly fewer commercials and more unsponsored features than the average, but a completely different type of service designed to suit the needs of a national society with unique problems.

Perhaps the most important difference between the facts of Canadian and American television (apart from the basic one of public ownership) is that revenues from advertising are insufficient to pay the expenses of all but the most modest of Canadian-produced programmes. Many expensive shows are "sponsored" by companies who may pay less than a quarter of the actual cost. It is not only Tories who object to the idea of the taxpayer "picking up the tab" (as the cant phrase goes) for the balance unpaid by General Motors or Lever Brothers. But the intelligent solution would be not to cut down on programme budgets or to raise advertising rates, but to abandon the dishonest pretence that the "sponsor" presents anything but the commercial announcements. Since the CBC itself produces all domestic programmes, sponsorship is really a myth, and one which benefits no one but the advertiser. The CBC should cease to perpetrate this deception, and should separate advertising from programme content as is the practice on the Independent Television Network in Great Britain.

Once this has been done, the way will be open for a number of vital reforms. Television is expensive in terms not only of money, but also of talent. At the moment the television cameras of the world are consuming creativity at an alarming and inhuman rate. Before the rise of the media, two or three basic routines could sustain a musical hall or vaudeville performer throughout a lifetime on the stage: three or four good plays might be the lifework of a successful dramatist; costumes and stage settings might serve unchanged for a run of two or three years. By contrast, television demands constant novelty: it makes stars overnight, drains off their fund of originality in a few months, and may then reject the spent personality as "overexposed"; it gobbles up original dramas at the rate of dozens a week, so that there is little wonder that most of them are merely slick applications of a few tested formulas.

By any standards and under any conditions, this is a wasteful way of going about things, but it is especially so in Canada where we are not blessed with an over-abundance of talent, and lose much of what we do produce to the lusher pastures of Britain or the United States. Why, therefore, should major television productions not be given "runs" like other theatrical enterprises? An opera, a 90-minute drama, or a special documentary ought not to be shown once and then disappear into the film library; it should be repeated several times at different hours and on different days over a period of a couple of weeks or a month so that it will reach the largest audience possible. Since no sponsor will be able to claim ownership of a programme, there should be no technical obstacle to this practice which would enliven weak spots on the schedule, cut down on expenses, and alleviate a prodigal waste of talent and energy.

Putting an end to sponsorship would also make it possible to adopt a more humane and creative attitude towards programme timing than the present rigid and inartistic system allows. What dramatist of the past would tolerate the absurd condition that his play should be exactly twenty-six, fifty-three or eighty minutes in length? Should documentaries, situation comedies, and concerts really be fitted together like so many identically shaped interchangeable prefabricated units? Is it rational to offer a programme called "Great Movies" (ironic though the title may be), then to edit the classic to fit the schedule so that such subtlety as the original possessed is almost totally obscured, and to interrupt the film's flowing action with triple commercials of the utmost vulgarity? Even Hollywood at its very worst would not expect the director of a feature film to conform to such conventions. If television is ever to achieve maturity, the schedule must be made flexible. Live programmes should be cushioned from succeeding items by interludes which would protect both writer and producer from an absurd bondage to the clock. Above all, if commercial announcements cannot be banned completely from the middle of programmes, they should be rigidly restricted in number and confined to "natural" breaks in the action.

Though the argument against commercially sponsored television may be theoretically unanswerable, the dependence of the CBC on programmes from the United States may mean that, in practice, there would have to be some exceptions to any regulation which outlawed the system in Canada. Likewise the privately owned stations within the CBC system and the new competitive stations authorized by the BBG would, under the circumstances, have to be allowed more freedom in this respect than the publicly owned stations of the national network. But programmes emanating from CBC production centres ought clearly to be labelled what in fact they are, enterprises in which both the viewer and the advertiser share costs.

One of the chief criteria adopted by the Board of Broadcast Governors in the award of television broadcast licences to private operators has been the proposed percentage of Canadian programmes. The most favoured figure is 55 per cent. It is certainly important to guard against the excessive use of American material, but it is possible to doubt whether the Board's policy in this respect is either realistic or desirable. Even the CBC, with all the resources at its disposal, barely meets this condition, and some of the programmes produced are no credit either to Canada or to the CBC. If private stations attempt to do the same, we can therefore expect some very shoddy fare to be offered up in the name of Canadianism. This will have the doubly unfortunate effect of increasing the volume of tripe to which the public is exposed and of nurturing the national inferiority complex about matters involving mass entertainment. The real concern of the BBG should be with standards rather than cultural nationalism. Self-interest can be relied on to convince the private operators of the value of programmes with a local appeal: the BBG's job is to ensure an appropriately balanced schedule whether the programmes originate in Hollywood, Toronto, London, or Moscow.

Our survey of the mass media in the Western world in general and Canada in particular has shown that they have all tended to be pressed into the service of the salesman: the information or entertainment they present is often offered not as an end in itself but as a means to manipulate the audience to serve private interests. If one had the power to re-establish the whole system of mass communication from scratch, one would surely try to find another principle to build upon. However, the opportunity to start afresh does not exist, and the task of reorganizing such a vast and politically sensitive area of public life is one which any democratic socialist party might well boggle at. Moreover, the alternative examples offered by the publicly owned systems of the communist countries do not encourage one to believe that complete nationalization of the media would do much more than replace one set of deficiencies with a new one. In the foreseeable future, the present mixture of public and private ownership will have to form the basis of government policy, whether of the left or of the right.

Nevertheless, there are many reasons why it would be desirable to limit the role of advertising not merely in the media but everywhere in society. Fifty years ago, it was a valid defence of most advertising that it expanded the market for goods, and thus made mass production and lower prices possible. In the affluent society of today that task has been largely accomplished. Most advertising in the mass media is devoted to competition for a larger share in an already limited market. It is designed either to stimulate wants where none were previously suspected, or to reveal imaginary distinctions between identical competing products. No longer can it be said to serve the interest of the consumer. As J. K. Galbraith has shown in *American Capitalism*, the advertiser whose sales campaign is successful is now far more likely to spend his increased rate of profit upon more advertising than to pass the savings on to his customers.

A very high proportion of the money and creative energy expended upon advertising is thus wasted, in the strictest sense of the word. Millions of dollars and the efforts of some of the ablest minds in the world are devoted to devising silly jingles, inculcating irrational anxieties, and concocting monstrous lies. And on whose behalf is this rather sinister fooling carried out? The manufacturers of beer, soap, automobiles, patent medicines, cigarettes, cosmetics, soft-drinks, and breakfast foods. It is intolerable that those who control this bizarre segment of our economy should continue to dominate the media of communication.

A measure which would automatically reduce this dangerous predominance and eliminate some of the worst excesses of our huckster's economy is a tax upon the advertising budgets of corporations. There is no harm in the kind of publicity which might be called "commercial intelligence" — department store advertisements in newspapers, announcements of new products and the like — but most people would agree that we suffer from a surfeit of the objectionable type of irrationally persuasive advertisement. Against this the tax would be directed. Properly adjusted, it would serve both to discourage needless and wasteful advertising campaigns and provide revenue for the government of the country. It would be an appropriately poetic justice if the proceeds were applied to the support of the CBC, the National Film Board, the Canada Council, and other public agencies concerned with maintaining a high standard of communication and discussion.

In the long run, if not in the short, the public gets the kind of communication system it deserves. There is a limit to what can be accomplished from the top even if there is, as there certainly is *not* in the House of Commons Committee on Broadcasting, a deep understanding of the problem. The future of the mass media in Canada rests with public opinion. Fortunately, effective public opinion is not a matter simply of counting heads, but of views expressed through voluntary associations or by citizens whose role in the community gives their opinions a special weight. Socialists in particular exert an influence of this kind out of all proportion to their numbers. So far as the mass media are concerned there can be no substitute for a small but vocal minority audience who are prepared to make their views felt not only negatively, but also positively by praising and supporting what seem to be worthwhile achievements. Alert and intelligent opinion of this kind may gradually transform the media beyond recognition. If this seems a slim hope, it is perhaps the only real one.

Canadian Education:
A Utopian Approach

ADAM GREENE

In the best old socialist posters of the thirties, a family was seen looking to the co-operative commonwealth of the future, a city which rose effulgently out of an unreal dawn. It was assumed, and quite properly, that in this new commonwealth the whole order of society must be changed. Some of these changes were indeed visible, even at a distance, partly because of the convenient lettering which appeared on the city's walls. EQUALITY OF OPPORTUNITY, GOOD HEALTH, DECENT PAY FOR DECENT WORK: these were not idle messages in the thirties, and they are not now. And if there was room on the walls to write of education, the message of course was, EDUCATION FOR ALL. But what kind of education, and just how much? If all is to be changed in the new commonwealth, will not our education be transformed as well? This leads to a more important practical question: can we hope to bring about extensive changes in society, without at the first changing the educational system in which the members of society are brought up?

Questions such as these, of course, cannot be asked or answered in a poster. Amid the troubles of the thirties, there was hardly time to ask them at all. Most socialists assumed that they could ignore the problem of educational reform, but not because they belittled the importance of education. On the contrary, the more education there was for everyone, the better. It was almost irreverent to ask just how good our education was, by its own standards; and even more so to ask what these standards should be.

At bottom we all have a well-grounded prejudice against questioning the contents of education in a social or political context. It smacks of totalitarianism: we are more accustomed to speak of education, either as an end in itself, or as a means to enable the self-development of the educated individual. Yet to talk this way is already to accept one theory of education. We may call it *the liberal theory*; for, like liberalism in general, it accepts individual values as ends in themselves, and in so doing it explicitly isolates them from their social context. The liberal theory is the only possible justification of the modern liberal arts faculty, in which different courses of "subjects," with differing and often contradictory frames of reference, compete in a more or less open market for the time and attention of the individual college student. The greater the competition of ideas, big and small, the more the student is supposed to have developed his powers of judgment. The liberal theory, in short, believes in absence of plan; and that not as a necessary evil, like the international situation, but as a value in itself.

At the other extreme we see *the Marxist approach* to education as it has evolved in the Soviet Union. Marx himself wrote little on the theory of education: this is one of the most noteworthy lacunae in the Marxist system. But theory is often an impediment to the mind, and indeed the Soviet experiment has been more revolutionary in the field of education than in any other. It is not always easy nowadays to tell capitalism from communism; the Soviet Union and the United States have much in common besides a desire to produce steel and launch Sputniks. But we have seen the land of Chekhov's peasants, the most feudal state in Europe, become a modern technological nation in a generation and a half; and the Russians have clearly not stopped going. This is an educational revolution for which we have no counterpart. Some Westerners have viewed this spread of light with a strange despair. Alternatively, it can encourage us in a faith, once central to the Western thirst for education, of which in recent years we have become tired and even forgetful. I mean the faith that education, properly pursued, will revolutionize society.

Of course we cannot simply admire the Soviet example, for their schools have evolved for narrow ends, in the context of a crude ideology and crude indoctrination (though this was once a noble word). We take this ideology very seriously, perhaps more so than the Russians themselves. Will ideology of any kind obstruct the truth, as has certainly happened on occasion? Or is some form of ideology always present, even if it is only the anti-ideology of liberalism? In Russia it seems that courses in dialectics are losing their importance, but other factors have reinforced a more socially oriented education. One is the Soviet faith in their ultimate historic destiny, the surviving element in Marxist ideology, which apparently inspires an extra effort in the classroom as well. Another is the concentration of the Soviet system on short-term objectives, such as the production of engineers, whose usefulness can be easily understood. Recently not only goals but the educational process itself have been adapted to the social context; and factory work has been linked with classroom training. This attempt to prepare youth for factory life, which is not unlinked to the labour shortage, has been attacked as retrograde. But as long as factory life exists it may be cruel to ignore it: is it enough to offer the worker's son a few terms of Shakespeare and Molière, and forty years at a lathe thereafter? Is it not both fairer and more realistic to follow the Soviet example, by setting up a meaningful youth and adult education programme within the confines of every major factory?

In any case, just as a liberal education may breed confusion or disaffection, a Marxist education may breed narrowness or fanaticism. In the West, of course, we are not really faced with a choice. In Canada as elsewhere we have inherited a valuable and complex heritage; we could not if we wished go as far as the Soviet Union in concentrating on explicit and largely short-term goals. But here we come to the most astonishing feature about Canadian education: the lack of any sustained discussion concerning what it should be. We discuss the constitutional issues, the financial issues, and issues of academic freedom. But when we hear statements about our education in general, these are usually tailored to some short-term goal. For example, there was the remark which made headlines a few years ago about there being nothing wrong with our education that a great deal of money will not cure. What is worst about Canadian education may well stem from precisely this approach — which no amount of money can do anything about at all.

One well-known dissident voice in Canada has been that of Dr. Neatby. With an inspired patience, she has gone through what is technically known as the "literature" of current education; and she has shown that much of it can be dull, uninspired, foolish, and even illiterate. More important, she has attacked certain specific practices which deserve to find no defence. But she has confused and clouded the central issues, just where light is most badly needed. She blames "progressivism" for the decline in standards; and those she attacks have replied by disowning "progressivism." In fact there are only a very few progressive schools in Canada, but their standards are usually very much higher than the average. It seems strange that she would attack one of the few forces that are attempting to cope creatively with our serious problems. But Miss Neatby has an exaggerated nostalgia for the recent past. What she really wants, one feels, are schools like the ones in which grandma used to teach. Thus she makes a revolutionary bogey out of that eminent post-Victorian, John Dewey.

A more coherent and practical approach to the same problems has been made by Dr. Frank MacKinnon in his recent book, *The Politics of Education.* According to Dr. MacKinnon, who is a political scientist as well as a teacher, the degree of direct governmental administration of public school education is "without parallel" in any other modern state activity; and this is probably the "anomaly that causes most of the difficulties of the educational system." Provincial Ministries of Education, he recommends, should be reconstituted as lay Educational Councils; and such schools as are ready for the responsibility should be turned into self-governing "public trusts," appointing their own employees, administering their own funds, and even determining their own curricula. (Of these proposals, only the last raises doubts as a goal in itself: in some parts of a school curriculum, standardization and even textbooks are not wholly disadvantageous — especially in a highly mobile society such as our own.) Decentralization is certainly a goal, if we are to attract better teachers and to allow them to teach. It is a goal, of course, that can be worked towards either inside or outside the present system of accountability to a central ministry. If we abolish the powers of the central authority, we shall still wish to provide guarantees that central and universal standards are, as far as possible, maintained. In fact Dr. MacKinnon's proposed Council would seem to have the powers to meet this requirement, as it would distribute large amounts of public funds according to its own formulae, and would even have sanctions to enforce the levy of local funds.

Local autonomy plus central, de-politicized, regulation is indeed a worthy model — which suggests that British experience in this field should be studied very closely by Canadian reformers. But the foundation of the wealthier schools as independent trusts, without adequate machinery for the maintenance of universal standards, would suggest a more anachronistic and controversial model — the original establishment of the British "public schools."

One way or the other, one suspects that there are sharp limits to the good effects of purely structural changes. However much Dr. MacKinnon may dislike the training and outlook of the educational administrator — who ought always, we agree, to be a man with teaching experience — the administrator will have some valid functions as long as decent standards have not been established in all our local schools. We must work to improve the quality of schools, and above all the qualifications of teachers, to the point that the *educational* responsibilities of administrators can be diminished and perhaps virtually dispensed with. Dr. MacKinnon advocates a closer relation between teacher training and a regular B.A. degree, with a correspondingly smaller emphasis on training in teaching techniques. Here one must surely agree. Teacher training should be a means of bringing good teachers in; and not, as it so often is now, a means of keeping them out. Hitherto we have insisted on training our teachers, but not on educating them. A measure of normal undergraduate education should be the chief requirement for qualifying any teacher: it is indeed surprising that teaching is one of the few professions where this is not already established. To improve and to broaden the qualifications of our teachers is not an easy programme, but it is a relatively simple one, and, of all the proposed remedies for our schools, perhaps the most likely to succeed.

For better or for worse, our educational system is the imperfect result of an extraordinarily ambitious, largely successful, and by no means completed experiment: the creation of a universal education system. In North America this experiment has been doubly difficult: for here we have expanded the educational system within our society at a time when our society itself has been rapidly expanding. All American educational philosophy and techniques — pragmatism, functionalism, the innovations of Professor Dewey and of Teachers' College — must be considered primarily as a response to the special problems of this accelerated expansion. Some of the innovations must probably be regarded as permanent. There has been new emphasis on secondary education, and above all primary education, as ends in themselves. The median or average intelligence of those attending schools has very possibly declined, and the basic curriculum has certainly been adapted to the capacities of the average intelligence. These trends are both inevitable and, when rightly construed, desirable: it is within this context that we must work for higher standards, attend to the needs of the exceptional student, and struggle to see that university and professional entrance requirements are maintained.

Some of the features of recent changes are, we trust, transitory. We have seen a tendency to disregard what is difficult or exceptional in education, a tendency to rely on mechanical, even assembly-line methods, for the teaching of children, and for the teaching of teachers as well. Much of what is drab in our schools and normal schools is there because, in the past, it seemed impossible to do better. This is particularly true in the United States, where breakneck expansion has been most harmful to American public education, just as it has not helped the structure of American democracy. In Canada the growth of population has not been as violent: the excuse, therefore, is not quite as valid. Authors Neatby and MacKinnon are quite right to question the domination of Canadian education by American ideas — not always the best or most recent American ideas. It is unfortunate that we have uncritically adopted American educational ideals and techniques, when these have often been culturally diluted, deprived of content, to an extent which in Canada is neither desirable nor necessary.

Of course we can learn a great deal from American experiments as well, but only if we understand clearly that our own society is one with different problems and even different goals. Education is one of the few fields in which we might legitimately hope to set higher standards for ourselves than does our neighbour, if only for the reasons outlined above. It is true that the best American schools have not their equal here; but neither have the worst. Taken as a whole, our educational system, especially in its public aspects, is quite possibly more sound. Certain American ideals, such as the attempted creation of a single homogeneous and independent culture, are not and cannot be ours.

This should be a point of particular interest to the Canadian left. The assumptions that underlie American education are, by and large, the assumptions that underlie the American political system. Many American educators have often been radical in their criticism of day-to-day affairs. They have not usually questioned, until very recently, the American way of life itself. Dewey, for example, was always proud of his ultimate faith in democracy as it had been conceived of by Jefferson. The ideal Dewey classroom is both modelled on, and designed for, the town meeting which is its adult counterpart. That part of education which does not produce or flow from this ideal is correspondingly ignored.

Such an approach is pragmatic in theory, but in practice it is self-defeating. The democratic process will hardly prosper when it is put forward as an article of faith rather than as a thesis for dispassionate examination. Dewey was a critic of the American scene, but a naive enthusiast concerning American ideals. As a result he had no great conviction that society should be radically transformed. In this respect he differs from the great men who have shaped the history of educational theory: Plato, St. Augustine, Erasmus, Vives, or Rousseau.

Dewey's attitude is an understandable response to the American predicament of success: a society that is so immense, so powerful and temporarily so prosperous, that to challenge it is quixotic. This predicament alone might explain the present difficulties of the American left. But perhaps we should also blame, in part, the very approach which we have just been describing: what we might call the naive *immanentism* of the Dewey tradition in matters of politics and education alike. This charge of immanentism may be clearer if we look from American to European ideals of education, or at least to certain European ideals.

Whereas American democracy is often taught as an end in itself,

Europeans are more conscious of their society as a moment in time. This historic sense is a liberating one. If one can admit both the general sordor and the occasional greatness of the past, then one can see the present in a more dispassionate light. This is not simply a defence of history in the curriculum. It is an appeal for socialists to reconsider the importance of all those elements in the curriculum which, by following American example, run the risk of being discounted because of their low pragmatic value. An historic sense demands that pragmatism, in education or elsewhere, be restated. One need not dwell on our loss if the feudal ages had taught only those subjects which were of "use" to that particular time and social structure. But there are advantages even in barbarism: perhaps the chief advantage of mediaeval barbarism was the creation of the European intellectual class. They did not accept, still less would they have taught, that one should become "adjusted" to a society based on war, pillage, and exploitation. Men of learning were notoriously prone to differ among themselves; at the same time they were conscious that their own ideas, whatever these might be, were not those of the society around them. The lamp of learning was fed at the darkest times by the hope that the patient spread of education might lead in time to a better society. Thus traditional learning was a link, not only with the past, but with a possible future as well. Socialists, more than any other group, have a vested interest in the preservation of that link.

This is not meant as a defence of Dr. Neatby. Miss Neatby's greatest weakness is that, while purporting to defend tradition and culture, she defends them only in their late and not wholly edifying incarnation: the Victorian gentleman. There is more to tradition and culture than Miss Neatby lets us know: Dewey too, for example, is part of our tradition. But we must be careful in the use of these words. By "tradition" we can mean either the unconscious habits and customs of a people, or the conscious heritage of learning that is transmitted with great pain and difficulty to such individuals of every generation as may wish to receive it. Tradition is usually a slogan of the conservative; but (what Miss Neatby and some socialists tend to forget) our conscious tradition is above all a revolutionary one. From its earliest days it has had before it the idea of a new and different society: an idea that has been challenged, refuted, lamented, but not hitherto ignored. The periods of great intellectual ferment in western Europe have been the time when this idea moved men with particular intensity. I am not suggesting that this idea was or should have been taught by the educational system itself. What matters is the maintenance of a cultural level at which man can be inspired by *ideas* of society, as well as restrained and guided by the *facts* of society. At every one of Europe's revolutionary periods, we see the presence of a class of men, often very few, a *sancta quaedam societas* as Erasmus described them, who were moved by ideas as well as guided by facts.

It would be foolish to suggest that only learned men can be, for example, socialists; and in fact the social impact of learned men is narrowly circumscribed. At the same time, no culture, and no social movement within that culture, will continue to be vital if it does not maintain a group of individuals who have been educated to a certain remoteness from day-to-day events. There is a sense in which anyone can hold what we loosely call an "idea." However, when these ideas are not being constantly reinterpreted in the light of our whole experience, and at some remove from the thick of fact, then these ideas decay. And when ideas decay, "the people perisheth."

Perhaps the chief idea which inspires and encourages the Soviet Union is that of the improved society which science and technology will create for man. The West has not failed to catch sight of these prospects either, and recently we have seen imaginative American innovations to help create the kind of scientific secondary education our changing society will need. It is not the function of a layman's article to suggest what form scientific education should take. We can however warn against that isolation between scientific and humanist education which has assumed the proportions of a social problem, known rather misleadingly as the problem of "the two cultures." But whatever the present situation in our country, the greater long-term dangers are faced not by scientific but by humanist education. In recent years, fortunately, the most successful defenders of humanist education have turned out to be certain leading scientists themselves.

But humanism and remoteness have not always held the same appeal for the socialist left. I remember a challenging article on society and alienation in the *Universities and Left Review,* in which it was somehow accepted, not only that alienation from society was in itself a bad thing, but that the literature of alienation, the "highbrow" tradition of Eliot and Joyce, was also a bad thing. In fact education and the whole of our conscious tradition are intimately connected, almost no more than two different ways of naming the same process. There is much to criticize, but no need for partisan rejection. In our dialectic, not only can tradition liberate, but alienation can adjust.

Luckily, as we have already said, the Canadian socialist is less likely to be doctrinaire in his views on education. There is rather the tendency to treat education as a fixed good, a commodity like natural gas or bread, for which the only plan is an ever greater distribution. Of the two alternatives, the latter is certainly preferable; but it seems in its turn to underestimate the shortcomings, and the vitality, of the present status quo. I do not think we can avoid a more considered answer to the question with which we began.

The original inspiration of socialism was a vision not just of a better society, but of a changed one. Traditional attitudes to wealth and power were to disappear, along with the society on which they were based. In the rather bloody struggle of continental European politics, the idea came to prevail that political measures were both necessary and insufficient to bring about this change. The alteration in the emphasis of socialism is now so pervasive as to arouse little controversy. In the nineteenth century, however, the controversy was a real one. The Marxist doctrine, which became fashionable, was that revolutionary changes in modes of ownership and production would themselves be accompanied by revolutionary changes in human relations and attitudes, since the latter (according to the materialist concept of history) were determined by the former. From this point of view the apparently utopian socialism of an older generation — with its "duodecimo editions of the New Jerusalem" — seemed unrealistic. With our own experience of communist revolutions, however, there are grounds for re-examining the verdict passed by the *Communist Manifesto* on the so-called Critical Utopians. After all, hardy visionaries like Fournier and Owen soon learned that a long road lay ahead. They attached considerable importance, not only to the political institutions of their New Society, but also to the educational changes that would bring it about. Their goal was a new kind of society for a new kind of man: politics and education must progress together in the achievement of this goal. If it was utopian to suggest that education, as much as economic progress, is a powerful medium of social change, I suggest that this notion is not so very foolish. Modern socialism, perhaps, is not utopian enough.

Since about the turn of the century, socialism, in its new incarnation of a mass political movement, has tended to ignore the long-term task of reforming education and to concentrate on political ends, many of them short-term ends. I think it is fair to date the intellectual crisis of democratic socialism from just this period, and from just this one-sided concentration. In fact, I would go further. Today our newspapers speak of an intellectual crisis in the West as a whole, an attitude of uneasy paralysis in the face of world revolution. This wider sense of loss is linked with the loss of which we have been speaking. It just is not true (as some academic enthusiasts would like us to believe) that our history is that of a "liberal" tradition, at war with ideology in all its ugly forms. Quite the contrary. However conscious or unconscious it may have been, the vision of a new man in a new society is not a private socialist vision, but has been a special goal of Western civilization from almost its earliest days.

The communism of Plato and the Christian apostles, of the philosophic city and the City of God, of the monastic orders and the new learning, of Utopia, Arcadia and the Second Jerusalem: all this cannot be lightly cast aside. By "revolution" we sometimes mean a great upheaval in a short period of time; but it is possible to think of revolution as having a longer span and if we take a longer view, we can see that our tradition is truly (and by its achievements, as well as its ideals) a revolutionary one. Nor, above all, is it a matter of evolution, as opposed to revolution. What we propose is still a scandal, however distant it may be. It is sure that, left to themselves, neither the passage of time, nor even piecemeal political reforms, are enough to bring it about. If we still want the vision, the new city where wealth is held in contempt and co-operation is not just a matter of law and taxes, then we must be interested in more than political economy. We must work for that education which our new order will demand.

This is a difficult challenge. Even if we accept it, we are not very far ahead: a five-year plan for education will not help. On the contrary, we have suggested that headstrong amendments, discontinuous changes of any kind, in fact, are likely to do our education far more harm than good. To talk of planning our education at all is misleading, if it suggests in anyone's mind something analogous to economic planning. Such an over-all reform or purification of our education as that which we must contemplate is too vast to be entrusted to any single commission or statute. And yet I think we can, and perhaps must, talk of a socialist programme in education, if there is to be any vision of a new man in a new society.

First, we can see our ideals more clearly. We must understand that our ideals are neither liberal nor Marxist, in the mutually exclusive, ideological sense which I have used in this article. I think that our ideals should be blatantly and explicitly utopian. And why not? More's *Utopia* is one of the greatest, wisest, and most saintly books to be written on education. Let us therefore be utopian proudly. Our goal should be nothing less than a society in which none are rich but all are leisured, where work is tolerable but a means to an end, where proper education has radically reduced our need for material goods, where learning is no longer a special profession but a universal pursuit, and where the cultivation of the mind and its powers is the highest end of the state.

One cannot think for a moment that a visitor to our land from Utopia would bless the contents or structure of our educational system. But what would shock him the most would be the fact that, in a society with respectable pretensions to be civilized, intelligent individuals are prevented from being educated as far as they have the wish and power to be. He would expect the correction of this evil to have the first priority in anyone's educational programme: to arguments about cost he would stubbornly reply that education is no longer a luxury; it is a need, not only for the individual, but even more for society as a whole. While ignorance leads to a host of social costs, education is the key to the rapid augmentation of social capital. This is a point which even our business men are coming to understand; there is no need to dwell upon it here. Whether we wish it or no, the white-collar revolution is taking place under our eyes: we are becoming a society of mental workers. The speed with which this happens is one easy criterion of industrial progress.

It is, therefore, not utopian to ask for universal schooling, a process which is (albeit slowly) beginning to show fruit in our own epoch. It is important, however, that these schools be used to educate, and not merely to provide the various forms of technical training which an advanced society needs. The word "school" comes from the Greek word for leisure, and this is no accident; it would be tragic if the school became a mere training-ground for work. A new society will be not just a community of wise men (as the Stoics imagined), but a community, like Utopia, where all have been taught to admire the wise. This means that all students must have been intimately exposed to the free life of the mind, those pursuits which, by their remoteness from our special modes of work, make us universal men. We must learn both to work well and to play well.

Utopia was, as we know, a great academy of the liberal arts. In our own day we might enlarge the list of pursuits, laying still greater stress on the creative arts. But for socialists, the utopian stress on amateur education, learning for its own sake, is an important one. Learning for its own sake is the only sure basis for a psychological transformation of man. The Platonic truth, that through education we become free from ourselves, is as important to socialism as the Marxist truth, that through the smashing of the class-state we become free from society. Neither truth, in fact, means very much for us without the other; but it is the first which requires re-emphasis today. To be a citizen of Utopia it is not necessary to conquer original sin; but only that (by and large) one's mental or spiritual appetites be more actively developed than one's material desires. A certain sacrifice, no doubt, but not an unusual one: we have probably enough such people in our own country to found a dozen Utopias. What was comic about the nineteenth-century utopian experiments was not the idea that men could live together without property — our own Mennonites and Hutterites can settle that point. It was the attempt to build a new society *de nihil* — in despite of social background — that was "comic." But should we laugh at New Harmony? We now see that England's misery in that period was surely no laughing matter.

Even technical training is enough to change a man's behaviour. It has made the Russians more civilized than they used to be, but not yet so very much better than ourselves. I suspect that only education, the cult of learning for its own sake, can train what there is in us of the old Adam. But this is only half the story. The idea of liberal education, which is sometimes attacked as "aristocratic," is an important factor in the shaping of a free intelligentsia, that class which, in each succeeding modern revolution, seems to play a larger role.

Hence the modern socialist has a vested interest in defending old-fashioned notions of liberal education against the very intense financial pressures to turn our schools into brain-factories for the Brave New World. Take, for example, some of the recent changes by which the universities have become more "integrated" into the community. There are signs that graduates are coming to be better "integrated" as well. A generation ago they had useless Arts degrees, were unemployed, and joined the LSR. Today they study social science, learn more about their own society, and qualify as high-priced industrial consultants. Should we really rejoice at the union of theory and practice which produces the psychology of modern advertising and the sociology of audience research? A liberal education is a means, however inefficient, of transformation and of political reform. Hence the utopian will not blush when he asks that the universities produce a social class who are learned as well as trained.

I think it is the particular concern of the socialist to see all educational reforms in the light of their usefulness for educating the community as a whole. This does not lead automatically to notions such as mass university education, even though everyone who qualifies for such education should be helped to have it. On the contrary, the more we think about educating everybody, the less we can afford to think of education as accomplished through a special profession or class. Education in Utopia was an amateur pursuit; in defending this approach, we may as well ask what other is equitable. Both by their origin and by their present structure, the universities are designed for the training of a restricted class of professions, to which by definition not everyone can belong. If we send everyone to university, the type of education and selection which they now afford will have to be sought at some higher level. If, as seems more likely, we send only the most intelligent, there is the danger of a new, intellectual stratification of society. One way or the other, it would be absurdly limiting to make the universities, with their intensive training over a relatively short period of life, the machinery of a new programme of universal adult education.

A socialist has the important goal (not just a utopian one) of a redistribution of leisure. In Utopia work and leisure are normally part of every man's day, each giving meaning to the other. To achieve this goal it is not enough to work for larger schools and more scholarships. It is not enough to hire some people to teach and be taught; we must encourage a society in which everyone can be helped to devote his leisure hours to education. Hence we must look with a great deal of interest to developments such as the adult education work of the trade union movement. This field is still a new one; it has not yet been explored long or energetically enough to know its full potentialities. Unlike the utopians, we still tend to think of education as something for children, or else for professionals. In fact, one present danger of mass education has been, with the professionalization of this function, the danger that its essentially amateur status be lost. A vast new industry has been created, the education industry: even the so-called liberal arts departments of the universities have become, in their graduate schools, more and more like training grounds for future teachers. But scholarship and education are not at all the same thing; a development of university "work" can even lead to a decline in the cultivated use of leisure. If this were to happen— in some places it *has* happened — we should be farther from ancient Athens — and from any hope hope of Utopia — than we were before.

This is why it is so important to keep in mind what it is we want from education: why the philosophical question of our goals must be considered as urgently as the practical question of reforming the local school board. Other countries feel even more urgently the relevance of educational thinking to political survival. They are closer to the challenge of the Soviet bloc, which may soon be training more of its workers than we do ours, and which plans seriously for an intelligentsia drawn from every class and group in society. The Soviets know roughly what they are doing: while they have suggested that every student should work, they have also suggested that every worker should study. At home we seem to have no such vision: in fact our plethora of wasted opportunities is becoming more and more embarrassing to us. We have leisure in greater and greater abundance; we can think of nothing to do with it; and, because we can think of nothing to do with it, we call it unemployment.

So many of the West's problems, economic, psychological, and social, arise from a failure to balance the improved organization of our work with an improved organization of our resulting leisure. We talk of planning to meet the unemployment crisis, but no long-range planning will succeed which does not recognize education and unemployment as two aspects of the same problem. In Russia, for example, the unemployment statistics are not rising, only the education statistics.

I say this to give only one example of the growing relevance, whether we like it or not, of educational thinking to our political thinking, and hence to our political planning. We should of course take heart rather than despair at whatever the Russians have been able to achieve: our enemy is ignorance and not those forces which overcome it. The true advantage of the West is still, as it always was, its educational advantage. Our military and industrial advantages, which we have lived without in the past, will decline and very possibly disappear. We may be surpassed in steel production, and we may even be surpassed in the percentage of our youth we send to school. But mass technical training, though it can do much to humanize manners and morals, has its limits as well. And the new societies, such as the Soviet Union, will see more and more that they cannot educate as easily as they can train. New schools alone cannot educate a country, for education, especially at its highest levels, is only to a limited extent a matter of institutions and institutional progress. We must be conservatives and admit these limits; but we must also be radicals and take up the problem nonetheless. If we cease to provide leadership in the field of education, then indeed the role of the West in the world will have changed forever.

Thus it seems to me that a utopian approach to education is not an idle one. The utopian model allows us to formulate our criticism of both liberal and Marxist educational theories; and indeed it emerges as a synthesis of what is best in both of them. Against the liberal theory, it establishes a profounder and more coherent goal — not just of the educated individual, but of the educated and self-educating community. Against the Marxist approach, it treats education, not just as a means to practical social ends, but as a higher autonomous end in itself. Indeed we shall only make progress towards the implementation of the utopian ideal by insisting that education is *the highest autonomous end to be envisaged in our political thinking.* The goal is education for its own sake, and not for the sake of the more decent political society which may follow as a consequence.

This idealized conception of the role of education seems to me to be deficient from all approaches to our Canadian educational problems, even the approaches of our most outspoken critics. That is why we have doctoral dissertations about the ideal size of the Grade Seven classroom, and so little thought as to what should be taught inside it. But the Grade Seven classroom has become part of a much more general problem. I view the order of priority in this fashion: whatever we may do as a stopgap, we can only have good schools when we have good teachers; we can only have good teachers when we have better training; and we can only have better training when we have done a great deal more about the familiar scandal of the liberal arts degree. And to do this last without fear, we must be willing to educate ourselves, as many of us as far as we can, to qualify ourselves as defenders and as critics of our educational heritage. We must swell the ranks of those whose interest in education is *amateur,* to preserve the centre of our academic system from professional and scholastic encroachment, and to expand it in concert with all the varied social possibilities of our society. A class of amateurs, utopians before their time, is necessary in any nation. It is they who keep alive the intellectual debate, necessary not only to the understanding of our educational problems, but to the vision of the good society towards which our education leads.

I do not myself believe in the likelihood of the Brave New World, such

as Huxley described it. It is a shore towards which we sometimes seem
to drift; but one of two alternatives will probably intervene before we
get there. The first is the destruction or decay of our rather precarious
ship. The second is that, with better steering, we educate ourselves
beyond such an awful possibility. Universal education is not merely an
opportunity. It is a need; in privileged countries such as Canada it has
become a more urgent need than better food and clothing and many
times more urgent than the many trivial types of luxury that we now
produce. Certainly it would be foolish and complacent to think that the
Brave New World, if it exists at all, is a storied country somewhere
east of the Elbe. The Russians are beginning to train all of their citizens; more and more, their intelligentsia is drawn from every class in
society. Once we heard about the Soviet military threat, then it was the
economic threat; now some people talk about their educational threat.
There is even some ground for shuddering at the thought of an educated
Russian. Because of its confusion and inertia, the West is now challenged for leadership in its own traditions of education, technology, and
culture. If it loses that leadership, as the Greeks once lost it, then its role
in history will never be the same.

But how are we to respond? Drop the Arts courses and train more
engineers? There are some voices of panic which imply we should be so
foolish. But we cannot win this contest by cutting back; our only chance
is to live up to our own best intentions. We need the training of technology to enhance not only our production, but the value (already high)
of our human labour. Above all, however, we need education; for the
modern mass state is an extraordinary mechanism, and only an extraordinary citizenry will be able to make it work.

This may not sound like a practical programme. In truth it is not, it
is rather the order of priorities which we should keep in mind as we
turn to the host of practical problems which will beset us. For these
will be legion: our task is not that of a five-year plan or a ten-year plan,
but a thousand-year plan, insofar as it is a plan at all. The length of
time involved does not make the programme any less revolutionary.
History has shown that although men will always seek what they
want, the years can see these wants change, and the centuries can see
them improve. The public still, properly, demands its circuses; but the
gladiators have gone, and the difference is due to education. The more
temperate manners of a civilized society, which the world has never yet
seen, may be difficult to achieve and impossible to maintain; but, however faint and ephemeral its chances of success, our utopian objective
should not be called impractical. For our present difficulties seem to
suggest that, in the long run, it may be easier to establish a society
where man's desires are temperate, than to establish a just and peaceful
society, where man's desires are not so.

Social Class and Education

JOHN PORTER

Modern education has been given its shape by two dominant historical trends — the increasing industrialization of economies and the more intensified egalitarian ideologies of political systems. These trends have affected both the availability and the quality of education. The effect on the latter can be seen in the attempt, particularly in North America, to create an educational system for masses of individuals who, because they enjoy some political equality, are thought also to share an intellectual equality. In its extreme form the egalitarian ideology results in a devotion to the statistical average or norms of performance in which the vast range of human intellectual capacity is drawn centripetally towards a common standard of mediocrity. It will be argued later in this paper that this development is a misapplication of the value of equality, and that what is required of democratic education is to treat equals equally by recognizing differences in intellectual capacity, and to remove as far as possible social and psychological barriers that interfere with the sharing of educational experience by intellectual equals.

Industrialization has affected the content of education because of the tremendous emphasis put on the practicability of knowledge, or — more precisely — on the marketability of certain kinds of skills. Knowledge for its own sake is ignored; knowledge which will yield an immediate income, either for the individual or for the society, is highly valued. This emphasis pervades the entire educational system. Some governments suggest that young people should borrow money to go to university because the knowledge they gain can yield a future income which will in a short time eliminate the debt. It must not be thought, however, that in this respect we have fallen from some high horse. There never has been a widespread desire for knowledge for its own sake. At the most education was confined to the leisure classes or priestly castes of earlier historical periods, where societies based on agrarian economies were organized on an aristocratic or sacred principle. Although modern mass education up to now has been little more than the transmission of knowhow of varying complexity we could be moving towards a stage where there is more for the mind and less for the market.

The market, however, is always with us. Our high standards of living and leisure depend on our industrial system being supplied with trained workers. In the rapid development of industry since the Second World War Canada has imported large numbers of skilled and professional workers,[1] while many of her own people remain untrained for technical roles. It can scarcely be said, in a country where only two in five of those between fifteen and nineteen years of age are still in school, and where less than one in twelve of the college age group are in college, that the demands of a modern industrial society are being met.

Industrialization and the egalitarian ideology are not independent of each other in their past social development. An industrial economy requires a free labour force as contrasted to one which is legally tied, as in a caste or estate system, to specific kinds of occupations inherited from kin. Consequently industrial societies have "open" class systems consisting of a hierarchy of skills ranging from the casually employed unskilled labourer to the highly trained professional worker. Education is an important determinant of one's ultimate position in this system of skill classes. Theoretically an industrial system sorts and sifts masses of people according to their interests and talents into the multifarious range of tasks which have to be performed. Social development based on industry means constantly emerging possibilities for innovation in which new skills are required. The richness of its educational system will determine an industrial society's chances of growth and survival.

The egalitarian ideology holds that individuals should be able to move through this hierarchy of skill classes according to their motivations and abilities. Such an ideology reinforces the needs of an industrial economic

[1]Royal Commission on Canada's Economic Prospects, *Skilled and Professional Manpower in Canada, 1945-1965* (Ottawa, 1957), pp. 56–7.

system. A society with a rigid class structure of occupational inheritance could not become heavily industrialized. On the other hand the industrial society which has the greatest flexibility is the one in which the egalitarian ideology has affected the educational system to the extent that education is available equally to all and careers are truly open to the talented.

Modern education should be examined against the kind of model which is here being suggested, that is, an ideal social system in which the allocation of individuals to social tasks and access to educational resources is determined by ability. Thus two ends are served. The occupational structure will reflect a more rational allocation of ability; and individuals will have the greatest opportunity to develop their talents and make their contribution to the social good. Where those who survive to the upper levels of the educational system are less able than many who drop out of it, the investment in educational capital is being wasted and the most valuable resource of human talent is being squandered. A society which refuses to remove barriers to educational opportunity is falling short of the democratic ideal. The principle of equality and the principle of the rational use of economic resources thus reinforce one another. A system which does not provide equal opportunity is inefficient as well as undemocratic.

SOCIAL BARRIERS TO EQUAL OPPORTUNITY

The barriers to equal opportunity are both social and psychological. Although it is analytically useful at times to keep the social and the psychological separate, they are in fact intricately interwoven. Social barriers have been built into our social structure as it has developed. None of them is beyond the control of social policy. Psychological barriers are the attitudes and values which individuals have and the motivations to become educated with which they are either endowed or inculcated. The removal of the psychological barriers raises practical and ethical problems which are not so easy to solve.

Of the social barriers the most obvious is the inequality of income and wealth. Education costs money and regardless of how "free" it may be, lower income families tend to take their children out of school at an earlier age and put them to work. Lower income families are obviously penalized when it comes to higher education, which in Canada, with the exception of the veterans' schemes, we have consistently refrained from making free. A second social barrier is family size. The larger the family the more difficult does it become for parents to keep their children in school, or even to make choices — if this is possible — about which of their children should remain in school as far as university. In the large family children can be put to work early to help meet the heavier expenses of child rearing. Here there is a doubly depressing process at work because invariably in industrial societies lower income groups have larger families. The child, therefore, born into a lower income family has almost automatically a greatly reduced horizon of opportunity.

A third social barrier to equality of education lies in the regional differences in educational facilities in Canada. Some are fortunate enough to be reared in areas where educational facilities and the quality of teaching are good; others are brought up where educational standards are low. For many the institutions of higher learning are a long way from home and for them the costs of going into residence and of paying fees are prohibitive. Although these regional inequalities are in large measure the result of our federal system there should be more consideration given to policies which could overcome them. Accident of birthplace should not limit a person's opportunity. Associated with regional differences is the occupational and ethnic homogeneity of some regions. The social milieu created by a region's geography and ethnic composition determines to some extent the kind of educational facilities that are available. Regions that are predominantly agricultural will have educational systems which serve this particular economic function. In the urban milieu there is a concentration of similarly appropriate facilities. While all this has a logical appeal it does not necessarily relate talent to training.

Although it is not possible here to examine the full implications of the fact, surely a fourth source of inequality arises from the great influence that religion has had on educational policy. The least adequate educational facilities for an industrial society, as census data later presented show, are those of Quebec where education for French Catholics is not only costly, but also at the secondary level concentrated within the tradition of the classical college. Professor Tremblay has found for example, that Catholic boys in Quebec leave school much earlier than Protestant boys. Even as early as twelve years of age there is a greater proportion of Protestant than Catholic boys in school. While for each age beyond twelve there are fewer of both groups at school, the difference between Catholics and Protestants increases. At sixteen years one-quarter of Catholic boys are at school compared to one-half of Protestant boys.[2] Other investigators have established that for every 100 pupils in Grade 6, Quebec Protestants keep 42 in school until Grade 11, but Quebec Catholics keep only 18.[3]

It may be argued that the earlier school-leaving age of Catholic children in Quebec can be accounted for on economic grounds, and that the religious variable is by itself of no importance. It is true that the average French Catholic family has more children to educate than the

[2]Arthur Tremblay, "Quelques Aspects de Notre Problème Scolaire," *Bulletin de la Fédération des Collèges Classiques*, vol. I, no. 5, April, 1956.
[3]"The First Report of the Canadian Research Committee on Practical Education," *Canadian Education*, vol. IV, no. 2, March, 1949, Table 2, p. 42.

average English Protestant family, and that on the average the socio-economic status of French family heads is lower than that of English family heads. But Quebec Catholics are not penalized, as are Catholics in other provinces, by tax and grant structures through which money is supplied for education. In Quebec, tax revenue, including that from corporations, is shared with the minority (Protestant) school board according to the number of resident children of each religion between the ages of five and sixteen in the community. In a province where 82 per cent of the population is French-speaking and 88 per cent is Catholic it must be accepted that the resources made available for education are a reflection of the dominant values.

Public educational policy for Catholics is entirely in the hands of the Roman Catholic Committee composed *ex officio* of the bishops in charge of dioceses and an equal number of laymen appointed by the cabinet. As one official of the Department of Education in Quebec has said:[4] "The presence of the bishops adds considerable prestige to the Roman Catholic Committee: all are eminent men who thoroughly understand the school situation in their diocese, and several are in addition experienced educators. Parents are thus assured of a thoughtful and stable educational policy." The Catholic view that religion and education are inseparable means of course that the content of education must be affected by religious ideology, and for this reason clerical control over education must be maintained. It is not unlikely also that in Quebec the availability of education is a reflection of the values of the Catholic hierarchy.

Charles Bilodeau points out the differences in Quebec for Catholics and Protestants, in the availability of education.[5]

. . . the present secondary course exists in two separate forms; one public, of five years' duration, *often free*, but leading only to certain university faculties (science, commerce, agriculture, etc.); the other private, of eight years' duration taught by the classical colleges and *comparatively expensive*, but giving admission to all faculties. French-speaking parents have not failed to notice that English-Canadian pupils are able to take a secondary course in the public schools at no or almost no charge, and to enter all university faculties, while their own children do not have the same opportunities. (italics added)

No one is seriously going to suggest to the French or to Catholics that they should abandon their cherished belief in the inseparability of religion and education. It is, however, legitimate to point out how the educational system which has developed in French Canada does not conform to the democratic industrial model which we are here constructing.

[4]Charles Bilodeau, "Education in Quebec," *University of Toronto Quarterly*, April, 1958.
[5]*Ibid.*

It is probably true that the Christian humanism which pervades French-Canadian education is to be highly valued, but on the other hand French Canadians cannot make their full contribution to Canadian society without reforms, many of which are recognized by French-Canadian educationalists. These reforms need not be inconsistent with an education based on religion.

In provinces other than Quebec the economic factor may be more important. Catholic separate schools suffer unnecessary impoverishment through tax and grant structures. If separate school education is a recognized right, the right becomes vitiated if funds are not made available for it in proportionately equal measure as for public school education. Catholic children are then at an educational disadvantage — a fact which accounts in part for the concentration of Catholics in lower occupational groups.

Religion then along with socio-economic status, ethnic affiliation, size of family and region is an important variable affecting the availability of education. The inter-relatedness of these variables must be kept in mind. It is the socio-economic variable which this paper seeks mainly to examine. The religious and other variables cannot here be examined beyond these remarks and the census data later presented.

PSYCHOLOGICAL BARRIERS

The psychological barriers to equality in education are much more vague. If suddenly education became as free as the air, many would not choose it. In a free society such a choice is everyone's right, but there is a great deal of evidence that the motivations to stay in school and continue to university are related principally to the position which the family occupies in the general social structure, particularly its class position. In other words, in an environment of limited choice, the appropriate motivations are not forthcoming and if they were they would probably lead to frustration. Those who are reared in a milieu indifferent to education are not likely to acquire a high evaluation of education, a situation which, although difficult, is not impossible to correct through social policy. There is evidence also that intelligence as measured by the standard type of intelligence test is closely associated with social class position, size of family and size of community. There is no convincing evidence, however, that motivation and intelligence are a genetic endowment of the middle and upper classes or of particular ethnic stock. What is more likely, and this is what is meant by the interweaving of the psychological and the social, is that there is an appropriate social milieu in which these psychological qualities are acquired. It would, of course, be foolish to assert that all are born with an equal intellectual capacity. It is more reasonable to assume that in any given human population there is a wide range of general ability depending for its development on the appropriate social environment, and it should be the aim of educational policy to remove from the social environment those conditions which frustrate and inhibit the development of intelligence and ability.

The relationship between the principle of equality and educational opportunity now becomes more clear. We need educational methods by which all children are encouraged to overcome their particular environments and to pursue the educational career which best suits their talents. In this respect much more research into the problems of selection is necessary. The general criticisms now being levelled at the "eleven plus" examinations in the United Kingdom would suggest that techniques are not yet adequate, but the principles underlying the British reforms of 1944 are sound. In Canada little has been done to remove the barriers imposed by social conditions on the individual's educational opportunity. The remainder of this paper will be an attempt to present empirical material which will help us to understand the relation between our social structure and education.

SURVEY OF CANADIAN EDUCATION, 1951

The most general picture of Canadian education can be found in the census. Although all Canadian provinces require children to remain in school until the age of fourteen, seven per cent of the age group ten to fourteen were out of school at the time of the 1951 cenus. Almost one-half of those in this age group who were not in school lived in Quebec. Saskatchewan had the best record of school attendance for these ages. Rural children up to fourteen years of age do as well in school attendance as the urban children of their province.[6]

If the proportion at school of the age group ten to fourteen years is taken as the index of the availability of some kind of schooling for Canadian children, the system then is 93 per cent complete. As would be expected there has been some progress since 1911 when the proportion at school for these ages was about eight out of ten. However, the ten to fourteen age group attending school shows the educational system at its best. For a more complete picture it is necessary to examine the age distribution for the usual school years — five to nineteen — of those in and out of school.[7] When all these school years are considered, the proportion of five- to nineteen-year-olds at school is only two-thirds, a not too substantial increase since 1871 when the proportion was one-half. Very little progress was shown between 1921, when the proportion was 61 per cent, and 1951, although during this period there was a

[6]DBS, *Statistical Review of Canadian Education, Census, 1951*. Unless stated otherwise census data on education have been taken from this document.

[7]Although the age groups used in this analysis may not correspond precisely to the normal years of school attendance they must be used because they are the groupings used by the census.

significant shift in the occupational structure as the Canadian economy became less agricultural and more industrial. At the same time, within industry the occupational structure became more complex and higher degrees of technical competence were required.

Compulsory school attendance up to the age of fourteen catches almost all children, but the drop-out from school after that age is alarming. As can be seen from Table I, at every school year beyond fourteen there was a considerable loss of students so that a little more than one in five of the eighteen-year-olds was in school in 1951. Of those between twenty and twenty-five years — a rough indication of those who go on to higher education — the proportion was about one in twenty. Although for the high school ages there has been more improvement since 1921, the question arises whether or not an industrial society can afford to have 60 per cent of its children aged fifteen to nineteen out of school.

Although the drop-out from school after fourteen is common to all provinces, it is greater in some than in others. In Quebec, for example, of the sixteen-year-olds only four out of ten are in school compared to more than seven out of ten in British Columbia. The percentages of those in school through high school ages by province can be seen in Table II. Throughout these years the three western provinces are able to keep a greater proportion of their children in school, while Quebec consistently lags behind.

For the high school ages, if both sexes are considered together, urban children do slightly better than do rural children. There has been an improvement in rural high school education since the 1941 census when only 30 per cent of the fifteen to nineteen age group were in school. Quebec has less than one-quarter of its rural children of this age group in school compared to about one-third of its urban children. Smaller cities — those with a population between 30,000 and 100,000 — have a slightly higher proportion of the high school ages in school

TABLE I

PERCENTAGE OF POPULATION IN SCHOOL FOR AGES 14 TO 19 YEARS, CANADA, Census 1921 and 1951

	1921			1951		
Age	M	F	Total	M	F	Total
14 years	73.1	73.7	73.4	90.3	86.9	88.6
15 "	49.4	53.2	51.3	75.8	75.7	75.7
16 "	29.4	35.9	32.6	54.1	56.7	55.4
17 "	17.0	22.2	19.6	36.0	37.4	36.7
18 "	10.0	12.5	11.2	23.5	21.5	22.5
19 "	6.9	6.8	6.9	15.4	11.5	13.5
20–24 "	3.1	1.5	2.3	6.5	3.3	4.9

SOURCE: DBS, Ottawa, *Statistical Review of Canadian Education, Census, 1951,* Table 5.

TABLE II

Percentage of Population, Ages 14–18, in School by Sex, by Province, 1951

	14 M	14 F	15 M	15 F	16 M	16 F	17 M	17 F	18 M	18 F
Newfoundland	92.3	91.6	78.1	77.6	54.6	55.6	32.0	31.7	15.1	16.2
Prince Edward Island	93.3	94.5	76.2	83.9	45.8	59.9	26.2	37.0	15.5	21.4
Nova Scotia	93.1	93.3	83.2	85.6	59.3	66.2	37.1	44.8	20.1	24.3
New Brunswick	90.3	90.9	77.3	80.1	52.6	58.1	32.1	36.3	19.3	17.6
Quebec	82.2	77.2	62.1	56.6	41.8	37.6	27.8	23.1	18.6	13.0
Ontario	91.8	91.9	82.0	83.7	58.6	62.3	38.0	39.6	25.5	23.4
Manitoba	91.7	92.6	77.3	82.1	57.8	65.1	39.9	44.0	25.0	23.6
Sakatchewan	94.5	95.6	83.2	87.5	60.4	70.9	41.5	52.9	27.6	34.9
Alberta	95.0	95.3	86.3	89.0	64.6	73.6	43.8	54.3	29.1	32.2
British Columbia	94.0	94.0	86.5	88.7	70.1	76.8	51.9	54.5	32.4	30.9

Source: DBS, *Statistical Review of Canadian Education, Census, 1951*, Appendix, Table 2.

(44.6 per cent) than do cities of over 100,000 (41.4 per cent), no doubt because large cities have more attractive job opportunities for young people than smaller ones.

Of the thirty-four Canadian cities with more than 30,000 people Hull, Quebec, has the lowest proportion (37 per cent of boys and 30 per cent of girls) of children between fifteen and eighteen years in school. Montreal, Canada's largest urban centre, has a record scarcely better. There is a remarkable difference between Montreal proper and Outremont, within the metropolitan area. The latter community has an outstanding record of keeping its young people at school. This tends to support the view that the social and cultural milieu is an important determinant of educational experience. Almost one-third of Outremont's population is Jewish and this ethnic group has a higher educational record for its adults than any other. There are other cities with contrasting records of keeping their children in high school. Oshawa, for example, has only 44 per cent of boys and 45 per cent of girls aged from fifteen to eighteen in school, while Fort William has 64 per cent and 58 per cent respectively. It would be valuable to discover what there is about these communities which accounts for the difference. It can be inferred, of course, that Oshawa is a part of the Southern Ontario industrial structure which

TABLE III

PERCENTAGE OF POPULATION IN AGE GROUPS 15–18 AND 19–24 AT SCHOOL IN
SELECTED CANADIAN CITIES WITH MORE THAN 30,000 POPULATION, 1951

| | Percentage at school | | | | Percentage of adult population not at school with 13–16 years of schooling |
| | 15–18 | | 19–24 | | |
	M	F	M	F	
Outremont	72.2	62.7	31.7	11.4	10.0
Saskatoon	72.0	64.2	15.6	12.7	11.5
Vancouver	66.7	60.6	14.6	6.5	9.6
Calgary	64.6	64.4	10.9	7.5	10.7
Winnipeg	63.6	52.8	12.8	6.5	6.9
Port Arthur	62.1	57.4	9.1	6.1	8.6
Windsor	59.1	55.4	12.2	7.9	10.0
Sydney	58.6	58.5	9.2	3.0	6.0
London	57.0	50.9	11.2	10.7	12.1
Toronto	53.7	47.8	11.7	6.4	10.5
Quebec	51.4	38.5	13.8	6.7	7.3
Trois-Rivieres	50.7	35.9	11.8	6.2	6.3
Oshawa	43.9	44.8	5.3	2.6	7.9
Montreal	42.9	33.8	9.3	4.0	5.9
Hull	37.1	30.4	5.2	2.3	5.1
Canada	47.1	47.3	7.8	4.6	

SOURCES: DBS, *Statistical Review of Canadian Education, Census, 1951,*
Tables 17 and 18; and Appendix, Table 1. *Census of Canada, 1951,* vol. II,
Appendix.

makes employment for boys, both local and migrant, more attractive than staying in school. Table III gives for selected cities the proportions of the fifteen to eighteen and the nineteen to twenty-four age groups of both sexes who are still in school. It also gives the percentage of the adult populations not at school who have had thirteen to sixteen years of schooling. The level of education of those who are or will become parents is an important factor in the transmission of values about education. Although the relationship between school attendance and the educational level of the adult population is obscured because of the geographical mobility between cities, the low educational level of Hull, for example, seems to be stabilized, as do the higher levels of Saskatoon, Vancouver and Calgary.

All Canadian cities with a population of more than 30,000 have more boys in the fifteen to eighteen age group in school than girls, which would suggest that the urban environment is less conducive to education for girls than for boys. However, for Canada as a whole boys and girls in this age group remain in school in relatively the same proportion, the sex balance being restored by girls from smaller cities and farms. In all provinces farm families keep girls in school longer than boys, which would suggest that the structure of the labour force in larger urban centres is an important factor in taking girls out of school earlier. However, cityward migration of young people, particularly girls, makes it difficult to tell from census data, which do not separate the urban and rural reared, the relative importance of urban and rural influences on educational experience of the sexes. In the university age group (nineteen to twenty-four) there are many more boys (49,783) than girls (30,427) or roughly 8 and 5 per cent respectively of this age group in the population.

Although girls do better on average at school than boys, they are less likely to stay in the educational stream after high school. As Professor Fleming points out,[8] if we plan to replace the less able in university by the more able it would mean changing the sex ratio in the universities with the possible result of forcing changes in adult sex roles. However, there are many professional roles to which, if the experience of other countries is a guide, women are as suited as men. We seem to be excluding on the basis of sex a considerable amount of intellectual capacity from the higher professions, for example, when we have as engineers 28 women to 27,013 men, as lawyers 197 women to 8,841 men, as physicians and surgeons 660 women to 13,665 men, as dentists 68 women to 4,540 men, as professors, 812 women to 4,610 men.[9] Many professional women have shown that it is possible in our culture to combine

[8]W. G. Fleming, *Background and Personality Factors Associated with Educational and Occupational Plans and Careers of Ontario Grade 13 Students* (Toronto: Ontario College of Education, 1957), p. 22.
[9]DBS, *Census of Canada*, 1951, vol. IV, Table 4.

professional roles with family roles, although obviously family life assumes a different form with mothers working. We do, of course, permit women, married or not, to work in the sub-professions or in lower status occupations. It is their traditional exclusion from the higher professions which is a measure of our intellectual wastage.

The main conclusion to be drawn from this brief review of census data is that a large number of young people leave school as soon as it is legally possible for them to do so despite the fact that there are generally no fees to pay to complete secondary education. While the drop-out from school is country-wide some kinds of social environments appear less conducive than others to staying in school. Very large cities, for example, although often thought to have superior school systems, do not have as good a record of school attendance as smaller cities. As we have seen large cities vary in their records depending on such things as ethnic composition, industrial structure, traditions and so forth.

CLASS ORIGINS OF HIGH-SCHOOL STUDENTS

One aspect of social life which is common to all communities is their division into different social classes. Differences in income, property, power, social status, level of education and prestige can be found in rural areas as well as urban centres of all sizes. Social class position can also be related to membership in particular ethnic and religious groups even though ethnic and religious communities will themselves be divided into classes.

The index of social class position which is in most general use is an individual's occupation or the way in which he earns a living. Thus if all occupations can be ranked in some way as being higher or lower than one another we would have a scale of occupations by which individuals could be assigned to different social classes. Such a scale has been designed for Canada by Professor Blishen.[10] With the use of census data he has constructed an occupational scale which includes 343 occupations ranked on the basis of average years of schooling and average income for those in the occupations. High in the scale are the highly trained professional jobs: low in the scale are the unskilled manual jobs. Blishen divided the 343 occupations into seven classes. Although his dividing lines between the classes are arbitrary, his scale is a very useful tool for sociological analysis.

Fortunately it is possible also from census data to discover the occupations of fathers of children who are in or out of school and thus with the use of Blishen's scale to find out something of the relation between social class position and continuation in the educational stream. In Table IV the 343 census occupations have been reduced to the seven classes,

[10]B. R. Blishen, "The Construction and Use of an Occupational Class Scale," *Canadian Journal of Economics and Political Science*, vol. XXIV, no. 4, Nov., 1958,

except that Class V — generally the class of skilled workers — has been shown with and without farmers. The first column gives the number of children aged fourteen to twenty-four years old who are living at home and the second column the proportion of these children who are still at school. The children are, of course, assigned to one of the seven classes on the basis of their father's occupation. It can be seen from the Table that Class I fathers, who are in the higher professions have almost three-quarters of their children in this age group at school whereas fathers in Class VII, unskilled manual workers, have a little over one-third of their children in the same age group in school. The gradient of the increasing proportion of school leavers from Class I to Class VII can also be seen from the Table. The evenness of the gradient is destroyed by Class V because it includes all farmers as a homogeneous occupation. When farmers are included, the Class does scarcely better than Class VI; when they are excluded the class does as well as Class IV.

Despite the distortion caused by assigning all farmers to one occupational class, the data clearly indicate that staying in school and university can be associated with father's occupational status. It should be remembered, of course, that subsumed in the term "occupational status" is a complex of factors of which family income is only one. Since Blishen's scale is based on education as well as income, the varying proportions of children at school by class show to some extent the transmission of educational values through the family(This association between social class and school leaving supports the findings of the Canadian Research Committee on Practical Education that "people from families below average

TABLE IV

CHILDREN AGED 14–24 LIVING AT HOME AND AT SCHOOL, 1951
(Blishen Occupational Scale*)

Occupational Class	Number of children aged 14–24 living at home		Percentage at school	
Class I	13,502		71.0	
Class II	173,937		55.2	
Class III	40,130		50.6	
Class IV	60,739		45.6	
Class V (with farmers)	573,095		38.9	
(without farmers)		237,925		45.6
Class VI	200,517		38.2	
Class VII	186,862		34.8	
Occupations Unstated in Census	41,316			
	1,290,098			

SOURCE: DBS, *Census of Canada, 1951*, vol. III, Table 141.
*B. R. Blishen, "The Construction and Use of An Occupational Class Scale," *Canadian Journal of Economics and Political Science*, vol. XXIV, no. 4, Nov., 1958.

TABLE V

OCCUPATIONAL LEVEL OF FATHERS OF ONTARIO GRADE 13 STUDENTS

Occupational level	Students by occupational level of father			Percentage of Ontario males 35 years and over by occupational level	
	No.	%	Accumulated %		Accumulated %
Professional, managerial, executive	3506	39		16	
Sub-professional, minor supervisory, proprietors	970	11	50	7	23
Skilled manual	2429	28	78	29	52
Semi-skilled manual	869	10	88	19	71
Unskilled	321	4	92	12	83
Father unknown, disabled, etc.	720	8	100	17	100
Total	8815	100		100	
Father dead	589				
Total	9404				

SOURCE: Adapted from W. G. Fleming, *Ontario Grade 13 Students,* Table 11.7.

in economic status are likely to be drop-outs and more likely to be early drop-outs."[11]

Further evidence of the effect of social class on educational experience can be found in the Atkinson studies prepared by Professor W. G. Fleming of the Ontario College of Education. His study includes all grade 13 students in Ontario in 1956. Although Fleming's method of classifying occupations is different to Blishen's, the social class bias of these students was evident from their fathers' occupations. Thirty-nine per cent of them had fathers in the professional, managerial or executive occupations whereas these occupations made up only 16 per cent of the labour force.[12] At the other end of the class spectrum fathers in the two lowest categories, semi-skilled manual and unskilled workers, who made up about one-third of the labour force in Ontario, had only 14 per cent of the grade 13 students. The over-representation of the two top classes in the Fleming study can be seen from Table V. Although they made up less than one-quarter of the labour force they produced one-half of the grade 13 students. The lowest class of unskilled labour, 12 per cent of the labour force, accounted for only 4 per cent of the students at this level. The class which came closest to equal representation — that is, which sent its children to school up to grade 13 in about the same pro-

[11]"Two Years after School," a Report of the Canadian Research Committee on Practical Education, *Canadian Education,* vol. VI, no. 2, March, 1951, p. 34.

[12]Fleming, *Ontario Grade 13 Students,* p. 7. The proportions of the Ontario labour force are of males thirty-five years of age and over since that is the group more likely than the total labour force to contain fathers of grade 13 students.

portion by which it made up the labour force — was the class of skilled workers. Since the Fleming data take no account of the larger families in the lower status occupations, as was possible with the data of Table IV, it is likely that the representation of children, as opposed to fathers, of these classes is less than has been shown. The combination of several variables with social class — religion, ethnic affiliation, and large families, for example — can be seen in Quebec where early school leaving is so frequent, and where also, as Professor Tremblay points out, there is probably a low parental evaluation of education, because of the number of children taken out of school but kept at home rather than put into the labour force.[13]

CLASS ORIGINS OF UNIVERSITY STUDENTS

If social class position with its sociological and psychological elements is an important factor in attendance at high school it follows that university students would be an even more class-biased group. Motivations for the longer educational haul must be transmitted, and the higher cost, which includes immediate income lost, must be met. Some evidence is available on the relation between university attendance and social class position.

In 1956 the Dominion Bureau of Statistics conducted a national sample survey of university students' income and expenditure. The students included in the study were in various faculties, at various levels of their university careers, from all regions in Canada and of both sexes.[14] Two of the questions asked in the survey — occupation of chief wage-earner in the parental family and parental family's total yearly income — can be taken as indicators of the social class position of the respondents.

Although a student's knowledge of his parental family's total yearly income may not be too accurate, it is interesting that just over one-half of those surveyed reported incomes of less than $5,000. To many $5,000 a year may seem a modest income, but in 1956 seven out of ten Canadian families had incomes of less than that amount. In the DBS Survey more than one-quarter of the students stated that their families had more than $7,000 a year whereas just over one-tenth of Canadian families fell into the $7,000 and over income group. The tendency for university students to be drawn from higher income families can be seen from Table VI which shows the distribution of students by family income groups. The median family income of all students was $4,908. Education for the higher professions is even more of a privilege of upper income classes. In law and medicine the median family incomes of

[13]Tremblay, "Quelques Aspects."
[14]DBS, *University Student Expenditure and Income in Canada, 1956–57.* The details of the sampling procedures used are given in Appendix B of the cited document.

students were $6,293 and $5,663 respectively. Twenty-eight per cent of
the law students and 22 per cent of the medical students came from
families with incomes of more than $10,000 compared to 15 per cent of
all students in the survey. Only about three out of one hundred Canadian families had incomes greater than $10,000 in 1956. The lowest
median family income was for the faculties of education which would
suggest that greater student aid in these faculties makes it possible to
recruit students from lower down the income scale. Women students on
the average came from higher income groups than did men. There is
little doubt that direct financial assistance to students from lower income
families is essential to make our educational systems democratic. It is
clear too that this aid should not be confined to the shorter and less
expensive courses. Access to the higher professions should not be cut off
because of the more expensive training.

Further evidence of the class bias of university students can be seen
by looking at their fathers' occupations (Table VII). One-half of the
students had fathers whom the researchers classified as "proprietors and
managers" or "professionals," whereas these occupations made up only
15 per cent of the labour force. Only one in twenty of the students'
fathers was classified as "labour" compared to one in five of the total
labour force.

The occupational groups employed in the DBS survey are crude socio-
economic classifications. Moreover, it is not realistic to measure the
representation of the various occupational classes in the university student population by taking the total labour force. Instead that segment

TABLE VI

PERCENTAGE DISTRIBUTION OF STUDENTS' PARENTAL FAMILIES AND ALL
CANADIAN FAMILIES, BY FAMILY INCOME GROUPS

Family income group	Percentage of students with families in income groups	Percentage of all Canadian families in income groups
$10,000 and over	15.2	3.3
7,000–9,999	12.2	8.4
5,000–6,999	21.3	18.7
4,000–4,999	14.8	15.7
3,000–3,999	17.5	22.9
2,000–2,999	11.6	17.0
Under 2,000*	7.4	14.0
	100.0	100.0

SOURCE: Adapted from DBS, *University Student Expenditure and Income in
Canada, 1956–57*, Table 6.
*Includes parents on pension, out of work, father deceased and mother working,
etc.

of it which is likely to contain fathers of children near university age should be used. For these reasons an attempt was made to reclassify, by going back to the original schedules, fathers' occupations according to the Blishen scale. At the same time the number of children at home in families with the male head in the labour force was substituted for the total labour force in order to obtain a more accurate measurement of the representation of the various classes in the student sample. The results are presented in Table VIII but in order fully to appraise the Table, attention should be paid to procedures followed in the reclassification.[15]

Table VIII gives for each occupational class in the Blishen scale proportions of the fathers of students in the sample; proportions of the total labour force; proportions of the total labour force who are male heads of families with children; proportions of all children at home in families where the male head is in the labour force, and proportions of such children fourteen to twenty-four years old. The last two columns, since they refer to children at home, obviously do not include all the children belonging to families with fathers in these classes. Since as we have seen the higher classes have a greater proportion of the fourteen to twenty-four age group at home and in school than the lower classes the proportions of children of lower class origin would probably be understated in the Table. For that reason the "ratios of representation" in Table VIII are probably higher than they should be for the lowest three classes. What we are seeking to measure is not the representation of fathers of the various classes in the student sample, but rather the representation of children. Although still not satisfactory, the "children at home" columns are a more adequate index than the occupational class

[15]The DBS schedule asked each student in the sample the occupation of the chief wage-earner in his or her parental family. In the DBS processing the responses to this question were combined into 64 occupational categories. Thirty-one of these categories fell readily into occupations on the Blishen scale. The remaining 33 categories were too broad in socio-economic level to be placed on the Blishen scale. Accordingly all the schedules placed originally in these 33 categories were re-sorted. Altogether 5,992 schedules (those that did not require re-sorting plus those that did) could be placed on the Blishen scale. Of the remaining schedules an effort was made to combine occupation and parental income as criteria for placing into one of Blishen's seven classes. However, in a fair number of cases father's occupation was not given (or was too vaguely stated) nor was parental income stated. These schedules were discarded as were those of foreign students whose mothers' occupations were given. 1,955 schedules were placed on the Blishen scale on the combined criteria of occupation and income. Thus altogether 7,947 schedules were placed in the seven classes. As a result of discarding some schedules the original DBS sample was reduced from 12.7 per cent to 10.2 per cent. The bulk of the discards were the schedules of foreign students and of married students who were not required to answer the income question. The largest proportions of married students were in the faculties of medicine, law or graduate studies. The direction of the bias in terms of social class origins created by the removal of married students is difficult to estimate. Apart from this possible bias the representativeness of the reduced sample is not likely to be less than the original. I am very grateful to the Education Division, DBS, for permission to re-sort the original schedules.

distribution of the total labour force. To use the latter is to overempha-
size the under-representation of Classes VI and VII. Similarly, farmers
are over-represented as a proportion of the labour force, but under-
represented when measured by "children at home." This difference
arises because Classes VI and VII clearly contain many young men starting out to work; whereas the "children at home" columns, based on male
heads with families, has an older age group as its base who have, on the
whole, been at work long enough to have in some degree moved up the
occupational ladder. The ratios of representation in Table VIII simply
measure the extent to which each class has over- or under-produced its
share of the university population, or in other words the extent to which
this particular social right is unequally distributed. A ratio of one would
be equal representation, greater than one, over-representation and less
than one, under-representation. Children of the top four classes are all
over-represented, while those of the lower three classes and farmers are
all under-represented. Class I children, whose fathers are in the highly
paid professions, have ten times more students in the sample than they
would have if representation were equal. Together Classes I and II provide 46 per cent of the students while children of these classes make up
only 11.5 per cent of children of the labour force population. Classes
VI and VII together provide 11 per cent of the students but they contain
31 per cent of the "labour force" children. Once again we see that the
children of skilled workers, Class V, although under-represented, do
reasonably well. Farm children do little better than do children of
Classes VI and VII, although it is probable that the children at home
total is more complete for farmers than it is for Classes VI and VII.

Since farmers are not a homogenous economic group some effort was
made to distribute students who were children of farmers by parental

TABLE VII

OCCUPATIONAL LEVEL OF STUDENTS' PARENTS

Occupational level	Percentage parents of students	Percentage of total labour force
Proprietors and managers	25.7	8.3
Professionals	24.9	7.1
Clerical and sales	12.3	16.5
Skilled and semi-skilled	21.1	30.6
Agriculture	10.9	15.7
Labour	5.1	20.5
Not stated	—	1.3
	100.0	100.0

SOURCE: Adapted from DBS, *University Student Expenditure and Income in
Canada, 1956–57*, Table 11.

TABLE VIII

SOCIAL CLASS ORIGINS OF 7947 CANADIAN UNIVERSITY STUDENTS
(Blishen Occupational Scale)

Blishen Occupational Class	Percentage of students (a)	Percentage of labour force		Percentage of children at home with fathers in labour force‡		Ratio of representation (a)/(d)
		total* (b)	male heads of families† with children (c)	all children (d)	aged 14–24 (e)	
Class I	11.0	.9	1.4	1.1	1.0	10.0
Class II	34.9	10.7	14.7	10.4	13.5	3.36
Class III	4.8	6.3	4.0	3.5	3.1	1.37
Class IV	7.1	7.0	5.0	4.9	4.7	1.45
Class V	19.7	23.9	24.8	22.6	18.4	.87
Class VI	5.8	19.6	15.1	16.1	15.5	.36
Class VII	5.3	21.3	13.8	14.9	14.5	.36
Farmers**	11.4	10.3	16.8	20.7	26.0	.55
Unclassifiable§		4.4	4.4	5.7	3.3	

*Computed from Blishen, "An Occupational Class Scale," Table 11b, and DBS, Census of Canada, 1951, vol. IV, Table 4.
†Computed from DBS, Census of Canada, 1951, vol. III, Table 141.
‡Census occupational class of "Farmers and stock raisers."
§"Others" and "not stated" in Census.

income groups. About one-third of them reported parental income of less than $3,000 while about one-fifth reported incomes of more than $5,000. Since it is difficult to find a satisfactory measure of farm incomes, ratios of representation of students from various farm income groups have not been computed.[16]

If the children of farmers are taken out of all columns in Table VIII, the inequality of representation, although basically of the same pattern, changes slightly with Class I children 8.86 times what their numbers would be with equal representation. Classes V, VI, and VII are all slightly farther away from equality of representation. In this group in which those of farm origin have been excluded, the two top classes have just over half of the university students compared to the 14.5 per cent of the children at home that that class has. The last two classes with 41 per cent of the children at home have only 12.5 per cent of the students. These data are found in Table IX.

It can be seen then that the unequal distribution of educational facilities which begins in high school is more marked in the institutions of higher learning. There is no reason to suppose that if account could be taken of the magnitude of the error introduced by the methods employed this general picture would change. However, some further evidence can be brought to support these general conclusions. Professor Fleming divided all the Ontario grade 13 students in his 1956 study — which was a total enumeration, not a sample survey — into three groups: those who went to university, those who entered other institutions of further education such as teachers colleges, and those who went into immediate employment. With the university group, children who had fathers in the higher status occupations were markedly over-represented. "It is evident," Professor Fleming remarked, "that education at this level is to a considerable extent the privilege of a numerically small occupational class."[17]

A further piece of evidence of the class bias of university students can be found in the study of the class origins of their fellow students undertaken by a group at the University of Montreal and published in their weekly paper *Le Quartier Latin*.[18] The data were taken from the records of 3,104 students in various faculties, and although the occupational categories used were not strictly socio-economic and the section of the labour force used to measure representativeness excluded those working on their own account, the inequality of representation is indisputable. Twenty-two per cent of the students had fathers in the liberal professions compared to 4 per cent of the provincial labour force. On the other hand 14 per cent of the students had fathers classified as

[16]In the Blishen occupational scale all farmers are included in Class V.
[17]Fleming, *Ontario Grade 13 Students*, p. 8.
[18]J.-Y. Morin, "Le Problème social et l'Université" in *Problèmes d'Etudiants à l'Université* (Montreal: Institut Social Populaire, 1953).

TABLE IX

Non-Farm Social Class Origins of 7042 Canadian University Students

(Blishen Occupational Scale)

Blishen Occupational Class	Percentage of students (a)	Percentage of labour force*		Percentage of 5 children at home* with fathers in labour force		Ratio of representation
		Total† (b)	male heads of families‡ with children (c)	all children‡ (d)	aged 14–24‡ (e)	(a)/(d)
Class I	12.4	1.0	1.6	1.4	1.4	8.86
Class II	39.4	11.9	17.6	13.1	18.2	3.0
Class III	5.4	7.0	4.9	4.35	4.2	1.24
Class IV	8.0	7.8	6.0	6.0	6.4	1.33
Class V	22.2	26.8	29.8	28.5	24.9	.78
Class VI	6.5	21.9	18.8	22.0	21.0	.34
Class VII	6.0	23.7	16.6	18.7	19.6	.32
"Others", and "un-stated" in Census			4.7	5.9	4.3	

*Excluding census occupation of "Farmers and stock raisers."
†Computed from Blishen, "An Occupational Class Scale," Table 2(b).
‡DBS, Census of Canada, 1951, vol. III, Table 141.

skilled and unskilled workers compared to 43 per cent of the provincial labour force. The author of the report, J.-Y. Morin states, "the intellectual and commercial classes, in the broad sense of the term, are represented at the University of Montreal in a proportion which greatly exceeds the proportion of their members in the Province. . . . The working class — or perhaps more exactly the less fortunate class — is represented by a very small proportion of its sons."[19]

[19]*Ibid.,* p. 8. The system of private fee-paying classical colleges which is so important in the educational system of Quebec is almost certain to produce inequality of class representation both among the students who remain in them until the BA years, and among those who leave to go to the universities.

Since the fees for this secondary education vary between $450 and $600 a year it is not surprising that in the Bureau of Statistics survey of student income and expenditures 22 per cent of classical college students in the BA years reported parental incomes of more than $10,000 a year — a proportion greater than for all medical students in the sample. As well, the median family income for these French-Canadian students was very close to that of all medical students. Moreover, less money was available for scholarships and bursaries for classical college students than for all other undergraduates, and almost twice as much student income came from parents than was the case with all other undergraduates.

Some care should be taken in any comparison of the University of Montreal data with that previously presented which was based on a national sample in which Quebec universities were represented. As Table VII shows, 21.1 per cent of students' fathers were classed as skilled and semi-skilled compared to 30.6 per cent of the labour force. Morin combines skilled and unskilled workers. If this is done with Table VII the proportions for the national sample would be 26.2 per cent "workers" as against 51.1 per cent of the labour force. The actual proportion of children of unskilled workers (ouvriers en général) at the University of Montreal was 4.55 per cent, and of skilled workers (ouvriers de métiers) 9.38 per cent. However, these are very crude socio-economic categories and that is why we have preferred the more refined social classes of the Blishen scale. If the fathers' occupations given in the Morin study are distributed through the seven classes the percentages are as follows: I, 11; II, 32.4; III, 11.2; IV, 11.7; V, 13.2; VI, 6.3; VII, 1.8; unknown 12.3. These proportions were arrived at by excluding from the total "cultivateurs," "retirés," and "décédés," and distributing the category "marchands et commerçants" equally over Classes III, IV, and V, and "autres ouvriers de métiers" and "autres ouvriers et journaliers" equally over Classes V, VI, and VII. This class distribution might cautiously be compared to Table IX. Ratios of representation cannot be computed, but if we assume that the general level of skill of fathers in the French-Canadian labour force is lower than the general level of skill of the total labour force the working class representation at the University of Montreal would be lower than that of "all Canadian universities."

A very different comparison emerges if we consider students at the University of Montreal as graduates which strictly speaking they are since most will already have a BA from a classical college. In the Bureau of Statistics survey, working class representation at the graduate level was 14.2 per cent (combining skilled, semi-skilled and labour) against 51.1 per cent of the labour force. This method makes working class representation at the University of Montreal (14 per cent "labour" against 43 per cent of the labour force) better than that at "all Canadian universities." Thus it would seem that at the peak of the educational system French-Canadian working class students do as well as those from the rest of Canada. Obviously much more investigation is necessary to discover the full effect of a fee-paying secondary education on university attendance. The one safe conclusion that can be made is that for both French and English Canada working class representation in the universities is abysmally low.

FINANCIAL CONSIDERATIONS AND SCHOOL LEAVING

If, as this analysis implies, social class differences with their economic inequalities are important in determining an individual's continuation in the educational stream it should be possible to find evidence that financial hardship has a direct bearing on leaving school for the labour force. Such evidence is not easy to obtain, partly because the myth that all can work their way through if they really want to has led investigators to overlook economic inequality, but also because what studies there are are based on those at school or university rather than those who have left. At this level of the educational system financial hardship has probably already taken its toll. It is, however, worthwhile to look at what evidence there is relating to financial hardship at the higher educational levels. In one study of school-leavers, based on a sample of about 20 per cent of pupils who left school during 1948 from Grade 7 up (excluding Quebec Catholic and Newfoundland schools) it was found that for boys 30 per cent and for girls 35 per cent of the reasons for leaving could be classed as "economic."[20]

In the Fleming study of Ontario grade 13, the students were asked if they intended to go to university or not, or whether they were uncertain. Thirty-one per cent stated they did not intend to go, and some of the reasons they gave were interesting. They were, of course, responding to a structured questionnaire in which a variety of reasons were provided for them to check. They could indicate more than one reason. The reasons given, either alone or in combination, in order of frequency were: "other plans for further education," "lack of money," "lack of interest," "studying too difficult," and "attractive employment opportunities." The students were then asked their main reason for not going to university. The rank order of reasons was the same as before with 60 per cent saying they had other plans for further education (67 per cent of the girls, a large number of whom would likely go to teachers colleges), 10 per cent said lack of money, 8 per cent lack of interest, 5 per cent studying too difficult, and 2 per cent said attractive employment opportunities.[21] It is interesting that attractive job opportunities, which are commonly thought to be one of the reasons why students are kept from university, are not really significant at least for Grade 13 students. It may be surprising, too, that lack of money was a reason in only 10 per cent of the cases (boys 14 per cent and girls 8 per cent), but it should be pointed out that we are here dealing with only those who expressed their intention of not going to university. It may be that financial problems intervened for those who said they were going to go or were uncertain and who finally did not go. There are grounds also for considering that many of those intending to go into other education did so because the courses

[20]"Two Years after School," p. 32.
[21]Fleming, *Ontario Grade 13 Students*, p. 31.

which are short and direct avenues to employment such as public school teaching are less of a financial burden. It is not possible, of course, with the data available to give firm answers to these questions.

In a similar study carried out in 1956 with Alberta grade 12 students, to whom almost the same questions were asked, the rank order of all reasons in combination for not intending to go to university were: other educational plans, not interested, studying too difficult, employment plans, and lack of money. With those who were uncertain about going the rank order of reasons was the same except that "lack of money" replaced "not interested" as the second most frequent reason. However, as has been suggested, economic reasons may enter into plans for non-university further education. Furthermore if "employment plans," "lack of money," "needed at home," and "university too far from home" were combined as reasons which may be based on economic considerations, economic reasons would have ranked second with the group not intending to go, and first with the uncertain group.[22]

In another Alberta study, all the students who graduated from grade 12 in 1949 with university entrance requirements, but who did not go, were sent a questionnaire designed to discover why they did not go. There were 201 usable responses out of 399 people polled. In almost half of the responses there was some indication that "financial difficulties prevented individuals from attending a university or a college.[23]

Although the magnitude of the financial problem is difficult to gauge from these studies they leave little doubt that for a good proportion of those who remain in school to university entrance standard, further education beyond that point is determined by financial considerations. In the DBS survey on student incomes and expenditures, 23 per cent of the students in the sample indicated that they had either to postpone their entrance, withdraw at some time from university, or attend part-time courses because of lack of funds.[24] It is not possible to review here all the material on how students pay for their years at university, but some indication of the inadequacy of our financing the training of young people in this highly technological age can be seen from the fact that scholarships, prizes and bursaries accounted for only 5 per cent of undergradu-

[22]*Progress Report*, Alberta Matriculation Study Sub-Committee, Feb., 1958 (mimeo), Table XXI. Matriculants and non-matriculants have been combined in these calculations.

[23]W. Glynn Roberts and A. O. Ackroyd, "Post-School Occupations of Alberta 1949 High School Graduates with University Entrance Standards," *Alberta Journal of Educational Research*, vol. I, no. 3, Sept., 1955.

[24]The acquisition of a working wife or joining the Armed Services can both be devices for meeting the financial costs of university. About 10 per cent of the students, most of them in law, medicine and graduate studies, in the DBS survey were married. Almost 5 per cent received income from the Department of National Defence or the Regular Officers Training Plan. DBS, *University Student Expenditure and Income in Canada, 1956–57*, Table 59.

ate student income in the DBS survey.[25] On the other hand, 37 per cent of student income came from the parental family (sometimes in the form of "loans"), gifts or loans from relatives and friends, or from investments and endowments. About one-third of student income came from savings from summer jobs. The inadequacy of summer employment as the way of working one's way through college can also be seen from the survey. Against an undergraduate median expenditure of $1,209 for the educational year there was a median savings of $507 from summer jobs.

INTELLIGENCE AND SOCIAL CLASS

So far in this analysis the emphasis has been on the economic aspects of social class as a factor determining educational experience. With planning and increased government funds these economic barriers could be removed at all levels of the educational system. Although their removal is necessary to achieve equality it would be naive to think that this would be sufficient to change the class composition of students in the higher grades and in university. What we have to deal with is the set of inter-related sociological and psychological variables which make up the social class position of the family and thus influence the individual's chances in the educational system. Economic and social factors set the boundaries within which, at the psychological level, values and attitudes are formed. These values and attitudes become transmitted from generation to generation and help preserve the various social milieux of class. Where parents have high occupational status they will also have more education, higher incomes and smaller families.[26] Their children will have a greater chance to complete their education and inherit parental status than children with parents of lower occupational status will have to improve their position. The lower class family does not value education so highly. In part it is a privilege beyond their horizons of opportunity, and at the same time, lacking education themselves they fail to appreciate its value and thus to motivate their children.[27] Social policy to be successful cannot ignore these psychological factors.

The inequalities which characterize Canadian education could be justified if those who were in the senior grades and in college were the most intelligent. The number of trained people the educational system should produce depends on the forecasts of the kinds of skills the society needs, but, whatever the number, the system is wasteful as well as inequitable if those who are trained are not the most intelligent. Intelligence is a slippery word in anybody's vocabulary and in order to make this quality objective so that we may talk about it we must resort to definitions

[25]*Ibid.*, Table 58.
[26]DBS, *Statistical Review of Canadian Education, Census, 1951*, ch. x; Enid Charles, *The Changing Size of the Family in Canada* (Ottawa, 1948), p. 95 *ff.*
[27]Some evidence on the importance of the family in the transmission of educational values can be found in Fleming, "Ontario Grade 13 Students," ch. II.

based on the tools used to measure it. There are three such indexes available: standard IQ tests, academic performance, and teachers' ratings. On all these scores Canadian schools show an appalling waste. While on the average those who continue through school and into university are better by these measures than those who do not, the spread of intelligence among both drop-outs and survivors is so great that large numbers who stay should be replaced by some of those who have left. It is not possible to deal with all this evidence here, but in reviewing some of it Professors Jackson and Fleming said, "We seem to be doing an admirable job of squandering the priceless human resources available to us. In fact it can be argued on the basis of the fragments of information at hand that we are utilizing to the full the talents of no more than one-third of our academically gifted young men and women."[28]

The Canadian Research Committee on Practical Education estimated an annual drop-out from Canadian schools of 100,000 of whom 10,000 are above average, 60,000 average and 30,000 below average in general ability. The Committee in its report remarked, "Undoubtedly a great deal could be done to keep the average and above average in school longer. Opinions differ as to which group represents the greatest loss to the nation, but the total loss is indeed serious."[29] Fleming points out in his study of Ontario grade 13 students that more than one-quarter of those who did not go to university (1,432 out of 5,099) had better records than nearly half of those who did go (1,535 out of 3,281). He concludes, "The pool of good academic material not being attracted to the universities would appear to be very large."[30]

What is distressing from the point of view of the social reformer is that low IQ scores and poor school achievement can be associated with lower social class position. Thus it may appear that the class bias of educational institutions is a kind of natural order based on the inherent differences of intelligence of a class-structured society. Certain kinds of evidence can be presented to support this point of view. Robbins,[31] for example, found in his study of Ottawa public school children that those with high IQs (130 or over) on the average came from more expensive houses, were from smaller families, had fathers with higher incomes and more education and higher status occupations than did children of low IQ (under 90). In fact, a gradient of children's IQ scores corresponded on the average with the gradient of social class as measured by these

[28]R. W. B. Jackson and W. G. Fleming, "Who Goes to University — English Canada" in C. T. Bissell (ed.), *Canada's Crisis in Higher Education* (Toronto, 1957), p. 76.

[29]"Two Years after School," p. 34.

[30]Fleming, *Ontario Grade 13 Students*, p. 22.

[31]John E. Robbins, "The Home and Family Background of Ottawa Public School Children in Relation to Their I.Q.'s" *Canadian Journal of Psychology*, vol. 2, no. 1, March, 1948.

indicators of class. The Research Committee on Practical Education also found some association between economic status of the family and school performance.[32] Although for Canada the evidence on the relation between social class and measured intelligence is meagre, there is enough of it from other industrial societies to suggest it may be a characteristic of industrial societies as such. However, it can never be known with present methods which of the elements that go into intelligence are the result of genetic or environmental factors. There may be a "cake of class," corresponding in a way to the "cake of custom" at a lower stage of social development, in that lower class status creates such a circumscribed learning environment that only the highly intelligent lower class children succeed in breaking out of it. It is fairly safe to assume that there is a reservoir of good native ability which never shows up in measured intelligence because the social milieu is not one in which the requisite motivations and values are acquired. If these speculative remarks have any validity, many of the reasons given for school leaving which are classed as relating to school experience, such as poor achievement, may also, along with financial and economic reasons, be attributed to social class differences. As we have said social class is a complex interweaving of the social and the psychological, and any policy designed to bring on the native ability found throughout a population must heed the psychological factors as well as the social. In fact it may be said that education policy cannot be viewed apart from social policy generally. Educational equality can probably not develop without corresponding advances in other areas of the social system. No society in the modern period can afford to ignore the ability which lies in its lower social strata. Whatever may be said about average intelligence and social class, the fact remains that in absolute numbers there are more of the highly intelligent in lower classes than in the higher.[33] It is a disgrace that this intelligence should be wasted because it lies in an inhospitable environment.

Canadians can scarcely boast of their educational systems. If the principles of efficiency and equality are to be upheld, the nation must be prepared to put a great deal more money into education and educational research than it has up to now. Not only must accessibility to educational institutions be greatly enlarged, but efforts must be made to overcome those psychological barriers which cut so many young people off from both the material and spiritual benefits of education.

[32] Two Years After School," p. 12.

[33] A. H. Halsey, "Genetics, Social Structure and Intelligence," *British Journal of Sociology*, 1958.

Social Welfare Services in Canada

JOHN S. MORGAN

It is an event of some note when the Toronto *Globe and Mail* in its leading editorial makes the welfare services the distinguishing feature of modern industrial society:

If one seeks the basic difference between capitalism and communism today, the answer is probably not to be found in the extent of the ownership of industry, but in the attitude toward welfare. The Soviet rulers are free to appropriate the entire production of the nation, above what is required for the bare subsistence of the population and apply it however they choose.

In Western countries, on the other hand, social welfare constitutes a first charge on the nation's wealth; only when the majority of people have been assured a comparatively high standard of living, with security against unemployment, old age and sickness, is a surplus available for any other purpose.[1]

There is, in this pronouncement, much to challenge the prevailing economic, social and political assumptions of many Canadians as well as the practical policies of governments and industrial leaders. It is, nevertheless, a current echo of a variety of statements by writers of many backgrounds in the past twenty years. A similar note is struck in Arnold

[1] Sept. 19, 1959, p. 6.

Toynbee's observation that "the present age will be known not so much for its terrifying inventions or its horrifying crimes but for the fact that for the first time in the history of mankind it is possible to conceive of the welfare of all human beings as an attainable objective."[2]

The significance of this positive attitude to welfare in the daily press is that it marks the growing acceptance of a new scale of human values by the public at large. "Welfare" is no longer a mere palliative in the scale of economic, political, social and moral values. One aspect of this change is summarized by J. Maurice Clark:

The present system of social security [in the United States of America] is so firmly established and taken so much as a matter of course, that it is not easy to realize that within the memory of middle aged persons the method of socially assured provisions ran counter to strongly entrenched moral conceptions of the way in which these contingencies (such as the lack of income due to unemployment, sickness, old age, or disability) should be met. They were regarded as things the individual should handle on his own responsibility; anything else was undermining the basic virtue of self-reliance.[3]

It is, of course, arguable whether the present system of welfare is "firmly established" or "taken as a matter of course" by all Canadians. If, however, a powerful newspaper dedicated to the virtues of private capitalism is prepared to say that society's attitude to welfare is the distinguishing mark of capitalism and that "social welfare is a first charge on the nation's wealth," it is clearly important to examine the extent to which this country's social welfare services are adequate to their purposes.

The facts show that Canada has many expensive welfare programmes but few coherent welfare policies; that, while the majority of Canadians do have a comparatively high standard of living, they are not adequately protected against the insecurities of unemployment and old age, and that they are not adequately protected against the hazards of sickness. A substantial minority of them are not protected at all against some of the normal insecurities of industrial society; and the majority are exposed to a variety of risks against which the protections are only partially adequate.

THE CONTEXT OF WELFARE IN CANADA

The nature and extent of a country's welfare services depend greatly on a wide range of factors which themselves derive from the economic, political, and social forces at work in society. A country's demographic structure, for example, determines some of its social needs. Canada, in 1960, had an estimated 5,975,600 children under the age of 16 years out of a total population estimated at 17,814,000. The age group of

[2]*New York Times*, Weekly Magazine, 1949.
[3]In his *Economic Institutions and Human Welfare* (New York: Alfred Knopf, 1957).

65 and over who are currently reckoned as "above working age" (although in fact a very large number of Canadians over 65 are gainfully employed in the labour force) represented about 7.5 per cent of the total population and numbered approximately 1,335,600.[4] It is not surprising, in the light of these facts alone, that some of the heaviest expenditures on welfare services are for programmes related to children and older persons.

The nature of provincial and local government in Canada is another important element in the background of welfare services. Provincial governments generally still conduct their affairs as though the communities they serve were settled agricultural societies. The distribution of seats in provincial legislatures gives a substantial preponderance of seats to thinly populated rural areas and thus greatly underrepresents the urban industrial areas. The legislatures themselves still normally meet only in the period between Christmas and Easter, as if the members could not neglect the service of their farms for the remainder of the year. The machinery of provincial government, in spite of strenuous efforts in many areas, necessarily reflects the kind of constituency and the socio-economic and political attitudes of those who compose the legislatures.

Municipal government suffers perhaps even more from inadequate adaptation to the rapid spread of urban industrialization. Units of government appropriate for the limited concerns of a rural municipality are being overwhelmed by the complex needs of an urban society for utilities and services.[5] The transference of responsibility to specific boards and commissions has been one way of adapting the machinery of provincial government to the changing conditions of the twentieth century, but it has the disadvantage of removing large areas of the public service from the scrutiny of the elected representatives, and has further confused the administrative tangle.[6] Metropolitan Toronto, Metropolitan Winnipeg, and Metropolitan Montreal are examples of different *ad hoc* solutions to the peculiarly intractable problems of local government in the exploding metropolitan areas. In general it may be said that although there is a profusion of forms and units of government, the machinery of local and provincial government in Canada is inadequate to the tasks of managing

[4]Canada, Dominion Bureau of Statistics, *Weekly Bulletin*, vol. 28, no. 37, *Estimates of Population as at June 1, 1960* (Ottawa, Sept., 1960).

[5]The complexity of local government in Canada can be studied in K. Grant Crawford, *Canadian Municipal Government* (Toronto: University of Toronto Press, 1954). The inadequacy of local government to the pressing demands of industrialization was a recurrent theme in the Round Table on Man and Industry, 1956–8, and is referred to in the brilliant analysis of this exploratory meeting in the book by Sir Geoffrey Vickers, *The Undirected Society* (Toronto: University of Toronto Press, 1959).

[6]*Report of the Committee on the Organization of Government in Ontario* (Toronto: Queen's Printer, Sept. 25, 1959).

public affairs in the rapidly developing industrial urban Canada to which the Gordon Commission's Report looks forward.[7]

The Gordon Commission has analysed in detail and with persuasive clarity the rapid changes now going on in Canada's economic and social patterns of living. The majority of Canadians are dependent on regular employment in industry for wages and the country is irrevocably committed to the urban way of life. The human needs arising from the tensions and complexities of metropolitan living and industrial employment are thus, inevitably, among the major determinants of the kind and extent of welfare services. The best analysis of these needs is still that of Lord Beveridge,[8] in which he identifies the "Five Giant" evils of modern society as Ignorance (or inadequate education), Idleness (or lack of gainful employment), Disease (or inadequate provision for health services), Squalor (or inadequate and sub-standard conditions), and Want (or inadequate monetary income to maintain a minimum standard of living). It is not surprising that Canada in 1960 is devoting increasingly large sums to education, health services, and housing and living facilities, or that its welfare services are heavily concentrated on alleviating the consequences of unemployment and inadequate family incomes.

Canada is a federal country with a written constitution. This is a fruitful source of discussion and dissension in many fields of national policy. Its consequences for the welfare services are particularly unfortunate. The Fathers of Confederation, when they drafted the British North America Act, were not dealing with a modern industrial society of workers living in towns, dependent on wages, and linked by effective communications across the whole country. Their concept of welfare, inherited largely through their forbears in Great Britain and the United States, or pre-revolutionary France, was related to a "settled people" in relatively self-sufficient localities. Welfare services as such were scarcely mentioned,[9] and were apparently relegated to the jurisdiction of the provinces, and by them in most cases unthinkingly assumed to be largely municipal and local matters. These views were reinforced by decisions of the Privy Council in the nineteenth century, when the social conditions and the available fiscal resources all seemed to support the view that welfare measures were appropriately matters of provincial and local concern.

The constitutional position was confirmed in the twentieth century by

[7]Canada, Royal Commission on Canada's Economic Prospects (Gordon Commission), *Final Report* (Ottawa: Queen's Printer, 1958).

[8]W. H. Beveridge, *The Pillars of Security* (London: George Allen & Unwin, 1942), p. 42.

[9]Subsection 7 of section 92 of the British North America Act assigns jurisdiction over "The Establishment, Maintenance and Management of Hospitals, Asylums, Charities and Eleemosynary Institutions in and for the province other than Marine Hospitals."

the acceptance in 1925 of the opinion of the Department of Justice that the collection of contributions for social insurance would be an infringement of provincial property and civil rights and by the decision of the Privy Council that the Unemployment Insurance Act of 1936 was *ultra vires*. Although the Family Allowances Act was introduced in 1944 without any constitutional amendment, in the case of Unemployment Insurance in 1940 and Old Age Security in 1951 the federal government was careful to secure appropriate amendments to the British North America Act.[10]

In the same period the federal government has progressively accepted financial responsibility for an increasing proportion of the expenditures until it is now estimated that 75 per cent of all the public expenditures on health and welfare fall on the federal government.

This dichotomy between political and financial responsibility is a serious weakness in Canada's welfare arrangements. It means that every attempt at improvement becomes part of a complex bargain between federal and provincial governments in which, almost invariably, the needs of people are subordinated to political and administrative expediency.

Traditions and fundamental religious attitudes have also a continued relevance to the quality and character of welfare services in Canada. The close relation between the Protestant ethic and capitalism has been clearly recognized since Max Weber's classic analysis.[11] The attitude of the community to the "poor and needy" and the moral connotations of self-dependence already mentioned still affect the welfare services established within the strongly Protestant background of the Anglo-Saxon and Scottish settlers in the Maritimes and Ontario. The position in Quebec is quite different and is clearly set out in Esdras Minville's memorandum to the Rowell-Sirois Commission:

However, a proper understanding of the specific character of social conditions in Quebec province requires a definite and clear comprehension of two absolutely essential points of Catholic doctrine: social justice and charity. Here indeed the nature and character of social institutions are the concrete expression of a doctrine, not merely the result of historical evolution.[12]

Thus, federal intervention in a field which by tradition comes under provincial jurisdiction is opposed not only by many powerful political

[10]The effect of these interpretations on the financing of welfare services is the subject of quite a number of studies. One of the more recent is that by A. H. Birch, *Federalism, Finance and Social Legislation* (London: Oxford University Press, 1955), where the situation in Canada is treated in a comparative way as a problem of federalism as well as a problem of welfare.

[11]Max Weber, *The Protestant Ethic and the Spirit of Capitalism*, trans. Talcott Parsons (5th ed., New York: Charles Scribner's Sons, 1956).

[12]Esdras Minville, "Labour Legislation and Social Services in the Province of Quebec," App. 5 of the *Report of the Royal Commission on Dominion-Provincial Relations* (Rowell-Sirois Commission), (Ottawa: King's Printer, 1939), p. 45.

interests in Quebec but also by the forces of religious belief. The need to scrutinize any proposal for a national programme of health and welfare services for its impact on the complex matrix of Quebec opinion as well as the remainder of the country is a phenomenon of welfare policy which is quite peculiar to Canada. It is a phenomenon which should not and cannot be ignored.

THE GROWTH OF WELFARE SERVICES

The development of welfare services in Canada has not been extensively studied or fully documented[13] and much research remains to be done to establish its full extent and character.[14] Nevertheless it is possible to detect four main phases.

At the time when Canada was primarily an agricultural country, welfare was essentially a local problem. For example, Nova Scotia and New Brunswick, settled largely by United Empire Loyalists and emigrants from Great Britain, had the Poor Law on the British model on the statute book at the time of Confederation.[15] Ontario, while specifically excluding the Poor Law from its statutes at the time of Confederation, inherited all the traditional attitudes and practices of local poor relief. In varying degrees the western provinces, while not enacting the Poor Law, relied upon municipal administration. This was the time when relief in times of personal disaster was largely a matter of neighbourly action or of local municipal responsibility. It was also the period when institutions were built, often with provincial support, to provide welfare services. The county poor-farm, the mental hospital, the children's orphanage were characteristic of the time.[16] The buildings are many of them still in existence, although most are now put to less archaic uses.[17]

[13]Margaret K. Strong, *Public Welfare Administration in Canada* (Chicago: University of Chicago Press, 1944); S. D. Clark, *The Social Development of Canada* (Toronto: University of Toronto Press, 1942).

[14]The researches of Mr. R. B. Splane, who is currently at work on a study of "The Role of the Provincial Government in the Development of Social Welfare in Ontario in the Nineteenth Century" for a dissertation for the degree of Doctor of Social Work at the University of Toronto have already shown that there is a rich mine of undiscovered material available.

[15]In 1949, when engaged on a survey of welfare services in New Brunswick, the author was intrigued to find that the basic statute was the Poor Law of 1786 (An Act Respecting Support of the Poor, Consolidated Statutes 1927, c. 204); it was repealed only in 1960. In 1958, Nova Scotia replaced its Poor Law by a General Assistance Act. For the development in Nova Scotia up to 1945 see George F. Davidson, *Report on Public Welfare Services*, for the Royal Commission on Development and Rehabilitation (Halifax: King's Printer, 1944).

[16]One of the author's students told him of an institution in his home municipality which still bears engraved in large letters on its pediment "The Home for the Indigent and the Mildly Insane."

[17]For example, the County Homes of Ontario are now the backbone of that province's expanding programme of Homes for the Aged.

One characteristically Canadian welfare service emerged toward the end of this period. The work of J. J. Kelso, a Toronto newspaperman, led to the passage of the Children's Protection Acts of Ontario in 1893. These acts were the basis for the establishment of Children's Aid Societies throughout Ontario, and resulted in the passage of similar legislation in other provinces, accompanied by the creation of Children's Aid Societies in most of the main populated areas of the country. This combination — private initiative and privately supported services combined with support from public funds and public responsibility to administer the law of the provinces — placed Canada among the pioneers of child welfare. More and more the services for the care of children have become a public responsibility, although Ontario and New Brunswick have retained the form of the private Children's Aid Society as have some of the larger cities and towns in other provinces.

The second phase of growth reflected the beginnings of industrialization as well as a growing interest in social services in Great Britain and the United States. The agitation for old age pensions in Great Britain at the time of the Royal Commission on the Aged Poor of 1895 and the Royal Commission on the Poor Law of 1906 was reflected in debates in the Canadian House of Commons in 1907 and at intervals until 1927 when the Old Age Pension Act established a non-contributory programme based on federal sharing in provincial schemes.[18] Even this might not have occurred if the late James S. Woodsworth had not been shrewd enough to compel the elusive Mackenzie King to promise in writing that legislation would be introduced as the price of Woodsworth's support after the critical election of 1925.[19] To the Old Age Pensions thus provided on a means test basis were added pensions for the blind in the same form in 1937.

The influence on Canada of events in the United States of America is shown by the enactment in 1916 of the first Mothers Allowance Act in the province of Manitoba. This reflected the agitation, expressed at the White House Conference of 1911, to provide "Mothers' Pensions" to enable a mother, deprived of the support of the family breadwinner, to rear her dependent children at home rather than place them in public care or leave them uncared for while she went out to work. This particular form of public assistance has been enacted in all the Canadian provinces and is still part of the pattern of welfare services.

[18]See John S. Morgan, "Old Age Pensions in Canada: A Review and a Result," *Social Service Review*, XXVI, no. 2, June, 1952; and Elisabeth Wallace, "Old Age Security in Canada: Changing Attitudes," *Canadian Journal of Economics and Political Science*, XXV, no. 2, May, 1952.

[19]K. W. McNaught, *A Prophet in Politics* (Toronto: University of Toronto Press, 1959), p. 218. This biography of James S. Woodsworth provides an admirable analysis of the changing social, political and economic background from the beginning of the twentieth century.

The emergence of industry in Canada led directly to the adoption in 1914 of Workmen's Compensation legislation in Ontario, largely based on the legislation of Chancellor Bismarck in Germany, and resulting from a full-scale inquiry by Mr. Justice Meredith of the Supreme Court of Ontario. The legislation also was repeated, with minor variations, by all the provinces. The effect of the First World War was to be seen in the provision of allowances for the families of service men and in the establishment of pensions and medical care services for the returning veterans as a federal responsibility.

The third phase was marked in its first stage by the economic depression of the 1930's. Canada's welfare services were quite inadequate to deal with the human consequences of the economic blizzard. Private social agencies were engulfed and municipalities went bankrupt under the burden of relief costs, while the provinces found it impossible to rescue them from their plight. The federal government was compelled to pour money into the provision of emergency relief. In both Great Britain and the United States a similar state of affairs led to a complete reorganization of the welfare services. The Social Security Act of 1935 marked the massive intervention of the federal government of the United States in the field of welfare for the first time in its history. Income maintenance programmes were placed on a planned basis of social insurance, supported by federally assisted state programmes of public assistance for designated categories. In Great Britain the establishment of the Unemployment Assistance Board in 1934 marked the first stage of the process which eventually led to the complete reorganization of income maintenance programmes under the National Insurance Act and the National Assistance Act of 1948. In Canada the impetus of the depression gave rise to a period of inquiry, investigation, and ferment but it did not result in any fundamental change in the pattern of welfare services. An attempt by the Government of Prime Minister Bennett to introduce unemployment insurance in 1935 was abortive, for in 1937 the legislation was ruled *ultra vires* the British North America Act upon appeal to the Privy Council. This decision confirmed, at least by inference, the constitutional responsibility of the provinces for welfare and uncovered the shoals upon which any attempt to create a social insurance programme might be wrecked.

The Second World War intervened before any decisions had been made. Canada was swept out of its third phase with breathtaking speed into the new age of industrial manufacture, urbanized populations, increasing wealth, and all the complexities of a twentieth-century industrial society.

Under the pressures generated by depression and war, much careful. study was undertaken upon which subsequent developments in welfare services have been based. The depression produced the efforts of the radicals like the League for Social Reconstruction[20] and the intergovernmental conflicts on costs and constitutional responsibility as revealed in the Rowell-Sirois Report, in which serious efforts were made to place the welfare services on some logical, integrated plan. The war period, and especially the astonishing popularity of the Beveridge Report, led to active consideration of ways and means of establishing and developing health and welfare services in Canada. Among the prominent writers of this period was the late Harry M. Cassidy, who made precise proposals for an integrated programme of health and welfare.[21] The Canadian government commissioned the Marsh Report[22] on social security and the Heagerty Report on health insurance.[23]

Meanwhile the course of the war had induced the federal Government to make a start, even before the reports were filed. In 1940 it began to be apparent that Germany would eventually be defeated. Foreseeing an awkward period of readjustment, with the probability of large-scale unemployment, and faced with the urgent current need for national administrative arrangements for selective service, the Government introduced a constitutional amendment in 1940 to permit the enactment of the Unemployment Insurance Act of that year.[24] In 1944, actuated as much by motives of economic policy[25] as concern with social policy, the Government introduced an act for the payment of family allowances, which Marsh had described as the "key to consistency" in a social security policy. As the war drew to a close, Canada, like every belligerent, began to make plans for the re-establishment and resettlement of the returning veterans. The Veterans' Charter, as it became known, provided extensive pensions, medical care provisions and resettlement benefits for all members of the armed forces, and a new department of state — the Department of Veterans Affairs — was created to administer the programme. The Department of Health and Pensions, deprived of its "pensions" duties, became the Department of National Health and Welfare, with a Deputy Minister of Welfare for the Welfare Branch.

Finally, at the Dominion-provincial conference of 1945, the federal Government submitted proposals to the provinces in which the re-

[20]*Social Planning for Canada*, prepared by the Research Committee of the League for Social Reconstruction (Toronto: Thomas Nelson & Sons, 1935).

[21]Harry M. Cassidy, *Social Security and Reconstruction in Canada* (Toronto: Ryerson Press, 1942); and *Health and Welfare Reorganization for Canada* (Toronto: Ryerson Press, 1946).

[22]L. C. Marsh, *Report on Social Security for Canada* (Ottawa: King's Printer, 1943).

[23]J. J. Heagerty, *Health Insurance*, Report of the Advisory Committee on Health Insurance Appointed by Order in Council (Ottawa: King's Printer, 1943).

[24]A more detailed criticism of the inadequacies in the current operation of this Act can be found in John S. Morgan, *Unemployment Insurance* (Toronto: Woodsworth Memorial Research Foundation, 1958).

[25]Harry M. Cassidy, "Children's Allowances in Canada," *Public Welfare*, Aug., 1945.

arrangement of fiscal resources, economic policies, and health and welfare services was included in a proposed "package deal." The conference collapsed on fiscal issues and the prospects for an integrated programme of health and welfare services disappeared.

The Liberal Government, defeated in its intentions of developing a comprehensive welfare programme, proceeded, as public opinion, electoral strategy, and fiscal resources gave it opportunities, to add piecemeal to the welfare services. In 1948 a programme of national health grants was announced to provide the basis of information and improved facilities upon which a national health insurance scheme might be built; in 1956 the Government introduced proposals for a national hospital insurance plan which is now being implemented by all the provinces; in 1950 the Government, in response to widespread criticism of the inadequacy of the old age pensions legislation, established a Joint Parliamentary Committee on Old Age Security.[26] After an exhaustive inquiry had been made into the systems in operation in other countries throughout the world, and representations heard from a wide variety of interests, the Government secured the consent of the provinces to a constitutional amendment and then introduced the present system of old age security allowances and old age assistance allowances. A new category was added when provision was made in 1955 for a federal-provincial programme for permanently and totally disabled persons.

The passing in 1956 of an act providing for federal participation in unemployment assistance did not merely add one more to the categories in which the federal government is prepared to assist the provinces to fulfil their constitutional responsibilities for welfare. The new Act makes no distinction, as was done in the 1945 proposals and in the Rowell-Sirois Report, between the employable and the unemployable. It leaves to the provinces full responsibility for determining the needs of their own people, and sets no maximum limits on benefits. The adherence of Ontario (in December, 1956) and Quebec (in 1959) to this Act brings its benefits to all of Canada. It is too early yet to determine exactly what the consequences of this legislation will be. It closes a major gap in the social services and marks another large-scale transference of financial responsibility to the federal government. It could be used as a means of reorganizing public welfare services in Canada, but much will depend on the vision and leadership of the federal and provincial authorities.

A new period seems to be opening in the sixties. Agitation against the inadequacy of the $40 a month basic benefit of old age security, established in 1951, led to the increase of this figure in April, 1957, to $46 as the Liberal Government faced a general election, in which it was defeated. In November, 1957, the victorious Progressive Conservative

[26]*Report of the Joint Committee of the Senate and the House of Commons on Old Age Security* (Ottawa: King's Printer, 1950).

Government, with a precarious hold on power and itself facing an early election, increased the figure to $55, which also became the basic maximum for the other "categorical assistance" programmes. Concern about the drain on the Treasury, and the attractions of the Old-Age and Survivors Insurance scheme in the United States, which does not depend on the general tax revenues, have led to considerable demand for revision of the system. Organized labour, interested in securing retirement benefits that bear some relation to previous earnings rather than the inadequate flat rate benefits of the existing scheme, began to press for consideration of an additional wage related pension financed by a social insurance programme. The introduction of such a scheme in Sweden and in Great Britain, after exhaustive studies, served to increase the pressure for a new look at old age security. Professor Robert M. Clark was appointed to make a study of the American and Canadian systems and his report has been in the Government's hands since 1959.[27]

The federal government's contribution to Canada's welfare programmes can be seen from this account to be both illogical and untidy. Not until 1944 did it formally acknowledge welfare as a matter of federal concern by establishing a Welfare Branch in the newly created Department of National Health and Welfare. This branch has been responsible for the extremely efficient management of the two universal allowances — family allowances and old age security — through the adoption of automation and skilful planning. On the other hand, federal participation in the public assistance programmes has been limited almost entirely to *ex post facto* audit of provincial operations. Unlike the social security system in the United States, the Canadian legislation makes no provision for the maintenance of sound administration, and the national department provides no consultation services. Very little use is made of advisory committees or boards, except that provincial departments are called into consultation at irregular intervals to discuss proposed amendments in the regulations of the various assistance programmes. This lack of supervision and direction is undoubtedly due in large measure to political considerations, since the parties that have been in power in Ottawa have, especially since 1945, leaned over backwards to avoid any appearance of intervention in matters which appear even to touch on the jurisdiction of the provinces. The Welfare Branch shares with the Health Branch the services of a Division of Research and Statistics, which has already made a notable contribution to welfare by providing the essential information on many aspects of welfare service on which policies heretofore have been decided largely on the basis of political intuition.

In addition to its direct responsibility for certain welfare programmes

[27]"Economic Security for the Aged in the United States and Canada" (2 vols., Ottawa: Dept. of National Health and Welfare, 1959) (mimeo.). Hereafter cited as Clark Report.

the federal government is also deeply involved in financial expenditures for a number of welfare programmes that are established and administered by the provinces. These are the "categorical assistance" programmes for persons who can demonstrate "need" within the terms of the legislation providing for old age assistance to persons between 65 and 69 years of age, blind persons' allowances, disabled persons' allowances for the "permanently and totally disabled," and, more recently, unemployment assistance. Each province, if it wishes to participate in these programmes, must pass its own legislation which conforms to the minimum conditions of the federal legislation. Even within the limits imposed by the federal legislation there is a wide variation between one province and another. For example, in 1959 the percentage of persons between 65 and 69 years of age in receipt of old age assistance varied in March from 61.11 per cent in Newfoundland and 37.63 per cent in New Brunswick to a low of 13.28 per cent in Ontario.[28] These variations are further widened by the practice followed by some provinces of paying supplementary allowances to recipients of old age assistance.[29] These wide variations result partly from local economic and social conditions as they are reflected in provincial legislation and local administration, and partly from the fact that in some provinces part of the burden carried by old age assistance may be carried by other elements in the public welfare programme. Much wider variations would undoubtedly be evident in the impact of the Unemployment Assistance Act if the figures for case loads were available. Professor Clark notes in his report:

The provisions [of the Unemployment Assistance Act] enable the Federal Government to share . . . in the Supplementary Allowances paid to recipients of Old Age Security and Old Age Assistance in Ontario and in Manitoba. The same provisions exclude Federal participation in costs of Supplementary Allowances or assistance paid in Saskatchewan, Alberta and British Columbia.[30]

Similar inconsistencies can also be found in the treatment of mothers' allowances under the federal Unemployment Assistance Act.

There is one social insurance programme which operates at the provincial level. Workmen's Compensation was first introduced into the province of Ontario in 1914. The system established then is based on acceptance of responsibility for full medical care of those affected by industrial injury or disease as well as compensation for loss of wages at

[28]Dept. of National Health and Welfare, "Public Health and Welfare Services in Canada," a report prepared for the *Canada Year Book*, 1960, by the Research and Statistics Division, March, 1960, Table 4, p. 28.

[29]See Clark Report, par. 1203 and Table 70, pp. 421–2.

[30]*Ibid.*, par. 1208, p. 423. It will not escape the notice of the percipient reader that the two favoured provinces had Progressive Conservative governments, whereas the other provinces had governments of a somewhat different political complexion from that of the party in power in Ottawa.

a reasonable percentage of previous average earnings. This service has been successfully operated and improved since its inception and copied in its essentials by all the provinces as they became industrialized.

The relations between provinces and their municipalities are infinitely more complex. The financial pressures of the depression of the 1930's and the unsolved fiscal problems of federal-provincial relations during and since the Second World War have left their mark. The proportionately weak fiscal position of the municipalities in the provinces, which by tradition have regarded welfare services as local matters, has led to a ⇠ wide variety of administrative and financial arrangements. In Newfoundland, for example, the welfare services are almost wholly provincial, while in most of the other provinces there have been two major trends. One trend has been the gradual assumption by the province of responsibility for the operation of programmes; the other has been the development of cost-sharing arrangements by which the municipalities administer the programme but are reimbursed by the province for a large proportion of the cost of benefits paid, and in some instances for administration. Each province has a department of government specifically charged with the administration of welfare services, but the range of services in a given province varies considerably from province to province. In every province there will be found programmes for the income maintenance of persons in need of financial assistance, for child welfare and protection, and services (including housing) for the care of old people. In all provinces, until recently, there were mothers' allowances programmes, but there is a trend now to merge these into the general assistance programmes. In addition, there may be services for disabled persons, for the mentally disabled, and for certain groups of sick persons, such as those suffering from tuberculosis, poliomyelitis, cancer, and other long-term diseases. In one province the care and treatment of offenders and of juvenile delinquents may be a welfare programme; in another it may come under a department of reform institutions, or that of the law officers of the province. The extent to which welfare services, even when a programme is in existence, are actually available to those who need them, will depend on the nature and adequacy of the local provincial and municipal organization. The general tendency is to create, within the provinces, larger units of administration under provincial auspices rather than depend on the structure of municipal government.

It will be evident from this brief description that it is quite impossible to make an accurate estimate of the numbers of people affected by Canada's welfare services.[31] Even in the public sector where services are mostly those of money payments to individual persons, there are no

[31]All families with children, and all persons aged 70 and over are, of course, affected by family allowances and old age security allowances respectively.

agreed procedures for reporting on services rendered except for the federal programmes and the federal-provincial assistance programmes. No standard definitions exist to provide the basis upon which case loads can be reported; no common periods of report or agreed dates of reporting exist. From time to time a major piece of research is done in respect of a particular social problem, as a result of which a particular phase of welfare is illuminated for a short period by relatively adequate information.

The most recent example of this type of study is the Clark Report. This report, of course, deals only with a programme which is substantially federal in character and requires adequate reporting of case loads as a necessary instrument for determining shareable costs. Nevertheless, it is clear from the information which is available that a substantial percentage of Canadian people do benefit at some time or other from the welfare services. There is a great need for the development of regular statistical reporting on a comparable basis, and for continuous research into the results of welfare programmes.

The Canadian Welfare Council, which has maintained a careful watch on Canada's welfare programmes, called a conference of experts in January, 1958, on certain aspects of income security. From the work of this meeting and the resultant discussions the Council prepared and adopted in June, 1958, a public statement of policy[32] which serves as a convenient commentary on social security in Canada today. There can be no question that the time has come when the accumulation of piecemeal amendments should give way to a comprehensive redesigning of Canada's social security arrangements.

Any review of the government services that can be classified as "welfare services" soon runs afoul of the difficulty of confining the phrase to any agreed definition. For example, the care and treatment of offenders against the law can be regarded, as it is by many people, as a function of the administration of justice. But in recent years, from the early stirrings of the Archambault Report[33] to the most recent Fauteux Report,[34] it has become more and more accepted that although the determination of guilt is a function of the administration of justice, the care and treatment of offenders is more appropriately conducted as a service to people with a wide range of human needs. This is so whether they are placed in the custodial care of penal institutions, or released on parole after a part of their sentence has been served in custody, or returned to the community on probation. All the indications are that

[32]*Social Security for Canada* (Ottawa: Canadian Welfare Council, 1958).
[33]*Report of the Royal Commission to Investigate the Penal System of Canada* (Ottawa: King's Printer, 1938).
[34]*Report of the Committee Appointed to Inquire into the Principles and Procedures Followed in the Remission Services of the Department of Justice of Canada* (Ottawa: Queen's Printer, 1956).

the developing service of "corrections" will increasingly come to be classified as a welfare service.

A somewhat different situation arises in relation to public housing. In many parts of Europe the need to provide from public resources for adequate minimum shelter for large sectors of the population has long been recognized. Canada has been singularly tardy in developing this type of environmental support of minimum standards of living.[35] The Central Mortage and Housing Corporation is a government agency through which substantial amounts of public money have been channelled into the encouragement of home-building, but relatively little has been achieved in slum clearance or the provision of subsidized rental housing. The last of these might be classified as a welfare service, but it is most improbable that loans to support home ownership would be regarded as a welfare service.

Other activities of the federal government in welfare are ancillary to the fulfilment of obligations to special sections of the community for which it has direct responsibility. The care of Indians and Eskimos and of immigrants is a typical example, where specific welfare services are included among the activities of the Department of Citizenship and Immigration; the welfare and recreation of members of the armed forces and of their families on service falls within the orbit of the Ministry of National Defence.

It is difficult, therefore, to trace any orderly development of social services provided by the various levels and types of government; it is quite impossible to do so for the services provided by private agencies.[36] Many private agencies owe their origin to the church, and in the province of Quebec this is still the primary form of welfare service. In the nineteenth century particularly, many private agencies were established, often with a measure of subsidy from public funds. They sprang up, usually in the first place on a local basis, in response to specific needs recognized by socially responsible groups of citizens in particular communities. Many of them were extensions of similar services in Great Britain, or were created in emulation of similar services in the old country. They cater to every variety of human need from that of a transient in need of food and shelter to that of a community in need of recreational facilities. Some of them, like the Canadian Red Cross Society, or the Salvation Army, or the YMCA or YWCA are Canadian counterparts of organizations in countries throughout the world. Some of them are national societies concerned with services — varying from

[35]See Humphrey Carver, *Houses for Canadians: A Study of Housing Problems in the Toronto Area* (Toronto: University of Toronto Press, 1948); and Albert Rose, *Regent Park: A Study in Slum Clearance* (Toronto: University of Toronto Press, 1958).

[36]Their complexity is well illustrated in D. V. Donnison, *Welfare Services in a Canadian Community* (Toronto: University of Toronto Press, 1958).

education and research to service programmes — connected with specific disadvantages, as for example the Canadian National Institute for the Blind or the Canadian Tuberculosis Society. Most private agencies, however, are local in character, organized and supported by groups of citizens in the municipality or area in which they operate. With a few notable exceptions they are confined to the urban areas and serve a selected clientele.

Private welfare agencies have greatly changed their character in the past half-century. Originally much of the actual work was done by volunteer citizens who gave direct service to those in need. While there is still a vital need for volunteers in modern welfare services, the "private agency" today is more likely to be staffed by salaried workers and differentiated from public agencies by the fact that it is financed largely by public subscription and governed by a private board of directors. The boards are usually self-perpetuating, even when nominally elected.

There has always been, especially in Canada, a close association between private agencies and the public authorities. The outstanding example is the Children's Aid Society, which is a private agency in form, but is often wholly supported by tax funds and carries out an esssentially public function in the care of neglected and dependent children. In many fields of activity the private agency, having pioneered a service and demonstrated its value, relinquishes its responsibility to the public authorities. This is happening today in the field of recreation. A recent and significant development in Toronto is the new arrangement at the University Settlement, where the city authorities have built a modern community centre but have deliberately committed its social and recreational direction to the private agency which had until 1959 been wholly responsible for the service.

The greatest change in the private welfare services in recent years has been in the way they are financed. In North America the creation of fund-raising organizations designed particularly to tap the corporate wealth of the new industrial order has been examined in great detail. The federation of private welfare agencies, first for fund-raising and also for joint planning and co-operation, dates back to the early part of this century in Cleveland, Ohio.[37] The most recent development in this field is the emergence of the United Fund as a lineal descendant of the Community Chest. In essence this movement divorces the raising of funds for welfare purposes from the actual organization and operation of the services, and replaces the separate fund-raising efforts of the agencies by a professional campaign, dominated by the task of raising enough each year to maintain all the member agencies at or above their current level of service.

[37]J. R. Seeley *et al., Community Chest: A Case History in Philanthropy* (Toronto: University of Toronto Press, 1957), p. 19.

There are now more than one hundred campaigns of this kind, collecting for 1,700 social agencies in all the major cities and larger towns of Canada. They are essentially local in character, just as the services they finance are essentially local in character. There are arrangements for the support of national agencies but these are not wholly satisfactory.

The organization of consultative and co-ordinating services is well developed on a national scale in the Canadian Welfare Council, which has made a notable contribution to the discussion and development of national policies through its studies and inquiries, its consultant services, and its provision of a steady flow of information on welfare matters. The continuous work of the Council is supplemented by the biennial Canadian Conference on Social Work which provides an opportunity every other year for administrators and interested laymen in both public and private welfare services to exchange ideas and information. The Canadian Association of Social Workers provides the essential nucleus of the professional workers, establishing standards for admission to the profession and maintaining contact with the field.

Except for the Ontario Welfare Council, the only organization of welfare services is at the local level, where the welfare council or the social planning council in the larger cities and towns ensures some measure of co-ordination among the multifarious agencies.

An important factor in the changing social services is that as the income maintenance programmes have grown more effective in both coverage and benefits, it has become increasingly clear that the provision of a minimum income, while essential, is not in itself enough. Along with the maintenance of income must go the development of services, such as, for example, adequate recreational services; medical care and after-care for the physically and mentally ill; homemaker services; skilled social work services to meet the infinite variety of social situations and social malfunctioning that are often the by-products of the stresses of modern social life; housing for those who are at an economic disadvantage (particularly for older people of small means and for large families with unstable and low incomes). All of these require the increasing attention of qualified professional staffs, especially of qualified social workers.

The emergence of social work as a discrete profession, with its own professional organization, and an established academic discipline of study and research, has been a mark of the second quarter of the twentieth century. The *Survey of Welfare Positions* conducted by the Department of National Health and Welfare and published in April, 1954, shows that there are gross deficiencies in the available supply of properly qualified workers.

In recent years public departments have shown a very substantial increase in the establishment of programmes designed to ensure that their staffs are qualified to deal, as they do, with the intimate affairs of so many thousands of citizens. British Columbia has had since the early 1940's a staff training programme intended to provide a steady flow of professional social workers and in-service trainees to its offices throughout the province. Other provinces have exploited the possibilities of educational leave for professional training and in-service training programmes in varying degrees. Nevertheless, it is still true to say that a great deal of welfare service is being administered in Canada by staffs who are neither qualified nor trained for this delicate and difficult work. Not all of the provinces have yet forsworn the relics of political patronage in making appointments, or recognized that technical competence and economical operation are not sufficient qualification for the administration of welfare services.

An entirely different type of health and welfare service which ought properly to be included in the private sector is the "fringe" benefits of the modern wage contracts which provide extensive health insurance coverage, retirement pensions, and other benefits which are, in all their essentials, welfare services of the same kind as those provided by the public schemes. Table I shows something of the range and extent of benefits in one major sector of Canadian industry. It is based on information drawn from the *Annual Survey of Working Conditions* and covers only one part of the field, and it does not provide any assessment of the actual coverage of these benefits or the degree to which they provide effective protection against the risks covered or the extent to which coverage extends beyond the immediate period of employment. The extent of coverage, however, is very clearly significant as part of the whole picture.

TABLE I

PERCENTAGES OF WORKERS IN PLANTS PROVIDING FOR CERTAIN FRINGE BENEFITS IN MANUFACTURING INDUSTRIES IN CANADA

Benefits	Office employees	Plant employees
Pension plans	82.8	69.3
Group life insurance	93.8	89.7
Cash compensation for wage loss due to sickness	62.6	81.6
Hospitalization	92.1	88.4
Surgical benefits	93.1	89.7
Physicians' services in hospital	83.8	78.6
Physicians' home and office calls	56.2	51.9
Major medical (catastrophe insurance)	18.9	9.7
Number of workers in surveyed plants	226,973	758,424

SOURCE: Dept. of Labour, Economics and Research Branch, *Working Conditions in Canada, 1958* (Ottawa: Queen's Printer, 1959), pp. 6–8. It is important to remember that these benefits are reported in respect to industrial plants; therefore, while it is true to say that 69.3 per cent of workers in manufacturing are employed in plants which have pension plans, it is *not* known what percentage of actual workers are covered by those plans.

In addition to these benefits secured in wage contracts, a whole range of social security benefits for upper income classes is provided by the personal income tax exemptions, provisions for full salary during sick leaves, substantial tax free perquisites and expense accounts (such as the provision of cars, holidays, club subscriptions) and generous retirement provisions for salaried employees, particularly in the upper ranks of industrial management. Professor Titmuss[38] has recently drawn attention to the fact that these provisions do greatly raise the standard of living of those who benefit from these perquisites of office and do protect them against the same contingencies as those covered by public schemes for wage earners. In a very marked degree they are financed indirectly by the taxpayer, since they are deductible expenses of industry.

The pattern of welfare services in Canada, then, is essentially that of the kaleidoscope. It is rich in variety, uneven in quality, and constantly changing in design. It reflects the rapidly changing society of which it is a part and demonstrates the truth of the aphorism that the social and political organisms of society tend to lag behind its industrial and economic development. There is, none the less, a general direction. Welfare services requiring large expenditures in relation to conditions generic to urban industrial society tend increasingly to demand the financial backing of federal tax resources. Provincial governments are tending to take a larger degree of responsibility for welfare from their municipalities and to reorganize their welfare services in larger units of administration. Private agencies tend to coalesce, both locally and nationally, as the complex interrelations of welfare compel more effective co-operation and more co-ordinated activity. Private business is being called upon to provide, for both its managerial employees and its operatives, a range of income security benefits which either substitute for gaps in the public programmes (as in the case of sickness benefits) or add differential benefits (as in the case of retirement pensions) to those now available in public programmes.

THE COST OF WELFARE SERVICES

It is impossible to make accurate estimates of the cost of welfare services in Canada for a number of reasons, some of which are inevitable and some of which can and should receive the attention of the responsible authorities. This aspect of welfare, like many others, is one which cries aloud for research.

The most recent estimates show that in 1959–60 public expenditure on health and welfare services was some $3 billion. This represents about 11.4 per cent of the net national income for that year. There are no reliable figures on the amounts raised and spent from non-

[38]Richard M. Titmuss, *Essays on the Welfare State* (New Haven: Yale University Press, 1958).

governmental sources. The United Funds and Community Chests in the same year raised and spent about $29 million, but this represents only a fraction of the total of private expenditures on health and welfare services. If to this figure are added the total annual expenditures[39] on social benefits made by employers and employees in industry and commerce, it can be seen that a substantial fraction of the nation's annual income is spent on health and welfare services.

By far the largest part of the public expenditure of $3 billion is spent on welfare services, the amount estimated for health services being only $0.825 billion. As the hospital insurance programme goes into effect in all provinces, the proportion spent on health services may increase. Of the $2.2 billion spent on public welfare programmes, over $2 billion, or more than 90 per cent, went to income maintenance programmes, about three-quarters of this expenditure going on old age security, old age assistance, family allowances and unemployment insurance.

These gross figures need to be seen in the context not only of the national income but also of the demographic facts.

In 1913 public expenditure on health and welfare stood at $15,215,000 or $2 per capita, of which the municipalities' share was $8,000,000 and that of the provinces something in excess of $4,000,000. In 1926 the corresponding figures including pensions and after care for veterans of World War I had risen to $88,000,000 or $9 per capita, of which $50,000,000 was carried by the federal government and the balance about equally by the provinces and municipalities.[40]

The corresponding figures for 1959–60 show a striking contrast — an expenditure of 3.0 billion, of which 71.2 per cent came from federal resources, 25.6 per cent from provincial resources (including payments

[39]The return on trusteed pension plans issued by the Dominion Bureau of Statistics for 1959 shows the income of the 841 plans "reporting" to have been $476 million or about 1.5 per cent of the net national income. A study by Industrial Relations Counsellors of Toronto on "Fringe Benefits in Canada" of 100 companies in Canada in 1959 showed that the cost as a percentage of payroll came to an over-all figure for all the companies of 22.2 per cent. The main items in these "fringe benefits" were: paid time off (for vacation pay, holidays with pay, rest breaks, compassionate leave, etc.) 10.6 per cent; payments required by law (unemployment insurance, workmen's compensation, old age security) 2.7 per cent; pension and welfare plans 6.4 per cent; year-end and special bonuses 1.5 per cent; other non-cash benefits 1.0 per cent. While there are wide variations among companies, the firms reporting appear to be a reasonably representative cross-section of Canadian employers. These figures are indicative of the very substantial amounts being spent on welfare (even under a much narrower definition than the very inflated definition of "fringe benefits" adopted in the above study) over and above payments from public funds and private charitable funds. A comparable study of United States industry by the Economic Research Department of the United States Chamber of Commerce is quoted as showing a figure for "fringe benefits" of 21.9 per cent in 1959 as compared with the 22.2 per cent for the Canadian companies studied.

[40]George F. Davidson, "Canadian Social Welfare" in *Social Work Year Book, 1957* (New York: Council on Social Work Education, 1958).

from workmen's compensation funds) and 3.2 per cent from municipal taxes. These figures illustrate a number of important changes in the pattern of welfare in Canada.

The shift of the burden of cost to the higher levels of government following the depression of the 1930's and the shift in taxation sources during and after the Second World War are plainly evident and illustrate at least one reason why the federal Government in 1961 forced upon the provinces the onus of raising additional taxes, while retaining its own priority over receipts from personal income, corporation, and sales tax. The effects of returning to the jungle of competition in the raising of tax funds cannot yet be measured, but it seems likely that provinces will be even more cautious than they were before about expanding provincial responsibilities — however badly they are needed — in their health and welfare departments. The fall in the proportionate costs of welfare to the provinces and municipalities raises serious questions about the validity of the claim of those governments for greater relief from the costs of health and welfare. They have, in fact, been relieved of substantial burdens by the federal government and it is pertinent to ask whether they have, in fact, devoted anything like the amounts "saved" to the improvement of their share of the welfare costs. For example, a calculation made in 1952 showed that the introduction of the old age security allowances relieved the provinces of income maintenance expenditures of the order of $17,683,000,[41] excluding the further decreases in their relief expenditures which were achieved when large numbers of those on relief were placed under the jurisdiction of the old age assistance programme, half the benefit costs of which were paid by the federal government.

On the other hand, there is evidence to show that any attempt to enlarge the financial responsibilities of municipal and provincial authorities would discriminate heavily against the Atlantic Provinces, where the need for improved and expanded welfare services is at its greatest.[42]

A second pertinent question which arises is whether the administrative arrangements, which leave both the responsibility and the burden of administration to the provinces and their municipalities, are adequately related to the financial responsibilities that are now so largely assumed by the federal government.

These very large sums of money, and the increase in recent years of per capita expenditure[43] on health and welfare services, all suggest that

[41]Personal communication to the author by C. D. Allen of the Research Division, Dept. of National Health and Welfare, Nov. 1957.

[42]Hugh J. Whalen, "Recent Municipal Fiscal Trends in the Atlantic Provinces," *Canadian Public Administration*, vol. II, no. 3, Sept., 1959.

[43]In 1954–5 this was $122, rising sharply in 1957 with the effect of the increased benefits in the old age security and other income maintenance programmes.

Canada is making continuous and rapid improvements in her welfare services. They also raise the question of how far and how fast further programmes can safely be initiated. To see these questions in their proper perspective it is necessary to see the expenditures in relation to the great growth in national income since the Second World War. In the years between 1947 and 1954 the percentage of net national income diverted to government expenditures on health and welfare in Canada varied from 7.2 per cent to 9.8 per cent. The figures for subsequent years show the effect of the two increases in 1957 in the benefit rates under old age security (from $40 per month to $46 in April, 1957, and from $46 per month to $55 in November, 1957) with the consequent readjustments to the same levels in the maximum rates under the various federal-provincial assistance programmes. Another major item of increase was the greatly increased amount of benefit payments under the Unemployment Insurance Act, as a result of heavy unemployment in those years. These were accompanied by the much slower rise in the net national income resulting from the recession of 1957–9, and its virtual standstill in the depression of 1960–1.

The question is often raised whether Canada can afford to divert a much larger proportion of her national income to health and welfare. This question can be answered in a variety of ways. In the first place it should be noted that the programmes requiring the heaviest expenditures — those for dependent children and the dependent aged — are already in effect.

Secondly it can be demonstrated that a large proportion of the costs of many of the needed services will not increase the amount diverted from the net national income and therefore the amount available for essential investment or consumption expenditures. For example, all Canadians now pay physicians' and dentists' bills from their personal incomes. The institution of a national programme of medical care would only redistribute this burden across the whole population and add the cost of care needed by those who cannot now afford it. Such a programme would constitute an investment in healthy people, which would be a more profitable investment for Canada than the same dollars sunk in the production of many current goods and services which contribute to the personal profit of individual promoters and hucksters.

The figures for Canada's expenditures on health and welfare may usefully be compared with those of other countries. The most recent available study suggests that Canada, in the year 1953–4, stood rather low in the list of countries examined. The figures are not strictly comparable with the more exhaustive analysis of the Department of National Health and Welfare, but they are useful as a measure of present achievement and a guide to future development (see Table II).

If the experience of other nations is any guide, it would appear that

TABLE II

EXPENDITURES IN SOCIAL SECURITY IN SELECTED COUNTRIES
AS PERCENTAGES OF NATIONAL INCOME, 1953–4

Country	Expenditures as percentages of national income
Germany (Federal Republic)	19.2
France	18.5
Belgium	16.2
Italy	14.7
Sweden	11.5
Denmark	11.1
United Kingdom	10.7
Netherlands	9.6
Canada	9.1
Norway	8.8
Australia	8.1
Switzerland	7.6
Israel	6.2
United States	5.4

SOURCE: International Labour Office, *Costs of Social Security* (Geneva, 1958) (adapted from Table III).

Canada can safely afford to increase the proportion of the national income devoted to social welfare, without serious consequences to the balance of her economy.

Lastly, it should be observed that Canadians already pay the cost of disease, social breakdown, inadequate housing, unemployment, and disability. The fundamental question is whether the cost should be paid by individual Canadians in the form of physical, social, or economic incapacity as well as accumulated family debts or whether, by an intelligent rearrangement of the nation's affairs, those most able to do so will pay the costs of preventing avoidable distress and alleviating the human burdens now loaded on the backs of those least able to bear them.

There are a number of serious questions about the proper balance of welfare programmes in relation to need. About $560 million is now spent on persons over 70 years of age, who number 854,284, while another $475 million is spent on family allowances in respect of some 6,035,256 children.[44] Meanwhile large numbers of people in need must rely for income maintenance on assistance programmes, and the amounts available for these programmes are at present inadequate. Furthermore, since these programmes are related either to matching expenditures by the provinces and municipalities, or wholly taken from provincial and municipal funds, the possibilities of expansion are limited by the degree to which local tax resources, already strained in many cases by the physical demands of urban expansion, can be made available for welfare.

[44]"Public Health and Welfare Services in Canada" in *Canada Year Book*, 1960. The figures are for 1959.

Thus far no mention has been made of the question that gave rise to the Clark Report on economic security for the aged and which has caused considerable agitation in connection with the Unemployment Insurance Fund. The suggestion is often made that there is a vital distinction between the financing of welfare services from the use of tax funds and the financing of welfare services from the contributions of those most nearly affected by the specific social risks against which protection is to be provided. It has been adequately demonstrated that, although there may be important values in establishing a contribution system, the contributions made and the taxes collected for welfare both constitute a significant diversion of current income for that purpose. The creation of separate funds, of which the Unemployment Insurance Fund and the Old Age Security Fund are the only examples in Canada, does little more than cushion the operation of the schemes against temporary fluctuations in the economy. The accumulation of a larger fund, either as a protection against economic recession in future years or in the belief that such a fund would constitute "savings" from which future pensions or benefits could be paid, raises a hornet's nest of problems which are the proper sphere of research for the economists. This research, however, is necessary if welfare services are to be financed in the most economical and effective way, with due regard to the balance of the total national economy. With more than 10 per cent of the net national income flowing into the health and welfare services provided by governments, it is clearly not a minor question to determine how and in what degree the necessary funds should be raised.

In this connection, another interesting question occurs for study by the economists. Since the bulk of welfare payments are made to persons in the lower income groups,[45] it is certain that most of these funds will at once be spent on consumer goods, probably on the immediate necessities of food and clothing. These payments, therefore, move very rapidly from the public sector of the economy into the private sector. It is an intriguing thought that the food chain stores are probably cashing the cheques for family allowances in their cash registers before they have paid their share of the taxes from which the government must derive the resources to issue the cheques. The effect of this rapid movement of large amounts of cash within the economy adds a new dimension to the economic value of welfare payments which has not been studied. It is not impossible that the retail traders in consumer goods receive

[45]See, e.g., Clark Report, par. 1721: "Income taxpayers reported a total of $31.2 million received in Old Age Security pensions payments in 1956. This amount is 8.2 per cent of Old Age Security payments of about $379 million in the fiscal year 1956–7. Thus, only a small proportion of recipients of Old Age Security pensions were in receipt of sufficient income to pay income tax. Also an unknown number of those who did pay income tax would not have done so if they had not received Old Age Security."

at least as much advantage from welfare benefits as do the original beneficiaries.

The financing of welfare services from private sources is not of the same order as that required for public programmes. There is no reliable estimate of the amounts of money involved. Many private agencies are in receipt of a proportion, often a very large proportion, of their income from public funds. A recent careful estimate for the United States[46] suggests that about five-tenths of 1 per cent of the gross national product was raised from philanthropic contributions for health and welfare purposes. Applying this formula to Canada, the figure for 1959 would be about $160 million. It is probably nearer $100 million, since Canada does not have the substantial income from foundations which is available in the United States. In 1959 the United Community Funds and Community Chests in Canada raised about $29 million.

The major question raised by the available information on private financing of welfare services is whether the methods adopted are adequate or appropriate to their purposes. The massive study by J. R. Seeley and his colleagues (already referred to) has raised a number of serious doubts about the monopoly in fund-raising attempted by the United Funds. These authors are particularly concerned over the increasing dependence of these organizations on corporate givers and their doubts are echoed by Professor Cohen: "What effect a significant shift from individual to corporate giving will have on our voluntary institutions and agencies merits very careful reflection and review."[47] The fact is that corporate wealth is rapidly replacing individual wealth as the source of the main flow of private income in the society of today. If private agencies are to get the support they need for continued existence, this flow must be tapped at the point of interlocking corporate management, where it is controlled. The problem for private welfare lies in the wide gulf which now exists between responsibility for raising the money and responsibility for the direction and operation of welfare services.

A more fundamental question is whether there is any real difference between donations, corporate and individual, to these fund-raising organizations, and taxes paid to governments. The donations are made annually on the basis of some more or less arbitrary assessment by a power group in the community, which exercises a substantial measure of social compulsion on the donors. Taxes are paid on an assessment made by public officials on a scale established by governments responsible to the electorate through the legislatures. One difference, of course, is that donors are free, in some measure, to refuse contributions to United

[46]Wilbur J. Cohen, "Trends in Social Welfare Expenditures and Programs" (an address before the National Conference on Sound Welfare, Chicago), *Commercial and Financial Chronicle*, July 31, 1958.

[47]*Ibid.* Mr. Cohen is now the Assistant Secretary for legislation of the US Dept. of Health, Education and Welfare.

Funds, or to underpay (or overpay) their assumed "fair share." They are not free to refuse to pay their taxes. Since the services for which these funds are raised are necessary to society it is extremely questionable whether individuals or corporations should be allowed to choose whether or not to support them. A further complication is that since substantial reliefs from taxation are accorded to charitable donations, it can be argued that a large proportion of the so-called private funds are in fact indirect subsidies from the taxpayers.

This question cannot really be answered in terms of efficiency or economy but only in terms of fundamental beliefs about the functions of government. Those who believe that it is the duty of government to provide essential services for the people it serves will press for increasing assumption of public responsibility, through public taxation, for all those services which are in the public interest. Those who believe that the government should only provide services that experience shows are necessary and which cannot be provided by private means will seek to find more and better ways of financing certain welfare services from privately raised funds.

Experience has in fact, provided the answer: it has shown that it is practically impossible today to raise the amount of money needed by the private agencies, although in financial terms these are relatively small, perhaps 5 per cent of the total. The much greater resources of governments are being called upon to carry an increasing share of the total cost. Political philosophies will, as usual, have to conform to financial reality.

PROBLEMS AND POLICIES IN CANADA'S WELFARE SERVICES

The context of welfare changes so rapidly that only a prophet can foretell the form that developments in welfare will take in order to be politically, economically, or socially acceptable in the next quarter-century. Nevertheless, it is also true that whatever is done in the next few years will alter the pattern of welfare services irrevocably, just as the decision in 1951 to provide a universal old age security allowance must control and predetermine any future developments, not merely in retirement policies but in the whole field of public policy on social security. It is, therefore, desirable to attempt the task of selecting for discussion one or two areas of welfare in which it appears that some choices exist and where changes of policy are likely to be of major significance.

Several questions are now looming before the governments and people of Canada which are related to the design and operation of income maintenance programmes. The International Labour Office, which maintains a constant oversight of social security throughout the world, prepared in 1952 a Draft Convention concerning Minimum Standards of

Social Security.[48] This document lists the major risks against which it is now recognized that provision can be made through public programmes. The contingencies covered by this convention are: medical care, sickness, unemployment, old age, employment injury, maintenance of children, maternity, invalidity, death of breadwinner. The fact that Canada is not able to sign this convention is a mark of the special problems which Canada has to face. The principal reason, of course, is not that Canada's social security programmes are wholly inadequate, but that so many of the contingencies are still considered to lie within the jurisdiction of the provinces. The federal government, therefore, is not in a position to join the other industrial nations of the world in adherence to this important document. The convention, however, provides a useful criterion of minimum adequacy against which to measure the current Canadian programmes.

On this criterion, Canada still needs to provide for the cost of maternity and for loss of income due to sickness of the wage earner or to the expenses connected with his death and burial. In connection with the needs of survivors, a recent study has concluded: "It is also important that more attention be paid to the survivors' provisions of public and private pensions. In a real sense, these provisions are not the fringes of a pension program but the heart of it."[49] In the area of health services, Canada has moved into hospital insurance programmes and has a number of provisions for meeting the special needs of certain long-term illnesses such as poliomyelitis. Only in Saskatchewan is there any visible plan for the provision of health services as part of an integrated social security programme.

Income maintenance programmes in Canada, though they do provide in some fashion against most of the contingencies, are deficient in two ways. They do not provide for all those who could be covered by an adequate programme and there is so much variation in the amounts of benefit available that it is difficult to say that the benefits provided meet minimum standards of health and decency.

The unemployment insurance system of Canada would certainly meet the minimum standards of the ILO convention. Its coverage has been steadily, if slowly, extended until the major gaps are the exclusion of agricultural workers and domestic servants. The deliberate exclusion of persons with incomes over $5,460 a year and of government employees and certain other classes is quite indefensible in principle.[50] The main weaknesses of unemployment insurance in Canada are caused by its having been distorted to meet other income security problems for which

---

[48]Convention 102 (Geneva: ILO, 1952).

[49]Peter O. Steiner and Robert Dorfman, *The Economic Status of the Aged* (Berkeley: University of California Press, 1957).

[50]John S. Morgan, *Our Unemployment Insurance System* (Toronto: Woodsworth Memorial Foundation, 1959), p. 13.

it is not an appropriate device, and by abuses arising from a misunder-standing of its essential purpose. For example, the regulations now permit a person who becomes sick after qualifying for unemployment insurance to continue to draw benefit although he may no longer be available for work, but they do not permit a person who becomes unem-ployed because of sickness to claim benefit. This is really a half-hearted and inadequate concession to the absence of a programme of sickness benefits. Again, it is almost certain that many people in older age groups are drawing unemployment benefits who have really retired from the labour market but for whom there is no adequate income mainten-ance programme. Another kind of abuse is the use of the fund to provide "seasonal benefits" in the winter period outside the normal requirements for eligibility and of the "fishermen's scheme" to provide for special problems of unemployment caused by local economic conditions which can only be dealt with by the adoption of economic policies.

The extensive use of the public assistance method of providing for income maintenance leads to many gaps in effective coverage. The creation of categories of persons in the federal-provincial assistance programmes gives, as it were, preferential treatment to certain groups and discriminates against others whose actual needs may be as great or greater. This anomaly arises from the fact that the provinces are, inevi-tably, more likely to develop programmes that attract federal support than to develop programmes that are entirely dependent on provincial revenues. The form of the federal Unemployment Assistance Act leaves it open to wide interpretation and it is not impossible that it could be used as an omnibus programme to offset the preferential aspects of the other categorical assistances.

Another weakness in Canada's provisions for income maintenance arises from the assumption that a recipient of benefit from one public programme should not receive benefits from any other. This assumption rests on a failure to distinguish between the different purposes of social insurance or universal benefit programmes and the purposes of public assistance programmes. The former are designed to provide benefits based on "average need" for large numbers of people, whereas the latter is designed to provide benefits based on an assessment of the individual needs of the eligible applicants. Thus, for example, old age security pro-vides a flat rate of benefit on the basis of age, and is not related to the needs of individuals upon their retirement from gainful employment — which vary in relation to personal circumstances and not in relation to age.

What is needed is to integrate the various programmes in such a way that the programmes based on average need do make reasonably ade-quate provision for the large proportion of those affected and that assistance programmes are also available to take care of an individual's needs whether or not he is already in receipt of benefits from the more general programmes. The task of providing for specific needs is clearly one which requires careful investigation at the level of the applicant and is best carried out by properly qualified provincial and municipal welfare staffs as part of a total programme related to the infinite variety of local circumstances. It is administratively impossible to achieve effective individual care unless the case load can be reduced by adequate general programmes which do provide for the majority of those in need. The integration of income maintenance programmes, therefore, can be effectively carried out only if there is close co-operation among the various authorities, national, provincial, and local, and if there are certain common standards as well as provision for flexibility in operations.

The present Canadian programmes each have their own patterns of benefit rates, and it is both illogical and inherently unjust to meet human needs at different levels which are set according to the particular cause and occasion of need rather than on the income which is required to maintain an agreed level of living. There is urgent need for some careful research, and for decisions on policy, to establish a level of benefit for all income maintenance programmes which is derived from knowledge about need rather than fiscal and political expediency.

Income maintenance programmes in Canada could be integrated only after the most careful exploration of the existing arrangements. Integration of this kind would require certain basic changes in public policy. In the first place, the federal and provincial governments would have to abandon their abortive controversies about the constitutional and fiscal responsibilities for welfare and recognize that each has an important part to play in an integrated system. The federal government, which has already accepted financial responsibility for the major part of income maintenance, would have to recognize that there are responsibilities for leadership, for expert consultation services, for the improvement of administrative arrangements, and for the maintenance of standards, which can no longer be evaded. Provincial governments, with their municipalities, at present display wide and often contradictory variations in policy and practice; they will have to recognize that they, and where appropriate their municipalities, have an essential contribution to make to an effective partnership in which they will develop common standards for Canada while retaining the flexibility and responsibility necessary to adapt common policies to local circumstances. This recognition of responsibility inevitably implies the acceptance and use of federal resources of advice and leadership as well as the acceptance and use of standards in common with other provinces.

The adoption of basic policies of this kind could lead to the reorganization of income maintenance programmes into a coherent and effective system to replace the present complex and inchoate pattern. Needs which are capable of being met on the basis of average need could easily become federal responsibilities, as indeed they already are, except for the historical accident of workmen's compensation. The categorical assistances could be replaced by a national assistance programme operated as a federal-provincial partnership with certain common standards which would be basically the same for all Canadians and which would be primarily concerned with meeting need, without reference to its cause.

Whether or not the time is yet ripe for major changes in policy of this kind, it is clear that the time has now come when a major reorganization of Canada's existing welfare services is required. They have grown up, as welfare services necessarily do, haphazard, in response to a variety of pressures. Public recognition of a social need, whether it be the provision of a minimum standard of living for old people or basic conditions of child care, is followed by the establishment of services within the social, political, and economic framework of the community at the time the service is inaugurated. Human needs change, governments are defeated, the economy develops, but welfare policies and their administration lag behind the times.

At present the federal government either issues cheques in payment of "universal benefits" such as old age security and family allowances, or is content to issue cheques to provincial governments for grant-aided programmes which the provinces administer with little or no guidance and no supervision except *ex post facto* accountancy.

The time has come for the federal government to give more direction to welfare services for which it is so largely responsible and to provide central services for those programmes in which it acts in partnership with the provincial governments. Canada needs a strong and effective federal Department of National Welfare, with expanded responsibilities and without the distraction of sharing administrative and political leadership with the health services. Not only does the present Minister of Health and Welfare have to defend, at budget time, one of the largest fractions of the federal budget from his colleagues as well as the Opposition, but the span of his interests prevents adequate concentration on the tasks of leadership in welfare development over the next twenty-five years.

The welfare functions of the present Department of National Health and Welfare should, therefore, be separated from the health functions and two separate ministries established. The great expansion of federal interests in the field of health, following the successful inauguration of hospital insurance, creates an administrative unit and a sphere of budgetary interest as well as political responsibility quite large enough to engage the full energies of a minister of the Crown. Progress in this area is not likely to stop at hospital insurance and diagnostic services, and the undivided attention of a strong political head will be needed to create effective partnerships with the health professions and to cope with the increasing administrative and technical pressures. Developments in the field of health require skilful and sustained leadership if the nation's health is to be effectively guarded and improved.

Another useful reform would be to separate the responsibility for payment of unemployment insurance benefits from the job-finding and employment functions of the National Employment Service. The present arrangement appears logical but in fact is not so. The payment of unemployment benefits is essentially a welfare function and is more closely allied to and needs to be related to unemployment assistance, disablement allowances, and old age assistance. Job-finding and the over-all deployment of labour resources in a rapidly changing industrial society would be more appropriately located in the Department of Labour, where the objective — employment — would be clear. Under the present arrangements, the time when there is the greatest need to concentrate on finding work is also the time when the staff are most heavily engaged in the adjudication and payment of claims for unemployment benefits. In this conflict of demands it is inevitable that the payment of benefits takes precedence over all other work, to the detriment of effective policies on employment.

There is little substance in the belief that the Unemployment Insurance Commission is "insulated" from politics, and there are real administrative deficiencies in an administrative triumvirate which is not directly responsible to Parliament. It seems highly likely that the result of the Clark Report on old age security will be the introduction of some form of old age contributory insurance. It would be possible to develop sickness and other benefits on a contributory basis. A social insurance branch should be established in the new Department of National Welfare which would undertake the management and expansion of the nation's social insurance programme to cover all the major contingencies cited in the ILO convention of 1952. At least three other federal government departments are actively engaged in welfare programmes, and there is much to be said in logic for consolidating all the federal government's responsibilities for welfare under the direction of the proposed Department of National Welfare.

There is, after every major war, a strong reason for distinctive government responsibility for the well-being of veterans. Canada's Veterans' Charter was one of the most generous and all-embracing provisions of this kind after the Second World War and covers a wide range of benefits from education to housing and from health to pensions. However, once veterans are resettled in civilian life, and their needs, as well as their status in the community, more nearly approximate those of their fellow Canadians, there is less and less reason for their segregation as a favoured group in the community.

As the number of veterans decreases, the Department of Veterans Affairs must inevitably be reduced. The best staff will not want to join a department which is being run down and the time to reorganize and distribute its functions is before the reductions become too drastic and while morale is still good.

The medical care facilities of the Department of Veterans Affairs include a substantial number of active treatment beds in some of the best hospital accommodation in Canada. They are being used at present very largely (70 per cent or more) for the care of elderly chronic sick recipients of war veterans' allowances, whose condition is not "war-connected" but is similar to that of the less fortunate members of their age group in the general population. The hospital and medical care facilities of DVA ought, for reasons of economy and effectiveness, to be transferred to the newly organized Department of National Health and thus added to the national resources for health care.

The various income maintenance programmes for veterans should be administered by the proposed federal Department of National Welfare, which would have programmes of a similar kind under its jurisdiction. The remnants of veterans' housing provisions could easily be absorbed in the ongoing work of the government's housing authority, while education and resettlement seem properly to belong to a revitalized Ministry of Labour, which, as part of its programme for the effective development of Canada's manpower, will need all the successful elements of the experience of the past fifteen years in its task of retraining and resettling members of the labour force in a changing society.

A proposal to wind up the Department of Veterans Affairs and distribute its functions in this way is likely to be opposed by the vested interests of the Department itself and by the embattled legions of veterans' organizations. This was certainly the case in Great Britain when a similar reorganization was undertaken in 1953 by Sir Winston Churchill, who could hardly be accused of lack of sympathy with ex-service men or anything but conservative political affiliations. If it is agreed that the services to veterans in Canada are better organized and more generous than those available to civilians, it is contrary to democratic principles, as well as being poor policy, to segregate veterans permanently at a higher level of service than the working members of industrial society, upon whom Canada's future now depends. In any event it is plainly uneconomical and administratively inefficient to have several ministries fulfilling functions which are exactly parallel. The spreading to the civilian community of all the lessons learned in caring for veterans could hardly be other than beneficial.

Two other classes of people have been the recipients of welfare services from federal government departments. Indians and Eskimos outside the areas administered by the Department of Northern Affairs and National Resources are at present the responsibility of the Indian Affairs Branch of the Department of Citizenship and Immigration, and immigrants have been given considerable attention in a series of make-shift arrangements under the general guidance of the latter Department. As efforts increase to regard and treat these Canadians as full citizens, it is undesirable to maintain welfare services which imply, if they do not actually encourage, their segregation as second-class citizens.

Among the many other internal administrative changes envisaged by this suggestion, one of the most desirable would be the creation of appropriate devices for regular and privileged consultation within the welfare field. There are at present no regular channels for communication between the federal government and the public and private organizations engaged in the administration of welfare services. This lack of consultation deprives both the federal government and the responsible administrators in the field of many valuable resources of advice and information.

At least two types of co-operation are needed. In the first place, there is room for advisory committees, with statutory recognition, through which the non-political, non-expert community, representing the many-sided constituency of welfare, can bring a wealth of knowledge and experience to the task of administering the complex welfare services. A Dominion Council of Welfare, analogous to the existing Dominion Council of Health, might be one appropriate device, but each major area of programme would greatly benefit from the existence of appropriately constituted advisory bodies.

The second kind of consultation required is that of experts in particular aspects of welfare. There would, for example, be great value in regular meetings of provincial administrators on technical aspects of the welfare services, and in the establishment of an advisory committee on social security both to review on a continuous basis the complex operational questions and to provide a wide range of technical competencies in the early stages of developing new programmes.

It is true that much of this consultation already goes on in government departments, but it lacks precision and authority. Too often provincial administrators meet only in the light of some emergency or some already determined policy. Too often the welfare community is faced with *faits accomplis* which are less adequate and less effective than they would have been with more effective consultation. The lack of continuity and of responsibility in these advisory consultations deprives them of much of their potential value. These advantages can be obtained without in any way contravening the essential responsibility of government for policy and administration. There is a good deal of useful experience and valuable analysis of the machinery of government,[51] relating to the best use of both technical and non-technical advisory bodies, of which little use has yet been made in Canada.

A reorganization of the kind implied here would change the character of federal participation in the administration of welfare in Canada. Each level of government would have to develop a welfare policy to replace the medley of programmes now in operation. New programmes would then be developed out of coherent policy instead of being established, as is now the case, for reasons of administrative or political expediency without any connection with any discernible policy. In place of a kind of grandfatherly interest in welfare, sweetened continuously from the tax funds, there would be active engagement in provisions of certain kinds: responsibility for active development of wider coverage and more effective administration in the universal benefit and social insurance programmes; integration and co-ordination of welfare services, with special emphasis on professional leadership; the provision of consultant services to the provinces in a genuine federal-provincial partnership in public assistance, with particular emphasis on adequate accessibility and equivalent standards of welfare across Canada; and the development of an adequate programme of study and research upon which future services could be built.

Another aspect of welfare services which seems likely to receive increasing attention in the years ahead is the development of skilled services both to handle income maintenance payments and to add a new dimension to the present pattern of public services, which have so far been largely concentrated on income maintenance. In the period when social security systems were first emerging out of the experience of the depression years of the 1930's, the great argument was whether benefits should be paid in cash or in goods. It was successfully demonstrated that to give food and clothing, or vouchers for particular types of food and clothing, was an unnecessary invasion of the applicant's capacity to manage his own most intimate affairs. It is a procedure which often leads to attitudes of increased dependency, and it is not either economical or efficient, except in rare cases when an applicant is completely unable to manage his own affairs. It is now increasingly recognized that the provision of a substitute income is not in itself enough, and that even the necessary tasks of investigating eligibility and assessing need are themselves part of extremely sensitive human relations, which require in the worker a high degree of knowledge and skill if the services are to be fully effective.

The result has been that welfare programmes are now developing

[51]See, e.g., Kenneth C. Wheare, *Government by Committee* (Oxford: Clarendon Press, 1955).

services to meet needs which cannot be met by the award of a cash allowance. For example, the constructive way to take care of a person with a physical disablement is to ensure that he is assisted to develop his fullest possible potential capacity for self-dependence and self-support. The Workmen's Compensation Boards and the medical services for veterans have made rapid strides in the development of rehabilitation services to accompany the payment of compensation allowances or pensions. Modern rehabilitative medicine has made great progress in this field, and the same principles can be applied, and are being applied in Great Britain and elsewhere, to the needs of old people. These constructive services should be available to all who need them. In the same way it is clear that social needs can be constructively met partly by the provision of such services as homemaker and home nursing services and partly by the employment of skilled staff in the administration of income maintenance and other welfare programmes.

The development of Canada's health services will throw new burdens on social workers, whose numbers are already inadequate. As the mental health services move from custodial care to preventive and rehabilitative treatment they need large numbers of qualified staff to work with patients and their families on the social readjustments that often determine the success or failure of the treatment. The advent of hospital insurance has thrown into high relief the need for medical social work as part of the essential services of modern care. The growth in demand for social workers in the health services is likely to be repeated in other fields, such as corrections, public housing, and education.

The development of qualified staff for the social services poses new problems of great difficulty. For a long time the private welfare services for families and for children were the main types of service in which professional social workers found their most effective practice. It was clearly recognized that help in the complex problems of human relations can be given only by persons who have been appropriately educated. The profession of social work emerged from the depression years with a nexus of discrete professional knowledge and skill which became the basis upon which modern education in social work has been developed in North America as post-graduate professional education. The depression and the Second World War revealed an increasingly wide area of human need in which the giving of help required the professional skill of social workers, not merely in situations of individual need, but in the application of skills in group relations and community organization to the social needs of groups and communities as they adjusted to the mechanical complexities of urban life in the industrial age.

Even when the principal fields of skilled endeavour were the relatively small and selective programmes of private welfare, it was difficult enough to ensure adequate numbers of qualified workers for the tasks involved.

When the large-scale public programmes began to recognize the need for properly trained staff, the supply of qualified workers became quite inadequate to meet the demand. This is clearly demonstrated in the *Survey of Welfare Positions* published by the Department of National Health and Welfare in 1954. The addition of new services, notably the expansion of social services as part of the care and after-care of the mentally ill, and of the care and after-care of offenders against the law, has greatly exacerbated the situation. Much is being done in the development of in-service training[52] and in the development and expansion of facilities in the eight schools of social work in Canadian universities, but there seems to be little chance that the supply of fully qualified professional workers will even begin to meet the need for staff in the foreseeable future.

The only solution seems to be the one that other professions, notably the health professions, have adopted — a careful analysis of the tasks and a carefully developed pattern of delegation to technical and auxiliary staffs of functions for which full professional qualifications are not essential. The public social services now need to be carefully studied, not only to discover at what points the services of professional staffs are essential, but how and in what ways to provide the necessary qualifications for those who, though not professionally qualified, are engaged in the delicate task of meeting the needs of people. The British government undertook an inquiry of this kind some three years ago, and examination of the report of this inquiry[53] suggests that only a similar exhaustive exploration of the problem of skilled manpower for the social services of Canada will provide a firm basis on which progress can be made in staffing the welfare services of Canada. An important part of any inquiry of this kind will be a searching analysis of standards of remuneration and conditions of employment in comparison with those available in other professions. Unless salary scales and prospects of a career are at least commensurate with the investment in university and post-graduate education, and competitive in relation to other professions, the social welfare services will be starved of the skills on which much of their usefulness depends.

So far neither the profession nor the employing agencies in Canada have shown any signs that they are prepared to face the realities of the situation and to take the bold corrective measures that are required. The profession is concerned with the defence of a very narrow perimeter of

---

[52]See, e.g., Martha Moscrop, *In-Service Training for Social Agency Practice* (Toronto: University of Toronto Press, 1958); and John S. Morgan, "An Experiment in Staff Training for Social Welfare Administration in Isolated Non-Urban Areas" in United Nations, *International Social Service Review*, no. 4, Sept., 1958.

[53]*Report of the Working Party on Social Workers in the Local Authority Health and Welfare Services, Ministry of Health and Department of Health for Scotland* (London: HMSO, 1959).

established professional practice and does not dare to look out over its battlements at the needs of thousands of people who cannot be helped without the use of staff who, though not professional social workers, are appropriately qualified for their part in the task. Employers — public and private agencies alike — are too content to do what they can with inadequately qualified staff and inadequate budgets because they are not prepared to engage in the vigorous scrutiny of their operations that would be needed or to face the opposition of the vested interests whose positions and prerogatives would be challenged by an inquiry of this kind.

The private sector of the welfare field is in need of drastic reform. There is still a large body of support for nineteenth-century attitudes which result in the perpetuation of soup-kitchen philanthropy. The religious organizations, in particular, still tolerate, as part of their daily work, the maintenance of activities which ought to have been thankfully transferred long ago to properly organized and operated community services. Private agencies, jealous of their past, continue to struggle to provide services for which they no longer have the resources in money, equipment, or manpower. The "takeover bid" in which corporate business has largely assumed control not only of the fund-raising apparatus of private welfare but also of the social planning field is fraught with danger. It could place control of the private sector of welfare in the hands of an oligarchy whose knowledge of welfare is, with a number of honourable exceptions, limited in the extreme and whose objectives are less those of public policy than of commercial convenience. Or it could be a great opportunity to work out a new medium of social responsibility in which corporate management can take its full share of the social problems of the modern state.

The essential problem for welfare in Canada at the second half of the twentieth century, however, does not lie in the reform and refurbishment of existing programmes, urgent and important as these are for the comfort and care of today's clients. The trouble in Canada is that Canadians cannot make up their minds about welfare. Welfare is too often thought of at best as a service to the unfortunate members of society who have been unable to compete as individuals. The prosperous, middle class payer of income tax does not think of his tax concessions for his wife and children as a welfare measure, although they are precisely that. The wealthy corporation executive does not think of his company car or his substantial pension as a welfare service, although these are largely paid for by the community and their justification is precisely the same as the justification for old age pensions, or the fringe benefits in his company's wage contracts with its employees. The "Welfare State" has been converted by the advertising consultants into a term of abuse to cover a sense of unease about the failure of society to care adequately for the casualties of economic and commercial expansion.

In fact, the Welfare State is now as out of date as the Model T. It represents a stage in the growth of industrial society when provision had to be made to adjust the technological reorganization of industry and commerce to the needs of the individual human beings who live and work in the context of modern corporate enterprise.

It is always more difficult to change attitudes than it is to change programmes. What is needed now is a new concept of welfare as a necessary part of human affairs in the large-scale operation of modern technological society. All members of society have human needs which they cannot meet from their own resources. The problem now is to organize the available skill, resources, and knowledge in such a way that they are accessible to all who need them, without reference to economic or social class. Rather than waste time in defending the past, Canadians should honour their pioneer heritage and strike out boldly in search of a socially responsible state in which the development of good welfare services will be as normal as good roads and good education were in previous generations.

The Economy

On the Economics of Social Democracy*

J. C. WELDON

What is the nature of the economic policy of social democracy? On what economic principles does it depend, by what methods and to what goals is it directed? I have in mind Canadian problems and Canadian institutions, for I want to discuss these questions in a familiar environment and with the facts of a specific system at hand. There is a reasonable unity to social democratic thought here and abroad, but its economic expression is dominated by the variety of circumstances that distinguishes Ottawa and London, to say nothing of the extremes that separate Ottawa and New Delhi. It is necessary to stay within a Canadian context. At the same time I want to talk about broad themes of economic policy, rather than anything so complex and immediate as the clauses of a political programme. It is policy in its simplest form that I want to consider, policy idealized to show sources and tendencies.

*This began as notes for a talk to a CCF study group in 1958, was turned into a paper for a staff seminar at McGill, and after revision makes this third appearance. Revision owes a good deal to ideas borrowed from the other contributors.

Only in its choice of goals is a social democratic party fundamentally different from other political parties. Because of this, what follows is mostly given to an account of economic goals, and to the economic choices that social democrats are likely to make. But there are also differences, of course, in economic technique and methodology: in particular the view that our economic affairs can be controlled in detail and with efficiency continues to distinguish the democratic left from the democratic right. The differences here are undoubtedly narrower than they were at the time the Regina Manifesto was published. Then, indeed, with other problems dwarfed by unemployment, the contrast between the newly established CCF and the older parties may well have been seen as resting primarily in methods rather than in goals. This predominance has disappeared, but the issue of methods is still very important; and since the issue is remarkably topical it is probably better treated as an introduction to a discussion of goals rather than a sequel.

Most observers would agree, I suppose, that in Canada not only has there been a narrowing of differences on the question of economic technique, but that this has been the result of changes from both sides. Seen from the right the root cause of change has simply been the great expansion in the economic role of government that was prefaced by the depression and imposed by the Second World War. Whatever one's theoretical preconceptions, economic events have in fact been reshaped by government intervention, drastically during the war but notably still in these later years. Effects have here been seen to follow causes even as they must in the rest of nature. The evidence has been plain that government can give stability and direction to the economy, and to avoid unendurable waste must choose to do so.

On the left, too, ideas have been modified by this direct experience of the creatively regulated economy, although on the left there has been an equal influence from the successes and failures of Britain's Labour Government, and from a generation's advance in technical economics. In the main the social democrat has found his expectations confirmed by events, but he has also found the methods of control advocated in the 1930's to be in some measure unwieldly and incomplete. They are methods now seen to have given an exaggerated emphasis to ownership as such, the left in a sense having accepted a fiction of the right by equating ownership with control. They are methods that did not properly distinguish between the virtues and vices of the price system, and that because of this failure gave too little weight to the use of the market place as an instrument of policy. They are methods that under-estimated the complexity, the interdependence and the administrative cost of regulatory devices conceived of in the small, and directed to control of an item-by-item kind; and although they are methods that prescribed a social democratic future for agencies such as the federal budget and the newly established central bank and the yet to be established federal housing authority, they only partly anticipated the value of control in the large, the flexibility of regulation that these massive central agencies would allow. Perhaps inevitably, until so-called big government had made its appearance, the tendency in imagining a planned economy was to overvalue fiat and specific legislation, and to undervalue operations in the open market and intervention of a general kind. It was a tendency that would have been corrected in practice by the restraints of a federal state, but it was also a tendency that had paternalistic implications at odds with the individualism of social democratic goals, and that unnecessarily alienated sympathetic opinion.

For many social democrats revision has been a troubling process. They fear that it has meant a dwindling of goals and the dilution of principle, especially where the new techniques have lessened the role seen for nationalization and direct controls. I think that in this they are, for a number of reasons, admirably but clearly mistaken.

In the first place the new techniques have made possible an extended rather than a reduced range of goals. What is economically possible to a nation is finally limited by its wealth and natural resources, by the state of its arts and by the terms on which it can deal abroad. No choice of social or economic philosophy can surmount these facts. But within such natural limits the economic pattern can appear in vastly different forms. Employment can be high or low, goods can be produced of one kind rather than another, distribution can favour this group and not that. From these manifold possibilities we can and should choose what actually happens to us. That at least is the social democratic view, and has historically distinguished the social democrat from those to his right. Since its effect is to define a wide area of governmental responsibility it goes a good deal further than simply to stipulate the existence of responsible government. Within ultimate limits economic events can be controlled, so the assertion is. From the range of events a best choice can be made, far superior to unplanned alternatives; and since this is so, responsible government must accept responsibility for the outcome of events, never pleading a lack of authority or power. It is a sweeping commitment, of course, and can never be fully satisfied. Accomplishment will inevitably fall short of the postulated responsibility. But the likely deficiency has been reduced. The new methods of economic control augment the old, and allow planning that is more efficient on the one hand and more detailed and discriminating on the other.

Nationalization and public ownership and economic planning have not been renounced. It is as irrational as it ever was to base policy on a natural superiority of private to public ownership, subordinating public interests and public enterprise whenever a choice is to be made. That principle only leads to such typically expensive absurdities as the use of the smaller Canadian Pacific Railway to measure the financial needs of the Canadian National. At the same time there is no reason to invest nationalization and public ownership with moral qualities, as processes that make a more than technical contribution to the good society. They are instruments of economic control, neither good nor bad in themselves, and are to be used pragmatically and without hesitation whenever they promise advantage over other instruments of control. More specifically, they are still the indicated remedies wherever the market mechanism is absent or impossible to regulate. Where, for example, industrialization must take place in jumps, as in the opening of a new region, or the development of a new industrial complex, the market mechanism cannot be expected to allocate resources efficiently or to protect the public against exploitation. Quebec and British Columbia may well net something from the private ventures now pushing back the frontier, but it does not follow that they will simply because the frontier is indeed pushed back; and certainly no market force exists to ensure the provinces of more than a fraction of the return available from public control of those ventures.

A strong case still exists for nationalization in the financial field, and of the insurance companies and chartered banks in particular. It is not a matter of the day-to-day and local affairs of these institutions, which nationalization need not touch, nor even of the uneconomical use they must make of the community's savings, for that can be remedied by new rules of investment and a reform of the capital market. It is the fact that more and more these institutions are the channels through which economic controls of a general kind are transmitted. The more freely they can be used in this way the less is intervention required in other parts of the economy. But one result is that their fortunes are sharply affected by the calculated accidents of policy, often to their disadvantage. They must lose or gain, for example, with any imposed change in interest rates, and lose or gain the more the larger the size of the change. Here and elsewhere their private status inevitably comes to inhibit policy, limiting the action the federal authorities would otherwise take. For once ownership as such is the crux of the matter. The situation is increasingly anomalous, rather as it would be if the Bank of Canada or the Central Mortgage and Housing Corporation were privately owned and constrained by commercial motives. To nationalize financial intermediaries is really to extend the historic evolution of central banking.

As one further case in point, nationalization remains an ultimate solution to concentrations of economic power. No doubt such problems are as much social as they are economic. Business is so interwoven with press and radio, with pension and health plans, with public and political relations, that excessive economic power entails excessive power throughout the social order. On technical grounds it may be undesirable or impossible to dissolve a given concentration of power, and no way may appear to limit its exercise to the economic sphere. Where this is so nationalization has at least the corrective virtue of bringing power that is irresponsible, and so inherently dangerous to the rest of the community, under responsible political control. It becomes a decisive resource of the democratic society.

But planning does not rely in an exclusive way upon nationalization and public ownership. Nothing, for example, can be done by nationalization to redistribute wealth and income that cannot be done more easily and equitably by taxation, by transfer payments, and by the provision of social capital. An anti-combines policy can depend on nationalization, and no doubt sometimes must; but I think that where it is directed to monopolistic conditions of an artificial kind, to the effects of the ordinary combine, say, or of equivalent "horizontal" mergers, conventional anti-trust provisions are probably all that is needed, given a heretofore unknown intention to apply them in a rigorous way. I might add that it would be a serious error to under-estimate how radical such an intention is, no less radical than a *bona fide* commitment to full employment or to low-income housing. Social democratic thinking has had to adapt itself to new problems and changed techniques, but it should not be deluded by the myth that its traditional programme has been exhausted.

The immediate point is that regulation has its costs and is committing, so that it is not sensible to use as strong a remedy as nationalization where a weaker remedy will do. It is not sensible, either, to increase the number of regulatory agencies and statutes if existing instruments can be used more intensively to the same purpose. In making a cautious use of nationalization the new methods of control reflect the wise theological maxim that entities should not be unnecessarily multiplied.

In principle nationalization (and public ownership generally) might be used to guarantee full employment, or to allocate resources, or to determine investment and economic growth. It is possible to imagine nationalization as the direct solution to almost any economic problem. The difficulty is that the projected solution may easily be question-begging, a solution by definition rather than anything of real consequence. Let something be brought under public ownership and there is no doubt the actions that can now be enforced include whatever is closest to the public interest. But the real problem may be, and may always have been, to find out what that best action is and to have it performed at the smallest possible cost. It would be pointless nowadays to base employment or investment policy on nationalization because the needed controls are much the same in the public sector of the economy as in the private. The critical decisions—how much spending there is to be, and in what industries, and in what regions—have the same form after nationalization as before, and can be best implemented by methods that have very little to do with ownership as such, by adjustments of the budget, the licensing of investment, monetary controls, and so on.

As to the allocation of resources, public ownership is better regarded as a regulator of the price system than a substitute for it. Undoubtedly the system has to be regulated. It has to be regulated in the sense that a framework is set for its operation: it is an instrument of planning, and we are free to choose what we want it to do. It has also to be regulated within these chosen limits, so that it operates in practice with something of the efficiency it is conceived to possess in theory. Public ownership is essential at both levels of regulation. The public must *own* the regulatory agencies, for whatever their form, from planning board to exchange fund, they must respond only to the public interests; while within the price system the public must be prepared to use nationalization when other correctives fail to preserve efficiency. The use of the price system in allocating resources takes nothing from the final responsibility of government. The point is, however, that under proper conditions the price system is indisputably efficient and economical, achieving just the results that rational planning would demand. Within a given system of goals and properly policed, it is automatic, sensitive and pervasive beyond comparison with other devices. The great bulk of economic decisions can safely be left to its care, and certainly those that are only local in their effects. Rational planning must take all major economic decisions into explicit account, but there is really no way the infinite total of minor decisions can be regulated except through the price system. Any scheme of direct controls would soon become an impossibly expensive alternative.

This has all been by way of comment on the fears some social democrats have expressed of revision. I want to add a word about revision and planning proper. Responsibility for what happens in the economy must be accepted by government, and finally by the federal government; and since responsibility is complete, *planning must also be complete*, and finally too at the federal level. The federal authorities must systematically study the state of the economy, and estimate its likely development. They must decide the range of goods the economy can achieve, and plan the goals that should actually be chosen. They must determine the structure and powers of the regulatory agencies, and plan the activities of those agencies so that the chosen goals can be realized.

Critics of the planned economy charge that it predicates a moral and administrative perfection found only in the seraphim. (Some then appear to argue that the fallibility of planners proves that less planning is better than more.) There would be a good deal of truth to this criticism if the federal authorities had to undertake even a major proportion of the actions on which a planned economy depends. Undoubtedly social democratic planning would enlarge the status and responsibilities of many parts of the civil service, and undoubtedly it would seek to increase the flow of first-class minds to government work. But there would be no need for it to accept tasks that lie beyond talents and techniques as they are. As I have just observed, much can be left to the price system. In our federal system much can also be left, much must be left to the provincial authorities. The boundary is political and constitutional, and allows federal pre-eminence in times of crisis. It also allows joint activities and co-ordinated planning, since obviously such arrangements often enlarge what any level of government can accomplish. But within these not inflexible limits the decisions of the provinces must be accepted as a natural part of the total economic plan. The federal authorities must take account of provincial programmes of resource development and provincial decisions on the form of welfare benefits and social capital; they must take account of these things so that they can be treated as a predetermined part of their own planning, a part with which other aspects of the federal programme must be reconciled. Is such a reconciliation always possible? Probably it is, granted the federal financial power, and with less difficulty in the economic than in the political sphere. Basically the relation of federal planning to provincial economics is the same as it is to the price system. Economic decisions are made—collectively in the one case, individually in the other—which, because of their origin, need no testing, and can be incorporated as a self-determining, self-fulfilling part of the federal plan.

The actions which the federal authorities themselves must take are those which *complete* the general plan. They are in part actions in which the government has an entrepreneurial role, activities paralleling in principle those of the provincial governments, but sponsored at the federal level because that is the most efficient place—perhaps the only place—for them to be undertaken. I have in mind the classical illustrations from defence and commercial policy, but also the long list of modern examples, the great acts of social reconstruction and lesser changes, federal expeditures on radio and television, transfer payments in pensions and allowances, the use of taxes to redistribute real income, the provision of marketing boards and research councils, and all other actions that in their own right have an immediate place in federal planning.

The further actions required at the federal level are those that are residual or compensatory, the very important activities undertaken to bring the total achievement of the economy into conformity with federal responsibility and planning, and deliberately varied to accommodate events in the rest of the economy. Management of the national debt, and of the exchange fund, the operations of the central bank, changes in the operations of the housing agency, changes in the tax structure, even nationalization itself, these are all actions which usually belong in this second category. With some allowance for the entrepreneurial activities of government, it does not oversimplify the social democratic position to say that while responsibility and planning must be complete, action should only be, can only be, residual.

To the renewed inquiry whether this is a consistent position, I believe a "yes" can again be fairly answered, even on the basis of our experience with existing regulatory agencies. Their present practice would, of course, be very much changed under social democratic auspices, and use would be made of their extensive latent powers; there would be some nationalization; but except for effective co-ordinating bodies, an all-essential planning board or ministry, and a related commission to license major investments, the instruments of a planned economy are already at hand. A social democratic budget would after all be in itself a radical instrument of reform, and so would a social democratic central bank.

I have one theme more in this discussion of methods. The social democrat contends that economic events are chosen rather than imposed, and this distinguishes him from those on the democratic right; he also contends that rational choice depends only on *individual* preferences and this distinguishes him from those on the non-democratic left. The mechanics of choice must reflect this judgment. If economic changes occur which in some sense are to the general benefit of society, then society should *compensate* persons and groups to whom the changes are substantially damaging. This is true whether the changes occur in the natural order or as the result of some deliberate action by government. Why? Because if there are advantages that can be shared so that there is disadvantage to no one, there has clearly been progress only if they are so shared. Such "compensationist" notions have been part of the labyrinth of theoretical welfare economics for a great many years. They are not complete tests of progress, and like other economic abstractions can be pressed to paradoxical results; but at the practical level they are safe and useful guides to what social democratic policy should be. Examples that come to mind include the recommendations on automation by the Canadian Labour Congress, recommendations which praise progress but properly enough only progress fully compensating those who are displaced; the single reference to compensation in the Regina Manifesto, compensation for properties taken under public control (a curious choice for the founders of the CCF to make, when one thinks of it, since it is compensation to the "right" rather than the "left" that they select); and again more recently, the response of the CCF parliamentary group to events like the cancellation of the AVRO contracts.

Social democratic goals are of an individualistic kind, but progress towards them need not depend on perverse lotteries in which a few lose heavily even when most of the community gains. It can be conceded at once that only economic changes in the large could or should be related to a principle of compensation, changes producing heavy and continuing damage to particular persons or groups, damage unlikely to be offset by benefits accruing from other changes. In the long run the random effects of economic changes are likely to balance out from person to person, and in a sense constitute a single, protracted, but generally beneficial event. This is not true of the repercussions from large and irreversible adjustments which, being uneven in their incidence, invite a perfectly rational resistance from those whose interests are harmed. Equity and progress are both served when compensation for such changes is made. It can be monetary compensation or take some other form, but it should be compensation as of right and compensation that is complete. In Canada partial compensation has usually had the appearance of a timid attempt to deflect the just severities of natural law. The costs of progress are in fact accidental, and should in reason and compassion be a first charge against the progress that is achieved.

There are endless instances against which the principle can be tested. As difficult as any in terms of public sympathies, but a very good test in logic, is the settlement a year or so ago between the railways and their diesel firemen. There is no doubt that dieselization was an enormously productive change. There may be dispute on almost any other point, but let it be agreed that the firemen were skilled workers, and that their skills were entirely lost to the new technology. Let it also be agreed that whatever its defects of form, anything offering *less* than the final settlement (which was a solution by attrition—virtually no discharges but no hirings) would not have been full compensation. Would anything less than full compensation have been just? Could the firemen have been expected to accept anything less? Society no more than the firemen foresaw dieselization, and had no better claim than the firemen to its benefits; but without compensation the firemen were to lose a great deal and society to gain. The settlement required what was reasonable, that enough be set aside from the improved product to compensate the firemen for their loss.

Take as another illustration the mines and miners at Springhill. Surely compensation in such situations is more logically applied before a crisis than after. To bring submarginal production to a halt is a gain to society, and need not be achieved by worsening the position of those who were submarginally employed. Or consider the social benefit that could accrue from a compensated increase in the mobility of the labour force, from the reduction of trade union rigidities by the use of severance allowances and transferable seniority and pension rights. The trade unions have no interest in the rigidities as such, and must make use of them as a second-best protection of the equity the members have in their jobs,

Uncompensated change is almost impossible, but compensated change, initiated by government, is there to be arranged as soon as government accepts the task.

If we look to the farmer instead of the trade unionist, and ask how to overcome the rigidities in agriculture, how to adapt to a technology that needs fewer farmers, we come to the same prescription: compensated change means that progress is shared and not resisted. Or consider even such wide issues as trade and immigration. There is a strong presumption in favour of freer trade and greater immigration. Yet as every period of recession proves, it is quite unrealistic to expect particular groups to subsidize those changes. If there is to be unemployment the auto workers and the auto industry or the textile workers and the textile industry have every reason to press for protection, regardless of the case for trade and immigration. Society must determine that the costs of progress do not fall upon the individual. They are costs that are uninsurable—uncertainties rather than risks—and only society should bear them.

I come now to the economic goals of social democracy. As I said at the beginning, I think it is here that fundamental issues are found and not in technique. Social democracy is after all *ideological*. A social democratic party is not simply an alternative route to agreed ends, the purely administrative coalition that the older parties represent, but a party seeking a changed social order. Its character is legislative quite as much, even more than it is administrative. The recent record of the democratic left in Canada would otherwise be bleak indeed. There would be Saskatchewan and nothing else. But an ideology can be advanced from a minority position, a party can legislate at second hand by being a potential administration: the experience of the CCF has shown how many specific goals have been attained without any share in government. The tests of success are not symmetrical with those that apply to the older parties: years in office, seats won, appointments made, these have to be counted but they have to be counted in an index that gives chief weight to social change and reform.

There are many ways in which goals might be classified, but the most useful I can think of is to use aspects of the national income as a continuing theme. On this principle the goals of social democracy can be placed in four categories, thus, goals that determine the size of the national income, that determine the rate of growth of the national income, that determine the distribution of the national income, and that determine the quality of the national income. The categories of size, growth, distribution, and quality are not independent, of course, and goals selected under one heading will ultimately modify and be modified by goals selected under another; but they seem to me to be sufficiently independent to be useful units of thought and to allow one to reflect about goals of one kind without at every stage having to recast one's appraisal of goals already noted. A devotion to economic absolutes is not needed: the conflict of one goal with another is in any case likely to be very distant from existing practice, and it is not difficult to keep in mind the need for possibly arbitrary compromise when a conflict of goals does appear.

What are the particular issues that these four categories embrace? It is worth going into some detail (indeed into more detail than I shall use) because to put things in co-ordinate groups is itself a kind of analysis, and shows something of the values on which the categories are based. Under the first heading, the category dealing with the size of the national income, it can go without saying that income is to be maximized. The leading item is therefore employment: on the one hand the amount of employment and (voluntary) leisure—leisure deliberately chosen can be given a full place in real income; on the other, the residual of employment and leisure, the amount of involuntary unemployment, both that of the unemployable and unemployment that actually reduces the national income. Then, since the national income is determined by trade as well as by production, and includes as a critical intangible our sense of national identity, there is the nature of commercial policy and the flow of international capital. There is the regulation of monopolies and combines, listed here because the economic problem is how to enlarge the national income by forestalling "monopolistic" misdirection of re-sources without limiting "monopolistic" efficiencies of large-scale pro-duction. (Some would argue, I think correctly, that here the economic problem is dominated by the social and political problem of power.) There is the issue of price stability and inflation, added not because on its merits it ranks with these other entries—under Canadian conditions it surely does not—but because again and again it has provided a rally-ing point about which economic conservatives have chosen to gather.

The issues relating to economic growth turn upon the rates of change in total and per capita real income. Here the leading item is the division of the national income into investment and consumption goods, since the proportion of investment goods is the simplest variable upon which growth depends; there is the further division of investment goods into growth and welfare components—it might be better to say into com-ponents affecting growth in the short run and the long, plant and equip-ment on the one hand and schools and houses on the other; and closely related to the welfare components of investment, there are those con-sumption goods that have at least a long-run effect upon growth—books, research, the services of doctors, of teachers. There are then two matters it is nowadays of considerable importance to distinguish, the size of the gross contribution to Canadian economic growth made available from abroad, presumably large and undoubtedly positive, and the size of the net contribution, inevitably smaller and conceivably negative. There is the relation of Canadian growth to growth abroad, and to the capital needs of the underdeveloped countries. These issues all arise from the single fact that if full employment is achieved, as from time to time in post-war Canada it has been, *growth and expansion are not free goods* but must be borrowed or paid for. The price in either form shares the property of all other prices that it can be excessive.

Questions dealing with the distribution of income—and of wealth—define the third category. I add "wealth" to "income" even though wealth is finally significant only because of the income that flows from it. There are difficulties of a statistical kind: wealth is sometimes part of the ordinary economic record where the corresponding income is not, and vice versa—the most important case is the failure of the usual records of income to give any account of the power that wealth confers. Statistics on wealth and statistics on income have thus an independent usefulness.

As to the category proper, economic equality is the central theme, although not equality mechanically or narrowly construed. It is equality considered in relation to families and households rather than to individuals, and then not at a particular point of time, but in relation to the full cycle of their economic history. The issue appears in the first instance at the national level, but it obviously has its specifically regional aspects; it has its specifically industrial aspects, of which an efficient road to farm parity is the most pressing example; it has its specifically ethnic aspects in the contrasting income patterns of French and English Canada; it has its specifically institutional aspects in the role of the trade union as an instrument of equality; and it has its specifically international aspects, more nearly fundamental than any of the rest, in the disparity between incomes here and in the rest of the world.

The final group of issues are those that bear on the quality of the national income, the worth of the goods and services of which the national income is composed. In one way or another the community has to decide what resources are to be set aside to produce economic growth, but once that decision has been made the investment of those resources is essentially an engineering problem; for any pattern of wants, investment should simply be embodied in whatever is technically efficient. The quality of the national income raises no issue over how the machinery of the economic process should be chosen, but only over the kinds of goods and services the machinery should be set to produce. It is finally determined only by the extent to which the wants of consumers are satisfied: wealth, investment and growth have no independent value.

What are the specific issues? I think the concept of consumers' sovereignty can be used to identify three substantial and largely separate questions. There is what might be called the "Madison Avenue"

question, the extent to which consumers' sovereignty has been in-
fringed by modern methods of marketing products, ideas and men. Do
remedies that respect individual choice exist? The question that logically
follows is the proper scope of consumers' sovereignty in situations where
the consumer is in fact uninformed or uninstructed. What should be
done to provide a basis for rational choice? Put in this way these
questions implicitly equate excellence in the national income with
sovereignty rationally exercised by individual consumers. As far as it
goes this equation is not only acceptable to social democratic sympathies
but vital to their emphasis on the welfare of persons rather than of
states and other collectives. Yet it is also true that the quality of the
national income depends in many ways upon choices that can only be
made collectively, and upon other choices that are much better made
collectively. There is the range of choice that goes from hospitals and
public architecture to town planning and national television and from
there to research councils and public support for the arts. There is in
brief the immensely important problem of the amount and kind of social
income needed to maximize the quality of total income.

To take these categories in turn let me begin with the size of the
national income, and with the flat assertion that the social democratic
commitment to full employment is complete. Everyone who wants a job
should either have one or be able to find one in a short space of time.
As always, of course, I have in mind only the Canadian situation and
no wider context. Admittedly there is nothing distinctively social democratic in the advocacy of full employment, but it is clear from the series
of post-war recessions (in 1949, 1954, 1958 and again in 1961) and
the growing totals of seasonal unemployment that the pledges of the
older parties are of a *pro forma* kind. Is an unqualified pledge possible
to honour? I think it is. Unemployment is a more difficult problem for
an open economy than a closed, more difficult on this count for Canada
than for the United States; but it seems to me that such interventions as
have been made—the housing expenditures of 1958, for example, or
even the various programmes of winter works—have had effects direct
and substantial enough to confirm that a full solution is possible. As
unemployment is reduced to its chronic elements they will probably
prove to be regional and structural. For efficient remedy the classical
prescriptions of deficits, easy money, and the rest, will then have to be
supplemented by controls of a more selective kind. But the evidence so
far available is that both the classical prescriptions and the specific controls do very much what they are expected to do, and are not particularly
difficult to adjust to changing requirements. The real need is determined
and systematic intervention, in brief, the acceptance of economic
planning.

It is not so much the technical possibility of full employment that needs discussion as the balance of social gains and losses. (In the last analysis the government could always maintain employment by operations in the open market, on the pattern of bond and exchange dealings.) The existence of some losses has to be conceded. It is inexcusable but true that no comprehensive survey has yet been made of Canadian seasonal unemployment, an expanded sampling of the labour force that would reveal who and where the seasonally unemployed are, what skills they have and what their employment history has been. But I imagine it is more than probable that in the winter months many of the unemployed are in a market sense unemployable, and in specially created jobs would add less to the statistics of real output than their jobs would cost to create, even with allowance for existing payments to the unemployed. Indeed the total elimination of seasonal unemployment would likely add little or nothing to the real statistics, and certainly an amount in negligible proportion to the man-hours now lost. But if these things are true it would still be social democratic policy to apply whatever "seasonal discrimination" is needed to provide jobs from November to April, devices such as seasonal depreciation and tax allowances to transfer work from summer to winter as efficiently as possible. The commitment would not be based upon the doubtful chance of a small gain in production, but upon the income outside the scope of the national accounts that is given in the assurance that all who want to work can find jobs. The worth of this income, like other dimensions of security, is to be conjectured rather than measured, but the social democratic estimate is that people value it very highly indeed.

The net advantage from eliminating other forms of unemployment (cyclical, structural) is even clearer, since here the same contribution to personal security is normally supplemented by impressive additions to real output. I recall a chilling computation from the 1958 recession that the steel the United States had *not* been producing totalled more than the steel the Soviet Union had been producing. It would be easy enough to find equally picturesque consequences of recession now. And yet anyone who has read the submissions of the financial houses to the Senate's committee on inflation, and anyone who has studied the utterances of the Bank of Canada will agree that inflation, and even the prospect or anticipation of inflation, is proposed in some quarters as an equal danger with unemployment, and as requiring remedies that would nullify or reduce the prescriptions for recession whenever a rising price level is seen or expected. If employment and the price level were in fact related so that to maintain employment greatly sacrificed real output to inflation then the pledge of full employment would be unreasonable. It would be better to accept unemployment, and improve the doles to the unemployed. But it seems to me there is not the slightest evidence of such a hazard, and that attempts to place inflation in the same scale with unemployment can be confidently rejected.

It is not necessary to assert that in itself inflation is ever a good thing, although I would guess that as a lubricant and limited to a percentage point or two a year it probably is. We can agree that when inflation is rapid, ten or fifteen percentage points a year or more, as sometimes in post-war Europe it has been, its dislocative and speculative effects may become so burdensome that control is a prerequisite to economic progress of any kind. The point is that inflation in North American magnitudes has had effects that can only have been incidental in relation to the state of employment they have accompanied. In Canada wholesale prices are about where they were in the Korean War. The entire cycle of consumers' prices from the recession of 1954 through the investment boom of 1956, the further recession of 1958 and the abortive recovery of 1959, has been compressed in a range of about 10 per cent; and even in the lushest days of expansion, with investment rising from a 1954 total of $4.4 billion to a 1956 total of $7.6 billion, with inherently inflationary defence expenditures running to $1.8 billion, with a politically courageous but still modest response to those pressures by the central bank, even in those circumstances inflation amounted to only some 3 per cent a year. If a guarantee of full employment does press upwards on the price level, it is hard to imagine a result exceeding the pressures of the exceptionally buoyant days of 1956 and 1957, and in that period surely nothing intolerable or even notably onerous was experienced.

Can we price ourselves out of world markets? We may find foreign competition toughening, but not because of inflation restricted to the magnitudes of 1954–60. On the one hand it is only the differential between inflation here and inflation abroad that matters, and that has been and is likely to be negligible in comparison with other factors affecting trade; and on the other, whatever differential may appear tends to be offset by the cushioning effect of the exchange rate. We should remind ourselves that we are not world bankers, and need not imitate (or exceed!) the fears of inflation of those who are. To accept a little unemployment as a protection of trade would be the most arid kind of reaction.

But what about the impact of even mild inflation upon those least able to afford it, the pensioners, the widows, and so on? I think the social democratic answer is simple and decisive. It is absurd *not* to have pensions and the like largely fixed in real terms. Basic payments from government should be adjusted to match rising prices as a matter of course (and should be adjusted, too, to match improved national productivity, although that is a separate issue). The forms in which private savings can be stored should be regulated with the same end in view, payment in real terms for those who need that protection. Society either decides in a deliberate way the proportion of national output that pensioners and the others are to have, and modifies their incomes accordingly; or it allows that proportion to be the unplanned result of changing prices. It would be utterly fallacious to think of these things in terms of actuarial soundness or unsoundness. The payments that society makes may be high or low but unless they are borrowed from abroad they are meaningfully reckoned only on a "pay as you go" basis—their accounting basis is quite incidental.

In an erratic and discontinuous way adjustments that balance welfare payments against prices are part of the existing process, and from time to time are applied on an impressive scale. The best example is probably the political freak of the two-stage adjustment of the general pension from $40 to $55 a month. It is an example that shows, too, that a systematic policy of adjustment as contrasted with *ad hoc* changes would not constitute anything like a proportionate addition to inflationary pressure. No doubt welfare spending would increase in some measure, but an equal result would be to make rational a policy that the older parties have applied awkwardly as events have forced it upon them.

The redistributive effects of inflation are often wildly exaggerated. Within the limits of our recent experience, the limits of anything that might be attributed to full employment, I do not think the statistics show any really important problem except for the welfare payments we have just discussed. The expropriation of the savings of bondholders and similar repercussions are not real possibilities. Reference to the surveys of liquid assets conducted by the Dominion Bureau of Statistics shows that the inflationary redistribution of wealth must be almost nil for the majority of families, and of slight consequence for most of the rest. In 1956, for example, the average family (non-farm and with "unattached individuals" counted) had only $1,525 in liquid assets and an additional $476 in mortgages and personal loans, while the median family had corresponding totals of only $234 and $28. To find a *total* of monetary savings various insurance and pension funds would have to be added in, but judging by the experience of the United States these would certainly fall short of doubling the sums already counted. Even without an allowance for the offsetting effects of debt, real losses to inflation can only have been small, not more than a few dollars a year for most families. Persistent mild inflation might eventually induce people to *transform* their savings—hence the bankers' fears?—but since the change would favour equity investment it might even improve the capital market. As for redistribution via salaries and wages, again it is only differentials that matter, and again inflation on the Canadian scale can hardly have produced important differentials. Moreover, there are few groups whose bargaining position is weakened by moderate inflation in the way it is checked by the smallest touch of unemployment.

In setting out questions bearing on the size of the national income I listed other issues than employment and inflation, and suggested that inflation really had more importance as a political than an economic theme. But since I am not going to try to give equal treatment to equal themes, except to declare their equality, I shall let these further topics pass with a few dogmatic sentences apiece.

There is the choice of commercial policy. Under Canadian conditions I think the logic of social democracy leads to an active sponsorship of free trade, or at least of trade much freer than trade now is. The theoretical credentials of free or freer trade are not so impressive that we have to accept its value misty-eyed; but at the practical level there is really no better peg on which to tie international co-operation. It is an instrument of rational economic planning, just as the price system is in the domestic economy. Its role goes much further, though, because in the international economy so little else can be used. In such terms the Canadian case for freer trade has been a strong one for many years. With the emergence of the new trading blocs, and the danger of our economic isolation, it has become urgent. Our clear interest now is to free our trade with Europe, with the Commonwealth, with the United States, to press for the exchange of markets with any of these and with other trading areas as well. Yet although it is a policy promising the greatest general advantage it can hardly be pursued except within the framework of the planned economy. The pace of transition must be controlled, compensation must be devised for areas and industries that are dependent on the old arrangements. Even after transition the guarantees of planning are essential. A shift to free trade lengthens the list of forces affecting the domestic economy. Their inevitable fluctuations must be offset, or else those they threaten will insist on protection, no matter what the general benefit from trade. To realize the gains from trade, economic security must be assured at home. As I said before, it would be quite unrealistic to expect any industry willingly to subsidize trade by unemployment. But if there is such an assurance of security, if disruptive changes are cushioned and employment maintained despite the vagaries of events abroad, I think the persuasive part of protectionist arguments largely disappears.

Acceptance of the controlled economy also allows a coherent attitude to the inflow of capital from the United States. If we agree that it is desirable to regulate the total and distribution of investment financed at home, we are bound to agree that investment financed from abroad must also be regulated, and by the same test of national interest. But we are then freed from the appeals to economic nationalism that have come to be a crude substitute for planning. In this area national identity can be preserved by a general control of capital markets without the dangerous adjuncts of discrimination and anti-American sentiment.

One further brief subheading: there is the social democratic approach to monopoly and anti-trust problems. I am afraid that this is an issue of the first importance on which agreement can be reached on final goals of policy, but for which the known machinery of policy must be regarded with meagre faith in its efficiency and purpose. In the light of recent jurisprudence—beer and sugar—it is tempting to say that only those who believe in planning have any real confidence in the price system. One object of social democratic policy is certainly to reduce the wide difference between promise and performance in the conventional anti-trust programme. Partly this is a matter of adding to the resources of the enforcement agencies; but to a greater extent I think it depends on substituting administrative for juridical procedures in testing business behaviour. Rules of mechanical application, so-called *per se* rules, are not much use, for example, in examining a complex merger, for though they may be predictable and objective, they still fail to distinguish the good merger from the bad. The defect is fatal and so "rules of reason" are required; but then the ordinary court cannot be expected to provide them in so specialized a field. The need is for an administrative court or commission as specialized in its processes as the problem itself. It might be empowered, say, to review all mergers above a certain size and to act as a kind of licensing agency, accepting some as being in the public interest and rejecting others. This would not bar either appeals to or enforcement in the ordinary courts, but it would allow an economically meaningful determination of the facts. Such an administrative emphasis is normal enough in social democratic thinking, in a context where economic controls do not have to be regarded as either reproof or punishment.

I want to turn now to the second major issue, the rate at which the national income is to grow. With due allowance for leisure the size of the national income should be as large as possible. There is no correspondingly simple presumption about growth. A buoyant and fully employed economy may show a very low rate of growth, while a depressed and stagnant economy may, with less likelihood, show a high rate. The ideas are easily confused, and often produce unwarranted hymns to growth.

There is no reason to accept either the rate of investment or the rate of growth that the market grinds out as having a natural claim to superiority in even the sense that ordinary market prices have over non-market prices. The *repercussions* of growth are often large, and may greatly modify and even reverse its immediate effects upon welfare. For example, the unregulated inflow of United States capital in the past decade has undoubtedly been of immense benefit to particular regions of the economy, but at the same time it has conditioned our economic development for many years to come, limiting the routes we can follow in the future. The restraint is likely to prove costly, not because of its American origin or a considered subordination of Canadian interests, but simply because its effects are haphazard and unforeseen.

But more nearly fundamental than the external cost of growth is what can be called the "horizon" problem. Growth is good or bad, depending almost entirely on the persons whose welfare is taken into account. The great-grandchildren of those in the Chinese communes may gain from the misery of this generation and the next, but no comparison of rates of growth can say much about the worth of the substitution. Growth generated in the market is less harsh in its results, but it is equally arbitrary in its valuation of persons. There is no natural boundary within which growth is to come to fruition.

Since the market can give no guidance it follows that the best rate of growth has to be determined by society. It certainly cannot be taken for granted (as it was in the Bank of Canada's *Report* for 1956—there have have been afterthoughts) that the object of economic policy in the world of today is "to facilitate economic growth at the highest rate that can be sustained for years at a time without endangering the stability of the currency. . . ." On that severe principle we would at once abolish pensions. It seems to me that the typically social democratic view of how this determination should be made is that all persons must count, and all must count equally; and that the estimate of people's wants that follows from this view is that they prefer welfare to expansion, that they value many of the things growth displaces more highly than growth itself and are prepared to accept a low rate of growth—in per capita terms— because of its concomitant benefits in consumption and social capital.

I will have to qualify this in a moment because it would be unrealistic in an open economy to press for goals that might be ideal in a closed one. In practical terms the qualification is important. I would emphasize, too, that this estimate of wants presupposes a technically advanced economy where living standards are already tolerable and where the individual who wants to save can always do so. In the underdeveloped countries I suppose the social democratic estimate would join the rest in judging that hope is to be found only in a high rate of growth, although high even then by New Delhi's standards and not those of Peiping.

Let me be quite clear that there is nothing deliberately ascetic in this view of growth. Other things being equal, of course the more growth the better. Where growth is a free good, as it is in a recession of any depth, it should always be accepted and encouraged. When equipment is to be replaced or reinvestment undertaken, there is no reason to choose less than the most profitable and efficient of techniques. Innovation is at least as welcome as it is under any other choice of programme, and though the emphasis on welfare expenditures is directed to the present good of those affected, there is no hint of austere regret that spending on health and housing will in the long run also enhance growth.

Growth for its own sake, or solely for the welfare of those yet to be born, or for the fame of the state as something apart from its people, is an essentially totalitarian goal. If all persons are to count, and to count equally, and if the claims of posterity are not in some mystical way to be ranked above our own, it is a necessary consequence that a high standard of living in the present should not be sacrificed to a still higher standard in the future. The alternative is a kind of regressive tax paid by one generation to the next. The logic of the social democratic position, I think, is that expenditures for *per capita growth* in an economy like our own should be a residual of other expenditures, a slack variable that ensures the full use of our resources but that is not applied until current needs have been satisfied. I have never been able to imagine future benefits that most people are likely to rank above the value of good housing *now*, of first-class and easily available medical services *now,* of free education *now,* and of the other entries in the catalogue of the welfare state.

With some reluctance I must come to the qualification I spoke of, the limit to our choice of growth that is set by Canada's role in the world economy. It is unlikely that we can insulate ourselves from the pattern of growth in the United States, unlikely that we can insulate ourselves from the competitive growth of the totalitarian economies, unlikely that we can, or should choose to, insulate ourselves from the capital needs of the underdeveloped countries. Each of these forces operates to require investment rather than welfare expenditures. Growth in the *open* economy cannot be left as a mere residual, but must include a calculated defence against external pressures. In response to American needs and Soviet growth, social democratic planning must accept whatever rate of development is necessary to preserve national identity, so that to this extent at least it must accept growth as an autonomous object of policy. In addition to this necessity, in addition to adapting to growth in the advanced economies, social democratic planning must offset such transfers of wealth as *are* made to the underdeveloped areas, thus narrowing further the range from which growth can be chosen, in the long run perhaps more decisively than anything else.

Does it make any practical difference to emphasize welfare rather than expansion if expansion must nevertheless be accepted and even encouraged? I think it does. If we think of expansion that is pressed upon us by external forces rather than deliberately chosen, if we think of such expansion in the same way we think of spending on defence, as something to be reduced and minimized when circumstances allow, then our policies have a different and more rational direction than if we indulge in an endless eulogy of growth. To admit that *some* response has to be made to external pressures does not prevent a systematic effort to enlarge consumption and social capital even when those pressures are greatest. Given such a view of growth, it would not be necessary to think of the federal housing expenditures of the past few years as an emergency programme required only to compensate for an unfortunate lapse in normal spending, inherently wasteful policies to be eliminated from the accounts as soon as normality returns, but as social contributions of great value in their own right that should have been expanded to exclude any element of slack, and then continued for many years to come without a sense of shame.

At the practical level how are the benefits of the welfare state to be paid for? At the practical level I think the social democratic answer to that durable question from the right is to turn first to the slack in the home economy and to the funds that can be diverted from the more wasteful follies of our military budget. When there are idle resources, the limits to policy, of course, are again internal to the home economy, and welfare becomes just as much of a free good as expansion. Only when those limits have been reached is it necessary to determine a margin between welfare and expansion, a margin as I say that is to be determined as a balance to external pressures.

The practical result would be a fully employed economy, a rationally employed economy. In all probability it would also be an economy in which the rate of growth is low. I think this consequence would follow not so much because of the substitution of welfare for growth—there *is* slack to be taken up, the military waste exists—but because of the one external pressure that would be difficult indeed to balance, the call upon our resources to support development in the new economies. That transfer is bound to take place, whether it is volunteered or enforced, for it would be naïve to imagine that expansion in the advanced economies can continue to have priority over the pyramiding claims of the rest of the world. Our choice is the basis of the transfer. I would guess the great majority of persons are ready to support large-scale assistance to the underdeveloped countries as a matter of right. If that is so, it would be disastrous to reduce its quality by sponsoring the transfer as national defence cleverly disguised.

I want to add only a comment or two under the subheadings of this category of growth. One very specific point is the social democratic attitude to the division between work and leisure. Unless the economy is regarded as a factory or a barracks, leisure is as much a component of the national income as any other consumption good. The difficulty is that both the total of leisure and its annual distribution—in daily leisure, statutory holidays, and summer vacations—are determined even more by convention and statute than they are by individual preferences, inevitably enough in view of industry's dependence on standard patterns of leisure for the efficiency of its operations. As a result industrial arrangements for leisure have to be recognized as being as much an object of policy as the level of employment. Where individual preferences can be expected to have had a determining effect, as in the collective bargaining of the "pattern-setting" industries, the role of policy is clearly to be guided rather than to guide. But this is not the general rule. It simply is not known, for example, whether most people prefer a shorter workday to longer vacations, or the extent to which they may prefer a shorter workday to the goods for which leisure has been traded. There is no presumption in favour of any given arrangement, and nothing in market forces that would automatically produce a best selection. The role of policy in such circumstances is to investigate what individual preferences actually are. It is an exercise in democratic planning. The conventions and statutes controlling leisure can then be changed as the facts suggest, quite possibly producing a notable improvement in welfare at almost invisible cost.

A more general point is the fact that goals with respect to growth obviously depend on a much finer classification of goods than a simple division into investment and consumption, although that is a useful first reference. The social democratic stress on welfare gives a very high rank to social spending, to the provision of goods that are used collectively. But that is a category that overlaps the division between investment and consumption, and that in each has markedly uneven effects upon growth. It is probably true that in the short run very little public spending makes a contribution to growth, whether the spending is on capital or current account. On the other hand, it is at least arguable that in the long run nothing would assist growth as much as extra spending, capital or current, on education and research. Discussion in these terms becomes increasingly tenuous as attention is turned to public spending on transportation, from there to spending on communication, to spending on health, on entertainment, on the arts. No doubt in every case there are long-run effects upon growth, but as one goes through the list these effects become more and more complex and remote, and less and less likely to deserve much weight in deciding policy.

Does this blurring of lines as specific goods are examined much affect the assertion that welfare is to be preferred to expansion? Not really. It would if welfare generally assisted expansion, but that fortunate case is exceptional. Social democracy must regularly make choices in which welfare is *substituted* for expansion in a quite deliberate way. As I have just observed, there is no bleak presumption against leisure, the consumers' good *par excellence*. Its total is to be whatever the bulk of individual preferences want it to be. Subject to external pressures there is no presumption either against light industry, against consumers' durables, no presumption that saving is to be encouraged or is of special merit. There is no presumption that consumers' credit is of less social worth than commercial credit. This is all in contrast with the existing puritanical presumption in favour of investment. But I think the most important (domestic) substitution of welfare for expansion contemplated in social democratic thought is the diversion of resources to those leaving the work force, to those pensioned or retired. The substitution offers a choice of earlier retirement, it increases the income of those who have retired, and it extends the opportunities and services society makes available to them. It is an enlargement of the *unenforceable* but basic contract between the productive and no longer productive members of society. To the charge that it is sentimentality to widen the contract I suppose the social democratic reply is that it is one further act of civilization. In any case, it is as clear a test as there is of the competing claims of welfare and growth. The planned transfer to welfare spending is very large, and at the same time is a transfer that can contribute nothing whatever to growth.

The third of the major themes that I set out earlier was the distribution of the national income. There is no reason to expect that social democrats will depart from the traditional goals of equalization and equality. Admittedly, faith in equality must have some other source than economic doctrine, if we set aside the assistance to faith that lack of support for a counter-faith provides. There is nothing within the compass of theoretical economics that passes an accepted judgment on the worth or efficiency of comparative patterns of distribution. No doubt the social democratic position rests directly on the same value that affirms the political equality of men, a belief in the equal worth of human beings and a disbelief that any overwhelming advantage flows from an uneven pattern of social benefits. I must be content to leave deeper explanations to the political scientists.

It is not the article of faith as such that I want to discuss but the sense in which it is to be interpreted, and the qualifications that are to be attached to its practical implementation. One sense in which it is *not* to be interpreted is as mere equality of opportunity. I think that variant appears because a mechanical interpretation of equality, conceived in terms of individual income tax returns or some similar measure, would be obvious folly. To have a conceptually consistent basis the idea of equality of income must admit a great many varieties of purely monetary inequality. The considerable variation in the cost by which individual incomes are attained must be recognized, the time given to acquiring skills, the particular risks and uncertainties attached to specific occupations, even the rate at which given money incomes have increased or decreased. (Even in the redistribution of income a compensationist approach has its value.) Similarly, the variation in non-monetary components of income must also be recognized, the availability of leisure, the pleasure to be found in particular kinds of work, the elements of status and authority. Of the same importance, equality cannot reasonably be sought in terms of individuals but in relation to families and households, and then only in relation to families and households considered by size and age distribution and other distinguishing features of the needs that income is equally to satisfy.

To clarify the concept not unexpectedly reveals that there are insurmountable difficulties in the way of its unqualified attainment. If equality were set as an obsolute goal, the repercussions on the size of the national income would be fabulously expensive simply because of the energies that would have to be applied to equalization as such. "Equality of opportunity" instead of "equality" avoids most of these difficulties, the conceptual as well as the practical, but it is really a quite different principle and leads to a different choice of goals. A parent may hope equally for the welfare of his children, the dull as well as the clever, but if he does, it is the attainment and not the opportunity of their equal welfare that concerns him. Although the difference is obscured in a society where there is a great deal of inequality by either test, it may already be a matter of critical importance for at least one decision, the resources to be set aside for education. Education on the principle of equality is directed to the needs of the individual and only then to society's interest in those who are educated. It is mass education, education as a free good and to the limit of individual capacity, and not education for an élite, however meritorious and productive and self-sacrificing that élite may be.

The difficulties with "equality" as a goal of policy are inherent, and cannot be defined out of existence. Equality is complex to measure, and it interacts with other goals. But despite this, I do not think we have to retreat very far from absolutes before we come to systems of equalization that would be administratively feasible in a closed economy. Larger transfer payments, to persons, regions, and industries, a wider system of social services, the subsidization of housing and other "necessities," these like other items of spending represent reasonably cost-free methods of equalization, while widened tax exemptions for low-income groups are probably an even more economical device. As for taxation, although the expense of income tax collection undoubtedly accelerates as rates are raised, it would be surprising to find that it has yet reached a limiting level, the more so if rates are raised by discontinuing exemptions of a typically "high-income" kind. If equalization does have to depend more on increased spending than on increased taxation, then balance can be restored by monetary controls and other restraints on investment. The social democratic concern for equality is in harmony with its attitude to economic growth.

In practical terms equalization must stop well short of equality. But note that the compromises with pure principle so far accepted do not depend on disadvantages in equality itself, supposing equality to be attained, but on the prohibitive cost of equalizing processes used in an unlimited way, on the cost of *administering* unqualified equality. Indeed I am not ready to agree that within a closed economy there *are* net disadvantages to equality as such, in the sense of repercussions that would clearly subtract from the size of the national income. The usual marginal arguments—a high income tax dulls incentive and limits effort, welfare payments dull incentive and limit effort—must meet the objection that at some levels these things sharpen incentive rather than dull it, and the further objection that many occupations cannot be entered on marginal terms but must be accepted or rejected as they stand without any variation of their requirements. Admittedly the force of this second objection is less clear cut in respect of entrepreneurship than for less "dynamic" factors, but I think even there it has some weight; and I am certainly not convinced that entrepreneurship is encouraged or rewarded by anything as much as it is by power and responsibility. There is the point, too, that equality presumably diminishes wasteful, emulative effects of a Veblenesque kind.

Statistical evidence on either side of these issues is, of course, very thin. The range of our experience is too narrow and spread over too long a time to decide such effects as the impact of tax rates on incentives. But whatever the worth of speculative argument on these points there is one qualification to goals of equality that makes much of the discussion academic. Pretty clearly the easily crossed frontier a few miles to the south and the distribution of incomes found beyond that frontier are determining factors in the extent to which equalization can be pressed within our own economy. Extensive measures to equalize income can be sponsored even though the much wider United States market is generally open to Canadian factors of production; but the predictable result of such measures, seen in the movement of factors across the border, is the index of what it is reasonable to propose and what it is not.

There is a considerable simplification of policy in this outcome. As with the choice between welfare and expansion, so here the governing fact of policy is the situation abroad. Most of what I said under that earlier heading could be repeated here without change. It is important once again to establish that departures from ideal conditions are enforced rather than chosen. This at least allows policy to be redirected in an automatic way when changes in the controlling conditions occur. Social democratic policy, I would judge, is to move as far as possible towards an equal distribution of incomes. How far is that, and what in fact limits policy? Evidently the effective limit is set by the influence of the United States economy. Equalization can be pursued up to the point where American arrangements have become unduly disruptive of our own, a limit that has to be set pragmatically and tested politically.

The one subheading under which I have a comment to make is the role of the trade union in redistribution. The trade union has a certain function in redistributing money incomes in the market place, but it also contributes other elements to its members' incomes, thus, independence, security, a share in the power structure of the nation. Many would even argue that these latter functions exceed the first in importance. They are functions that are remarkably sensitive to the institutional framework within which they operate, to trade union structure itself, to the laws limiting or encouraging trade union activity, to the boards and agencies the laws establish. Historically, both the bursts of energy the movement sometimes shows and its long periods of stagnation have been closely related with the question of whether or not outmoded institutions have been reformed. On this view the trade union movement needs nothing today so much as institutional change. The basis of the favour with which social democracy regards the union movement is partly the movement's narrowly economic role, but much more its role in giving its members an equal place in society. In that respect the movement has gradually but undoubtedly lost much of its vigour. Remedial policy is simple enough to state, if decidedly less simple to implement. It is to assist the movement to make institutional changes, and in particular, to help it follow its members as they advance in the new technology from blue collar to white collar and semi-professional status. One element of reform is to have laws that regard unionism as beneficial to society, as something to be encouraged rather than merely permitted wherever it can be instituted.

Let me be very brief in dealing with the last of the four main categories with which I began, the quality of the national income. I want to be brief to bring an overly long paper to a close, and because the tests of quality have already been suggested by the discussion of other goals. I do *not* want, though, to subordinate the issue of quality itself for if the categories must be ranked it may be that correct choices here are vital to a degree they are nowhere else.

I suggested earlier that discussion in this area could be made to turn on the concept of consumers' sovereignty. As item one of a short enumeration: social democracy is obviously prepared to restrict attempts to make consumers' choice less rational. Policy goals include selective and much heavier taxes upon advertising, much more stringent rules about labelling and advertising copy, perhaps devices in the BBC fashion which separate advertising from communication proper. The needed qualification is always that the rules by which the consumer is defended do not themselves intrude on his freedom.

Social democracy, I think, is also prepared to commit itself to measures intended not only to preserve but to widen the rationality of consumers' choice. Education as a free good is the obviously predominant example, but at a more humble level there is the provision of public funds to consumers' associations and research agencies. Social democracy is also prepared to accept the responsibility of multiplying the flow of social income, of implementing collective choices in the many areas where individual choice cannot be effectively realized. In this its position is taken not in order to override consumers' sovereignty, as though it were entitled to provide a paternal authority, but to extend consumers' sovereignty to decisions from which the consumer would otherwise be barred. In both aspects—the increased flow of social income, the deference to the authority of the consumer—this endorsement of collective choice is basic to the social democratic position.

Social democracy, that is to say, looks for its economic values to consumer opinion that as far as may be is undistorted, that as far as may be is informed and instructed, and that often seeks expression in social choices—in all of which the essential thing is that it looks to consumer opinion. I speak of "economic values" and "consumer opinion" because this paper has been limited to economic issues, and more honorific terms are therefore not available. But I imagine that if social democracy is to command sizeable support it must be as ready on wider issues to accept the values of the consumer-as-citizen as it is to accept his values as mere consumer on purely economic questions. I suppose this amounts to saying that social democracy must above all else be democratic in its socialism.

Concentration and Monopoly in the Canadian Economy

G. ROSENBLUTH

How important are large corporations and how high is the degree of concentration in Canadian business today? Unfortunately the statistics needed for an accurate answer to this question are not available. We are therefore forced to make do with partial and out-of-date statistical guide posts.

CONCENTRATION OF OWNERSHIP AND CONTROL

A. Large Firms and High Concentration

There are today in the Canadian economy well over half a million separate business firms (excluding those that are too small to come to the notice of the Department of National Revenue).[1] Among them there are something of the order of one hundred corporations with assets of over $100 million each.[2] These will be called "giants" in our discussion.

[1]This chapter was written early in 1960, and the figures used are the latest that were available at that time. The methods and sources on which the estimates in this section are based, are shown in the Appendix, where the measurement of concentration is discussed in detail. For the number of firms see Appendix, §1.

[2]Appendix, §2.

About fifty-seven of the giants are non-financial corporations, and it is with them that we shall be primarily concerned. A financial corporation is one whose main assets are not real means of production but the stocks, bonds, mortgages, and other debts of business, governments and individuals. To include the financial institutions in any simple statistical measure of concentration would thus involve considerable duplication of asset values. But wherever a financial institution has a strong interest in two or more non-financial firms there is a further concentration of control that is not reflected in our figures.

The fifty-seven non-financial giants owned in 1956 about 38 per cent of the total value of what we shall call "real" assets — land, buildings, equipment and inventory — of all non-financial corporations. A very rough calculation suggests that they own about one-fifth of all the "real" business assets in Canada, including those of unincorporated firms. Four of these fifty-seven corporations are federal Crown companies. If we exclude them we are left with fifty-three giants which control about 29 per cent of the real assets of all privately owned non-financial corporations, one-quarter of the real assets of all corporations, and roughly one-seventh of the whole business economy.[3]

These estimates understate the degree of concentration, because corporations that are subsidiaries of others must appear in the *Taxation Statistics* as separate entities. "Corporations are not permitted to file consolidated returns."[4] Thus A. V. Roe and Dominion Coal and Steel Corporation will appear as separate manufacturing corporations in the returns even though, since their merger in 1957, they constitute one firm. Where a "holding company" owns a controlling block of shares in each of a group of corporations they become, in fact, one firm, but this fact is not reflected in the statistics. The Argus Corporation, for example, is not included in our group of giants because its total assets are valued at less than $100 million and because it is technically classed as a financial corporation, its assets consisting mainly of stocks. Yet it owns controlling blocks of shares in six large industrial corporations — BC Forest Products, Canadian Breweries, Dominion Stores, Dominion Tar and Chemical, Massey-Ferguson, St. Lawrence Corporation — with total assets of nearly $900 million in 1957. Its control extends even further since, for example, Dominion Tar and Chemical controls the Howard Smith Paper Mills with assets of $89 million, which in turn controls the Donnacona Paper Company with assets of $22 million.[5]

By examining the individual published accounts of large companies

[3]Appendix, §§3,4. We measure concentration in terms of real assets, omitting financial assets, in order to avoid the duplication that arises when financial assets are counted.

[4]Department of National Revenue, *Taxation Statistics, 1958.*

[5]*Moody's Bank and Finance Manual, 1958*, p. 1015. BC Forest Products is controlled jointly with Scott Paper.

and consolidating those of subsidiaries with their parents, we have attempted to construct an estimate of the relative importance of giant corporations that takes into account the fact of inter-corporate control. We find that in 1956 forty-four privately owned non-financial giants accounted for 44 per cent of the value of "real" assets held by all privately owned non-financial corporations. This is a much higher degree of concentration than would appear from the figures cited above. The estimate may be slightly too high because some assets of foreign subsidiaries are included. On the other hand it may be slightly too low because the assets of large so-called "private companies," such as Eaton's and General Motors, are not included since they do not publish their accounts. Moreover it was not possible to include the real assets of *all* subsidiaries with their parents among the giant corporations. While all our figures are subject to error, therefore, they do indicate the dominant role of giant corporations in the economy.[6]

We must now examine the relative importance of giant corporations and the concentration of market control in the major sectors of the economy. The largest sectors of the Canadian economy are manufacturing, trade, and the service industries, which account for 30 per cent, 14 per cent and 11 per cent respectively of the total output of goods and services (excluding government and defence). Agriculture (including forestry and fishing), transportation (including storage and communication) and finance (including insurance and real estate) each account for 10 per cent. Construction, mining and public utilities are the smallest sectors, accounting for only 6 per cent, 5 per cent and 3 per cent respectively.[7]

In 1956, twenty-eight "giants" in manufacturing had about 29 per cent of the "real" assets of all manufacturing firms, both incorporated and unincorporated. One hundred and forty-three corporations, worth over $25 million each, had 53 per cent of these real assets. These figures again understate the degree of concentration since accounts of parent corporations and subsidiaries are not consolidated. It is clear, however, that a small number of large corporations dominate this leading sector of the Canadian economy.[8]

At the same time there is an enormous number of small firms, most of them very small indeed, in the manufacturing field. It is a safe guess that there are well over thirty thousand separate business firms in this sector.[9] The great inequality of firm sizes means that, on the one hand, the "typical" firm is very small, on the other hand the average employee

[6]Appendix, §5.
[7]Figures for 1956 from Dominion Bureau of Statistics, *National Accounts, Income and Expenditure, 1926-56*, Table 21.
[8]Appendix, §6.
[9]Appendix, §7.

and the average dollar's worth of sales or assets are connected with a giant corporation.

Both the relative importance of large firms and the degree of concentration of market control vary greatly from one manufacturing industry to another, but the average level of concentration is quite high. A comprehensive study, based on figures for the year 1948, shows that in half of a large sample of industries, nine firms or fewer accounted for 80 per cent of employment. Most of the industries based on metals, chemicals and non-metallic minerals had still higher concentration while most of the industries in the wood, paper, textiles and clothing groups had lower concentration. Food processing industries contain examples of both very low and very high concentration.[10]

In retail trade, wholesale trade, and services, while there are well-known examples of giant corporations, small firms are the dominant form of business. In 1958, twenty-one chains with over 100 stores each, accounted for less than 11 per cent of all retail sales and 509 chains (with over four stores each) accounted for only 20 per cent. In a few lines of trade, however, concentration is very high; the leading example is the grocery trade, where forty chains accounted for 44 per cent of sales in 1958, and four chains accounted for 31 per cent.[11]

Agriculture, too, is still in the main a small business area. The 6,728 largest farms, in terms of acreage, had just 15 per cent of all farm land in 1951. The 4,409 largest farms, in terms of sales, had only 5 per cent of all farmland. Farms with sales of less than $5,000 in 1950 had over two-thirds of all farmland.[12]

In the field of transportation, communication and storage, concentration is much higher and giant firms dominate, but many of the largest firms are government-owned.[13] The government-owned Canadian National Railways and the privately owned Canadian Pacific Railway together have 89 per cent of the operating revenue of all railways. They also dominate the air transport industry where their subsidiaries, Trans-Canada Air Lines and Canadian Pacific Airlines, have 69 per cent of the assets of all Canadian companies. The telephone industry is dominated by the privately owned Bell Telephone Company, which accounts for 66 per cent of the operating revenue of the industry. The British Columbia Telephone Company, also privately owned, has 9 per cent of the operating revenue, and the three provincially owned systems on the Prairies account for 12 per cent. In radio and television the government-owned Canadian Broadcasting Corporation incurs about

[10]G. Rosenbluth, *Concentration in Canadian Manufacturing Industries* (Princeton, 1957), ch. II.
[11]Appendix, §§8,9,10.
[12]Appendix, §11.
[13]Appendix, §12.

one third of the operating expenses of the radio industry, and four-fifths in the case of television.[14] There is no readily available information on the degree of concentration among private stations, but local monopolies or duopolies appear to be the typical pattern.

Large government-owned and private units also dominate the urban transit field. Information is much less adequate for the road transportation industry, but it would appear that here concentration is somewhat lower and the leading firms are not hundred-million-dollar corporations. There is no statistical information on concentration in water transportation, but the field of inland water transportation seems to be highly concentrated.

The "newest" sector of the transportation field is the rapidly growing pipeline business. In this field, concentration is high and giant firms are of major importance. Among oil pipelines the two giants — Interprovincial and Trans Mountain — have 72 per cent of the assets, 58 per cent of the gross operating revenue and 65 per cent of the net operating revenue.

The financial sector of the economy is marked by large firms and high levels of concentration in its major branches. Commercial banking is carried on by only nine large chartered banks, of which only one had assets of less than $100 million in 1956.[15] The Canadian assets of nine leading insurance companies constitute three-quarters of all Canadian life insurance assets.[16] The assets of other financial institutions (fire and casualty insurance companies, trust and loan companies, savings banks, etc.) are quite small in comparison with those of the chartered banks and life insurance companies.[17]

The most important branch of the mining industries is metal mining, and here output is concentrated in the large integrated firms which combine mining with the smelting and refining of nonferrous metals. In 1954 there were only six firms in nickel-copper production, and the same number in iron ore mining, while in copper-gold production six firms account for 88 per cent of value-added and in lead-zinc production six firms account for 86 per cent of value-added. Uranium was produced by 21 companies in 1958, but the number has since declined.[18]

[14]Based on figures for 1956 in DBS memorandum, *Radio and Television Broadcasting Stations, 1956.*

[15]*Canada Gazette*, Supplement, February 2, 1957.

[16]Canadian assets of nine largest companies and all Dominion-registered companies in 1956, from the *Report of the Superintendent of Insurance, 1957*, vol. I. Assets of provincially registered companies, estimated on basis of life insurance in force for Dominion and provincial companies, are from the same source, p. 101A.

[17]See *Canada Year Book, 1959*, pp. 1111–26, 1137–49.

[18]Data for 1954 from I. Brecher and S. S. Reisman, *Canada–United States Economic Relations* (Ottawa, 1957), Appendix B. Number of uranium producers from *Canada Year Book, 1959*, p. 497.

Petroleum production has become the second most important branch of the "mining" industries and it, too, is concentrated in the hands of large integrated producers that combine crude petroleum production with refining. In 1954 the six largest firms accounted for 69 per cent of value-added in crude petroleum production.[19]

Public utilities are traditionally the domain of large firms and high concentration. It should be noted, however, that in 1958, more than three-fifths of the output of electric utilities came from government-operated stations.[20] For our final sector, the construction industry, there is no statistical information on the business structure, but there is little doubt that in this sector small firms and low concentration are still the rule, with the possible exception of specialized fields of industrial construction.

Conclusion. Our survey has shown that major sectors of the economy are dominated by hundred-million-dollar corporations while at the same time a vast number of very small business firms operate in many economic fields and handle the bulk of the business in important sectors. Making a rough and ready breakdown, we can say that about three-fifths of Canada's output (excluding government administration and defence) originates in sectors dominated by large corporations (manufacturing, transport, finance, mining, utilities) while two-fifths originates in sectors in which small firms predominate (agriculture, trade, services, construction). These figures are very rough and would be modified by a different grouping of industries into sectors. Publicly owned units are included in both sectors and are of major importance in the fields of transportation and utilities.

We have to remember also that many "firms," particularly the largest corporations, operate in a good many different industries. Thus the Canadian Pacific Railway Company is a leading firm not only in railway transportation, but also in air transport, shipping, highway transport, non-ferrous metals mining and smelting, hotels, the manufacture of rolling stock. The Dominion Steel and Coal Corporation was involved not only in the primary iron and steel industry but also in mining, shipbuilding, bridge construction and many other manufacturing fields. Since its merger with the Avro interests in 1957 this diversification has greatly increased. There are many examples of "vertical integration" such as the combination in one company of logging, pulp and paper mills, and secondary industries based on paper and wood, or the combination of flour milling and bakeries, of food processing, wholesaling and retail distribution. There is the combination of technologically related products or processes, such as pulp and paper with electric power, or meat with hides and fertilizer. There are also many examples of the combination

[19]Brecher and Reisman, *Canada–United States Economic Relations.*
[20]DBS *Electric Power Statistics,* 1958, Table 3.

of quite unrelated economic activities under a common firm, as in the Argus Corporation.

Many individual lines of business are substantially controlled by large corporations, and in many more, markets are controlled by just a few sellers, who may not be corporate giants. Problems due to "bigness" in business, problems due to extreme inequality of firm size, and problems due to monopolistic control of markets by a small number of sellers are therefore of major importance in the Canadian economy.

B. *Who Owns and Controls the Large Corporations*

We have seen that a large proportion of Canada's capital is concentrated in a small number of large corporations. Those who control these corporations wield enormous power over Canadian economic life. Who controls the large corporations?

The answer suggested by the public relations departments of large corporations and stock exchanges is that in North America "the public" owns the large corporations so that under the new "people's capitalism," "government by the people" in the political sphere is matched by "government by the people" in the economic sphere. A more sophisticated answer, first suggested by Berle and Means, is that while ownership of the giant corporations is widespread, it has become divorced from control, which it exercised by a separate group of executives. As a result, they argue, "the explosion of the atom of property destroys the basis of the old assumption that the quest for profit will spur the owner of individual property to its effective use."[21] Neither of these views is correct.

Corporate common stock, which constitutes the ownership certificate of corporations, is held by only a very small proportion of families. A survey by the Dominion Bureau of Statistics shows that only 9 per cent of non-farm "families and unattached individuals" own any publicly traded common stock at all, and only 2 per cent own more than $5,000 worth.[22] The percentage owning more than $5,000 worth of the stock of one corporation is obviously much smaller still. Thus even if every block of $5,000 of common stock in a giant corporation constituted a share in effective control, this control would be in the hands of a relatively insignificant percentage of the population. It would be an unrepresentative segment also, since the data indicate that "the ownership of stocks . . . is concentrated in the very high income groups."[23]

Actually, of course, the vast majority of even the holders of $5,000 or more of stock are separated from control of the large corporations as effectively as if they were bondholders. The available evidence leaves no

[21]A. A. Berle and G. C. Means, *The Modern Corporation and Private Property* (New York, 1947), p. 9.

[22]DBS, *Incomes, Liquid Assets and Indebtedness of Non-Farm Families in Canada, 1955* (Ottawa, 1958), Table 26. Data are for March, 1956.

[23]Wm. C. Hood, *Financing of Economic Activity in Canada,* a study prepared for the Royal Commission on Canada's Economic Prospects (Ottawa, 1958), p. 145.

reasonable doubt that control of Canada's large corporations is much more highly concentrated. We can usefully classify those in control into two groups: (1) foreign and particularly United States business interests; (2) a small and interlocking Canadian "economic élite."

1. *Foreign ownership and control.* In a high proportion of Canada's leading corporations a controlling interest is held by United States parent corporations. Others are controlled by foreign individuals and some by parent corporations in Britain and other countries. The distribution of control among large manufacturing corporations (with total capital of $25 million or more) is shown in Table I.[24] Table II gives estimates for all firms, not only the largest corporations.[25] The figures show that foreign control is of major importance in manufacturing and mining, and is significant in merchandising and public utilities. It is also known to be an important factor among insurance and finance companies,[26] but is not significant in agriculture, transportation, and, probably, the construction and service industries. There is a rising trend in the percentage of foreign control in manufacturing, mining, and even in merchandising, but a decline in public utilities. Over-all, there appears to have been a very great increase in the relative importance of foreign control.

TABLE I
CONTROL OF LARGE MANUFACTURING CORPORATIONS

	End of 1946		End of 1953	
	Number of enterprises	Percentage of total investment	Number of enterprises	Percentage of total investment
Canadian-controlled	11	40	31	42
US-controlled	}		23	52
UK-controlled	12	60	4	6
Total	23	100	60	100

SOURCE: DBS.

In particular industries the importance of foreign control is much greater than these over-all figures indicate. A very incomplete survey shows that by 1957 Canadians controlled less than one-quarter of the capital employed in petroleum and natural gas (including refining), rubber manufactures, automobiles and parts, and electric apparatus and

[24]DBS, *Canada International Investment Position, 1926–1954* (Ottawa, 1956), p. 26. Concerns under foreign control are defined as those "which are known to have 50% or more of their voting stock held in one country outside Canada. In addition a few instances of concerns are included where it is known that effective control is held by a parent firm with less than 50% of the stock. . . . There are a relatively small number of Canadian Companies included . . . where there is not a parent concern. These exceptional cases are confined to instances where control is believed to rest with non-residents." (p. 24)

[25]*Ibid.*, pp. 30, 35; and *Supplement to the Canadian Balance of International Payments, 1958*, pp. 2, 3.

[26]*Canada's International Investment Position, 1926-1954*, p. 38.

TABLE II
FOREIGN CONTROL OF MANUFACTURING FIRMS

Sector	Percentage of sector total capital employed in US-controlled companies			Percentage of sector total capital employed in foreign-controlled companies		
	1926	1953	1957	1946	1953	1957
Manufacturing	30	43	43	35	50	56
Mining and smelting	32	55	64	38	57	70
Steam railways	3	2	2	3	2	2
Other utilities	20	11	4	20	12	5
Merchandising	5	8	n.a.	5	10	n.a.
Total	15	24	27	17	28	33

SOURCE: DBS.
n.a.—not available.

supplies. Less than one-half of the capital was under Canadian control in the pulp and paper industry, transportation equipment, chemicals, and other industries. On the other hand, such major industries as textiles and beverages remained with more than 80 per cent Canadian control.[27]

In many industries foreign control is particularly important among the largest firms. One of the Gordon Commission staff studies points out that "in almost every sector of Canadian industry where there is a significant degree of non-resident investment, the average size of enterprises controlled outside Canada is considerably larger than their Canadian counterparts."[28] The importance of foreign control among the leading firms is illustrated by Table III.

When Canadian companies are controlled by United States or British parent corporations, control is based on ownership. In most cases ownership of all, or a majority of the common stock is involved, but cases where the controlling group owns a minority of the stock are also included in the statistics. In any case, control is based on ownership so that, where Canadian companies are controlled abroad, there is no "separation of ownership and control."[29]

2. *The economic élite.* A study by John Porter[30] examines the directors of 170 "dominant corporations" in manufacturing, mining, transportation, communication, public utilities, and trade. There are 1613 directorships in these companies, of which 1304 are held by 907 Canadian residents, whom he classified as the "economic élite." Through

[27]*Supplement to the Canadian Balance of International Payments, 1958,* pp. 2, 3.

[28]Brecher and Reisman, *Canada–United States Economic Relations,* p. 278.

[29]Ownership of the *parent* company may of course be separated from control. The discussion below (pp. 209–11) suggests that this situation is exceptional.

[30]"Concentration of Economic Power and the Economic Elite in Canada," *Canadian Journal of Economics and Political Science,* vol. XXII, no. 2, May, 1956, pp. 199–220; and "The Economic Elite and the Social Structure in Canada," *CJEPS,* vol. XXIII, no. 3, Aug., 1957, pp. 376–94.

interlocking directorates — the practice of one individual holding direct-
orship in two or more companies — these "dominant corporations" are
closely linked with one another and with smaller corporations. Moreover, through this practice directorships are concentrated. Of the "Canadian" directorships in dominant corporations, 45 per cent are held by
203 individuals with two or more directorships (in dominant corporations) each, and 28 per cent are held by ninety individuals with three or
more directorships each. Interlocks also link the control of "dominant"
industrial corporations to the banks and insurance companies. The directors of nine chartered banks hold 297 of the directorships in "dominant corporations" and the directors of ten large Canadian life insurance
companies hold 188 directorships in dominant corporations. If we include all chartered bank directors in the economic élite, a controlling
group of 985 Canadian residents is obtained. For 760 of these individuals, 611 of them Canadian-born, Porter was able to tabulate biographical
data. His findings indicate that the corporate controlling group displays

TABLE III

FOREIGN CONTROL OF LEADING FIRMS

Industry	Percentage of value-added accounted for by six largest firms 1954	Number of foreign controlled firms among the six largest	
		U.S.	Other Foreign
Crude petroleum	68%	5	1
Petroleum refining	93	4	1
Mining, smelting and refining			
Nickel-Copper	100	3	–
Lead-Zinc	86	1	1
Copper-Gold	88	2	–
Iron Ore	100	3	–
Aluminum (one company only)	100	1	–
Asbestos	94	2	1
Gypsum	97	3	1
Manufacturing			
Pulp and Paper	46	1	1
Fertilizers	92	2	1
Acids, Alkalis, Salts	63	3	2
Electrical Apparatus and Supplies	52	4	–
Primary Iron and Steel	84	1	–
Automobiles	97	6	–
Railway Rolling Stock	84	3	1
Synthetic Fibres (five companies only)	100	3	2
Other Primary Textiles	90	0	–
Agricultural Implements	91	2	–
Rubber Goods	77	4	1

SOURCE: I. Brecher and S. S. Reisman, *Canada–United States Economic Relations* (Ottawa, 1957), pp. 278–85.

a high degree of homogeneity and interaction, and that it is recruited from a very small section of the population.

Of the Canadian-born sample of the élite, 64 per cent have had more than high school education; most of them have been to university and a few have had specialized professional training (for example as chartered accountants) outside university. At the time they were trained, less than four per cent of those aged 18–21 were college students, and there is little doubt that college attendance was substantially confined to members of the middle and upper classes, as it still is in large measure. More than one-third of the Canadian-born élite attended private secondary schools.

The élite is almost entirely of English-speaking British origin, although this ethnic group accounts for less than half of the general population. Less than seven per cent of the élite are of French origin, while French Canadians account for more than 30 per cent of the Canadian population. The representation of other groups is negligible. Of those élite members for whom a religious affiliation could be ascertained (583 individuals) 86 per cent are Protestant, 13 per cent Catholic and one per cent Jewish. In the population as a whole Catholics account for 43 per cent and Jews for 1.4 per cent.

Nearly two-fifths of the 611 Canadian-born members of the élite sample have an origin that can be defined as "upper class" and more than four-fifths can be classified as of middle or upper class origin.[31] The narrowness of the class and cultural base of the élite is even more pronounced among a group of a hundred individuals whom Porter selected as "top-ranking members of the élite."[32] Fifty-five per cent of these are of upper class origin and 85 per cent of upper or middle class origin.

Common class and cultural background make for coherence among the élite group, which is further promoted by their numerous points of contact with one another in business, professional and social life. Apart from the common membership on boards of both "dominant" and smaller corporations and financial institutions, members of the corporate élite meet in social clubs, and on the boards of universities, hospitals, cultural and philanthropic organizations. Moreover, many of them have been classmates, not only at the same universities but in the same faculties. Twenty-two per cent of the élite had their training in engineering and science, and 14 per cent in law.

It is thus evident that Canada's domestically controlled dominant

[31]Porter defines "upper class origin" as involving a father in an élite group, wife from élite family, or father in control of a large business. "Upper or middle class origin" is indicated, in addition, by attendance at a private school, attendance at university, or father in a middle class occupation.

[32]For the method of selection see "The Economic Elite and the Social Structure," p. 391, n. 42. These hundred men hold 324 of the directorships in the "dominant corporations" identified by Porter.

corporations are in the care of a small and fairly homogeneous group representing, by class and social background, a very narrow segment of the population. The question arises whether this control is, as Berle and Means suggested, divorced from the ownership interest. There is no specific Canadian information on this point, but British and United States studies suggest that such a separation is likely to be exceptional.

Those who maintain that owners of large corporations do not control them point to the fact that the typical large corporation has thousands of stockholders, most of them owning, individually, a negligible proportion of the stock and deriving only a small part of their current income from stock of one corporation. The typical stockholder is thus neither able nor willing to exercise control. What this analysis ignores, however, is that stockholdings in a large corporation are typically extremely unequal in size, and at the top of the pyramid there is generally a small number of very large holdings, few enough to permit consultation and co-ordination, large enough to be decisive in a vote, and large enough in size to justify strong interest in the company's affairs. While it is true, therefore, that *most* owners cannot control and have no wish to do so, a few large owners *can* have effective control and generally want to exercise it.

Studies of share ownership in large corporations, summarized by P. S. Florence,[33] show that in the typical case the twenty largest owners have a sufficient share to constitute working control, and that *within* the group of twenty, ownership is very highly concentrated. In all but four of 132 large American common stock issues the twenty largest holders had more than 10 per cent of the stock, in more than two-thirds of the cases they had over 20 per cent of the stock, and in nearly one-quarter of the cases they held more than half the stock. In all but seven of eighty-two large British companies the twenty leading owners held more than 10 per cent of the stock, and in two-fifths of the cases they held over half the stock. On the average, in the US sample, the largest *five* owners hold 13 per cent of the stock, and in the British sample 17 per cent of the stock.

When the rest of the stock is widely held, concerted action by owners of 10 per cent or even less of the stock is sufficient to give control. Florence points out that case studies of the twenty largest holdings often reveal a single dominant owner (who may be another corporation or financial institution), family connections among leading owners, and identity or connection among leading owners and directors. He concludes that in two-thirds of the US sample and more than three-quarters of the British sample, control by a dominant owner-group is fairly clearly established, so that "proclamation of the managerial revolution should

[33]*The Logic of British and American Industry* (London, 1953), pp. 189–90, 201–03. The US data are from TNEC monograph, no. 30, and the UK data from Parkinson, *Ownership of Industry*.

perhaps, for the present, be postponed!" It is hardly likely that the pattern in Canada is significantly different from that discovered in Britain and the United States.

In the minority of cases where no dominant ownership interest can be identified and the paid "managers" of the company in fact control the Board of Directors, they are still typically under strong incentive to operate the company in the interest of maximum profit. They often own stock or stock options in amounts which may be insignificant in terms of the percentage of control that they represent, but are still large in terms of their own income. Their salary and bonus is not independent of the profitability of the company. More important, however, is the fact that, whatever may be the relation between their income and their own company's profit, they are members of the propertied class and operate in a world in which the increase of property values is the only criterion of success. The American sociologist C. Wright Mills sums up the position of the "managers" of large corporations as follows:

Under the owners of property a huge and complex bureaucracy of business and industry has come into existence. . . . But the top man in the bureaucracy *is* a powerful member of the propertied class. He derives his right to act from the institution of property; he does act insofar as he possibly can in a manner he believes is to the interests of the private property system; he does feel in unity, politically and status-wise as well as economically, with his class and its source of wealth. . . .

To say that managers are managers of private property means, first, . . . that they use their power in the interest of maximizing profits. Secondly, it means that . . . "they are responsible to the effective clique of owners" . . . and to the "large property class in general." Managers have not been known to act intentionally against the property interests of the large owners.

At least two thirds of the $75,000 a year and up incomes of corporation managers are derived from property holdings. Top level managers are socially and politically in tune with other large property holders. Their image of ascent involves moving further into the big propertied circles . . .[34]

Thus the apparent "separation of ownership and control" does not mean that the operation of large corporations is freed, for better or worse, from the profit motive. That this is so is admitted, in the last analysis, by even so extreme a protagonist of the "new look" theory of corporate management as Herrymon Maurer.[35] He first asserts that the modern giant corporation is run "not primarily for the stock holders . . . but for the enterprise itself." He immediately adds, however, that "a profit test, whereby the company's affairs are subjected to a constant and strict accounting in terms of income and outgo, has great effect. It is the measuring instrument whereby managers decide how well they are operating in the present and also planning for the future."

We may conclude that the traditional assumption of economic analy-

[34]*White Collar* (New York, 1951, 1956), pp. 100–5.
[35]*Great Enterprise* (New York, 1955), p. 186.

sis, that business firms are motivated by the desire for profit, is not invalidated by the new patterns of ownership and control in the large corporation. We can therefore safely use this assumption in analysing the problems resulting from corporate bigness and the concentration of market control.

C. Conditions of Entry for New Firms

The effects of concentrated market control depend to a considerable extent on the ease of entry for new firms. Under "easy" conditions of entry the expectation of exceptionally high profits in a given field will lead to the establishment of new firms (unless, of course, the conditions giving rise to the high profits are purely temporary), or the entry of firms operating in other fields, into the market in question. Ease of entry therefore acts as a check that prevents firms from exploiting their monopoly positions by charging high prices.

Ease of entry depends on (a) technical conditions, which determine the minimum scale of operations, and hence capital, required for technical efficiency; (b) market conditions, which determine the capital outlay required to build up the new firm's market (e.g., advertising outlays, time required for customer acceptance of product, establishment of working relations with suppliers and customers); (c) conditions in the capital market which determine the difficulty and cost of obtaining the necessary capital; (d) the framework of laws, regulations, and contractual rights in which business operates. Tariffs, licensing requirements for firms, patents, grading regulations and many other aspects of government regulation of business clearly have a bearing on the conditions of entry.

Concrete studies of entry conditions in Canadian industry are sadly lacking, but inferences can be drawn from well-established facts, and since Canadian industrial and business techniques are largely drawn from the United States, United States studies of entry conditions throw some light on the conditions that are likely to prevail in Canada.

It is clear that in many lines of business in which concentration is high, the entry of new firms is obstructed by high initial capital requirements and the high concentration in the capital market. A large scale of output is frequently required for efficient operation and in many industries capital requirements are raised further by the defensive tactics of existing firms. These tactics include high expenses on advertising and on customer relations generally, a readiness to engage in price wars, and other devices. At the same time banks and investment dealers who are financing the operations of existing firms are likely to find their interests adversely affected by the entry of new competitors, and the high concentration in the capital market, which has been described in Section IA, means that the aspiring new entrant can be obstructed in his attempt to get capital from domestic sources on reasonable terms. The combination of these factors gives firms in highly concentrated industries considerable protection from the competition of new entrants.

Dependence on the Canadian capital market can of course be avoided by foreign firms or by domestic entrepreneurs who can raise funds abroad. In many cases, however, high concentration in Canada matches high concentration in the United States, so that there are similar obstacles to the entry of new firms with US capital. It is significant, nevertheless, that a great deal of the competition injected into various long-monopolized industries since the war has been due to the entry of new firms with United States, British or European capital.

In a country as highly dependent on foreign trade as Canada, tariff policy can have a major influence on the entry of foreign goods and hence the conditions of competition in the domestic market. There are numerous Canadian industries in which high concentration and high entry barriers domestically are reinforced by high tariffs which prevent the entry of foreign goods at low prices. In these cases monopolistic price and output policies can be pursued behind the tariff wall.[36]

To a considerable extent barriers to entry result from policies of established firms that have the obstruction of entry as their objective. These policies will be discussed in the next section.

PROBLEMS DUE TO HIGH CONCENTRATION AND FOREIGN CONTROL

A. Monopolistic Business Policies

When markets are controlled by a small number of firms and entry of new firms is difficult, the way is open for monopolistic price and output policies. The general characteristics of such policies — though not the details — can be deduced from simple economic models on the assumption that firms seek profits. This is, as we have seen, a reasonable assumption. Concrete examples of such policies in Canada come to light in the reports under the Combines Act, and sometimes in other government investigations. On the whole, however, the secrecy surrounding the operation of modern private business forces us to deduce the nature of these policies from the basic characteristics of the business system, and the circumstantial evidence of concentration data, entry conditions, characteristics of prices and price changes, and so on. In the paragraphs that follow, a few leading types of monopolistic policies will be discussed.

Price agreements. The most basic and best known type of monopolistic policy is the price agreement. Firms selling the same or related com-

[36]Apart from tariffs, import competition is greatly restricted by the fact that in many industries leading domestic and foreign suppliers are controlled by the same firm or, in some cases, participate in international cartel arrangements. See section IIA.

modities agree on the prices they will charge, thus preventing a competitive bidding for business. Price agreements are not likely to be effective when there are many small firms and entry is easy, unless there is an elaborate apparatus for "enforcement." The reason is that a small firm or new entrant has strong incentive to gain business by slightly undercutting the agreed price. On the other hand when the market is substantially in the hands of a small number of large firms, an agreement can be effectively maintained without much administration, since each firm knows that an undercutting of the price would have a substantial effect on the business of its rivals and would therefore be followed by immediate retaliation. Such agreements are therefore often maintained by conversations and telephone calls, leaving no documentary evidence that the Combines Administration could take to court.

The majority of the cases reported upon under the Combines Investigation Act have been price agreements under conditions of moderately high concentration, where enforcement of the agreement was sufficiently difficult to result in documentary evidence. For example the Canadian National Millers' Association maintained a system of price control in Eastern Canada described as follows: "Briefly, the system of control over prices has been exercised by the establishment of separate selling structures for Ontario, Quebec and the Maritime Provinces. This involved, within each structure, agreement upon prices and terms of sale, price differentials for the various grades of flour, price differentials for the different types of packaging and classification of customers. . . . In addition . . . indirect methods have also been agreed upon to prevent individual mills from reducing prices. . . . Agreements of this nature . . . related mainly to terms of sale and discounts. They have also included such matters as cash discounts, time limitations on shipments, non-repricing and non-cancellation of contracts except under certain conditions, cartage charges, legitimate storage points and storage allowances, carrying charges on undelivered balances and the effective dates of price changes. . . . Similar agreements were in force in Western Canada."[37]

In recent years there have also been reports under the Combines Investigation Act on price agreements in the sale of rubber goods, paper products, wire and cable, and in other industries.

Monopoly and oligopoly. When a market is substantially controlled by one firm or a very small number of firms, monopolistic prices can be maintained without agreement or any communication among firms. Such situations have not become the subject of combines investigations, except in a few cases where a deliberate policy of establishing a monopoly position was involved. There are however many important industries in

[37]*Flour Milling Industry*, Report of Commissioner, Combines Investigation Act (Ottawa, 1949), pp. 16, 17, 49.

Canada where the degree of concentration is so high that monopolistic prices can be maintained without agreement.

Price discrimination. When competition is restricted by high concentration and obstacles to entry, price discrimination flourishes. This term denotes establishment by a seller of price differentials between different classes of customers, differentials which do not correspond to differences in cost. A firm can make higher profits if it charges each class of customers "what the traffic will bear" than it would if all customers paid the same price, but this practice cannot be maintained if the customers can shop around in a competitive market or can buy from one another. Discrimination between different classes of customers is very often a feature of price structures established by agreement. Discrimination in favour of a large buyer also frequently serves the purpose of giving this buyer an advantage over his business competitors in the markets in which he sells. In the groceries trade, for example, it is urged by representatives of small retailers that the competitive strength of the large chains is due in part to discrimination by suppliers. A Combines Branch inquiry showed that in 1954 chain stores and "voluntary chains" received "special discounts and allowances" amounting to 2.1 per cent and 2.3 per cent of their purchases, while wholesalers and other accounts received 0.9 per cent and 0.6 per cent.[38]

Policies designed to change the market structure. Since profits are to be gained from a market position that permits monopolistic practices, a great deal of the skill and energy of businessmen is directed to the establishment and protection of monopolistic business positions and the suppression of competition. Much of the business conduct that looks at first sight like failure to seek maximum profit is in fact directed at the development and protection of monopoly positions.

Where imports are freely available even a highly concentrated business structure does not permit monopolistic pricing. Much energy is therefore devoted to the suppression of import competition. In many cases, of course, import competition is controlled by the fact that the Canadian producers are subsidiaries of United States or other foreign parent companies. In other cases Canadian producers are themselves the chief importers and thus control the price of imports. Often strenuous efforts are made to ensure that tariffs are kept high enough to permit monopolistic pricing. Imports of radios, television sets and other electronic equipment are prevented by the operation of a patent pool,[39] which has become the object of US anti-trust action against the parent companies of the participants. In other industries Canadian producers

[38]*Discriminatory Pricing Practices in the Grocery Trade* (Ottawa, 1958), Table 5–1, p. 115.

[39]See e.g., Royal Commission on Canada's Economic Prospects, *The Electronics Industry in Canada* (Ottawa, 1956), pp. 24, 25.

have participated in international cartels which have generally assured for the producers of each country a monopoly of their home market.[40]

A major way in which the number of competitors has been reduced, or its expansion slowed down, has been the merger of two or more existing firms. There is hardly a firm among today's giant corporations that has not grown to a significant extent by merger. In many mergers, of course, the improvement of market control is not the main object, and often it plays no part at all in the motivation of the merging firms. There are, however, many instances where a reduction in competition is at least one of the objectives, and still more where it is the result. The merger of the Toronto and Dominion Banks in 1956 significantly increased concentration in commercial banking (and the merger, announced in 1961, of the Imperial Bank and the Bank of Commerce, raised it further). Canadian Breweries was formed in 1930, with the purpose, according to a document found in the company's files "of ultimately acquiring the ownership or control of a sufficient number of selected brewing corporations in the Province of Ontario to establish itself as a dominant factor in the brewing business within that province." After a number of mergers had been completed its founder wrote: "I am sure that we now have the power to control prices and sales practices of the industry, and while it may be necessary for us to start local price wars here and there to discipline a small competitor, I am sure the profits will prove most gratifying to the shareholders."[41] Many post-war mergers have involved the acquisition of Canadian companies by United States or British firms and have thus further increased the importance of foreign control in the Canadian economy.

Price wars, local price cutting and other restrictive practices have been used to prevent new firms from getting a foothold, to drive out existing competitors, or to soften them up for a profitable merger. Thus, a merger of zinc oxide firms was preceded by a price war that had the specific objective of eliminating competition. Similarly the record of the Eddy Match Company shows that it maintained its monopoly by repeated local price cutting followed by absorption of independent firms. These price wars usually involved price discrimination. For example, "when . . . independent manufacturers quoted lower prices, Eddy Match generally met their competition, not by lowering the price of its standard products, but by introducing special brands, sometimes called "fighting

---

[40]*Canada and International Cartels,* Report of the Commissioner, Combines Investigation Act (Ottawa, 1946).

[41]*Report of the Director of Investigation and Research, Combines Investigation Act, 1956* (Ottawa, 1956), p. 10. In a recent court decision the company was acquitted of the charge of having violated the combines legislation. The acquittal was based on the grounds that the merger had not achieved a virtually complete monopoly, and that the price of beer was under some degree of provincial control. See section IVB.

brands," at reduced prices. These were sold only in the areas affected by the new competition, and only in limited quantities and for limited periods."[42]

Advertising and other promotional activities are of course a common method of competition, but they often serve the purpose of building up or defending a protected market for a particular product or brand. As has been pointed out, in some industries, such as cigarettes, the heavy advertising expenditures of existing firms raise the capital requirements of a new competitor far beyond those called for by technological conditions, and thus greatly increase the barriers to entry of new firms.

Numerous legal devices designed for other purposes have been used to restrict the number of competitors or to regulate competition. The use of patents to bar imports has already been mentioned. Patents have also been used to restrict the number of domestic producers, to control their selling prices, to control resale prices, and to control the use of unpatented articles in conjunction with the patented one. While the purpose of patents is often interpreted as the stimulation of invention by granting a temporary monopoly to the inventor, in practice patent monopolies have been extended far beyond the period of validity of a single patent, and patent rights have been used to restrict the supply and raise the price of patented and unpatented articles.

Close ties between existing firms and their suppliers have on occasion provided these firms with the support of their suppliers in their attempt to eliminate competitors. Thus the Zinc Oxide Company of Canada was given secret price concessions by its supplier of zinc, Hudson Bay Mining and Smelting Company, in support of its price war which ended in the elimination of one of its competitors by merger.

Monopolistic pricing policies and attempts to restrict entry are not confined to conditions of high concentration or giant firms. Small firms, particularly in retailing services, and contracting, have attempted to control prices through trade associations or by inducing suppliers to enforce minimum resale prices. The entry of competitors in a given locality is often obstructed by licensing requirements which may have had the original purpose of safeguarding the quality of the service rendered or sold (for example, skilled trades). Finally there are the well developed arrangements for eliminating competition in the sale of farm products many of which operate under provincial marketing legislation.

B. Inequality and Inefficiency

Monopolistic business policies have important effects both on the distribution of income and on the efficiency with which the economy operates. Receipts of the firms that benefit from such policies are higher

[42]*Matches*, Report of Commissioner, Combines Investigation Act (Ottawa, 1949), p. 124.

than they would be under more competitive conditions and these higher receipts are mainly reflected in higher profits and higher incomes of corporate executives. Higher profits benefit the stockholders, either in the form of dividends or in the form of retained profits that raise the values behind the shares. We have already seen that stock ownership is highly concentrated in the top income groups, apart from the ownership of Canadian stocks by foreign corporations and individuals. The benefits derived from monopolistic policies therefore both in the form of profits and in the form of executive salaries, tend to increase the inequality of the income distribution, to raise the proportion of income going to the top income groups and to United States and other foreign owners. In some cases a part of the benefits of monopoly income can be shared by the employees of the monopolistic firm if, for example, they have a strong union.

The effect on the distribution of incomes is what is usually in the critic's mind when monopolistic practices are condemned. Similarly, the defences made of monopolistic pricing usually involve the argument that it is socially desirable or just to raise the income of a particular group by this device. What is often not realized is that monopolistic policies also render the operation of the economic system inefficient. First, they permit and therefore tend to promote technical inefficiency in the firms enjoying monopoly profit. Under competitive conditions, when profit margins are narrow, technical inefficiency is punished by the disappearance of profit in the backward firm. Under monopolistic conditions, however, a certain degree of inefficiency will reduce but not eliminate profit, and the fear of lower profits is a much weaker incentive to efficiency than the fear of losses.

Secondly a good deal of the advertising and promotional activity which is fostered in oligopoly situations represents a socially wasteful use of labour, materials and capital. It is of course useful and indeed necessary, in any complex economy, to spread information about the goods that are available and their prices. A good deal of advertising and promotional activity is, however, not designed to convey information, but rather to change the buyers' tastes or to induce irrational behaviour. Generally speaking the pursuit of either one of these objectives does not represent a socially useful employment of labour and resources. Moreover, a good deal of advertising expenditure does not even succeed in influencing buyers' tastes, since to a considerable extent the competitive promotional efforts of rival firms neutralize one another.

Finally, monopolistic policies lead to *economic* inefficiency. An efficient economic system requires not only that goods and services be produced without waste of resources, in the technically most efficient manner, but also that the relative quantities that are produced be responsive to "what people want." The precise meaning of this requirement has been the subject of much discussion by economists. It is customary and useful to separate the question of economic efficiency from the question of the distribution of incomes by assuming that "what people want" corresponds to what they are willing to pay for. On that basis the high profit margins or inflated costs of the monopolized industries indicate that the system is producing too little of the monopolized output in relation to the output of more competitive industries. The prices people are willing to pay for additional supplies of the monopolized items are much higher in relation to the cost of the labour and resources required to produce them, than is the case in competitive industries. The systems would therefore be more efficient if it allocated more of its labour and resources to supplying the goods presently monopolized and less to those produced under competitive conditions.[43]

Inequality and inefficiency must therefore be expected in an economy in which monopolistic conditions are widespread, as is the case in Canada. Monopolistic conditions are not, of course, the only source of inequality and inefficiency, and it is doubtful whether they are the most important. We do not, in fact, know "how much" inequality of incomes or inefficient use of resources is to be attributed to monopoly. Recently it has been suggested that the problem is not serious. Suggestions to this effect have been made by the economist J. K. Galbraith in two successive books that have received much publicity.[44] In the first he suggested that both the inequality and the inefficiency due to monopoly are reduced by the development of "countervailing power." A monopoly on one side of a market leads to defensive organization on the other, and when both sides of the market are monopolized, the result of bargaining will be more like that emerging from competition than the result of one-sided monopoly would be. Certain historical trends seem to be in agreement with Galbraith's theory. Monopolistic organization of big business was followed by the development of co-operative marketing and finally government controlled marketing in agriculture, and by the growth of labour unions. It is, however, hardly realistic to suggest that the power

[43]A reader of the manuscript has objected to this conclusion on the grounds that the demand for monopolized goods may be "inflated" by advertising so that in the absence of monopoly *and advertising* the efficient output might be *less* than the monopoly output. However, the criterion of efficiency based on "what people want" is violated by monopolistic market structures, regardless of whether these wants are conditioned by custom, education, government propaganda, advertising or anything else. Moreover, the view that demand for a particular product is "inflated" by advertising implies a judgment that the influence of advertising on consumer tastes is undesirable. I would agree with such a judgment in some particular cases, though on the average there is no reason to suppose that the quality of consumers' tastes is either damaged or improved by commercial advertising. Even if it were damaged, however, it would not follow that to deprive consumers of what they want through monopoly is a suitable remedy.

[44]*American Capitalism* (Cambridge, Mass., 1952); *The Affluent Society* (Cambridge, Mass., 1958).

of such organizations rivals that of big business. Much propaganda to the contrary notwithstanding, a labour union cannot control the supply of labour. Its only real bargaining weapon is the strike, and its financial resources are slight indeed compared to those available to large corporations. A union's leadership cannot "order" a strike; it can strike only if a large number of workmen, with insignificant individual savings and small collective savings, individually vote to sacrifice their livelihood temporarily in the uncertain expectation of a longer-run gain. A large corporation, by contrast is centrally directed by its board or an even smaller group, and the major beneficiaries of its operation, executives and stockholders, have, individually and collectively, high incomes and considerable wealth which render their livelihood independent of temporary interruptions in the firm's operation.

Moreover, the theory of countervailing power breaks down completely when it comes to the consumer. Particular groups of workers or farmers may be sufficiently strongly organized to gain a share in monopoly profits, but in their capacity as consumers, all members of the public are exploited by monopoly.

The great majority of individuals participate in the economic system as sellers of their labour and as buyers of "consumer goods." Hence anything that raises the price of goods relative to their labour cost is against the interest of the majority of the public, though it may benefit a particular minority. Monopolistic business policies and inefficiency clearly have this effect.

Galbraith further suggests that economists lack a sense of proportion in emphasizing the inefficiency and waste due to monopoly, since output can be raised much more effectively by stimulating innovation, increasing the rate of capital investment, and reducing cyclical unemployment than by curbing monopoly. This judgment cannot be put to an empirical test at present, but even if it is correct, it would not furnish reasonable grounds for complacency about the problem of monopoly. Moreover, as indicated in subsequent sections, there are reasonable grounds for the view that the prevalence of large corporations and high concentration in an economy renders the stabilization of employment more difficult and does not promote technological progress.

C. Depression and Inflation

The prevention of serious cyclical unemployment has become a generally accepted goal of government policy in Canada and the United States. Fiscal and monetary policies by which governments can pursue this aim all involve an increase in government-induced spending when serious unemployment threatens, in order to prevent or reverse a decline in total spending. If such policies are to be effective, an increase in spending must be promptly reflected in an increase in output and employment. They are rendered ineffective to the extent that the business response to increased spending is an increase in prices while substantial unemployment remains.

In a flexible and competitive economy substantial price increases will not occur until the volume of unemployment is very low. Where large firms predominate and concentration is high, however, firms have substantial control over their prices and can raise them in response to the pressure of increased demand instead of expanding output.

The behaviour of the "administered prices," controlled by large firms under conditions of high concentration, attracted considerable attention in the thirties. The evidence available at that time suggested that such prices had a tendency to be "rigid" — to fall less than other prices in the downswing of the business cycle and to rise less in the upswing. The behaviour of "administered prices" in the last decade, however, suggests a different pattern. They have shown a tendency to rise more than others when business is improving, and to fall less when conditions are relatively slack. Table IV shows recent United States price increases for steel, machinery and "motive products" (automobiles, railway rolling stock, etc.) compared with price increases for other industrial products. This evidence suggests the possibility that the behaviour of administered prices has changed, because businessmen now expect the government to stabilize demand and underwrite reasonably full employment, whereas before the war they had to contend with violent fluctuations in demand and employment which rendered "price rigidity" a sensible defensive strategy. Thus, where "administered prices" are a major factor in the price structure, government policies to raise or maintain employment are likely to operate in an inefficient manner and to achieve their objective only at the cost of persistent upward pressure on the price structure.

Where a strong union exists it may secure for its members a share of the gains resulting from rising administered prices. Indeed, it has frequently been suggested that the pressure for higher wages is the main *cause* of the rise in prices. Strong unions have, however, developed only in response to high concentration in business and the greater-than-average wage advances have been secured in highly concentrated indus-

TABLE IV

CHANGES IN "ADMINISTERED" AND OTHER PRICES IN THE UNITED STATES

| | Percentage price increase | | |
	1947–51	1951–55	1955–58
All commodities other than farm and food products	22	1	8
Iron and steel products	37	14	20
Machinery and motive products	29	8	17

SOURCE: O. Eckstein and G. Fromm, *Steel and the Postwar Inflation*, Joint Economic Committee (Washington, 1959), p. 5.

tries in which, typically, profit margins too have risen.[45] Thus, high business concentration may reasonably be considered as the basic factor in the inflationary pressure from administered prices.

D. *Political and Social Implications*

A small firm has relatively little scope for influencing the technological, economic, political and social environment in which it operates. In most respects it will either be impossible for the firm to exert such influence, or else the cost involved will exceed the financial benefit to be expected. As a firm grows, however, the range of aspects of the environment over which it can profitably exert an influence increases.

Economists have analysed the difference in the firm's power to influence price, and in the profitable extent of its "selling costs" (expenditure on advertising, salesmen, etc.) that comes with a difference in firm size in relation to the market. The analysis can, however, be extended to many other aspects of the environment. Large firms find it worth while to engage in research, to devote a considerable expenditure to "public relations" and "employee relations," to operate training programmes, to influence governments, educational institutions and media of mass communications. These are aspects of the firm's environment where no influence can be exerted unless the expenditure is large, and where such expenditure is not worth while unless the benefit to the firm is applied to a large output. The employment of specialized personnel for functions of this type is only worth while for firms operating on a large scale or for co-operating groups of firms.

The distinction we are making between the range of functions of small firms and large firms is essentially a matter of degree. Even quite small firms find it worth their while to exert political influence at the municipal government level but a firm has to be larger before it can profitably perform this function at the federal level. Firms that are large in relation to the government of Newfoundland may be small in relation to the federal government, and firms, domestic and foreign, that are large in relation to the federal government may be small in relation to the government of the United States.

A good case can be made for the view that all the functions of business firms that are directed at influencing the environment are either socially undesirable or better performed by other agencies. In the case of monopolistic practices — those operations on the business environment that are commonly considered "economic" — the undesirable features have been adequately discussed in the literature, and we have referred to them in the preceding section. Here we shall select certain other aspects of business policy for more detailed review.

[45]O. Eckstein and G. Fromm, *Steel and the Postwar Inflation*, Joint Economic Committee (Washington, 1959), pp. 14–21, 32–3.

Political influence. There is no doubt that the activities of government have become a major factor in influencing the fortunes of business firms. Correspondingly the function of influencing government activity must be an increasingly important aspect of business policy. With the increase in government expenditure at all levels, taxes have become a dominant element in the business cost structure, and government contracts an increasingly important market for firms in a growing range of industries. In other industries — such as residential construction — the indirect effects of government expenditure and the government's monetary and fiscal policies have become major determinants of market conditions. Governments are called upon to help businessmen in securing foreign markets and to protect them from foreign competition. Government legislation and regulation establishes the legal framework in which business operates and many industries are subject to a good deal of regulation.

Little is known in detail about the way in which governmental processes are influenced in the interest of business firms. Corporate contributions to the campaign funds of both major parties appear to be standard practice, and are commonly divided in the ratio of 60 to 40 between the government and the opposition.[46] These contributions form the background for the use of techniques of persuasion that range from formal briefs and argument before commissions, committees, etc., to the most informal personal contacts.

The official attitude of governments and politicians to these activities is variable and often not clearly defined. Personal gifts of money or in kind designed to secure favourable action are generally considered improper, but contributions to party funds are fairly openly solicited. Politicians seem to differ in their evaluation of the use of stock options or inside information permitting favourable operations on the stock exchange. "Lobbying" and other persuasive techniques not coupled with offers of personal advantage are generally regarded as justifiable business activity.

How far is the exercise of political influence by business firms compatible with the values underlying democratic government? No serious student of politics would suggest that the citizen's attempt to influence government should be confined to the ballot box. In the modern theory of democracy the attempts of various interest groups to *organize* in order to gain favourable political action is recognized as part of the democratic process. The underlying value judgment remains, however, that expressed in the principle, "one man one vote;" political power should be approximately equally distributed.

If concentration were low and business firms small, the exercise of political influence by business firms would not be in conflict with this principle. When, however, economic power is highly concentrated in

[46]R. M. Dawson, *The Government of Canada* (Toronto, 1957), p. 567.

large corporations, as it is in Canada, those in control of these corporations exercise political power far out of proportion to their number. Hence highly concentrated private economic power conflicts with political democracy. This conflict is probably a far more serious consequence of the rise of great corporations than the economic inefficiency and inequality of incomes discussed above.

It should be stressed that the exercise of political influence does not reflect any "sinister machinations" on the part of corporate interests, but is simply the result of the rational pursuit of profit, within the bounds set by law and current moral standards, in an age when legislation and government activity are important features of the business environment. In fact, it often does not require any political activity at all, on the part of the corporation, beyond the standard contribution to campaign funds. Since the party machines are in fact dependent on large business contributions, the interests of large corporations are bound to be very influential in both legislation and administration. Politicians must constantly strive to achieve a balance between the aspects of legislation and administration that appeal to a large number of voters, and those that appeal to the sources of campaign funds.

In federal politics the influence of concentrated business power is probably a somewhat less serious problem than in provincial politics, since a greater variety of business interests is involved and the government is financially stronger in relation to the financial power of large corporations. Provincial governments on the other hand, are in many cases financially much weaker than individual giant corporations. At the same time their control over natural resources combines with their financial inability to exploit these resources themselves to render them most profitable targets for the exercise of influence by large international corporations. In this respect they are in fact in exactly the same position as the Middle East oil kingdoms.

Public relations. Political influence is exerted not only directly but also indirectly by influencing the views of the electorate. Such influence is an important aspect of the increasingly important public relations activities of large corporations. More generally, public relations activity has the objective of rendering the public sympathetic to the corporation concerned and to business in general, as well as to policies favoured by business groups. Public relations includes the guidance of the conduct of the corporation's employees and the performance of corporate good works. A great deal of it, however, is concerned with influencing the public through the media of mass communication — newspapers, periodicals, television and radio. Here again, the influence of the large corporation is to a considerable extent indirect. Its advertisements are generally confined to selling its goods, but since this advertising constitutes the major source of revenue for newspapers, periodicals and broadcasting stations, these media must strive to satisfy the advertisers in their choice of material for publication and broadcasting.

The efficiency of public relations activity is increased by the fact that the mass media themselves are a highly concentrated industry. Over the years mergers of newspapers have brought matters to the point where in most areas there is only one local paper. Moreover, many papers are linked by common ownership in a "chain." Radio and television stations are local monopolies or duopolies, often under common ownership with the local newspaper. Public ownership of the CBC constitutes an exception of major importance to the concentration of private control over the mass media.

Independent and critical views can reach the public only through a few periodicals of limited circulation or on some of the CBC programmes. On any controversial issue, large sums will be spent to put the view favoured by large corporations before the public through monopolized channels of communication, and other views get only a very limited hearing. A good example is the current tendency of communications media to impress on the public an unfavourable picture of labour unions.

The public relations interests of large corporations present formidable obstacles to the efficient operation of the democratic process. On major issues of public policy the public does not get a balanced presentation of alternative views. Some slight counterbalance to the corporate point of view is provided by the socialized element in broadcasting (although here, too, as has recently been shown, the presentation of "controversial" points of view is severely limited) and by a few periodicals with very small circulation.

Social services and education. In Canada governments do not accept full responsibility for social services and higher education. Hence funds required for the operation of "charitable institutions" and universities must be laboriously collected from private individuals and corporations. The undistributed profits of large corporations constitute a major source of such funds. The "charitable contributions" of such corporations are almost negligible in relation to their total profits, but constitute an important element in the revenues of universities and social service agencies.[47] Naturally enough, this situation is reflected in the control of these institutions; the large corporations and their executive staffs are well represented on the governing boards of universities, hospitals and charitable institutions. Naturally also, the activities of these institutions are influenced by the corporate scale of values. Funds are more readily available

[47]In 1958 corporate grants to universities and colleges constituted only 0.36 per cent of corporate profits, but were 7.2 per cent of the capital and operating expenditures of these institutions (*Financial Post*, September 12, 1959, p. 13, quoting a report by the Industrial Foundation on Education).

for facilities and fellowships in the natural sciences, engineering, and commerce than in the humanities and social sciences.

Thus, as governments have refused to accept what should be their responsibility, the large corporations have in some measure become "private" government agencies. They levy their own private "sales tax" which is included in the controlled price of their product and apply the proceeds to the provision of social services, education and research. They differ from government agencies only in one respect, but it is of major importance: there is no social control over their activities.

E. Problems arising from Foreign Control

There has been considerable debate about the implications of foreign, and particularly, United States control in Canadian industry. As has been shown, United States control is particularly prevalent among the largest corporations. A number of economists have argued that no deleterious economic consequences flow from the fact of United States control. Some of the "evils" ascribed to foreign control are, in fact, the consequences of concentration and monopoly, so that there is no reason to assume that they would be remedied if the companies in question were domestically controlled. Others, it is claimed, are imaginary.

There are, however, important implications of foreign control that are serious and not imaginary. The United States parent companies are subject to United States law and are responsible, in the United States, for the acts of their Canadian subsidiaries. Hence foreign economic control is in fact a link through which United States policies and legal decisions are imposed on the Canadian economy. Some of the resulting problems have received considerable publicity. United States–controlled companies cannot trade with China and have been subject, in the case of Canadian Industries Limited, to dissolution by United States court decree. It is obvious that a serious loss in autonomy is involved.

The importance of this problem is emphasized when it is considered in conjunction with the great political influence of large corporations discussed above. When there are close links between government policy and business policy, in both the United States and Canada, the United States control of substantial segments of Canadian business is bound to be reflected in the political sphere, and to reduce substantially the degree of real political independence enjoyed by Canada.

Foreign control also makes it more difficult for Canada to pursue independent economic policies. For example, in a period of inflation, Canada's attempts to restrict business capital expenditures by a "tight money" policy can be frustrated by the access of foreign subsidiaries to their parent companies' funds. Similarly, if the Canadian Combines Investigation authorities ever decided to pursue a vigorous anti-merger policy, their aims could be frustrated by mergers or agreements among foreign parent companies.[48] In countless ways foreign control of Canadian firms weakens the freedom of Canadian governments to pursue independent economic policies, as well as exposing Canadian governments to powerful foreign pressures.

Does foreign control lead to a direct economic loss to Canadians? A recent investigation suggests that there is little concrete evidence of this.[49] One type of situation is, however, sufficiently important to deserve comment: many United States–controlled firms produce raw materials for United States industry. "It has been suggested by responsible Canadian businessmen that certain non-resident controlled firms in a dominant market position have responded to political and other pressures abroad by pricing important Canadian exports at abnormally low levels."[50]

F. Conclusions

Large corporations have concentrated a considerable amount of economic, social and political power in the hands of a small group. The activities of most of these corporations are not subject to significant social control, although they vitally affect the economic, social and political life of the nation.

In the economic sphere this structure promotes inefficiency, inequality of wealth and income, and economic instability. In the political sphere it conflicts with the basic principles of democracy. The importance of foreign control among leading firms involves a significant limitation on the national freedom of independent decision.

The question naturally arises whether it is realistic to look for ways of improving a business structure of this kind. Many commentators, aware of the shortcomings discussed above, would contend that there are substantial benefits from corporate concentration which would be lost if the present structure of ownership and control were altered in a significant way. This question will be examined in the next section.

ARE LARGE CORPORATIONS "NECESSARY"?

Champions of the modern business structure involving high concentration and large firms have stressed two related lines of argument. According to one, large firms are a technological necessity and the tendency of technological progress is to increase the most efficient firm size. Any attempts to limit or reduce firm sizes below those desired by the businessman in control is therefore bound to lead to economic inefficiency.

[48]When the British aircraft firms, De Havilland and Hawker Siddeley, merged in 1960, the small number of independent aircraft producers in Canada was further reduced, since both had Canadian subsidiaries.

[49]Brecher and Reisman, *Canada–US Economic Relations*, chaps. 8, 9.

[50]*Ibid.*, p. 158.

According to the second, more recent, line of argument, only giant firms with monopolistic markets can afford to take the risks involved in innovation. Limitation of firm size must therefore slow down the rate of progress.[51] Neither of these lines of argument is well founded.

There is no doubt that the "economies of large scale" are of major importance in the modern business system. The available evidence suggests, however, that they reach their limit at a scale of operations that is generally well below that of the giant industry leaders, and the evidence does not suggest that improvements in technology inevitably or even predominantly tend to increase the minimum efficient scale. In most industries firms greatly different in size exist side by side. In some cases it has been suggested that monopolistic prices enable inefficient firms to survive together with the efficient. But great inequality of firm size is found in many industries where this explanation is not likely to hold, and cost studies, which unfortunately are not numerous, suggest that medium-sized firms are generally as efficient as the largest firms, and often more efficient.[52] What is relevant, in the present context, is of course efficiency from the standpoint of society, not profitability for the firm. Large firms have advantages due to their superior bargaining power and more efficient use of advertising and other marketing tools. Such advantages are, however, not advantages to society and therefore do not furnish an argument for the protection or conservation of large firms as a matter of government policy.

Technological progress has not, by any means, had the one-sided effect of only increasing the advantages of large firms. Many innovations, indeed, have created new opportunities for small firms and there is no indication that this trend is coming to an end. For example, the widespread replacement of steam power by electricity has liberated firms from the costly investment in steam plant and made it efficient to install small-capacity machines run by purchased electricity. The widespread replacement of railway by truck transportation has greatly increased the range of cheap but efficient locations available to small firms with limited capital. New materials, such as the light metals and plastics, are efficiently fabricated by small firms and new machine processes have further increased the small firm's opportunities.[53]

[51]For a version of the first view see, for example, B. S. Keirstead, *The Theory of Economic Change* (Toronto, 1948), p. 239 *ff*. For the second view see J. A. Schumpeter, *Capitalism, Socialism and Democracy* (New York, 1953), ch. 6, and other sections; and other recent works.

[52]See C. A. Smith, "Survey of the Empirical Evidence on Economies of Scale" in National Bureau of Economic Research, *Business Concentration and Price Policy* (Princeton, 1955), pp. 213–38. See also G. J. Stigler, "Monopoly and Oligopoly by Merger," *American Economic Review*, May, 1950, pp. 23–34, esp. p. 26.

[53]See J. M. Blair, "Technology and Size," *American Economic Review,* May, 1948, pp. 121–52.

Recently the defence of the large corporation has shifted its ground to the claim that the rate of technological progress depends on research, which, in view of its cost and uncertain pay-off, only large corporations can finance. The theoretical foundations of this line of argument are unconvincing, while the empirical evidence is scanty and conflicting, but on the whole tends to refute the argument.

In the long run the rate of technological advance depends on progress in basic rather than applied research, and basic research is an activity in which even giant corporations do not engage to any significant extent, precisely because of the uncertain direction and amount of the pay-off. Basic research is, in fact, already in the main a socialized activity, financed by governments, universities and other non-profit institutions. In a good many fields, moreover, this socialized research even now extends a long way into the applied areas. Agriculture, housing, and defence are obvious examples.[54] There is no good reason why an increasing area of applied research should not be taken over by the socialized forms, and it is evident that this would in fact increase the rate of technological progress.

The rate at which the information resulting from research — both basic and applied — is put to use in industry depends in large measure on the difficulty and expense of getting the information into the hands of potential users. Progress is most rapid when the information is available without charge and steps are taken to publish it widely, while progress is minimized when the information is kept as a "trade secret," sold at an appreciable cost, or made available to only a select group of firms. Business firms carrying on research for profit are impelled to withhold discoveries from actual or potential competitors, to patent processes and products that can be patented and to make patented or "private" knowledge available, if at all, only for a fee or to a restricted group of firms. The results of socialized research on the other hand can be made freely available.

Moreover, research resources employed by monopolistic private firms are bound to be used in a socially inefficient manner. Secrecy leads to duplication of research efforts; concern with a firm's strategic position leads to lines of research that will strengthen and extend the power of patent control rather than those that are socially most promising; concern with the market means that research is largely devoted to changes in the product that will promote obsolescence and to new products, rather

[54]It is not generally realized that even a substantial proportion of the applied research carried out "by business" is financed by the government and therefore involves no risk or financial burden to the firms concerned. "A recent study of scientific research in American industry conducted by the Research and Development Board indicates that approximately half of all research engineers and scientists employed by industry in January, 1952, were on contract research with either the Department of Defense or the Atomic Energy Commission." (W. R. Mac-Laurin in *American Economic Review*, May, 1954, p. 188)

than to improvements that will make products cheaper and more durable.

It is sometimes argued that "applied" research cannot in fact be planned and carried out by governments and non-profit institutions because they lack the knowledge of production processes and market conditions that is required. But knowledge is held and used by individuals, not institutions, and the scientist in a giant firm's research department has the same problems. He can acquire the necessary knowledge by talking to production engineers and sales staff, but so can a government scientist. If it is objected that firms will not disclose such information to government personnel, the answer is that they will, if this constitutes an economical way of getting research problems solved.

Thus the research operations in which large firms are alleged to have a decided advantage over the small — i.e., projects that are both large-scale and risky — are more efficiently carried out on a socialized basis if the benefit to society is the criterion of efficiency.

A recent study of the case histories of important twentieth-century inventions concludes that:

1. The large research organizations of industrial corporations have not been responsible in the past fifty years for the greater part of the significant inventions.
2. These organizations continue to rely heavily upon other sources of original thinking.
3. These organizations may themselves be centres of resistance to change.[55]

A variant of the defence of the large firm on grounds of "innovation" argues that the risks which only a large firm can shoulder are not in the field of research expenditure, but involve rather the investment required to apply a new process or produce a new product once it has been invented. The record suggests, however, as George Stigler points out, that "there is no evidence of any unwillingness of entrepreneurs to undertake the risks associated with new industries or old industries revolutionized by new processes. There are numerous industries to be sure, which for a considerable time had only one or two firms. . . . But in almost every case, patents or other contrived restrictions on entry were available and actively exploited. Where the new industry did not have such barriers, there was an eager host of new firms — even in the face of the greatest uncertainties. One may cite automobiles, frozen foods, various electrical appliances and equipment, petroleum refining, incandescent lamps, radio, aircraft, and . . . uranium mining."[56]

Stigler's statistical study compares, for forty-two manufacturing indus-

55J. Jewkes, D. Sawers, and R. Stillerman, *The Sources of Invention* (London, 1958), p. 185.

56G. J. Stigler, "Industrial Organization and Economic Progress," in L. D. White, ed., *The State of the Social Sciences* (Chicago, 1956), pp. 269–82.

tries, the decline in labour requirements per unit of output between 1899 and 1937 with the concentration ratio of the industry at both the beginning and the end of the period. No significant correlation between high concentration and rapid technological progress is found. In fact, the average decline in labour requirements per unit of output is considerably greater in the industries with declining concentration and the industries that have low concentration throughout the period, than it is in the industries that have high concentration at both the beginning and the end of the period.[57]

We may conclude that there are no sound theoretical grounds and no convincing empirical evidence that would make it reasonable to regard the giant corporation as a "necessary," or even a particularly convenient, vehicle of technological progress. To this general conclusion a specific Canadian footnote should be added. There has been considerable discussion of the fact that Canadian giant corporations have not distinguished themselves in research and innovation, and that they tend to lean on the research efforts of their foreign parents. Thus in Canada tenderness to the giant corporation on the grounds of its contribution to progress is particularly misplaced.

The belief that changing technology makes giant firms and increasing concentration necessary or "inevitable" is also in conflict with the sketchy information that is available on actual trends in firm size and concentration in the United States and Canada. On the average there appears to have been a rising trend in typical firm size over the long run, but to a considerable extent this has been the result of mergers, and in general mergers involve improvements in financial strength, bargaining power and market control rather than technical improvement.[58] Technological progress may well have facilitated such growth by removing obstacles which previously made large-scale operation in many respects less efficient than the operations of medium-sized plants. Improvements in communications, office procedures, data processing, and the science of management are relevant here.

In spite of the increase in average firm size the statistics for the United States and Canada do not suggest on the average any significant increase in the degree of concentration since the First World War. The

[57]*Ibid.*

[58]J. F. Weston, *The Role of Mergers in the Growth of Large Firms* (Berkeley, Calif., 1953), studied a sample of 74 dominant firms in the US and found that one-third of the growth in assets of the firms between the turn of the century and 1948 is growth by merger (p. 13 *ff*). Moreover, the *relative* position of these oligopolists in their respective industries is almost entirely due to mergers at the turn of the century (p. 48–9).

[59]See G. W. Nutter, *The Extent of Enterprise Monopoly* (Chicago, 1951); M. A. Adelman, "Measurement of Industrial Concentration," *Review of Economics and Statistics*, Nov., 1951, p. 269; G. Rosenbluth, *Concentration in Canadian Manufacturing Industries* (Princeton, 1957), chap. v; G. Rosenbluth, "The Trend in Concentration and its Implications for Small Business," *Law and Contemporary Problems*, winter, 1959, pp. 192–207.

reason is that the expansion of markets has more than kept pace with the increase in firm size.[59] If mergers involving leading firms had been successfully resisted, a significant decline in the average degree of concentration would no doubt have been observed.

This conclusion has important implications for present and future government policy. Spectacular growth of the Canadian economy over the next quarter century has been forecast by the Gordon Commission. The actual figures mentioned may be little better than guesses, but the present population structure makes a significant growth a safe bet. Given appropriate policies, this growth of the whole economy can provide the basis for a significant growth in the number of firms, a decline in the concentration of market control, and an increase in competition. It could also mean, if appropriate policies are followed, a decline in the importance and influence of individual large corporations in economic, social and political life, and a decline in the relative importance of United States influence.

PRESENT GOVERNMENT POLICIES

A. No Significant Controls over Large Corporations

The most important feature of present government policies in the field of business regulation is that they do not treat the giant corporation as a phenomenon calling for social control. Corporations are legal devices which enable small groups of individuals to concentrate power over large segments of national wealth and income with, as we have seen, a consequent concentration of political and social power. It is clear that such concentrations would not be possible without the special rights and privileges that governments confer on corporations. Yet the view implicit in the present structure of government regulation is that, in general, the way this power is used is entirely the private business of the individuals in control; the public interest is not affected. This view is hardly realistic. "The influence of limited companies upon the whole economy of the country is now so profound that they can no longer be left in the ambiguous position of being "persons" but without personal responsibilities; their organization and control can no longer safely be left as a purely domestic matter."[60]

In fact, there are few effective restrictions on the activities of large corporations, and they do not have to give an account of their activities to anyone. Their policies are shrouded in secrecy, except for such pictures as the public relations experts consider it expedient to reveal. In the case of companies offering securities for sale to the public, the statutes require the publication of financial statements which, however, can be made to reveal a minimum of information. "Private" companies, which have not over fifty shareholders and do not offer securities to the

[60]C. A. Ashley and J. E. Smyth, *Corporation Finance in Canada* (Toronto, 1956), p. 19.

public, do not have to provide any public information at all. A considerable number of Canada's giant corporations are organized as "private" companies, being either closely held foreign subsidiaries or closely held family concerns. General Motors and the T. Eaton Company are outstanding examples. Their freedom from publicity has drawn unfavourable comment.[61]

While there are no general controls over the activities of large corporations, certain specific types of activity are subject to some measure of regulation. The chief of these are discussed below.

B. The Combines Investigation Act

Canada's main legislative defence against monopoly is the Combines Investigation Act. The Act was drastically amended by the Conservative government on August 1, 1960, but at the time of writing we have had no experience of the operation of the amended legislation. Our account of anti-combines activity will therefore refer to the act *as it stood up to August 1960*, and the legislative changes will be outlined in a final paragraph.

The Act prohibits agreements among business firms to control prices, output, entry, as well as "mergers, trusts or monopolies," if they operate against the public interest. It applies only to commodities, however, not to services. Since 1952, the practice of resale price maintenance is also prohibited. Price discrimination is banned, but is defined only for sales of the same item "in like quantities," a provision which has rendered the ban ineffective.

Under the administrative system established in 1952, suspected violations of the Act are to be investigated by the Director of Investigation and Research who, if his findings warrant further action, places a Statement of Evidence before the Restrictive Trade Practices Commission which then holds a hearing at which argument is presented by both the Director and the firms under investigation. The Commission's Report is then presented to the Minister of Justice and published. The Minister decides whether a prosecution is called for.

Despite this impressive machinery and the sweeping clauses in the Act, its impact on the economy has most likely been slight. Between 1923 and 1959 only sixty-five formal reports were made (not all of them published), of which twenty-five were made since the establishment of the new administrative machinery in 1952. Up to 1957 there had been less than thirty court cases and only twenty-two convictions. "Either Canadian business has been very good, or our administration has been very loose. In either case business seems to have little to worry about, whether or not the law be strictly construed."[62]

[61]*Ibid.*, p. 6.

[62]D. G. Kilgour, "Combines — Fine Papers," *Canadian Bar Review*, vol. 35, no. 9, (Nov., 1957), pp. 1087–1100, esp. p. 1096.

No machinery has been established for checking up on the discontinuance of violations after conviction or investigation, and the fines levied on conviction have been very slight indeed. It is thus very doubtful whether the fear of conviction is a significant deterrent. Nor has the fear of publicity resulting from the publication of reports, on which Mackenzie King laid great stress when he put through the legislation, proved to be an important factor. As a matter of fact the reports receive very little attention in the mass media, and no effort is made by the government to attract publicity.[63]

The bulk of the cases reported on, and a still higher proportion of those that have gone to court, have dealt with a price agreement among a group of firms, or resale price maintenance. Moreover, the price agreement cases handled have been those involving documentary evidence, and hence as a rule cases involving a considerable number of firms. It is likely that in relation to formal agreements of this kind the Act has had some deterrent effect.

Many of the most important types of monopolistic structure and practices have, however, been left virtually untouched. Single-firm monopolies, oligopolies involving informal or "tacit" agreement among a few firms, price discrimination and related practices, all these are areas to which the Act has not been applied in any significant degree. Moreover — and this is a related phenomenon — remedies other than conviction and fine (lately supplemented by "orders of prohibition") have rarely been applied, although the law provides for the reduction of tariff and patent protection in appropriate cases, and government policies in such fields as finance, taxation, government purchasing, and trade promotion, could have considerable impact on particular monopolistic situations.

Mergers, although clearly covered by the Act, were long neglected by the administration. In the last few years a number of merger cases have been investigated, but the court decisions in two recent test cases suggest that the typical monopolistic merger is beyond the reach of the legislation as it stands. In the case of the Canadian Breweries merger (described on page 215 above) the company was acquitted, mainly on the grounds that the merger had not achieved virtually complete monopoly and that there was some degree of provincial control over beer prices in Ontario and Quebec.[64] In the second case, decided in August, 1960, the BC Sugar Refining Company was acquitted although it had bought out its sole western competitor, the Manitoba Sugar Company.

Neither the Director of Investigation and Research nor the Commis-

[63]On the contrary, since 1957 the press releases announcing Commission reports no longer even summarise the contents of the reports.

[64]Judgment of Chief Justice McRuer, Supreme Court of Ontario, February 8, 1960. Evidence previously presented to the Commission had indicated that the Provinces did not effectively control the price of beer.

sion has an economic research staff (the Director had one research economist for a number of years; the Commission has recently acquired one) and in fact no basic research in the field of monopoly and industrial organization is carried on. The operations under the Act were closely scrutinized by the MacQuarrie Committee in 1952,[65] and while a good many of its suggestions relating to the mechanics of administration (e.g. the separation of "investigation" and "reporting") were implemented, its most important recommendations, relating to research, to remedies other than conviction and fine, and to co-ordination of combines policy with other government economic policies, were ignored.

In summary, administrative activity under the Act has lacked the scale and vigour required to make a significant impact, and neither Liberal nor Conservative governments have shown any desire to change this basic situation. Business interests have constantly fought the Act, both in the lobbies and in the courts. Their campaign has been successful since the administration of the Act has not come to grips with the major problems arising from concentration.

The amendments passed in 1960 will almost certainly have the effect of further weakening the administration of the Act. Combinations and agreements are now exempt if they relate "only to the export of articles from Canada" and do not "lessen competition unduly" in the domestic market. With regard to domestic agreements the wording has been changed in such a way as to render prosecution and conviction much more difficult. The ban against resale price maintenance has been rendered virtually ineffective through the introduction of defences that make successful prosecution extremely unlikely.[66]

C. Regulation by Administrative Agencies

In this section we are concerned with only one aspect of regulation: the use of regulation as a substitute for competition in the case of large corporations in monopolistic situations. One cannot find pure cases of this kind in Canada since in any particular case the aims of regulation are mixed and, very often, are not clearly formulated. However, the regulation of railways and public utilities by federal and provincial governments has the control of monopoly policies as a major objective.

The Canadian railway system was financed in large measure by means of government grants and government guarantees, and one of the two major companies is now owned by the government. Nevertheless, both companies are operated for profit, and have therefore been subjected to external regulation. The Board of Transport Commissioners has the

---

[65]*Report of the Committee to Study Combines Legislation* (Ottawa, 1952).

[66]House of Commons, 24th Parliament, 3rd Session. *Bill C-58.* See also H. of C. Committee on Banking and Commerce, *Minutes of Proceedings and Evidence,* no. 13, July 18, 1960, pp. 731–2, and H. of C. *Debates,* July 26, 1960, p. 6973.

power to regulate not only the rates charged by the railways, but also some aspects of their investment policies and many details of operation. Its powers have been extended to cover express, telegraph and telephone lines, water transport, and interprovincial pipelines. Its decisions can be appealed to the Supreme Court, and can be amended or rescinded by the Cabinet.[67] Airlines were regulated by the Board of Transport Commissioners from 1938 to 1944, when the Air Transport Board was established. Provincial governments regulate the rates charged by privately owned public utility companies operating within the province and in most cases exercise some control over investment policy.[68]

We lack analytical studies of the process of regulation in Canada, but certain conclusions are suggested by a consideration of the basic objectives of the regulated group and the regulating authority and the relation between them. Effective regulation of monopolized industries would mean that all important decisions are passed upon by at least two groups: the management or directors of the regulated firms, and the regulating authority. When, as is usually the case, there is provision for appeals to the courts or the government, a third group will be involved. Hence, at best, the decision-making process would be extremely slow and cumbersome.

The decisions subject to regulation would have to be the basic decisions of business policy, those concerning the scale of operations, the types of products or services, and the prices or rates to be charged. Moreover, if regulation is effective, the interests of the regulated firm would diverge from those of the authority. The firm is interested in maximum profit while the authority would be interested in a level of profit no higher than "necessary." The authority would want to promote technical efficiency and the reduction of costs, but the interest of the firm in cost reduction would be slight, since the benefits would not accrue to the firm but would be passed on to the customers.

It follows that the regulated firm has a strong interest in rendering regulation ineffective as a curb on monopoly policies. Since the determination of the "correct" price level involves a detailed study of costs, and even then is largely a matter of judgment (in the absence of competition), the firm has a strong and central interest in seeing to it that the information that is available to the regulating authority, and the rules it adopts in evaluating the information, will lead to the conclusion that the prices desired by the firm concerned are correct. Similarly the firm will have a strong interest in seeing that the decisions regarding relative prices, investment policy, the type of service, and such matters are in line with its own wishes.

[67]A. W. Currie, *The Economics of Canadian Transportation* (Toronto, 1954), chap. 16.
[68]A. W. Currie, "Rate Control on Canadian Public Utilities," *CJEPS*, vol. XII, no. 2, May, 1946, pp. 148–58.

The chances are good that the firm will succeed in influencing the regulating authority. A large firm will have considerable financial and manpower resources to devote to this task. It is worth its while to go to a great deal of trouble, since the decisions concern the vital aspects of business policy and the stakes are high. It will therefore devote a considerable effort not only to the presentation of information and argument to the authority, but also to the formal and informal presentation of its views to the government as regards the legislation under which the authority operates, its personnel, and its budget. Public relations activity will also be worth while if a change in the process of regulation is desired.

The regulating authority, on the other hand, depends on the regulated firm for detailed information and is therefore not likely to be able to operate without the co-operation and goodwill of the regulated firm. Moreover, governments, under pressure from business interests to minimize "interference," and under pressure from all sides to economize, are likely to appoint regulating authorities with budgets that are inadequate for the task of effective regulation and hence with inadequate personnel in respect of both quantity and quality. These authorities will find the case for the policies that the regulated firms wish to follow well prepared and backed with facts and figures, while the elucidation of the public interest is left to their own inadequate resources. In such a situation the easy and safe solution for the regulating authority is to refrain from exercising initiative, and to take up a "judicial" role, dealing with issues that are brought before it and leaving the public interest to become apparent through presentations from members of the public who feel sufficiently strongly about the matter. The process of regulation thus becomes even more slow and cumbersome, more and more like a court trial, so that it is only likely to be applied to selected major issues. Moreover, on most issues the gains or losses at stake will be very great for the firm, but much less significant for any one group of their customers or other members of the public. The basic information necessary for the elucidation of the public interest is in the hands of the regulated firms, and even if made freely available, its processing and analysis is a costly business. In view of all these considerations it is probable that in general the regulatory authority will simply sanction the policies of the regulated firms, or modify them in relatively minor respects.

This conclusion must be qualified in an important respect where the monopoly in question sells a commodity or service that is of basic major importance to other firms that are also in the giant class, or to large numbers of smaller firms grouped together in an industry or region. In this case the customers' interest in the outcome is likely to be great enough to justify considerable expense on their part in the presentation of their point of view, and their political importance is likely to be great enough to give their views a considerable weight in determining the decision. In Canada railway rates on Prairie wheat or Maritime coal are clearly in this category.

A recent summary of regulatory experience in the United States indicates that the features of the process that we have deduced from the general characteristics of business firms and governments are prevalent in practice.[69] The author concludes that "the economic stakes are sufficiently significant to render the control of regulatory practice an important, and sometimes crucial, political objective of regulated groups." He describes regulation as a "two-way process, in which the regulatory commission and the regulated group try to control each other." He adds that "the failure of political leaders to formulate regulatory goals and give support to regulatory policies paves the way for acceptance by the agency of the philosophies and values as well as the specific regulatory proposals of the affected groups."

The administrative structure of control in Canada appears to differ from that in the United States in one important respect. The United States procedure places great emphasis on making the regulatory body "independent of politics," while in the Canadian practice the subordination of the regulating body to the elected government is an important element. Both procedures have their weaknesses, and the forces tending to render regulation ineffective persist in either case. Bernstein points out that the notion that regulation in the public interest can be made nonpolitical is unrealistic, and that attempts to isolate a commission from politics leave it more exposed to the attempts of the regulated groups to gain control. On the other hand the Canadian practice may lead to the overruling of regulatory bodies by *ad hoc* government decisions which are based on short-run political considerations and not on a careful study of all the facts and the consideration of the public interest in the long run.

The scanty descriptions that are available of regulation in Canada suggest that the major conclusions of the United States studies are applicable also to this country. A. W. Currie's review of the Board of Transport Commissioners' personnel, although very cautiously worded, makes it plain that Canadian governments have not provided the Board with Commissioners equal to the task of effective regulations.[70] "Appointment of incompetent men for purely political reasons has doubtless discouraged able men with experience in transportation from seeking or accepting position . . . the Board as a whole has not been as able as other comparable groups, such as the deputy ministers of government departments, the Board of Directors of the Canadian Pacific, or the top execu-

[69] Marver Bernstein, *Regulating Business by Independent Commission* (Princeton, 1955), p. 280 *ff*.

[70] *Economics of Canadian Transportation*, chap. 16. Quotations are from pp. 426–35.

tives of either major railway. . . . The high retiring age has led to positions on the Board being considered a sort of pension."

Currie further points out that the Board itself is too large and its staff too small for effective operation. A large board leads to conventions regarding "representation" of regions and interest groups and hence second-rate appointments. Moreover, it tends to "become a debating society" and cannot function expeditiously. Inadequate staff has led to the Board itself having to handle a high proportion of routine work. The Board's work has been piecemeal and *ad hoc*. For example, "During hostilities, when it had comparatively little work, it had not seriously tried to anticipate post-war problems or formulated tentative plans for meeting them."

The Board has emphasized judicialized procedures; "hearings" are the typical preliminary to important decisions, and in these proceedings the scales are weighted in favour of the railways. The public interest is ascertained by hearing representations from shippers, the provincial governments, and others as well as from the railways, and "before the Royal Commission of 1951 several witnesses and provincial counsel suggested that the Board should be more generous in lending assistance to the public in preparing rate cases and in advising shippers on the intricacies of rates."

The incomplete nature of the Board's control is indicated by much of Currie's discussion. The Board does not appear to take the initiative in changing the rate structure and in regard to many details of the structure it in fact leaves the railways free to formulate their own policy. "To emphasize the judicial or semi-judicial quality of the Board's work," Curries says elsewhere, "makes clear its fundamental weakness. It is unable to formulate a constructive policy or even to carry one through unless it is laid down in fairly definite terms by Parliament."[71]

Currie concludes a review of public utility regulation by both Dominion and provincial authorities by remarking that "Canadian experience with rate making is characterized more by routine than by originality. . . . In the main Canadians have relied on public ownership rather than on regulation for ensuring good utility service at reasonable prices."[72]

NOTES ON PUBLIC POLICY

It is not proposed to attempt here a blueprint for the solution of the problems discussed in preceding sections. We can, however, present certain basic considerations which may be helpful in the evaluation of policy proposals.

[71]"The Board of Transport Commissioners as an Administrative Body," *CJEPS*, vol. XI, no. 3, Aug., 1945, pp. 355–6.
[72]"Rate Control on Canadian Public Utilities," p. 158.

The problems we have discussed have their origin in the existence of concentrations of economic power that are not subject to social control. The policy alternatives that arise for consideration can be classified as those that eliminate these concentrations through public ownership, those that subject them to control by regulation, and those that reduce the degree of concentration. It is important to bear in mind that policies are not applied in a static environment. The economy as a whole is likely to grow at a rapid rate over the next ten or twenty years, and centres of economic power will shift, grow, or contract, while new ones arise, even in the absence of specific policies.

A basic and reasonable requirement for policies in this area is that they should not be guided by an unreasoning prejudice in favour of private enterprise. The organization of economic activity through private profit-making firms is a social device for which alternatives are available, and a sensible choice between the alternatives is made in a particular situation by studying the manner in which each is likely to operate and evaluating its probable operation from the point of view of the public interest. The point has been well put by Sir William Beveridge: "The list of essential liberties . . . does not include liberty of a private citizen to own means of production and to employ other citizens in operating them at a wage. Whether private ownership of means of production to be operated by others is a good economic device or not, it must be judged as a device."[73]

It is evident that the political representatives of the Liberal, Conservative, and Social Credit parties do not take this unbiased view. Their speeches abound in statements that indicate an unquestioning preference for private enterprise. In its mildest form this prejudice expresses itself in the view that "in the absence of special circumstances" private enterprise is to be preferred to public enterprise. The "special circumstances" usually amount to situations in which private enterprise is not profitable.

4. Public Ownership

In Canada there are and will continue to be many industries in which high concentration and giant firms render private enterprise socially inefficient, while a "breaking up" of the leading firms would introduce technological inefficiencies. "Regulation" of the policies of such firms has been, as we have seen, a cumbersome and ineffective device and it may be suggested that this inefficiency and ineffectiveness is inherent in the structure of the relation between the regulator and the regulated. Moreover, regulation is not likely to come to grips with the political and social problems arising from the power of large corporations; in fact its ineffectiveness is in large measure due to the political power of the regulated groups.

[73]W. H. Beveridge, *Full Employment in a Free Society* (London, 1944), p. 23.

The remaining remedy is then the elimination of these centres o
uncontrolled power through public ownership. We do not propose to
review here the whole extensive debate regarding the relative merits o
private and public operation of industry. Certain aspects of this con
troversy will, however, be selected for discussion.

One of the problems most frequently mentioned in connection with
public ownership is that of maintaining a system of incentives and con
trols within a large public organization which will ensure intensity o
effort, efficiency and honesty on the part of employees. This is by no
means a trivial problem. It must be emphasized, however, that thi
problem exists within the large privately owned corporation just as i
does in a publicly owned enterprise and its character is not changed by
public ownership.

The widespread impression that there is more inefficiency and waste o
manpower in government employment than in the large corporation is in
the main attributable to the fact that information on government opera
tions is more readily available and to the effectiveness of the public
relations efforts of large corporations. Where a real difference exists, i
can be ascribed to the fact that government salary rates are notoriously
lower than those prevailing in private business — largely owing to busi
ness pressure for "economy" in government — and in a free labou
market levels of efficiency tend to adjust to salary levels. But any result
ing loss of efficiency in government would not be due to the inheren
characteristics of government operation, and can be remedied by a
adjustment of employment conditions.

There is no doubt that the spread of public ownership would throw a
considerably increased burden on the political process and would requir
some reform of the political machinery. The major policy decisions o
nationalized industries or firms, decisions concerning the scale of op
erations, type of product, and prices, have implications in terms of "who
gets what" and are therefore bound to be the object of political pres
sures. They cannot be made "non-political" by such administrativ
devices as an "independent" Crown corporation. The important point i
that these decisions should be made in a socially responsible manner
They should take political pressures based on voting strength into ac
count, but not pressures based on concentrated economic power. The
should be based on a careful consideration of their full implications
both short-run and long-run, and not on considerations of immediat
political gain.

The Canadian political machinery, as it is constituted at present, can
not make such decisions efficiently because it lacks facilities for th
examination of the implications of government decisions in the economi
sphere in an integrated manner; in other words, it lacks facilities fo
economic planning. This deficiency exists at the federal level, and th
problem is magnified by the division of economic functions betwee

federal, provincial and municipal authorities. It constitutes an obstacle to socially responsible policy making at present, and it would constitute a much more serious problem if the area of nationalized economic activity were enlarged. Hence any extension of nationalization must be accompanied by the development of machinery for economic planning under democratic control. "Machinery" means not only an administrative structure, but also principles and procedures.

The difficulties obstructing the extension of publicly owned business which have been discussed so far have to do with the operation of nationalized industry. They are not fundamental, because their solution is a matter of developing the right kind of administrative machinery; it is a matter of exercising sufficient ingenuity. A more fundamental difficulty arises because the resistance of the owners may be so great that the transfer of existing firms to public ownership may not be feasible in many cases. In fact, since public influence and political power are major consequences of economic concentration, one may find that the greater is the need for public ownership, the stronger is the resistance to it. In Canada the problem is further complicated by the importance of United States control among the leading firms. Attempts to nationalize corporations having United States parent companies would be sure to encounter the resistance not only of these parent companies, but of the United States government as well. In view of the qualified character of Canada's political independence, it is likely that nationalization of existing firms could not in fact be carried through on any appreciable scale.

There is a much better chance of preventing the spread of the power of large corporations into new areas. Canada's growth involves the development of new industries, as well as the expansion of the industries that exist today. Government policy can assure that these new fields will not become the monopoly of large private corporations. In recent years the transportation and distribution of natural gas has been handed over to private interests (with a public subsidy in the form of public construction of the unremunerative part of the transcontinental pipeline) with large capital gains for promoters and friendly politicians built into the capital structure, just as in the days of railroad promotion. There has also been a considerable acceleration in the rate at which provincial authorities are handing over the development of natural resources under their control to foreign and domestic private groups. Wenner-Gren in the west, Eaton and Krupp in the east, are outstanding examples. It is widely recognized that the terms on which these privileges have been granted are extremely favourable to the private groups concerned. What is not so generally realized is that these grants involve the establishment of new concentrations of corporate power and the consolidation and growth of existing concentrations with consequent aggravation of the economic, social and political problems that result from such concentration.

The readiness of provincial governments to hand over resources to private groups has sometimes been ascribed to the difficulty such governments would have in acquiring capital and "know how" for the development of resources under public ownership. It is likely that new forms of federal-provincial co-operation must be developed in order to enable provincial governments to check the further consolidation of private power over natural resources.

Since the war large new areas of economic activity have been opened up by technological advances based on government research or government-financed research in various countries. Most of these advances have been connected with "defence," but have also had important "peaceful" applications. Atomic energy, jet propulsion, radar, computers, are major examples. In all these cases the government is initially in complete control, both as the source of research funds and as sole buyer of the product. The government is therefore in an excellent position to prevent the monopolization of the resulting new industries by corporate big business and to ensure their development on either a socialized or a competitive basis. This course has, however, not been taken by governments in either the United States or Canada. The bias in favour of free enterprise has combined with the defence chiefs' bias in favour of monopolistic business to promote the extension of corporate concentration to these new areas. Research contracts as well as contracts for the new products have been highly concentrated and in some cases corporations have been permitted to patent the results of government-financed research. Government defence policy has become subject to the pressures of large corporations whose major markets are government procurement. The development of applications of atomic energy is passing into private hands.

This survey suggests the directions in which government policy could move in order to reduce the degree of corporate concentration. To a very considerable extent federal and provincial governments have the power to keep the new economic areas developing in the course of Canada's growth out of the hands of large private firms. Even if it proves difficult to go very far in eliminating existing concentrations, such a policy would reduce the relative importance of existing concentrations as the economy grows.

B. Anti-Combines Policy

An effective anti-merger policy would also be required if economic growth is to reduce concentration. In view of the recent court decisions the anti-merger clause of the Combines Investigation Act would have to be rewritten to effectively prohibit mergers that significantly increase concentration, and would have to be vigorously enforced.

The administration of the Act with respect to price agreements, price discrimination, and other monopoly practices could play an important part in preserving competition, freedom of entry and mobility in the many sectors of the economy where an anti-merger policy can maintain a sufficiently low degree of concentration. Our review suggested that here too a much more serious administrative effort and a larger staff would be required.

C. Conclusion

Private enterprise is a useful and efficient way of organizing economic activity when it is competitive, when entry is open, and when business firms are not so large as to exert a significant social and political influence. The large corporations which dominate the economy today constitute a system of organization that is economically, socially and politically inefficient. These corporations are, in large measure, the result of uncontrolled merger and they do not appear to be "necessary" in terms of either technological efficiency or technological progress. With the rapid growth of the economy that is to be expected, one may look forward to a decline in the *relative* size of the business unit "required" by technological considerations, that is, a decline in its size in relation to the size of the economic areas in which it operates. Government policy can take advantage of the resulting opportunity to reduce the degree of corporate concentration by abandoning the bias in favour of corporate private enterprise in resource development, procurement, research, and other spheres of activity under government control, as well as by seriously applying an anti-combines policy, especially in relation to mergers.

The problems created by existing concentrations of economic power cannot be effectively solved by regulation, which, at best, is bound to be limited and specific in its application and cumbersome in its operation. Moreover, regulated corporate concentrates display a strong tendency to regulate the process of regulation, thus rendering it ineffective.

In some situations the dissolution of corporate concentrates may be technologically feasible and may promise a sufficient increase in competition to render it worthwhile. In general, however, the transfer of these corporations to federal and provincial ownership is required to solve the problems of concentration. Moves in this direction are bound to encounter strong resistance from the business interests involved, and indeed from the business community generally, and this resistance can have recourse to all the techniques of economic, political and social influence at the disposal of large corporations. Particularly where United States ownership is involved, this resistance may prove a decisive obstacle to large-scale nationalization. These considerations serve to emphasize the point that at least the opportunities for reduced concentration presented by economic growth should not be neglected.

APPENDIX

THE MEASUREMENT OF CONCENTRATION

1. *Number of firms*. The estimate is for 1956. Dept. of National Revenue, *Taxation Statistics, 1958*, records for the 1956 taxation year a total of 630,000 farmers, fishermen and forestry operators, independent professionals, other "business proprietors" and corporations. The number of separate business firms must be less since many businessmen and professionals are partners and some corporations are subsidiaries of others. Data for earlier years show that about 26.5 per cent of all business proprietors are partners. We can get a "lower limit" to the number of business firms by making the extreme assumption that there are on the average four partners per business partnership, that the same proportion of partners and number of partners per partnership holds for professionals, and that half of all corporations are subsidiaries of others. These assumptions yield a "lower limit" of 521,000 for the number of firms.

2. *Number of giant corporations. Taxation Statistics, 1958*, shows sixty-nine corporations with total assets (gross of depreciation reserves) of $100 million or more each, in 1956. This figure excludes banks, insurance companies and Crown corporations. *Canada Gazette*, Supplement, Feb. 2, 1957, shows that eight of the nine chartered banks are in the same size-class and the *Report of the Superintendent of Insurance, 1956*, vol. 1, pp. 25A, 51A, shows fourteen life insurance companies whose assets in Canada were over $100 million. An examination of the accounts of federal Crown corporations in *Public Accounts of Canada, 1956,* vol. II and *1957,* vol. II, together with the description of their functions in *Canada Year Book, 1957–58,* pp. 86–91 yields a list of five with primarily business activities and assets of over $100 million each in 1956 (Canadian National Railways, Central Mortgage and Housing Corporation, Polymer Corporation, Trans-Canada Air Lines, Canadian Wheat Board). *Financial Post Survey of Industrials, 1956,* shows one savings bank with assets of over $100 million. We thus have data for ninety-seven giant corporations.

3. *Number of non-financial corporations*. The *Financial Post Survey of Industrials, 1956,* shows eleven trust companies, two mortgage companies and three finance companies with assets of over $100 million in 1956. These are presumably included in the sixty-nine companies recorded in *Taxation Statistics* in the giant class. Four of the five Crown corporations listed in paragraph 2 are non-financial corporations. The estimated total number of non-financial corporations in the giant class is thus $69 - 16 + 4 = 57$.

4. *Concentration of assets*. (a) Value of inventory, land, buildings and equipment is taken net of depreciation and depletion reserves. Minimum value owned by fifty-seven non-financial giant corporations in 1956 is calculated as total for sixty-nine "giants" less total for *all* trust, mortgage, loan and finance companies (both figures from *Taxation Statistics*) plus total for CNR, Polymer Corp., TCA, and Wheat Board (from *Public Accounts*). Result: $10,861 million.

(b) Value owned by all non-financial corporations is estimated as follows: total for all "fully tabulated" companies less total for all fully tabulated financial companies, excluding real estate firms (from *Taxation Statistics*). Result is adjusted for incomplete coverage by dividing by 98 per cent for "profit" companies and 82 per cent for "loss" companies. These adjustments are based on the ratio of profits or losses of fully tabulated companies (which exclude banks, insurance companies, Crown corporations) to the profits or losses of fully tabulated companies plus companies with incomplete returns, inactive companies, co-operatives, personal and exempt corporations, Result: $25,164 million. Figures for four large Crown corporations (see §4,a) and seven smaller Crown corporations are added (*Public Accounts*). The seven smaller Crown corporations are the CBC, Canadian Arsenals, Northern Canada Power, Canadian National Steamships, Canadian Overseas Telecommunication Corporation, Eldorado, Northern Transportation. Result: $28,723 millions.

(c) To estimate real assets for all business firms, we first add an estimate for real assets owned by financial corporations. This is the total for financial corporations shown in *Taxation Statistics,* plus chartered banks (*Canada Gazette,* Feb. 2, 1957), plus Central Mortgage and Housing Corporation (*Public Accounts*), plus an estimate for insurance companies based on *Report of the Superintendent of Insurance,* vol. 1. The latter gives data for real estate holdings of Dominion-registered insurance companies. They were adjusted for the holdings of provincial companies by using the ratio of value of policies in force, total to Dominion-registered, for life insurance companies and the corresponding ratio of net premiums written for fire and casualty companies. Next, real assets of unincorporated firms are estimated. There is no comprehensive information on the assets of this sector and not even any data on its relative importance in terms of income and output. In order to obtain a rough estimate we are driven to the desperate expedient of assuming that real assets per dollar of income of unincorporated proprietors are the average of real corporate assets per dollar of corporation profit and real corporate assets per dollar of "investment income." The former is likely to be an over-estimate since the income of unincorporated business contains a large element of labour income that is excluded from corporate profits. On the other hand the latter may be an under-estimate since some of "investment income," namely part of interest and rent paid to "individuals," originates in the unincorporated sector. Data for unincorporated income, corporation profits, and investments income, 1956, from *National Accounts, 1926–56.*

5. *Consolidation of parent and subsidiary companies.* A list of companies was developed by examining John Porter, "Concentration of Economic Power and the Economic Elite in Canada," *Canadian Journal of Economics and Political Science,* vol. XXII, no. 2, May, 1956, pp. 199–220, and W. H. McCollum, *Who Owns Canada* (Ottawa, 1947) as well as other sources. Data on the value of assets (1956) were obtained from *Moody's Handbooks* and the *Financial Post* surveys of corporate securities. These sources also contain information on parent-subsidiary relations. The denominator of the percentage given in the text is the figure of $25,164 million estimated as shown in §4,a.

6. *Concentration in manufacturing.* The proportion of real estate, equipment and inventories of all "fully tabulated" manufacturing companies, concentrated in the "giant" class in 1956, is computed from *Taxation Statistics.* The figure is 31.1 per cent.

The "fully tabulated" companies have 99 per cent of the profits and 97 per cent of the losses of all "active taxable" companies in manufacturing. We assume that they have about 99 per cent of the real assets (losses are only about 4 per cent of the profits).

The relative importance of "active taxable" companies as compared with all companies is shown only for all industries together in the published statistics. The "active taxable" companies have 98 per cent of the profits and 92 per cent of the losses of all companies. The weighted average (treating both profits and losses as positive) is 98 per cent (Crown companies are omitted). We assume that the "active taxable" companies in *manufacturing* have 98 per cent of the assets of all companies in manufacturing.

Incorporated manufacturing companies had, in 1956, 96 per cent of both the value of shipments and the "net value added" (value of shipments less cost of raw materials, fuel and electricity) of all manufacturing plants (DBS, *Type of Ownership, Manufacturing Industries of Canada, 1956,* p. 6). We assume they have 96 per cent of the assets.

It is thus estimated that the "fully tabulated" companies have 99% × 98% × 96% = 93% of all manufacturing real assets.

Assuming that all of the largest firms are "fully tabulated," the percentage of assets concentrated in the largest size groups among the "fully tabulated" companies must be multiplied by a factor of 93 per cent to obtain the estimated concentration ratio for all manufacturing firms. Figures for the concentration of total assets (including investment in affiliated companies) are about the same as those for real assets: 28 per cent for the largest 28 companies and 53 per cent for the largest 143 companies.

7. *Number of firms in manufacturing. Taxation Statistics* shows over 15,000 "active taxable" corporations in manufacturing for 1956. In addition, DBS, *Type of Ownership, Manufacturing Industries of Canada, 1956* shows that there were over 19,000 "establishments" (plants) operated by unincorporated businesses. Even if account is taken of the fact that some unincorporated firms may operate more than one plant, and some corporations are subsidiaries of others, a minimum of 30,000 firms is a safe guess.

8. *Concentration in retail trade.* Sales of chains are from DBS, *Retail Chain Stores, 1958.* Total retail sales are from DBS, *Retail Trade, 1958.* The figures in the text again understate the degree of concentration since they do not take account of all intercorporate connections and the common ownership of retail outlets in unrelated types of business.

TABLE A

CONCENTRATION OF WHOLESALE TRADE, 1951

"Size" of firm (number of establishments per firm)	Number of firms	Percentage of all wholesale sales	Average sales per firm ($000)
1	14,716	46	431
2	587	10	2,303
3	224	6	3,645
4–5	202–253	9	4,985–6,250
6–10	98–163	10	8,820–14,670
11–25	39–88	9	14,500–32,750
26–50	14–88	5	21,500–40,000
51–100	3–5	1	31,600–52,600
100 and over	4 or less	3	111,600 or more

SOURCE: *Census,* 1951, vol. VIII, Table 15 (grain elevators excluded).

Number of firms and sales per firm are estimates in the form of ranges within which the correct figure must lie. Number of firms is estimated by dividing th number of establishments, as reported in Census Table 15 by the number o establishments per firm that characterizes the class interval concerned.

More detailed information is available for 1951. In that year there were 140,869 "independent" firms (with one, two, or three outlets each) accounting for four-fifths of retail sales, and 479 chains (computed from DBS, *Census of Canada, 1951,* vol. VII, Table 13 and Appendix B).

9. *Concentration in wholesale trade.* Relevant statistics are available only for 1951 and are even less satisfactory than those covering manufacturing and retail trade. They clearly indicate, however, that by far the greater part of the business is done by small firms (Table A). Petroleum bulk tank stations are the exception. Here 44 per cent of the sales are made by four firms, or fewer, averaging over $100 million of sales per firm (*Census, 1951,* vol. VIII, Table 15).

10. *Concentration in the Service Industries.* Over two-thirds of the labour force in this sector is in non-profit organizations, professional services and domestic service, where there is clearly no question of large firms or high concentration (*Census, 1951,* vol. IV, p. 16–9). Government is excluded from the calculation. The services *not* considered "non-profit, professional, or domestic" for this calculation are Recreation, Advertising, "Other Business Services," and Personal (except private households). In these latter fields three-quarters of the total business was done by single-unit firms in 1951, and only 15 per cent by large regional or national chains (Table B).

11. *Concentration in agriculture.* Figures are computed from *Cenus, 1951,* vol. VI, part 1. They may understate concentration slightly since there may be cases where different farms are under joint corporate ownership. This cannot be an important factor, however, since only three per cent of all farm land is on farms operated by hired managers (*Census,* Table 46).

12. *Concentration in transportation, communications and storage.* The relative size of the different components of this sector in 1951 is indicated very roughly by the percentage distribution of the labour force (1951) as follows:

Steam railways (including express and telegraph)	43%
Truck transportation	15%
Telephone	12%
Water transport (including incidental services)	9%
Taxi cabs	6%
Urban and suburban transit	6%
Air transport	3%
Bus and coach transport (interurban)	2%

TABLE B

RECEIPTS OF SERVICE ESTABLISHMENTS BY TYPE OF FIRM, 1951

Type of firm	Percentage of receipts
"Independents"	
Single stores	75
Two-store multiples	4
Three-store multiples	2
"Chains"	
Local	1
Provincial	3
Section and national	15
	100

SOURCE: *Census,* 1951, vol. VIII, Table 27.

(Based on *Census, 1951*, vol. IV, Table 16. Grain elevators are excluded, since these are included in wholesale trade.) Concentration figures in the text and below relate to the year 1957 and are computed from annual DBS reports.

In urban and suburban transit, the publicly owned Toronto and Montreal systems together account for 55 per cent of the gross operating revenue.

Highway bus passenger transport may also be fairly highly concentrated. Forty-seven large companies have 94 per cent of the gross revenue. In trucking, however, 103 large carriers account for only 68 per cent of the total gross revenue.

In inland water transport Canada Steamship Lines "controls the most important part of the passenger and freight transportation between Canadian ports on Great Lakes and Montreal and Quebec on the St. Lawrence Seaway" (*Moody's Transportation Manual, 1959*, p. 1427).

No industry-wide statistics for the natural gas pipeline industry are as yet available, but the annual report for all pipelines (DBS) shows that net operating revenue plus salaries and wages (a figure roughly equivalent to income generated in the industry) amounted to $62 million in 1957, which may be compared with a corresponding figure of $112 million for truck transportation and $79 million for civil aviation.

Four pipeline firms had assets of over $100 million in 1957: Trans Mountain, Interprovincial, Westcoast Transmission, and Trans-Canada Pipe Line.

Planning for Economic Progress: Resource Development and Capital Investment

H. SCOTT GORDON

There are two great facts of modern economic life that most people know so well that they are hardly aware of them. The first is the fact of economic progress — the remarkable rise in man's capacity to satisfy his material wants and needs that has taken place over the past century or so. The second great fact, and perhaps the more surprising when one reflects upon it, is the great disparity in the distribution of the means and benefits of economic progress among the nations of the earth. Each nation not only carries within itself "two nations — the rich and the poor" as Disraeli pointed out more than a hundred years ago, but the world as a whole carries within itself two *groups* of nations — the advanced and the backward or, in the modern euphemism, the developed and the underdeveloped. The United States and Canada enjoy material standards of living that are at least ten times and may be as much as thirty times those of countries such as Burma, Ethiopia, or Bolivia.[1]

[1]International comparisons of this nature are of course very difficult and any effort at precise measurement would be quite misleading. However, rough comparisons based on national income statistics are probably safe enough as indicators. For figures on per capita incomes in various countries, together with some discussion of their usefulness in this respect, see Charles P. Kindleberger, *Economic Development* (New York, 1958), chap. I; Henry H. Villard, *Economic Development* (New York, 1959), chaps. I, II; Harvey Leibenstein, *Economic Backwardness and Economic Growth* (New York, 1957), chaps. I, II.

Moreover the rate of economic *improvement* is very different in different countries. In North America, output per capita has been increasing at about 2½ or 3 per cent a year, that is, doubling in a single generation, while in other parts of the world there has hardly been any growth at all. Necessarily, the result is that the disparity in the world's living standards, great though it already is, is growing even greater.

THE DYNAMICS OF PROGRESS

A good deal of attention has been paid in recent years to the study of the causes of these international disparities and perhaps the most striking thing that seems to emerge is how obscure the causes of economic wealth and progress seem to be. One might have expected the rich countries to be those that are well endowed with the natural resources on which modern economic life is based. But there are many anomalies: Switzerland and Israel are relatively rich but have very few natural resources; Venezuela and Brazil are poor but have many natural resources that are more or less unexploited; Saudi Arabia is desperately poor though it has at least one resource and it *is* exploited.

Canada is a country with excellent natural resources and it is exploiting them to a steadily increasing extent. It is also a country that enjoys, at least relatively speaking, a very high and rapidly rising standard of living. But the foregoing cursory illustrations should make it clear that one ought not to trace any simple and direct connections between a country's resources on the one hand and its wealth and progress on the other. We are fortunate in having rich natural resources. That makes the task of providing a comfortable life for all our citizens easier than it is for many other countries; but it does not assure us that a progressive standard of living will inevitably be ours simply by waiting for it. The land is rich, but it must be used with energy, intelligence, and foresight if it is to yield us what we wish.

The Elements of Economic Progress

To answer the insistent question, Why is one nation rich and another poor? is beyond both the scope of this chapter and the understanding of this writer. There are many causes of poverty, and it is almost impossible to say what specific collection or combination of things would be sufficient to generate a high standard of living in any nation or region. Undoubtedly, we would discover that different countries have different economic problems and require different policies. However, it seems fairly clear that there are certain basic elements that must be present whenever a high and rising standard of living is manifest.

The first of these basic elements is the one that has already been mentioned — natural resources. A nation must have, or have access to, the great resources that are the foundation of modern industry if it is to achieve a high standard of living. If it does not have minerals, forests, and energy resources of its own it must obtain them from other nations by trade. The fact that a country is dependent on foreign supplies of natural resources does not at all mean that it is doomed to poverty. But it does mean that it has a more limited ability to direct its own economic life and development. A country such as Canada that has rich and diversified natural resources within its own boundaries is in a much better position to plan its economic development in a comprehensive and long-sighted fashion than one that is dependent on foreign suppliers.

The second requirement is capital. Either machines or men must be slaves, one or the other. If men are to be emancipated from the domination of hard physical toil and economic necessity then machines must be bound over to the task. These machines, the buildings that house them, the railroads and highways that carry their raw materials and finished products, the dams, harbours, warehouses, shops, and offices that serve the modern production process in their own various ways, these things constitute the productive capital that is perhaps the most distinguishing mark of an advanced economy.

There are other elements of economic wealth and progress, rather less tangible than resources and capital, but not less important. The first of these is knowledge. A rich endowment of natural resources is of no use without the knowledge of how to use it. Capital, slave as it is, must be directed, and the quality of that direction will determine whether the output obtained is much, or little, or nothing at all. The advances in man's knowledge have been so great in recent years, and their practical economic results have been so astounding that one might say almost without exaggeration that knowledge is the basic element of economic progress. Or, to put it differently, there is but one ultimate cause of poverty and that is ignorance. Therein lies at once the great hope and the great despond of man, for the history of civilization is a story of great advances of knowledge and great areas of intractable ignorance existing side by side.

Another factor of considerable importance is the institutional structure of society. If a society is so ordered that its economic, social, political, and legal systems act as barriers to economic innovation, it will progress only with difficulty, if at all. A caste system that prevents people of ability from entering occupations for which they are best suited; a financial system that channels the nation's savings into nothing but safe, conservative investments; a political system that makes the discovery and exploitation of natural resources an occasion for nothing more important than the personal aggrandizement of politicians and their friends; a legal system that permits private property interest to stand immovably in the way of national development; a constitutional system that permits one section of the nation to prevent developments that are for the general good — these are but brief examples of institutional structures that are inimical to economic progress. A progressive society continually re-examines its institutional structure and readjusts it to changing needs and changing circumstances. A society that regards its institutions as sacrosanct will effectively prevent the other elements of economic progress from working.

Finally, we must consider a factor of progress that is the most intangible of all. Lacking a better term, I will call it the "energetic spirit." It is a very important fact that different countries and different epochs have varied enormously in the amount of creative and productive energy that their people have been able to put forward. No one really knows why one country may be bustling with activity and innovation while another continues to plod dispiritedly in the worn pathways of ancient practice. No one knows why there have been, in the Western world, vivid epochs of great intellectual and practical ferment and others that have been dull and stuffy, dominated by closed minds and by tried, conservative ways of doing things. Yet the facts are plain enough. Whenever and wherever man has made significant progress, it has been when his society has been endowed with many people who have the energy and desire to search and experiment, to innovate and build, and to knock down in order to build anew.

Although I have here presented these basic elements of economic progress as if they were separate and independent, it is quite clear that the relations among them are close and important. When we talk of the natural resources "available" to a nation we are talking about materials that have been brought within man's grasp as a result of the capital that has been invested in developing them and the knowledge that can put them to use. An unknown ore body consisting of materials that geologists and chemists do not yet understand is not a resource. It is a curious thing about many mineral resources that although the amount of them used up increases steadily from year to year, the "proven reserves" still available seem to increase at the same time. It is not the physical mineral stock itself that is growing, of course, but the capital and knowledge that turn unknown and useless material into valuable resources. This was never more true than it is in Canada at the present time. Many of the resources that will clearly be the foundations of our future prosperity were not even proven to exist a generation ago. Others that were known were too inaccessible to be exploited. Alberta oil is a great resource only because geologists have recently broken some of the earth's mysteries. Labrador iron is a resource because the transport facilities have been constructed that enable it to be used. And similarly, the deposits of base metals at Great Slave Lake will not constitute "resources" until we invest the capital that is necessary to bring them within reach. To do all this requires that we should *want* to progress and that our society should manifest a spirit of creative energy that will produce the searching and investing by which resources are discovered and developed.

Consider knowledge as an element in progress. To increase knowledge requires a great deal of capital investment — in schools and universities, laboratories and equipment. It also requires an energetic pursuit. If the student is to learn what is known and the scientist is to investigate what is unknown, two things are necessary: physical facilities and mental vigour. The first of these is capital and the second is a manifestation of what I have been calling the "energetic spirit." It is clear then that the various basic elements of economic progress are closely interrelated and dependent upon each other.

The Energetic Spirit and the Social Structure

It is apparent from the foregoing that I would place a great deal of weight on the intangible factors of knowledge, institutional structure and energetic spirit, in accounting for the economic wealth of the "advanced" nations of the world. The history of the Western world itself provides sufficient evidence of their importance but the point is further reinforced today by the awakening of nations and peoples in heretofore "backward" areas of the world. China is probably the most dramatic example of a country that is shaking off the sloth and complacency of ancient practice and is moving into the foreground of the world scene as a vigorous, dynamic, and growing economy. But China's experience is not unique; it is being repeated also in numerous other countries of Asia and Africa.

The dynamic force that seems to be the main source of the creative and constructive changes that are manifesting themselves in these emerging countries is nationalism. We have to recognize the great creative energies that nationalistic fervour is capable of generating, but it would be a mistake, in my opinion, for Canada to seek to further its economic progress through this channel. Canada is perhaps, as yet, rather less nationalistic than many other countries, but to anyone with a liberal, humanist point of view we are surely quite nationalistic enough. If we wish to do something to dissipate the cloud of fear that darkens the horizon of mankind we can do so by trying to base our civilization on the things which all men hold in common rather than those, like nationalism, which are sources of conspicuous distinction and invidious comparison among peoples.

We can, however, learn some lessons from the economic dynamism that nationalistic fervour has apparently been able to release. The most important of these, in my own view, is that the creative energies that are latent in man and that have occasionally in the past burst forth with such a marvellously variegated display are fostered best by a society that can give its people a sense of communal achievement. A great deal of the economic mythology of our time is founded on the belief that the great industrial advances of the nineteenth century were the result of an individualistic, competitive society where each man sought his own private gain and nothing more. No interpretation of social history could be shallower than this. One need only dig beneath the surface a little to discover that the great industrialists and business men who played the leading role in nineteenth-century economic development were builders as much as they were moneymakers. Pride and pleasure in the work done and in the thing created were the mainspring of their energetic spirit, more so than the amassing of personal fortunes. The same is true of the great business and industrial leaders of our own day. No less than artists and scientists, they pour out their energies primarily for achievement's sake.

But herein lies the deep criticism that has to be levied at modern capitalistic society: it affords this sense of creation and achievement to business men, but to few others. Most of our citizens are reduced to the status of mere sellers of labour services; they have no hand in shaping the future and can feel no sense of achievement in performing the tasks they are required to do. This is the great challenge to the social organization of modern society. If we can create a civilization in which many more members share a deep sense of their contributions to the communal life, we will have one in which the energetic spirit is greatly enhanced. Here is the great division that lies between the socialist and the competitive concepts of society. In the socialist concept, man is conceived as a being wise enough and co-operative enough to be capable of forming a society of mutual help and to seek a life that is rich in its communal experience. In the competitive concept, man is unalterably egotistical, life is unremitting struggle and conflict, and the only purpose of social organization is to restrain an unregenerate humanity.

Who Plans for Progress?

In studying the question of economic progress it is just as important to examine the processes by which economic changes are brought about as to consider what the preceding pages have called the elements of progress. The first step in understanding these processes is to recognize that economic change does not just happen; it is the result of decisions taken by human beings.

In the economist's picture of the competitive economy, events are presented as resulting from the impersonal play of the forces of demand and supply. But competent economists have always recognized that this picture must be significantly qualified when we consider economic activities that either (a) are carried out under "imperfectly competitive" conditions, that is, where only a small number are engaged in the activity in question, either as suppliers or demanders; or (b) involve large and basic economic decisions that, once made, alter the whole economic environment in a significant way. To illustrate: (*a*) it would be silly to contend that the production of steel in Canada is determined by "market forces," if this were meant to imply that the decisions of the small number of producers (STELCO, DOFASCO, and a handful of other firms) were not of overriding importance; and (*b*), it would be silly to discuss the particular decision to build a steel mill in Montreal as if that were a "marginal decision," that is to say, a decision that would have no significant effect on the conditions which, in the future, would face the steel industry, and industry in general, in the Montreal area.

These considerations are particularly important in Canada, for the industries that make these economy-altering "non-marginal" decisions are precisely those that are also characterized by high degrees of concentration of control. Decisions to build steel mills, or transportation facilities, or communications systems, etc., may be viewed by those who make them as "private business," but it is quite clear that what is occurring is that the shape and direction of the whole Canadian economy of the future is thereby being determined.

This is a matter on which socialists have long held fundamental and distinctive views. These economic decisions, which are of such great importance to the welfare of the whole nation, must not be left to a small number of private individuals, but must become the specific and elaborated concern of government. There are two grounds for this viewpoint, one political and the other economic or technical. First, it seems quite clear that business men cannot accept and cannot be expected to accept a national responsibility for their decisions. In the modern large business corporation, those who have the power to formulate policy are often responsible in only a tenuous way even to the corporation's own shareholders. The responsibility that corporate policy-makers can acknowledge to all the other people, outside the corporation, who will be significantly affected by their decisions, is much less again. The general public can apply no sanctions to the corporate managers. They cannot vote them from office. This is one of the main reasons why the extent of government control over these important private economic decisions must be enlarged. Where decisions are made that will significantly affect the speed, direction, and distribution of economic progress, it is a necessary part of the democratic conception of society that those who make these decisions should be subject to the control of the public through its elected representatives.

Secondly, if these important decisions are made by separate and independent corporate managers, it is inevitable that they will not be sufficiently integrated to make the best and most efficient use of the nation's resources. Under such a system, the nation's resources as a whole are sometimes under-employed and sometimes over-employed, and almost always they are distributed in ways that are not in the best long-run interest of the nation.

Modern governments, of the sort we have had in Canada under both Liberal and Conservative party leadership, have accepted a large measure of responsibility for the regulation and control of important economic processes. There is however still a distinct and fundamental difference between their approach to economic management and that envisaged by socialists. The key concepts of the approach of Conservative and Liberal administrations in Canada are the concepts of forecast, and compensation. The government attempts to forecast what the economic future will bring if it is left to work itself out without interference, and the result of this forecast is used to indicate the nature and extent of government action necessary to compensate for the deficiencies of private decision-making. The result of this approach is that government economic policy lacks coherent objectives of its own. It is simply devoted to patching and filling the inadequacies of the private sector of the economy. The government is not the architect of the economy but merely its repair man.

The key concept of the socialist approach to economic control is public planning. The government, it is felt, should accept the task of being the architect of the nation's economic future. It should plan what it wishes to come to pass, not merely forecast what might or probably will occur. Its plans must be explicit, detailed, and public. They must be decided upon at the highest level of government and must be made the most compelling item of political responsibility on the part of the cabinet as a whole and, through it, the party in power. There should not be just a single minister of economic planning in the federal government but a committee of cabinet, similar to the present Treasury Board, composed of the most senior ministers who must jointly build and jointly be responsible for the economic plan. The programmes and policies of the individual departments of government and of the institutions in the private sector of the economy must be subservient to the over-all objectives of the economic plan. A great deal of the economy must nevertheless be left to private enterprise. Nationalization of industry and business on anything more than a very modest scale would probably make the achievement of coherent and efficient use of the nation's resources more difficult rather than easier. But this does not mean that the private sector of the economy should be left to operate according to principles of laissez-faire or that the government ought not to be responsible for the results of these operations. The economic plan built by the cabinet must take the private sector of the economy as fully into account as the public sector, and the government must be as responsible for the results of what it leaves in private hands as for its own direct operations.

Finally, it is of the greatest importance that the economic plan should be made public, in detail. The public must have an opportunity to evaluate and criticize the government's projected use of the nation's resources, as well as the opportunity to manifest its general approval or disapproval at elections.

The object of this chapter is the discussion of economic policy in two important areas: the development of natural resources and the investment of capital. This is a more limited task than the examination of the principles and methods of economic planning in general but the preceding few paragraphs were needed in order to make clear the defects of present policies respecting resources and investment. In the following pages it will repeatedly be found that the main deficiencies of current practices are traceable to the lack of a coherent general economic plan that would provide meaningful criteria for economic policies in particular areas. What I am trying to show is that these deficiencies do not spring from mere administrative difficulties that can be easily corrected by a small change in organization. They can only be eliminated by the acceptance of the principle of economic planning.

NATURAL RESOURCES

The Changing Resources Bases of the Canadian Economy

Up to the Second World War, Canadians (and foreigners also) tended to think of Canada as a farming country. Even at that time such a viewpoint was rather out of date, for the importance of agriculture in the Canadian economy had been on the decline for some time. In terms of output there has been no absolute decline in Canadian agriculture but its rate of growth has been a great deal slower than that of other sectors of the economy. In the later 1920's agriculture accounted for about one-quarter of the total output of the economy, but while the economy as a whole has more than doubled its output since then, agriculture has only increased by about 10 per cent. The result has been that agricultural output is now less than 15 per cent of the gross domestic product. (See Tables I and II for the data referred to here and in the following paragraphs.)

In terms of the number of people engaged, the change that has taken place is even more marked. While the labour force engaged in all industries has grown by almost 40 per cent since the later 1920's, the number engaged in agriculture has actually declined by almost 30 per cent. These trends, moreover, will probably continue. The Royal Commission on Canada's Economic Prospects (the Gordon Commission) forecast that by 1980 agricultural output would constitute only some 6 per cent of Canada's gross domestic product.

What has been happening in Canada is that we are becoming more of an industrial and manufacturing nation and the natural resource bases of our economy have been undergoing a marked and rapid change. The output of the manufacturing sector of the economy rose from about 23 per cent of gross domestic product (excluding the government sector) in 1926 to 32 per cent in 1955. The new resource bases of the Canadian economy are indicated by the fact that mining output has more than trebled since the later 1920's and electric power has increased almost six times. The Gordon Commission estimated that the natural resource industries would grow more rapidly than any other sector of the Canadian economy during the next twenty-five years. By 1980, the total output of the economy is expected to be three times what it is today and the natural resource industries are expected to contribute a substantially larger share to it than they do at the present time. Indeed, it is quite clear that the prospects for Canadian economic growth are as bright as they are largely because we possess within our own borders many of the resources that are important to modern economic life: oil and natural gas, uranium, iron ore and base metals, forest resources and water power. While agriculture will continue to yield rich benefits to the Canadian economy, there is little possibility of bringing new land under cultivation[2] and it seems clear that the possibilities of economic growth in Canada do not lie in this direction.

TABLE I

GROSS DOMESTIC PRODUCT IN AGRICULTURE AND RESOURCE INDUSTRIES

Annual averages	Agriculture		Resource industries	
	(Billions of 1949 dollars)	% of total GDP*	(Billions of 1949 dollars)	% of total GDP*
1927–29	2.01	25.8	.55	7.0
1937–39	1.85	24.2	.77	10.1
1947–49	1.89	15.4	1.04	8.5
1950–52	2.32	16.3	1.34	9.4
1953–55	2.22	14.2	1.64	10.5
Forecast 1979–81	2.91	6.2	7.85	16.7

SOURCE: Based on Wm. C. Hood and Anthony Scott, *Output, Labour and Capital in The Canadian Economy* (Ottawa, 1957), p. 315.
*Excluding residential rents and the GDP arising in the armed forces and the civilian government and community services sectors of the economy.

Agriculture is not the only industry that will lose in relative importance as the economy develops. The shifting resource bases of the economy are having similar effects in other directions as well. Consider the coal-mining industry, for example. The diesel locomotive, together

[2]W. M. Drummond and W. Mackenzie, in their study prepared for the Gordon Commission, expect a continuation of the decline in the amount of land occupied for farming in eastern Canada, and an increase, but only by a small amount, in western Canada. *Progress and Prospects of Canadian Agriculture* (Ottawa, 1957), p. 97.

TABLE II

GROSS DOMESTIC PRODUCT AND LABOUR FORCE IN RESOURCE INDUSTRIES, 1926–9 AND 1952–5

	1926–9 Annual average		1952–5 Annual average		Change 1926–9 to 1952–5	
	GDP ($ 000,000)*	Labour force (000)	GDP ($ 000,000)*	Labour force (000)	GDP %	Labour force %
Agriculture	2,013	1,210	2,303	859	+ 14.4	− 29.0
Forestry, fishing, trapping	271	115	470	120	+ 73.4	+ 4.3
Mining	210	64	783	99	+272.8	+ 54.7
Electric power	51	16	307	52	+502.0	+225.0
Total, all industries†	7,609	3,342	15,512	4,617	+103.9	+ 38.2

SOURCE: Hood and Scott, *Output, Labour and Capital in the Canadian Economy*, chap. v, App. F.
*1949 dollars.
†Excluding the government and community services sector of the economy.

with the development of oil resources in Canada, has meant that one of
the principal users, the railway transport industry, has shifted to other
fuels. Within a few years, virtually no coal will be used by Canadian
railways. Meanwhile, coal for space-heating is in sharp decline and the
high cost of Canadian coal is restricting its industrial use as well. It has
sometimes been suggested that the long-term outlook for the coal
industry is brighter than the immediate prospects, for supplies of competing sources of energy (oil, gas, hydro-electric power) are not unlimited and coal will come into its own again as these are used up.
Expectations of this sort appear to rest on the belief (or hope) that new
large discoveries of other fuels will not be made and, perhaps more
important, that nuclear energy will remain as costly as it is at the
present time. These expectations, in my view, are highly questionable
and it is more realistic and more sensible at this time to act as if the
decline of the Canadian coal industry will prove to be permanent.

This is, of course, far from a complete story of the changes that are
taking place in the resource bases of the Canadian economy, but it may
be sufficient to serve as preamble to the important considerations that
must underlie a successful policy of economic development in Canada.
The main point I wish to make is this: it is impossible for us to undertake the intelligent planning of our economic development unless we are
willing to recognize that economic progress involves large changes in
the industrial and geographic structure of the economy. Some industries
and regions will grow, while others will remain static or even decline.
Some occupations and skills will strongly increase in demand, while
others will go into the doldrums. This is an issue that political leaders
seem to be very unwilling to face. They appear to regard it as politically
impossible for them to admit that economic progress may involve the
decline of certain activities or certain regions of the country. As a result
of this deliberate blindness, Canadian economic development has not
only been hampered, but its costs have been much greater than they
need have been, and these costs have usually been imposed on those
members of the community who are little able to bear them. The necessary changes have taken place just the same, but they have been both
more difficult and less efficient than they would have been if political
leaders had faced them squarely and prepared for them in a sensible
fashion.

In the past we have had two kinds of policies on economic change in
Canada — to do nothing about it, or to do the wrong thing about it. The
wrong kind of policy is amply illustrated by the two industries discussed
above, agriculture and coal. Successive Canadian governments have
attempted to maintain a dying coal-mining industry by tariffs and subsidies that impose the cost of doing so on the Canadian people as a
whole. But these policies have not been accompanied by the necessary

effort to plan for the inevitable long-run changes in the industry and to ensure that an orderly shift of its labour force into other occupations would take place. The federal government's policies have only *delayed* the impact of economic change on the coal industry; they have done nothing to ease the industry's adjustment. As a result, the coal industry, especially in Nova Scotia,[3] is as much of a problem today as it was a generation ago. If present policies continue, it will still be a burden and a problem to us a generation from now. (The report of the Rand Commission, made public after this was written, is a move, though a disappointingly timid one, in the direction of a sensible coal policy for Canada.)

Many of the government's policies on agriculture are of a similar nature. Supporting the prices of certain agricultural commodities in the face of a long-term condition of over supply is a policy that prevents agricultural resources and farm labour from shifting to other activities that are more in demand. This type of agricultural policy has the clear effect of magnifying the problem with which it is supposed to deal. The result is that Canadian agriculture is probably less well adjusted to the effective world demand for agricultural products now than it was fifteen years ago.

There are still some unregenerate believers in laissez-faire who suggest that policies such as price supports and coal subventions should simply be abandoned, and nothing erected to take their place except the so-called "competitive market." This, of course, would ensure that economic change would take place very rapidly. When coal became uncompetitive as a fuel, the mines would simply shut down, and the miners would become diesel-drawn hoboes; or farmers caught in a disequilibrium of demand and supply would follow a straight and rapid route from the market place to the poor house without any temporary stopover at the prices support board. The trouble with the laissez-faire theory of economic progress is that it will not face the question: Who pays for progress? It lays so much emphasis on the great benefits that are to be derived from taking advantage of technological development or discoveries of new resources that it does not recognize that economic changes involve costs, and that these costs are borne largely by those who are caught in the declining industries with obsolete skills or obsolete productive assets. It may, for example, be taken for granted that the dieselization of the railways and the development of Canada's oil and gas and hydro-electric resources will bring great benefits to all our citizens, but is there any reason why the coal miners should pay such a large share of the cost?

[3]The fact that there are greater opportunities for other employment in western Canada than in eastern Canada has meant that western coal miners have been leaving the coal industry at a faster pace than eastern coal miners.

The social problems that attend economic change call attention to the fact that this is an area in which positive policies of a comprehensive nature must be developed. These policies should, in my view, be founded on two broad principles. The first of these is that we should not hamper economic progress through self-deception. It may be perfectly sensible for us to subsidize a declining industry or a relatively poor region in Canada either on social or political grounds but it can do no good for us to pretend that this does not involve costs for the economy as a whole. The political prophets who rise regularly to preach that Newfoundland, or Nova Scotia, for example, should be made over into great industrial regions, can only lead their followers to further disillusionment. Because they are part of the Canadian nation, these regions can validly claim a right to share in Canadian growth. But if they are to do so, policies should be pursued that permit growth to take place and that will succeed in integrating these regions economically with the more rapidly developing centres of the country.

A digression is necessary at this point to answer a crucial question: If the "poorer" regions of Canada lack the resources and the locational advantages that would give them good foundations for economic development, on what can a continuing growth of their living standards be based? The economically correct answer to this question will appear at first sight to be a paradox: a rise in their living standards can be based on wage rates and salaried incomes that are lower than those obtaining in the more favoured centres of the economy. Lower wages and salaries can give these regions cost advantages in certain manufacturing lines that can compensate for their natural disadvantages. These regions can specialize in industries that are relatively heavy users of labour, where their wage advantages would be the greatest, leaving the heavy capital-using and resource-based industries to other regions. By being integrated in this way with the main developing centres of the Canadian economy, these poorer regions will necessarily share in the general economic growth that is taking place. Their wage rates, even though they may be 10 or 15 per cent below those of other regions, ought nevertheless to be rising at 3 per cent a year or so, just as those of other regions are doing when the economy as a whole is healthy. This is a prospect that may fail to satisfy those who value parochial pride at an unreasonably high price, but it can provide the material elements of a comfortable, satisfying, and enlarging life for those who make their homes in those regions of the country that are less favoured by nature and geography.

The second principle upon which economic development policy should be based is that of retraining, and relocation. When certain industries, occupations, and regions decline, it should be the full responsibility of government to provide for the retraining of workers and, if necessary, their geographic relocation. When a mine shuts down, for example, the present government renders the displaced miner some assistance, but by and large, he is responsible for finding his own job, equipping and training himself to handle it, and transporting himself and his family to it. Moreover he is expected to do all this and provide for his family's ordinary needs with no income beyond his small severance pay and unemployment benefit. It is no wonder that the displaced worker usually makes an adjustment that is both unsatisfactory to himself and inefficient from society's standpoint. The proper reintegration of the displaced worker into the economy requires a considerable capital investment and it is ridiculous to expect that such an investment can be made by people who have little or no savings, little borrowing power, and whose incomes have just been reduced. We would not attempt to handle any other kind of capital investment in the economy by such absurd methods. Government has already accepted a considerable share of the responsibility for the financing of "human capital expenditures" in the form of primary, secondary, and university education, technical training, and vocational schools. It must now go a step further and make itself responsible for the retraining and relocating of older workers whose occupations have been rendered obsolete by the directions of economic change.

The chief point that must be kept in mind in planning for economic progress is that in the long run the whole Canadian nation will benefit from policies that are designed to achieve swift and efficient adjustments to changing economic conditions and opportunities. Since the whole nation benefits, the costs should be borne by the whole nation. The industries, regions, and occupational groups that are faced with decline have a right to expect the nation as a whole to bear the financial responsibility for reintegrating them into the new economic structure. However, they have no right to ask that the progress of the nation should be halted in order that their old positions should be maintained intact. There is one condition of economic progress that must be accepted by individuals — a willingness to change and adapt themselves to new conditions. Canadian economic policy in the past has erred seriously both by omission and commission. On the one hand, the funds made available to finance the shifting of economic activities that progress requires have been grossly inadequate; on the other hand people have been encouraged to believe that they should look to the government for protective subsidies when the winds of economic change turn cold against them. This is a double error. The sums now spent by government on price supports and subsidies, and indirectly by the community as a whole through such devices as tariff protection, should be used to encourage economic mobility and change, rather than hamper it as they do now.

The Development and Conservation of Resources

According to the British North America Act, the natural resources of Canada are placed under the jurisdiction of the several provincial governments. This arrangement has imposed special difficulties in developing policies that would contribute to the greatest economic welfare of the country as a whole. A province or region in which a resource is located may not, in itself, provide a market large enough to take up the full output of the resource. In such a case, the provincial authorities tend to regard that resource and behave towards it as if the aim were to sell as much of it as possible at the highest possible price, without regard to the interests of the other Canadians that are the buyers. In this respect, provincial governments are frequently found in the position of acting as lobbies for their local industries. The oil industry of western Canada, for example, would like to see legislation adopted that would shift the Montreal petroleum market from foreign crude oil to domestic (higher priced) oil and in this object they have the full and active support of the Alberta government. Similarly the steel and coal interests of the Atlantic Provinces are supported by their governments in efforts to get special considerations from the federal government that would enable their products to compete in the central Canadian markets.

These examples are mentioned in order to illustrate the necessity of developing comprehensive *national* policies with respect to our natural resources. Quite apart from the constitutional problem, Canadian governments have shown very little disposition to develop or adopt such policies — a surprising reluctance in a country whose economic wealth and progress are so clearly bound up with the use of domestic natural resources. The current problems of particular industries or regions have been dealt with piecemeal, but no effort has been made to develop a coherent programme of long-term development.

The Borden Royal Commission on Energy, which was appointed in the early days of the Diefenbaker Government, promised to be a refreshing departure. However, the results so far have been disappointing. The term "energy" is very comprehensive, but the work of the Commission was almost exclusively concerned with oil and gas. Similarly, the National Energy Board which was recommended by the *First Report* of the Royal Commission on Energy and enacted by Parliament in 1959[4] has a comprehensive-sounding name, but it would appear from the Act that its functions are to be limited in both scope and extent. The Gordon Royal Commission on Canada's Economic Prospects had previously emphasized the necessity of comprehensiveness in Canada's energy policies and had suggested the creation of a "national energy authority"

[4]An Act for the Establishment of a National Energy Board, 7–8 Eliz. II, c. 46. The Commission reported in two parts, the *First Report* is dated October 1958 and the *Second Report* July 1959.

with such an end in view.[5] The Energy Board that has recently been established seems to have been created primarily to act as an agency for the administration of existing policies and legislation, and there is no indication that the Government appreciates the necessary enlargement of vision that a national energy policy would require. The Energy Board Act does give the Board certain research and advisory functions that could be made the foundation of a broad national policy but it remains to be seen how much importance the Board as constituted will attach to these particular powers, and if it does take advantage of them, it remains to be seen what use the Government will make of the proffered advice.

TABLE III

CONCENTRATION OF CONTROL IN SOME LEADING CANADIAN RESOURCE INDUSTRIES, 1954

	Proportion of net value added accounted for by six largest firms %
Petroleum	
Crude production	68
Refining	93
Mining, smelting, and refining	
Nickel-copper	100
Lead-zinc	86
Copper-gold	88
Iron ore	100
Aluminum*	100
Asbestos	94
Gypsum	97

SOURCE: Brecher and Reisman, *Canada–United States Economic Relations*, p. 110.
*One company only.

The lack of a coherent policy of government control over the development of resources in Canada does not mean that these important decisions are left to the interplay of the dispersed and impersonal forces of a competitive market. This is, in fact, an area of the Canadian economy that is concentrated to an unusually high degree (see Table III), and the important decisions therefore rest in the hands of only a few firms. The ultimate, of course, is the aluminum industry, which consists of only a single company. Iron ore production is entirely in the hands of six companies. Other minerals are almost entirely in the hands of a very small number of large companies. Even the production of crude petroleum, an industry in which the technical conditions are not

[5]See this Commission's *Final Report* (Ottawa, 1957), pp. 143–7. For example, it recommended that when a national energy authority was established, the existing Dominion Coal Board should be merged with it.

especially difficult or capital-consuming, is dominated by the large companies. Concentration is, of course, also high in other Canadian industries,[6] but in the natural resource industries it is especially great. Moreover, it seems more likely to grow rather than diminish in the foreseeable future.[7] It is clear therefore that if the governmental authorities in Canada choose not to exercise control over our natural resources, they do not thereby place them under the influence of a competitive market but simply abandon them to the discretion of the monopolistic firms that dominate these important sectors of the economy.

The lack of a policy for the long-range development of resources in Canada as part of a comprehensive economic plan is reflected in the disorderly volatility of investment activity in this field: in 1956 the amount rose more than 60 per cent above that of the previous year, continued to rise in 1957, though at a somewhat reduced rate, and then fell quite sharply in 1958. The Bank of Canada in its annual reports for 1956 and 1957 made special reference to the great growth of expenditure on resource development, and in the latter report (p. 6) noted that "Resource development was in fact the basic reason for the intensity of the 1955-57 boom in Canada — and for the degree of inflation experienced." The subsequent decline of this type of investment was, similarly, an important cause of the recession of 1958. Such uncontrolled and disorderly investment detracts from the best long-range development of our natural wealth and also contributes substantially to the shorter-range fluctuations in business activity that are so damaging to personal welfare.

The fluctuations in investment in Canadian resource development reflect in large part the volatility of world markets for raw materials. Especially important for Canada is the United States market for these commodities. Canadian resource industries are very closely connected with the secondary manufacturing industry of the United States. There has been considerable debate among economists over the extent to which economic fluctuations in Canada are a result of fluctuations in the United States.[8] In general there does not seem to be much ground for blaming the United States economy for all our economic fluctuations but, so far as our natural resource industries are concerned, the tie-in with American industry is so close that fluctuations in American economic activity have clear repercussions on this sector of our economy.

The extent to which the natural resource industries of Canada are dependent on foreign markets is indicated by Table IV. Some com-

[6]See I. Brecher and S. S. Reisman, *Canada–United States Economic Relations* (Ottawa, 1957), p. 110.

[7]This is the opinion of the Royal Commission on Canada's Economic Prospects concerning the minerals industry. See its *Final Report,* p. 226.

[8]See, e.g., Brecher and Reisman, *Canada–United States Economic Relations,* Part I, where the important literature on the subject is cited.

TABLE IV

EXPORTS OF CERTAIN NATURAL RESOURCE PRODUCTS, 1955, AS
PERCENTAGE OF CANADIAN PRODUCTION EXPORTED

	%
Wood pulp	
Mechanical	5
Chemical	48
Iron ore	89
Aluminum and products	90
Copper and products	71
Nickel and products	99
Zinc and products	95
Uranium	100*
Asbestos	94
Petroleum and products	14

SOURCE: R. V. Anderson, *The Future of Canada's Export Trade* (Ottawa, 1957), pp. 163, 175, 181, 206–7, 217, 225, and 245. These estimates are all, apparently, on a quantity basis.
*I.e., *virtually* 100 per cent.

modities, such as uranium, nickel, zinc, and asbestos, are virtually all exported; others are exported to a major extent. The United States market is the most important destination of these exports: in 1959 it took virtually all of our exports of uranium and petroleum, about 75 per cent of our exports of iron ore, and about 85 per cent of our exports of wood pulp; it was less important but still our largest single market for most non-ferrous minerals and mineral products.[9]

The nature of the connections between Canadian natural resource enterprises and foreign firms varies a great deal from industry to industry. In the petroleum industry for example, six large international companies hold 75 per cent of Canada's proven reserves.[10] This is an industry that sells the greater part of its output in the domestic market. Although exports of petroleum (all to the United States) have risen sharply in recent years, it is questionable whether the international companies are as interested in selling Canadian oil abroad as they are in exploiting quickly the reserves of countries where political conditions are less reliable than in Canada. On the other hand there are industries such as pulp and paper which are owned by foreign interests whose main concern is to build up Canada's exports of these commodities, for they have invested in Canada principally in order to acquire raw materials for their own domestic operations.

The development of the large iron ore deposits of the Ungava region is a good illustration of our apparent dependence on the United States in our resource development. This project was originally undertaken by

[9]Dominion Bureau of Statistics, *Trade of Canada: Exports*, 1959.
[10]These figures refer to the end of 1956. See Royal Commission on Canada's Economic Prospects, *Final Report*, p. 130.

Canadian interests, but the problem of providing capital and ensuring markets made it necessary for them to include some of the American steel companies. The result has been that, today, the development is oriented directly to the needs of the United States steel firms.[11] On account of this intimate connection, which extends to other sections of the Canadian iron ore industry as well, Canada's future production of iron ore will probably be determined by the demands of the United States market. In making its forecasts, the Gordon Commission assumed this to be the case and predicted that Canadian output of iron ore would expand at the same rate as our exports to the United States. The Commission forecast that these would increase by some 600 per cent between 1955 and 1980, but that domestic consumption would only expand by about 300 per cent in the same period. In other natural resources, similarly, the trade between Canada and the United States is mainly a trade between Canadian subsidiaries and their foreign parents and this in-the-family kind of trade is likely to grow in the future.

These close connections raise some important questions for Canadian economic policy. In the case of in-the-family trade there can be little assurance that the prices paid by foreign buyers for Canadian raw materials are fair to Canada. The ultimate sharing of this wealth between the two countries involved is dependent on prices that are simply matters of administrative arrangement between a firm and its subsidiary. Even where foreign firms act "at arm's length" in purchasing Canadian raw materials, the traders are usually so few in number that the price arrived at can hardly be described as "competitive."

The share that Canada gets of the ultimate value of the things created out of its natural resources depends on the prices paid for these resources. It is not necessarily true that Canada would be wealthier if we processed our own raw materials at home. It is quite possible and, at the present time, highly probable, that both Canada and the countries to which we export can be better off by continuing the present kind of specialization. It is necessary to emphasize this point because of the red herring that has been drawn across the path by politicians and business men who deplore that we are "hewers of wood and drawers of water." Hewers of wood and drawers of water can be very wealthy — provided they are efficient hewers and drawers and that they charge enough for their wood and water. While it is true that we are rapidly becoming an industrial nation, we still export large quantities of our natural resources abroad in the raw or semi-processed state and are likely to do so for some years. The fact that so much of this trade operates under tight monopolies, or is simply an in-the-family exchange between an American

[11]The Royal Commission on Canada's Economic Prospects noted (*ibid.*, p. 386) that even this degree of Canadian participation in the development of our natural resources "is something of an exception. More often such projects are financed entirely by non-residents who control the enterprise completely."

firm and its Canadian subsidiary, means that we have some special need to see to it that we do not come out on the short end of the bargain. The following passage from the *Final Report* of the Royal Commission on Canada's Economic Prospects, which refers to natural gas, is of interest in this connection:

No doubt, as time goes by, more attention will be paid to the terms under which gas is exported. In our opinion, Canadians hitherto have been insufficiently aware of some of the influences that have been operative in setting prices. In one instance, Canadian gas is being supplied to industrial users across the border at very low prices under the terms of a contract negotiated with a supplying company in Canada which forms part of the same corporate structure as the public utility purchasing the gas and the industrial enterprise that is the principal user. In other cases, a pivotal role in setting prices has been played by the United States Federal Power Commission, which has the duty under the Natural Gas Act, in its own words, "to protect the American public in all possible respects through the regulation and control of the transmission and wholesale sale of natural gas." If the Federal Power Commission with its public and quasi-judicial procedures for investigating both the engineering and economic aspects of proposals for importing gas into the United States finds against a Canadian proposal, the would-be suppliers in Canada may have no alternative but to come to a different agreement with prospective purchasers in the United States on terms less advantageous to themselves but more likely to be approved by the Commission. The present system of export licensing by the Canadian Government would seem to be an inadequate counterweight to this bargaining advantage held by United States companies wanting to purchase Canadian gas; and in our opinion, the bargaining position of Canadian suppliers might well be strengthened by stronger institutional arrangements within the Canadian Government. . . . (p. 135)

Some surveillance of the prices charged in in-the-family trade is at present exercised by the federal taxation authorities who must see to it that they are not cheated of corporate income tax revenue. The new National Energy Board also seems to be paying some attention to the problem.[12] This surveillance however is not yet sufficiently penetrating or comprehensive to reflect adequately the importance of this problem to Canada's economic welfare.

The close connections between Canadian resource industries and foreign buyers raise some other issues of considerable importance. United States firms are, of course, significantly influenced in their behaviour by the economic and political policies of their government. This influence is transferred to the Canadian subsidiaries of these firms, making them, in effect, subservient to United States policy on trade,

[12]Five companies applied to the Board early in 1960 for permission to export natural gas to the United States. One of these applications, by Niagara Gas Transmission Ltd., was rejected partly because the Board did not feel satisfied that the price Niagara proposed to charge the buyer, the St. Lawrence Gas Co. (both firms are subsidiaries of Consumers Gas Co.), was "just and reasonable in relation to the public interest" (*Globe and Mail*, Toronto, April 4, 1960).

defence, and foreign affairs. To the extent that Canada and the United States share common objectives in these areas no appreciable friction is likely to arise. There is little question of conflict between us on the question, say, of the *ultimate* aims of foreign policy, but our *immediate* aims, objectives, and methods may be significantly different. This is a problem that runs far beyond the question of the use and development of Canadian resources and it is touched on in other papers in this volume. So far as natural resources are specifically concerned, we have been content to complain about this or that decision of American firms and governments but have steadily avoided setting out a definite Canadian policy in these areas. Until we are prepared to do so we will continue to be subservient to American policies and decisions to a quite unnecessary extent.

The discovery and development of natural resources is an area of economic activity that calls for a more delicate balance of public and private enterprise than is necessary in most other industries. We have had ample experience in both Canada and other countries with unrestrained private enterprise in this area and the attending evils of waste and corruption have been so manifest that all but the most unregenerate supporters of private enterprise are prepared to concede the necessity for substantial measures of government regulation and control. It would be a great mistake, however, if we were to conclude that this is an area of economic activity that must be operated directly and exclusively by the state.

Even though the search for resources and their subsequent exploitation are much more scientific activities than they once were, they are, apparently, still fraught with the kind of risks and indeterminacies that make it difficult for governments to engage in them directly. The development of western Canada's oil stocks illustrates this point. Private companies drilled extensively for some years before the Leduc field was discovered. It has been estimated that some two thousand dry holes were sunk at a cost of $125 million before success was achieved in 1947.[13] This investment represents a degree of faith in geologists that is easier for private companies to entertain than for governments. The public's attitude to the dry holes drilled by private companies seems to be that if they want to waste their money it is their own affair. If a government were to do the same thing, as for example the government of British Columbia did before the Second World War, the public's reaction is almost certain to be condemning.

The distinction that public opinion draws in these cases between private money and public money is spurious from the general economic standpoint. In both cases the nation's resources are being invested in risky ventures, but it would be unrealistic for us not to recognize that

[13]L. M. Fanning, *Foreign Oil and the Free World* (New York, 1955), p. 176.

democratic governments are not perfectly suited to such ventures. We will need, therefore, to devise special techniques and policies that will bring about a successful partnership of private enterprise and governmental control. The initiative of the venturesome prospectors and developers must be retained without permitting the present activities of financial promoters and stock salesmen who milk the resources of all their value before production starts.

The principles that apply to the search for new resources and their development also apply to the conservation of existing resources. The present status of conservation policy in Canada stands, however, as a vivid example of the basic inadequacy of a piecemeal approach to such problems. We have forestry policies whose avowed object is to maximize the gross output of the forests, regardless of what other resources are used up in the process. We have fisheries policies which seek to maximize the catch of fish regardless of the other resources that are used up in doing so. The same statement can be repeated for each of our natural resource industries. The result of this is a chaotic situation in which the various conservationists are engaged, in effect, in a competitive struggle in which each is attempting to sacrifice the others' resources for the benefit of his own.

It would be hard to find an area of economic policy in which there has been more nonsense and folly than in the field of conservation. Examples could be given almost *ad infinitum*, but perhaps one will suffice. The conservation of Pacific salmon is based on the principle that catching them should be made so difficult that it will not be worth while. The regulations that govern where and when fishing can be carried on thus compel fishermen to spend much more for boats, gear, fuel and other things than is actually necessary to bring in the catch. The result is that conserving salmon involves a gross waste of other valuable resources. A study of the details of the regulations can lead one only to believe that they were drafted by a salmon. They give neither short-run nor long-run benefit to the fisherman nor to the economy as a whole.

The basic error is a failure to see that conservation is just a particular way of developing and utilizing a resource. To conserve, either by positive effort or by refraining from present use, is simply to invest valuable resources today in order to obtain larger values in the future.[14] The chief import is that it is a mistake to establish conservation policies on the piecemeal basis that characterizes present policy. This kind of conservation policy probably does more harm than good to the long-run welfare of the economy as a whole. I come back then to reiterate that

[14]The principle that conservation is investment is clearly advanced in A. D. Scott, *Natural Resources: The Economics of Conservation* (Toronto, 1955). A brief statement of the basic economics of resource conservation can be found in my article "Economics and the Conservation Question," *Journal of Law and Economics,* Oct., 1958.

we need to construct a coherent, comprehensive economic plan for the long-range development of resources. As part of such a policy, conservation efforts can be made sensible, but not otherwise.

CAPITAL INVESTMENT

The most distinct mark of a modern "developed" economy is not only that it has machines to do the work of man but that it has machines to do work that man could never do at all. A thousand men might accomplish, in a day, the same results as one giant earth-moving tractor, but not even tens of thousands of men, without elaborate capital equipment, could generate and transport electric power or harness atomic energy or smelt bauxite into aluminum. An economy, if it is to be wealthy and progressive, *must* be "capitalistic" in the sense that it must possess and use large quantities of capital equipment.[15]

This capital comes in a great variety of forms and types. It includes schools in which knowledge is acquired, hospitals in which health is restored, homes where comfort and shelter are provided, factory buildings where workers and machines are housed, machinery which shapes raw materials into finished goods, trucks, roads and railways to transport them, warehouses to store them, and a host of others too many to specify. All these things however have one characteristic in common — they provide a perpetual stream of services that either directly or indirectly can be devoted to the wants and needs of human beings. The capital of a society, viewed as a whole, creates value enough to maintain and replace itself and something over to add to the annual income of society. Capital is not merely an obedient and uncomplaining slave but one endowed with the potentiality of perpetual life.

The Canadian Pattern of Capital Investment

In terms of degree of economic development the Canadian economy presents a rather ambiguous face. Canada can be regarded as an underdeveloped country judged in terms of its great potentialities for future growth. However, in terms of the capital stock it now possesses (which is a fairly good index of the degree of a country's development) it is already among the most highly developed nations of the world. In Table V, estimates of the total gross value of the capital stock of the Canadian economy are given. The first section gives the stock of "industrial capital" — the plant, equipment, etc., used by industry which, broadly speaking, renders "indirect" services by assisting in the production of other commodities. The latter section records the nation's stock of housing, which renders its services directly to consumers, and the capital

[15]Numerous studies have found that in the most advanced economies, the ratio of capital to output is between two and three; that is, it takes a stock of two or three dollars' worth of capital to enable a continuous flow of final goods of one dollar's worth a year to be produced.

of governments and public institutions, which renders both direct and indirect services.

Measured in terms of 1949 prices, the stock of industrial capital in Canada amounted to more than $40 billion in 1955. Approximately three-fifths of this was in the form of buildings and other construction works (such as dams, land improvements, railway roadbeds, etc.) and the remaining two-fifths in machinery and equipment. Of these two categories of capital, the big growth in recent years has been in machinery and equipment. This has grown by about two and a half times since 1945, while the buildings and construction category has increased by less than a half. This difference reflects the fact that in the early days of Canadian economic development the big task was to build large construction projects, such as railways,[16] which were of fundamental economic importance. In more recent years we have been able to shift our efforts to equipping the economy with capital in the form of machinery and tools.

TABLE V

GROSS CAPITAL STOCK IN CANADA, 1955
$ million at 1949 prices

	Plant, buildings and construction works	Machinery and equipment	Total	
			$	%*
Industrial capital				
Agriculture	1,237.2	3,316.0	4,553.2	5.8
Resource industries	5,082.6	2,176.6	7,259.2	9.3
Primary manufacturing	1,728.5	2,056.6	3,785.1	4.9
Secondary manufacturing	3,790.8	3,868.6	7,659.4	9.8
Transport, storage and communications	7,625.8	3,506.5	11,132.3	14.3
Trade, services and construction	4,362.2	2,385.8	6,748.0	8.7
Total industrial capital	23,827.1	17,310.1	41,137.2	52.8
Social capital and housing				
Government	9,608.2	1,334.2	10,942.4	14.0
Institutions	3,804.4	266.3	4,070.7	5.2
Housing	21,742.1		21,742.1	27.9
TOTAL	58,981.8	18,910.6	77,892.4	100.0

SOURCE: Hood and Scott, *Output, Labour and Capital in the Canadian Economy*, Tables 6B.2 and 6B.5.

*Figures in this column do not add to 100 per cent due to rounding.

There is not enough space in this chapter to make an analysis of these recently provided estimates of Canada's capital stock. However, the data, which are given in considerable detail in the volume cited as

[16]The haphazard nature of the economic development of the time is reflected in the fact that this task, hard as it was, we made even harder for ourselves by *excessive* building of railways.

source to Table V, reveal many important aspects of the development
of the Canadian economy and merit careful study.[17]

The ability of a country to build up its capital is dependent on two
main factors: (a) its willingness and ability to devote part of its current
production to capital investment rather than to direct consumption, and
(b) its ability to borrow from other countries by importing more goods
and services than it exports. Since the end of the war, these two conditions have been well met in Canada. High national income, together
with the high saving propensities of Canadian corporations and individuals have provided substantial domestic funds for capital investment and,
in addition, foreign firms and individuals (mainly American) have
invested heavily in Canada. Table VI shows the capital investments
made in Canada from 1956 to 1959. In those years capital expenditures
usually amounted to more than one-quarter of the gross national product
and about one-fifth of this amount was financed by foreign borrowing.

TABLE VI
Capital Investment in Canada, 1956–9*
$ million

	1956	1957	1958	1959†
Business capital	5,004	5,654	4,869	4,720
Housing	1,547	1,430	1,782	1,759
Institutional services	402	455	515	531
Government departments and waterworks	1,083	1,178	1,198	1,401
TOTAL	8,036	8,717	8,364	8,411
Total as percentage of GNP	26.3	27.4	25.7	24.3

SOURCE: Dept. of Trade and Commerce, *Private and Public Investment in
Canada, Outlook 1960*, pp. 5, 7
*These figures do not include expenditures for the repair and maintenance of
the existing capital stock.
†Preliminary

By almost any comparison, Canadian investment is large. Over the past
several years in fact, the rate of capital investment in Canada as a proportion of GNP has been one of the highest in the world. The Canadian
rate has been substantially above that of the United States, the United
Kingdom, France, and Germany. The rate of investment in the USSR
has only been a few percentage points above Canada's and this of
course is in a country where capital development is the central aim of
economic policy and is implemented by the full force of dictatorial
power.[18]

[17]An example: the investment of Canadian agriculture in machinery and
equipment is almost as large as that of the secondary manufacturing industry,
and has been more rapid since the end of the war than that of almost any other
industrial sector. Canadian agriculture is becoming a highly mechanized industry.
[18]See the Chase Manhattan Bank, *Business in Brief* (March–April, 1960)
where some interesting international comparisons of investment and growth rates
are made for the period 1950–7 using data from the United Nations and the
Pan-American Union.

These great capital investments in Canada have not, of course, been spread evenly over the economy. Some areas of the country have been developing much faster than others. Estimates of the geographic distribution of aggregate capital investment for the period from 1951 to 1958 are given in Table VII. It is clear from this Table that the principal development poles of the Canadian economy are located in central Canada, the west coast and the prairie petroleum region being secondary centres. It is impossible to predict the future pattern of investment with certainty but there does not seem to be any reason to expect that its high concentration in the central provinces will be altered in the near future.

The Significance of Investment

The decisions that are made with respect to capital investment are of vital importance to the economy and to the welfare of the Canadian people as a whole. The magnitude of the total investment made annually is the most important of the tangible factors that determine the rate of growth of the economy, and the industrial and geographic distribution of that investment will determine the shape and structure of the economy for years to come. Especially important are investments in basic industries such as transportation, natural resources, and certain primary manufacturing activities, for the capital creation decisions made there impress their influence very strongly on the investment and production plans of all other segments of the economy.

The great fallacy that pervades private enterprise thinking with respect to capital investment is the belief that investment decisions are regulated by the forces of the classical competitive market. However,

TABLE VII

CAPITAL INVESTMENT IN CANADA, BY PROVINCES, 1951–8

	$ million	%
Newfoundland	678	1.3
Prince Edward Island	168	0.3
Nova Scotia	1,286	2.4
New Brunswick	1,126	2.1
Quebec	12,486	23.7
Ontario	19,346	36.7
Manitoba	2,465	4.7
Saskatchewan	3,014	5.7
Alberta	5,811	11.0
British Columbia*	6,317	12.0
CANADA	52,697	100.0

SOURCE: Dept. of Trade and Commerce, *Supplement to Private and Public Investment in Canada, Outlook, Regional Estimates*, various issues.
*Includes Yukon and Northwest Territories.

many of the decisions that are made concerning capital development are so large and important that the influence they exert on the economy as a whole is far from "marginal." Moreover, they are subject to especially large degrees of uncertainty.[19] In addition, the number of business enterprises that are involved in these basic decisions are too few and too closely connected with one another for this activity to fit the economist's requirements of a competitive market.

The choice then is not whether to regulate and plan capital investment or to leave it to the competitive market. The latter is no real alternative. The important questions are: who should do the planning, and according to what criteria? At the present time the planning of capital investment in Canada takes place in the head offices of a limited number of Canadian and American firms. Despite the close financial and commercial relations of these firms to each other the result is not a coherent programme of capital development but a confused jumble of (frequently incompatible) private plans and policies.

The conclusion is inescapable that the capital development of Canada must be placed under the control and direction of governmental agencies that are charged with the duty of implementing a definite and comprehensive plan respecting the long-run development of the Canadian economy as a whole. The heart of economic planning is investment planning, for it is this that will determine the future economic character of our society.

It is unfortunate that in recent years this fundamental issue has become obscured by the great amount of public discussion of foreign investment in Canada. Many people talk of foreign investment as if that were an evil in itself. In my view, that is an erroneous and misleading belief. It is true that American investment in Canada, being concentrated so heavily in direct investments in subsidiary firms and in the ownership of shares of Canadian corporations, carries with it more power of corporate control than the same amount of money invested in bonds or debentures. But the heart of the issue is not that Canadian industry is controlled by persons who are citizens of another country. Have we any reason to think that any substantive differences would result if the investment decisions were made in Toronto and Montreal rather than in New York and Chicago? The real issue is that these investment decisions, whether made by Americans or Canadians, are not sufficiently

[19]The following statement by an economist who is a strong defender of the competitive order is of interest: "It is unfortunate that the theoretical argument defending the price system as an efficient regulatory mechanism becomes least satisfying when it treats of the regulation of investment decisions. Investment decisions characteristically involve large, indivisible blocks of real assets and always they require the assessment of distant and uncertain prospects. Indivisibilities and uncertainty comprise two of the principle conditions over which the theoretical justification of the price system falters." Wm. C. Hood, *Financing of Economic Activity in Canada* (Ottawa, 1958), p. 271.

subject to the policies of a publicly responsible government. We should, in my view, stop our nattering about *foreign* control of the economy and consider instead the need for *public* as opposed to *private* control of these fundamental economic decisions.

Capital investment has another economic dimension, in addition to its implications for the future wealth and character of the economy. It is an important factor in the problem of short-term fluctuations in economic activity and, consequently, in the problem of unemployment.

The expenditure that is currently made for investment goods determines the amount of employment there will be in the industries that produce these goods. A sharp reduction in investment creates unemployment in these industries and, indirectly, in other sectors of the economy as well. Our experience has been that capital investment expenditures are considerably more unstable than other categories of the gross national expenditure. The recession that began in mid-1957, for example, was largely caused by a decline in business investment. It is, of course, impossible for government to *force* businesses to invest but it has long since been accepted that the federal government must stand ready to compensate for these fluctuations by its own fiscal policies. Government expenditures on public works and other projects have been used in the past as a weapon against recession but these programmes have invariably been thrown together hurriedly and belatedly when the recession was already upon us. Until we accept the necessity of planning ahead for the achievement of enduring objectives, governmental capital expenditures will always have this haphazard and wasteful character.

The Problem of Social Capital

In the bottom of Table V (already mentioned) is shown the capital investment made in Canada by the various levels of government and by public institutions such as universities, hospitals, and churches. This kind of capital is usually called "social capital" in order to distinguish it from the "industrial capital" that results from the investment expenditures of business enterprise.

Social capital includes a wide variety of things — school buildings, water and sewerage facilities, parks, roads and bridges, hospitals, churches, museums and concert halls, and so on. There are few, if any, characteristics that *all* of these things share so it is difficult to say exactly what makes a thing a part of social rather than industrial capital. However, we may say that, broadly speaking, social capital is constructed in order to meet certain needs that large numbers of the general public have in common; it usually serves these needs directly; and it is not usually operated on the profit criterion.

The importance of social capital in our society has been increasing markedly in the last generation or so. Some of this growth has been caused by the development of new products — the automobile, for example, has made necessary the construction of roads and streets; and some by the desire for higher standards of culture and welfare — thus schools, hospitals, civic centres, etc. When one considers social needs as a whole however it is remarkable how much is attributable, directly and indirectly, to the increased urbanization of our society. The concentration of hundreds of thousands and even millions of people in cities and metropolitan areas brings great need for water supplies, sewage disposal facilities, recreational facilities, government and civic services of a variety of kinds, etc. Even the recent development of national and provincial parks where people may go to camp and tour is largely due to the increased value that an urban society has begun to place on the enjoyment of nature.

The degree of urbanization in Canada has been increasing steadily over the last thirty years. Even in the provinces that are already the most heavily urbanized (Ontario, Quebec, and British Columbia, where some two-thirds of the population now live in urban areas) the trend to the cities still continues.[20] Our needs for social capital in the future will consequently be even greater than they have been in the past.

Thus far, our record for the creation of social capital has not been a good one. Between 1945 and 1955, the gross stock of social capital increased by less than 40 per cent.[21] The stock of industrial capital by comparison, increased by 70 per cent in the same period.[22] Compared to that of previous periods, the rise in our social capital since the war has been rapid but it is still far too low in terms of our needs. Large backlogs exist in practically every area of social investment and a substantially increased rate of construction will be required in the future if these are to be filled.

One of the chief reasons for the inadequacy of our social capital is that a large part of it is the responsibility of municipal governments which seem to lack both the financial means and the inclination to make sufficient expenditures of this nature. In terms of the importance of cities in our way of life the funds available to municipal authorities are ridiculously small. In my own city, where thousands of homes depend on wells and septic tanks for water and sewage disposal, where there is no civic auditorium or theatre, where the streets and sidewalks are broken and filthy, I pay annually in municipal taxes an amount only as large as I pay to heat my home, or, to take another comparison, an amount substantially less than the depreciation on my automobile. For this pittance

[20]See Y. Dubé, J. E. Howes, and D. L. McQueen, *Housing and Social Capital* (Ottawa, 1957), p. 24.

[21]Hood and Scott, *Output, Labour and Capital*, Table 6B.5. Total figures given here include housing which is eliminated in arriving at the percentage given in the text above.

[22]*Ibid.*, Table 6B.2.

I presumably am to expect the civic authorities to provide streets and sidewalks, water and sewage disposal, schools, police and fire protection, and a host of other services. Is it any wonder that many of them are provided in a fashion that is shabby to a degree?

A thoroughgoing reform of the foundations of municipal finance is essential if we are to meet the problem of providing the kind of social capital that a modern society requires. There is no area of modern life in which it is more necessary for us to elevate our vision to a new plane and to display some imagination and foresight.

Financing Capital Investment[23]

In the preceding sections I have paid attention mainly to the question of the physical use of the nation's resources. In our type of economy, however, this physical allocation is very closely connected with the operations of the financial system. A corporation or a municipality can only purchase capital goods if it has the necessary funds. The way in which the financial system allocates investment funds determines in large part the way in which the physical resources of the community will be employed.

A large part of the funds that make investment possible does not necessarily, however, flow through the financial institutions at all. Corporations acquire large amounts of money from their ordinary business operations which they retain possession of in the form of depreciation accounts and profits which are not distributed to shareholders. In the years from 1956 to 1958, for example, these undistributed profits and depreciation accounts amounted to $13,554 million or more than 75 per cent of the total national savings of that period.[24] Although it is true that corporations may lend these funds to each other, or to other borrowers, the fact remains that they have a steady source of funds which they can use if they wish for their own business purposes. The funds which they must seek outside are of minor importance compared to those they generate themselves.

The fact that corporations have such large amounts of money under their direct control means that the allocation of capital investment is largely divorced from the process of competitive bidding for funds. Nor is business investment as a whole quickly responsive to the monetary control measures of the central bank, for the same reason.

The present form of corporate income tax collections is such as to accentuate the effects of business investment on economic fluctuations. The tax is not collected on a pay-as-you-earn basis, as personal income tax is, but is averaged back over a period of years. The effect is that

[23]The reader is referred to Hood, *Financing of Economic Activity in Canada*, which contains a great deal of useful information on this subject.

[24]See DBS, *National Accounts, Income and Expenditure, Fourth Quarter and Preliminary Annual*, 1958, Table 10.

corporations pay relatively larger taxes during the recession phase of the cycle and relatively smaller during the revival. Thus, during recession, when investment should be stimulated, corporations are drained of funds, and during a boom, when investment should be checked, their funds are supplemented. For example, in his Budget Speech of April 9, 1959,[25] the Minister of Finance predicted that the GNP would rise by 7 per cent over 1958 and that personal income tax collections would increase by 13 per cent. He predicted virtually no increase in corporation tax payments despite the clear expectations of a large rise in corporate profits. Where did this money go? Because of the method of tax collection it remained in the hands of the corporations. It was really a loan (interest free) by the federal government to corporations which added to their available funds and supported their plans for investment expenditure at a time when the Government and the monetary authorities were pursuing an anti-inflationary policy.

I have given this illustration in order to show how little attention has been given in Canada to the problem of corporate taxation in its relation to basic economic policy. Two lines of attack on this problem are necessary: first, a tax on undistributed profits that would be sufficiently high to reduce substantially the amount of investment that corporations are able to finance from this source,[26] second, a revision of the existing corporate income tax law with the object of (*a*) putting the tax collections on a pay-as-you-earn basis and (*b*) permitting depreciation allowances that are more in accord with the true depreciation of corporate property.[27]

The funds made available for capital investment by the savings of private individuals do not approach the amounts businesses accumulate through their internal saving, but they are quite substantial nevertheless. In 1958, for example, personal net saving amounted to over $2 billion.[28] Some of these funds are invested directly by their owners in the form of loans to investors, in bonds or stocks, and in unincorporated businesses in which they may be interested. However the great bulk of these funds are handed over by their owners to financial institutions such as banks, life insurance companies, trust companies, pension funds, etc. Statistical information on this matter is not as complete as one would wish but the

[25]See *Hansard* for that date, pp. 2414, 2406. The percentages given are on a fiscal-year basis and omit consideration of the effects of changes in tax rates announced in the Budget.

[26]In 1956, corporation profits after taxes amounted to $1,816 million, of which $1,012 million remained undistributed. D.B.S., *National Accounts, Income and Expenditure, 1926–1956*, Table 50.

[27]These measures should be coupled with a reduction in the general rates of corporate profits tax which, I would argue, are too high for a number of reasons.

[28]D.B.S., *National Accounts, Income and Expenditure, Fourth Quarter and Preliminary Annual, 1958*, Table 10. This item includes the savings of unincorporated businesses.

following figures will serve to illustrate the point. From 1946 to 1954, private individuals furnished $2,156 million to the life insurance companies, and $4,026 million to banks and other similar deposit-holding institutions. By contrast, private individuals furnished only $1,655 million directly to corporations and provincial and municipal governments by the purchase of their bonds and stocks.[29] The significance of all this is that the actual decisions concerning the use of personal savings are made in very large part not by the individuals themselves but by the large financial institutions that handle them. Consequently, the influence that private individuals actually exercise over the use of investment funds in Canada is very much less than might be suggested by the total of personal saving.[30]

The use that these large financial institutions make of the funds deposited with them is governed extensively by legislation. In the case of insurance and trust companies in particular the main purpose of the legislation is to guarantee safe and conservative investment practices. The actual behaviour of these institutions is however even more conservative than the legislation. They seem to take fright at any thought that their funds might be used to develop new and dynamic areas of the economy. The chartered banks, though not as conservative as the insurance and trust companies, are also restricted in their investment practices to a degree that significantly limits their participation in the market for capital funds. The capital market, as a result, is characterized not only by limited numbers of lenders but also by the operation of ossified conventions which are especially inappropriate to a dynamic economy such as Canada's.

The federal government has, from time to time, attempted to rectify the inadequacies of existing institutional practices by inducing the financial institutions to expand their lending functions. Thus, for example, the chartered banks were either threatened or cajoled into extending medium term loans to farmers in 1944 and mortgage loans to house builders in 1954. Similar influences have been exercised from time to time by the Bank of Canada.

[29]Hood, "National Transactions Accounts" in his *Financing of Economic Activity in Canada,* pp. 497–505. The figure given first is the savings portion of life policies less policy loans. Life insurance savings amounted to 25 per cent of total personal savings in this period. Because of their contractual nature, life insurance savings vary much less from year to year than total personal savings. In 1947, life insurance companies received more than 46 per cent of the latter, which were small in that year.

The second figure is net of bank loans to individuals. It includes the increase in cash holdings of individuals, which is not separated in the accounts.

[30]The growth of these financial institutions, and in particular their growing ownership of corporate common stock, raises some very important questions concerning the meaning of property ownership in our society. These questions are well stated and explored in Paul P. Harbrecht, *Pension Funds and Economic Power* (New York, 1959).

Once again however it is necessary to recognize that these governmental influences have not been part of a coherent policy of progress and development. In capital market reorganization, as in most other fields of economic policy, the motto of successive governments has been "Sufficient unto the day are the problems thereof." The result is that the legislative and administrative regulations of our financial institutions are a hodge-podge that is quite without meaning so far as Canadian economic development is concerned.

Policies for a Stable Economy*

ALBERT BRETON

The concept of stability in relation to the economy as a whole is one of the most difficult concepts in economics for at least two reasons. First, it does not and cannot mean the stability of every firm or industry in the economy, for obviously the more efficient must replace the less efficient and the more desirable the less desirable, so that some firms or industries will be declining and disappearing while others are growing. Secondly, the concept of an "absolutely stable" economy, that is, one that would move without oscillation along a smooth course, breaks down on any but the most superficial analysis. Indeed, the idea that a man can work day in and day out at the same level of efficiency or that no errors will ever be committed in the economy is completely untenable. And it is highly possible that such errors and inefficiencies will generate oscilla-

*I am grateful to Professor Robert M. Solow of the Massachusetts Institute of Technology and to Mr. Lauge Stetting of the University of Copenhagen for helpful comments on a draft of the model underlying the present proposals. I am also thankful to Mr. Marc Lalonde for discussions of many points as well as for his comments on an earlier draft of the paper. I am grateful also to the other writers in this book who have read this chapter and made useful comments, especially Professors Gordon, Rosenbluth, Weldon, and Mr. P. E. Trudeau.

tions of one kind or another. Moreover, these are probably the less serious causes of fluctuations. There is a further difficulty arising from the fact that public or private efforts to stabilize one phenomenon or another can be self-defeating or even destabilizing for other phenomena in the economy. For these reasons one should acquire a clear notion of the factors that should be stabilized as well as an idea of the essential workings of the economic system.

Should stabilization then mean the constancy of an economic phenomenon through time or its growth at a constant rate? And if the economy as a whole is envisaged and not only a single factor, does stabilization still mean the same thing?

Asking such questions may not be a very useful way of approaching the problem, since it really creates more problems than it solves. For, if the economic phenomena to be stabilized are prices and output, it should be remembered that these are aggregates. Output, for example, is the sum of the value added to each and every product in the economy by all the factors of production. Among other things it includes the value added to such products as wheat, bread, textiles, automobiles, and TV sets. Some industries producing one or other of these products may be declining while others may be growing. They may be declining for a number of reasons. For example, it may be that consumers want less of the products of that industry or that they want so much more of another product, which is very expensive relative to their income, that they cannot afford the first one any more. Or it may be that new firms producing the same product but at a lower cost have developed somewhere so that the older industry can no longer compete for the consumers' dollar. The disappearance of this industry is undoubtedly a good thing from the social point of view. Stability should not therefore mean the maintenance of output or its growth at a constant rate in all industries. Examples could be developed for prices, but this is surely unnecessary. As long as some production is falling and some growing and some prices declining and others rising, the variables to be stabilized must be averages. It is the average level of output and the average level of prices that will occupy us in this chapter. The fact that some components of the averages will be rising while others are falling will create problems of their own, but not problems specific to stabilization policy. If, however, the government or private groups take measures to "stabilize" the output or the price of some individual product, a policy aimed at stabilizing the economy as a whole will have to take these measures into consideration. It will still be true, however, that the concern of stabilization policy will be with averages.

But what is the meaning of stabilization? No one would propose a constant level of aggregate output, because with a growing population, this would mean a falling average per capita output. On the other hand a constant level of average per capita output implies absence of growth; although this does not mean a constant composition of consumption budgets, it does imply non-growing budgets. This cannot easily be made an end of policy.

A stable level of aggregate output must therefore mean a rising level of aggregate output. It really does not seem too important that it should rise at a constant rate. But, this rate of growth should be large enough that the growing potential of the economy should at all times be fully utilized. When we come to prices the case is not as clear-cut. Some will argue—for reasons that it is unnecessary to explore here—that a rising level of prices, if moderate, will constitute a favourable environment to a stable output; others will argue that a moderate increase in the level of prices, if it is expected to be permanent, is really not possible since once this rate of increase is built into the economy it will — in terms of the environment — be equivalent to a constant level of prices which by the initial assumption is not as favourable to a stable output as a rising level of prices. To recapture a new favourable environment will require a further rise in the level of prices and so on.

For the purpose of this chapter it will be taken for granted that the proper object of policy is a constant level of prices. This does not mean that such an objective is absolute; it must still be co-ordinated with a stable level of output. But there can be a contradiction in trying to maintain both a stable level of output and a stable level of prices. What should be the outcome in such cases? Because the level of output is closely related to the level of employment and because the level of prices is only very indirectly related to it, it is submitted that the stability of output should always have priority over the stability of prices. This may give rise to a form of "creeping inflation" which may, however, become excessive especially if repeated stabilization of output means continuous increase of prices. To prevent such a thing from happening, autonomous measures to stabilize some prices may have to be implemented. This will be discussed later on.

Strictly, stabilization policy proposals would require a statement of the essential workings of the economic system; but this is an exceedingly technical and specialized task into which we need not enter in a paper like the present one. A statement of the underlying ideas is sufficient.

The first is that the economy contains enough mechanisms to correct initial oscillations or disturbances, but that many of these mechanisms are so weak or impeded in their operation by rigidities and imperfections of all kinds that to rely on them alone would be too costly on economic grounds alone and prohibitive on social, political, and spiritual grounds.

Another idea underlying this chapter is that it is generally correct to concentrate most efforts on policies designed to affect demand conditions; but when the output of the competitive sectors of the economy is small relative to the total output or if a substantial fraction of the competitive output is not substitutable with the non-competitive or administered output, then it is imperative to have policies designed to affect price-cost relations in the economic system.

Further, this chapter deals exclusively with policies for internal stability, not on the principle that external disturbances acting through exports or imports or both are not a significant source of fluctuations, but on the principle that, whatever the source of oscillations, external stability must be subordinated and above all preceded by internal stability brought about in large part by fiscal and monetary measures.

The recent tendency to link the attainment of internal equilibrium to tariffs and other commercial policies is in the case of Canada the most short-sighted, costly and irrational sort of thing that could be done. A perusal of different policy proposals made in recent years relating internal stability to tariffs reveals incorrect reasoning, incomplete arguments, emotional biases and downright ignorance.

In the Canadian context stability is above all a problem of internal stability. The subsequent sections consequently deal with fiscal, monetary and price policies for internal stability.

FISCAL POLICIES

Fiscal policies are the policies governing the income-expenditure relations of all levels of government in so far as these are related to the income and expenditure of the economy. Fiscal policies have their effects on demand conditions.[1] In other words, by nature they regulate the positive or negative excess demand that may exist in the economy. Stated differently, if total expenditures in all the private sectors of the economy fall short or exceed full employment or capacity income, government expenditures should be made to exceed or to fall short of government revenues. A budget deficit or a budget surplus should be incurred.

This way of stating the question makes clear that the budget to balance is the economy-wide budget and not just the government's budget. The foregoing argument in effect implies that the deficit or the surplus will set up forces strong enough so that after a period of time the economy-wide budget will be balanced without a current deficit or a current surplus in the government's budget. If the forces set up are strong, the balance may be overshot; the previous deficit or surplus in the government's budget then may be partially or totally compensated.

[1]Although fiscal policies can be devised to deal with supply problems, the policies known to the writer are based on the assumption that competitive and monopoly cost curves are identical or that cost curves can be estimated by the government, or on other similar assumptions, which cannot very well be taken for granted.

Preoccupations with the government's budget should therefore always be subordinated to preoccupations with the economy's budget.

This seems an obvious point, yet it is constantly neglected. It seems that, mostly because of public opinion, it is very difficult for a government to incur a deficit in periods of recession and a surplus in prosperity. In Canada, since the end of the last war the federal government has from time to time incurred small deficits and surpluses. In most cases, the "informed" opinion of newspapers has been to ask when there was a surplus for a reduction in taxes and to frown on the deficits. The causes of these opinions is well known: people think that the central government is nothing but a large household. And there are always some politicians (who probably honestly believe this themselves) to accentuate this point of view. If in some way or other this idea is not broken down, a rational fiscal policy becomes impossible as it has tended to be in Canada in recent years.

One question has been left unanswered. Is the federal government alone or are all levels of government the makers of fiscal policies? To answer this question it must be borne in mind that a deficit is an excess of expenditures over revenues, while a surplus is the opposite. This implies, of course, that a deficit will increase the debt while a surplus can reduce it.[2] Furthermore a debt must be serviced at a cost; and the taxpayer is the one who pays this cost. Herein lies the answer to our query. Fiscal policies are policies of the federal government. For if it were not the case, let us imagine what could happen. Suppose that aggregate demand falls, generating unemployment. Suppose that the federal government is totally inactive or confidently rests on the principles of the balanced budget. Suppose further that a provincial government decides to create a budgetary deficit by borrowing from the banks or by issuing a bond in New York. The deficit will generate an increase in expenditures giving rise to secondary income effects. However, the income-generating process cannot be contained in the province, but will spread to the other areas to an extent determined by the fraction of its expenditures made in the other areas. For any Canadian province this is surely very large. However, the population of the deficit province alone would be paying the charges on the debt.

This example helps clarify a few points. First, different levels of government can offset each other's actions. If the federal government creates a deficit to alleviate a fall in demand, one or more provincial governments by creating a surplus can wipe out the effects of the federal government's deficit. Secondly, it is for reasons not directly related to stabilization, but for reasons of costs, that fiscal policies are primarily policies of the federal government in co-ordination with the provincial

[2]The monetary and debt policy implications of this problem will be discussed in a subsequent section.

governments.[3] Thirdly, that if a deficit or a surplus is needed and if the federal government sticks to the principle of a balanced budget, one or more provincial governments can always create an "unbalance" in their budgets if the cost to the provinces of doing this is smaller than the cost of keeping labour and other resources idle. Obviously, policies such as the last one are not optimal and should only be used when all other means have been exhausted. The co-ordination of provincial and federal budgets is therefore an essential element of a consistent and cost-minimizing policy of stabilization. This point will be taken up later on, in the section on monetary policies. Most of the following discussion will assume that co-ordination can be achieved and that it is sufficient therefore to consider policies at the federal level.

In the current context, however, this is not a very good assumption, because the federal-provincial fiscal discussions disregard stabilization problems altogether, mostly, I suspect, because all those concerned believe that stabilization through fiscal policy is a federal problem. Since it is not, the federal-provincial fiscal negotiations should be broadened to include budget policies.

How can a deficit or a surplus be brought about? A deficit is caused by an increase in expenditures (revenues being held constant) or by a reduction in revenues (outlays constant) or by an increase in expenditures greater than the increase in revenues. And a surplus if revenues are increased (expenditures constant) or expenditures reduced (revenues constant) or revenues increase more than expenditures.

Rises and falls in expenditures and revenues come about in two different ways. These are usually referred to as automatic and discretionary. If the change in government revenues comes about because of a change in national income and if the change in government revenue is larger and in the same direction as the change in national income (expenditures being held constant), this change is automatic and stabilizing. In other words, a fall in the national income will mean a *larger* proportionate fall in government revenue and therefore a deficit. Similarly, a change in government expenditures brought about by a change in national income is automatic if the change in government expenditures is *smaller* than the change in national income, (revenues being held constant); this is also stabilizing. These policies are built in the system by previous discretionary policies; once built in, they operate automatically. It is only in this sense that they are automatic. Discretionary policies are policies voted and applied to a specific problem at the time it arises.

Automatic policies should be more efficient and more numerous than

[3]Co-ordination will reduce the costs of stabilization. In the case of "non-co-operation," the federal government can always offset the action of any provincial government, since it alone has the power to print money. But this is hardly economical.

they now are, but discretionary policies should always be employed when it appears that the automatic policies are not sufficient.

Three reasons may be advanced to justify this mixed position. Automatic policies reduce the need for prediction and forecasting; and since economists are not and may never be able to predict future magnitudes accurately, automatic stabilization policies makes forecasting less of a problem. But, since variations in aggregate activity are not always of the same magnitude nor of the same nature, automatic policies which may do the job nicely in one case may not be able to do so in other cases. Thirdly, automatic stabilization policies can never prevent fluctuations and are not generally capable alone of returning the economy to its equilibrium level; they can only reduce the size of fluctuations.[4]

What should be done to make the behaviour of revenues and expenditures more efficient automatically? Also, what type of discretionary policies should and what type should not be implemented? The automaticity of fiscal policies can be increased both in revenue and expenditure. Let us discuss these questions in order.

It is not my intention to propose a new streamlined tax system, since this is hardly the object of this chapter. At the same time, one must remember that if the only purpose of taxation were stabilization a highly regressive[5] tax system would be the ideal one, on the only assumption that the proportion of income consumed is larger for lower than for higher income groups.[6] Since this is unacceptable on grounds of equity,[7] it follows that equity considerations cannot be by-passed when making recommendations for a stabilizing tax system. Various aspects of the personal income tax, of the capital gains tax, of the undistributed profit tax, and of the corporate income tax will be considered in turn, showing their contributions to stabilization.

The personal income tax should not be made more progressive. If all the other features of the tax system proposed here were implemented, it

[4]Recently, some economists have become concerned about the many kinds of lags which are involved in the application of stabilization policies. They believe that fiscal policies, either automatic or discretionary, may more often than not spell disaster. It cannot be denied that there are some grounds for this pessimistic view. But we know from experience that absence of policies is also disastrous. What are we to do but try what has not yet been tried?

[5]A tax system or a tax is progressive if the rate of taxation increases as we move to higher income brackets, and regressive in the opposite case. If the tax rate is ten per cent for the $1000–$2000 bracket and twenty per cent for the $5000–$6000, then the system is progressive. If the rates were twenty per cent for the $1000–$2000 bracket and ten per cent for the $5000–$6000, it would be regressive. Finally, if it were ten per cent or twenty per cent for both brackets, it would be proportional.

[6]This is an empirically well-substantiated fact.

[7]This point is taken as a self-evident truth. Even if the proposition cannot be proved, it can certainly be made acceptable to all social groups by referring alternatively to justice or brotherhood, or simply in some cases to social and political revolution.

should be made less progressive. This would reduce the incentive to evade the tax and furthermore divert some of the energy now spent on evading the tax to socially more profitable ventures. More important from the stabilization point of view is the change that should be made in the bracket structure. The number of brackets should be increased. Instead of $1000 brackets, $500 brackets should be introduced; the greater "sensitivity" of the structure would cause revenues to be substantially increased. In other words, changes in government revenues resulting from changes in national income would be greater. This is true because of the progressive nature of the tax structure.

Secondly, an averaging system should be implemented to compute personal income tax; with such a system taxable income would not be computed on the gross income of one year but on the gross income of a number of years. The method implemented should be the cumulative assessment method.[8] The advantages of such a device are many.[9] In addition to equalizing the tax liabilities of individuals whose incomes have different time-shapes, it makes possible with a minimum of complications the introduction in the tax base of incomes which are presently exempt (such as capital gains). Furthermore such an averaging device would tend to increase the stability of the economy and make the compensatory automaticity of the budget greater than under the present system.[10]

[8]Given the accumulated tax balance of any taxpayer, his cumulated income balance and the date at which cumulative assessment was initiated, it is possible to assess the whole income of that taxpayer and to tax it at rates graduated with considerations given to the period over which the income was received. To compute his tax liabilities for any year, the taxpayer first computes his accumulated taxable income. To do so, he adds to his accumulated income, the income of the current year and the present value of taxes paid (obtained by multiplying the accumulated tax paid by a legally set rate of interest and by adding this new amount to the accumulated tax paid. If T is the accumulated tax paid, and if r is the rate of interest, $(1+r)\ T$ is the present value of the accumulated tax). To this taxable accumulated income he applies tax rates which are a function, *inter alia*, of the number of years over which his income is averaged. This yields his total tax liabilities from which he substracts the present value of past taxes to obtain his current tax liabilities. See W. S. Vickrey, *Agenda for Progressive Taxation* (New York, 1947), 164–97; also "Averaging, Cumulative Assessment and Retirement Income Provisions" in *Federal Tax Policy for Economic Growth and Stability* (Washington, 1955), 871–6.

[9]The difficulties of application, which are not as bad as it would seem after reading the previous concentrated footnote, are further compensated by reducing the number of present laws required to close (or open!) loop-holes for certain types of incomes like capital gains and dividends. It also reduces complications at the level of exemptions.

[10]Indeed, a reduction in current income below the average of past years reduces the (average) amount of income for those past years and accordingly reduces the tax liabilities for those years below the amount already paid. If the fall in current income is large enough and if the income brackets are small enough, it is even possible for the taxpayer to receive a tax refund. In any case his current tax liabilities will be falling with falling income and rising with rising income. This is so, even if the amount of income subject to the current rates is increased. The gist of this

A last feature that should be incorporated in the personal income tax structure, is the following: whenever employment falls below a certain percentage of full employment for a number of months—three, for example—then, automatically, income taxes should be cut across the board by a specified percentage. Suppose that employment has remained at five per cent below full employment for the last three months and that five per cent is the percentage of permissible unemployment incorporated in the law, then a fraction of the taxes of the fourth month should be remitted for individuals paying income taxes. If employment stayed below five per cent during the fourth month, taxes of the fifth month should be reduced by the same fraction or by a larger one and so on. As soon however, as employment reached ninety-five per cent, tax payments would be resumed. This is a very potent measure which would certainly have a great stabilizing influence on the economy.

In periods of excess demand,[11] something like the opposite should be done; that is, income taxes would be raised "automatically" as soon as demand was greater than supply. If demand exceeded supply for three consecutive months by some percentage then in the fourth month taxes on personal incomes should be raised across the board. If excess demand did not fall, the tax increase would be maintained; but it would be dropped as soon as excess demand fell.

What about capital gains and undistributed profit taxation? The absence of taxes on capital gains has led to all kinds of practices such as paying salaries in stocks valued at, or at less than, market prices; purchasing the corporation's stocks at a low pre-issue price with funds borrowed from the corporation's till, holding the stocks after the market issue until the price has risen, selling the stocks at a large profit, repaying the loan, and by this very simple expedient accumulating a large non-taxable income and increasing destabilizing speculation in the stock market.

Capital gains should be taxed as ordinary income. Practices like the above would be greatly reduced, the stock market would be made con-

---

argument rests on the fact that a fall or increase in current income affects the average of all past incomes and therefore makes the taxes paid on these amounts larger or smaller than they would have been had current income been taken into account when the tax liabilities on these past incomes were computed. This is not a feature of other averaging devices such as carry backward–carry forward, or moving averages. These last are destabilizing and should never be implemented; when in force they should be discarded.

The general stabilizing effect of the cumulative assessment method of taxation could also be increased still more by speeding up the tax refunds for taxes witheld at source.

[11]Periods of excess demand are not as easy to identify as periods of excess supply; this is due mostly to the fact that very little work as yet has been done on the relationship of income, productivity, prices, etc., which are all crucial to excess demand.

siderably less buoyant since a taxation of capital gains would greatly reduce the number of transactions, but not very much the liquidity of the market. Furthermore, it would make all incomes from manual labour to speculative labour exactly alike.[12] Without an averaging device, taxing capital gains like ordinary incomes has very serious disadvantages, since it taxes with very high rates in years of high income, but with an averaging technique it makes the economy more stable at the same time as it does away with gross injustice.

If capital gains are taxed like ordinary income, is there a need for an undistributed corporate profit tax? A capital gains tax is not sufficient to make an undistributed profit tax useless, but coupled with a succession tax, it is. Further, since in all probability an equitable succession tax would be one that did not compute the succession's taxable income from the gross income of the deceased but from the gross income of the person or persons receiving the succession,[13] an undistributed profit tax would be completely unnecessary.

If capital gains are not taxed an undistributed profit tax could be a substitute for it, but it would be a much less efficient way of attaining the goals of stability and equity. This is a consequence of the way claims are layered in the economy, that is, of the pattern of property ownership.

What about the corporate income tax? So much debate exists about the behaviour of this tax, that one hesitates to propose anything. If the tax is shifted to the consumer, and if one prefers progressive to regressive taxation, then the tax should probably just as well be eliminated and "replaced" by the progressive personal income and succession tax. If the tax is not shifted or if it is only partially shifted, the tax to implement depends on the degree of shifting. Whatever may be the case, the stabilization possibilities of the corporate income tax are very limited: first, because investments do not seem to be very responsive to corporate income during depression; secondly, because dividend payouts are virtually constant or move very slowly over the cycle; and thirdly, because dividend receivers are higher-income individuals with a relatively low marginal propensity to consume and in depression a still lower "propensity to invest," while in prosperity this propensity is presumably very high, so that the net result is destabilizing.

When consideration is given to deductions from gross corporate income again little is really important for the stability of the economy as

[12]One should always keep in mind that as long as the government needs a certain income — over a period of years — and that this required income and not more is collected, every privilege in the tax system is equivalent to a transfer of real resources or real income from the community to the privileged group, over and above the price paid for the services this group renders to society.

[13]I need not go into all the possibilities of evasion that come to mind in thinking of such a tax; but I feel that an applicable tax on heirs could be devised.

a whole. FIFO valuation[14] of inventories is more stabilizing or less destabilizing than LIFO, but the magnitudes involved are quite small indeed. In terms of long-run stability and certainly in terms of equity the case is different. Whatever we consider, be it expense accounts or paid "passive" directors waiting calmly for one or the other of their "active" colleagues to falter in the call of duty but in the meantime living quite gracefully, most of these practices require legislation since they are slowly undermining the tax system. Legislation of course should be gradual and experimental. A consideration of the large number of existing exemptions, deductions and allowances may at first lead one to believe that businessmen are rather greedy to claim yearly such large hidden subsidies, because this is what many of these things in effect amount to. Further consideration, however, encourages one to think, all the verbal ballyhoo notwithstanding, that these hidden subsidies may be a necessary "incentive" for the businessman to do his job. In other words, the businessman may not be the aggressive, risk-loving, adventurous, dedicated individual of *Fortune* and *Time,* but more simply the ordinary guy who is "willing" only if assured of the carrot or of the stick. Since for philosophical reasons the stick is condemned (at least for the businessman), then large subsidies are needed to assure him of the carrot. If this is so, one should be careful lest, in removing the subsidies, one is obliged to grab the stick. If subsidies are necessary they should not be hidden but should be incorporated in the law and voted annually with the budget. To remove them altogether and all at once would be disastrous, since it would create a big slump in activity. Take for example expense accounts. If they were removed—as they should certainly be for all entertainment, which include yachts, call girls, hunting lodges, private use of company cars, club dues and other things —then, it is quite a bit of fun to imagine the other things that would have to go.

The bearing of all these points on stabilization is only indirect; it is real, however, in that they all accelerate expansion but also accelerate depression.

As long as government expenditures do not vary with changes in national income, automatic deficits or surpluses arise only from the revenue or tax side of the budget. The expenditure side could, however, possess automatic features of its own.

The present recommendation is very similar in form to one proposed earlier and to that proposed by others.[15] Basically it consists of increasing unemployment compensation by an amount which would be a func-

[14]FIFO stands for "first in–first out" and LIFO for "last in–first out."
[15]See J. K. Galbraith, *The Affluent Society* (Boston, 1958) 296–307. My proposal resembles Professor Galbraith's in its essentials but differs from it in detail.

tion of the percentage of unemployed over a stated fixed number. Suppose that this number is five per cent. Then as soon as unemployment exceeds five per cent, monthly compensations would increase by a stated percentage of the basic compensation. Another possibility is to increase compensations to make the unemployed's income equal or almost equal to the wages earned before unemployment. So that there will be no incentive to abandon work, unemployment, for the purpose of this policy, should be defined as the number of persons out of work and seeking work over and above the number of jobs available. This last statistical series exists only in very imperfect form presently but could be made quite good by giving some incentive, in the form of a bonus, to employers to declare all jobs available. Any tendency to declare more jobs than are really available could be counterbalanced by charging a small fine, or by forcing the employer to accept employees for each job declared. However, since the mobility of labour is not at all perfect and since it cannot easily be increased sufficiently in the short run, the country would have to be divided into regions; so that the above recommendation is in effect only valid for the regions; if this were not so, excess demand would very soon arise. To the extent that unemployment comes not from the demand but from the supply side of the economy, the central bank or the government should initiate policies which would remove from the economy as much money as is actually introduced through this automatic unemployment compensation scheme.

A Digression

There are many other questions related to fiscal policies which should be discussed. Only a few will be mentioned. First, there is the question of farmers' incomes and the best ways to stabilize them. Although not all will agree, it seems that like the incomes of other groups income of farmers should be maintained in depression. However, it is probably not a very good policy to tamper continually with the price mechanism, at least as long as the tampering is always in the same direction. As long as this is the case it is probably better to maintain farmers' income by direct income payments. These would be put in effect as soon as incomes fell below some legally defined limit. What should be done if the incomes persistently remain below the legal limit? A fascinating hypothesis which was given to the writer on the process of rural-urban mobility has bearing on this question.[16] It goes as follows. On the average, the people who leave the farms are the younger ones, and among these, mostly those who have been to school for any significant time. Constant incomes over a considerable period are required to make it possible for parents to send their children to school. The government should therefore pay a

[16]This hypothesis was privately submitted to the writer by Professor Walton Anderson of the University of British Columbia. Professor Anderson's hypothesis was not, however, intended for this context.

fraction of the income to farmers in the form of vouchers which would have value only for educational purposes. In this way the income supports would not have to be maintained for ever, since a reduced number of farmers will mean increasing incomes. If all educational costs were paid by the government, the government could distribute its vouchers to children attending school in the form of a so-called *pré-salaire*.

As it has already been mentioned a few times, stabilization is not an absolute norm; so that all policies that do not increase stability should not necessarily be rejected. Two cases come to mind. First, family allowances; in real terms these have dwindled to almost nothing since they were implemented. Introducing a price index in them would be destabilizing to the economy in periods of excess demand, but it should command support on other grounds. The second point is more difficult. Governments, labour unions and business now all have an economic policy of immigration. This policy in effect boils down to the fact that in good times we parade what we have as a nation so as to interest foreigners with the hope that they will come to us. As soon as a mild depression or recession hits us we put a stop to our propaganda and even to the incoming of immigrants by such devices as lengthening the bureaucratic process and by insinuating to the foreigner that it is now his turn to parade and to interest us. This is a short-sighted policy, detrimental to the progress of the country. Furthermore, it is an anti-social policy for it really amounts to exporting our unemployment abroad. The comments made previously about tariffs apply with equal force in this case. We should favour or disfavour immigration on other than economic grounds.

Turn now to discretionary policies. Are there special policies that should be implemented? The answer to this question is very difficult, since the required policies should differ substantially if the fluctuations to be corrected were minor or if they were major. But since it is not possible to forecast that a fluctuation will be a minor or a major one, the first general rule is to be ready for major movements. This problem of prediction is a very serious one since, if remedies to offset a major fluctuation are applied and if the fluctuation turns out to be but a minor one, very serious problems will be created for the future; and to combat a major movement with tools appropriate to minor ones is bound to be disastrous in the present. It is for this reason that so many permanent automatic measures of anti-cyclical policy have been proposed above.

If a fluctuation threatens to be a major one then a determined government can always stop it by throwing all it has into the machine—that is, by incurring very large deficits or very large surpluses. It has become a belief of many—especially among those in public life—to advocate public works as a standard way of incurring a deficit in slump periods.

In periods of major slumps, as has just been said, everything possible should be done, but in periods of minor fluctuations an anti-cyclical policy of public works is ridiculous. First, it is not efficient for a number of reasons among which the following can be mentioned: it takes a long time to get the projects started; they cannot be stopped as they are started; they are for the most part relatively capital-intensive and, given the dividend policies of corporations, tend to generate relatively little disposable income; but over and above all, the importance of public works is too great to be the object exclusively of anti-cyclical policy. Hospitals, schools, public housing, urban renewal are needed not because the economy is slumping, but for other reasons. If they are needed, then they should be built. A public works stabilization policy would then go as follows: in periods of major depressions public projects which could have waited should be undertaken. If major public work projects are undertaken, because it is felt that the depression is going to be a major one, but that it turns out to be but a very mild one, what then? Obviously the projects cannot be stopped so that the only thing for the government to do is to raise taxes high enough to pay for the projects.

Fiscal policies are only one tool available to stabilize the economy, but they are the most efficient as well as the most flexible, since they can be made to reach anywhere in the economy in a short time.

However, fiscal policies do not exist in a vacuum; they are related to monetary and to debt policies. These must now be discussed.

MONETARY POLICIES

Like fiscal policies, monetary policies have most of their impact on demand. This happens in two general ways. First, they change the relative cost of most of the components of aggregate demand: investment and consumption (in the latter by affecting the price of consumer credit). A restrictive monetary policy, say, will increase the earnings of interest-bearing liquid assets relative to the real or imputed returns from goods. Second, monetary policies can change the capital value of liquid assets. Monetary restriction will cause capital losses to the owners of liquid assets. These capital losses are brought about by a fall in the market value of the asset and by a rise in the price of goods.

There is still much debate on the efficiency of monetary policies as well as on the reallocation effects of these policies. All participants in the debate recognize, however, that measures of different kinds could be implemented which would make monetary policy more efficient. This is the point of view taken here.

On the reallocation effects of monetary policies unanimity is probably impossible. Some would argue against the existence of monetary policies themselves because of the "bad" allocation effects of such policies. The position adopted in this chapter is that monetary policies have strong allocation effects and that much of the justification for monetary policy rests on that fact. If, however, it is found that all the reallocations are systematically biased in a direction which is socially non-optimal then special measures changing the pressure of monetary policy to other directions should be implemented.

In summary, monetary policies should be made as efficient as possible, while measures should be taken to correct reallocation of resources judged socially non-optimal.

To obtain an efficient monetary policy, there is no reason why more stress should be given to the liquidity than to the cost aspect of the policy. Both are important. More concretely this means that much importance should be accorded to the banking system, even if not all the importance. Finance companies, insurance companies, trust funds and others are also very important. All institutions providing liquidity are important. Within this broad framework some of the proposals for more efficient monetary policies are presented.

The first of these in that the banks be required to hold a substantial fraction of their non-cash assets in reserves. These assets would constitute the effective reserve requirements of the banking system. The present liquidity ratio of fifteen per cent is a step in that direction, but a higher ratio may be still more beneficial to the economy. To have a liquidity ratio instead of a cash ratio as the effective reserve requirement has the advantage that the banks will hold interest-bearing assets instead of the non-interest-bearing ones which are assumed in most plans to meet increased cash requirements. The prospect of interest should make such a proposal more easily enforceable.

But why should the liquidity ratio be set higher than fifteen per cent? The main reason has nothing to do with the stability of the banks themselves, but with the lack of a mechanism in the banks which would impede the creation of new deposits by the banking system when the accumulated sum of these plus the accumulated sum of other credit instruments equal the total amount of savings that the community desires to perform. There is no magic number at which the liquidity ratio should be set, however; in fact, this ratio should be varied as economic conditions warrant: increased in periods of inflation and inflationary pressure and reduced in periods of recession and depression. I think that variations in reserve requirements, although politically more difficult to apply, could be the most efficient of the tools of monetary policy.

A second proposal is that interest rates on consumer credit, sales finances, and instalment credit be as strictly regulated as rates on bank loans. This proposal does not stem from a general belief that fiat rates in the capital market are "better" than market rates, but from the fact that the Canadian capital market is an oligopolistic market with strong taints of collusion. There is no reason to believe that an oligopoly capable of impeding entry over the present high barriers would behave as if it were a competitive industry. For this reason, a maximum legal rate should be specified as well as a method of computing the interest costs. The law should also set the maximum service charges that could be imposed on the borrower. These maximum service charges would of course vary with loan sizes.

It is sufficient to justify such a proposal on the grounds that it increases the effectiveness of monetary policy. The interest inelasticity of the demand for consumer sales and instalment credit makes it possible to shift cost increases as well as capital losses to borrowers, so that the fraction of aggregate demand which is financed by these credits remains unresponsive to monetary action.

And what about the bank rate and the discount policy? The problem here is that a discount policy can dampen the effects of the open market operation of the central bank. There are a certain number of ways to handle this problem. First, the discount window can be closed. Second, the discount window can be a two-way market in which bankers can lend as well as borrow. Thirdly, the bank rate can be left to fluctuate freely so that it will be pushed upwards whenever bankers sell treasury bills and downwards when they buy. These different possibilities are not equivalent; but, apart from the first one, they have the advantage of leaving the system flexible as well as dampening the neutralizing effects on open market operations. Since it is not easy to choose among these various practices, the current practice of leaving the bank rate to be determined at .025 per cent above the average of three-month treasury bills could be continued long enough to permit a good analysis of its effects. Should it be found inefficient, the discount window should be closed and the burden of a flexible monetary system displaced towards variable reserve requirements, open market operations, and the government's debt management.

The third instrument of monetary policy is open market operations, which, if used properly, can have a substantial impact. Through open market operations carried on in the long as well as in the short markets, the monetary base as well as the liquidity of the economy is affected.

That the monetary base is affected is obvious since the process of buying or selling implies exchange of bonds against money, so that money necessarily enters or leaves the economy.[17] Open market operations will also affect the liquidity of the economy because buying or selling pushes interest rates downwards or upwards. But for this control to be efficient, that is, to reach all lending institutions and not only banks, the entire rate structure must be altered. The central bank must

[17]The central bank is not included in this definition of economy.

therefore buy and sell in all maturities, since that will affect all credit institutions and raise the chances of efficient control. This is the third proposal.

In periods of substantial and sustained inflation monetary policies should be coupled with direct controls. These would consist of controls applied to consumer and sales finance and also to the stock market. They include changes in initial down payment and in period of repayment, and also changes in margin requirements.

The last instrument of monetary policy to be discussed is debt management. That debt management should be considered a tool of monetary policies follows from the fact that debt management can undo open market operations especially in a capital market in which the share of government bonds is as large as in the Canadian market; and also from the fact that debt management can increase the efficiency of monetary control generally. This is brought about by the fact that debt management is in effect negative or positive monetization. Like central bank open market operations monetization should be carried in all maturities so as to affect the structure of interest rates generally. To the extent that short debt is more liquid than long debt, funding policies— that is, policies designed to affect the average maturity of the entire debt —are clearly also an aspect of open market operations.

It is customary to think that monetary policies must be under federal supervision because it is alleged that only the federal government can create money. This is not correct. That monetary policy should be under federal supervision follows from the fact that only the federal government can efficiently initiate co-operation between different levels of government. And only co-operation will insure that stabilization policies will have some efficiency as illustrated by debt policies. It has already been shown that provincial governments could—deliberately or otherwise—offset fiscal measures introduced by the central government. It is now possible to see that these same provincial governments could offset monetary policies. Again, however, the central bank and/or the federal government—these by structure are closely related[18]—could always have their way, but this could only be done at an extra cost and with some hardships. It follows that a federal-provincial permanent committee should be created to co-ordinate budget and debt policies as well as all stabilization policies generally. Such a committee could make the workings of a general fiscal-monetary policy quite efficient in coping with problems of excess demand.

PRICE POLICIES

In the previous sections policies which could regulate excess demand —positive or negative—have been discussed. Once excess demand has

[18]E. P. Neufeld, *Bank of Canada Operations, 1935–54* (Toronto, 1955), 315.

been reduced to zero, it is possible that prices may keep on increasing and generate unemployment of labour and other resources. In such cases, the authorities—government(s) and/or the central bank—should avoid increasing demand, since this will not cause a substantial fall in unemployment but only a further rise in prices. What should be done? This is not an easy question and it will not be possible to give a very satisfactory answer to it. To be sure, two general solutions are open: price and wage controls or structural alterations. To enumerate alternative solutions does not solve anything since there are a number of ways of controlling prices and wages and of altering the structure of the economy.

Would price and wage controls be an improvement? They would most certainly not be better than no controls if controls were unnecessary. This sort of tautological statement is given to indicate that controls carry with them rather unpleasant aspects. The question can now be framed as: Are controls necessary? Again to be a little paradoxical, one can say that the theory of competitive prices is a theory of price controls! However, when competition falters, so do the inherent controls, so that others have to be found to replace them. As a rule in the administered sectors of the economy, big business controls prices, and big labour wages. But since business and labour are bound to control these prices to their advantage and not to that of the economy, it follows that this control should be altered. There are a number of ways to go about doing this. Some would advocate that big business as well as big labour be broken up so as to make competition possible once more. The inherent virtues of all-around competitive behaviour are still hidden to the writer, although he has spent many an hour trying to discover them. Of course, competition to the extent that it is limited to prices is "good," but it seems to have an inherent tendency to spill over to other phenomena as well and when this happens the optimal solutions of price competition are much less optimal for society as a whole. Since industrial organization is not discussed in this chapter, the existence of big business and big labour is taken for granted and policies for such a context are devised. Obviously price and wage controls should be limited to the administered sectors of the economy.

The government should create a price and wage commission. The role of this commission should for a substantial period be limited to analysis. If the analysis showed that price and wage controls were necessary, then the commission should recommend controls for those prices and wages requiring them. The commission should study the pricing process in the economy. By this I mean that investigations should be conducted to discover the steps which entrepreneurs (or maybe employees) follow in setting prices.[19] To assume marginal cost pricing is valid in some cases,

[19]This must be understood to include all prices, including therefore wages, interest rates, etc.

but it seems obvious to the writer that a knowledge of how entrepreneurs actually go about doing these things is needed if any progress is to be achieved. The writer is convinced also that such a task should be performed by economists, aided by sociologists. The latter are in many ways less ruthless with reality than economists often are! The results of these investigations, discreetly clothed in anonymity, should be published.

The commission should furthermore have the power to investigate demands[20] for wage and price increases in large industries, make a judgment on these demands, and publish the judgment as well as the information on which it is based. The publication of the judgment as well as of the information by this independent commission is proposed in the belief that it would have enough impact on public opinion to prevent undue price and wage increases.

As a very long-run policy, there is a structural change that would considerably improve the prospects of price stabilization from the supply side of the market: the introduction of consumer co-operatives which, when big enough, could prevent price increases. Co-operatives are not the only possible structural changes in the economy that would increase long-run stability, but they have the advantage that very little in terms of material transformation would have to be done to install them. Where they exist to any extent, as they do in Scandinavia, they have apparently substantially reduced the problem of stabilization. This would require further study, but if it should prove to be true, the government should encourage their inception by the means at its disposal.

[20]These demands are not explicit demands made either by business or labour, but implicit demands arising at the occasion of collective bargaining or other such events.

Agriculture

MEYER BROWNSTONE

Agriculture, in 1961, has few rivals as the nation's social and economic conscience. Not only does it contain within itself characteristics which militate against well-being, but it is the unfortunate target of some of our most vicious economic instruments. This chapter will consist of an attempt to expose the root causes and manifestations of this public malady and will (with considerable optimism) suggest relevant treatment.

Agriculture is an industry within a nation of industries and the aims and needs of the people in agriculture are fundamentally the same as those of all other citizens. The fact that agriculture may have special problems because of its industrial[1] characteristics and its rural setting,

[1]The issue of family farms *v.* factory farms will not be debated here. Apart from reference to co-operative farming, which is a consistent and useful development of family farms, the family farm is assumed to be the typical form of agricultural organization. The whole analysis is thus really focused on improving the family farm as an economic and social unit. Relatively few farms in Canada today qualify as adequate family farms if level-of-living and productivity criteria are applied. See Saskatchewan Royal Commission on Agriculture and Rural Life, Report no. 5, *Land Tenure* (Regina, 1955); and B. H. Kristjanson, "Maintaining Family Farming as an Objective," AES Workshop, 1960 (mimeo).

does not militate against common social goals, and similar, if not common, public policies. Throughout this chapter it should become evident that basic farm and non-farm problems have common roots and their solution requires similar attitudes and treatment. We have far too long placed agriculture in a rather special, rather precious preserve instead of recognizing its interdependent and integrated position in the economy. The popular concept of rugged individualism, self-reliance, and isolation has surely been shattered by the facts of commercialization, government and co-operative activity, transportation and communication, and urbanization. The recent impact of automation has virtually an exact counterpart in the mechanization of agriculture. Labour displaced from the land is no different in essence from labour displaced from a factory. We can under such conditions proceed with some assurance that fundamental policies have a broad social base and as such have application, not just to agriculture, but to society as a whole.

We can begin by exposing our basic concerns. In our materialistic environment,[2] income, or better still, level of living, is of fundamental concern. But we need to go into the details of level of living before judgments can be made. One important specification is the constitution of level of living. In the present treatment, this includes not only income earned in the market place but also "socially derived income" stemming from public expenditure in the whole range of public services. It also includes the values derived from living in particular environments.

A second specification vital to our analysis is comparative level of living. Equality is a central socialist goal; consequently, the essential criterion in judging economic well-being is the degree of equality in our society. Equality is a difficult and elusive notion; but to accept present inequality as a permanent state is to perpetuate a divisive force within our communities, our nation, and throughout the world.

Third, we must be concerned with the stability of level of living.

The status of some of the above concepts may be illustrated statistically. We can, for instance, with regard to level of living, use data relating to farm living conditions. In 1951, the last year for which data are available, the census classified 23 per cent of our rural (compared with 17 per cent of our urban) homes as being "crowded." A home is considered crowded when the number of persons exceeded the number of rooms in the dwelling. In 1951, 20 per cent of our farm homes required major repairs; 44 per cent of our farm homes did not have electricity, 77 per cent were without piped-in water supply, 87 per cent did not have an electric or gas range. Compared with urban standards, the level of living in rural areas generally is deplorably low.

This is illustrated further by a comparison of farm and non-farm

---

[2]It is not argued here that materialism should be our sole concern. The subject has been dealt with more usefully in earlier chapters.

incomes. Table I contains historical data grouped on the basis of periods of relative national prosperity and depression. The data are in terms of average farm income. Further insights into the comparative level of living are provided by an examination of the distribution of income within agriculture. Unfortunately, our only usable measure is based on gross income. In 1950, 62 per cent of our farms had gross sales of less than an average of $2,500. Obviously an average income figure grossly distorts the welfare situation in agriculture.[3]

TABLE I

COMPARISON OF FARM AND NON-FARM NET INCOME PER CAPITA,
ANNUAL AVERAGES FOR SELECTED YEARS, CANADA, 1926–1954
in constant 1935–9 dollars

Period	Farm income as a percentage of non-farm income
1926–28	41.6
1929–41	22.9
1942–50	40.7
1942–53	42.8
1954	30.7

SOURCE: Saskatchewan Commision, Report no. 13, *Farm Income* (Regina, 1955), p. 27.

Finally, the problem is compounded by the absolute and relative instability of farm income. Table II reveals that, on the average between 1935 and 1955, annual variations in farm income were six times greater than variations in non-farm income.

It is clear that, by whatever income measure one applies, the historical position of agriculture in Canada's developing economy has been one of chronic depression and uncertainty. Moreover, despite absolute improvements in level of living, the relative position of agriculture has failed to improve materially. It will be apparent from the analysis below that the roots of the problem are closely entwined with our total economic and social structure. It is contended here that agriculture cannot be successfully treated as a "special" problem, in isolation from the many forces which impinge upon it. And fundamental to the remedies proposed is a radical extension of public responsibility in the economic sphere.

AGRICULTURE IN THE NATIONAL ECONOMY: PEOPLE,
PRODUCTION AND PRODUCTIVITY

One of the better known characteristics of agriculture is its long-run tendency to employ fewer and fewer people while its output is maintained or grows. This tendency is almost a measure of the maturing

[3]This analysis requires a much more searching treatment such as those provided in the Royal Commission on Canada's Economic Prospects, *Progress and Prospects of Canadian Agriculture* (Ottawa, 1957); and J. B. Rutherford, "The Small Farm Problem," CAES Workshop, 1957 (mimeo).

TABLE II
VARIABILITY OF INCOMES: AVERAGES OF PERCENTAGE CHANGES
FROM PRECEDING YEAR
in constant 1949 dollars

Period	Non-paid farm worker	Non-farm worker
1936–39	13.2	3.0
1941–45	32.4	2.9
1946–50	7.2	1.5
1951–55	20.6	3.4
1935–55 average	18.3	2.7

SOURCE: Royal Commission on Canada's Economic Prospects, *Progress and Prospects of Canadian Agriculture* (Ottawa, 1957), p. 343.

process in modern societies. The demand for food is shaped by total population, disposable income, and the propensity to spend for food. This may well appear as an unlimited demand if we view the world scene. But, in terms of our domestic population, rising real incomes, and present export prospects, there are some real limits to the demand for food.

At the same time the limits to our demand for virtually every other good are not so closely circumscribed. People have an endless capacity to consume clothes, cars, houses, and services of various kinds. Coupled with this, improvements in the technology of agricultural production permit the transfer of labour out of agriculture into other types of production without threatening total food output. Thus, as the economy grows, relatively more and more of our resources, both human and material, are allocated to other than food production.[4]

These long-term developments on the demand and technology side provide the basis for population and labour force changes in agriculture. There is certainly little doubt that these changes have occurred. Our basic questions will be: are these changes generally desirable; are the experienced rates of change adequate; is the process itself satisfactory?

People

First let us explore these developments by noting the population characteristics of Canadian agriculture and its changes both in the short and the long run. We are concerned here with all people engaged in agriculture and dependent on farming for at least part of their income.

[4]In technical terms the income elasticity for food is relatively low. R. E. Caves and R. H. Holton in *The Canadian Economy* (Cambridge, Mass., 1959), pp. 443–5, estimate that the income elasticity of food at the retail level is 0.4 and at the farm level between 0.20 and 0.25. The latter means that as disposable income rises 1 per cent, food consumption per capita rises by 0.20 per cent. Caves and Holton quote Rex F. Daly. "Some evidence suggests that income elasticities tend to decline at . . . higher income levels and may decline as income rises over time." In contrast, income elasticity of tobacco and alcohol, furniture, automobiles, and durable goods generally, is well over 1.0. It is also very important to note that the elasticity of demand for food processing services is very high. This means that while food expenditures may remain high, gross farm incomes may be falling.

For other purposes it may be useful to differentiate within agriculture as to subsistence and commercial farming, full-time and part-time farming, and rural or urban residence of farmers.[5] Here we will use farming population in its broadest sense as people who produce farm products which go into our national food consumption.

Table III shows three kinds of farm population change. First, we can measure how farm population itself has changed over time by applying the index of change of farm population. The long-run trend is unmistakably downwards. There have been interruptions and even regional reversals to the trend. The major cause of such short-run fluctuations has been general economic depression with its absence of any superior employment alternative for farm people.

TABLE III
FARM POPULATION TRENDS, 1931–1956

Year	Index of change (1931 = 100)	Farm population as percentage of total population	Farm labour force as percentage of total labour force
1931	100	32	33
1941	96	27	26
1951	89	21	19
1956	83		

SOURCES: *Census of Agriculture* and *Census of Canada*.

Regional analysis would point up how the problem of rural adjustment differs with the rate of depopulation and the accompanying farm changes. It may be noted, for example, that the consequences of adjustment on the prairies, and in Saskatchewan particularly, have been, quantitatively if not qualitatively, more serious than in either the Central and Maritime provinces or in British Columbia.

Second, the trend in farm population expressed as a percentage of total population is a useful measure of the transfer of population from one industry and environment to another. Finally, the third tabulation, relating to the labour force, shows the implications of this transfer for production. These latter two indices show a more rapid rate of change than the first index, indicating that the increase in non-agricultural population and non-farm labour force in Canada in recent years has been augmented by new non-agricultural entrants into the population and labour force. In our earlier economic history the reverse was true. Farm population showed a greater rate of increase than total population as most of the new immigrants worked on farms.[6]

[5]See Rutherford, "The Small Farm Problem." It is recognized that the general treatment provided here requires specification based upon the distinctive characteristics of each situation. But the broad treatment is both relevant and unavoidable in a chapter of this length.

[6]In 1926, for instance, 57 per cent of immigrant arrivals were classified as farm immigrants. In 1952 only 10 per cent were so classified (*Canada Year Book*, 1955).

The over-all long-run trend appears clearly. In its broadest economic terms it is a desirable shift since it characterizes a developing and maturing economy, utilizing human resources with increasing effectiveness and thus providing for a potential general improvement in the Canadian standard of living. However, not only has the population adjustment to date fallen short of an optimum rate and level, but it has taken place aimlessly and haphazardly. Historically, adjustment of farm population in Canada is a classic example of the unplanned impact of impersonal economic forces on an exposed sector of our economy. As such, farm adjustment as we have known it is quite inconsistent with the essence of socialism. The planless disruption of the rural family and community, the socially questionable drift of people from rural poverty to urban slums, the painful adjustment to urban employment and urban life, the irrational "selection" of movers and non-movers — all are heavy social costs that would not be tolerated in a socialist context.

The emphasis thus needs to be placed on policies based on a thorough knowledge of the social choices involved in terms of the individual families, the community, and the national welfare. Without denying the basic proposition of a declining farm population, and in fact admitting the desirability of a greater rate of decline (something which Canadian socialists have evaded), the whole process should be identified and accepted. Then, measures should be taken to facilitate adjustment by means of clear public responsibility for such diverse programmes as farm credit, urban housing, adjustment grants, training, and rural services.

Production: The Broad Perspective

The efforts of agriculture as an industry in terms of physical production have been outstanding. Apart from the largely unavoidable effects of natural conditions, agriculture has faithfully, year in and year out, produced in growing abundance for the Canadian consumer. Despite economic fluctuations, which in other industries have produced anti-social effects, farmers have rarely, if ever, consciously withheld food from the market in order to exploit a particular price situation.[7] Typically, agriculture's production performance has gone unheralded except when surpluses appear.

When we turn to production as an economic component within the national economy we find agriculture in a position of long-run relative decline (see Table IV). The decline is a direct function of the over-all place of agriculture in a developing economy, as defined earlier. The point is not that food production is less essential today, but simply that in general the economic value of farm production is of declining impor-

[7]Without minimizing the positive contribution of the industry, it must be recognized clearly that the organization of agriculture itself is an important deterrent to output adjustments which might have anti-social effects.

TABLE IV
AGRICULTURE'S SHARE OF THE NATIONAL OUTPUT,* 1926–1955
millions of 1949 dollars

Year	Agriculture's share
	%
1926	25.2
1931	20.7
1936	18.9
1941	15.4
1946	12.3
1951	14.0
1955	12.0

SOURCE: A. Scott and Wm. C. Hood, *Output, Labour and Capital in the Canadian Economy*, report for RC on Canada's Economic Prospects (Ottawa, 1957), p. 212.
*Expressed in terms of Gross Domestic Product.

tance in a maturing economy. If necessary, one could extend the argument to include all the secondary industries directly stimulated by agriculture. The portion of consumer food prices accounted for by food processing, packaging, and distribution has risen steeply, but this is quite independent of the demand for farm production. The farm implement industry has continued to grow, but in large part because of expanded foreign markets and technological improvements in Canadian agriculture rather than because of an expansion in food output. It is evident then that in the long run, except for extraordinary population expansion nationally or extraordinarily large increases in the exports of food, agriculture will continue its long-run decline as a factor in Canada's national product.

There are nevertheless some important and persistent qualifications to the broad evaluation just given. There are still significant effects on regional and industrial sectors which hinge on the value of farm output. Obviously in areas where agriculture is the predominant economic activity, fluctuations in farm output and income have important short-run effects not only on farmers themselves but on the many services within such areas which depend directly on farm income. This problem is compounded where agriculture is depressed chronically. There is a more widely dispersed effect on extra-regional industries which depend on agriculture for a market. Prominent among these is the farm implement industry which finds itself quite exposed to fluctuations in farm output and income. In 1952, for example, employment in this industry reached a peak of 19,400. By December, 1954, after a year of sharp decline in farm income, employment dropped to 8,000. It rose to 13,200 in the following April only to drop back again to 10,700 in November, 1955.[8] These fluctuations are seasonal in part, but they also reflect annual sensitivity to farm income and demand.

[8]Saskatchewan Commission, Report no. 13, *Farm Income*, p. 37.

Another widely dispersed effect may be found in Canada's international trade sector. Here again, while food exports have declined as a portion of total exports, they have remained an essential and basic element of Canada's export trade.

The foregoing analysis suggests two implications. First and most important, agriculture in terms of the total economy is more and more dependent on domestic conditions, and its welfare can be provided for when necessary with a smaller and smaller drain on the total economy. Thus, there is increasingly less justification for the traditional position that agriculture's problems are uncontrollable because they arise outside Canada and that their solution would constitute a major drain on the entire economy. Second, there is still ample justification in terms of the regional and industrial impact of agricultural fluctuations on the national economy to warrant concern for farm problems.

These implications are made explicit primarily to satisfy those whose consciences require more stimulation than that induced by the bare facts of poverty and inequality in a rich society.

Production: Problems and Answers

Over the next few decades we will be faced with a number of problems in agricultural production. Perhaps the most important is the redirection of production. This is based on our growing population and improvement in levels of living. A number of recent forecasts of the changing nature of demand are available. They indicate a shift towards greater production of meat products, fruits, and vegetables, and a decline in the relative importance of cash grain production.[9]

There are, in contrast, chronic production problems that are a function of either production decisions or of uncontrollable conditions of production. The difficulties about decisions lead us to a vast and complex area which ranges from the price system itself to the organization of agricultural production. It encompasses the impact of support price policy on food surpluses or deficits and the current issue of contract farming and vertical integration. We will leave all those problems having to do with the market place for later development, for we are concerned at the moment with problems relating to the total output of food and the composition of the food basket. We are also concerned with the effects of changing production on farm income. There are important techniques, not concerned with costs and prices, for dealing with production problems, and we can list both positive and negative techniques. To expand food production along lines suggested by demand projection, it is possible to employ more credit for individual farmers, public resource development programmes, technological research, technical education for farmers, and grants for

[9]Caves and Holton, *The Canadian Economy*, pp. 432–52; RC on Canada's Economic Prospects, *Canadian Agriculture*.

specific production programmes. These are the main tools for a positive public policy to encourage needed food production.

There are in addition a whole set of activities which may be classified as negative production controls, whose object is to avoid gluts in total output by directing or encouraging individual production decisions. These include acreage controls, marketing quotas, soil banks, and conservation measures. Here it is necessary to face squarely the fact that, when thousands of individual producers each make their own independent production decisions, the total tendency is always towards decisions leading to extremes in production. To aggravate this problem, resources used in agriculture are in many cases rather inflexible so that activity cannot be switched in the short run from one form of production to another in keeping with market requirements.[10]

Preventive measures are thus strictly limited in character because of the economic and production organization of agriculture. This may be viewed in sharp contrast to highly administered non-farm industries which have for many years effectively controlled their total production and marketing. As agriculture itself becomes more concentrated, however, under the impact of technology and economic incentives (the recent interest in vertical integration is a good demonstration; vertical integration and a closely related form, contract farming, have emerged in segments of agriculture where technical conditions were conducive to a high degree of concentration), supply can become more "rationalized" and production control quite workable. But even under such conditions control is effective to the extent that the industry as a whole is in fact concentrated in the monopolistic sense. As long as many small, uncommitted firms remain, production control is uncertain.

There is, however, another method of achieving more effective production control. Offsets are designed to smooth out variations in supply and to counteract the economic effects of such fluctuations on consumers and producers. Offsets include such diverse measures as public storage, marketing quotas (and farm storage) and crop insurance. These offsets are justified in cases of unavoidable production fluctuations caused by natural hazards or marketing fluctuations caused by temporary lack of capacity in central marketing storage and other facilities. When offsets are combined with a positive programme of food disposal, preventive and controlling measures become much less important.

The main contention here is that emphasis should be placed on offsets and disposal rather than on production controls alone to mitigate the problem of production fluctuations. There are available a number of possible programmes as yet either unexploited or under-exploited in Canada. A positive programme of public storage or publicly assisted

[10]Machines, buildings and other resources of the straight grain farmer, for example, are not readily adaptable to large-scale cattle production.

storage would provide a useful device for smoothing out supply variations of storable commodities. Where commodities cannot be stored in their natural form or transformed into storable condition then controls must be used.

Crop insurance, an important offset technique, is now making its début in Canadian agriculture but is largely confined to the prairies. Unfortunately, crop insurance is not being given an effective foundation even in these areas. The Prairie Farm Assistance Act provides such a foundation and should have been modified and extended to (1) permit zonal differentials in premiums and indemnities, to (2) raise the level of insurance, and to (3) include a wide range of commodities throughout Canada. A modified PFAA would provide important advantages including federal financial strength, centralized administration and standardization, superior experimental facilities, efficient collection and inspection facilities. In contrast, the present provincial schemes pose a financial threat to the provinces if the schemes are expanded to significant size. They are extremely expensive to administer, and they do not provide for a desirable sharing of risks among farmers.

National food disposal programmes such as universally applied school lunch programmes and food disposal programmes to low-income groups have been demonstrated to be feasible in other countries, notably the United States. They have had important nutritional effects[11] in addition to helping use up the farm surpluses. At the same time they have limited application as purely stabilizing measures since they should become "built-in" aspects of consumption.

International food disposal programmes have been largely neglected by Canada. Yet they have much to recommend them on both moral and economic grounds. That food surpluses and hunger should exist side by side in the world is a paradox which has evoked protests from humanitarians everywhere. At the same time, a sound and effective means of disposing of surplus food stocks would alleviate a recurring production problem for Canadian agriculture. Too often, however, proponents have been more idealistic than realistic in their proposals. Certainly there can be no argument with the emergency distribution of food to forestall starvation wherever it may occur. But beyond this, food disposal in the underdeveloped countries can be effective only if it is closely integrated with and contributes to an indigenous programme of government and economic development.[12] It should be viewed, in other words, strictly as a development tool.

In any other context, food disposal will probably accomplish little and may even be harmful. In many underdeveloped countries a combina-

[11]Cf. M. Southworth and M. I. Klayman, *The School Lunch Program and Agricultural Surplus Disposal* (Washington, DC, 1941).

[12]See J. K. Galbraith, "A Positive Approach to Economic Aid," *Foreign Affairs,* April, 1961.

tion of the need to improve local agriculture, weak administration and outright corruption results in resistance to food distribution programmes and a tragic misuse of food. In many cases it helps to entrench forces which inhibit real development.

Food can be transformed into capital, and so help development. Proceeds from food sales in the recipient country, for example, can be diverted to specific capital projects. Or, under some conditions, food can be used in lieu of cash for wages. In any case

The ultimate value to a recipient country will still depend in large measure upon the development program and how well [food disposal] assistance is geared in with it. Economic development in low-income countries is an intricate and complicated undertaking — much more so than most economists have realized. . . . In large measure the people of a country, themselves, have to assume responsibility for economic development.[13]

Recognition of the problems need not preclude action. Ideally, food disposal should be administered by an international agency in order to maximize receptivity and to minimize friction between commercial rivals. But, short of that, Canada should proceed independently to plan and execute her own programmes of national and international food disposal.

In summary, then, some of the emerging production problems of agriculture lend themselves to effective treatment by non-market techniques. To encourage needed food production, credit, public resource development, technological research and technical education programmes for farmers can be employed.

Offsets rather than restrictive controls offer the most effective means for dealing with production fluctuations. Public storage would be one useful means of smoothing out supply variations of storable commodities. Crop insurance, if soundly based, could ease the income effects of crop failure. Positive programmes of domestic and international food disposal are important counterparts of offset measures.

Productivity: Difficulties and Possibilities

We come now to one of the central issues in farm policy productivity. It is an issue which has been misunderstood and misused. In large part this has been so because we have failed to treat productivity in the context of comprehensive social and economic policy. In this light an adequate treatment of the productivity problem on the one hand lays bare many fundamental faults of our economic system, and on the other hand its solution requires drastic modifications of that system.

In the context of a classical market economy, labour productivity is the basic determinant of labour income; wage rates and income become equalized in all directions by a process of labour mobility flowing from

[13]John H. Davis, "Surplus Disposal as a Tool for World Development — Objectives and Accomplishments," *Journal of Farm Economics*, Dec., 1958.

low marginal[14] productivity with low rewards, to high marginal productivity with high rewards. Agricultural adjustment is a prime example of the classical process. Unfortunately, as a process it has lacked timing, has proceeded at an inadequate rate, and has epitomized the harshness so characteristic of our economic system.

Despite such shortcomings, this should not discourage a positive approach to productivity; far from it. The problem is best met by assisting those individuals who are far down the productivity scale to increase their output and have their rewards. Agriculture, despite recent improvements, has a labour productivity below that of most industries.

Productivity of labour may be defined as the output per unit of labour and its marginal productivity as the output of an additional unit of labour. Productivity, however, is the result of the interaction of a host of factors besides labour itself. One main factor is the resources available to farmers individually and as an industry. The productivity of a given resource is itself of obvious importance to the individual and national income. A drought- or rust-resistant wheat will clearly make the farmer more productive; a labour-saving machine will permit increased output per farmer. In short, the quality of resources as well as their quantity is of significance to labour productivity.

If the quality of resources, whether it be land or machines or seeds, is lower on one farm, then that farmer will need more of them than a farmer whose resources are of higher quality. Thus, a farm with good soil may be smaller in area than a farm with poor soil and yet yield the same or, more likely, more in terms of output per unit of labour. In terms of values of resources or resource investment this means in general that farms yielding equal output per unit of labour may have widely differing resources but quite similar investment in resources. The "large" prairie grain farm will have a resource investment similar to the "small" eastern fruit farm.

TABLE V

RATES OF GROWTH OF OUTPUT

per cent per annum

Period	Agriculture	Non-agriculture (excluding government)
1926–47	.60	1.71
1926–53	2.37	1.85
1947–53	8.82	2.35
1949–53	11.23	2.64
1949–55	7.59	2.68

SOURCE: Hood and Scott, *Output, Labour and Capital*, pp. 215, 217.

Recently agriculture has shown an enormous increase in labour productivity, greater in fact than most industries (see Table V). But despite

[14]Marginal productivity here refers to the increment in output resulting from the addition of a unit of labour.

such progress, agriculture as an industry is still less productive per unit of labour than other industries and appears destined to remain so under predictable conditions (Table VI). The main villain in the piece is an inadequate diffusion of technically potential productivity throughout the industry. To put the matter as succinctly as possible: under prevailing conditions of technology there are too many people in agriculture and too few resources per farmer. When this is coupled with the weak position of agriculture in the market place the result is chronically low farm income.

TABLE VI
OUTPUT PER MAN-HOUR
in 1949 dollars of gross domestic products

Year	Agriculture	Non-agriculture (excluding government)
1926	.52	.98
1931	.44	—
1936	.40	—
1941	.51	—
1946	.58	1.38
1951	.91	1.51
1955	.99	1.70

SOURCE: Hood and Scott, *Output, Labour and Capital*, pp. 214, 216.

Agriculture's low productivity in relation to non-farm industries persists to a greater or lesser degree in every province. We can take one province which shows relatively high productivity — Saskatchewan — and look at the problem in concrete terms of numbers of farms and people. A Royal Commission on Agriculture and Rural Life in that province had as an important objective the establishment of family farms. Among other prescribed characteristics to qualify as a family farm, the farm needed sufficient resources to provide at least a modest income of $2,000 per annum (plus home-produced commodities valued at $1,000). Using this income criterion the Commission estimated that 56,000 — more than one-half of the farms in Saskatchewan — had insufficient resources to yield the income standard. Put in another way, there were sufficient resources in Saskatchewan agriculture to provide the "standard" income for roughly 75,000 farms, and not for the total of 100,000 farms in existence now.[15] There were 25,000 too many farm units.

To this point nothing has been said about prices. Productivity measurements are made on the basis of assumed price levels both for resources bought and products sold. What if the prices of resources were lowered and prices of products raised? This would surely raise farm income and "make" agriculture more productive in value terms. It is not intended to argue the entire point here except to point out the following possibilities: (1) Society could decide to pay more for food and

[15]*Farm Income*, pp. 77–82.

therefore raise farm incomes. No more food would be produced, and farm population would be encouraged to stay on the land. (2) Society could decide to pay no more for food, but could lower production costs by rationalizing or subsidizing the industries producing farm production goods: machines, chemicals, seeds, etc. If subsidy were involved, this would mean a transfer of income from one sector of society to another. (3) Society could concentrate on creating conditions for depopulating agriculture by offering more attractive alternative employment and a reasonable adjustment process. Remembering that labour is less productive in agriculture than elsewhere, this could result in: as much food being produced and at least as cheaply; fewer people to share in total farm income; higher incomes for those leaving agriculture; additional non-farm production by those leaving agriculture. (4) Resources available in agriculture could be increased without increasing the farm labour force as much. Such additions could either increase efficiency (lower costs) without increasing output, or increase output, or both. Here we admit all the possibilities of technological improvement, intensification of land use and expansion of the land base. But the limiting factor is the market for agricultural products. The danger is that gains in labour productivity may be wiped out by accumulation of surpluses and depressed prices.[16]

All of these possibilities have merit and require implementation to correct particular conditions, but on balance, and considering that our concern here is with labour productivity, the third possibility mentioned above is surely deserving of primary emphasis, not only with reference to the problem of low productivity in agriculture, but with reference to the broad social policy required with respect to virtually every kind of labour-saving technological improvement. (We will deal with (4) below and (1) and (2) in other contexts.)

Productivity: Population and Resource Adjustments

Before proceeding to a discussion of how to achieve a greater rate of depopulation in agriculture, it is helpful to examine the basis of the concept and to enquire about the receptivity of the farm population.

First, it should be stressed that the basic concept justifying the process of adjustment is individual freedom, a freedom which is now severely circumscribed by the restricted number of real choices open to many farm families. The function of the state in this context is to provide practical opportunities consistent with an optimum combination of individual and social welfare. Such a policy must include an important

[16]It should be noted here that although the individual farmer has much to gain from increasing his own productivity and output, farmers in the aggregate may have little to gain. This is because of the inelastic demand for many farm products wherein a small increase in output will result in a much larger relative drop in prices.

element of government discretion, but its intent is to widen the possibilities of human satisfaction and to substitute genuine choices for the phantom "freedoms" of today's random adjustment process.

What of farm attitudes? It may be said that a policy of deliberate depopulation in agriculture runs against the stream of traditional views on farming and rural living. But the stream itself has lost much of its force, although this assertion cannot be made unequivocally. One might argue, for instance, that rural people everywhere in Canada have voluntarily joined in an exodus from the farm and have in this process disintegrated rural communities. Therefore any programme that makes adjustment less painful is quite consistent with the inclination of rural people. However, there is much evidence to suggest that this movement away from the farm is rarely "free" except for younger people. In most cases it is more of a forced ejection with a small margin of improvement between moves. Thus the fact that farm people have left the farm in great numbers cannot by itself be taken as conclusive evidence of satisfaction on the part of the movers.

There is, however, other evidence, fragmentary but significant. The urbanization of farmers, particularly on prairie farms, is such evidence. In the past two decades many farmers have permanently moved to town. This suggests strongly that the tradition of rural living has broken down to a significant extent. One might argue that improved rural services would correct this. However, such services would need to be of an extraordinarily high quality and would be very costly to maintain. In any case, rural services have improved in recent years, but this has had little effect on the growing tendency to "farm from town."

TABLE VII

MOTIVATIONS AND MOBILITY AMONG SASKATCHEWAN FARMERS

Question and answer	Percentage of respondents
A. *Why have you stayed on the farm?*	
Preference for farm	43.8
No other choice	32.1
Economically sound	17.7
Good for children	3.5
Independence	2.9
Total	100.0
B. *In general, what do you think might lead you to move off the farm?*	
Retirement	42.5
To obtain better financial set-up	33.3
If schools close	11.9
Isolation	7.9
Obtain conveniences	4.4
Total	100.0

Further evidence is provided from studies of farmers' views on the question of movement. In a Saskatchewan study[17] a sample of farmers was asked the question, "Why have you stayed on the farm?" Table VII shows that nearly one-third of the respondents, in the absence of a positive rehabilitation programme, felt trapped on the farm, with no alternative or other trade to turn to.

Other evidence may be cited. Fortin's analysis of an agricultural parish in Quebec is revealing:

En opposition à l'équilibre relatif d'il y a 20 ans, c'est un climat de tension qu'on retrouve actuellement à Ste-Julienne. Même si le désir d'un niveau de vie tend à remplacer le système de valeur antérieur, les anciennes valeurs n'ont pas encore complètement disparues. Le degré d'intériorisation de ces deux systèmes contradictoires varie d'un individu à l'autre et demeure pratiquement imprévisible. Des conflits éclatent aussi bien au sein des familles qu'au sein de la communauté. Le vieil habitant qui croît encore à l'agriculture voit ses garcons refuser la ferme. De plus en plus, de jeunes couples s'établissent au village pendant que les rentiers doivent rester sur leur ferme dont personne ne veut. Les garcons continuent de laisser l'école à 13–14 ans mais ne trouvent rien à s'occuper avant 17–18 ans, âge où ils partent pour le bois ou la ville. Les jeunes villageois ne vont plus dans le bois mais passent directement à la ville. Les garcons et les filles qui s'attendent encore à ce que leur père les établissent, refusent de lui donner leurs salaires et même de participer aux travaux de la ferme. Les plus âgés reprochent aux jeunes de dépenser sans considération pour le vêtement, l'automobile ou la boisson, mais plus souvent qu'autrement, les plus âgés font de même. Le dancing et le grill sont des institutions reconnues et attirent autant de gens que l'église. Le leadership passe dans les mains des marchands et des contremaîtres en forêt. En général donc les patterns traditionnels sont en conflit avec les nouvelles valeurs mais persistent toujours (Toussaint) alors que de nouveaux patterns tendent à s'imposer à une bonne partie de la population qui les rejettent. Sans doute un nouvel équilibre finira-t-il par s'instaurer, mais il est possible aussi que Ste-Julienne soit pratiquement une paroisse fantôme avant que cela se produise.[18]

Haviland discusses the larger scene in Quebec:

Quebec agriculture is on the move. The industrial thrust of the economy and urbanization are becoming more powerful and pervasive in their influence upon agriculture. The rural community and the farm family are subjected to pressures from within also. Farming is becoming more commercial and mechanized. The farmer is paying increasing attention to economic efficiency and he is demanding greater economic welfare. Fewer and larger farms are symptoms of these important economic adjustments. The adjustments are accompanied by notable sociological changes. The horizons of the farm family extend well beyond the rural community. The adaptable habitant exhibits no special reluctance these days to cross the mental threshold into this bigger and busier world, or even to desert farming altogether in its favour. Nevertheless the family farm, evolving and expanding,

[17]Saskatchewan Commission, *Movement of People*, ch. 5.
[18]Gerald Fortin, "Mobilité occupationnelle d'une paroisse agricole," Laval University, 1957 (mimeo).

of course, remains the vital socio-economic unit in Quebec agriculture. The central problem of family farm policy in our province is to strike a new balance between the rich social traditions and economic progress.[19]

This evidence suggests strongly that a broadening of choices in employment and residence will be of considerable appeal to farmers. It suggests furthermore that adherence to farming and rural living — if it is significant — cannot be explained by the romantic notions so popular among non-farm people.

What then is necessary to accomplish a rational population adjustment in agriculture? Two broad avenues of approach are indicated: one is designed to adjust labour and other resources within agriculture; the other is designed to provide reasonable conditions for families to leave agriculture.

Farm Credit. Resource adjustment within agriculture is reasonably well conceived and formed in public policy. The main device is farm credit,[20] and we have developed in Canada federal and provincial schemes which have virtually all espoused the goal of "economic farm units." Perhaps the main criticism of present credit programmes lies in the concept of the economic farm and how it is to be attained, given the conditions of the various credit clients. The economic farm unit is extremely difficult to define, but it must be defined if the scale of credit made available is to be determined. In Canada there is a deplorable lack of research on this question. As a result the scale of credit provided in most legislation is based on *ad hoc* judgment plus the usual dose of political acumen. In the Saskatchewan Commission study referred to previously, investment required to yield a modest $3,000 net income (including subsistence) was estimated conservatively at $20,000 in terms of 1950 conditions. In 1960, the minimum investment required would be close to $35,000.

Turning from the scale of credit to the potential consumers of credit, we find a number of characteristics which should condition the credit programme. Given objectives of maximizing labour productivity and of selecting a limited number from the total agricultural population, the programme must emphasize competence in farming as a prime criterion. Thus, the traditional emphasis on *existing* security must be discarded in favour of *potential* security flowing from a combination of the borrower's competence and the resources which credit creates. A credit programme should provide: an adequate level of resources capable of being transformed rapidly by a competent farmer into a reasonable level of living; technical advice and, if necessary, supervision which will help in the

[19]W. E. Haviland, "The Family Farm in Quebec: An Economic or Sociological Unit?" *Canadian Journal of Agricultural Economics*, vol. 5, no. 2, 1957, pp. 83–4.
[20]Greater public participation in the ownership and renting of land is another important and under-utilized technique for adequate resource allocation.

application of credit and thus benefit both the borrower and the lending agency; and a repayment schedule geared to the income potential of the credit provided and to the income flow. There should be less adherence to a dogma of ten-, fifteen- or twenty-year repayment period if the achievement of the programme requires forty years. Consideration should be given to utilizing a perpetual mortgage as an alternative to ownership. "This would give more flexibility to providing the necessary working capital particularly in the earlier years of the farmer's career. Present conditions too often require a schedule of forced savings for land purchase that impedes resource allocation in agriculture."[21]

Present programmes have incorporated provisions which partially meet the listed requirements; none of them really does the job effectively. Perhaps the best example is the Veterans Land Act, but it falls down on one aspect — the level of resources made available. Nevertheless, VLA introduced adequate selection, advice, supervision, and flexible repayments — techniques which are still absent from most provincial programmes. Ontario, for example, provides advisory services, but through the agricultural representative. He, in most cases, is too busy and lacks the specialization to perform the task adequately.

Perhaps the best example of a credit programme which meets the suggested provisions is the Farmers Home Administration in the United States. There the size of the loan is based on need and the personal integrity of the borrower rather than on the amount of security available. For land, loans are made up to 100 per cent of the normal productive ability of the farms when fully developed. Supervision and guidance are applied where necessary.

Re-establishment. The second broad avenue which must be travelled on the road to agricultural adjustment is outside agriculture. Since it is desirable to provide real choices for redundant farmers outside of agriculture, public policy must be focused on non-farm opportunities. It must focus, not narrowly on the prime requirement, job opportunities,[22] but on the whole range of problems which relate to human mobility and social adjustment. It must therefore be based on an understanding of the entire complex process and a realistic development of alternatives.

Such a programme should not be construed as having narrow applicability. Agriculture and rural life do have some important unique characteristics, but the broad problems of labour adjustment and mobility are general in character. They are relevant to labour in agriculture, labour in the textile industry, and labour in the railway industry. In each of these cases, and others, the public and individual interest may be best served, not by callous ejection of people who become redundant, but by

[21]Kristjanson, "Maintaining Family Farming as an Objective."
[22]Full employment, essential to this process, remains a politically proclaimed but unattained goal in Canada.

public policies which comprehend the necessity for adjustment and ensure serious attention to the twin goals of public and individual welfare.

The present process is reasonably well known. It has been illustrated vividly by the Arrow aircraft incident, the Elliot Lake problem, the plight of the Maritimes. These all dramatize a much more widespread if not widely publicized situation. For the farmer, adjustment is not a new experience, but it has become much more common in recent decades. In most cases he departs from agriculture with great reluctance, and not only because he is leaving a familiar, if unsatisfactory, environment. To a large extent reluctance is based on insecurity. Typically, the farmer who leaves agriculture, whether young or old, is in the low-income group. He is trained for little except farming and probably ended his schooling early. Again, typically, he moves to the bottom rung in the labour market as an unskilled labourer or a helper. In a society which has provided few amenities such as housing for low-income groups, the farm expatriate often winds up in an urban slum far less satisfying than his inadequate rural home. In addition to these crucial economic and social deficiencies, he faces the problems associated with a shift from a rural community to an urban milieu.

But all of these problems can be alleviated by a specific public policy. Thus, generous provision could be made for training movers, for specific rehabilitation, for moving grants and loans, and for careful job counselling. Policies could be devised for minimizing shifts by developing alternative full- or part-time employment in rural areas, as is now being done in the United States. Urban housing designed to ensure the needs of both a mobile and a permanent population is an essential element in a labour adjustment programme. Public policy has neglected this kind of emphasis in its housing programme.

The process of increasing farm productivity through reducing the labour component and providing more resources per farmer is postulated as the main solution to the problem of low productivity. Two other related possibilities deserve comment.

Co-operative farming. Labour productivity can undoubtedly be improved through joint use of modern large-scale equipment and through specialized use of individual skills in a joint farming organization. Co-operative forms of farming have demonstrated their economic and social effectiveness in other parts of the world. Their formal application has been extremely limited in Canada despite the fact that rural areas have a lengthy tradition of informal co-operation. In form, co-operative use of machinery and fully fledged co-operative farms are consistent with the objectives of socialists. There is no denying that their widespread growth from a base of "independent" single family type of agriculture is difficult to achieve. Not only is it difficult for the individual to adjust to sharing resources and decision-making and to living in a close settlement, but such groupings find themselves isolated and surrounded by the traditional type of rural environment.[23]

Nevertheless, the potential economic and social benefits are impressive. Production co-operatives can take advantage of the economies of large-scale production and member specialization to provide enviable levels of living of its members — levels far greater than each member could obtain using his resources as an individual farmer. Social and service potentials stemming from close settlement are enhanced in a farm co-operative. For those interested in an efficient agriculture and a maximum rural population, widespread co-operative farming offers a solution consistent with a goal of increased farm labour productivity.

Resource development. On a somewhat different plane, and assuming no concomitant rise in population, another important way of increasing resources per unit of labour in agriculture is to add new resources. This possibility is tied firmly to other considerations largely related to the size and composition of our demand for food. Some salient points may be sketched here:

1. The demand for food includes domestic and foreign elements. The former is far more subject to Canadian discretionary action than the latter; with respect to foreign markets there is little we can do to make demand more effective. Within Canada, however, it is possible to have school lunch programmes or food distribution schemes and to exercise controls over the total food market to prevent disruption. This difference in foreign and domestic conditions suggests that a projection of demand in domestic terms can be based on an optimum level of food consumption. However, foreign demand must be predicated, not on known food needs, but rather on market experience. None of this means that we reject the problem of world malnutrition and hunger. It suggests that other developments need to take place before we can assume a widening demand for food exports, the prime development being economic growth within underdeveloped countries.

2. Evidence suggests that there are dietary gaps in Canada today. These gaps are determined by income deficiencies in our society and by inadequate knowledge of nutrition. Unfortunately current data on these aspects are not available for Canada. In the United States, where consumption characteristics are similar, public policies have been in effect for many years to provide school lunches and to redistribute food to low income groups. There can be little doubt that the problem exists in Canada and that remedial action would have the effect of changing the

[23]For an excellent analysis see H. Cooperstock, "Report to the Saskatchewan Federation of Production Co-operatives," Saskatchewan Department of Co-operation and Co-operative Development, March, 1960 (mimeo).

composition of consumption and output and increasing their scale even with existing population.

3. Population is increasing at a fairly rapid rate in Canada, and projections by the Gordon Commission and other groups suggest a continued expansion. Similarly it is expected that disposable income will increase. These two factors will provide the nutritional and economic base for an expansion of total output and a change in the composition of food consumption. The latter will occur because of the well-established shift as income rises from grains and potatoes to meats, fruits, and vegetables. The estimates of the Gordon Commission are given in Table VIII. It should be stressed that any improvement in income distribution will accentuate these trends, as will deliberate public programmes designed to improve nutritional levels.

TABLE VIII

TOTAL CONSUMPTION OF MAJOR FOOD PRODUCTS
(1951–55 = 100)

	Cereals	Potatoes	Fruits	Vegetables	Red meats	Eggs
1951–55	100	100	100	100	100	100
1965	122	119	138	134	140	143
1980	140	134	237	193	218	231

SOURCE: RC on Canada's Economic Prospects, *Final Report*, p. 164.

When these aspects of existing and projected food needs are translated into supply requirements it is clear that output must rise through an increase in land resources and/or an intensification in present land use. Any additional demand made effective through international economic development will accentuate this rise in output.

There are therefore important possibilities for increasing productivity based on rising demand for food. But the gains in productivity and overall national welfare will depend on how the expansion in output is attained. The issue is not posed in terms of physical possibilities. We can attain physical production goals through bringing new land into production by clearing and breaking forested soils, by draining large areas, or by intensifying use through irrigation, fertilization or improved seeds and breeds. The real problem is to translate the physical production possibilities into forms of production most desirable economically and socially.

Historically, resource development in agriculture has in many instances not been related primarily to production goals. One can point to recent colonization and settlement programmes which were and still are based on such goals as "back-to-the-land" resettlement of veterans and rehabilitation of farmers from submarginal land. One can also find many irrigation and drainage programmes designed to stabilize and diversify farming or to resettle farmers from drought-ridden areas.

This is not to say that such developments have failed to improve productivity, but the validity of the development framework is questionable. For example, the "back-to-the-land" movement in Quebec was based firmly on an effort to maintain the romantic image of traditional rural Quebec — an image which was tied to social, ethnic and religious factors. But this image now has practically no reflection in reality. The real trends in Quebec are towards the mechanization of agriculture, a decline in farm population, and growth in urbanization. A resource development policy which does not comprehend this fundamental adjustment cannot succeed any more than a policy which is unrelated to the over-all demand for food. Similarly, settlement schemes in other provinces which are not sensitive to alternative urban opportunities will encounter difficulties. In most cases such schemes have required a degree of sacrifice on the part of settlers in terms of hard work and limited rewards which makes settlement relatively unattractive.

Resource development as a whole requires a national framework based on demand possibilities and an appraisal of alternative national production possibilities. Under existing constitutional arrangements a joint federal-provincial approach seems most feasible. At present the main barrier to the development of stable federal-provincial relationships has been the reluctance of the federal government to assume even partial responsibility for resource development as a national policy. This is not to say that the federal government has been inactive. Through the PFRA, MMRA, and Eastern Rockies Forest Conservation Board a number of *ad hoc* and often inconsistent policies have evolved. These policies contain a wide range of degrees of federal participation — financial, developmental and administrative.

What is needed now is a national policy and a national agency which could provide a consistent programme in and for all provinces. Such a programme would be predicated on a national concept of development and implemented with a minimum of inconsistency with national goals. A standardized relationship could be developed between the provinces and the federal government encompassing such matters as planning, development, settlement, and cost-sharing.

Of particular importance in any resource development programme is the problem of river basins. The main issue is the maximization of benefits from resources of such basins taken as a whole. As stated by the Royal Commission on the South Saskatchewan River Project: "The Commission finds that the future demand for water for irrigation could be such as to exhaust the available flow . . . and recommends, therefore, that without delay a comprehensive, long-range program be developed that would result, over the years, in the most beneficial use being made in the interests of the people of Canada of the waters of the Saskatchewan River from its head waters to the sea." The Commission went on to suggest: "The Government of Canada make available appropriate administrative and other machinery for collecting and correlating relevant data for making the required studies and for developing and coordinating a basin program."[24]

No doubt constitutional problems must be faced in securing integrated development of river basins. It appears, on the basis of the constitutional division of powers, that the federal government has no jurisdiction over interprovincial streams except for special circumstances, such as navigation or "works to the general advantage of Canada." If this is a real block, it may be overcome by agreement between the provinces and federal government or possibly by constitutional amendment. The fact remains, however, that the federal government has major discretion over development in Canada at any given time, because its financial participation is essential.

To review the argument of this subsection: mainly because of improved technology, agriculture today has too many farm people combined with too few resources per farmer. The remedy — and the basic step in improving labour productivity — lies in (1) creating conditions for increasing the rate of depopulation in agriculture and (2) readjusting resources within agriculture.

Despite popular conceptions to the contrary, there is evidence that a deliberate policy of agricultural depopulation would be welcomed by farm people provided alternative employment were attractive and the adjustment process reasonable.

Readjusting resources within agriculture can be accomplished mainly through appropriate, supervised credit programmes. Rational depopulation implies the specific focus of public policy on a wide front: full employment, job training and counselling, rehabilitation grants and loans, appropriate urban housing and, perhaps, development of non-farm employment opportunities in rural areas. Similar measures are appropriate — not only for farm workers — but also for re-establishing redundant workers of all kinds.

Co-operative farming offers the opportunity to combine the goals of efficient farming and the maintenance of a maximum rural population. Widespread acceptance of the co-operative farm, however, is beset by many difficulties.

In the light of increasing and changing domestic food demand, the development of new agricultural resources offers important possibilities for increasing productivity. What is required here is a national development framework based on national planning and carried out by federal-provincial co-operation.

[24]Royal Commission on the South Saskatchewan River Project, *Report* (Ottawa, 1952), part I, pp. 7–8.

THE FARMER AND THE MARKET PLACE

Apart from such aspects of the market place as the exploitation with which the farmer has to contend, his greatest difficulty lies within the farm industry itself. For agriculture has been and will probably remain an atomistic industry containing thousands of small firms that not only have no individual effects on the market but find it exceedingly difficult to organize effectively. Superimposed on this condition, the unpredictable nature of production further complicates the rationalization of the farm economy. Finally, many sectors of agriculture depend on external markets for sales, and this plunges agriculture into the vast complexities of international political and economic relations.

For these reasons it can be argued that improvements in productivity have not resulted in the attainment of farm income objectives. Because agriculture is so exposed in the market place, gains in productivity are passed quickly on to other elements in the marketing network, and agriculture operates more or less at a cost-of-production level with minimum returns to the producer. As pointed out so clearly by the Stewart Commission on Price Spreads, in the past decade food processors have been in the enviable position of forcing lower prices on the farmer and higher prices on the consumer. And so the farmer, for his part, has been engaged historically in a struggle to develop market power either through industry devices or government intervention.

Farmers and governments have taken two main kinds of action to contend with farm problems in the market place. First, farmers have attempted to organize in order to confront the market as one large force rather than thousands of small ones. This has taken many forms. Second, governments have intervened either to fortify farmers' group strength or to substitute the direct power of the state. Again, such intervention has taken many forms.

Market Power

Ideally, the co-operative movement taken as a whole is capable of developing market power both as a bargaining device and as a means of increasing marketing efficiency. And, on the production side, farmers have organized a very wide range of marketing co-operatives with these ends in view. These devices have enjoyed considerable success to rationalize marketing in terms of quality, stable flow of commodities, and efficient handling. Their accomplishments include, in varying degree, an expansion of markets, a reduction of the impact of seasonal fluctuations and a reduction of handling costs. Through such advances marketing co-operatives have bolstered and, in some measure, stabilized farm income.

But as bargaining agencies in the market place co-operatives have, almost without exception, been quite unsuccessful. At no time has the co-operative form developed enough member support to be able to command enough product consistently to obtain real market power. The kind of frustration which co-operatives have faced is illustrated by this description of efforts in British Columbia thirty years ago:

> In the Okanagan Valley the fruit growers turned to central marketing only after many other selling devices had been found wanting. Co-operatives were formed and re-formed. Co-operatives were strengthened by buying out some of the independent shippers and hiring their ablest personnel. Associations were formed based on solemn contracts. Shippers cartels were organized to set and maintain prices. All manner of free-will schemes were tried and failed.
>
> In the end one grower summed up the general feeling as follows: "The silly farce of attempting voluntary control must stop. We must make it impossible for the self-destroying competition among growers to continue. We must demand from our government compulsory legislation with real teeth in it to prevent the wasteful conditions that are killing the industry.[25]

The almost universal shortcomings of co-operation as a form of marketing power cannot necessarily be ascribed to co-operation *per se*. Rather it lies in the nature of the farm industry itself with its many unspecialized, limited-output producers who have neither the economic or social incentives nor the discipline to organize voluntarily and remain organized. In sharp and ironical contrast, disciplined voluntarism is carried out far more effectively in those large industries which exploit producers and consumers.

Frustration with co-operative effort has led to the utilization of powers of the state provincially and federally. There is little doubt that this leads to a market power of two main forms: monopoly bargaining power and outright price-fixing power.

Monopoly bargaining power can be of two sorts: producer power supported by and sanctioned by the power of the state; and state power exercised directly by the state — in other words, the familiar producer marketing board and the government marketing board. Over the past forty years there has been a rapid development of producer boards under provincial legislation and more recently by extension of federal powers to provincially organized boards. Largely as a result of wide differences in conditions, provincial producers boards across Canada differ widely in their form and function. In the West and Maritimes a relatively full range of controls has been provided in legislation. In the central provinces legislation was relatively "mild" in form. In fact, activities in Quebec are based largely on co-operative foundations. More recently, the central provinces have moved in the direction of far more

[25]R. J. Leslie, "Marketing Through Boards," *Proceedings of the Canadian Agricultural Economics Society*, 1950, p. 101.

stringent controls. In Ontario, furthermore, a very recent development has been the introduction of more direct government activity on producer boards.

Producer boards have achieved notable success in some areas under certain conditions. But the goal of significant market power is far from being achieved generally, even through this powerful device. What are its limitations? (a) Producer boards organized provincially rarely command their relevant markets. They either must sell extra-provincially where they may have limited control because producers from other areas compete, or they must face competition from imports which they cannot control. (b) To overcome these disabilities boards can avail themselves of federal legislation. However, in order to do this effectively provincial legislation must be made identical with respect to strategic powers, and this is not achieved easily in the face of the bewildering array of provincial laws now in effect. Perhaps more fundamentally, producers in certain provinces may well enjoy the protection of their sovereignty which would be given up in an interprovincial system. (c) Processors of some farm commodities may frustrate the efforts of producers to attain market power by developing their own sources of supply which are not subject to marketing controls. This is done through the now familiar process of vertical integration.

Apart from these basic limitations, the question of public welfare might well be raised. Is it in the public interest to facilitate the development of a farm producers' power bloc in our society? The proposition that producers are exploited in the market place is well established. But is the cure producer power? In the long run it may not be necessary to make a conscious decision since it is doubtful that producers will achieve their goals through this device. The historical drift is towards government rather than producer boards, as exemplified by the process of nationalization of grain marketing.

This is not to deny the improvements achieved by the wide range of devices reviewed, from the co-operative to the central selling agency. With respect to farm income, improvements flow from marketing economies, quality grading, and seasonal stabilization. Furthermore, co-operatives and boards have provided an important educational medium for the achievement of objectives beyond the scope of the devices themselves. They have served finally as necessary and unavoidable steps towards wider goals and, as such, have been important organizational media for farmers.

In broad terms the whole issue of market power has shifted from the bargaining area to direct price intervention through price support policies. Here the ultimate discretion lies not with producers *per se* but with Parliament. In many ways this has been the fundamental ultimate concern of farmers. It appears to lie behind the organization of co-operatives and marketing boards. These have not proven wholly effective because of organizational problems and because of the nature of supply and demand for given products. Therefore, farmers have continued to press for price support, the obvious form of effective intervention.

Costs

Before examining commodity price supports let us turn briefly to the input side of agriculture. This is the familiar cost side of the price-cost squeeze. Although a prominent issue historically, the possibilities for action on the cost side have not received as much attention as commodity prices. And yet we find here arrayed forces which in some respects are more powerful in exploitative potential. As the mechanical revolution has overrun agriculture, cash outlays have risen and have been built into the farm budget. The farmer has less and less opportunity to control cash costs by substituting labour for machines and by growing feed for horse labour. Today the farmer must contend with the vast and highly organized industrial complex which provides him with his means of production. What does he find? He finds what most consumers find — few companies, no price competition, administered prices, "hidden persuasion," prices which are flexible upward but rarely downward, credit sales at exorbitant interest costs.

It is impossible to review here every component of farm costs, but it may be useful to examine briefly the field of farm machinery and its allied costs as a representative case. The importance of farm machinery may be gauged by its growth as an element in farm capital and farm costs. In 1901, for example, machinery capital was only 6 per cent of total farm capital in Canada. In 1951, it was 20 per cent of total capital. Every region shared in this development although there have been important variations. In 1951, the percentage in the Atlantic region was 16.8, while in the prairie region it was 24.4.

Machinery costs in Canada in 1957, exclusive of depreciation, were 30 per cent of total operating costs. In Saskatchewan, machinery costs were almost 50 per cent of total costs. The farmer is now vitally concerned with the price and quality of farm machinery and every indication points to an increased concern as mechanization continues. His concern is not alleviated by the nature of his supplier, the farm machinery industry. The monopolistic or oligopolistic character of this industry has been described on a number of occasions by various bodies of public inquiry. The virtually complete absence of price competition among the few firms in the industry is well documented. As pointed out by Phillips, the degree of inter-firm control in the implement industry is being extended: "The experience of the implement industry during the depression . . . may have prepared the way for the inclusion of distribution and credit, along with price, in quasi-agreements within the industry. In a sense, the change in distribution in 1945 might be interpreted as a step in this direction."[26]

Serious as industry administered prices are, other characteristics reinforce the impact of this attribute. Foremost among these is the duplication of major lines of equipment which, technically, are virtually indistinguishable from one company to the next. There are of course exceptions, but there is little basic justification, for instance, for the existence of some seventy distinctive sizes, types, and makes of tractors when ten or twelve would be ample for farm needs. Flowing from such duplication are heavy costs of selling and distributing new machines, and perhaps even heavier costs of repair parts and servicing associated with individual types.

We have, then, in the farm implement industry an excellent example of mature capitalism which has enough market power to force its own deficiencies on the mass of farmers through the existing market mechanism. Ironically, an important public programme, the Farm Improvement Loans Act, has made it easier for farmers to participate in its relationship with the implement industry without reducing the degree of exploitation significantly. Public objectives should be the rationalization of the entire industry and the transfer of price administration powers from the private to the public sector.

There are examples throughout the farm supplies field of efforts to reduce exploitation. An outstanding example is in the fuel field. Here farmers on the prairies through co-operative organization have succeeded in modifying exploitation. They have done so by building from very small beginnings a fuels enterprise which now extends from the exploration and production of crude oil to a modern refinery and a developed distribution system. They have succeeded in improving the real income of all users of fuels on the prairies directly through payment of dividends to members and indirectly by their effect on prices generally. It is significant that this co-operative development has proceeded with active assistance from government in the form of financial assistance and conscious concessions of proven oil properties. In somewhat similar fashion progress has been made with feeds and fertilizers on a national scale.

Ventures into farm implements have been far less successful. Perhaps the major problem has been failure to acquire plant. A secondary problem has been inability to compete with the highly developed and extravagant system of distribution in the industry generally.

Nationalization would appear to be a worthwhile alternative technique in the case of farm implements. The twin objectives of rationalization and market control could be achieved far more effectively with public

26J. W. G. Phillips, *The Agricultural Implement Industry in Canada* (Toronto, 1956), p. 164.

ownership than with co-operative ownership. Under national ownership standardization of an adequate range of equipment would lead directly to economies in production, distribution and maintenance of equipment. The public would assume a direct responsibility for the cost conditions in the farm industry. With basic nationalization it would be possible to initiate and develop a growing role for co-operative activity in the implement industry.

Price Policy

The destruction of the free market has evaded farmers for many decades. That this is the ultimate objective is difficult to deny. That it has not been achieved is fundamentally due to the weakness of farmers as an economic and political force, the inappropriateness of many farmer-sponsored policies and the powerful forces that defend the status quo. It is quite clear, in 1961, that farmers have a long way to travel before they attain their price policy objectives. The Royal Commission on Price Spreads of Food Products in its recent report pointed up the fundamental fact that the Canadian farmer in the post-war period has been unable and continues to be unable to benefit from his increase in productive efficiency. It revealed that between 1949 and 1958 real net operating income per farm as measured in 1957 dollars had actually declined by $251 per farm, or almost 8 per cent.[27] Taking the entire period from 1949 to 1958, income per farm in real terms in Canada declined at an annual average rate of 0.8 per cent while personal real income per capita for consumers generally rose by 2 per cent per year. As the Commission puts it, "The significant conclusion is that, in a period when real incomes generally were rising, farm real incomes were not."

Some argue that these observations are biased by the existence and inclusion of large numbers of non-commercial, subsistence and part-time farmers. However, in western Canada, the larger well-established commercial farmer is having his standard of living seriously affected and assistance is being sought not for the average (lower income) farmers but the *modal* or typical (higher income) farmer. These comments mean, in no uncertain terms, that farm policy has in fact failed on many fronts in its most fundamental task, the maintenance of adequate farm income.

The role of price in farm policy is still problematical. But until public policy develops in the comprehensive fashion suggested previously and becomes obviously reassuring to farmers, there is little point in assailing their central concern with prices. Insistence on parity prices (that is, output prices that are tied to input prices) may well be the political road to more satisfactory approaches, as it has been, in part, in the United States.

[27]*Report* (Ottawa, 1960), vol. II, p. 16.

A price support programme is important first because it fixes public responsibility for a critical factor in income determination and distribution. But, given this, price support must be recognized for what it is and what it can and cannot do. Let us take four commonly accepted goals for a price support programme and evaluate the possibilities of a pricing programme by itself to attain such goals. A price support programme should: (1) stabilize prices both seasonally and from year to year; (2) provide direction to producers in their production planning, that is, by reflecting demand; (3) provide a return which is based on a reasonable balance between productivity and income goals; (4) ensure an optimum distribution of food without creating maldistribution of income.

Clearly goal (1) is attainable by any variety of price support system. Goal (2), on the other hand, cannot be attained by price policy alone, although it will be quite effective in some cases. The limitations arise because of prediction problems and commodity production characteristics as well as the organization of agriculture itself.

The first requirement of direction is obviously knowledge of demand conditions or demand objectives. For some commodities, based on short production periods and limited investment in plant, forward pricing can be carried out with confidence. Where production periods are longer, for example, with cattle or orchards, and where decisions to produce involve significant long-term capital investment, then demand predictions must be long-run in nature. Here the possibility of error in prediction and price-setting becomes significant. However, if the price-directing agency can depend on a generally stable price situation on the demand side and can arm itself with suitable offsetting devices, such as storage, then the prediction problem may not be too limiting. To be workable, then, a forward pricing system needs technical accuracy in prediction, an economy which has reasonable stability, and offsets to dampen the effects of error.

A second requirement is that the target of price information be receptive, that is react in the desired manner. Agriculture rarely meets these criteria. Because there are so many producers a "right" response individually is invariably an extreme response in the aggregate. (This is compounded by the insensitiveness of nature to price.) This means that only in rare cases is a price signal adequate. Rather it must be reinforced by wide information on production targets, quotas and storage. In certain branches of agriculture where concentration has taken place, price by itself may be more effective. This occurs because the industry is more "commercialized," perhaps "integrated," and generally "rationalized."

There are other factors. One of these is the fixed nature of many agricultural enterprises militating against easy shifts suggested by price manipulation. On the prairies, farmers can and do shift from one grain to another but a shift into livestock is not accomplished with ease. Such a shift requires resources such as water, heavy investments in buildings, and results in redundancy of investment in grain farming equipment. In Ontario and British Columbia shifting from one crop to another in orchards is extremely difficult. Admittedly many shifts are not short-run and resources do become more flexible given the right incentives. But here other techniques such as farm credit, public resource development and grants are probably more effective than price. Where price is used it should be a secure commitment and should be accompanied by other programmes.

Another factor is the unresponsiveness of many individual farmers for a variety of reasons. Management is one of these. With hundreds of thousands of managers involved, improvement of skills and changes of habits are extremely difficult undertakings. Poor management, for one thing, will mean misinterpreting and ignoring price movements. Lack of resources on many individual farms is another reason. The farmer may interpret prices correctly and may desire to make the "right" adjustment, but he may have no means other than his own management skills.

With reference to goal (2) then, price by itself cannot be entrusted with the task of directing production, the elegance of the classical position notwithstanding. This does not mean that price should be abandoned as a directive instrument. But it should be used in conjunction with the many techniques sketched above.

In the case of goal (3) the ranges of income and productivity in agriculture are so great that no single average price support can strike a significant balance between productivity and income goals. Perhaps the best that can be accomplished with this goal is to base supports on the budget of a farm of desired scale and productivity, by type of farm and region. That is, society would be prepared to ensure through prices an adequate income for an acceptable degree of productivity. Such support could be limited in such a way as to prevent undue gains by farms above the standard. But the problem of farms below standard cannot be solved by this kind of pricing system. Prices will be below the level required to provide them with socially acceptable incomes. And so the need for productivity adjustments becomes crucial and in a real sense more pressing than price supports.

Goal (4) brings us directly to the non-farm economy and really poses some requirements within an adequate price support policy. Parity pricing, to take one system of price supports, is not consistent with the goal since it obliges all consumers to pay higher prices for food than they would pay "normally," that is, when parity prices are above market prices. The result, in crude terms, is either a reduction in food consumption or a reduction in other expenditures. Clearly, for the low-income consumer this is a regressive step which is aggravated where the result is a transfer of income from a low-income consumer to a high-income farmer.

In essence, this is why, first, price supports should be of the deficiency payment variety. With deficiency payments, prices to the consumer are "free" within the conditions of the consumer market. Prices to the farmer are established on the basis of goals (1) and (3) and the difference between these two prices is paid directly to farmers. In this form price supports are producers' subsidies, but consumers' subsidies could be an acceptable variant.

Second, price supports should be administered so as to prevent income redistribution which is regressive, that is, tending to inequality. The subsidy involved should not result in income transfers from low to high income groups. It may be possible to design a support system which will pay a higher subsidy (price) to a low-income farmer than a high-income farmer but unless it were done very crudely it would be an administrative monster. The most feasible approach would be to limit support to a reasonable level of output per farm.

We can now pull together elements of a price support programme suggested in the preceding paragraphs, and add some further needed aspects. The programme is based on a public responsibility for farm prices. It is a programme which is complementary to a wide range of programmes reviewed previously.

It is suggested here that prices be established annually with productivity, income and costs as factors. If this can be done successfully then price support will not only provide stability and acceptable income but also identify productivity targets. Such support will be based on a hypothetical standard farm unit for each particular product and will allow for regional differences. On the basis of existing cost conditions for such a farm and planned output, price supports will be set on the basis of a desired level of farm income. When necessary and if effective, the levels of support can be adjusted to provide guides for production. This may involve some long-run guarantees. Deficiency payments should be used and support per farm restricted to a defined level of output.

Supports should be applied for commodities consumed domestically and internationally. This may involve troublesome multi-pricing systems in the case of export commodities, but the less desirable alternative is to discriminate against large sectors of agriculture. The programme should contemplate use of industry-wide quotas, but should emphasize consumption programmes.

With such a programme of price supports the problems of farm income, production and consumption may be alleviated. However, it is possible that either producer or consumer subsidies may be captured by the food processor and distributor or the farm implement manufacturer or others. Certainly price support does nothing to diminish their market power and ability to exploit both producer and consumer. In the end, then, price support, as an income device, no matter how well designed, may benefit the producer less than his opposites in the market unless the conditions of the market itself are changed.

We can conclude this section then by noting that, confronted by well disciplined and powerful market forces on both the farm supply and farm marketing sides of his operation, the Canadian farmer has been and is subject to severe exploitation. He has sought to counteract these pressures through the building of co-operative organizations and through the establishment of producer and government marketing boards. Neither co-operatives nor producer boards have been sufficiently effective in a bargaining sense to achieve the requisite power in the market. Even if such power were attained by producer boards, it is doubtful that the public interest would be served.

Direct public intervention in terms of price supports is an essential requirement, primarily because it fixes public responsibility with respect to one critical factor in achieving farm income objectives. But its limitations must be recognized and its implementation geared to public as well as industry goals. Further, its objectives can be assured only if integrated with action on a broad front to achieve the production, productivity and stabilization goals set forth earlier.

RURAL SERVICES AND THE RURAL COMMUNITY

To this point we have been discussing adjustments which are largely relevant to the individual farm family as an economic unit. If all the programmes are implemented we may still be some distance from the ultimate goal of equality. We can get closer by applying public programmes which directly equalize opportunities and level of living. This is of critical importance,[28] because not only are incomes lower in the rural scene, but costs of service are higher. Thus, even if incomes were on a par with urban incomes, services might continue to lag.

It is often argued that to attempt farm adjustment on the one hand and to provide rural services on the other is inconsistent, since the latter will tend only to immobilize farm people; if this takes place general national growth goals are threatened. The argument is weak on several counts. First, adjustment may well be facilitated by provision of better services, such as education and provision for the aged. Second, even with recent improvements in rural services the rate of depopulation has been impressive. Third, in many parts of Canada rural services are becoming increasingly services for farmers and also for non-farmers who are establishing rural residence. Fourth, if the argument is ultimately a choice between economic growth and welfare, then surely welfare deserves a higher priority.

[28]Unfortunately space limitations dictate a much too sketchy, categorical discussion here.

The development of equitable rural services is resolved in many minds simply by a transfer of income through established government channels. This is a vast oversimplification of the nature of the problem and its treatment. Redistribution is vital, but so are government and administration for planning, choosing and implementing rural services. All of this is based on an effective and continuous understanding of the historic, present and potential rural environment. It is based also on consideration of the place of our political institutions in the provision of services.

An objective observer would be appalled by the vast lag between rural change in farming, in family and community life and in the institutions which provide services. In rare instances institutional adjustment has kept pace, but in general there has been a deplorable inertia.

The main implication for most of Canada has been an unmistakable erosion of rural local government with a commensurate transfer of responsibilities to provincial governments and an increase in provincial control over local government. This is best described by the term "drift" since it is rarely planned and in many cases rarely recognized. What we are left with are anachronistic local institutions with little real responsibility.

The first requirement is to arrive at a clear decision to reconstruct an effective local government based on broadly political grounds and on the grounds of providing effective services. Rural local government in the context of the modern and anticipated environment requires areal and fiscal expansion, geographic conformity with planning and service requirements, integration of interdependent jurisdictions into multi-purpose forms, integration between increasingly interdependent rural and urban areas, professionalization of administration and sharper separation of policy and administration, reform of the tax base, and greater contributions from senior governments on a basis of equalized grants.[29] Nothing less than this sort of comprehensive reconstruction will provide for (a) meaningful local government as a viable political institution, and (b) effective rural services.

Given such reorganization it will be possible for local governments to begin the task of planning and implementing services which are now of a dangerously low order. It will also be possible to begin to reverse the tendency of provincial governments to absorb more and more local responsibilities. Where this kind of adjustment in local government has taken place, as it has, for example, in Alberta and in the school system in Saskatchewan, the above possibilities are well on their way to realization. Programmes are being carried out consistent with the needs of the environment and provincial controls have relaxed.

[29]See also Jean-Marie Martin, "The Socio-Economic Implications of Extensive Consolidation of Small Farms Into Efficient Family Farm Units" (Laval University, 1957), (mimeo), pp. 16–21.

The rural community has been affected by the same forces that have weakened its formal institutions of local government. The traditional informal organization based on the rural school, the rural church and the local baseball team is literally disintegrating. This is as true in Quebec as it is on the prairies.

Decisions to make economic adjustments are individual decisions, but many of the consequences are communal in impact. The baseball team cannot exist when one or two members leave, and baseball ceases to be a socializing factor in the community. The local gatherings in the school house or in the church can no longer retain community identification when the facilities close and relocate in a much larger community.

But the main difficulty is not the disappearance of old forms and old communities. The vital question is to constitute communities in keeping with the changed environment. Fundamentally it is a problem in community development predicated on the people themselves understanding the nature of the problem and organizing their resources to overcome it.

Community development is by now a familiar phrase. Typically, it is viewed primarily as an export commodity intended for the underdeveloped countries. It is, however, needed quite desperately here to perform a number of essential functions. First it is a process of research. Community change is extremely complex and requires our best efforts in the social sciences. Second, it is an educational process which equips people in a community with tools and techniques for analysing their own situation. Third, it is a training process for the development of local programmes of study and action and for extension activities in communities.

Saskatchewan is now pioneering community development as a systematic field of study and activity through its Center for Community Studies at the University of Saskatchewan.

Broadly conceived as an informal unit within which human beings interact, the community consumes the energies of thousands of leader-citizens and influences the investment of a large share of public and private funds. In this sense, it performs a major role as an informal planning and development influence. Witness what happens when schools are to be consolidated, hospitals relocated, roads rerouted, municipal government reorganized, churches merged, co-operatives re-grouped, railroad stations closed or industries located. Citizens respond to the challenge as they perceive it. They give of their leadership both in striving to maintain what *is,* and in absorbing, assessing and selecting or rejecting what *might be.*

There is, then, a special sense in which the influences of the larger national and world society cannot be separated from any consideration of local Saskatchewan communities as a resource capable of meaningful development. To the extent that the larger — or mass — society is dominated by influences which distort, limit, or destroy the informal responsiveness of citizens in local communities, there must follow greater recourse to the formal machinery of centralized decision and control. There is already substantial evidence of a growing incapacity to be even articulate about the role of voluntarism in our modern society. To choose only two examples, note the inability to come to grips with the care of the aged or with juvenile delinquency except in terms of institutional, formal, and often punitive measures. Traditionally, these have been problems which could be dealt with almost wholly on an informal, community basis.

It is a glaring fact that we are barely literate about this essential interplay between mass society and the informality of the small community. There is a commonly acknowledged drift in the direction of a centrally dominated and conforming society with its prospect of what C. Wright Mills has called "the cheerful robot." The survival of a democratic society guided by humanitarian principles demands an enlargement of our knowledge of the informal responsiveness of communities. Paradoxically, we know a great deal more — though not nearly enough — about the larger bureaucratic structures of government, industry and commerce than we do about communities. Social scientists in their pursuit of knowledge have tended to reflect the influence of dominant interests. The exception appears to be found in the work of the social anthropologists and rural sociologists. Anthropologists have concentrated upon the small primitive community; only in recent years has there been a turning to the study of modern communities. Rural sociologists have studied the small community but the analysis has been largely descriptive rather than dynamic.

There is, then, much to be gained by a renewal of interest in the study of small communities as a development resource. Such studies, however, must be more than merely descriptive. They must strive to understand communities in the midst of change; communities in a state of becoming. A central assumption is that the informal and many-dimensioned planning of the community environment is an organized process. If so, then it can not only be studied; it can also be taught and learned. This offers the very large promise that communities as a development resource can be made immensely more productive for human welfare.[30]

SUMMARY

No group in our society has more to gain from a socialist approach to social and economic problems than our farm group. For it is furthest from the goals of socialism on virtually every count and it now functions within a system which provides little hope for improvement. In the chapter a selective and systematic analysis of the most significant farm problems has been attempted. In this summary an effort will be made to focus on solutions (programmes) and to place these in order of priority.

It should be obvious by now that the analysis rejects rather completely the existing economic order as it impinges on agriculture. Given economic goals of equality and stability in level of living, stable and adequate production, and productivity equalization, it will be necessary to transform much of our existing economic structure and function.

The place to begin is at the vital centre of the existing system, the market, and the institutions which form it. Thus public responsibility for

[30]*Second Annual Report,* Center for Community Studies, University of Saskatchewan, 1959, pp. 1–2.

equalization of incomes via market intervention should rank high. This involves: (1) a system of price supports for all farm commodities which is consistent with income, consumption and productivity goals. In essence price supports would be predicated on a socially desirable income level for family farm units of reasonable productivity, having in mind such factors as type-of-farming differentials and the demand situation. Price supports would include provisions for deficiency payments. (2) consumption programmes based domestically on nutritional goals and internationally on humanitarian and developmental objectives; (3) an extended system of public marketing responsibility on domestic and external markets; (4) related co-operative activity which should be extended vertically and horizontally but should not be expected to play a significant bargaining role; (5) nationalization of farm supply industries, such as the farm implement industry, for the purpose of rationalizing the production and distribution of implements and machinery. Fertilizer and farm chemical industries should also be considered for nationalization.

In conjunction with market intervention as a means of attaining fundamental goals, increased emphasis should be placed on improved rural services based on a reconstruction of local government; greatly increased investment in social capital, and more expenditures on an equalized basis for the whole range of health, welfare and educational services.

The third group of programmes is directed towards another important means of attaining economic goals — productivity equalization. Essentially the task is to increase farm productivity by increasing resources per farm and per farm family and by encouraging the movement of population from agriculture to more productive occupations. This may be done by means of farm credit programmes whose objective is the rapid development of fully productive farm units based on modern technological standards but retaining essentially family operation and decision-making, and by the provision of real alternatives to farming through re-establishment grants, training, urban housing and full employment programmes. Similar, but more limited means for attaining our production goals are co-operative agricultural production developed with full appreciation of the difficulties involved in transforming the traditional type of farm organization; and public resource development programmes based largely on changing and expanding food consumption and implemented jointly by federal and provincial governments within the framework of a national resource development policy.

Fourth, a set of stabilization measures is required to ensure a desirable flow of food and to stabilize farm income. These include: (1) the use of forward pricing as part of the price support system wherever such prices can be predicted and where they can be effective at the farm level; (2) direct use of information, credit, resource development and grants to encourage shifts in production; (3) crop insurance, essentially as a federal programme; (4) public storage programmes as part of the price and marketing responsibility; and (5) broad national economic policies to ensure stable full employment and adequate income distribution.

Finally, a comprehensive approach to our rural society should provide for a systematic approach to the problems of community change and development.

Labour Unionism and Collective Bargaining

STUART JAMIESON

Trade unionism in Canada has undergone enormous changes in size, power and influence over the past twenty years, from the relatively small, divided and ineffectual organizations of the 1930's to the much larger, more unified and influential movement of today. The Canadian Labour Congress, as the main central labour federation in this country, is now taking active steps to found and support a democratic socialist political party, as has already been done in most nations in the British Commonwealth and in Western Europe.

These developments have given rise to rather ambivalent attitudes among wide sections of the public. While trade unionism is generally accepted today as an important, legitimate and permanent institution — a status that it never enjoyed in this country prior to the Second World War — its new importance and power have given rise to certain misgivings.

This ambivalence has arisen mainly, perhaps, from a rather over-idealized image of trade unionism in the past, based on a widespread sympathy for the underdog. Trade unionism was pictured as a movement of selfless, dedicated men, struggling, against the entrenched power of capitalist exploiters, to win a better life for a powerless and impoverished working class. Much of the moral drive and idealism of the socialist movement, and the wide sympathy and support that it won from the public, lay in the fact that it was closely identified with the struggles and objectives of organized labour. Under socialism, it was argued, social justice would ultimately be achieved and costly industrial conflict would disappear. Labour would, in effect, own and operate the means of production, at least indirectly, through its elected representatives in government. There would be no clash of interest between workers and employers, and trade unions would become primarily instruments of administration and co-operation for achieving maximum efficiency in industry, rather than agencies of opposition and conflict as under capitalism.

There is now a serious danger that wide sections of public opinion are swinging to the other extreme, from an over-simplified and somewhat romantic view of the nature and role of trade unions to an attitude of excessive cynicism or hostility. And, to the degree that democratic socialism is identified with trade unionism, it too may suffer in moral prestige and support from the public. The widespread publicity given to Senate Committee findings of dictatorship and corruption among certain unions in the United States has magnified such problems out of all proportion to their real importance and seriously weakened the prestige of the labour movement, in Canada as well as the United States. Perhaps more important in the aggregate is the fact that the trade union movement on the North American continent today no longer fits the traditional public image of the weak and exploited underdog. Organized labour in Canada has undergone tremendous expansion during the past twenty years, and union members have enjoyed far greater improvements in wages and working conditions than in any comparable period in the past. Total union membership now accounts for more than one-third of all non-agricultural workers in Canada, and is centred in the largest and most important industries and firms in the country. The influence of the labour movement extends far beyond the limits of its own membership. Representatives of all major political parties, in principle at least, uphold unionism and collective bargaining as the fairest and most efficient means for regulating relations between workers and employers. For more than a decade, the federal government, and the provincial governments with the exception of Newfoundland and Prince Edward Island, have had legislation prohibiting employers from engaging in various anti-union activities and requiring them to recognize and bargain with unions deemed to be properly representative of their employees. After decades of bitter and sometimes violent opposition, major employers in virtually all industries, whether from necessity or choice, have come to accept unions as an unavoidable part of the modern industrial scene.

The tremendous increase in size, militancy, bargaining power and legal status of trade unions during and since the Second World War has, however, tended to make them a main target of attack by groups who feel threatened. Spokesmen of major business organizations in particular have been prone to lay the blame for such complex economic problems as inflation, foreign trade deficits and unemployment largely on unions. By means of widespread publicity and propaganda, and by direct lobbying in the halls of government, they have been exerting growing pressure, in the United States and in Canada, for new legislative restrictions aimed at curbing the activities of unions and weakening their bargaining power and effectiveness.

In view of the confusing image that the trade union movement presents today, it is perhaps necessary to reassert some time-worn (but by no means universally accepted) platitudes. The survival and growth of a vigorous labour movement is vital for the preservation of democracy in modern industrial society. The role of trade unions is many-sided: economic, political, social and psychological. In the context of an industrial system dominated to an increasing degree by large and powerful aggregations of capital, unions are necessary as a "countervailing force" to protect workers from exploitation and to ensure them a fair share of the proceeds from industry. Fully as important is their role of protecting and enhancing the individual worker's sense of identity and self-respect against the arbitrary exercise of authority by management, and encouraging their greater participation in decision-making processes, in the large, centralized and increasingly complex bureaucratic structures characteristic of modern business concerns. And beyond this, representative organizations such as trade unions must engage in a broader and more vigorous programme of political action, if democratic government at all levels is not to be subverted and undermined by the growing wealth and power of major business concerns on the one hand, and the growing apathy of a bemused citizenry on the other.

In this perspective, the recent legislation in British Columbia, which prohibits an open and effective way for trade unions to contribute funds to a political party, must be seen as damaging to democracy as well as discriminatory.

It would be foolish, however, to dismiss all criticism of trade union policies as mere "anti-labour propaganda," or condemn any criticism as contributing to such propaganda, just because the most vocal and influential critics have been the spokesmen of prominent employers and business concerns. Any democratic government, socialist or otherwise, must or should devise its main policies primarily in terms of the needs and interests of the majority of citizens. The trade union movement in

Canada still represents only a minority of the adult working population in most provinces, and within its ranks there are numerous conflicts of interest and ideology. The organizational and bargaining policies of some unions have in the past created, and may continue in the future to create, economic and social problems that no government, whatever its political complexion, could rightfully ignore.

The major "labour problems" that have developed as a by-product of organized labour's rise to a position of power and influence will not automatically disappear with the election of a socialist government to office. A socialist administration should be dedicated to a system of economic and social planning along democratic lines, in which government assumes the main responsibility for maintaining full employment, stable but sustained economic growth, equitable distribution of income, and the socially most efficient use of resources. Such a government would be under a special obligation to ensure that no private group — whether business concern, trade or professional association, farm organization or trade union — could, in the pursuit of its own special interests, use its special bargaining power to disrupt the economy unduly, or to exploit other elements in the community.

It is necessary, therefore, to undertake as objective as possible an examination of the major policies of the unions, their impact on the Canadian economy since the war, and appropriate policies with regard to them in a planned economy. Any precise analysis along these lines is exceedingly difficult to undertake, however, owing to the serious lack of reliable knowledge about the effects which trade unionism and collective bargaining have had, and are likely to have, upon the national economy. Most public discussion of the subject takes place in a highly emotional atmosphere, and is usually based upon conjecture, hearsay or prejudice. Employers attack unions, and unions attack employers, neither group having much in the way of reliable factual evidence or scientific analysis on which to base its assertions. Very little research has been done in this field in Canada. There has been a great deal of research of one kind or another in the broad field of "industrial relations" in the United States since the War, but there is a notable lack of agreement among scholars and experts in that country about the nature and importance of the "labour problem," and the impact which unions generally have had upon various sectors of the national economy.

It is in this rather uncertain context, then, that we must attempt to discuss a number of questions that have been of major public concern and controversy in recent years, and that any government, socialist or otherwise, will be called upon to face. Among the more important of these are: the impact of strikes; the effects of various union restrictions on economic efficiency; the union wage policies and the distribution of income; the effects of union demands upon capital investment and the rate of economic growth; and the connection, if any, between collective bargaining and inflation.

None of these questions can be proved or answered conclusively, one way or the other. Nor can the specific impact of any one type of union policy be measured precisely enough to give definite answers, for in every case there are too many other variables involved. All that can be done here is to discuss each question in terms of the knowledge available.

STRIKES AND LOCKOUTS

No reliable method of analysis has as yet been devised by which to determine the economic gains or losses from strikes.[1] Wide sections of the public tend to look upon all strikes as being entirely *negative* in character, and causing wasteful and unnecessary losses of output and employment. What is often overlooked is the fact that strikes are only one, *overt* form of conflict between workers and employers. Industrial conflict, however, can and does frequently take a variety of *covert* forms, such as: tension, apathy and deterioration of morale or incentive; high sickness and accident rates; unconscious or deliberate carelessness and sabotage; excessive tardiness or absenteeism; high labour turnover; and so on. In the aggregate these can be far more damaging to the community and the nation, in decreased efficiency and output, than are strikes. Strikes, or merely awareness of them as a possibility, in most cases are necessary for reaching agreements by voluntary means, through collective bargaining, to settle outstanding issues and conflicts between workers and employers. The very knowledge of the hardships and losses in wages, output and profits that strikes entail in itself encourages unions and employers to be more moderate and realistic in their demands, more willing to compromise and make concessions. Severe legal restrictions on the right to strike or outright prohibition as advocated in some quarters would not, therefore, be likely to create better labour-employer relations, improve industrial efficiency, or increase output. If underlying conflicts cannot be settled by overt means, they are likely to remain in a covert or hidden, and probably more damaging, form.

This is not to say that all strikes are justified, by any means, particularly where a strike arises because one party insists upon making unreasonable demands, or offering unreasonable resistance to the reasonable demands of the other. Nor do all strikes necessarily settle conflicts, and even where they do, in some cases the cost of settlement to the community may be excessive in relation to the benefits gained by one or both parties to the conflict. But over the economy as a whole, in the long run, greater efficiency and output are probably achieved through relatively "free" collective bargaining, including freedom to carry out

[1]The term "strike" is used in the text to include disputes which technically may be in the category of "lockouts."

strikes and lockouts, than if governments were to sharply circumscribe or prohibit their use.

The widespread tendency to exaggerate the cost of strikes also arises from an improper "time perspective." It is unrealistic to compare a period of prosperity and a high incidence of strikes, such as we have had for several years, with a purely hypothetical situation of prosperity with a complete absence of strikes. It would be more realistic to compare the losses of output and income due to strikes during periods of prosperity with the much heavier losses of output and income during periods of depression and unemployment in which strikes are almost absent. Strikes to a large extent are a by-product of prosperity, and tend to be concentrated at or near the peak of a boom. Union bargaining power with employers is increased because of high demand and relatively scarce supplies of labour. At the same time, other accompaniments of boomtime prosperity — rising prices, large and widely publicized profits, spectacular "killings" in real estate and the stock market, conspicuous expenditures by the newly prosperous at all levels — create unrest and dissatisfaction among workers, who press their union leaders to demand large wage increases or other benefits from their employers.

Strikes are probably an unavoidable cost of prosperity and full employment. Accounting as they generally do for considerably less than 1 per cent of total man days of employment per annum, they are a small price for the nation to pay for the benefits received, certainly far smaller than the price involved if the alternatives were adopted: (i) unemployment severe enough to weaken union bargaining power and render strikes virtually impossible in every industry; or (ii) severe legal restrictions upon, or outright prohibition of, strikes, with the attendant deterioration of morale and consequent inefficiency.

JOB SECURITY AND RESTRICTIVE PRACTICES

Another question for which there is no answer that one can "prove" conclusively is the aggregate effect of various types of restrictions that unions place on employers in order to protect the bargaining power and security of their organization, and the job status and livelihoods of their members. Among such practices are, for instance: closed shop, union shop and preferential hiring clauses; seniority rules governing layoffs and rehiring, promotions and transfers; work-sharing arrangements during periods of slack employment; and restrictions, via "grievance procedure," on employers' freedom of action to discharge workers.

Such practices are widely alleged by prominent business spokesmen and others to have reduced the over-all level of productive efficiency, imposed unnecessarily high costs upon industry, and generally to have kept the national income below its potential maximum.

Quite different conclusions have been reached by some scholars who have made the most comprehensive studies of the whole question. The noted Harvard University economist, the late Sumner Slichter,[2] for instance, concluded that the impact of union pressure for higher wages and fringe benefits has been far greater than the impact of restrictive practices, and has had the net effect, in the aggregate, of raising rather than reducing productivity, by forcing management constantly to seek improvements in production methods by technological change and other means. His conclusions generally seem to be supported by the fact that, in the United States and in Canada during and since the war, the period of most rapid expansion in union membership and bargaining power has on the whole coincided with a period of most rapid technological change and rising productivity.

Many critics of union policies on job security are prone to reason, erroneously, from the particular to the general, from the part to the whole, that is, to analyse the national economy as a whole in terms of the individual plant or firm. From the point of view of the management of any *one* plant, *by itself* ("other things remaining the same") maximum economic efficiency might be achieved if the employer had a completely free hand to hire and fire, promote or transfer his employees, and "weed out" old, slow or inefficient workers whenever and wherever younger, faster and more efficient ones were available to replace them. From the point of view of the *economy as a whole*, however, the end result would be self-defeating and inefficient. First, one must take into account the adverse effects of anxiety and insecurity on the morale of workers, with consequent losses of productivity. More important is the fact that there just are not enough young, fast, trained and efficient workers in periods of full or nearly full employment to go around, and managements would be neutralizing one another's efforts (and bidding wages up rapidly) in competing for a limited labour supply in the market. Furthermore, unrestrained management policy of this kind would lead to a highly uneconomical and wasteful situation in which a relatively small number of employees were working feverishly producing at a high rate of output per man *employed,* while they, and the taxpaying public generally, were obliged to support an inordinately large number of workers who were deemed "substandard" according to managements' criteria, and therefore permanently displaced from employment. For this reason, Slichter and others argue that union policies on job security have in the aggregate encouraged a *larger* volume of output, employment and income over the economy as a whole, though at a lower average output and income per worker *employed* than would otherwise be the case: when the job tenure of the older or slower workers is protected,

[2]S. H. Slichter, *Union Policies and Industrial Management* (Washington, D.C., 1941); also his "Economic Effects of Unionism" in E. W. Bakke and C. Kerr, eds., *Unions, Management and the Public* (New York: Wiley, 1948).

and operations are kept to a pace that such workers can stand, a larger proportion of the adult population is kept at self-sustaining and productive employment, and for a longer average "working lifetime."

On this basis there are arguments to support the principle that, in a properly planned economy, major industries and firms should be required, by union agreement and/or by law, to employ representative cross-sections of the adult working population, including a share of the aged and handicapped of various kinds. There are obvious limits to which this principle could be carried before "diminishing returns" set in, of course, but it is an issue that merits a great deal of careful research and planning.

Some union practices, however, while understandable in terms of the interests and motivations of the workers that engage in them, are difficult or impossible to justify by any rational criteria of economic efficiency or social welfare. Among these are: "featherbedding" and "make-work" rules (which require employers to hire more workers than are, by normal or accepted standards, needed to produce a given output); deliberate restriction of output (for purposes other than protection against excessive fatigue, sickness or accident); and prohibition or sabotage of technological changes that would increase the productivity of labour and reduce production costs. Various examples come to mind: the union resistance to eliminating firemen from diesel locomotives on the railroads; the daily quotas enforced by bricklayers' unions; the attempt by painters' unions in some cities to prevent the use of spray guns; and so on.

Such practices are engaged in by only a small minority of unions, and their impact is very minor in the total picture. That this is so, however, in no way justifies them, for they involve the inequitable principle of privileged minorities imposing economic losses on the community for their own private advantage — a principle even less acceptable under socialism than under capitalism. And, with the current threat of large-scale displacement of labour under so-called automation, unions may come under strong pressure from their members to apply such restrictive practices on a far larger scale than ever before.

Workers, however, are unlikely to abandon such practices merely by being told repeatedly that they are immoral, unethical or uneconomical. Probably no one can be expected voluntarily to give up his livelihood on the grounds that his work is redundant and his skills obsolescent. A worker's job is analogous in some ways to an employer's capital. It represents an investment of time, money and energy over a period of several years. And, like capital equipment, in a dynamic economy of shifting markets and rapid technological changes it is always potentially vulnerable to displacement and premature obsolescence. Where workers are forced to bear most or all of the costs of technological change and displacement, they naturally have a strong inducement to protect themselves, where possible, by restrictive practices, even if these are damaging to the economy as a whole. If they are to be persuaded to abandon such practices it will be necessary to ensure them opportunities for getting other jobs of comparable pay or status.

This plan would involve more than just a programme of "full employment" over the economy as a whole. More specifically, it would require the provision of such benefits as layoff or severance pay, travel grants and retraining facilities, to enable displaced workers to take full advantage of other job opportunities. Logically, an industry or firm that stands to make substantial gains through adopting new machinery or new methods of production should be required, by law and/or by union agreement, to pay the major part of such benefits, as costs properly charged against technological change. Declining industries, or regions faced with shrinking markets or depleted resources, in many cases could not afford such outlays. Here the costs of displacement would have to be spread amongst the tax-paying public.

DISTRIBUTION OF INCOME AND ALLOCATION OF LABOUR

Another question that is impossible to determine precisely is that of the effects, advantageous or disadvantageous, that trade unions have had upon the general distribution of income and the allocation of labour. For there is no generally accepted principle by which the "fair" or "proper" rate of pay for each and every occupation can be discovered unless it be the desirability of a trend toward greater equality of incomes. A basic ideal of democratic society is that of "equality of opportunity." In an increasingly large-scale, complex society that requires longer, more expensive education, training and conditioning to qualify for the jobs with the most prestige and pay, greater equality of opportunity increasingly means greater equality of income.

If such is the case, unions have contributed to a more efficient and equitable pattern of distribution. Some disparities in wages and fringe benefits have developed among certain industries and occupations as a result, in part, of unequal bargaining power among unions. But *in the aggregate,* the great expansion of trade unionism during and since the war has coincided with, and contributed to, a more equitable and efficient wage and salary structure and distribution of income. There has been a pronounced and relatively rapid narrowing of differentials in rates of pay and privileges or benefits (such as pensions, medical and hospital insurance, sick leave, etc.) among workers in different firms doing the same kinds of jobs; among unskilled, semi-skilled and skilled workers; between manual and white-collar workers; and between the lower-paid wage-earning and higher-paid salaried or fee-taking professional and executive classes.

This trend does *not* appear, as is so often alleged, to have reduced the work incentives of the higher-paid executive and professional groups, or discouraged new recruits from trying to enter their ranks. On the contrary, the economic and social gains of wage earners in recent years have enabled far larger numbers than ever before to afford the special education and training required for the more skilled, better-paid and higher-status positions. The numbers training for and seeking entrance into executive and professional jobs far exceed any previous number or percentage of the population, as evidenced by the swollen enrolments in our universities (particularly in such fields as law, engineering, and commerce or business administration). Shortages of personnel in executive and professional ranks are due, not to a lack of applicants, but to a shortage of educational and training facilities, along with the barriers imposed by the privileged incumbents against new recruits into their ranks. It is still generally true that the highest-paid jobs also enjoy the highest "psychic incomes" in terms of security, power and influence, status and prestige, comfort, creative satisfaction, and the like. Shortages of trained workers in such vitally necessary fields as education, social work, nursing and public service have, admittedly, arisen because of inadequate rates of pay. These, however, have been due primarily to shortcomings of government policy, to the unrestrained competition of "private enterprise" for scarce personnel, and to low rates of pay in comparison to those of other executive and professional groups, not to the gains of organized wage earners in wages and fringe benefits.

INFLATION AND UNEMPLOYMENT

Most difficult of all questions to analyse is the degree to which union pressure for higher wages and fringe benefits has contributed to the recurrent cycles of inflation and unemployment of recent years. Some of the most eminent economists reach diametrically opposite conclusions on this question. One group tends to place the main blame for inflation on unions, while another group maintains that inflation arises from causes entirely beyond and apart from union policy.[3] A few economists, such as Milton Friedman of the University of Chicago, even go so far as to maintain that unions have *no* important effects upon general wage levels over the economy as a whole.[4]

The "wage-push" inflation argument rests on the fact that, over the past decade or more, wages have generally risen more rapidly than increases in productivity, or output per man hour. The consequent in-

[3]For the fullest discussion of this subject see G. H. Hildebrand, "The Economic Effects of Unionism" in N. W. Chamberlain, F. C. Pierson, and T. Wolfson, eds., *A Decade of Industrial Relations Research, 1946–1956* (New York: Harper, 1958).

[4]Milton Friedman, "Some Comments on the Significance of Labor Unions for Economic Policy" in David McC. Wright, ed., *The Impact of the Union* (New York: Harcourt Brace, 1951).

creases in cost have had to be passed on to the buying public in higher prices. (According to official figures of the Dominion Bureau of Statistics for instance, the average hourly earnings of workers in manufacturing in Canada increased by 62.3 per cent, while output per man hour increased by 37.6 per cent from 1949 to 1956. The excess of wage increases over gains in physical productivity was about 18 per cent, which was approximately the same as the increase in the general price level during that period.)

The case for "wage-push" inflation in the United States has been presented in convincing fashion by a number of economists. Briefly, their thesis is that the centre of trouble lies in "key" capital goods industries, particularly steel, which are controlled by a few big firms and large industrial unions. The unions periodically demand, and win, larger-than-average increases in wages or fringe benefits that exceed increases in productivity, so that costs of production go up. Employers in these industries, because of their monopoly or "oligopoly" position in the market, are able to raise prices by more than enough to cover the higher costs. These lead to a "chain reaction" of higher wages, costs and prices throughout the economy.[5] Governments, faced with fixed commitments for defence, public works and other requirements, have to increase their expenditures, while private business men and consumers tend to borrow larger amounts of money from banks and other lending agencies, to pay for higher wages and higher prices for materials and equipment. Inflation thus becomes "induced" by union wage pressure. More money is brought into circulation by government deficit financing and bank credit expansion, to sustain output and employment at periodically higher wages, costs and prices.

The "wage-push" inflation thesis would seem to have a good deal of validity in the United States, for it is a largely self-contained economy. Foreign trade accounts for only 3 per cent to 4 per cent of the national income. Any expansion of the domestic money supply, therefore, is spent almost entirely for domestic output, while any decrease in exports and increase in imports due to higher costs and prices in the United States affect only a small part of the total economy.

The argument is not valid, however, for an "open" economy such as Canada's, in which foreign trade accounts for 20 per cent or 25 per cent of the national income, and in which large amounts of foreign (mostly American) capital investment have been depended upon in recent years to sustain economic expansion and full employment. Canadian firms generally have a more limited range within which they can raise their prices to cover higher wages and costs of production. On the one hand, major export industries selling in the United States and overseas markets, in competition with producers from other countries, have little or

[5]J. K. Galbraith, "Are Living Costs Out of Control?" *Atlantic*, Jan., 1957.

no control over their prices. (Wages *directly* account for only a small fraction of the total costs of most major Canadian exports, but general wage increases in Canada that exceeded increases in productivity would soon be reflected in higher costs for buildings, equipment, materials, fuel, transportation and other items.) On the other hand, those industries that produce primarily for the domestic Canadian market would face increasing competition from imports if they raised their prices to cover higher wages and costs (unless every round of wage and price increases were accompanied by higher tariffs, exchange controls, or other restrictions on imports, and these would create a whole new set of special problems). Therefore, if and when increases in wages and fringe benefits exceeded increases in productivity by too large a margin in Canada in comparison to other countries, Canada would rapidly find herself in difficulty. Exports would decline, imports would increase, capital investment (both foreign and domestic) would be discouraged, the Canadian dollar would depreciate in value in relation to other countries' currencies, and unemployment would become increasingly serious. In the face of such difficulties, then, any prospect of long-continued or permanent inflation in Canada, "induced" by trade union wage pressure, and at a rate in excess of that in the United States and other major trading nations, seems out of the question. In brief, excessive wage increases in Canada lead to unemployment more than to inflation.

Up to 1957, at least, such maladjustments showed no signs of having developed in Canada, except for brief periods immediately after the Second World War and again during the Korean War (and these were caused by excessive money and credit expansion as well as inventory speculation by business firms, not by excessive wage increases). On the contrary, from 1949 to 1956 Canada underwent one of the most rapid rates of economic expansion of any country. The national income increased by some 52 per cent in terms of money, and by almost 45 per cent in "real" terms, while the dollar volume of exports increased by more than 60 per cent. Similarly, both the annual volume of domestic savings and the investment in Canada of foreign (mostly American) capital more than *doubled* during that period. The Canadian dollar, far from depreciating, consistently maintained a premium above the American dollar after being freed from exchange control. Nor were Canadian workers "priced out of the market" by large wage increases or other such pressures; they may have been in particular firms or industries from time to time, but such losses of employment were more than compensated for by expansion in other sectors of the economy. Over the nation as a whole, total employment increased by more than 20 per cent (including the net absorption of several hundred thousand immigrants into the labour force).

Clearly, then, Canadian unions in general fell far short of reaching a danger point in their demands during the period 1949–56. Inflation in Canada, hitherto, has been mainly of the "demand-pull" rather than "wage-push" type. It arose from the unprecedented American and overseas demand for Canadian exports; the huge investments of capital, both domestic and foreign, in Canadian industry; and, accompanying these, excessive credit expansion to finance greatly increased consumer as well as capital expenditures. The huge increase in demand from these sources, rather than trade union pressure, was the main factor forcing up wages, production costs and prices. Or, to put it another way, increases in wages and fringe benefits in excess of increased productivity in Canada have been, in the aggregate, *responses to* or *by-products* of, rather than *causes* of, inflationary increases in costs, prices and incomes generally.

The analysis of trade unionism's impact upon the Canadian economy so far has been confined mainly to the period 1949–56 inclusive, when the economy was operating under unusually favourable conditions. Much of the expansion in Canada's exports, and of the capital investment in new resource development, arose in response to the accumulated shortages created by the great depression of the 1930's, the ravages of the Second World War, the rapid population increases in many countries immediately after the war, and the huge increase in military expenditures by the United States, Canada and other countries after the Korean War broke out. There was an almost insatiable demand in the United States and overseas for raw materials, semi-finished products and some manufactured goods of the kinds in which Canada specializes.

Expansion at the rate that occurred in the period 1949–56 may now have come to an end, though this is far from certain as yet. Most of the industrialized nations that suffered the greatest damage during the war have now more than recovered, and are producing at well above prewar levels, while much new productive capacity is being developed in many parts of the world, in the types of products in which Canada's exports are concentrated. In this situation, the possibility must be faced that the momentum of competitive upward pressure by unions on wages, if it forced wages higher than increases in productivity, *might* very well contribute to "pricing Canadian goods out of foreign markets" and "pricing labour out of the market" in Canada, in competition with more efficient or lower-cost producers in other countries.

A number of developments in recent years would seem to indicate, on the face of it, that this process has already begun, though the case is yet far from clear. A "recession" developed from late 1957 throughout 1958. The national income declined and unemployment increased, despite an inflationary (or "reflationary") policy of deficit financing by the Government to the extent of almost one billion dollars. Recovery and expansion during 1959 and early 1960 brought the national income to a new high, slightly above the record level of 1957. But the increases in export trade and in domestic investment and consumption were not large enough to absorb the rapidly growing number of workers in Canada, with the result that unemployment has remained within a range of 7–11 per cent of the total labour force. The deficit in "current accounts" in Canada's foreign trade reached record proportions during 1959. Total imports (including payments on interest and dividends on foreign capital, and other non-commodity items) far exceeded those of any previous year, and exceeded total exports by almost one and a half billion dollars. The premium on the Canadian dollar over other currencies has been declining.

Despite these adversities, the general level of wages and prices has continued to rise, year by year, since 1957. Comparative statistics on the wholesale price level would seem to indicate that prices in this country have not risen out of line with those of other major industrial trading nations. According to official statistics, the cost of living index rose by only 8.3 per cent in Canada during 1953–8, as compared to 9 per cent in Japan, 10 per cent in Germany and 19 per cent in the United Kingdom (see Bank of Canada, *Statistical Summary,* Jan., 1960, p. 61). The general price index in Canada, however, included a large and rising proportion of lower-priced imported goods. If these were subtracted from the index, it would probably be found that prices for domestically produced goods and services had risen more rapidly in Canada than in a number of other major trading nations in recent years.

Just who or what group should be held primarily responsible for the state of affairs that has developed since 1957 is a matter of intense controversy. Trade union pressure for higher wages and fringe benefits has undoubtedly been a contributing factor. But probably far more important, in the aggregate, have been: (*a*) the over-investment and "demand-pull" inflation of 1955–7, which raised labour, material and capital costs above a level that could be sustained, in terms of the potentialities of foreign and domestic markets; and (*b*) "administered" price increases by firms enjoying monopoly or oligopoly control in the Canadian market.

CURRENT TRENDS

What are the prospects of such trends in the future? What are the main factors that may lead unions to press continuously for increases in wages or other benefits beyond levels that the Canadian economy can afford, if full employment is to be maintained? What compensating trends are there, if any, that would reduce such pressures?

A special problem, perhaps, that will continue to face any administration in this country is the unique relation of Canada to the United States, and its effect upon Canadian workers. The overwhelming majority of Canadian unions and their members belong to so-called international organizations, the officers and members of which are predominantly American. This connection does not create any great problem of "domination" by American labour "bosses" over their Canadian subsidiaries, as is so often alleged by Canadian employers and newspapers. It does, however, contribute to a more intangible but none the less important problem — the "demonstration effect" of American wages, standards of living and patterns of consumption upon the attitudes and values of Canadian workers, and the influence which these in turn have upon trade union policies in Canada.

Like its American counterpart, the trade union movement in Canada for the most part has not developed a distinct ideology and set of values of its own. Most union leaders and members on this continent have been and are essentially pragmatic in viewpoint and policy, and merely reflect the more widely accepted values of North American society, with all its strengths and weaknesses. This is a society in which money income and conspicuous expenditure tend to be the main criteria of personal worth and social status. Workers and union members, like other groups, are subjected to the pressures of mass communication and mass consumption to provide ever larger markets for mass production industry. Business in the aggregate spends billions of dollars on this continent for advertising and high-pressure salesmanship, utilizing the most effective media of communication, in order to instil new wants among the consuming public in excess of its current income. (C. Wright Mills has defined trade union leaders as "managers of discontent." By the same token, modern business management could be defined as "agitators" or "instigators" of discontent.)

The philosophy and cultural environment of "free enterprise" are reflected in union policy. The many and diverse organizations that comprise the trade union movement undoubtedly do have many characteristics and traditions in common, and they do co-operate loyally in pursuing certain common objectives. But, in line with the prevailing business ethics and philosophy of the major employers with whom unions have to deal, they also tend to follow a policy of "free enterprise" or "business unionism" in pursuit of their private group interests. Individual union leaders often see their role and responsibility primarily in terms of maximizing the size, power and status of their own organizations, and the economic and social gains of their own members, in competition with, or if need be at the expense of, other groups.

One major effect of these forces, in the segmented structure of trade unionism and collective bargaining on this continent, is to generate an unusually strong competitive upward pressure for higher wages and fringe benefits, and a relatively high incidence of industrial conflict.[6]

[6]A. M. Ross and P. T. Hartman, *Changing Patterns of Industrial Conflict* (New York: Wiley, 1960).

Canada perhaps faces a special dilemma in this connection. It might be phrased in terms of the question: How can American standards of living be achieved and maintained on Canadian incomes? Canadian workers, for a variety of reasons, aspire to American rates of pay and styles of life in comparable occupations. Closer ties of transportation and communication (particularly in advertising) between the two countries; the increasing amount and proportion of Canada's trade with the United States; the large and increasing volume of American capital investment in Canada and the corresponding increase in the size and number of employer firms in this country that are branch plants or subsidiaries of American concerns; the affiliation of Canadian with American unions — all these factors conduce to a growing "Americanization" of Canadian standards of income and consumption. Average per capita output and income in *real* terms of goods and services of all kinds, however, is about 30 per cent lower in Canada than in the United States. Efforts by Canadian workers to achieve closer parity in wages and fringe benefits with their American counterparts face the barriers of lower productivity and higher costs in most industries in Canada. These efforts may lead periodically to prolonged and bitter industrial conflict or, as the price of avoiding conflict, to inordinately high wage, cost and price levels that may cause unemployment, trade deficits and attendant problems.

That is one side of the picture. On the other hand, there are a number of trends that are likely to have a counteracting or moderating effect. They may help to make industrial relations in Canada more stable, and to restrain union wage and other demands from becoming excessive in relation to changes in national income and productivity.

If, as has been argued, disparities in output and income as between Canadian and American workers have been a major source of tension and conflict, there is evidence to indicate that the gap is narrowing. Productivity and hourly earnings appear to be rising more rapidly in Canada than in the United States. According to the survey which Brecher and Reisman carried out for the Gordon Commission,[7] average hourly earnings in American manufacturing were 53.1 per cent higher than in Canadian manufacturing in 1939. By 1950 the differential had shrunk to 42.1 per cent, by 1955 to 31.9 per cent and by 1957 to 30.2 per cent.

Another important underlying development is the rapid change in the composition of the labour force itself, due to changes in technology, in business or industrial organization, and in patterns of consumer expenditure. Year by year and decade by decade, an increasing proportion of paid employees are "white-collar" professional, technical and

7I. Brecher and S. Reisman, *Canada–United States Economic Relations* (Ottawa: Queen's Printer, 1957) p. 217.

clerical workers who earn a salary, whereas a correspondingly smaller proportion are in the category of manual wage earners paid by the hour, day or week. Already it is estimated that the former account for more than one-half the total labour force in the United States, and that they will soon do so in Canada. This trend has serious implications for the status, importance and bargaining power of the trade union movement in both countries, as unions hitherto have had only limited success in attempting to organize salaried white-collar workers on this continent. In any case, it is likely to mean that unions will be forced to change their philosophy, objectives and bargaining tactics considerably if they are to succeed in organizing any large fraction of such workers in the future.

Important changes have recently occurred in this connection. They are chiefly a result perhaps of changes in the economic status of wage earners and union members, as these have become more "white collar" or "middle class" in viewpoint and style of life. One indication of this trend is the much greater emphasis that unions now place on long-run security of jobs and incomes, rather than short-run maximization of hourly or weekly wages. Union agreements now commonly include provisions for such things as pensions, medical insurance, sick leave, seniority and, to an increasing extent, guaranteed annual wage plans of one kind or another, benefits which were at one time the exclusive privilege of the office or administrative staff. Private, company-financed pension and welfare plans have serious limitations, but in the long run the change in organized labour's goals is likely to exert a moderating effect on union policies, and to reduce the incidence of industrial conflict.[8] Employees who have a permanent or long-term interest in their jobs, who are paid by the month or the year and who have accumulated sizable benefits of various kinds are likely to be less militant or extreme in their demands, and less preoccupied with short-run gains in wages and fringe benefits than are wage earners whose tenure of employment is insecure, and who are paid by the hour, day or week.

The much-discussed phenomenon of "automation" is likely to have much the same impact in the long run. Economists and others diverge widely in their predictions about the effects of automation on employment. Some maintain that it will lead to mass displacement and unemployment, whereas others foresee no such threat. Again, some experts maintain that it will virtually supplant all semi-skilled work and create large new demands for many types of skilled labour, whereas others predict the opposite results. Virtually everyone, however, agrees on certain major effects that automation is likely to have upon the economy: (1) it will greatly increase physical productivity per man hour or man day, and thus serve as one important factor compensating for large wage increases or equivalent benefits; (2) although it creates a threat

[8]Ross and Hartman, *Changing Patterns of Industrial Conflict.*

of large-scale displacement of labour in many industries, if properly planned and controlled it offers workers more leisure and other compensations; and (3) by the very nature of its operations (for example the need for careful "scheduling" of production) and the large investment of capital per worker, it is likely to place even greater emphasis than hitherto on stability of output and employment.

Such trends, however, while tending to reduce the intensity of union wage pressure and industrial conflict over the nation *as a whole,* provide no assurance that particular groups, whether employers or unions, will not exploit positions of strategic bargaining power to win disproportionately large gains for themselves at the expense of the rest of the community. Indeed, such trends as automation and an increase in the proportion of the labour force in the white collar category may tend to strengthen rather than weaken the bargaining power of unionized manual workers in some industries, in so far as a steadily larger superstructure of capital investment, management and white-collar personnel comes to depend upon their output. If the experience of the steel industry in the United States is any indication, the smaller but more heavily "capitalized" and "automated" work force of 1959 had every bit as much bargaining power as did its larger but less mechanized counterpart of earlier years.

ORGANIZED LABOUR AND DEMOCRATIC SOCIALISM

The whole problem of trade union policy and industrial relations in general presents a special challenge to socialism as a body of thought, a political movement and a system of planning and administration. The maintenance of full emloyment is basic to the socialist programme but, as noted earlier, full employment strengthens the bargaining power of organized labour and tends to generate competitive upward pressure on wages and prices by unions and employers. And, critics of socialism allege, in so far as a socialist government would have to depend upon organized labour as one of its main sources of support, it would be inhibited from taking effective action to control such inflationary pressures.

There are a number of reasons, on the other hand, for maintaining that a democratic socialist administration would be better equipped to deal effectively with the economic problems that trade unions present, and to exert a moderating influence upon inflationary wage pressures, than the so-called free enterprise system has been able to achieve so far.

Democratic socialism presupposes, in the first place, that the trade union movement will participate actively in politics and governmental administration, and support or be affiliated with a democratic socialist party (for example the present negotiations to form a new party between the CLC and CCF). The underlying factor contributing to this development is recognition by union officials and members of the fact that governmental rather than private business policies are or soon must be the main force determining the distribution of income, the level of output and employment, and the final uses to which the national income will be put. It would not be too naïve and idealistic, perhaps, to assume that as the trade union movement concerns itself increasingly with political action and governmental policy, its own demands, tactics and policies will be more far sighted and "responsible," in the sense that they will be geared to broader issues and take other group interests into consideration, rather than being focused exclusively on the narrower economic or occupational interests of union members. Furthermore, under socialism, conflict between unions and management will likely be carried out to a greater degree on the political rather than economic plane, focusing on demands for governmental social security programmes and protective legislation, rather than on higher wages and fringe benefits from private industry. Election campaigns and parliamentary debates will partially replace strikes, lockouts and picket lines.

Again, a socialist administration that plans and carries out programmes the main objectives of which are stability, full employment and a wider and more equitable distribution of opportunities would in itself help substantially to create greater stability in industrial relations. As stressed earlier, much of the instability and conflict between labour and management, and the at times excessive wage or other demands by unions, have been generated in large part by the feverish and unstable pattern of economic expansion under the auspices of so-called free enterprise, with its accompanying cycles of inflationary expansion and periodic recession.

In this connection, a government that made some sincere and consistent effort to ensure greater stability, to exert some effective control over prices, profits and conspicuous consumption, and to channel more capital investment into socially useful or necessary facilities would be better able to exert "moral pressure" (for want of a better term) upon unions to keep their wage and other demands within manageable bounds. Governments and private employers dedicated to the unregulated growth and profitability of "free enterprise" as an end in itself lack any moral basis for asking unions to be "restrained" or "responsible" in their demands. To act "responsibly" presumes that a person or group is able to foresee or predict with some degree of accuracy the effects of its actions (for instance, the effect of a given wage increase upon the costs, prices, output and sales of an industry's products) and to govern its demands accordingly. "Responsible" behaviour in this sense, however, would be possible only in a planned economy. It has not been possible under the more or less unregulated "free enterprise" system with its generally unpredictable cycles of expansion and contraction, in which the major decisions as regards prices, investment, output and employment are exclusively in the hands of private company management, and the pertinent data concerning productivity and costs are deemed confidential secrets not available to unions and the public generally.

Furthermore, a socialist administration could exert a moderating influence on conflicts of group interests like those of unions and business managements, by seeking to instil, and planning the economy to achieve, new and different priorities in the nation's scale of values. Much of the instability and conflict in the industrial system, as noted, has been generated by the North American cultural pattern of intense competition between individuals and groups in conspicuous consumption and display, as a measure of personal worth and status. The result has been that far too large a part of the nation's wealth, energies and resources has been expended on more or less trivial or useless consumer goods and services produced for profit by "private enterprise," while far too little has been devoted to "social" capital and public services that are vital for the health, welfare and efficiency of the people as a whole, particularly those in the lower-income categories — such facilities as better low-rent housing and community planning, more adequate hospital and medical services, wider and more equal educational opportunities, more liberal and comprehensive social security and the like. Much industrial conflict and inflationary pressure in Canada and the United States has been generated by the failure of governments to provide such facilities and services, and the consequent attempt by workers, through their unions, to compensate by demanding large wage increases and fringe benefits from private industry. The proliferation of private company-financed pension plans, many of them needlessly costly or inadequate in terms of coverage, is a case in point.

The limitations of the present system, and the contributions that a democratic socialist administration could make towards achieving greater stability in industrial relations, are brought out sharply in the field of social security. The weaknesses of private, company-financed plans are particularly apparent as regards provisions for superannuation. Prior to the war such plans numbered a few dozen in Canada. Today they number in the thousands, and have become a major issue in bargaining between unions and employers.

Whether paid entirely by the employing company or financed jointly by the contributions of employers and workers, contributions to pension or welfare plans represent a margin of income that could have been paid to, or received by, workers in other forms, such as higher wages, longer holidays, lay-off or severance pay, or other benefits. To the extent that a worker fails to receive the full amount of the company contributions to his pension, he sacrifices the investment of a wage increase or other benefit that he might have been enjoying over a period of time. Only in a properly "vested" plan can an employee receive the full amount of the contributions before retirement, and then only after a minimum period of time, of five, ten or more years. Not only are such programmes expensive in relation to benefits received as compared to more comprehensive government social security programmes. They also tend to tie workers to particular employers, prevent a more economic mobility of labour, limit the workers' freedom of movement, and inculcate attitudes of dependence and conformity, for to leave one's job prematurely means sacrificing a sizable investment.

In the broader view, and perhaps more important, private pension plans create wide disparities and inequalities, and hence widespread unrest and dissatisfaction, among various groups of workers. Such plans generally give the broadest coverage and most liberal benefits to the very types of workers who need them least, that is, to the already well-paid and secure employees of larger firms in such fields as manufacturing, transportation and public utilities. On the other hand, it is virtually impossible to provide and administer such plans for low-income and insecure workers who generally need such benefits the most, such as the intermittently or seasonably employed labourers in such industries as mining, logging, agriculture and building construction, as well as workers employed in a wide variety of small enterprises in many different fields. Many of the same limitations apply to privately financed medical, health and other welfare plans.

In general, a more comprehensive programme of social security financed and administered by the federal government, and providing more adequate old age pensions, sick benefits, medical services, and the like, would be more economical and more equitable than the present hodge-podge, bits-and-pieces system of privately financed plans. Those who wish to have more liberal benefits than the government programme would provide could, of course, work out their own arrangements with their employers to have supplementary benefits. There would seem to be no sound justification, however, for keeping the contributions to private programmes exempt from taxation (as they are now) at the expense of a more comprehensive government programme.

Although a broad programme of social security along such lines would be expensive in terms of the additional taxation that would be required to finance it, this drawback would be more than compensated for by the improvements in health, welfare and morale of workers, the lower incidence of industrial conflict and the greater general productivity that such a programme would make possible.

PUBLIC OWNERSHIP

No mention has been made so far of the role that "nationalization" or public ownership could or should play in bringing about greater stability in industrial relations and higher morale and productivity among workers. Public ownership of the means of production has, of course, long been one of the main foundations of socialist thought. Although no realistic socialist in Canada today would uphold a system of complete public ownership of *all* the means of production, any programme of democratic socialist planning would require a considerable extension of public ownership beyond its present boundaries if a better balance between public and private investment, a more socially efficient use of output and resources, and a more equitable distribution of wealth and income are to be achieved.

Public ownership and operation are not, however, in themselves a guarantee against attitudes of apathy or "alienation" on the part of workers to their jobs, restrictive union practices, industrial conflict and inflationary wage pressures. One need only point to such examples as the Canadian National Railways and the Toronto Transportation Commission in this country, and the nationalized coal mines and railways in Great Britain under both Labour and Tory régimes. The main problems of industrial relations today do not arise primarily over questions of *ownership*. They are by-products, rather, of maladjustments and inequities throughout the economic system as a whole, and of internal problems of labour-management relations endemic in the large, increasingly complex and bureaucratic types of organizations that dominate the modern industrial economy.

As suggested earlier, a broad programme of democratic economic and social planning would help bring greater stability in industrial relations to the extent that it could provide workers greater security, a more equitable distribution of income and more opportunities for achieving fuller and more meaningful lives. At the level of the individual firm or plant, whether publicly or privately owned and operated, a great deal of research and experimentation needs to be carried out for the purpose of providing greater interest and variety in jobs, and more democratic participation by workers or their representatives in control and decision-making, to inculcate better morale, more pride in their work, and a greater sense of identification with the means and purpose of the production process.

SPECIFIC MEASURES

So far the discussion of the role and impact of trade unionism and collective bargaining in the national economy has been dealt with in rather general terms. Long-term trends in production and employment and in the composition of the labour force, along with rational planning to achieve and maintain stable, full employment, a socially more useful allocation of labour, capital and resources and a more equitable distribution of wealth, income and opportunities will, it has been argued, conduce to greater stability in industrial relations and generally bring union objectives and policies into line with the needs and interests of the nation as a whole.

This résumé still leaves unanswered the question of just how, in terms of specific planning and legislation, trade unionism and industrial relations generally can be integrated in a system of economic and social planning. How, to repeat, are we to be assured that particular unions, private business interests or other organized groups will not use their strategic bargaining power to exploit the rest of the community, or unduly disrupt the economy, in pursuing their own private interests?

The great diversity in size and structure, bargaining power and labour relations in general among the thousands of unions and employers bound by collective agreements in Canada makes it impossible to lay down any blanket formula that will guarantee stability and efficiency in each and every case. It will be more fruitful, therefore, to focus on a few major "problem areas" and specific types of policies that offer some possibilities of being effective in particular situations.

MULTI-EMPLOYER BARGAINING: REGIONAL AND NATIONAL

It is a safe generalization, to begin with, that the larger and broader the area of bargaining between unions and employers, the more stable and "responsible" will be the bargaining relations and the agreements negotiated. In a comprehensive survey of fifteen countries recently completed by Arthur M. Ross and Paul T. Hartman of the University of California,[9] it was found that industrial conflict and competitive upward pressure on wage rates and fringe benefits were considerably more intense and widespread in the United States and Canada than in other nations. The authors attribute this industrial relations pattern partly to the fact that government welfare and social security programmes on the North American Continent are far less comprehensive in their coverage than is the case in Western Europe and most British dominions. Related to this is the fact that organized labour on this Continent, unlike its counterparts in other highly unionized and industrialized regions of the world, has not developed an effective labour or socialist political party (though steps are now being taken in Canada to bring this about). Another highly important factor, however, as Ross and Hartman stress, is the highly *sectional* pattern of collective bargaining on this continent. In both Canada and the United States more than 70 per cent of all collective agreements are negotiated between individual union locals and individual company or plant managements.[10]

In Britain, West Germany and the Scandinavian countries, by contrast, the vast majority of organized workers are covered by master agreements negotiated on a nation-wide scale between industrial unions

[9]*Ibid.*

[10]One should not over-emphasize this point, of course, or draw misleading conclusions from the raw statistics. Because of the extreme degree of monopolistic concentration in many Canadian industries, as brought out by Dr. Rosenbluth's study in this volume, one or two, or a few, firms constitute an *industry* in themselves, and their negotiations with local unions constitute, in effect, industry-wide bargaining on a national scale.

and employer associations or industry federations. Industry-wide or multi-employer bargaining makes possible greater stability in industrial relations for a number of reasons. It reduces or eliminates wage competition and forces employers to compete (where the industry *is* competitive) more on the basis of managerial efficiency and techniques of production. Trouble over disparities in rates of pay and fringe benefits, among workers doing the same types of work for different employers in the same industry, can be ironed out more effectively. Wages are more stable over the long run. During periods of expansion and labour shortages, unions are less able to play employers off against one another in pressing for wage increases or other gains, and in periods of recession and unemployment employers are less able to play union locals and workers against one another in seeking wage cuts or other concessions. (In this connection, paradoxical as it may seem, unions generally favour industry-wide or multi-employer bargaining even though, contrary to the popular impression, it tends to strengthen rather than weaken the bargaining power of employers over the industry as a whole, in periods of full employment at least.) Strikes are less frequent, partly because various troublesome disparities and sources of instability are reduced or eliminated, and partly because labour and employer organizations are more evenly matched at all times. For this reason, of course, when shutdowns *do* occur they tend to be long drawn out and costly. But the very awareness of this fact tends to induce the parties to go to greater lengths to avoid complete deadlocks, so that the losses from industrial conflict are probably less in the long run than under individual company-by-company bargaining.

Finally, and perhaps most important in the long run, industry-wide bargaining tends to induce union and employer representatives to adopt more rational and responsible attitudes and policies in their bargaining relations. Where collective bargaining involves only one or two local unions and employers in a limited area, the contending parties may feel free to adopt extreme or uncompromising positions on the assumption that the results of their actions are of relatively minor importance to the nation as a whole. Where union-employer negotiations involve an entire industry over a region or over the nation as a whole, however, they are a focus of wide public interest, and the impact of their policies on the economy becomes more apparent, to themselves and to the public.

It would seem appropriate for governments at both the federal and provincial levels to give the utmost encouragement, by legislation or otherwise, to multi-employer bargaining on the broadest possible basis, whether regional, interprovincial or national in scope, as determined by industry location and by labour and product markets. In some industries and trades, indeed, there are strong arguments for establishing, by legislation, administrative rulings or otherwise, a system of multi-union and multi-employer bargaining.

The construction industry is a case in point. In major urban industrial centres it comprises some twenty "craft" unions, each of which generally bargains with its counterpart association of contractors or subcontractors, as well as with individual employers hiring various types of construction labour. In many areas this structure of bargaining has given rise to a chaotic wage and employment pattern, due to wide inequalities in relative bargaining power and militancy among the various labour and employer groups. Troublesome disparities give rise to frequent and costly conflicts, and ensuing losses in output and employment are often out of all proportion to the issues or interests involved. A strike or lockout by any one union or employer association often shuts down virtually all major construction projects over a wide area. It would seem rational, in a situation of this kind, to require a system of "consolidated" bargaining among all unions and employer organizations on at least a regional scale, to require craft unions, in effect, to act as if they belonged to one industrial union.

In furtherance of the objective of multi-union and multi-employer bargaining it would seem particularly desirable to achieve greater uniformity in provincial legislation governing industrial relations. Even more important, perhaps, is the desirability of extending and broadening the role and jurisdiction of the federal government over labour relations by whatever means possible — by testing new legislation in the courts, by federal-provincial agreement, or by constitutional amendment. This would help achieve greater equality in organizational and bargaining rights and procedures, as well as in wages, hours and fringe benefits, among workers across the nation, thus eliminating many troublesome disparities and inequalities. It is a serious anomaly that, under the present system in Canada, in many industries and firms that have plants or subsidiaries in various provinces and that sell the bulk of their output in national or international markets, the jurisdiction over labour negotiations concerning wages and various fringe benefits, which affect production costs and prices, should lie exclusively with the various provinces. If union policies *are* an important contributing factor to inflation and other economic maladjustments in Canada, as the critics of organized labour allege so vociferously, such critics should be equally articulate in pointing out that no rational wage or price policies can be carried out to deal with labour problems effectively under the present fragmented system of provincial jurisdiction. We cannot have it both ways!

MONOPOLISTIC PRICE AND WAGE POLICIES

Extending the scope of collective bargaining, as suggested above, though it would bring greater stability in industrial relations and reduce the frequency and impact of strikes or lockouts, would not in itself ensure that excessive wage and price increase will not occur in some sectors of the economy. Indeed, it could be argued that in some industries it might encourage organized labour and employers to act in collusion to exploit the public. That is to say, employers in the same industry, selling the same product, are in many cases inhibited from combining to raise their prices to the most profitable levels for fear of running foul of the Combines Act. Negotiating with unions on an industry-wide basis, however, might give them an opportunity to increase their profits without the risk of illegality. Substantial concessions in wages and fringe benefits might give a ready-made justification for raising prices by more than enough to cover the increased labour costs. Unions and their members in such situations, while thus sharing in monopoly profits at public expense, would tend to get most of the blame for causing "inflationary" wage and price increases.[11]

Much the same situation can occur, and probably has occurred fairly frequently in recent years, in industries characterized by a high degree of monopoly or "oligopoly," where one or two large firms account for the major share of the nation's output and have a virtually free hand to raise prices (within the limits set by foreign competition). Outstanding examples of this kind are the basic steel, electrical equipment and heavy machinery industries of the United States and Canada. Indeed, as pointed out earlier, Galbraith, Ulman and a number of other prominent economists maintain that the inordinately high wage and price increases arising out of negotiations between strong unions in monopolistic or ologopolistic industries are the most important factor in the inflation of recent years. Galbraith, for instance, points out that steel prices have more than doubled during the past ten years, whereas the prices of clothing and textiles have remained virtually unchanged.

Short of compulsory arbitration, the only means of ensuring adequate protection of the public from union-employer collusion of this kind would seem to be some system of selective price control. J. K. Galbraith, among others, has suggested, for instance, that major corporations and employer associations producing goods and services that affect the welfare of any sizable fraction of the community be prohibited by law

[11]Theoretically, a union could win an inordinately high wage increase and force a corresponding increase in prices if it were fully organized in a highly competitive industry in which its bargaining power greatly exceeded that of the employers. This sort of situation has occurred, at times, in such fields as local service industries and in some branches of building construction. In most cases, however, wage increases have been smaller in highly competitive than in monopolistic industries, even where the relative bargaining power of unions has been greater, for highly competitive industries are generally characterized by large numbers of small firms requiring limited capital and few employees. Unions in such cases face a limit to the gains they can win at any one time, due to either (*a*) marginal operators being forced out of business, with consequent unemployment of union members, or (*b*) increasing competition from "working proprietors" and employers hiring non-union labour, in areas beyond union jurisdiction.

from raising their prices within a year after completing their bargaining negotiations with unions. (The purpose of such a provision, of course, would be to stiffen the resistance of employers to union demands, in so far as wage increases or other benefits would have to come directly out of increased productivity or other economies rather than paid for out of higher prices.) This proposal, by itself, has the obvious limitation that employers could adjust to, and anticipate, any such provisions. That is to say, they would have a strong inducement to raise prices after the first year by more than enough to cover the higher labour costs of the preceding year and to leave some margin for succeeding negotiations. Such a provision might be made effective, however, if it were backed up by a requirement that no price increases would be allowed until a full investigation was made by a public inquiry board or some such agency, armed with the full power to subpoena witnesses from unions and employers alike, to require submission of data, ordinarily considered "confidential," on production costs, productivity, profits, etc. and to give full publicity to all its findings and recommendations.

Here again, however, any such system of selective wage and price control, to be effective, would have to be part of a broad programme of economic and social planning. And it would require an extension of federal control over industrial disputes and other labour matters far beyond the present limits. The prevailing system of federal and provincial legislation on labour disputes, with its central theme of "compulsory conciliation," offers no real assurance of protection against exorbitant wage and price increases in monopolistic industries or combines, for the basic principle of conciliation is to bring the parties to a dispute into agreement on any terms that are mutually acceptable, whether or not the general public has to pay an inordinately high price for the settlement. A manufacturing firm in Ontario, for instance, may be enjoying a monopoly over the supply of a certain product to the Canadian market under the umbrella of tariffs on foreign competition. A major part of its output, let us assume, is sold outside Ontario. The legislature of that province has little incentive, therefore, to exert strong pressure against wage and price increases in this case, if the main costs are borne by consumers in other provinces for the benefit of Ontario capital and labour.

CONCLUSION

It is necessary to stress, in conclusion, that under a democratic system of government, regardless of the ideology and philosophy of the political party in power, there is and can be no over-all "solution" to the "problem" of industrial conflict, and the competition among major interest groups for larger rewards in income, power and status. Or, if there were such a "solution," it would almost inevitably create new problems worse than the ones it set out to solve, and in the process it would in all likelihood undermine and destroy our democratic traditions.

Specifically, the only means by which the nation could absolutely guarantee to eliminate all strikes and lockouts, and prevent unions in every and all industries and occupations from pushing wages and other benefits out of line, would be to establish some system of *compulsory arbitration,* on a nation-wide scale. The federal and provincial governments would have to pass legislation prohibiting all strikes or lockouts or other interruptions in production, and invoke severe penalties for any violations. "Labour courts," arbitration boards or some such agencies would have to be vested with the authority to fix wages and other conditions of employment, which workers and employers would be compelled by law to accept.

Compulsory arbitration along these lines has, with few exceptions, been opposed by unions, management and neutral observers of the labour scene in Canada and the United States, primarily because it would in all likelihood be inefficient. There is the probability, as pointed out earlier, that, while preventing *overt* conflict, it would give rise to more damaging types of *covert* or hidden conflict and sabotage, among unions and employers. Furthermore, in any system operating under democratic principles, the authority of labour courts or abitration boards to determine wage rates and other components of labour income would necessarily involve extending such authority over employers and owners of capital, to govern prices, profits and levels of investment in each industry. It is extremely doubtful whether judges or arbitrators are the people best suited to exert such authority, particularly if it were carried out on an *ad hoc,* piecemeal basis in the process of settling individual labour disputes. If such authority is to be exercised, it should be part of a comprehensive programme of economic and social planning.

Even in this case, however, there are strong arguments for limiting the role and intervention of public authority in collective bargaining. A programme of complete wage and price control almost inevitably involves rationing consumer goods and centralizing the allocation of labour, capital and resources. It is difficult and costly to administer, even in the exigencies of wartime, when the patriotic fervour of citizens might be expected to bring forth the utmost co-operation and compliance. No government can be so all wise and far seeing, and so well staffed, as to be able to plan and execute in detail every facet of labour-management relations in every industry, firm and plant in the country. Except in cases of extreme emergency, such as a nation-wide railway strike, issues and conflicts that arise between workers and employers are generally best settled between the parties themselves, through voluntary collective bargaining, rather than by governmental fiat.

Politics

The Practice and Theory of Federalism

P. E. TRUDEAU

A great democracy must either sacrifice self-government to unity, or preserve it by federalism.—Lord Acton

Goals have no more reality than the means that are devised to reach them. As every reformer discovers sooner or later to his chagrin, it is not sufficient to conceive ideals lofty enough, and to desire them strongly enough, for them to be automatically attained through some due process of history. And there exists no "Operation Boot-straps" whereby dedicated parties can lift themselves by sheer force of will into the realm of justice triumphant.

Therefore inevitably, the electoral failings of democratic socialism in most industrial societies have led the partisans of social democracy in recent years to reappraise their ends and their means in the light of changing social and economic reality. For example, the nationalization of the instruments of production is now being considered less as an end than as a means, and one that might in many cases be replaced by more flexible processes of economic control and redistribution.

In Canada, the Regina Manifesto of 1933 was replaced in 1956 by the Winnipeg statement of principles which purported to fit more adequately the social and economic temper of the times. Socialist strategy likewise has been radically altered, as is shown by the recent resolutions of the CCF and of the Canadian Labour Congress to launch a new party. But unfortunately socialists in Canada have seldom been guided in their doctrine and their strategy by a whole-hearted acceptance of the basic political fact of federalism.

Left-wing thinkers have too often assumed that fundamental reform is impossible without a vast increase, in law or in fact, of the national government's areas of jurisdiction; CCF parliamentarians have repeatedly identified themselves with centralism, albeit within the framework of a federal constitution; party strategists have planned accordingly; and the general public can rarely praise or damn Canadian socialism without referring to its centralizing tendencies.

In the present chapter, I will state my belief that the foregoing assumptions and inclinations have considerably harmed the cause of reform. Section I will show that, other things being equal, radicalism can more easily be introduced in a federal society than in a unitary one. Section II will claim that the dynamics of history are not urging the Canadian nation towards centralization any more than they are towards decentralization. Section III will argue that the theory of democratic socialism can make no unassailable case for centralization.

In consequence it should follow that Canadian socialists must consider federalism as a positive asset, rather than as an inevitable handicap. However, that is not to say — and I hope the point will remain present in the reader's mind throughout — that this chapter pleads *for* provincial autonomy and *against* centralization in absolute terms. My plea is merely for greater realism and greater flexibility in the socialist approach to problems of federalism: I should like to see socialists feeling free to espouse whatever political trends or to use whatever constitutional tools happen to fit each particular problem at each particular time; and if my argument is taken to mean that the present socialist preconception in favour of centralism should permanently be replaced by a preconception in favour of provincial autonomy, I shall have completely failed to make my point.

ON STRATEGY AND TACTICS

The revolutionary bases, in spite of their insignificant size, are a great political force and strongly oppose the power of the Kuomintang, which spreads over vast regions . . . Revolution and revolutionary wars proceed from birth to development, from small to large, from lack of power to seizure of power . . .—Mao Tse-tung

If the whole of the Canadian electorate could miraculously be converted to socialist ideals at one fell swoop, there would be no reason to discuss strategy in the present context. Socialism would be achieved with or without federalism, and socialist administrations would be installed at every level of governmental affairs, no matter the form of the constitution.

But such is not the case. In a non-revolutionary society and in non-revolutionary times, no manner of reform can be implanted with sudden universality. Democratic reformers must proceed step by step, convincing little bands of intellectuals here, rallying sections of the working class there, and appealing to the underprivileged in the next place. The drive towards power must begin with the establishment of bridgeheads, since at the outset it is obviously easier to convert specific groups or localities than to win over an absolute majority of the whole nation.

Under a system of proportional representation the argument might run differently, and indeed that is why so many reformers have stood for PR. But it is obviously unrealistic to suppose that the governing parties will introduce electoral régimes that would hasten the accession to power of the oppositions. Consequently radical strategy must be designed to operate under the present electoral system of one-man constituencies.

In the absence of PR it seems obvious that the multi-state system of a federal constitution is the next best thing. (Indeed the experience of that superb strategist, Mao Tse-tung, might lead us to conclude that in a vast and heterogeneous country, the possibility of establishing socialist strongholds in certain regions is the very best thing.) It is strange that on the one hand CCF tacticians often argue that the road to power at the national level might have to pass through the election of socialist administrations at the municipal level, but that on the other hand, by casting themselves as very unenthusiastic supporters of provincial autonomy, they make it difficult for themselves to follow the provincial highroads towards national power. Such subservience of the tacticians to the postulates of the "theory class" is amazing, in face of the fact that the CCF has become the government or the official opposition in several provinces, whereas it has never come within sight of such successes in the national Parliament.

True, the successes of socialism at the provincial level, especially around the middle 1940's, did stimulate somewhat more interest in the provincial cause. But, for all that, a change of attitude to federalism still seems to be required within the ranks of Canadian socialism. No longer must our federal constitution be regarded as something to be undone, the result of a costly historical error which is only retained at all because of the "backward areas" of Canada. Federalism must not only be accepted as a datum with which Canada is stuck, as is many another country of semi-continental size. Federalism must be welcomed as a valuable tool which permits dynamic parties to plant socialist governments in certain provinces, from which the seed of radicalism can slowly spread.

Economists readily accept the fact that different areas have reached different stages of economic growth, and consequently that theories cannot be implemented everywhere in identical fashion.[1] Sociologists accept similar facts with similar consequences. It is urgent that socialist politicians give wider recognition to the fact that different regions or ethnic groups in Canada are at vastly different stages of their political development,[2] and that it is folly to endorse strategies that are devised to swing the whole country at the same time and in the same way into the path of socialism.

I have heard socialist leaders in Canada state with indignation that they would never "water down" their doctrines to make them more palatable to this or that part of Canada. Such an approach, I must admit, always puzzles me; for socialism, like every other political theory, has been diluted at different times and in different places to a great variety of strengths. And in terms of political tactics, the only real question democratic socialists must answer is: "Just how much reform can the majority of the people be brought to desire at the present time?"

The main distinction between the conservative and the progressive mind is that, in seeking the solution to the foregoing problem, the progressive will tend to overestimate the people's desire for justice, freedom and change, whereas the conservative will tend to err on the side of order, authority and continuity. The true tactical position of the *democratic* socialist is on the left, *but no further*.

Such a line of thought leads to the conclusion — unpleasant only for the doctrinaires — that socialists must stand for different things in different parts of Canada. Of course there is a need for doctrinaires of a sort; or at any rate for theoreticians who will constantly expound what they think to be the nearest thing to "pure" socialism. For, as it has been often observed, the dreamers of today frequently become the realists of tomorrow; and the educational value of painting utopias has repeatedly been established by the eventual realization of such goals through the democratic process.

Yet, so long as socialism is to seek fulfilment through parliamentary democracy, with its paraphernalia of parties and elections, there will be a constant need for the tactician as well as the theorist. And both will have to be reconciled by the strategist.

[1]See Scott Gordon's chapter in this book, wherein he accepts the possibility that the wage rate in the Maritimes will be lower than the Canadian average, providing the rate of growth is not. See also W. W. Rostov, *Stages of Economic Growth* (Cambridge, 1960), *passim*.

[2]The author attempted to show this in his "Some Obstacles to Democracy in Québec," in the *Canadian Journal of Economics and Political Science*, XXIV, no. 3, Aug., 1958, pp. 297–311.

Now it should be obvious to all these groups that no national party can keep its integrity while preaching a gospel which varies as it moves *a mari usque ad mare*; neither can it keep its status as a national party if it seeks support only in narrow regionalism. Yet, on the other hand, if the party preaches the same gospel everywhere, its partisans in some areas will desert it as being too reactionary, whereas in other areas the party will fail to find adherents because it appears too revolutionary.

That dilemma can easily be solved by making full use of our federative form of government. Socialists *can* stand for varying degrees of socialism in the various provinces of Canada by standing in autonomous provincial parties. Indeed, since the strength of a national party is largely determined by the strength of its component parts, sufficient priority must be given to the building of such parts. In other words, in building a national party of the left consideration must be given to what is provincially possible as well as to what is nationally desirable. The policy of the national party will thus be the result of a compromise between the most and the least advanced socialist thinking in various parts of Canada.

It is perhaps no coincidence that during the twentieth century, that is to say during the period when Canada has effectively developed into a vast and heterogeneous nation spreading from coast to coast, the one national party that has been strongest and governed longest is the party that has traditionally stood for provincial rights and embraced in its ranks such provincial free-stylers as Taschereau, Hepburn, Angus Macdonald, and Smallwood. For even while the Liberals at Ottawa were riding the wave of centralism, Liberal leaders in provincial capitals were stoutly defending the cause of autonomy.

By contrast, the CCF has reaped little electoral reward for its studied application in speaking with one voice and acting with one purpose in all parts of Canada. In Quebec alone, where the socialist vote has usually hovered around one per cent of the total, a book could be filled with the frustrations of former members of the CCF who felt or imagined that provincial affairs must always be subordinate to the *raison d'Etat* of the national party.

In the post-war era the Quebec organization squandered its efforts and ridiculed itself by running spurious candidates in two or three dozen ridings at each federal election, partly in order to obtain free time on the air-waves, but mainly in order that the electorate of the rest of Canada might be momentarily fooled into believing that the party was strong in Quebec. Then in 1956 and 1957, when efforts were being made to enlarge the left in Quebec by grouping all liberal-minded people in the *Rassemblement*, members of the CCF — on the grounds that the CCF was here to stay — refused to envisage any orientation that might lead to the setting up of a left-wing political group, newer and stronger than the CCF. Finally, in 1958 and 1959, when the CCF had decided it was no longer here to stay but here to merge into a new party, the Quebec branch of the CCF—on the grounds that it had to wait for the new party — rejected the *Union des forces démocratiques*, with the consequences, in June, 1960, that the *Union nationale* party was defeated by the Liberals alone rather than by a coalition of the left and of liberal-minded people.

The historical events briefly recited in the foregoing paragraph were the result of discussion and decision by honest men. If I refer to them in the present context it cannot be with the intention of displaying hindsight; for who knows what good or evil would have followed from the contrary decisions? But such references are necessary to illustrate what great pains were taken by the CCF in Quebec in order to avoid "nationalist deviationism." In view of Quebec's past, such a course was not without some justification, but it obviously went too far when it precluded the Quebec left from exploiting the same type of elementary opportunity as that which permitted the launching by Mr. Ed. Finn of *a* new party in Newfoundland, even though *the* new party had not yet fired the starting gun.

In short, the CCF in and out of Quebec always seemed to take the position that once it had become a powerful party at the national level it would easily find support in each province. Such an approach smacks of paternalism, if each province is taken singly; and it obviously begs the principle, if the situation is considered as a whole.

A greater amount of freedom for the left appears to be necessary at the provincial level. Just as each province must evolve towards political and economic maturity in its own good time, likewise radicalism in different parts of Canada must be implanted in different fashions. For a time, parties with the same name may find themselves preaching policies differing in scope from one province to the other. Perhaps even parties with different names may preach the same ideology in different provinces. And for a time, the situation of the left in Canada will not be cut and dried. It will be confused and challenging; and its diversity from province to province will stimulate competition and perhaps even establish a system of checks and balances, while at the national level the left will adopt strategies and tactics based on possibilities rather than on mere desirabilities.

The socialist mind is a planning one, so in all likelihood it will not respond enthusiastically to the pragmatic approach to strategy which is suggested here. Consequently, it may be well to point out that the present argument does not do away with the possibility of, or with the need for, planning at every level of politics; but it does lend emphasis to the importance of the plan at the provincial level, and hence it makes planning more effective.

Obviously, a strategy limited to Saskatchewan (or Quebec, or British Columbia) will be less exciting than one covering the whole of Canada. But it will also be less exciting than a plan applicable to the Socialist International. And much more telling than either!

It is sometimes argued by Canadian socialists that their opposition to the United States is not based on narrow nationalism, but on the fact that complete American domination would tend to prevent Canada as a community from realizing values good for human beings. In other words they believe that socialism can more easily be established in Canada, as a smaller unit, than on the whole North American continent. Surely then they should not underestimate the importance of trying to realize socialism in the even smaller units of the provinces, which have, within the limits of the constitution and particularly of section 92, many of the prerogatives of sovereign states.

ON HISTORY, PAST AND FUTURE

In so far as matters requiring concerted action can be dealt with by co-operation among the provinces, or between the Dominion and the provinces, the case for additional centralization to promote efficiency or uniformity will not arise.—The Rowell-Sirois Report

Of the countries of the world, Canada has the eighth oldest written constitution, the second oldest one of a federal nature, and the oldest which combines federalism with the principles of responsible government.

Yet some of our fellow Canadians have an even more illustrious record as pioneers in constitution-making: the Confederation of Six Iroquois Nations was founded in 1570, or thereabouts, and is still in existence today. Anthropologists and sociologists have marvelled at the keen political sense of Canada's earlier inhabitants. And the question arises whether historians will have the same opinion of the subsequent settlers!

If it be true that the first hundred years are the hardest, I see no cause to despair of the future of Canadian federalism. True, its erratic advance has caused many misgivings. There has been endless discussion as to the nature of the British North America Act, whether it be of the essence of a law or of a contract; and we have heard much argument from the lawyers and the senators, deploring the provincial bias given to the constitution by the Privy Council.

In reference to practical politics, such discussions can become tedious. It should be a sufficiently workable proposition to hold that the Act of 1867 was a law of the Imperial Parliament, but a law based on an agreement between federating parties, and consequently a law which can best be understood and interpreted (and eventually amended) by referring to the spirit of that agreement.

As to the criticism of the Privy Council's interpretation of the BNA

Act, it is basically in the same category as the criticism of the Supreme Court interpretations by a late premier of Quebec. In the final analysis, the ultimate decisions of the courts in matters of public concern always affect someone's politics adversely and will always be attacked on that basis.

Such criticism of the Privy Council by socialists is of course a political right. But I wonder how useful it is to the cause of socialism when it can be fairly construed as an opposition to provincial autonomy. For, as I shall argue later on, in section III of this chapter, socialists do not stand to gain very much in theoretical terms from vastly increased centralization. And in practical terms, I have tried to show in section I above, that they stand to lose a great deal. In point of fact, had the CCF been less identified with centralization I doubt whether it would have been weaker as a national party. On the contrary, its national strength might have benefited from the improved fortunes of the provincial parties. And I do not see how democratic socialism could have been adulterated in the process.

True, in present-day politics, there exists a number of built-in centralizing forces. The combination of external pressure and of improved internal communication may tend to unify large countries to a greater extent than in the past. Legislation may tend to become as broad as the problem with which it is meant to deal, and a federal constitution may not appear to be the best instrument for dealing with a non-federal economic society. The countervailing power to a corporate élite which is nation-wide in strength may have to be a government which is nation-wide in jurisdiction. And for all these reasons, the socialist will be tempted to enhance the power of the central government at the expense of the provinces.

But the true socialist will also be a humanist and a democrat and he will be quick to realize that Canada is very much a federal society from the sociological point of view; people from various parts of Canada *do* hang together on a regional basis which very often supersedes the class basis. And the understanding of Canadian political history would be very incomplete indeed if it ignored the existence, for instance, of the Maritimer, the Quebecker or the Westerner. In the first part of this chapter I have argued that the existence of such regional fidelities provided a tactical asset to the spread of radicalism. But I add here that they may eventually, in times when cybernetic planning is becoming a possibility, prove to be the main bulwark of democracy against a central government's *New Despotism,* its *Law and Orders* or its "parliamentary bureaucracy."

For there are physical limits to the control which may be exercised over the central bureaucracy by the people's representatives and by the judiciary. The executive power may tend to increase its control by increasing the number of ministers; but the cabinet will quickly reach that size beyond which deliberation becomes useless and decision impossible. (Thus, in the United Kingdom, out of some five dozen ministers, perhaps only half of them will be of cabinet rank and only twenty-odd will actually sit in the cabinet proper.) The legislative power can increase its control over the bureaucracy by increasing the length of the parliamentary session, but there again British experience shows that the entire year eventually proves too short; besides in as large a country as Canada, members of Parliament would lose all contact with the electorate if they had to sojourn in the federal capital indefinitely.

As regards the judiciary, its terms of reference are limited by the statutes themselves, which are generally prepared by the bureaucracy before being adopted by Parliament; the judiciary is powerless to exercise an over-all control of the bureaucracy as long as our system of administrative law remains in its present embryonic state.

In time, it is hoped that administrative law will be expanded and perfected, that Parliament will learn to use the committee system with greater effectiveness, and that other devices will be developed to protect democracy against bureaucracy. But in the meanwhile, and even after, it would be folly to disregard the device of federalism which we already have in our possession and which may be the most effective of all, since it reduces the magnitude of the task allotted to one central government.

Furthermore, in the age of the mass society, it is no small advantage to foster the creation of quasi-sovereign communities at the provincial level, where power is that much less remote from the people and where political education (and general creativeness) is related to more homogeneous and manageable groups of citizens.

Finally it might be added that at a time when the uncontrolled production of thermonuclear weapons has made total war a gruesome possibility, the case for decentralization in terms of defence extends far beyond the mere scattering of industries.

Caught between centripetal and centrifugal forces, Canada's future like its past may continue to oscillate between times of federal and times of provincial predominance, depending upon the immediate needs of the people and the temper of their various politicians. (For it must not be forgotten that these latter have a vested interest in strengthening *that* level of government at which *they* operate.) Or — more likely — the political future of Canada will lie in the direction of greater centralization in some areas and greater decentralization in others. But at all times, co-operation and interchange between the two levels of government will be, as they have been, an absolute necessity. In that sense, I doubt whether federalism in the classical sense has ever existed, that is to say a federation which would have divided the totality of its sovereign powers between regional and central governments with such sharpness and adequacy that those governments would have been able to carry on their affairs in complete independence of one another.

Applied to Canada, the foregoing statement is easily proven. The constitutional provisions of the B.N.A. Act established intergovernmental relationship as indispensable from the outset, between the executive, the legislative and the judicial organs.

Concerning the executive, the office of Lieutenant-Governor was designed to ensure a permanent bond between the federal and the provincial governments: the Lieutenant-Governor was definitely a federal official, appointed, paid and in some cases dismissed by the Ottawa government. The powers of reservation and disallowance also provided a link between the two levels of government. Finally the financing of the respective administrations was established as an area of indispensable co-operation: by Confederation the provinces gave up the bulk of their sources of revenue, retaining only direct taxes and various fees; in exchange the central government pledged itself to make the four different types of payment referred to in sections 111, 118 and 119 of the BNA Act.

As regards the legislative function, relations were inevitable in the areas of subordinate jurisdiction and in those of divided jurisdiction. Under the first heading fall sections 93, 94 and 95 of the BNA Act, relating to education, uniform legislation, agriculture and immigration; in that area we might also add cases of conditional legislation or of legislation by reference (but not of legislation by delegation which is deemed unconstitutional). Under the second heading (jurisdiction divided between the federal and the provincial legislative powers) fall four types of laws: first, laws concerning matters which can be regulated either by criminal or by civil law, such as the Sunday Observance Acts; second, laws concerning matters which fall partly under the federal residual clause ("peace, order and good government") and partly under the provincial residual clause ("all matters of merely local or private nature"), such as Temperance Acts; third, laws concerning matters which, according to their extension, are either "regulation of trade and commerce" or "property and civil rights," such as company laws, marketing laws and industrial legislation; fourth, laws concerning matters allocated (without subordination) to both federal and provincial jurisdiction, either by the letter of the BNA Act, such as direct taxation, or by judicial interpretation, such as fisheries.

Finally, in judicial matters, co-operation was of vital importance. By section 92, paragraph 14, the provinces were given exclusive jurisdiction over the administration of justice; by 96 the Governor General appoints "the Judges of the Superior, District and County Courts in each Province"; and by 101 the central government may establish a general court of appeals and any additional courts. If these sections in their application had not been reasonably well integrated, the judiciary would have ceased to function: rival tribunals would have been set up, *res judicata* would have had no meaning, and clash between executive powers would have been inevitable.

From the foregoing analysis of the BNA Act it is obvious that intergovernmental co-operation is not only possible but that it is in many ways constitutionally indispensable. It is not surprising therefore that the federal and provincial governments have developed many instruments for dealing with subjects of joint concern.

First in order of importance are the meetings of governments at ministerial level: the federal-provincial conferences of 1906, 1910, 1915, 1918, 1927, 1931, 1932, 1933, 1934, 1935, 1941, 1945-46, 1950, 1960 (not to be confused with the interprovincial conferences of 1887, 1902, 1910, 1913, 1926, 1960).

Second come the meetings of departments at ministerial level. This category includes, for example, the agricultural conferences, the Ministers of Mines Committee, the tourist conferences, all of which are generally annual meetings of the appropriate ministers and other personnel. Also included in this group are the Old Age Pension Interprovincial Board, the conferences set up for the exchange of statistical material, and those convened to discuss the Trans-Canada highway.

Third, at the purely administrative level, there exists a great variety of agreements and continuing organizations to deal co-operatively with specific matters of common concern. Typical examples include the Canadian Association of Administrators of Labour Legislation, the Conference of Commissioners on Uniformity of Legislation, the Committee on Security Frauds Prevention Law, the Committee on Uniform Company Law, the Fisheries Development Committee, the Fur Advisory Committee, the Provincial Boundary Commission, the Canadian Council on Nutrition, the Canadian Wild Life Conference, the Vocational Training Committee. Other examples might include the recently established "Resources for Tomorrow" Conference; co-operation in the fields of agricultural and forestry research and control; arrangements concerning citizenship training classes; co-ordination of health programmes; agreements whereby provincial officers administer the federal Migratory Birds Convention Act or some of the fisheries regulations enacted by the government of Canada; agreements whereby certain provinces delegate the policing of certain towns and rural districts to the RCMP.[3]

Finally, and in a category apart, one must consider the various types of financial arrangements between the federal government and the

[3]The foregoing enumeration is apt to appear long and tedious to the layman. But in order that he truly grasp the tremendous scope of federal-provincial relationships, I will add that in 1950, at the request of the Privy Council Office, I made a summary of existing federal-provincial co-operative arrangements which covered more than fifty pages.

provinces. As we stated above, the BNA Act made provision for certain types of federal payments. But government finance remained ever a problem: the subsidy basis was thoroughly altered by constitutional amendment in 1907, and in various ways since then. Federal grants-in-aid to help the provinces with specific tasks were also resorted to, though rather sparingly at first, since it was generally felt that the spending of funds should not be divorced from the perception thereof. This category also includes the tax-rental agreements, first begun during the Second World War, and periodically renewed, with varying degrees of provincial acceptance, the history of which is fairly well known.

The purpose of the foregoing paragraphs is to show that the story of Canadian federalism is one of constant intergovernmental exchange and co-operation. It is also in part a story of sometimes subtle, sometimes brazen, and usually tolerated encroachments by one government upon the jurisdiction of the other. For instance, the federal government (which has always shirked from using the jurisdiction over education it held under section 93, paragraph 4, of the BNA Act) has used grants-in-aid to enter resolutely into the areas of technical and university education. Indeed the federal "spending power" or so-called "power of the purse" is presently being construed as a federal right to decide (at the taxpayers' expense!) whether provincial governments are properly exercising any and every right they hold under the constitution.[4]

On the other hand, examples can be given of provincial encroachments upon federal jurisdiction. The invasion, supported by legal fiction, into the field of indirect taxation might be one case. Another example is the appointment of judges of provincial courts whose jurisdiction far exceeds the limits beyond which only that of federal judges was supposed to go, under section 96 of the constitution.[5]

In short, it almost seems as though whenever an important segment of the Canadian population needs something badly enough, it is eventually given to them by one level of government or the other, regardless of the constitution. The main drawback to such an approach is that it tends to develop paternalistic instincts in more enterprising governments, at the expense of democratic maturation in others. In areas where there exists a clear division of responsibilities between the federal and provin-

[4]In a brilliant chapter published in A. R. M. Lower, F. R. Scott, *et al.*, *Evolving Canadian Federalism* (Durham, NC, 1958), Professor Corry finds it "extraordinary that no one has challenged the constitutionality of the assumed spending power before the Supreme Court" (p. 119). I share his wonderment; but I find it even more extraordinary that political scientists fail to see the eroding effect that the "power of the purse" will have on Canadian democracy if the present construction continues to prevail, and in particular what chaos will result if provincial governments borrow federal logic and begin using their own "power of the purse" to meddle in federal affairs. (For a discussion of these points, see the author's "Les octrois fédéraux aux universités" in *Cité Libre*, Feb., 1957, particularly pp. 15–20.)

[5]I first heard this point raised by Mr. Benno Cohen of the Montreal Bar.

cial levels, there is no doubt that the only proper censor of a government which incompetently discharges its obligations is the electorate of *that* government, and not some other government responsible to some other (level of) electorate.[6] And if, for example, federal politicians are convinced that by their very nature the totality of the provincial governments *cannot* discharge their duties in some area, surely the proper procedure is for those politicians to seek the overt transfer of such areas into federal jurisdiction, either by way of constitutional amendment (as in the case of unemployment insurance), or by invoking federal powers under section 92, paragraph 10 (c).[7]

It might be wise to labour this point further, since it will illustrate how certain policies, though conceived in terms of the general welfare and applied in a spirit of co-operation, can in reality be paternalism in disguise.

Thus far in this chapter I have studiously avoided making a special case for French Canada. But at this time it is necessary to discuss the special case English-Canadian writers sometimes make on its behalf.

It has been very ably argued that "the initial survival of French culture in Canada did not depend upon provincial autonomy"; and further that "the possession of provincial autonomy was a relatively minor factor in the growth of French culture and influence during the first half century after 1867."[8] Both facts are quite true; but not true is the inference that many people draw from them, to wit, that the survival and growth of French-Canadian culture do not (at the present time) depend upon the existence of provincial autonomy. Such an inference might only be true if culture were defined to exclude the art of self-government. As a matter of fact, if the ability to govern themselves is such a minor facet of the French Canadians' cultural make-up today, it is precisely because in the past French Canadians never learned to make proper use of their elective governments as servants of the whole community.[9]

Typically, Quebec's two most recent champions of provincial autonomy, Premiers Taschereau and Duplessis, were socially and economically

[6]I will consider the case of disallowance and of reservation later on. But it might avoid considerable misunderstanding if I state immediately and unequivocally that I hold equalization grants (enabling poorer provinces to keep pace with the richer ones) and counter-cyclical fiscal policies to be within the jurisdiction of the federal government.

[7]In this respect it might be remarked that if these latter means are infrequently used, it is partly because central governments, who occasionally like to meddle in provincial affairs, do not necessarily relish the prospect of being saddled with some new responsibility for ever. It is interesting to note that while it took over sole responsibility for unemployment *insurance*, the federal government has always scrupulously avoided the claim that unemployment *in general* was a matter within the jurisdiction of the federal government.

[8]Frank Scott, "French-Canada and Canadian Federalism" in Lower, Scott, *et al.*, *Evolving Canadian Federalism*, pp. 57 and 59.

[9]I have tried to explain the reasons for this in the article quoted in n. 2.

conservatives. They barely exercised many of the powers given to them by the autonomy they so loudly affirmed and, as a result, social and cultural legislation was the product of the central government over which the French-Canadian electorate had no absolute control.

Now there is no need to remind me that the central government is not foreign, but is the government of all Canadians. And I do not find good legislation distasteful merely because it originates in Ottawa as opposed to Quebec.[10] The real question lies elsewhere: can a cultural group, which by virtue of the Act of 1867 received the right to govern itself in many areas of jurisdiction, ever mature democratically if it persistently neglects or refuses to exercise its right? And are not such omissions or refusals inevitable if the lacunae they create are constantly and adequately filled up by a central government which is largely representative of another cultural group? To give but one example: from the Quebec point of view, the most serious objection to federal grants to universities was obviously not that the universities had enough money or that federal money had a peculiar odour; it was that once the universities had their bellies filled with federal grants they would see no reason to oppose that provincial government which had persistently failed in its constitutional duties by leaving education in such an impoverished state; and Quebeckers would chalk up another failure in their struggle to master the art of self-government.

At this point, a comment may well be forthcoming: should the universities of the poorer provinces be faced with starvation simply because Quebec is showing signs of embarking upon the slow process of political maturation? The objection is typical of all those which keep Quebec nationalism alive. For it is basically emotional and misses the point that the university grants were not equalization grants since they were handed to all provinces, rich and poor, on the same basis. Nor, for that matter, were they anti-cyclical in nature since they were initiated and continued in times of inflation, when the central government should have been trying to reduce its spending. To the average Quebecker therefore, the university grants appeared to be an invasion pure and simple of provincial rights.[11]

[10]As a matter of fact I might be prepared to argue that some day, if and when *inter alia* the political maturity of all Canadians had reached a very high level, a more centralized state would be acceptable for Canada.

[11]There is here neither time nor place to deal at length with the subject of federal grants to universities. However, I wish to make it quite clear that the Quebec argument is based on the explicit position of the federal authorities that they have no jurisdiction whatsoever over education. (*Cf.* Mr. St. Laurent's speech at Sherbrooke in October, 1956, and one on November 12th of that year.) Since the grants cannot be justified on grounds of federal jurisdiction over education, nor in terms of macro-economic stabilization, nor for reasons of equalization policy, there only remains the argument of "the power of the purse." That prerogative is interpreted to mean that any government can raise money by taxation for purposes outside of its jurisdiction, providing it gives the money without any

Most English Canadians fail to realize that it is their attitude (as in the above example) which exactly determines the extent and force of Quebec nationalism. Central government encroachments, which are accepted in other provinces as matters of expediency, cannot be so viewed in Quebec. For French Canadians are not in any important sense represented in the Canadian power élite, whether governmental or financial,[12] and any attempt at unilateral transference of power from the Quebec élite to the Canadian one will naturally set the corresponding defence mechanisms in motion. On the contrary, a scrupulous respect of the postulates of federalism — by rendering such mechanisms obsolete — will lend greater force to the efforts of those Quebeckers who are trying to turn their province into an open society. And perhaps more important still, it will create a climate where the debate between autonomy and centralization can be solved through rational rather than emotional discussion.

The upshot of my entire argument in this section is that socialists, rather than water down (to use a previous expression) their socialism, must constantly seek ways of adapting it to a bicultural society governed under a federal constitution. And since the future of Canadian federalism lies clearly in the direction of co-operation, the wise socialist will turn his thoughts in that direction, keeping in mind the importance of establishing buffer zones of joint sovereignty and co-operative zones of joint administration between the two levels of government.

The establishment of such areas of confidence is very important; for when parties stand as equals at negotiations, the results are invariably better and fairer. That perhaps is why there has been a great deal of effective co-operation between federal and provincial departmental officials; each feels that he is answerable only to his own "sovereign" government. Might not machinery be established to extend this feeling to meetings at the highest levels with similar beneficial result?

There have been many proposals for setting up machinery to ensure better co-operation between the federal and the provincial governments. The most frequent concern the desirability of having periodical federal-provincial conferences with a permanent secretariat to ensure their suc-

---

attempt to legislate. In my view such an interpretation is not only wrong but dangerous: for it would, for instance, authorize the provinces to tax in order to pay a large bonus to any federal civil servants or military personnel who could prove their mastery of the French language; or to any federal judge whose philosophy was "sound." And so on. (For lengthy argument on these and other points, see the article referred to in n. 4. This business of referring to my own writings is not particularly pleasant; but in some places I feel I am writing against the grain of certain readers and I find it only fair to refer them to the places where my arguments are substantiated at some length.)

[12]See John Porter's work on economic and bureaucratic élites, *CJEPS*, Aug., 1957, p. 386, and Nov., 1958, p. 491. For other references, see P. E. Trudeau, ed., *La Grève de l'Amiante* (Montreal, 1956), p. 77.

cessful functioning. A less frequent proposal advocates the establishment of a secretary of state for the provinces at Ottawa, and a department of federal relations in each province. It has also been suggested that if governments were constitutionally permitted to delegate legislative powers to one another there would be much greater co-operation between them.

Of course there exist many more devices for promoting co-operative federalism.[13] And others still await discovery. By way of example I might single out a rather neglected piece of co-operative machinery: royal commissions of inquiry could become a very important medium of co-operation between governments in Canada, rather than the causes of friction they sometimes are now. Reliable information upon matters of joint concern is essential to the pursuance of harmonious federal-provincial relations; it is therefore surprising that in such matters royal commissions tend[14] to be the exclusive creation of the executive branch of *one* government, which in effect exercises inquisitorial activities over acts within the jurisdiction of other governments. Surely in such cases, some method should be devised for the setting up of joint commissions of inquiry, appointed by the several governments and reporting back to them.

But unfortunately there is here neither time nor place to discuss these matters further. It would be regrettable, however, if Canadian socialists found too little time to discuss them. For if it be true that Canada's future lies in the direction of co-operative federalism, it will be guided there by those parties and politicians who will have proven themselves most realistic and farseeing in that regard.

ON THEORY

To seek to unify the state excessively is not beneficial. . . . The state, as its unification . . . will be a worse state, just as if one turned a harmony into unison or rhythm into a single foot. — Aristotle

It would seem at first glance that many of the more important economic policies of socialism can only be applied with thoroughness under

[13]Thus in Australia co-operative action has been greatly facilitated by such institutions as the Premiers' Conferences and the Loan Council. The United States, which, it might be argued, is more centrally controlled than Canada, has also experimented with many devices of inter-state co-operation: the Governors' Conferences, the Regional Conferences of Governors, the Council of State Governments, the American Legislators' Association, the different national associations of Secretaries of State, of Supervisors of State Banks, etc.

[14]Quasi-exceptions—too rare to create a contrary trend—have existed. For instance, Mr. Mackenzie King in 1909 obtained the approval of all provinces before proceeding with the appointment of a Commission on Industrial Training and Technical Education. In 1948 the Fraser Valley Commission included commissioners nominated by federal and provincial governments, and was asked to report to both.

a unitary form of government. Economic planning and control have little meaning unless they are part of a unified, well integrated process. Therefore, the argument goes, a socialist must, in essence, be a centralizer.

Fiscal and monetary policies, for instance, are bound to have little beneficial effect if various central and regional governments are at liberty to cancel out each other's actions by contradictory policies. Thus a deficitary federal budget would have but slight effect upon national deflationary trends if provincial surpluses added up to an amount equal to the federal deficit.

However, it must be pointed out that from that point of view socialists are no worse off than neo-capitalists or Keynesian liberals. The stabilization policies of these latter groups might also be easier to apply in a unitary state; but in its absence, those groups do not throw up their hands in despair, nor do they cast political caution to the winds by becoming crusaders against provincial rights. They merely set out to find ways of adapting their economic theories to the political realities.

In Canada, there exists no constitutional problem as regards monetary policy, since money, banking and the interest rate all fall under the single jurisdiction of the central government. However, regarding fiscal policy the difficulties are great, since provincial governments have autonomous budgets and consequent taxing, borrowing and spending powers. And, for instance, Canadian post-war inflation was no doubt aggravated to the extent that certain provincial deficits operated against federal surpluses.

It is to the credit of the Liberals that they devised and implemented tax-rental agreements between the central and regional governments which curtailed the degree to which the fiscal practices of the various governments might operate at cross-purposes. But as time went by it became obvious that Liberal logic, as expressed during the 1945 Conference (and in the Green Book), was in reality a vicious circle: the federal government — because it had greater financial resources — argued that it should bear greater social responsibility and therefore that its financial powers should be correspondingly increased.

It is to the credit of the reactionaries (I am referring to Mr. Duplessis and his *Union nationale*)[15] that they refused to be deceived by a system whereby the federal government could, in lieu of the provincial government, tax the citizen in all the provinces in order to spend monies (on a scale far in excess of that which might have been required for stabilization or equalization policies) for purposes within provincial jurisdiction. But it is not to the credit of the socialists that they should have been

[15]See the author's "De libro, tributo et quibusdam aliis" in *Cité Libre*, Oct., 1954, esp. pp. 6–9.

little more than by-standers, goading the Liberals on, during this whole episode.[16]

At the present time, when Canadian public opinion, led by the Liberal Premier of Quebec and the Conservative Premier of Ontario, apparently unopposed by the socialist Premier of Saskatchewan, seems to be running amok in favour of extreme provincialism, as witnessed by the federal-provincial conference held in the summer of 1960, there is a greater need than ever for an enlightened socialist approach to the fiscal problems of a federal form of government. If the swing towards centralism, which began with the Depression, is not now to be countered by a long swing towards excessive regionalism, there will be an urgent need for solutions based on co-operation.

It is quite conceivable that Canadian fiscal policy could be considered from month to month and year to year by a joint continuing committee of federal and provincial officials and experts. Confronted with comprehensive sets of statistical material and forecasting data, such a committee — if it were immunized against all forms of political interference — could make policy recommendations as well as any body of purely central officials; and perhaps even better, since they would take greater cognizance of such problems as regional bottle-necks, local unemployment, and immobility of labour, and since the hitherto purely federal control over money and banking would be examined in the light of provincial budgetary needs.

Of course, it would be up to the several provincial and central governments to decide what they would do with the policy recommendations. And this is where co-operation at the executive levels would appear to be of extreme importance and would have to be recognized as such. But one could count, in the first place, on some degree of moral suasion to which the governments might find themselves subjected. And in the second, the various electorates — when the time came to judge the financial policies of their respective governments — would be less inclined than now to condone incompetence or ignorance.

For there is no escape from politics, nor should there be. There is always one point where the most expert economic advice must be submitted for implementation to the political representatives of the people. "I know no safe depository of the ultimate powers of society but the people themselves; and if we think them not enlightened enough to exer-

---

[16]Exception should be made for the group which headed the Quebec Federation of Industrial Unions (CCL). Their *Mémoire à la Commission royale d'enquête sur les problèmes constitutionnels* (Montreal, 1954) was the first document or statement I know of, which reconciled the rationale of provincial tax deductibility with that of equalization grants and macro-economic stabilization. And the preface to the second edition showed that the formulae which had just been worked out by the St. Laurent and the Duplessis governments were wrong, in that they were based on unilateral action and in that they betrayed the very principles of anti-cyclical budgeting.

cise this control with a wholesome discretion, the remedy is not to take it from them, but to inform their discretion by education" (Thomas Jefferson). And as I have shown in sections I and II of this chapter, the people can "exercise their control" just as well under a federal state as under a unitary one, and perhaps even better.

Consequently the economic aspects of socialist theory might be a guide towards a more efficient distribution of powers under the constitution; but they need never be considered as an invitation to turn Canada, any more than all of North America or the whole world itself, into a unitary state. Planning is a possibility at any and every level of government. It may be more costly (in economic terms of outlay, leakage, multiplier effect, and so on) at one level of government than at another.[17] But the incidence of political cost (in terms of freedom, self-government, local pride and ingenuity) might be completely the reverse.[18] The true planner is the one who tries to minimize cost and maximize satisfaction, in every way and not only in dollars and cents.

The foregoing argumentation can be applied to every aspect of economic theory. Investment planning and resource development, for instance, both become in the last analysis matters for political decision. In economic terms it may be possible to compare the costs of building and operating a zinc mine at Hay River, a railway in Labrador, a steel mill near Verchères, a university in Prince Rupert, and the marginal productivity of each. But the social value of such enterprises can only be appreciated with reference to political realities. And the final choice will have to be a political one.

Consequently, in such matters, there is no reason to presume that the federal government will be more enlightened than the sum of the provincial governments, or even than one provincial government acting alone. Since ultimately the decisions are political rather than economic, it follows that they can be taken by provinces as well as by the central government. And a (socialist) province with a planning board might be more likely to plan wisely than a (reactionary) central government with no such board.

[17]Even in strictly economic terms, however, it is too readily assumed that planning should necessarily be a centralized function. Recent studies of planning in the Soviet Union underline "les nécessités de la décentralisation" and the importance of "des centres de décisions autonomes" (Cahiers de l'I.S.E.A. no. 86, (Paris, 1959)). And in this connection I am grateful to my friend Mr. Fernand Cadieux for having pointed out to me certain recent trends in the study of social institutions: in their book *Organizations* (New York, 1958), March and Simon invoke "the principle of bounded rationality as an important force making for decentralization" as opposed to central planning; in other words, "given realistic limits on human planning capacity, the decentralized system will work better than the centralized" (pp. 203–9).

[18]"Le premier effet de la centralisation est de faire disparaître dans les diverses localités d'un pays toute espèce de caractère indigène; tandis qu'on s'imagine par ce moyen exalter dans la masse la vie politique, on la détruit dans ses parties constitutives et jusque dans ses éléments." Proudhon.

In other words, economic planning must eventually be reduced to political planning. And the economic theory of socialism cannot be divorced from its political theory, which is largely bound to strategy and tactics.

Thus we revert to the first section of this chapter, which recommended pragmatism, condemned paternalism, and paid great heed to the different stages of political maturity. Since regionalisms do exist in Canada, such feelings should be exploited to further the cause of democracy: each community might enter into a state of healthy competition with the others in order to have better "self-government"; and thus the whole Canadian system of government would be improved by creative tensions between the central, the provincial, and even the municipal administrations.

Regarding such tensions and competition, it is not for the socialist to cast his lot irrevocably with one level of government as opposed to another. (It is not, for instance, because the reactionaries have in the main opposed centralization that socialists should necessarily favour it!) Since the sum total of governments has the sum total of powers, the first task of the socialist is to educate all of the people to demand maximum service from all of their governments. And his second task is to show how any unhealthy tensions can be resolved through co-operation.

Since every Canadian has a right to the good life, whatever the province or community he lives in, the socialist should define the minimum conditions required for that life, and make them a part of the socialist programme. But such goals must first be stated without any preconception as to whether they should be realized at the federal or at the provincial level. It is often said that the concept of provincial autonomy is favourable to corporate wealth, since it weakens the power of the (central) state. But it can just as easily be shown that it favours socialism, as in the case of Saskatchewan.[19] And, as was pointed out earlier, there is certainly no reason to believe that socialism in Canada is nearer to realization at the federal rather than at the provincial level.

Federalism then must be regarded as a *chose donnée* of Canadian politics; and in the debate which opposes centralization to autonomy, socialists should be as detached and pragmatic as they hope to become in the debate over public versus private ownership; those are all means, and not ends, and they must be chosen according to their usefulness in each specific case.

Of course it should not be adduced from the foregoing paragraph

[19]The riots that occurred in Belgium during the first days of 1961 underline the importance of a decentralized state to the cause of socialism. According to Jean Lambion, an outstanding socialist trade-union official, "federation [instead of a unitary state] would give us Walloons a socialist government to carry out long overdue social and economic reforms we desperately require. There is no other way we can get those things." (*Montreal Star*, Jan. 7, 1961).

that the division of sovereign powers under a federal constitution is held to be purely a matter of arbitrariness and indifference. Obviously some laws and some areas of administration should, by their very nature, come under one level of government rather than under the other. And there is surely some good trying to improve upon, or modernize, the rational but perhaps aging division of powers adopted by the Fathers of Confederation. I am inclined to believe, however, that Canadian socialists have exaggerated the urgency of rewriting or reinterpreting the BNA Act.

Personally I cannot share the views of those people who seem to feel that, had the trend of Privy Council decisions favouring provincial autonomy been different, the fate of the Canadian people would have been immeasurably improved in the past. Neither can I agree with those who, having read long-run centralizing trends into our political future, predict the virtual withering away of Canadian federalism and oblige the political party to which they belong to stand or fall on the fulfilment of such prophecies.

As I have shown above, most of the reforms that could come about through greater centralization could also follow from patient and painstaking co-operation between federal and provincial governments. And the remaining balance of economic advantage that might arise from forcefully transferring more power to the central government is easily offset by the political disadvantages of living under a paternalistic or bullying government.

Granted the foregoing statement, it is difficult to see why socialists devote such energy to constitutional might-have-been's or ought-to-be's, instead of generally accepting the constitution as a datum. From the point of view of "making available to all what we desire for ourselves," it is not of such momentous consequence that the subject matter of some particular law falls within the jurisdiction of the federal as opposed to the provincial governments, since in either case the governments are responsible to one electorate or another. In other words, laws — whether they issue from one central government or from ten provincial governments — benefit the same sets of citizens. The only important thing then, is that these latter clearly know which level of government is responsible for what area of legislation, so that they may be aroused to demand good laws from *all* their governments.

A sound rule for Canadian socialists would be to insist that, if need be, they are prepared to carry out their ideals under the present constitution. Thus they would be encouraged to educate and organize at *all* levels of the electorate. And the various federal or provincial socialist parties and programmes would tend to concentrate on that part of the socialist ideals that can be implemented at *their* level of government.

This would not prevent socialist parties from stating in certain limited cases that reforms might be carried out more efficiently if the constitution were amended. But in such cases, amendments would be clearly mentioned, and not sly encroachments which inevitably result in confusing the electorate as to which level of government is responsible for what. Nor would the proposed amendments all, and as a matter of course, tend to be in the direction of centralization.

For instance, provincial socialist parties should stand for provincial labour codes, and for co-operation between the various governments under the constitution to establish minimum labour standards from coast to coast. But that would not necessarily prevent the same men, as members of the socialist party at the national level, from standing for a constitutional amendment permitting Parliament to legislate upon a national labour code if and when the provinces should fail to arrive at one through co-operative action. There are even some cases where socialists at all levels could unite in advocating *joint* federal-provincial legislation.[20]

For example again, when socialists advocate a constitutional amendment enacting a bill of rights for all Canadians and all governments in Canada, they might simultaneously advocate the abolition of the federal right to disallow and to reserve provincial laws, since such safeguards would then be obsolete.[21] For example also, socialists might well prove their lack of bias between central and regional governments by proposing that the Supreme Court be really established as an impartial arbitrator in constitutional cases. This could be done by making the Court independent of the federal and the provincial governments, just as the Privy Council used to be. Thus the Supreme Court Act would cease to be a federal statute, and could be entrenched in the constitution. And the judges might be chosen alternately from panels submitted by the federal and the provincial governments.

To sum up and conclude this chapter, it might well be said that the basis of a socialist ideology is to work out a certain set of human values, for the fostering of which society is held collectively responsible.

The basis of a socialist programme is to state what minimum standards of the good life must ensue from that set of values, and to demand that those standards be made available to all, given the federal data that some like to live by the sea, some in the plains, and that some prefer to speak French.

The basis of a socialist critique is to state clearly what the provincial governments can do and fail to do, and what the federal government can do and does not do, each within its respective jurisdiction.

Finally, the basis of socialist action is to define the various ways of striving towards socialist goals under a federal constitution, and to lead each community towards such goals as it can hope to attain.

[20]This is spelt out in some detail on pp. 23–4 of the *Mémoire* cited in n. 16.
[21]Personally I would be prepared to argue that they are obsolete in any case.

To many an idealist, it may appear that socialism within a federal structure of government is not as pure, as exciting, and as efficient as socialism in a unitary state. That may be so, just as democratic socialism may be less efficient and far-reaching than the totalitarian brand. But just as democracy is a value in itself, which cannot be sacrificed to considerations of expediency, likewise at certain times and in certain places federalism may be held to be a fundamental value, and the penalty for disregarding it may be the complete collapse of socialism itself.

Social Planning and
Canadian Federalism

F. R. SCOTT

From the day of its founding the CCF party anticipated that the building of a socialist society would require constitutional change in Canada. A British North America Act drafted for a predominantly agricultural community in 1867 could hardly be expected to fit an industrialized economy operated on principles of economic planning. Yet the degree of change required was not at all clear. The Regina Manifesto in 1933 did not propose any specific shift in the distribution of legislative powers as between Ottawa and the provinces; it contented itself with the statement that "What is chiefly needed today is the placing in the hands of the national government of more power to control national economic development." All were agreed that there must be more central authority, for reasons obvious to anyone faced with the conditions in Canada at the time. But this was centralization for planning's sake, not for centralization's sake. Indeed, the Manifesto also speaks of "the increasing industrialization of the country and the consequent centralization of economic and financial power which has taken place in the last two generations." Private centralization had obviously already taken place in the hands of big business — a centralization before which the provinces were power-less. What was needed was a countervailing public power to restore the national interest. Only the Parliament of Canada was seen as big enough for this task. In CCF thinking, strengthening federal authority for this purpose therefore took away jurisdiction, not from provincial govern-ments, but from a "small irresponsible minority of financiers and indus-trialists." That the CCF opposed any extreme centralization is evident from its reference, in the Manifesto, to the historic distinction between "matters of common interest" and "local matters," adopted by the Fathers of Confederation at the Quebec Conference of 1864, and from its description of public ownership as being "Dominion, Provincial or Municipal." The party, despite its socialist objectives, always accepted the principles of Canadian federalism.

By 1935, when *Social Planning for Canada* was published, the fields where federal powers needed reinforcement were being clarified. In that book it was argued that a great deal of the supposed weakness in federal authority was due, not to the BNA Act, but to "long years of planned inactivity on the part of Liberal and Conservative governments" (p. 504). The non-use of existing powers was more striking than the absence of powers. Unquestioned authority existed to deal with interna-tional trade, interprovincial trade and communications, banking, cur-rency and interest; there was the declaratory power over local works which could bring them within federal jurisdiction; federal taxing powers were virtually unrestricted. The desire in the old parties for reform was obviously less than the constitutional authority for reform. Yet certain areas remained beyond federal reach and, in the opinion of the authors, required federal action. These were said to be related to (1) social legislation, particularly in respect of labour matters, where it was felt concurrent powers might be adequate for the Dominion, (2) aspects of intraprovincial trade and commerce given to the provinces by judicial interpretation, (3) insufficient control over corporations and insurance companies, and (4) lack of clarity in federal-provincial finan-cial arrangements. At that time, a federal power to implement interna-tional treaties was thought to exist; Mr. Bennett had just ratified three conventions of the International Labour Organization and had enacted legislation which was only later referred to the courts by Mr. King and held *ultra vires*. The constitutional aspects of national planning were already reduced to what seemed like manageable proportions, im-plying change but no drastic overhauling of the Canadian system of government.

It will be interesting now to contrast what *Social Planning* proposed with what has actually happened in the growth of the Canadian consti-tution since 1935. Many changes have taken place, both in the law and custom of the constitution. With a few notable exceptions, they have tended to be along the lines suggested in so far as the distribution of legislative power is concerned. In 1934 the central bank, demanded in the Regina Manifesto, was created, and by 1938 was made a wholly owned state bank. A national currency emerged, signed by public officials rather than by bank presidents. The Rowell-Sirois Report surveyed the experiences of the depression years and recommended a variety of changes in government responsibility; the provinces were to keep the lesser social services, but the Dominion was to assume unemployment insurance, contributory old age pensions, jurisdiction over minimum wages, maximum hours and minimum age of employment, and the power to implement ILO conventions; it was, in addition, to deal with marketing even when intraprovincial trade was affected, and to supervise all insurance companies except those confined to one province. These recommendations were thus specifically designed to overcome the Privy Council's disastrous decisions of 1937 on Mr. Bennett's "New Deal" legislation, which had struck down the first unemployment insurance and federal marketing laws as well as the statutes implementing the three ILO conventions.[1] In its financial recommendations the Rowell-Sirois Report was even bolder; all provincial debts were to be assumed by Ottawa, and provincial subsidies based on population were to be replaced by national adjustment grants calculated to meet the proved fiscal needs of the provinces. Future provincial debts were to be in Canadian currency only, unless approval was obtained from the Finance Commission. The provinces were also to withdraw from personal and corporation income taxes, and succession duties. The Report has passed into history, but it left behind, besides a reflection of the left-of-centre trend of opinion in the 1930's, the unemployment insurance amendments to the constitution of 1940 and a distribution of tax fields that was accepted in subsequent federal-provincial taxation agreements.

The war years changed Canada's constitutional position in international affairs, notably by establishing her independent right to declare war and make peace, but they did not compel a change in the distribution of legislative powers. They did, however, enormously increase the knowledge of what might be accomplished within the existing distribution. Perhaps most of the wartime economic planning could have been justified under the "emergency" doctrine which, as enunciated by the courts, permits extensive federal legislation based on the "peace, order and good government" clause of the constitution of a kind not permissible when there is no emergency. Indeed, given a sufficiently dangerous situation, Canada becomes virtually a unitary state; we possess a theory of the *état de siège* in our law, though no mention of it appears in the BNA Act. Apart from emergency powers, however, there were other

[1] The unemployment insurance reference will be found in [1937] Appeal Cases 355; the marketing reference, *ibid.*, 377; the ILO reference, *ibid.*, 326. Comments on the cases will be found in 15 *Canadian Bar Review* (1937).

sources of federal authority in the ordinary law capable of extensive use for economic planning during the war; classes of subjects such as defence, interest, banking, taxation and the spending power fully justified federal control of military production and monetary and fiscal policy at that time.

The emergence of monetary and fiscal planning was one of the major developments of the war experience of 1939–45. Maynard Keynes put more substance back into federal powers than Lord Haldane had ever taken out, and the techniques he suggested are now widely accepted if not always consistently applied. The federal Government after the war followed Keynesian policies with varying degrees of eagerness and success, and no changes in the law of the constitution were found necessary. Existing federal powers, supplemented by agreements with most of the provinces, sufficed. Parliament, having jurisdiction over "The Public Debt and Property," was competent to dispose of federal Crown money by gift or conditional grant, so long as the law providing for the expenditure did not purport to change any existing law in the provinces. This enabled federal spending to be directed to the achievement of a wide variety of social and economic goals. Hence, for example, were established family allowances,[2] pensions for the blind, a national housing programme, grants to universities, allowances for disabled persons and floor prices for agricultural products. Some of the federal grants are made direct to recipients without provincial intervention, as are family allowances; others form the basis of federal-provincial agreements, as does hospital insurance; both are instruments of social planning involving no constitutional change. A co-operative federalism can achieve much with this approach. The 1951 amendment defining federal jurisdiction over old age pensions was useful, but probably only clarified a power that previously existed. It introduced a new principle into the constitution, however, by specifically subjecting federal old age pension law to existing or future provincial laws.[3] In all other instances of concurrent powers in the BNA Act, a valid federal law prevails over any provincial law in conflict with it.

Besides constitutional amendment, judicial interpretation has been clarifying important aspects of federal jurisdiction. On four matters of serious national concern the courts have rendered decisions which denied federal powers and which have left us with unresolved governmental problems. These are judgments in the Snider case (to refer back to 1925),[4] which reduced federal jurisdiction in labour matters to federal

---

[2]The Family Allowance Act was upheld in *Angers* v. *Min. of National Revenue*, [1957] Ex. C.R. 83

[3]BNA Act, s. 94A.

[4]*Toronto Electric Commissioners* v. *Snider*, [1925] Appeal Cases 396. See F. R. Scott, "Federal Jurisdiction over Labour Relations—A New Look," *McGill Law Journal* (1960), at p. 153

undertakings; the Labour Conventions case (1937)[5] which reduced the power to implement treaties to matters otherwise within federal jurisdiction; the Marketing Act case (1937)[6] which overthrew a nation-wide marketing scheme supported by every provincial legislature; and the Delegation case (1951)[7] which held that a delegation of powers from Parliament to legislature or vice versa was unconstitutional. The first three of these decisions upset existing federal statutes; the last imposed a new limitation on all legislatures in Canada. The seeming victory for the provinces was a hollow one, except in so far as it fixed the status quo; the marketing situation is today very confused, and what positive use can provinces make of the power to implement treaties when they can have no diplomatic representatives abroad, or of the power to make laws on labour relations when more and more industries in each province are controlled by a single national board of directors which deals with a single trade union? The futile attempts of provincial governments to settle the Packinghouse Workers' strike in 1947, while the federal Government sat helplessly on the side lines, is a standing example of the danger of confiding large issues to small jurisdictions in a federal state.[8]

More recent judicial interpretation has suggested that some of these decisions may be modified and their more extreme effects overcome. When the Empire Treaty of 1919 which supported federal jurisdiction over aeronautics was replaced by a purely Canadian treaty, the courts found that the subject was one which fell within the "peace, order and good government" clause of the constitution, though there was no national emergency at the time.[9] If this clause, which was intended by the Fathers of Confederation to serve as the residuary clause of the constitution, and which Lord Haldane reduced to a war emergency power, could be restored to its original place in the law, a number of difficulties in national planning could be overcome. Matters which have "grown up" through social change to become truly national could then be legislated on in their national aspects. It would be rash, however, to imply that this point has been reached. In regard to delegation, some of the effects of the 1951 reference case have been overcome by a subsequent holding that delegation, not from legislature to legislature, but from legislature to subordinate administrative bodies, is permissible.[10]

---

[5]See n. 1 above.

[6]*Ibid.*

[7]*A. G. of Nova Scotia* v. *A. G. of Canada*, [1951] S.C.R. 31.

[8]The story of this attempt is told in Scott, "Federal Jurisdiction over Labour Relations." The strike in the Dominion Bridge Co. in 1960 was caused by the Company's refusal to accept nation-wide bargaining for certain items.

[9]*Johannesson* v. *Mun. of West St. Paul*, [1952] 1 S.C.R. 292, and note by Bora Laskin in 35 *Canadian Bar Review* (1957), at p. 101.

[10]See the *Willis* case, [1952] 2 S.C.R. 392 and note by John Ballem in 30 *Canadian Bar Review* (1952), at p. 1050.

The logic of this is unconvincing, but an example of its working may be seen in the federal delegation to provincial transportation commissions of the power, granted Ottawa in the Winner case,[11] to regulate trucking and bus services crossing provincial boundaries.[12] Delegation here produced decentralization; it could be used in the reverse direction. As pointed out above, the constitutional position of marketing legislation is very unsatisfactory, owing to the 1937 decision, but even here there are signs that the courts may begin to take a more realistic view of the trade and commerce clause. The notion of "interprovincial trade" is becoming clearer, and is more frequently found in federal statutes; of even greater significance is the acceptance of the notion that trade within a province may enter into a "current" or "flow" of trade, a "stream of commerce" which may take it out of provincial jurisdiction and bring it under the federal power. Germinal ideas of this nature are to be found in the Ontario Farm Products Marketing Act reference of 1957[13] and the Murphy case of 1958,[14] more especially in the masterly judgments of Judge Rand. What Professor Laskin calls the "thaw" in the frozen trade and commerce clause[15] seems to have set in, and Canada may be beginning to follow the trend of American decisions some fifty years later.

In another large field of constitutional law recent developments are of particular interest to socialists. This is the area of human rights. Unless these expand as society grows, the socialist goal is unattained, for no amount of economic security can make up for their loss. Freedom, like full employment, can be made a goal of planning; it is not accidental that the book of essays on planning published by the CCF in 1943 was called *Planning for Freedom,* or that it contained a special chapter on freedom. In a series of judgments during the 1950's the Supreme Court of Canada had occasion to take its stand on several issues involving fundamental liberties, and it made constitutional history by its elucidation of the basic concepts of freedom to be found in the BNA Act. The definition of sedition was narrowed in the Boucher case,[16] freedom of religion emerged triumphant over provincial limitation in the Saumur[17] and Birks[18] cases, freedom of speech and of the press were preserved in the Padlock Act case,[19] and the responsibility of public officials, even the highest, to the citizen whom they have illegally

---

[11][1954] Appeal Cases 541; [1954] 4 D.L.R. 657; note in 32 *Canadian Bar Review* (1954), at p. 788.
[12]Statutes of Canada, 1953–4, c. 59.
[13]1957 S.C.R. 198.
[14]1958 S.C.R. 626.
[15]*Canadian Constitutional Law* (2nd ed., Toronto, 1960), p. 318.
[16][1951] S.C.R. 255.
[17][1953] 2 S.C.R. 299.
[18][1955] S.C.R. 799.
[19][1957] S.C.R. 285; and see note by Andrew Brewin in 35 *Canadian Bar Review* (1957), at p. 544.

injured was sustained in the Chaput,[20] Roncarelli[21] and Lamb[22] cases.
Improvements in the statute law, for the better protection of basic freedoms, are seen in the growing adoption of Fair Employment Practices
Acts and Fair Accommodation Practices Acts. In 1960 came the Canadian Bill of Rights which, though making much less change in the law
than many have supposed, set out in one document enacted by Parliament a number of the traditional civil liberties.[23] There was only one
counter-trend observable in the decade, but it was a frightening one —
the attack on freedom of association which was launched by several
provinces in their anti-trade union legislation; this forms part of the
provincial picture which is dealt with below.

Other chapters in this book make clear the importance of the control
of investment in any form of economic planning. Is this control possible
within the present distribution of powers? To some extent, obviously so.
Monetary policy affects investment, at least quantitatively. Fiscal policy
provides different forms of direct public investment. Tax incentives can
be given to induce capital to flow into selected areas. All these devices
are being used by federal authorities today. Can more drastic controls
be exercised, for example to prohibit investment in undesirable enterprises or over-expanded industries? Could Ottawa, instead of subsidizing
the development of Elliot Lake, have forbidden the mining development
of that area? The answer in this instance might well be affirmative,
because the export of the ore can be controlled, and in addition all
mines for the production of uranium and other prescribed substances are
"works for the general advantage of Canada" under the Atomic Energy
Control Act. The unregulated development of uranium production in
Canada, with private capital being allowed to make its own decisions as
to investment, is a good example of bad planning; the Canadian taxpayer pays the cost of all the services the private investors require, and
allows them such quick profit that the risk of a collapsed market is
assumed by workers' families much more than by capital. The workers
do not receive equivalently quick wages.

If we ask ourselves about federal control of investment in a private
industry that is not producing a commodity specifically within federal
jurisdiction, we meet grave constitutional difficulties. For the Privy Council long ago laid down the ridiculous rule that federal authority to regulate trade and commerce did not include regulation of any particular
trades (for example insurance or margarine) in which Canadians would

20[1955] S.C.R. 834.
21[1959] S.C.R. 121.
22[1959] S.C.R. 321. See also F. R. Scott, *Civil Liberties and Canadian
Federalism* (Toronto, 1959), pp. 37 ff
23The legal nature of the Bill of Rights is analysed in 37 *Canadian Bar Review*
(1959), at pp. 1 ff.

otherwise be free to engage in the provinces. It would appear that the only particular forms of trade and commerce which Ottawa may directly control, regardless of their magnitude, are ones that can be brought within specific federal powers, such as banks and interprovincial communications. Any other kind of enterprise desiring to expand its plant by investing its own reserves or funds raised in Canada would seem to be free from federal interference, regardless of the social utility of the investment; such control as might exist would seem to be a provincial matter. While the flow of foreign capital can probably be federally regulated, a prohibition of its entry for a particular trade purpose might be considered as colourable legislation, designed to evade the constitutional prohibition, and hence *ultra vires*. The same danger would exist if export licences were used to control particular schemes. Companies with federal charters might be subject to special forms of investment regulation, but, according to another Privy Council decision,[24] a provincial company can do business across the country provided other provinces give it permission, so some large businesses might escape by this door. The "works and undertakings" of a company can be declared to be for the general advantage; here is a power seemingly available for investment control. But it bites off more than is needed, and is a clumsy device for the purpose. Short of constitutional amendment, or some form of delegation, the most useful legal basis for a national investment policy would be a further "thaw" in the trade and commerce power so that federal legislation could embrace regulation of a trade as a whole where it was carried on throughout the country by transactions that ignored provincial boundaries. But even if this occurs, a considerable area of investment remains within provincial jurisdiction, and provincial co-operation is therefore required.

Apart from federal regulation of investment in areas directly within federal jurisdiction, there is another method than can improve the possibilities of co-ordination and synchronization of national investment policies. This is the offer of financial inducements to provinces and municipalities to accept federal leadership and timing in the management of public investment.[23a] The offer by Mr. Diefenbaker to share the cost of municipal public works timed to relieve winter unemployment is an example. While it has its merits, this device has so far been little developed and only occasionally applied. A province may have plans of its own which it prefers, or may be actively opposing federal plans because of pressures from private investors: indications of this have been evident in the development of the Columbia River project in British

---

[23a]See on this, W. A. Mackintosh, "Federal Finance (Canada)," in Geoffrey Sawer, ed., *Federalism: An Australian Study* (Melbourne, 1952), pp. 100–5.
[24]The *Bonanza Creek* case, [1916] 1 Appeal Cases 566.

Columbia. Canadian federalism is more difficult to operate than that of
the United States where, because of the larger number of states, no single
state can exert any special influence on the central government.

This brings us to the role of the provinces as agencies of planning.
During the 1930's their helpless financial situation made them drowning
victims needing rescue rather than lifeboats bringing safety and security:
hence the CCF emphasis at that time on federal action. Another depression could reduce them to the same state. Alberta's bold attempt to
fight the economic battle alone fell foul of the BNA Act in 1937–8; as
Professor Mallory says, "the Aberhart programme provided the *reductio
ad absurdum* which was required to demonstrate the unsuitability of the
provinces as agencies of major fiscal and economic policy."[25] The
emphasis there must be on the word "major." When war expenditures
and wartime planning ended the economic depression, and as the capture of power in both Ontario and Saskatchewan seemed possible, the
CCF began to pay greater attention to provincial responsibilities and
opportunities. As early as 1943, E. B. Jolliffe reminds us, CCF members
of several provincial legislatures met to discuss mutual problems; he was
then the leader of thirty-four CCF members of the Ontario legislature as
against only thirty-eight Conservative supporters of the Drew Government. Writing in *Planning for Freedom* (pp. 74, 75), he says: "it is
generally recognised now in the CCF that there is an important job to
be done by a provincial administration. Part of that job, under our
present constitution, can only be done by the provinces; it cannot be
done by the Dominion." Also in 1943, the CCF book *Make This Your
Canada* (p. 151) declared that "central planning over the whole economy
must fit in with, take account of and give opportunity for regional, provincial and municipal planning. The last thing desired is complete
centralisation." Several further conferences of provincial representatives
were held in the following years, the Saskatchewan Government giving
first-hand information and advice. The CCF party was the first party in
Canada to initiate the "interprovincial caucus." While economic planning for Canada will certainly mean more action by the federal government, it does not mean less action by provincial governments; on the
contrary, their role increases proportionately. Economic planning will be
"even more essential and important than it is today," as *Make This
Your Canada* put it (p. 151). The charge of "centralization" against
the CCF, if used so as to imply a disregard of legitimate provincial
autonomy, is largely a fear-raising slogan put across by reactionaries in
order to keep capitalists in power, with the result that the economic
domination of our society by the power élite is further protected.

The most obvious example of the need for provincial planning is in
regard to natural resources. These all started (except in the Northwest

[25]*Social Credit and the Federal Power in Canada* (Toronto, 1954), p. 189.

Territories) as provincial Crown property, that is, in public ownership. Even today most of them remain in public hands. Under the BNA Act it is the provinces who must make the concessions, leases and sales that transfer them to private corporations. The terms of these grants largely determine the manner in which economic development will take place and the amount of return the public treasury will receive for the province's permission. Under a provincial Premier like Duplessis, heading a political machine universally recognized as susceptible to corruption and bribery, and confronted with vast sums of American capital seeking profitable outlet, the nature of a province's economic planning is easily imagined. In his case, not content with giving away huge resources for a minimum of return to the public, he even sold to a private corporation dominated by American capital the publicly owned distribution system for gas in Montreal which a previous Liberal administration had itself taken away from the old Montreal Light, Heat and Power Company. And all this was under the guise of preserving Quebec's autonomy. No wonder that a present Liberal cabinet minister has written that what Quebec needed was a Mossadegh.[26] All but one of the Canadian provinces rejected the CCF proposals for provincial socialization and planning; the resultant degree of Americanization and big-industry control is only now beginning to be appreciated. In Saskatchewan, the gas distribution system is a provincially owned public utility.

It is in the development of provincial resources that very large amounts of investment take place, and as has just been pointed out, provincial governments can exercise control, if they wish, over many of these enterprises. It is thus possible for the separate provincial investment policies to run counter to federal policy. Provincial administrations may be counted on to want to maximize investment at all times in their own province, even when national planning may require a slowing down. Quebec has special cultural reasons for wanting to control her economy. Provinces may borrow at will, either in Canada or abroad, and, as in the 1930's, may find themselves overloaded with a debt that must be repaid in a depreciated currency. All these forms of provincial autonomy will make over-all control of investment very difficult without co-ordinating machinery and a spirit of co-operation. In Australia, dangers of this kind led to the imaginative step of creating a Loan Council to control the borrowing of both the state and Commonwealth governments; each state is represented on the Council, but the Commonwealth has two votes and a casting vote. The rejection of the Rowell-Sirois Report in 1940 left Canada without any plan for co-ordinating federal-provincial financing, and since then we have proceeded by a series of *ad hoc* arrangements which have become so

[26]René Levesque (now the Hon. René Levesque, Minister of Natural Resources), "Pas plus bêtes que les Arabes," *Cité libre*, mai 1960, p. 17.

subject to individual exceptions and special deals as to make of Ottawa
a kind of United Nations seeking agreement among ten sovereign states.
In October, 1960, and again in February, 1961, the federal Government actually proposed as a "new plan" that the provinces should revert
to levying their own taxes to meet their own needs. Thus the pre-1940
anarchy would be restored, the rich provinces would become richer
and the poor poorer. Even Quebec was not prepared to accept this
degree of autonomy; Premier Lesage is reported as describing Mr.
Diefenbaker's proposals as a backward move that would "endanger the
satisfactory functioning of our federal system" and as liable to "increase
regional inequalities."[27] The equalization formula which formed part of
the revised proposals presented by Ottawa in February was still, according to Lesage, "unthinkable, unbelievable, utter and complete deception."[28] The failure of post-war governments, whether Liberal or Conservative, to grapple seriously with the financial problems of Canadian
federalism, or even to set up a permanent federal-provincial secretariat
as recommended by the Rowell-Sirois Report, is a reflection of their lack
of national purpose and their dominance by outmoded notions of free
enterprise.

Obviously federal co-operation is needed even in the development of
provincial resources. The federal government built the railway into
Labrador down which Quebec's iron ore is carried. The central Mortgage and Housing Corporation assists in the building of new towns without which the workers at remote provincial mines could not be housed.
Everywhere provincial development dovetails into some federal undertaking. The vaster the provincial resources, the more likely they are to
be beyond complete provincial control. If they require a market outside
the province, they cease in that aspect to be provincial. The planning
of new power dams on rivers is perhaps wholly a provincial matter if
the rivers are wholly within a province and the province happens to be
large enough to finance the projects. In poorer provinces this may be
impossible, and federal or other aid must be sought. The rivers may be
interprovincial or international, limiting the authority of one provincial
government, and requiring interprovincial agreements or federal-
provincial-American co-operation. In a federal state, whether planning
be by governments or private corporations, intergovernmental co-
operation is essential. In Canada we have made some but far from
enough progress in working it out.[29] There is a place also for purely
interprovincial co-operation, and for that reason the initiative of Premier

[27]*Montreal Gazette*, Oct. 27, 1960.
[28]*Ibid.*, Feb. 24, 1961.
[29]On the idea of "co-operative federalism" see J. A. Corry, "Constitutional
Trends and Federalism" in A. R. M. Lower *et al.*, *Evolving Canadian Federalism*
(Durham, N.C., 1958), chap. III; see also A. W. Macmahon, ed., *Federalism,
Mature and Emergent* (New York, 1953), *passim*.

Lesage of Quebec in calling the provincial governments together in December, 1960, is to be welcomed, though it is not yet clear what form of co-operation will emerge.[30]

A good example of a successful form of federal-provincial co-operation in Canada is to be found in the work of the advisory committees under the Prairie Farm Rehabilitation Act (1935) and the Maritime Marshland Rehabilitation Act (1948). The drifting soils of the prairies and the unreclaimed marshlands of the maritimes were wasting agricultural assets beyond the means of those provinces to restore. Federal initiative and provincial co-operation have resulted here in a truly impressive programme of agricultural planning. Agriculture is of course a concurrent power under the constitution, so Ottawa may legislate within the field; the trouble is that the field has been extremely narrowly defined by the courts. The form of co-operation now adopted, in which plans are mutually agreed on and cost is shared, avoids legal pitfalls. To March 31, 1958, PFRA provided the necessary assistance to construct 421 community projects for water conservation; it undertook major irrigation projects in southern Alberta and minor ones in British Columbia; it has promoted major reclamation projects in all four western provinces, notably on the South Saskatchewan River; and MMRA works constructed or in progress affect hundreds of thousands of acres in Nova Scotia, New Brunswick and Prince Edward Island.[31] Another example of a similar approach is the Eastern Rockies Forest Conservation Board (1947) which provides for co-operation between Ottawa and Alberta for the conservation of the forests on the eastern slope of the Rockies which is part of the watershed of the Saskatchewan River. As the value of these forms of co-operation becomes more evident, the willingness to embark upon them may be expected to grow.

Economic planning is only a small part of a province's responsibility for planning. Fields such as education, welfare and community planning provide even larger opportunities for provincial experimentation. These matters are more exclusively within provincial jurisdiction, though in each the federal government has an important role to play. Despite Quebec's change of mind, which finally led her to reject what she had first accepted, federal grants to universities are likely to continue in other provinces which feel that university autonomy in educational matters is great enough to permit them to decide for themselves whether

[30]See reports of the meeting in *Montreal Gazette*, Dec. 3, 1960. The idea was proposed in the Tremblay Report on Constitutional Problems, 1956. For comment on this Report, see: F. R. Scott, "French-Canada and Canadian Federalism" in Lower *et al.*, *Evolving Canadian Federalism*, chap. II; and A. Brady, "Quebec and Canadian Federalism," 25 *Canadian Journal of Economics and Political Science* (1959), at p. 259

[31]For a brief description of these projects, see *Canada Year Book*, 1959, pp. 408–11.

or not to accept a gift. So too the federal government's responsibility for large areas of social welfare needs no emphasis; here federal authority rests on a combination of specific powers (unemployment insurance, pensions, etc.) plus the spending power (family allowances, contributions to hospitals, etc.). Community planning remains wholly within provincial jurisdiction, but the federal government is not prevented from participation in specific schemes such as the development of new townsites (Elliot Lake) or slum clearance (Regent's Park). Ottawa alone can decide where airports and railway stations are to be located. In all these three fields, however, the provinces are primarily responsible, and are likely to remain so. The constitutional problem here is financial rather than legal: it is more difficult to find the money than find the legal authority. Socialist planning that envisages enlarged functions of provincial government in activities that are inevitably costly must make provision for the necessary funds. One place where provinces must learn to look, besides any arrangement they may have with Ottawa, is in their own treasure house of natural resources, at present exploited primarily in the interest of shareholders. Only under an unplanned capitalism would one find Canadian children receiving a scanty education in overcrowded schools while Texan shareholders reap huge profits from Canadian oil and natural gas. A proper system of redistribution, based on need rather than population, will also be needed to enable poorer provinces to keep pace with those more fortunately endowed.

There is another function of provincial governments, already mentioned, which concerns deeply all Canadians. This is their responsibility for many aspects of civil liberties. While the fundamental freedoms of religion, speech, association and the press are predominantly in federal care, there is a division of authority in the broad field of human rights which makes the provinces important agencies for the preservation of certain liberties. Although the criminal law is federal, it is administered by the provinces, and the way a law is enforced, particularly if police are involved, can expand or narrow the freedoms it guarantees. Municipal governments also play a large part in the creation of a free society, though their authority is derived from and can be no wider than that of the province. What a province may do to harass and confine the trade union movement is becoming evident from anti-union legislation in Quebec, Newfoundland, British Columbia and Alberta.[32] There are styles in freedoms as in clothes; it is fashionable today to oppose racial discrimination, so we have made considerable advances in the enactment of provincial Fair Employment Practices Acts, for example; but although the black man may work with the white, neither may be free to exercise

[32]For criticism of this legislation see 4 *Canadian Labour* (1959), nos. 4–5. The most outright attack on freedom of association is found in the Newfoundland legislation (Statutes of Newfoundland, 1959, cc. 1–2), commented on by Stanley Knowles, "The Facts about Newfoundland," 4 *Canadian Labour* (1959), nos. 4–5.

to the full his trade union rights. Capitalism does not worry about the colour of its workers so much as about their power.

When we have discussed the role of the federal government on the one hand, and of provincial and municipal governments on the other, and of the great necessity of continued co-operation among them, we have still left out a whole area of social and economic planning — the area which is supranational. For no nation state can live unto itself alone in the contemporary world, least of all a country with the peculiar geographical situation and political relationships of Canada. Neither the federal government, nor the provincial governments, nor both combined, can make foreign markets secure, or guarantee the bases of stable economic progress. Canada cannot isolate herself, even if she would, from world conditions, though by better planning she can cushion the shock of external influences and redistribute their burdens more equitably. It is sterile now to confine discussion to the old conflict of jurisdiction between Ottawa and the provinces; too many problems have grown outward beyond our frontiers. The principle that the size of government must be as large as the size of the problems with which government must deal not only leaves the provinces far behind as adequate agencies of planning but increasingly leaves the federal government behind also. Defence becomes North American defence and defence of the Western world; trade likewise takes on its global aspects. Even the subjects seemingly confined more easily within national boundaries, such as health, education and welfare, have their international relations. The old two-way federalism blends into world federalism the beginnings of which are evident in a multitude of specialized agencies of the United Nations and in the United Nations itself. To be a good Canadian citizen one must be a good world citizen; to be a good socialist one must be an international socialist. National constitutions are the bricks and stones in a world structure, and one contribution to world peace and stability which nation-states can make is to see that their constitutions render it possible for them to fulfil their international duties. That is why it is imperative that Canada's power to implement Canadian treaties should be defined as clearly as was her original power to implement Empire treaties.

Municipal Government

KEITH CALLARD

Many Canadians look upon their local government as inefficient, uninteresting and quite possibly corrupt. Certainly most who study the subject would agree that many features of our municipal institutions are out of date. Since each of the ten provinces makes its own municipal law it is not easy to make generalizations, but some municipal problems are widespread.

The boundaries of a large number of municipalities were drawn over a century ago. Since then changes have been made piecemeal — new municipalities have been established as new areas have been settled, new towns have been carved out of rural municipalities and many existing cities and towns have expanded their limits by the process of annexation. No province (except Alberta) has undertaken a systematic and radical overhaul of local government boundaries. The result is that the basic pattern was established when a local unit had to be based on distances that could be reached on foot or on horseback. The coming of the automobile and the telephone has changed the way we live but it has done little to the boundaries of the municipalities however seriously it has changed their budgets. The rural units — villages and rural municipalities — made sense when their inhabitants were isolated from their neighbours by distance and weather. There may still be regions where the very small community is the only possible unit of local government but this is no longer true in most parts of the country. Yet, out of 1,873 cities, towns and villages, 1,039 (55 per cent) had a population of less than 1,000 in 1956. The average population of Saskatchewan's 377 villages was 250. What can such a municipality do in the way of police and fire protection, road-building and public works, health and welfare? How can a province grant substantial powers to municipalities that have annual budgets of less than $10,000 and no full-time employees?

Where there have been boundary changes they have often made the problem worse. Small urban units have been cut out of the surrounding municipality leaving the latter looking like a piece of gruyère — as many holes as cheese. And many of the "urban" units are too small to be treated as modern towns capable of providing a full range of municipal services. Thus in 1957 Quebec had ninety-five towns with fewer than 5,000 inhabitants, and in forty of these there were fewer than 2,000.

From time to time Canadians are told that local self-government is the cradle of democracy. This may be true in the sense that municipal democracy has scarcely learned to crawl. In most provinces the franchise is limited by a property qualification; the vote is usually restricted to the owner or tenant of real property and perhaps his wife as well. To reinforce the point that it is the property that is entitled to the vote, nonresidents or even corporations may vote by virtue of the property they own. Indeed municipal law often goes further and insists that the incurrence of municipal debt must be approved by a vote of property owners by number and by value of property owned. It is rather as though the income, and corporation, taxpayers were asked to approve federal borrowings, according to the size of tax payments.

The very small municipalities have the virtue that every citizen can know the office holders and can be aware of their activity. But in the larger centres the citizens usually take little active interest unless some unusual issue arouses strong feeling. A few mayors of large towns are sufficiently well paid to make the job attractive and it may also be used as a stepping stone to provincial or federal politics. But the ordinary council member is unknown and badly (if at all) paid. Who, then, is willing to run? In some places the council seats go uncontested for years, some sort of nominating committee filling vacancies by co-option. A contested election costs money and a private citizen is unlikely to want to spend his own time, effort and cash to win a thankless office. Most urban councils are run by small business men who have real interests in the communal well-being of their community. These interests are to keep taxes low, to boost real estate values (but not valuations) and to increase trade.

There is usually a loud outcry against any suggestion of introducing parties into local politics. Good, clean, business-like administration is to be preferred to rhetoric and possible corruption. But the partyless system is an example of irresponsible government. If the province does something the voter does not like he can blame the party in power. But who is in power at city hall? A project may be buried in a committee and the voter has to be very alert to find out how his alderman voted on each issue. The party battle may often be a sham but it is better than the petty personal bickering that takes place in some municipalities.

The electoral system curtails mass participation in local affairs. But the fact that the property owner is in control has not meant that our municipalities are trusted as efficient and scrupulous guardians of local interests. In every part of the country there has been a tendency to remove many local functions from municipal control. Thus the public school system is normally run by special boards; the police are sometimes controlled by a commission; and instances can be found of parks, libraries and utilities that are under the jurisdiction of special-purpose bodies. In each case the municipality has not been trusted to do the job. And rather than reform the municipal system we have multiplied the sources of local confusion and rivalry.

It is to be expected that a municipality which has too small a population to sustain an adequate range of services will also lack financial resources. For example in Quebec in 1956 there were 33 urban municipalities spending less than $50,000 and 364 rural municipalities spending less than $5,000.[1] Five thousand dollars do not go very far in building roads, nor $50,000 in maintaining fire and police protection.

It may be argued that some localities prefer a low standard of services and a low tax rate. But the immense disparity in resources makes revenue-raising easy for some and almost impossible for others. A few examples are given in Table I. The first four towns are in Greater Montreal and the other two in the Lake St. John area. Essentially they represent rich and poor municipalities within a single urban combination; in fact they are all suburbs. This degree of disparity is likely to increase. A rich municipality is likely to have good services and moderate taxes and will thereby attract more residents of high quality. A poor municipality has poor services and relatively high taxes and yet it has the greatest need for services such as public health and social welfare.

The major source of municipal tax revenue is the levy upon real property. Yet this tax is clumsy in its application and highly inflexible. The process of assessment frequently gives rise to suspicions of bias and favouritism. And it was clearly proved in the early 1930's that, at the moment of greatest financial need, it was incapable of response. The

[1]These figures exclude education. In some respects Quebec represents the extreme case, but Ontario in 1953 had 310 municipalities spending less than $50,000, education included.

consequences of this failure were generally to remove some functions from local control (thus weakening the effectiveness of local government) and to increase provincial grants to municipalities. In some provinces half the municipal income is now provided directly by the province. These grants are seldom designed to relieve inequalities between municipalities. On the contrary they are often "matching grants," that is, they give more to the rich municipalities and less to the poor. In any event they lessen the autonomy of the municipality by guiding its spending programme into patterns determined by provincial policy. (Let it be added that this lessening of autonomy may, at times, be advantageous.)

Provincial control over municipalities has been steadily increasing. Before 1939 its main purpose was to maintain financial solvency. Thus provincial law limits both taxes that may be imposed and debts that may be incurred. More recently, greater control has been exercised over by-laws, and over programmes in such areas as health, housing, roads and water supply.

An increasing proportion of our growing population lives in the larger urban agglomerations and it is there that municipal problems are most serious. A typical large Canadian city consists of three zones. There is a central zone with the chief places of commerce and amusement — the "downtown area," frequently surrounded by older housing rapidly degenerating into slums. Then come the inner suburbs, either residential or industrial, but fully developed, reasonably stable areas. Finally there is the development fringe where the greatest increase in population is taking place. The downtown area faces problems of traffic congestion and slum removal; the fringe areas face the costs of constructing new roads, sewers etc., at contemporary inflated costs, for a population that is changing, heterogeneous and lacking in civic cohesion. Across the metropolitan areas run the lines of municipal boundaries, often those of rural units established many years ago.

Some stable suburbs have no downtown problems of congestion and no development costs. Their inhabitants are members of the upper

TABLE I

	Taxed real estate per head	Expenditure per head
Westmount (pop. 24,800)	$ 3,148	$100
Jacques Cartier (pop. 33,132)	1,210	56
Montreal East (pop. 4,607)	10,969	217
St. Pierre (pop. 5,276)	1,247	43
Arvida (pop. 12,919)	4,000	112
Chicoutimi North (pop. 6,446)	379	24

*The figures on population are for 1956, on finance, 1957. There may, of course, be wide disparities in the method of assessing real estate but these certainly do not account for more than a small part of the spread between the wealth of the various communities.

income groups who have contrived to isolate themselves in pleasant, well-run municipalities. They use the downtown area for work and amusement and are the first to criticize its traffic congestion and general inefficiency. But they pay no taxes to the central area and combine to resist any sharing of fiscal or administrative burdens. (Metropolitan Toronto was able to reach a partial solution of this problem only because the provincial government coerced the richer suburbs.)

The outskirts of our big towns are the ugliest areas in Canada. The roads leading to them are made hideous with billboards, hot dog stands, second hand car lots and cheap real estate developments. Thus new slums are being built in the countryside while we are just beginning to tackle the old slums in the centre of cities. These new slums cannot be controlled by the rural municipalities in whose territory they lie. The function of physical planning must be exercised on a regional basis, combining adjacent town and country areas into a satisfactory whole.

Does this rather gloomy assessment mean that municipal government has to be written off as a factor in improving social conditions? The broad answer is, certainly not, provided we are prepared to go back to first principles in deciding what local government can and ought to do in the age of the automobile and the telephone. It is impossible in a few paragraphs to lay down a comprehensive blueprint for reform but the direction of the required changes is clear. In any case the diversity of the Canadian scene makes uniformity unworkable and undesirable.

None the less we will need to redefine all our categories of local government. At the lowest level there should be a primary unit of true *local* government. It may vary in size from a small village of 200 souls to a suburban area of 50,000. But it should possess a sense of community and of physical cohesion — the kind of unit in which opinion can be continuously active on an issue of cutting down an old tree or improving the safety of school crossings. It should not deal with technical problems or large expenditures, its representatives should be part time and strictly amateur and lots of scope should be provided for mass participation. Clearly the powers and resources of the community units would vary with the size and location of the area but they should never become so great that the sense of neighbourhood is lost.

At a higher level there should be the all-purpose municipality capable of providing a full range of local services. It must be large enough to maintain professional staffs of engineers, architects, health officers, welfare workers and protective services and an adequate supply of equipment. The population of such a unit would never be below 100,000 and might exceed 2,000,000. At this level many of the functions that have been taken over by the provinces could be re-entrusted to local control and perhaps some new services added, for example police protection in rural areas.

So far no distinction has been drawn between urban and rural units. At the community level the difference is still necessary but at the higher level its significance is rapidly diminishing. Many services — road- and bridge-building for example — can no longer be allocated to small municipalities whether rural or urban. The modern automobile has made possible travelling health units, libraries, welfare workers. The farmer may now look as far away as fifty or a hundred miles for shopping, amusement, education and technical services. He wants good all-weather roads, and adequate parking facilities in town. He will certainly not accept the argument that because he lives on a farm he must expect markedly inferior public services. Of course, he does not want to pay for some of the benefits that only the town dwellers can make use of. A scheme of differential taxation, although complicated, can take care of this issue.

Another aspect of local government that needs a thorough overhaul is the role of the province. Up to now it has been a strange alternation of laissez-faire and paternalism. The provinces have let the municipalities sink or swim except that before one disappears for the third time the province will haul it out of the lake, pump some of the water from its lungs and throw it right back in again. Perhaps the time has come for the province to make sure that every municipality knows how to swim.

First the province must set municipal boundaries and review them as the population changes. Secondly it must ensure adequate resources. There are many formulae for adjusting grants so as to leave some discretion to the municipality and at the same time aid the less fortunate.[2] Thirdly the province can do much more by way of technical assistance and supervision. It can maintain advisory services in many fields. It should exercise strict control over municipal accounting and auditing. It should also establish standards for classes of municipal employees and perhaps establish conditions of transfer and exchange of municipal civil servants. It can establish and enforce much stricter codes of planning and building regulations, municipal contracting, fire hazard measures, health regulations, traffic control schemes. In short the standards of quality of local services should be accepted as a provincial responsibility.

In Canada today the citizen may well feel that he is more in control of his provincial or federal government than his municipality whose affairs are concealed behind a smokescreen of divided authority and personal rivalries. Local government has become a matter of cliques and vested interests and yet comprehensive municipal reform is a subject that seems to interest neither the voter nor the politician.

[2]See, e.g., J. F. Graham, "Fiscal Equity Principle in Provincial-Municipal Relations," *Canadian Public Administration*, III, March, 1960, pp. 24 ff.

Democratic Socialist Politics for Canada

MICHAEL OLIVER

The French socialist poet, Charles Péguy, wrote: "The revolution will be a moral one or there will be no revolution." This not only is the hope of the democratic socialist; it is a statement of the depth of his responsibilities. More than most other members of society, he believes that profound changes must be made in society if certain moral ends are to be achieved. But he should be vitally aware, as much as any conservative who continually harps on the subject, of the weight of responsibility which is carried by those who seek to change society. And it is perhaps just this consciousness of the far-reaching effects of the means which he chooses and the proximate ends which he seeks which distinguishes the *democratic* socialist from other kinds of socialist.

Utopia-building of a mechanical sort is no business of the social democrat; his reforms cannot be just a matter of fitting people and institutions into a pattern prescribed by an unchanging blueprint. Nor can he accept the comforting assumption that there are historic forces at work leading to an inevitable utopia. Rather he must be willing to admit that he is neither infallible nor all-knowing. He must recognize that he cannot determine all the consequences of his acts; that the institutions he seeks to change have great strength and persistence; and that in a dynamic world the situation he is trying to cope with may have changed before his remedy has been tried. The important part of his belief, however, is not that man is fallible, but that he has infinite worth. He therefore rejects the doctrine of adjustment; he refuses to accept as a norm that which is. His refusal of facile optimism is complemented by a monumental repugnance for pessimism.

The democratic socialist is thus bound to act. And to act responsibly he must have a clear picture of society as it exists and a vision of what is possible. This picture of present and future will inevitably be coloured by his values — by the order in which he ranks things like power, leisure, Cadillacs, health, poetry, freedom, and order — but it need not be clouded by them. Putting it another way: because any vision of that-which-is will be incomplete, the selection which a socialist makes for his partial portrayal of reality will be determined by what he thinks is important. But his preferences should not distort; the necessarily abstract quality of his description need not make it imaginary. Thus a conservative could describe Canada as a country in which the average standard of living is one of the highest in the history of the world; a socialist, as one in which a small élite enjoys many times more wealth and power than the average citizen. Both would be correct. But for the conservative to claim that Canada is the land of prosperity for all, or for the socialist to say that Canadians are oppressed by a brutal dictatorship, would be distortion. Particular and varying views of reality are the necessary result of differing values; but it is important that each of them, and especially in this context that of the socialist, be clear and accurate.

The first job of the social democrat is, therefore, to picture his society, in terms of his values, with the greatest possible clarity. He must then examine the institutional framework for social change which exists and decide: (a) what parts of this framework serve his ends; (b) what aspects of it can be adapted to serve his ends; (c) what replacements will be required; and (d) what different institutions seem to provide the best substitutes. In performing this second operation, certain principles are of great importance. They are not first principles in the sense of ultimate values; these have been discussed by George Grant in the opening chapter. Rather they are organizational principles which relate to the problems of politics — the public and collective application of moral values. Two of these principles are generally accepted as the fundamental bases of constitutional democracy. First, power must be limited; secondly, participation in making decisions must be maximized. Two others seem to me important, though they have none of the status of the first pair: it is unwise to link socialism with any particular institutional means to the goals it seeks to achieve; and more predictable results can be obtained by adapting existing institutions than by replacing them with new ones.

"Politics is the art of the possible." This irritating little cliché is also ambiguous for it is truer to say that politics is the art of making things possible. But it is a reminder that collective decisions are always made at a certain time and place. The eternal and the universal may also have their place in politics, but if they do (and this is the author's firm belief) they are criteria for choice between better or worse alternative lines of action in a given real situation. The politics of socialism in Canada in the 1960's cannot be identical with the politics of any other place in the 1960's or of Canada at any other time. If one besetting sin of socialists has been the belief that an institutional blueprint can be devised and followed solely on the basis of first principles, surely another has been to adopt uncritically the socialist model which has been worked out for another country.

These remarks give the perspective in which the politics of Canadian social democracy are going to be discussed in this chapter. The first job to be tackled is to sketch the partial description of Canadian society for which a pattern of change is to be proposed. This is an unenviable task, but it has been made somewhat easier by the chapters which precede. For our purposes, the most important items in this description seem to be the following:

1. Canadian society is dominated economically by an élite which controls the major industrial, commercial and financial corporations of the country.

2. From this economic stronghold, the power of the élite spreads to Canada's main social and political institutions.

3. Although the average standard of living in Canada is high, there are great inequalities in wealth and income between individuals and, to a lesser extent, between regions. Poverty, poor health, crowded and sub-standard living quarters, insecurity in employment, insecurity for the aged, for the ill and incapacitated, gross differences in educational opportunities, in leisure, in the availability of cultural and recreational facilities — all these persist.

4. The two political parties which have alternated in (or shared) power since Confederation have not attempted to alter the basic power position of the Canadian élite. Their programmes at present indicate that they have no intention of making such a change. Both parties obtain most of their funds from the individuals who make up this élite and from the corporations they control.

5. With the partial exception of the radio and television networks of the CBC, this élite owns and controls the mass media of communications — press, private radio and television, large circulation magazines.

6. Besides ensuring their own wealth and power, those who make up this élite have a disproportionate effect on the whole life of Canada. They are the major influence in deciding the rate of economic growth, the balance between industrial capital and social capital (that is, between plant and equipment for the production and distribution of commodities, and plant and equipment for schools and universities, hospitals, houses, parks, theatres, roads, recreation centres, police services, etc.), and the stability or instability of economic conditions. They do this directly through their control over investment funds; and indirectly through advertising which affects demand, through their moulding of tastes via the mass media, and through their influence on government and the political parties which control government. The economic élite has fashioned an economy with an irrationally fluctuating growth rate, a bias favouring industrial capital rather than social capital, and a high degree of instability.

7. Although Canadians enjoy a wide range of personal freedom, they do not participate at all equally in making the collective decisions which determine the social context in which this freedom is enjoyed. And if freedom means a power to act as well as a lack of restraint, differences in wealth — and in race and creed and influence — mean different degrees of freedom too.

8. Like other industrial, urbanized states, Canada is becoming in the twentieth century a mass society; its characteristic form of social and industrial organization is bureaucracy.

9. Canada is a federal state with parliamentary forms in both its central and regional governments. Both federalism and parliamentary institutions are deeply rooted.

10. The Canadian population is pluralistic in terms of ethnic and geographic origins. Its most fundamental division is, however, dual. Approximately thirty per cent of the population speak French as their principal language and are culturally different from the vast majority of the remainder, who speak English and are Anglo-American in culture. The French-Canadian minority has proportionately a much smaller representation than the English-speaking majority in the economic élite; it is also under-represented (in this sense) in the federal civil service and in several other key centres of power.

With this selective picture in mind, the next step is to examine the means to social change which are available and to try to assess their adequacy. There are many ways of going about this examination, and one very useful way is to take the traditional socialist proposals for reform as a starting point, and try to see to what extent they remain valid. For there is as little point in exaggerating the uniqueness of Canadian problems as there is in forgetting to allow for our real particularities. To some extent, the sketch of Canadian conditions which has just been made would describe any state in the group of highly developed Western countries in which the capitalist system has operated. It was in reaction against earlier and much more brutal conditions character- istic of capitalist society that socialist theory was developed. The eco- nomic stress of democratic socialism was based, not on any belief that material aspects of life were more important than any others, but on the conviction that the moral (and, in the judgment of a man like William Morris, aesthetic) shortcomings of society, as well as the ma- terial, could best be tackled by limiting the economic power which enabled a certain group to impose its values. This is still the contention of socialists.

It is hard to deny however, that the necessary economic emphasis tended to draw to socialist thinking and writing the sort of mind which gloried in the task of tidying and rationalizing the economic and social chaos which it saw so clearly. Such minds often assumed a little blithely that political problems would look after themselves. The Marxists were most guilty of this sort of thinking; witness the doctrine of the withering away of the state and the notion that, when class exploitation ended, the "administration of things" would automatically replace the coercion of people. But even within the much more politically conscious socialism of English Fabianism, preoccupation with the power of an economic class led to a certain neglect of the problems of power *per se*. Not that the socialist belief that control over the means of production meant immense social influence was wrong; the error was rather in concluding that once bourgeois class-ownership had been removed, the problem of limiting economic power and making it democratic would be simple and straightforward.

Much of this optimism about the creation of economic democracy was the result of the outstanding success of European states, and espe- cially Britain, in establishing political democracy during the late 19th and early 20th centuries. The extension of democratic control seemed to demand simply the addition of economic functions and responsibilities to a parliament and cabinet which, after centuries of struggle and experi- ment, had been made responsive to public desires. Nationalization meant just this; and so did national economic planning. From the per- spective of the mid-twentieth century, however, the simplicity of these solutions is lost. This does not mean that nationalization was a mistaken policy; at most it can be said that too much was hoped for from it. National planning is perhaps even more necessary. Only antediluvians believe that public intervention can be reduced (though the forms of intervention may be changed), and it is obvious that any goals, other than the enrichment of a minority in conditions of chaotic instability, demand increases in planning. But there are certain problems which loom larger in the 1960's than they did previously and force themselves on our attention.

George Grant and John Porter have isolated these problems and described them. More and more, men have become anonymous units in agglomerations which are not communities. The jobs most of us hold fit us impersonally into a hierarchy of posts in which initiative and responsibility have little meaning. Most of our dealings are with people who lack a personal involvement in the tasks they perform: the clerk in the department store; the checker in the super-market; the telephone operator whose trained unctuousness sets teeth on edge. Our pleasures bring us together without associating us: the moving picture audience slowly changes as we stumble in and out of the darkness. One of the first lessons we must teach our children is that the man who smiles out from the television screen is not really smiling at them and that he does not really mean what he says.

These are not entirely novel situations. Marx developed the concept of alienation a hundred years ago. The need to establish communities where men and women were persons, rather than categories or commodities, was felt by every utopian. Avoiding hierarchy, subordination and depersonalization was the central aim of a socialist like Proudhon; the guild socialists in England had the same preoccupations. But it would have been anachronistic to press the case against large-scale, routinized social activities too hard. Mass production had its stultifying side, but it also gave a decent standard of life to millions who had known nothing but poverty. Bureaucratic organization might offer little scope for individual creativity, but often it was clear that any other organizational structure would mean a much greater cost in men and materials (railways, postal service and dozens of other examples spring to mind) or would involve even greater sacrifices in freedom and equality (the thought of a police force run on any other than bureaucratic lines is a chilling one!).

The immediate aim of most socialists therefore became the taking over of large-scale enterprises. The problems of making concentrations of power and productive capacity — the modern corporations — responsive to the public will and interest took precedence over the transformation of personal relations within them. (Sometimes, indeed, it was believed that public ownership would of itself alter the status and outlook of the worker.) This approach cannot be discarded; but neither can it be deemed a sufficient base for mid-twentieth century socialism.

To sum up: three problems which were recognized in the past but often considered of secondary importance now must be treated on a par with those which most commonly concerned democratic socialists: first, the problem of limiting power and making it responsible, whether it be exercised by *private or public* bodies; second, the problem of spreading responsibility and increasing participation in public affairs — of avoiding excessive centralization of power, again whether public or private; and third, the closely related problem of limiting bureaucracy.

Let us be quite clear on what we mean by this last point. Bureaucracy is the most efficient way of organizing large-scale enterprises. It requires "specialization, a hierarchy of authority, a system of rules, and impersonality." It makes possible mass production and the quantity and variety of goods which go with it. But it also creates profound inequalities of power, due to its pyramidal structure which centres decisions in the topmost peak; and, as it is used in more and more spheres, it reduces opportunities "for acquiring experiences that are essential for effective participation in democratic government."[1] Because of these features of bureaucracy which are inimical to democracy, we cannot be satisfied with the goal of controlling and limiting bureaucracy. Democratic socialists seem required also to accept this proposition: when a non-bureaucratic or a less bureaucratic form of organization can be used to achieve the same ends as a highly bureaucratized form, it will be preferred.

The economic programme of socialism is of central importance; the economic remedies which are applied will be among the major determinants of the style of life we lead. A large part of our ingenuity will under any circumstances have to be devoted to finding ways of curbing existing bureaucratic power centres. If effective means of transforming our economic life without increases in an already extensive bureaucratization are available, so much the better. Let us seek out an economist, therefore, who is also a socialist, and engage him in conversation. We must insist on reasonable assurances that new methods of tackling economic problems are likely to be no less effective than those proposed by an older generation of socialists, even if it means pressing and harrying our economist rather unmercifully.

CITIZEN: Have there been any important changes in your views on the best methods for reaching the goals of socialism in Canada?

ECONOMIST: I suppose we should be agreed on what the goals are first of all, or at least on those goals which *economic* action is designed to further. Could you accept these as the main ones? First, a high degree of equality in wealth and incomes. Secondly, an approximately equal weighting of personal wants in determining the range and quantities of goods and services which will be produced. In addition, of course, there are some goals of economic policy which are not specifically socialist but which cannot be ignored — stability and economic growth, especially.

CITIZEN: That sounds reasonable to me. Nationalization plus a central plan for socialized industry promised these results. But I am concerned that these techniques may heighten the already pressing problem of

[1]Peter Blau, *Bureaucracy in Modern Society* (New York, 1956), pp. 19, 116–17.

bureaucratization of our lives. Still, there is one question any socialist must ask when he thinks about substituting other techniques for that of further concentrating economic control through nationalization. How can a more equal distribution of wealth and power be achieved unless the problem of *ownership* of capital is tackled directly?

ECONOMIST: I don't want to evade this question, but may I counter with another? Surely the reason a socialist wants to eliminate private ownership of capital is this. Ownership of capital gives title to income and therefore to goods and services and social influence, and it gives a right to the disposition of capital. Well, if by a variety of means, not excluding socialization, (a) the income from capital and the gains from its appreciation can be drastically restricted; (b) the types of non-economic advantages of wealth can be rigorously reduced (and I am thinking especially of influence on ideas, on politics, on social attitudes); and (c) the right to dispose of capital can be limited, its arbitrary *aspects* removed, so that its use corresponds fairly closely to the preferences of individuals taken as equals — if all this is possible, is the question of the ownership of capital still of paramount importance?

CITIZEN: Perhaps not of paramount importance, though I still have reservations about incomes which come from coupon clipping and dividend cheques when they are payments for non-existent risks, or sacrifices in consumption which are not real personal sacrifices at all. But why does your generation of economists in Canada think that privately owned capital can be retained and civilized while during most of the 19th and early 20th centuries almost all socialist economists felt this was impossible?

ECONOMIST: Probably for two reasons. The first is that the nationalization alternative began to look less simple and less complete; not only because of the bureaucracy problem you have mentioned, but also because it raised purely economic problems, such as the pricing policy to be followed, which were by no means easy to solve. The second reason is the multiplication of the tools of economic policy which resulted from better and fuller economic understanding. One fundamental aspect of this change in understanding deserves to be spelled out. The nationalization emphasis came in an era when the operation of the firm and the industry was the primary concern of orthodox economists, especially in England. Since that time, the focus has widened to include the national economy as a whole — the *general* levels of investment, employment, and income as well as investment, employment and profits, wages and salaries in a single industry. When most national economic problems were seen simply as the sum of a series of inadequacies in one industry after another, it was logical to think of taking over the industries as a means of solving the national problem. If, however, certain general problems could be handled as such — if for example, unemployment could be dealt with not by looking separately at unemployed miners, steel workers, transport workers, but by raising the national level of employment — then the need for nationalization was not nearly as pressing. With the working out of techniques of general economic control, the number of problems for which socialization had seemed a necessary answer had clearly been reduced.

CITIZEN: But this set of tools, while immensely useful, surely does not help with the problems which we agreed were fundamental to socialists — the concentration of wealth and the power flowing from wealth in the hands of a few, and their irresponsible and arbitrary use of it?

ECONOMIST: Agreed; although they are important for these goals too, they cannot do the whole job by any means. But perhaps the sort of thinking on which Keynesian economics was based affected economists' outlooks in a more general way. So far you have questioned me about nationalization almost exclusively; let us turn for a moment to socialist economic planning. You have admitted that the bureaucratic nature of large-scale industry, whether it was in private or public hands, bothered you. What about the type of centralized economic planning which actually was put into practice in the Soviet Union? Were the critics of this conception of socialism — and remember they included socialists like the guild socialists in Britain and syndicalists in France — completely wrong-headed? Are there not some dangers in putting too much power to make economic decisions in too few hands? With the development of computers, it may be possible some day to plan an entire economy simply and elegantly, but until that day comes I suspect that the machinery for total planning is necessarily so complex that it is uncontrollable and, by its very nature, irresponsible.

CITIZEN: Certainly there are dangers, though I doubt if they are so great as to make the élite-imposed decisions of our present situation preferable. But surely you are not suggesting a return to the "free market"? Keynesian economics cannot have made you and your colleagues suddenly go back to a nineteen-century fervour for free enterprise. Admittedly there is a certain attractiveness to an economic system which, in its Never-Never Land version of perfect competition, solves all problems equitably without one group of people having to decide for another. Mind you, even in its ideal form I have my reservations about it — about its unattractive acquisitive base, for instance. But, putting that sort of objection aside, can you reverse the judgment of practically every socialist up to the present that the task of reaching even a working approximation of the competitive market was a superhuman one, that from the outset the market had produced incredible contrasts of luxury and misery, and that even though it had succeeded in raising average living standards all the current trends were towards the perpetuation of inequality and the continuation of a selfish and short-sighted use of concentrated power?

ECONOMIST: The only way I can answer this is to give you, in as few words as possible, my conception of what economic planning should mean today, and then ask you whether it still seems to you a plea for the free market. To begin with, I am not going to pass over your reference to the obnoxious acquisitive basis of market economics. Frankly, I cannot see that competition for personal profit is an unmitigated evil, as long as it is not the dominant component of a social ethos, and as long as the sort of things which are allocated on the basis of competition for profit are limited. I entirely agree that a society which *values* people in terms of their success in accumulating material things, which permits almost every sort of prize — the warm glow of philanthropy, political influence, private lakes, seats on hospital boards — to be awarded for this sort of success is a debased society. And if I were convinced that the total elimination of private market activities was a necessary and sufficient condition for getting rid of this state of affairs, I would be only too happy to see every last trace of the market go. But I am not convinced. I think it is quite possible to put market activities in their proper place.

CITIZEN: This is what interests me. How do you propose to go about it?

ECONOMIST: By three sorts of action. First, by greatly increasing the number and variety of goods and services which are not procured on the market and which are not bought and sold for profit at all. This involves both devoting a much larger proportion of our total investment to social capital than we do at present and also taking off the market certain things which are now bought and sold there such as university education, medical and dental services, radio and television programmes. Second, by assuring to everyone, regardless of how they fare in market pursuits, sufficient income to maintain a decent standard of living. And third, by greatly reducing the spread between high and low incomes.

CITIZEN: But where does the "planning" come in?

ECONOMIST: Surely I have already gone part way in defining what I mean by "planning" by putting "market economics" in this perspective? Obviously, for those goods and services which are not to be produced and sold for profit, planned production and distribution is necessary. It already exists in a small, ineffective, piecemeal way: at the municipal level, when decisions are made to provide parks, libraries, sewage disposal, etc., in certain qualities and quantities; at the provincial level, for roads, law courts, various welfare services; at the federal level for defence, harbours, penitentiaries. Very considerable changes would be involved, of course, if *more* things were to be produced and distributed in this way, if greater co-ordination were desired, and if different criteria for making planning decisions were introduced. A socialist government would be dedicated to all these changes and more. But there would remain a large number of goods and services which were still produced according to market dictates. Must a socialist demand that planning totally replace the market? The answer I would give would be: no, socialist goals can be achieved by limiting the scope of the market and, once this has been done, by working through the market. But he must always insist that responsibility for the health of the economy rests squarely on the shoulders of government. Now admittedly this is a conception of socialist economics which sounds like rank treason to anyone brought up on the socialism of the thirties, but . . .

CITIZEN: May I interrupt you for a moment? I was thinking while you were talking of just this contrast and especially of one of the dozens of books on socialism written in the thirties which seems diametrically opposed to what you are saying. Do you know John Strachey's *The Theory and Practice of Socialism?* Strachey when he wrote it was very much a Marxist and to that extent it is perhaps not typical of the ideas which were predominant in English socialism. But it was widely read, and a remarkably clear exposition. One of his main points was that there could be no middle ground between capitalism and socialist planning . . .

ECONOMIST: Yes, and do you remember the chief proof of this which he offered? He had earlier dwelt on the most vicious and shocking facts about the failure of capitalism in the depression — the unemployment, the waste and destruction of goods, the idle factories and machines. How could a government, while retaining capitalism, do what was obviously necessary and urgent: get men back at work producing so that they could feed and clothe their families? What would happen, he asked, if the government "ordered the owners of the means for the production of necessities to employ the unemployed on unprofitable production"?[2] What would happen if they told textile mill owners to take back their men, pay them wages, and produce when they could not possibly sell for a profit? His answer was a perfectly correct one. "The owners of the textile mills must either disobey the planning commission or they must cease to be owners of the textile mills. For they will go bankrupt." Strachey's mistake was to assume that the only alternatives open to government were to force individual industries to operate unprofitably or to take them over and to plan production without reference to the market. He can hardly be blamed for this error, because no more than a handful of economists understood clearly that there was an effective third course. That course, as I said earlier, involved not industry-by-industry thinking, but fiscal and monetary action to raise the total level of demand for

[2]John Strachey, *The Theory and Practice of Socialism* (London, 1937), p. 67.

goods and services and to make increased production attractive. Once this outlook had been understood, it became plainly and simply incorrect to base the case for planning outside the market and public ownership on the claim that it was necessary for economic stability. But you hadn't finished what you wanted to say about Strachey.

CITIZEN: No, there were a couple of things I wanted to add, though your example clears up one point. Still, depression and unemployment were not the only capitalist ailments which socialist planning in the old sense promised to remedy, and which Strachey and others said could not possibly be cured by production guided by the market, production for profit. What about the misdirection of resources under capitalism? Strachey stated quite accurately that even during the boom years of the 1920's, there was desperate need for basic goods like decent food, clothing and shelter while there were plentiful supplies of "the foolish luxuries desired by a handful of the very rich." Things haven't changed all that much. Slums which people can't afford to move out of still exist in Montreal, Toronto and other Canadian cities while a few blocks away lies the world of mink and expense accounts. This sort of example brings us back to the ownership problem too, incidentally, for two factors enter into this situation. First, the capitalist weakness for *producing* ostentatious extras while neglecting to satisfy much more elemental needs; second, the capitalist system of distribution, which gives enormous rewards to those who own property, and very considerably less to labour. Socialists like Strachey claimed that planned production was the way out of the first problem and public ownership the answer to the second. You agreed that socialists must always insist that income differences be kept to a minimum and that the pattern of production reflect the consumption preferences of individuals taken as equals. I know you did not rule out public ownership as a remedy, but you obviously do not think that it is still the only, or even the best, answer to as general a problem as this. How then does your planning within the market structure, with a good deal of private ownership retained, handle this type of problem?

ECONOMIST: I cannot give you anything like a complete answer, but perhaps I can indicate the *direction* the answers would take. Let's deal with the allocation problem first, the way in which the shape of the productive process is determined. We are agreed that at present it is far from perfect. There are at least four reasons for this. The first is the differences in wealth and incomes. This means that the demand of the well-off is expressed effectively; it is a dollars and cents demand which promises profit to those who satisfy it, while the demand of lower income groups has comparatively little effect on the market because it does not have the same backing.

The second is the existence of the persuaders and the peculiar way in which they are concentrated. We have it dinned into our ears that we need soap and more soap, in every conceivable form, every time we turn on the radio, watch television, or glance around at billboards or bus advertisements. No one, as Galbraith has pointed out so clearly, implores us to buy art and more art; no one makes us feel guilty and unsuccessful if we have not a well-equipped concert hall to go to; and the public transit authorities have not tried very hard to make riding in *their* vehicles a status symbol or (Lord help us!) a means of releasing frustrated sexual urges. Modern advertising *induces* demand for an odd collection of goods and services — all of which are privately produced for individual consumption — and leaves us in ignorance, or at least fails to remind us, of our collective needs which can only be met by public, non-profit-seeking action.

The third reason is, of course, that variety of ailments which can be summed up by the seemingly innocent phrase "the imperfections of the market." This can refer to restricted production at high prices due to monopoly; to insufficiently rapid adjustments to changes in tastes or technology; to inadequate foresight; to the concentration of investment funds in the hands of corporation officials who may be interested in maximizing their institutional power and security rather than profits; and to a host of other things too.

And the fourth reason is mistaken governmental policy, or governmental policy which gives privileges to certain groups at the expense of others.

CITIZEN: So far so good. Now how would you propose that socialists cope with these sources of distortion if you reject wholesale public ownership of the means of production and planning with no reference to profit?

ECONOMIST: Let us take the problem of unequal wealth and incomes, both as a goal in itself and as a factor affecting the pattern of production. The traditional socialist said: eliminate property income by nationalization. If this means expropriation without compensation, then it serves the end of equality. If it means compensation — which is only equitable unless socialization of *all* capital is intended — then it does not. For the compensation either by itself produces an income comparable to that produced by the assets it replaces or, if it is cash, can be readily converted to some other income-producing property. To produce, with any degree of fairness, the wealth and income equalization which is desired, other steps must be taken. I am simply suggesting that these steps be taken immediately. They could include: a more steeply progressive tax structure; a capital levy; a considerable increase in the redistribution of income by transfer payments. Moreover, unless a high growth rate in industrial capital was desired, property incomes could be prevented from growing at their present rate and even gradually reduced by investment in social capital and by fostering a high consumption economy rather than a high investment pattern.

CITIZEN: The second reason for a distorted economy which you cited — the engineering of tastes by advertising — is perhaps a matter for direct legislative action rather than something which comes under the heading of planning in the usual sense. But before we move to the next factor in your list, I would like to ask you about something which occurred to me while you were talking. I do not think it can be called a market imperfection, rather it is a market inadequacy. I am thinking of certain preferences which the market cannot reflect because they are uneconomic, such as the desire because of social reasons to have secondary industries rather than primary ones; or the need to have railways run east and west instead of north and south.

ECONOMIST: Perhaps we can take this point and the other two I mentioned together. For these problems — market imperfections, uneconomic reasons for certain types of economic decisions, and altering previous government policies — all demand action which brings us to the very heart of economic planning. In part these problems can be met by legislative action which puts controls on market activity rather than replacing it. Rosenbluth's chapter suggests a number of ways in which perhaps the chief market imperfection — the concentration of capital in huge monopolistic structures — can be dealt with: vigorous anti-combines action against existing firms; a strict policy limiting mergers; public ownership of certain industries. But such measures are insufficient for the whole task which we have outlined. As you mentioned earlier, the goal of creating a perfect market system is superhuman, and even if it were possible, it would not solve the problems of economic activity which is desirable for non-economic reasons. Conscious and direct investment planning simply cannot be dispensed with if the socialist goal of an economy which satisfies the needs of people seen as equals is to be reached.

CITIZEN: A planning authority of some kind would still be an important part of the governmental structure of any socialist regime then?

ECONOMIST: Certainly; although, if you have Canada in mind, you should say planning authorities, for the provinces must be involved as much as the federal government. But notice that their responsibilities would not be quite as sweeping as those which John Strachey, for example, imagined a planning authority would have to undertake. They would be primarily concerned with (a) control of investment and the exploitation of resources and (b) regulating the rate of economic growth. Goals like stabilization and equalization would only very indirectly be within their terms of reference.

CITIZEN: What about the methods of the planning authorities?

ECONOMIST: This, I think, is the vital question. I see them functioning in two ways: first, as an overseer of private investment decisions with a veto power; secondly, as recommending public investment programmes which would fill the gaps left by private investors, either because the desired programme was uneconomic or because of rigidities in an imperfectly competitive private system of supplying funds and initiative for certain kinds of production.

CITIZEN: If private investors proposed to build new industrial plant at the expense of necessary hospitals, the planners might then forbid some projects?

ECONOMIST: Yes. Because they are not replacing the market, they will not be able to order private firms to undertake projects, but they will be able to forbid them from using resources which are needed more for other purposes. One likely use of the veto might be in preventing American investors from developing Canadian iron ore deposits solely as a source of supply for US steel mills.

CITIZEN: What about the positive recommendations of the planning authorities now? Do you see Crown corporations fulfilling these plans?

ECONOMIST: They would probably be necessary above all in cases where socially desirable enterprises were likely to be unprofitable. The whole field of social capital would, of course, then as now be exclusively public, and we have said that this must be enormously enlarged. But in addition there would be some public industrial and commercial enterprise. The Trans-Canada pipe line is a case in point. No socialist government would, because of a bias in favour of private enterprise, subsidize under such conditions rather than taking public action. But this is more because the creation of a monopoly was involved than because state action making private enterprise profitable is ruled out. In the case of housing, for instance, public action might well take the form of subsidy, or ensuring the availability of low interest mortgage funds, although the field of public housing would also be greatly expanded. It is in fact the likelihood of an expansion of public subsidy and loan policy being employed quite frequently that makes me favour strongly the nationalization of the banking system.

CITIZEN: That is interesting. I had thought that you might consider controls over banking sufficient. I remember, for example, that the CCF dropped public ownership of the banks from its programme several years ago.

ECONOMIST: My reason for advocating it is that the Canadian chartered banks are already to a great extent the agents for governmental monetary policy. Under socialist economic planning such as I have outlined they would be cast in this role even more often. Bank stockholders would thus be receiving profits for fulfilling public functions with no risk involved, and with no enterprise either.

But there is a limit to which banks as they are presently constituted, even if they were publicly owned, could fulfil the job of providing funds for desirable investments which might be profitable, but for which capital might be hard to come by. At present, a large proportion of investment is "planned" and directed by, first of all, corporations which simply re-invest accumulated profits, and secondly, by insurance companies, trust companies, and the like. Their control of investment funds is one of the chief sources of distortion in the capital market, because of their excessive conservatism, often legislatively imposed, and their desire to favour the inter-connected élite which controls existing industry, and enhance its power by diverting funds to it. To some extent, the planning authority's veto power over investment projects might ease the flow of funds to would-be investors outside the great corporations. Rather than having reserves lie idle, corporations which had been refused permission to carry out their own expansion schemes would loan their funds on the capital market. But two further steps probably would still be desirable: first, the nationalization of insurance companies; and secondly, the creation of a public agency as an alternative source of capital to compensate for the rigidities and bias of those institutions which at present finance new capital ventures.

CITIZEN: Wasn't the Industrial Development Bank intended to meet this last need?

ECONOMIST: Yes, but its functions were very limited indeed. A more ambitious project, similarly backed by public funds, could be created, but I am interested in the possibility of establishing a rather differently based institution. Have you read of the new phenomenon in North American business which has arisen over the past few years, the investors' mutual? Instead of buying stocks directly, private investors purchase shares of the mutual, which invests in a balanced range of securities and distributes its earnings in dividends to its subscribers. Besides providing certain advantages to the wealthy investor, who avoids the risks and headaches of handling his own investment portfolio, the mutuals seem to have attracted new money from the less affluent, who find this a safe and simple way of protecting their savings from erosion from inflation. I think that you can see that for many people a regular purchase plan of such shares would be a substitute both for annuity payments and bank savings. The mutuals have already become potent factors in the capital market, and show every sign of growing. My idea is to create a publicly sponsored and managed investors' mutual of just this sort, which could, in addition to its market purchases of shares in existing corporations, provide funds for new ventures which were deemed socially desirable by the planning authorities. I see no reason why such a public investors' mutual could not, over the years, have put at its disposal a considerable fraction of non-corporate savings. (What better place to put trade union strike funds, welfare funds, for example?) It could in certain cases purchase enough shares in a corporation to secure representation on the board of directors, and thus bring the public's voice into the firm's affairs. Just as important, it could inhibit behind-the-scenes decisions to seek private profit at the cost of public detriment. The English Labour party's scheme of "partial nationalization" was open to serious objections. Funds obtained by taxation, or from the public domain, were to be used for the purchase of stocks in private corporations. Since public responsibility for the use of monies so placed could not be assured, it was feared by many critics that the government would be compromised. These objections cannot be made against the scheme I have suggested, as all funds would be voluntarily subscribed. The plan also seems to me to have considerable advantages as a means of avoiding the constitutional dilemmas of action through the use of public funds. But this is something of a digression into particulars . . .

This discussion with a hypothetical economist could go on endlessly, but perhaps enough has been said for us to summarize, and try to answer the questions which provoked the conversation. We set out to get a picture of the methods which contemporary economists might propose for reaching socialist goals, and especially to estimate the sort of political problems that the carrying out of socialist policies would involve us in. Would an increase in bureaucracy be a necessary result of socialist policies in the 1960's?

The answer to this question is clear. The purely *economic* reasons for nationalization are much more restricted than they were deemed to be a generation ago. It would still be desirable to transfer to public ownership (federal, provincial and municipal) a sizable number of public utilities, the banks and the insurance companies;[3] new public enterprises would be formed without hesitation to fill gaps left by private industry; to handle politically sensitive situations where strict accountability to the public interest is essential (for example, munitions, atomic energy production, new space age industries and to strike out imaginatively in new fields of service to meet changing public needs). Furthermore, because of socialist concern for each person's chance to develop freely and creatively — the sort of concern described by John Porter — government would both encourage private attempts to replace the bureaucratic hierarchy with more humane organizational forms and,

[3]In his pamphlet, *Labour in the Affluent Society* (Fabian Tract 325, June, 1960), R. H. S. Crossman calls (p. 23) on the Labour party to "make it unambiguously clear that, if we are given a mandate, we shall overcome this crisis by deliberately reversing the balance of the economy and ensuring that the public sector dominates over the private sector." Mr. Crossman would probably not agree, but it seems quite likely that the nationalization of the banks and insurance companies would, in fact, mean the predominance of the public sector of the economy over the private sector.

with a real sense of urgency, sponsor on its own a wide range of similar voluntary experiments. Public industrial enterprise for the sake of social experimentation should, therefore, be a central feature of a socialist political programme; and this would require the purchase of existing plant, or the creation of new. These projects, of course, would have to be the very reverse of social manipulation from above. Rather, they would be designed to draw on the creative capacity of ordinary men and women, to use their experience and their imagination in working out new forms of co-operative activity in the field they know most intimately: their daily work activity.

The planning of a democratic socialist regime in Canada would be concerned to guide, redirect and massively supplement independent activities within the economy rather than to put them under the rigid control of a central body which reserved to itself all significant decisions. Planning authorities at the federal level would have to co-ordinate their schemes with those of similar planning bodies at the provincial and sometimes at the municipal level. This would undeniably produce friction and tension, and would demand the development of new skills in working a co-operative federalism.[4] But in such fields as hospital insurance, public assistance, police work and university education, forms of co-operative action have been worked out already with greater and greater refinement. Federalism is an asset in a country such as Canada as well as a necessity, and its virtues are particularly evident when the problem of avoiding excessive concentrations of power are under study.

In sum, therefore, it can be asserted quite confidently that, given the sort of socialist economics which have been outlined here, the bureaucratization of our society will not be increased and should gradually be considerably reduced.

But before we welcome the varied, pluralistic, socialist economic pattern which has been sketched, let us face squarely the charge that these new ways of shaping the economy are not preferred means of reaching socialist goals, but rather discouraged compromises with the seemingly invincible power of North American capitalism.

It would be redundant to go over again the reasoning of the economist in our dialogue, who suggested that a mixed arsenal of small and medium arms would answer the needs of social democracy better than the atomic blast of wholesale nationalization and over-all central control. It would also be an evasion of one of the critics' main arguments to remain at the level of economic relationships. For their challenge has another element in it. "Perhaps it is *logically* possible," they say, "to transform society by piecemeal adjustments, by pushes and prods, by

[4]For an interesting discussion of the co-ordination of planning see Gabriel Gagnon, "Pour une planification régionale et démocratique," *Cité Libre*, Aug.-Sept., 1960.

complementary and compensatory action; but practically this approach is useless. It ignores the fact that the entrenched power of privilege is so great that each reform will be countered or circumvented before it has had a chance to take effect. It may be true that the older socialist tradition ignored the dangers of centring economic power exclusively in the state, but this new socialism is even more ostrich-like in refusing to face the power facts of our *present* society and especially the immense power of resistance of an élite which hugs the status quo."

The answer to this argument is purely political and it is at this level that we must remain for the rest of this essay. The first step in rebuttal requires another look at the sources of strength of the power élite in Canada. In the summary view of Canadian society through socialist eyes sketched above, it was stressed that although the stronghold of this élite was the modern business corporation its influence was enormously reinforced by its predominance in the councils of both the old-line parties (and, for that matter, the Social Credit party) and thus, as long as these parties held power, by its predominance in government. Now if either a policy of extensive nationalization and a non-market economy *or* one of pluralist planning is to be applied, it must be assumed that a socialist party controls at least the federal government. Automatically, therefore, the political adjunct to the economic strength of the power élite has been partially removed. "Partially" may seem excessively cautious, but to say more is to beg an important question. For part of the critics' case is that a mere change in the parliamentary majority and the consequent accession of a new cabinet is not enough to alter the bias of government in favour of the capitalistic élite. Unless the party of the left in power strikes fast and hard at the very roots of corporate power, the argument runs, the effect of the change in government is going to be negligible. Why? Because the senior civil servants responsible for carrying out any less drastic policies will so deaden the impact of new legislation by their administrative decisions and will permit themselves to become so entangled in obstructive technicalities that the whole programme will be emasculated. The very variety and flexibility of pluralistic planning puts a premium on the dedication of civil servants to the new goals of economic policy. Even if they are not sluggish and reluctant in applying cabinet directives, will they provide that indispensable advice, based on intimate day-to-day experience with the working of new schemes, which will permit adjustments to be made and further advances to be projected? It is no secret that most government legislation has its origin in the recommendations of deputy ministers. Will they be willing, or even able, to feed to a socialist government the creative ideas which are necessary for it to achieve its ends?

There are two replies which can be made to these objections. The first is, of course, that changes can be made at the deputy-minister level and below, and men who have the aims of the party at heart brought in as replacements, but, because this would open the door to patronage politics, it should only be used in exceptional cases. Furthermore, new agencies, such as the planning commission can, with perfect propriety, be staffed by socialists. The problem, however, may not be nearly as serious as has been suggested. The Cassandras, one suspects, have the United States public service in mind rather than the federal civil service of Canada. In the United States, the turnover in administrative posts is extremely high, and a shuttling to-and-fro from business to government and back again is characteristic of almost all government departments. In Canada, the civil service is much more a career in itself, and within the service standards have developed which are intrinsic to it and not just, as in the United States, borrowed from a business community with which it is interlocked.[5] This is admittedly an oversimplified description of the situation in both countries: the US *does* have some elements of an independent career service; a few of Canada's senior government employees are linked with Canadian business. But it is equally an over-simplification to underestimate the capacity of Canadian administrators to give disinterested, competent and even imaginative service to a government of any political hue which behaved constitutionally. A senior deputy minister recently put this case very clearly. He said: "If I had no regard for the political facts of life when I make recommendations to my minister, I'd be completely worthless."[6] Admittedly he had in mind only the rather negligible differences between a Liberal and a Conservative minister, but the case is not completely invalidated if a more drastic change to a democratic socialist minister is assumed.

If a socialist government in Canada controls the federal administration, it has at its disposal the greatest single source of information and pool of talent in the country. It may be argued, indeed, that the right to choose the problems the civil service will work on, to set the subjects of its research and priorities in its use of time, is as important a cabinet power as the control of Parliament and the power to pass legislation. Recognition of this fact is vital if any sensible comparison of a socialist government's political power and the corporate élite's business power is to be made.

Yet another vital re-inforcement to the influence of the economic élite comes from its preponderant role in the media of communication, welfare organizations, the universities, and other centres where opinions are formed and to which prestige is attached. Because of their financial

[5]For a discussion of the social origins and the social contacts of Canadian government administrators, see John Porter, "Higher Public Servants and the Bureaucratic Elite in Canada," *Canadian Journal of Economics and Political Science*, XXIV, 4, Nov., 1958, pp. 483–501.

[6]Cited in Peter C. Newman, "The Twenty Men Who Really Run Canada," *Maclean's* (Toronto), June 4, 1960, p. 2.

contributions, wealthy individuals and corporations stake a claim to support from a whole host of institutions whose primary purposes are far removed from the world of buying and selling and producing. There is no logical reason why success as a banker should give one a greater title to sit on a university's board of regents than success as a trade union leader. There is only a reason based on wealth and social position. Limiting the things which private wealth can secure automatically limits the power of the wealthy. A socialist regime must, in its pursuit of equality, make such restrictions.

One immediate step which could be taken is the denial of tax benefits to corporations for their contributions to charity or to education. Another is Neil Compton's proposal to forbid the sponsorship of radio and TV programmes and confine advertisement to spot announcements. Further on the positive side, the extension of free education up to and throughout university, the expansion of public welfare programmes at all levels of government, the extension of activities of the Canada Council and the creation of provincial arts councils — all these are measures which lessen the social control which at present accompanies and reinforces economic position.

Many of these steps mean a transfer of influence from a certain fraction of society to government. And although this is undoubtedly preferable to non-accountable control, precautions must be taken against undue centralization of power. These safeguards can take a number of forms. The making of grants to private bodies rather than their replacement by public agencies was the formula used in federal aid to universities and it is capable of extension. The retention of provincial jurisdiction and the reinvigoration of municipalities are also vital elements in preserving a plurality of participation and control.

It seems clear, to return to the point at issue, that socialists who see no chance of real reform unless private economic power is reduced to almost nothing are distorting real power relationships as much as laissez-faire extremists who feel that any government intervention in the private economy sounds the death knell of personal initiative. A sensible view recognizes that the power of both government and the rulers of the private economy is great indeed. But the power élite are invincible only if they can maintain control of the apparatus of government as well as corporate institutions. Those who succeed in wresting government from their hands need not set about the destruction of their antagonist. Their task can safely be to clip their wings rather than to pluck them bare. Their role is fundamentally a positive one: to break through the limits of a narrow élite outlook and provide the imaginative leadership we need to give Canada the shape it could have in a world of automation, continuous scientific break-through and rapid social change; to organize the massive contributions we must make to the underdeveloped areas of the world; to fit our foreign policy both to our capacity and the new priorities of diplomacy in a nuclear age; to ensure the equal spread of the costs and benefits of change; and to receive and accept the stimulus of varied experience and new insights both from outside Canada and from the groups and individuals within our country who are now excluded from influence.

It should now be possible to go back to the questions which were set in the opening pages of this essay and see how complete an answer can be given to them. It was asked: what particular political problems would be faced by Canadian society altered according to social democratic principles; what institutions would be adaptable and along what lines; and what new institutions would be required.

In the sketch of present-day Canada which was made above, parliamentary institutions and federalism were singled out as the most deep-rooted of our political structures. F. R. Scott and Pierre Trudeau deal with the latter; the former require a few words here. They are already in real need of repair, and although the socialist economic programme which now seems necessary is likely to put less additional strain on them than that of a generation ago, the postponement of rehabilitation would invite a gradual breakdown. The greatest weaknesses centre in Parliament and the provincial legislatures themselves and especially in the down-grading of the individual member and the opposition relative to the government front benches. At present, the government has a crushing advantage. It has all the resources of the civil service behind it, and can be expertly briefed on short notice. In Ottawa and in every provincial capital, the opposition by contrast is desperately short of office space, stenographic help, research assistance and facilities — in fact all the modern apparatus which a firm's business representative would consider a matter of course. There is a strong case for increasing members' indemnities to enable them to fulfil their functions more competently, but a much more pressing one for establishing staff services which are available to all members, and especially to parliamentary standing and select committees.

The committees themselves have long been in need of reorganization and there are overwhelming arguments for assigning them a much larger role in the parliamentary process. In committees which had full access to the facts which give rise to legislation and a staff to assemble evidence, and which could examine much more carefully the operation of government departments and the delegated legislation which the executive constantly produces, the ordinary MP could regain his self-respect in the assurance that he is really involved both in deliberation and in the control of government. At present he acts all too often merely as an audience for his leaders' addresses and as the harried agent of interests in his constituency. The classical argument against strengthening the committees of parliament is that it would create rivals to the authority of the cabinet and obscure the clear lines of responsibility which at present exist. If Canada had weakly disciplined political parties and a multitude of them, as in France during the third and fourth republics, this viewpoint would be more impressive. In fact, we suffer from a very different ailment: overblown prestige for our prime minister and provincial premiers and their chief cabinet colleagues, and a tendency to executive arrogance which federal Conservatives found distasteful in their predecessors but easily assumed once they were in power themselves.

If the changes which a democratic socialist government would bring about are not to seem paternalistic, parliaments, which have traditionally linked the people with government, must be re-invigorated. Governments are kept on their toes, and responsive to public desires, by being subjected to a barrage of informed criticism. Secrecy is alien to both freedom and responsibility. MPs who, as individuals and as members of efficient committees, bring the citizen's grievances to light as well as urging the consideration of his particular problems, should have as important a role to play in the founding of social democracy as the most wonderfully expert planner. Bernard Crick, dealing with a similar situation in England, has summed up the case:

. . . while . . . the power of the executive has increased, is increasing and need not necessarily be diminished, yet the power of Parliament to offer informed and well-disseminated criticism has declined, is declining and should be increased. For there is no necessary contradiction between wanting a strong Executive and wanting a more effective and efficient House of Commons. The more power we trust a Government with to do things for us, the more need there is for it to operate amid a blaze of publicity and criticism. But there is such a contradiction at the moment because Parliament has not improved her own instruments of control, scrutiny and criticism to keep pace with improvements of efficiency and the increase in size in the departments of executive government. . . . M.P.s must be brought to remember that they are the only effective mechanism by which people's trust and distrust of government can be brought into equilibrium — and at the present time they are falling down on the job badly.[7]

It is undoubtedly true that in our society private power is wielded more irresponsibly than public; we are just not conditioned to resent the pollution of our air and water by factories and the debasement of our children's standards of truth and value by advertisers with the same bitterness we feel towards abuses by government. But whatever the source of the encroachment, individuals need protection from the arbitrariness of the powerful. Court action provides remedies in many cases but proceedings are expensive and protracted. Canada has shared

[7]*Reform of the Commons,* Fabian Tract 319 (London: The Fabian Society, Nov., 1959), p. 2.

in the reluctance of countries with a common law tradition to establish
a system of administrative courts which provides high standards of
justice, at the same time cheap and speedy, such as exists in many
European states. We lack too an adequate number and quality of "domestic tribunals," which ensure that rules of due process are observed
when penalties such as the loss of a dealer's franchise, refusal to supply
a cut-rate retailer, or expulsion from a professional or trade association
or a trade union, are imposed by private organizations.

A Bill of Rights defining personal freedoms still does not exist in
Canada in any real sense. The Diefenbaker Act can be superseded by
any subsequent legislation of the federal Parliament, and it does not
apply to provincial government actions. But even if rights were entrenched in the British North America Act and applied to encroachments from every level of government, a problem of enforcement would
remain. An integrated system of administrative courts might, as suggested, be one answer, but either as alternative or supplement another
device is available.

In Scandinavian countries, this problem is tackled in an ingenious
way, which deserves careful investigation in Canada. Sweden, Finland
and, most recently, Denmark have an official called an Ombudsman
whose only responsibility is to investigate citizens' grievances and, if
they are well-founded, to secure redress. He is appointed by parliament
and reports to a committee of parliament. His authority is great enough
to permit him to take to task the highest officials, including cabinet ministers in Sweden. Even if no complaint has been made to him, he still
can act: he makes unheralded visits to prisons and mental hospitals and
interviews those detained there in complete privacy. In most cases his
request that a wrong be righted is sufficient; the officials in question
have little desire to pit themselves against his great prestige. But if
necessary, he can himself initiate court action.

In a federal country like Canada, we would probably need not one,
but eleven such "citizen's defenders." The type of man who can fill
such posts is not easy to find. He must be of irreproachable integrity,
zealous yet discrete, thoroughly versed in both law and government.
But although these and other difficulties may be found, Donald Rowat's
conclusion stands: "If it is found that the Scandinavian Ombudsman
cannot be adopted directly, then we must develop our own form of
citizen's defender."[8]

If we are to plan democratically, new ways must be found to bring
Canadians who have hitherto had all too little influence into active

[8]"Citizen's defender" is the term suggested by Dr. Donald Rowat in his article
on an Ombudsman for Canada in the "For the sake of argument" column of
Maclean's (Toronto, Jan. 7, 1961). For further discussion of the Ombudsman
see the *Observer*, London, May 31 and June 7, 1959, and Brian Chapman, *The
Profession of Government* (London, 1959), ch. 12.

political participation. To some extent, this can be done by the political parties, and especially by the political party which stands for social democracy. It also demands the deliberate fostering of private groups which can, by balancing the power centres of the corporate élite, both reinforce state action designed for this purpose and reduce the extent to which it is necessary.

The internal structure of the CCF was well designed to bring citizens into political life with a sense of direct participation. In Saskatchewan especially it offered the reality of democracy to a wide range of people. But there is little doubt that it failed to attract to its ranks certain groups which, *a priori,* might have been expected to use it for political expression. Now that a new party is forming, deliberate steps should be taken to recruit from these sources. Three of them only can be singled out for mention here.

The first, organized labour, raises little difficulty, for the chief impetus to the formation of the new party was the merger of Canada's two largest trade union federations and the expressed desire of the new CLC to take direct political action. The worsening of an already chronic unemployment problem should do nothing to lessen their determination.

The second group must, for want of a better term, be called the "intellectuals" of Canada. While support for the CCF was never lacking in the Canadian university community, it tended to be tacit and inactive during the 1950's especially. In part, this may have been due to the conservative temper induced by the cold war, McCarthyism, the confusions and indecisions within British and European socialist parties and similar external forces. It may also have reflected the economic insecurity of academics who, in a period of inflation, found their salaries quite inadequate to maintain living standards comparable to those of the other professions. The desire to supplement university incomes with fees from government and business was wholly understandable, but it entailed certain costs. It directed time and research to problems set by the power élite rather than those chosen freely by academics themselves; it encouraged silence when outspoken opinion might jeopardize welcome additions to income. At the end of the 1950's, these conditions had changed. Not only had salaries increased appreciably, but there had been formed a national association of university teachers as a vehicle for further advances in security. There is thus a much greater likelihood that university people will be available for independent political action within the new party. The last period when Canadian university professors gave any considerable assistance to a left-wing movement was in the thirties. It took a special form, and one which seems peculiarly suited to the academic temperament. Intellectuals were grouped in the League for Social Reconstruction, which concentrated on research, discussion and publication, and kept in close liaison with the CCF. The Regina Manifesto, indeed, was drafted by Professor F. H. Underhill with the assistance of other members of the League. The new party would be wise, surely, to work for the formation of a new league and to establish similar links with it.

But only a fraction of the intelligentsia are found in the universities. Among scientists, teachers, the clergy, writers, the learned professions, there are reservoirs of ideas, skills, energy and social concern for which contemporary political life provides few outlets. A glance at the data on the backgrounds of our legislators, both federal and provincial, leaves one with the impression that only lawyers are fit for public functions. Obviously, the old parties of Canada have been unsatisfactory means for inspiring action outside a limited group. There are undoubtedly dozens of reasons for this political passivity, but one of them at least seems clear. The most valuable among these people who work with their minds are already involved in demanding, yet personally satisfying, pursuits. For them to be brought into political activity, a comparable challenge must be presented. The politics of adjustment — the brokerage function which reconciles interests within a basically unchanged framework — is unlikely to appeal. Yet the scientists especially are more and more realizing that they cannot pursue their specializations without so much as a glance at the society which is making use of their research. For reasons which need not be laboured, this moral unrest has been most noticeable among the nuclear physicists. As good a test as any of the vitality of Canada's new party will be its success in attracting scientists, artists and intellectuals to its ranks. C. Wright Mills' assessment of the role they can play is well worth quoting:

At just this point in human history, the role of intellectuals might well be crucial, for there is much evidence that political ideas could now become crucial. It is in terms of ideas — contained in ideologies and proclamations — that men seize upon the ends and the means supposed to be available within history and invite their pursuit and their use. A political idea is a definition of reality in terms of which decisions are formulated and acted upon by élites, accepted by masses, used in the reasoning of intellectuals. The structure of power and the role of élite decisions within it are now such as to open the way for ideas, and for their debate by publics. Ideologies and programs, arguments and critiques, handled by intellectuals, can make a difference in the shaping of our epoch and in the chances to avoid World War III. . . . The truth is that there has not been enough intellectual and political discussion since the thirties really to know how much effect it might have. . . . If we as intellectuals, scientists, ministers do not make available, in such organs of opinion as we command, criticisms and alternatives, clearly we have little right to complain about the decline of genuine debate and about the demise of publics themselves. Given our own continued default, we cannot know what effect upon either publics or élites such public work as we might well perform and refuse to perform might have. Nobody will ever know unless we try it.[9]

  [9]C. Wright Mills, *The Causes of World War III* (New York, 1958), pp. 136–7.

The third element which must be mentioned is hardly a "group"; it constitutes nearly one third of the Canadian population. All too few French Canadians ever did see the CCF as a place where they could be politically at home, although individuals made great contributions to the party. Not only does a party of the left seem a logical place for French-Canadian political action, given their almost complete exclusion from the top circles of the corporate world, but the party itself sorely needs them. This is true not only from the narrow standpoint of electoral success, but more important, because a socialist programme to which French Canadians denied support would be doomed to failure. The thesis which was advanced by certain Conservatives during the 1957 election that it is not necessary to win Quebec to gain power in Ottawa has no meaning for a democratic socialist party. A glance at the past suggests that at least twice, the electors of Canada *outside* the province of Quebec were on the verge of upsetting the monopoly of Liberals and Conservatives on control of the federal government. The first occasion came after the First World War, when a nation-wide farmers' movement formed the spearhead of an attack on the old parties' privileged position. United Farmers were organized in almost every province, and their success was surprising. Ontario led the way. In October, 1919, the United Farmers of Ontario elected forty-five members in the provincial legislature, and their leader, E. C. Drury, formed the government. In Manitoba, in June, 1920, a dozen farmers won seats and the Liberal government found itself in a shaky minority position. In Nova Scotia a month later the Liberal government was in only a slightly better position. In New Brunswick in October, 1920, the United Farmers of New Brunswick held the balance of power. Saskatchewan which had never faltered in its support of the Liberals since its creation in 1905, saw Progressive farmers elect twelve members in June, 1921, and force the provincial Liberals to repudiate their national party. And just a month later, the United Farmers of Alberta elected a solid majority and took over the province. Except in the two Western provinces of Saskatchewan and Alberta, the farmers owed much of their success to the fact that labour candidates were winning too. For in 1917, the TLC had once again temporarily given its blessing to political action, and organized labour began to register political gains. In Ontario, the Drury government was an alliance between labour and farmers, and, with eleven Labour representatives in the provincial legislature, the organized workers received two cabinet posts. In Manitoba, the Independent Labour party, riding on popular reaction to the suppression of the general strike, won eleven seats, only one less than the farmers. Five labour representatives had been strike leaders. In Nova Scotia and New Brunswick labour candidates shared the success of the United Farmers. Unfortunately, farmer-labour unity on the provincial level was only very shaky, and at the federal level, the farmers' political arm, the National Progressive party, made few overtures to labour. But even though it must be admitted that both labour and farmers' radical movements were split internally and had not worked out a solid programme of joint action, the chief reason for their failure to cause more than a temporary upset in Canadian politics must be sought elsewhere.

The 1919 provincial election results in Quebec, and the 1921 federal election returns between them tell the story of the defeat of the left at the end of the First World War. The Liberal party swept through Quebec in both cases. The radical ferment which stirred English Canada was lost in the nationalism of Quebec, the aftermath of the conscription crisis and the Ontario schools question. If one subtracts from the 1921 federal election figures the votes from Quebec, one can only conclude that Canadian politics would have been transformed, that they would have been re-shaped into a left-right division such as that which was forming in Britain and New Zealand at the same time. Without Quebec, the party totals would have stood: Progressive 65; Labour 3; Liberals 52; Conservatives 50. With its solid Quebec contingent, however, the Liberals were by far the largest single party and from this firm base, Mackenzie King could begin his successful campaign of luring the farmers back into the fold of the party which stood for bicultural nationalism and little else. The failure of English-Canadian radicalism to find in Quebec a French-Canadian counterpart with which it could co-operate doomed the post-war political movement of the left.

History repeated itself during and after the Second World War. The CCF was founded in 1932. The federal Parliament's "Ginger Group," composed of labour spokesmen led by J. S. Woodsworth and Progressives who had resisted the advances of the Liberals, had carried on the national radical tradition, and, especially in the western provinces, independent farm and labour movements continued on a provincial basis. The Great Depression provided the impetus for their forces to unite; and joined by eastern intellectuals from McGill and the University of Toronto, who grouped themselves in the League for Social Reconstruction, workers and farmers built a firm basis for united action in the CCF. By the end of the Second World War the time seemed ripe for success once more. The CCF had missed forming the government in Ontario by only a hair's breadth in August, 1943, and although the Conservatives had come back in 1945 CCF strength remained impressive. The CCF won Saskatchewan in 1944, and it became the official opposition in Manitoba and BC, forcing Liberals and Conservatives into coalition. Even in the Maritimes, it had some strength, and in 1945 hopes were high for the federal election.

The results of the election, however, show a pattern similar to that of 1921. Without Quebec, the Liberal party would have been sadly reduced, and the chances of a re-alignment of Canadian politics would have been enormous. But Liberals, in spite of some losses to Independent candidates and the Bloc Populaire, were the only national party which could claim the support of Quebec. The party of democratic radicalism in English Canada, the CCF, had polled few votes among French Canadians and won not a single seat. It is, of course, easy to oversimplify. The radical wave in Ontario had already largely subsided and, except for a Nova Scotia seat, the CCF strength was exclusively western. But it remains true, I think, that the fundamental weakness of the CCF was its exclusively English-Canadian character.

Quebec enters the 1960's as an urban and industrial province. It has already thrown aside the Union Nationale regime, a corrupt incubus which rode the province while clutching the past with both hands. The provincial Liberal party which replaced the Union Nationale appealed to the voters with a programme further to the left than the federal Liberals had dared to go, and there is no direct connection between party votes in Quebec elections and federal elections. Those who accepted the Liberal slogan in Quebec's election, "It's time for a change," may very well feel that changes in Ottawa require a party much more willing to take vigorous action than the federal party. Certainly in the near future, if not in the immediate future, the chances of a party of the democratic left striking roots in Quebec are better than they have ever been. An examination of the past suggests that once the base for a left-wing party has been laid in Quebec as well as in the rest of Canada, a time will come when it can quite readily oust one of the old parties from its position as alternative government. If the new party is to be an effective vehicle for social democracy in Canada, it must be bicultural and bilingual from the very outset. Equally important, it must show, as Pierre Trudeau has emphasized, that it sees federalism as an asset which must be preserved and augmented, rather than as an unavoidable liability. If the means to socialist goals which have been previously discussed are accepted by the new party, this should present no problem at all in principle, and in practice, no problems which imagination and goodwill cannot solve.

The political party itself cannot, however, fulfil the need for an invigoration and expansion of the base of public life sufficient to displace the power of the existing élite. The programme for social democracy itself must be an invitation to all Canadians to join in the pursuit of public happiness; to shift their eyes from the gaudy world which the advertisers paint as utopia and turn them to the real community of which they are a part; to see what Canada is and what it might be, with a vision directed by values which put persons before goods and human growth before accumulation. But the invitation is not only to see; it is also to participate actively in realizing this vision.

The clear location of ultimate responsibility for public policy in government, which is essential to the coherence of planning, need not be sacrificed while fostering public participation in collective enterprises. The way to prevent either the perpetuation of the hold of the present élite, or alternatively, its replacement by an official élite, is to open the way to full public contribution for as wide a range of groups, interests and individuals as possible.

There already exist associations which, in a small way, are attempting to modify élite decisions. Among them are the consumer groups who have fought a losing battle against trading stamps. Given present power relations, it is not surprising that their triumphs have been pathetically small: for example, eliminating red-stripe bacon packages and some progress towards standardization of clothing sizes. But with the co-operation of government departments and with budgets increased by matching grants (which are a useful way of ensuring that such groups do not simply become state agencies), much more could be expected of them.

A clue to another possible way of diffusing power comes from the practice of several countries regarding nationalized industries. For each of these industries there is established a consumers' council made up of independent individuals and representatives of groups affected by the industry's operations.[10] The feasibility of erecting similar councils for privately owned industries deserves careful study. They would report annually through the federal Minister of Trade and Commerce (or his provincial equivalent) to parliament, or perhaps directly to parliamentary committees. Operating with a small permanent staff, they could provide a continuous check on how the public interest was being served. Could not a council for the Canadian automotive industry, for example, make useful reports on built-in obsolescence, on the suitability of each model for Canadian road and climate conditions, and on the safety precautions built into both domestic and imported cars?[11] Equally appropriate reasons for surveillance of the drug and patent medicine industries, and a multitude of others, are not hard to find. Periodic Royal Commissions are a haphazard substitute.

The encouragement of co-operatives, experiments under public auspices in non-bureaucratic forms of economic enterprise, and even, in an indirect way, the proposed Crown-operated investors' mutual, all may be useful ways of serving the general ends which have been outlined.

[10]For a description and assessment of Britain's councils for publicly owned industry, see W. A. Robson, *Nationalized Industry and Public Ownership* (Toronto, 1960), ch. X.

[11]The American publication, *Consumer Report,* provides a small fraction of the information which might be made public through councils such as these, but there exists no satisfactory Canadian counterpart even for this limited, but valuable, service.

Moreover, a scheme for social democracy which does not stress techniques demanding centralization surely invites closer attention to existing provincial and local spheres of action. It would be surprising if a vigorous social democratic movement did not breathe new life in the institutions which already exist there.

In countries like China and Yugoslavia, social energies have been released for good or ill which no western state can match. It is ridiculous to suppose that force or propaganda manipulation alone explain what is taking place. These regimes have succeeded in breaking the shell of traditional apathy, in giving large numbers of men and women a feeling that they have a significant role to play in changing society. The brutal excesses of these governments, their lack of respect for the individual, and particularly of his right to dissent vocally and actively, need not blind us to the facts of renewed vitality.

Can we envisage a comparable dynamism in Canadian society? Few among us would want to buy it at the price which has been paid elsewhere, but there is no reason to believe that this price is necessary. What seems to have brought these countries alive is the dissolving of old, quasi-feudal power structures. In Canada, a different kind of élite dominates a power system which is corporate and bureaucratic. The politics of democratic socialism are designed to work profound changes in this pattern of control. They also promise new vigour for democracy.

Foreign Policy

KENNETH McNAUGHT

Perhaps the least well-defined area of socialist thought is that of foreign policy. In the British Labour party not even the question of nationalization divides the membership as deeply as do such problems as disarmament and the American alliance. The Fabians resolve these issues by publishing pamphlets expressing diametrically opposed points of view.[1] The election of 1959, moreover, cracked the thin plaster which had been hastily spread across the shattering split on nuclear arms. In the midst of the British debate, however, a comment by C. A. R. Crosland was particularly striking from a Canadian point of view, especially since it even greater validity if applied in the Canadian context. Crosland wrote: "Socialism now has more application to Britain's relations with other, poorer countries than to internal class relations within Britain. Viewed on a world scale, the British worker belongs to a privileged upper class and he should concede as well as demand greater equality."[2] Even if one takes into account the minimal nature of the

[1]For example, *Foreign Policy: The Labour Party's Dilemma*, Fabian Research Series, no. 121, 1947.

[2]*The Future of Socialism* (London, 1956), p. 12.

welfare state in Canada, and the vicious effects of seasonal and cyclical unemployment, there can be little doubt that the average Canadian worker is further up the social-economic scale than his British brother. If, therefore, Crosland's argument is correct in the British situation, it is even more applicable to the Canadian. The implications of the argument are very far-reaching indeed. If seriously pondered by Canadian socialists they must lead to a much closer integration of foreign and domestic policies.

I take it as axiomatic that a socialist foreign policy, either for Britain or for Canada, must be based upon the principle of equality. Equality in external, as in domestic affairs, must mean the provision of minimum standards of living and real equality of opportunity. Stated this way, international equality falls far short of absolute equality; but it presents a considerable challenge. It is a challenge which the political left of the Western democracies must define and meet if social democracy is not going to accept the fate depicted for it as long ago as 1942 by Franz Borkenau.[3]

Briefly, Borkenau argued that the nineteenth-century dogmas of socialism have been mocked by twentieth-century developments. As collectivism has increased, with its products of greater social security and higher living standards for the mass of the people, nationalism has tended to wax rather than wane in vigour. As more and more people apprehend that their income and welfare levels depend upon the treasuries and policies of national states, they are progressively inclined to acquiesce in or even push for protectionist and even expansionist policies developed by their national governments. This interpretation appears to be no less applicable to the American welfare state than to collectivized Russia. It might, of course, be argued that such *détentes* as NATO or the European Common Market invalidate this argument; that, in fact, Western protective nationalism is modified by the threat of armed communism. But NATO remains an old-fashioned military alliance with no sacrifice of national sovereignty and certainly no diminution in the protective attitudes of its national members. The anticipations of Article 2 have certainly not been realized. The attitudes of Britain and France, for example, have not become notably less protective or nationalist since 1949. The French vetoing of a Free Trade Area for western Europe was patently the result of her fear of British competition, while France's attitude to Algeria is far from internationalist. Britain's attitude to the Common Market, on the other hand, remains one of deep and dark suspicion, largely through fear of the remarkably revived productive capacity of West Germany. Indeed, the Common Market itself is, in not a few respects, simply an extension of western European nationalism. Many British commentators have feared that it "would be 'inward look-

[3]F. Borkenau, *Socialism, National or International?* (London, 1942).

ing', through excessive protectionism towards domestic agriculture and unwarrantable discrimination in favour of the raw materials and foodstuffs of members' overseas territories."[4]

It is interesting, of course, that much of the European social-democratic support for the Common Market stems from the guarantees of greater equality of welfare amongst the participating countries. To this extent, perhaps, the Borkenau thesis appears to be contradicted by the Common Market. But vis-a-vis the rest of the world the supranational government contemplated by the Rome Treaty would likely inherit a great deal from its protectionist founding governments. This threat, at the end of 1960, is so great as to compel in the United Kingdom a much more flexible attitude to the Rome Treaty. In the event of British accession to the Common Market the isolation of Canada within the North American market would be even more pronounced than at present.

Questions of this sort are far from irrelevant to a consideration of Canadian foreign policy. A Canadian social-democratic government, in its external relations, would have to concern itself with extending and underpinning international levels of social welfare just as much as with protecting national prosperity. Indeed, in the long run, the two considerations are inseparable. But such a government of Canada would have also to take account of the pattern of Canadian history. Since social-democracy is evolutionary by definition, a socialist foreign policy must be a growth based upon previous experience, if not necessarily upon previous purposes, as well as upon universally applicable socialist principles.

It is the purpose of this chapter to interpret the Canadian experience in external affairs in the light of socialist principles and to relate that experience to our position in the contemporary world.

The actual originating point of a Canadian foreign policy may be debatable. It is not debatable, however, that Canadians and their governments have entertained fairly definite ideas about the relationship of this part of North America to "outside powers." In one way or another, for example, we have decided on many occasions against a continental political union. Characteristically this tradition was begun, and begun vigorously, by New France. It was continued by Quebec under Murray and Carleton, and was reinforced in all of British North America by the Loyalist migration after 1783. The War of 1812, the border raiding of the 1830's and 1860's, the Manifest Destiny of the 1880's and 1890's all produced similar Canadian decisions against a political union with the United States. The clearest exposition of the Canadian attitude in the nineteenth century is to be found in the

[4]James C. Hunt, "Britain and the Common Market," *Political Quarterly,* vol. 30, no. 3, 1959, p. 297.

Confederation Debates of 1865. There the strongest argument against the opponents of federal union was that any other political programme would lead to annexation. It was an argument used equally by French and English supporters of the Quebec scheme. So deep-seated was the feeling, indeed, that the whole American political and constitutional experience was employed almost exclusively as a warning rather than as an example for Canadians.

It is true, of course, that there has always been opposition to this recurring majority decision; but it seems equally true that the dissenters have usually moved to the majority camp. Thus the signatories of the Annexation Manifesto of 1849 became either fathers or supporters of national confederation in 1864; and the Liberal quasi-annexationists of the lugubrious year 1891 soon followed Laurier into the extreme railway nationalism of 1903. Defection from this major policy has usually been the result of economic depression. But the disheartened merchants and farmers of one decade became the enthusiastic votaries of protection and the British connection in the next.[5]

In the history both of external relations and domestic developments we have been deeply affected by external influences—in particular by London, Washington and Rome. In each case of specific influence the external source has been applauded by some Canadian sections and classes and condemned by others. Canadians have divided frequently over the effect of British influence in matters ranging from the form of the constitution to fisheries protection, imperial organization and foreign policy commitments. And at nearly every point of our history the impact of American influence has produced varying reactions in Canada. We have feared the horrors of atheistic Jacksonian democracy, manifest destiny, railway inter-relationships and capital investment; we have tamely followed the American policy of non-recognition of the Chinese government. In the case of influence emanating from Rome the division of opinion has been even sharper: from the recurring schools questions to the Spanish Civil War and diplomatic representation at the Vatican. But much the most important fact to emerge from the chronic clashing of external influences is that Canadians have always succeeded, somehow, in resolving that conflict.

The methods of resolution have varied, but the essential goal has not. The goal is the achievement and maintenance of an independence in political, economic and cultural life. Competitive external influences, indeed, have not infrequently been used in the attempt to realize the goal. Markets in the United States were constantly sought in order to offset dependence upon the British market. Canada urged successfully

[5] A classic example of this experience is W. S. Fielding. In 1887, as premier of Nova Scotia he sponsored secession threats in the Nova Scotia legislature; by 1896, as federal minister of finance, he was helping Laurier take the Liberal party into the protectionist camp.

upon Britain the abandonment of the Anglo-Japanese alliance in 1921 because we insisted on having the United States associated in an Anglo-American Pacific policy. Conversely, when the United States and Britain appeared to be working in concert to Canada's detriment there were pronounced outbursts of Canadian nationalism. One example is the creation of the Canada First movement as part of Canada's reaction to the 1871 Treaty of Washington; another was the marked upsurge of national feeling following the Alaska boundary award—an award which was intimately related to the development of the twentieth-century Anglo-American *entente*.

But while the goal of independence, guaranteed by the balancing of external forces, is clearly one of the essentials of the Canadian experience, the purposes for which that independence was sought are open to debate. Throughout most of the nineteenth century the purposes were overwhelmingly domestic: the economic development of the country in the varying interests of merchants, manufacturers and farmers; the safeguarding of ocean fisheries; defence against American expansionism. By the turn of the century the purposes had become more complex. The South African War could not be avoided by Laurier in the same way that Macdonald had turned down the British request in 1885 for assistance in the Sudan. The Canadian debate which resulted from the Anglo-German naval race brought crisis and a compromise naval policy immediately preceding the First World War. That debate, and the war itself, while they were followed by the last-ditch stands of isolationism, introduced Canada to twentieth-century realities. It was more than symbolic that the Department of External Affairs was created in 1909.

Borden, Meighen and their supporters argued that Canada could not and should not remain aloof from world politics, and that the best way to use our growing independence was in close, voluntary association with the British Commonwealth. Mackenzie King and his Liberals after 1921 set this purpose completely aside. Insisting that the price of commitment to a common Commonwealth policy was too high,[6] they moved with increasing speed toward dissolution of the formal imperial ties.[7] The purposes behind this use of the right of independence were complex. Maintenance of "racial unity" inside Canada by isolating the country from serious participation in international affairs was undoubtedly the primary purpose. Canada's refusal to consider the League of Nations as either a desirable or a potentially effective instrument of collective security is another aspect of this purpose. But behind the unity doctrine lay many other considerations: the business man's desire for

[6]For King's attitude see the concluding chapters of R. M. Dawson, *W. L. Mackenzie King, A Political Biography* (Toronto, 1958), and J. W. Pickersgill, *The Mackenzie King Record* (Toronto, 1960).

[7]Beginning with the negative response to the Chanak crisis of 1922 the process has been unbroken, indeed, down to the present.

"normalcy" and profits undisturbed by the winds of European doctrines; the belief of many that Britain was still basically imperialist in the nineteenth-century sense; the left-wing view that a League dominated by Britain and France could only serve the interests of Neanderthal capitalism.

Looking back at the 1920's and 1930's it is difficult not to see considerable justice in some of these views. But the popular sense of isolationism which resulted was, in some of its aspects, merely irresponsible; irresponsible in assuming that Canada could dissociate herself from the results of British policy — or the policy of any other major state for that matter. King knew this also, but for domestic political reasons refused to discuss the matter frankly. Thus Canada, while exercising her technical independence, went to war at Britain's side in 1939 for the defence of policies in whose formation she had refused to participate.[8]

An equally important result of this use of independence (as well as of the shift in the world balance of power) was the manifest drift of Canada into the American orbit. Cordell Hull's reciprocal trade agreements overshadowed Bennett's ineffectual imperial preferences. American investment, both in the public and private sectors of the Canadian market, overhauled and then surpassed the British. Yet despite this fundamentally important shift in the balance of external influences two almost hidden facts remained even more important as determinants of policy. First, despite the public proclamations of independence and "no commitments," King realized the eventual political impossibility of that policy and Canada did not elect to follow a "North American" path in 1939; second, the fears of British dominance, paradoxically, continued to exercise so strong an influence on Canadian policy that the battle against imperial ties continued to be fought during and after the Second World War. It was a superfluous battle. It was also a battle which blinded Canadians to the rapidly changing nature of world power.

The battle (or perhaps one should call it the veiled process of decision-making) had two aspects. The first was traditional: no imperial war cabinet developed, no Commonwealth delegation to a peace conference was permitted, and Canada's entry into the United Nations was flamboyantly independent. The second was the encouragement of American influence upon and within Canada in total disregard of the fact that the United States already greatly outweighed Britain by any material measurement. This second aspect has frequently been described as the continuance of Canada's vital interest in balancing the North Atlantic triangle. It is difficult now, however, not to concede that it was

[8]I have discussed this more fully in "The Whig Interpretation and Canadian Foreign Policy," *Report of the Canadian Historical Association,* 1957.

in fact the maturation of an historical trend in Liberal thought. It has always been within the ranks of that party that one has found the closest approach to continentalism. Unrestricted reciprocity, commercial union, and continental defence agreements all bear the Liberal tag.

A closer examination of the years following 1939 is now necessary. But here it is worth summing up the argument to this point. Despite the tendency of various sections of the country to encourage or condemn external influences emanating from London, Washington and Rome, in the end a compromise has always been found between the directions in which these forces pushed. The compromises have been based upon a recovenanting between Canadian sections and classes to achieve and maintain an essential Canadian independence. Independence has been seen as guaranteeing sectional, economic, cultural and political advantages. In the twentieth century these internal purposes of independence have had to be enlarged for two reasons: first, the speed of technological advance in communications and military power, and, second, because the completion of independence (in this new context) implied decisions about peace and war and the nature of the international world. Finally, since the First World War, the process of removing all vestiges of any effective Commonwealth connection gathered such momentum that it could not, politically, be stopped. Indeed, the momentum varied inversely to the decline of real British power and was about equal to the growth rate of American power.

What of the past twenty years? Throughout there is an unbroken dominant theme. It is the total commitment to American leadership and influence. It is a theme only mildly modified by variations played on the engaging melody of a "balanced North Atlantic triangle." The lyrics inform us that the balance, for Canada, is achieved by our NATO and Commonwealth connections. While the variations sometimes catch electoral support, the basic theme has been unrevised, even by Tories. It is best analysed by Professor Frank Underhill who, with his enviable precision, declared in 1957: "In 1940 we passed from the British century of our history to the American century. We became dependent upon the United States for our security. We have, therefore, no choice but to follow American leadership."[9] It is of no little importance to perceive that this *has* been the unspoken assumption of Canadian policy since 1940. It is equally important to observe that, just as King in the 1930's resolutely steeled himself against revealing that Canada was committed to the support of British policy, so St. Laurent, Pearson, Smith and Green have refused to concede that Canada has become far

[9]"Canada and the North Atlantic Triangle," *Centennial Review*, vol. 1, no. 4, 1957.

more subservient to American tutoring than she ever was to British (since our commitment is, for the first time in our history, supported in advance by military pacts and establishments).

It is worth recalling the landmarks of the past twenty years in order to be perfectly clear about the extent of the revolution in Canada's international position. Beginning with the Ogdensburg Agreement for the establishment of a Permanent Joint Board on Defence in August of 1940, and moving with increasing wartime pace through the establishment of the Materials Co-ordinating Committee and the Joint Economic Committees to the Hyde Park Declaration, the base was laid for that extremely close integration of the economic and military life of North America which characterized the rest of the war period. Symptomatic of the nature of the rapid continental assimilation was the problem of Newfoundland. It may be, as Mr. Brooke Claxton said at the time,[10] that the destroyers-for-bases deal was "the greatest act of co-operation among the English-speaking peoples since the War of Independence." However, in the negotiation of the deal, Canada was excluded as a principal and has not been able, since the admission of Newfoundland to Confederation in 1949, to obtain withdrawal of American ownership of the Newfoundland bases. The specific guarantee in the 1947 Canadian-American defence agreements[11] excluding United States bases in Canada was thus ignored when Newfoundland joined Canada. The 1947 agreements provided the starting point for the immense radar-air defence system in the north. They also made official the policy of encouraging standardization of arms, equipment and organization which has led to a much increased Canadian dependence upon American patents and production, especially in the field of aircraft and missiles.

The logic of this course of development culminated in the retroactively debated and documented North American Air Defence Command—a process which shed light on the methods of foreign policy formulation and the cabinet's total lack of respect for the House of Commons. At regular stages in the emergence of this new pattern Canadians were informed that what was happening was not really happening at all. Mr. King announced that the northern programme envisaged in 1947 was not military but civilian and that the armed forces of the two countries would merely make contributions to it. Spokesmen for the Diefenbaker government maintained stoutly that NORAD did not place the RCAF on this continent under American command because a Canadian officer was named deputy commander.

Of equal importance to the growth of continental integration was the attitude of Canada toward the United Nations and the Commonwealth.

[10]Canada, *House of Commons Debates*, 1940, p. 6.
[11]Canada, Treaty Series, 1947, no. 43. See also the excellent discussion of this problem in R. A. Spencer, *Canada in World Affairs, 1946–1949* (Toronto, 1959), p. 306 ff.

In 1947 Mr. St. Laurent left no doubt that Canada was satisfied with the nature of the Commonwealth as it was, namely, a loose association of independent nations who had agreed to eschew any machinery for making prior commitments or agreements on high policy.[12] Thus, despite our relatively inexpensive participation in the Colombo Plan, the substantial recovery credits to the United Kingdom, and a series of conferences on specific subjects the negative aspects of Commonwealth relations remained of overriding importance. These included the elimination of appeals to the Privy Council, the acquiring of power to amend the BNA Act (in some respects) without reference to Westminster, the alteration of the Royal Style and Titles and the amending of the Letters Patent of the Governor General. Most Canadians have no difficulty in approving these steps in themselves; they appear as part of the logic of Canadian history. It is remarkable, however, that they were not justified in terms of increased efficiency but purely on symbolic grounds. The whole tenor of these moves to "complete our independence" was grotesquely negative. Furthermore, the significance of this continued status-seeking was accentuated by developments in other areas.

During the war, and despite the absence of a Commonwealth war cabinet, common policy was worked out satisfactorily from day to day by virtually continuous consultation. When the United States entered the war a new influence was brought to bear upon policy, and the effect was considerably to reduce the weight of Canadian views. This culminated in the almost total exclusion of Canada from the formulation of the minor peace treaties and from the negotiations for a German peace treaty. Despite Mr. St. Laurent's assertion that "Canada was proud to share the fortunes of war with her Allies" and that "she expects with them also to share the task of making a just and lasting peace," Canada was permitted no direct representations to the Council of Foreign Ministers or at the Moscow or London Conferences.[13] It was in the midst of this unhappy experience that Canada was moving erratically, and with markedly less vigour than Australia, to establish an independence which would be entirely unrelated to her Commonwealth connections. Lethargy seemed entirely to replace the vigour with which the war effort had been conducted. Coincident with the freeing of India and the stirring implications of a multi-racial Commonwealth the Canadian imagination broke down utterly.

After the United Nations founding conference both Mr. King and Mr. St. Laurent seemed proud of the acceptance of Article 106 of the Charter. This was an article which modified Article 43 nearly out of

[12]*The Foundations of Canadian Policy in World Affairs* (Toronto, 1947).
[13]Canada, *House of Commons Debates*, 1947, p. 7. It is true that Canada's early withdrawal of occupation troops was used as an argument against her direct participation in treaty-making, but it is equally evident that this was merely a great power device to maintain control.

existence and thus rendered more distant the time for establishing a permanent system of UN military or police intervention in disputes. Yet the Liberals continued to avow the hope that the UN would provide a new agency through which Canada could balance external forces and gain influence. Canada, said Senator Wishart Robertson in 1944, would appear "virtually as the leader of the smaller countries among the United Nations."[14] Mr. Brooke Claxton went further, stating that Canada would now be "in the shadow of no other land."[15] As Mackenzie King and Mr. St. Laurent worked out this new approach (heavily assisted by the permanent officials of the Department of External Affairs) it was given the sophistication of two new terms: "middle power status" and "functionalism." Mr. King defined the "functional idea of international organization" as one implying that initiative and influence must be strictly proportional to military power. He further suggested that "middle powers" such as Canada should have more influence than small states but should not expect to equal the influence of the great powers. This was an approach to world politics made novel only by the coining of new phrases; indeed, even some of the phrasing had been used before in a very different context. As Mr. Howard Green pointed out, "functionalism" was the "old hobby-horse that the Prime Minister trots out whenever he is faced with the problem of whether we are to work together as a Commonwealth or whether Great Britain is to carry the responsibility."[16]

Despite Canada's participation in all the agencies of the UN, in actual policy matters she was extremely reluctant to lead. Middle power functionalism remained a synonym for acceptance of big power, and increasingly American, decisions. Faced with big power refusal to give up the veto power the Canadian government remained skeptical of the UN's efficacy in security matters. Indeed, Mr. King, before, during and after the San Francisco Conference exuded no conviction at all, emphasized over and over again that we would make no military commitments, and in fact exploded the concepts of middle power functionalism. As Mr. Bruce Hutchison has remarked, King wrote off the UN "as a failure" within a week of the opening of the Conference.[17] This is the attitude that has been called realistic and it was inherited by Mr. St. Laurent who said in 1947: "There is little point in a country of our stature recommending international action, if those who must carry the major burden of whatever action is taken are not in sympathy . . . "[18] In this respect, also, there was a failure of imagination. The problem of

[14]Quoted in F. H. Soward, *Canada in World Affairs* (Toronto, 1950), p. 124.
[15]"The Place of Canada in Post-War Organization," *Canadian Journal of Economics and Political Science*, vol. X, no. 4, Nov., 1944, p. 421.
[16]Canada, *House of Commons Debates*, 1944, p. 5922.
[17]*The Incredible Canadian* (Toronto, 1952), p. 403.
[18]*The Foundations of Canadian Policy in World Affairs* (Toronto, 1947), p. 33.

"security" was seen exclusively in terms of military power and a short suit in military power was, *ipso facto*, justification for non-leadership. Rather, it could be used to excuse a nascent policy of putting all our eggs into the huge military basket to be fabricated by Uncle Sam. Responsibility had been put aside by Canada in the League of Nations in synonymous language and, then also, the fact was denied. Certainly pessimism was plausible in both cases and, in the UN, Canada did work for a modification of the veto power and a compromise solution in Palestine. But the most significant point is that her leaders never believed that UN could mean any real increase either in influence or security for Canada. Nor, apparently, did the majority of Canadian people.

The importance of this can scarcely be exaggerated. It affects basically our interpretation of more recent Canadian policy: the acceptance of a system of regional military alliances and the consequent promotion of a North Atlantic treaty. Since our role in NATO is the master key to the present situation it must be examined more closely.

The received version of the NATO background may be readily traced in every book which deals with Canadian policy since 1947.[19] Beginning with the exposure of the Soviet espionage ring in Canada, this version suggests, Canada became increasingly disillusioned with the United Nations. The growing rift between East and West, the crisis of the Berlin blockade, the frequent use of the veto to inhibit the Security Council—all these developments in 1946 and 1947 are said to have convinced Canada that she must bolster her security and independence by resort to a regional military alliance. As Professor Spencer puts it in his admirable review of the period:

When the history of the twentieth century is written from the vantage point of the twenty-first, Canada's signature of the North Atlantic Treaty on April 4, 1949, may come to be regarded as a more significant event than her entry into the United Nations four years earlier. Never before had she taken a leading part in working out so binding and formal a document. Yet the fundamental continuity of Canada's external relations was preserved.[20]

Here the emphasis is placed upon a return to the main theme of Canadian foreign policy. The context is an argument for the case that Canada had seriously accepted the UN and only after the developments

[19]R. A. Spencer, *Canada in World Affairs, 1946–1949* (Toronto, 1959); James Eayrs, *Canada in World Affairs, 1955–57* (Toronto, 1960); G. deT. Glazebrook, *A History of Canadian External Relations* (Toronto, 1950); F. H. Soward and Edgar McInnis, *Canada and the United Nations* (New York, 1956); W. E. C. Harrison, *Canada in World Affairs, 1949–1950* (Toronto, 1957); Edgar McInnis, *NATO and the Cold War* (Toronto, 1959); *Canada and the United Nations, 1948, and 1949* (Department of External Affairs). The virtual unanimity of interpretation extends to all the publications of the Department, to articles in the various journals of current affairs and, perforce, to such "foreign" observers as Nicholas Mansergh and Gwendolyn Carter.
[20]*Canada in World Affairs, 1946–1949* (Toronto, 1959), p. 243.

of 1946 and 1947 did she lose faith. The evidence suggests, however, that this is only one of two possible versions. On the part of the Canadian government the expectation of UN failure is fully evident. Canada's primary concern in the UN was with debating procedures, middle power status and non-security agencies. Her serious contributions in these years were made outside the UN: the considerable system of credits advanced for United Kingdom recovery, and the North American defence agreements. In retrospect Mr. Kennan's 1947 proclamation of a policy of containment and Senator Vandenberg's 1948 resolution on the necessity of regional alliances seem to have been received by Canada with an audible sigh of relief. During the second half of 1947 and the early months of 1948 Parliament, press and platform echoed with scarcely disguised intimations of Canada's desire to join a strong military alliance. In the tension of those months we were continuously assaulted by declarations about the fundamentally antagonistic forms of society and with growing boldness it was suggested that a system of alliances could be constructed without technically flouting the terms of the Charter.[21] The happy acquiescence of Canada in the soft-pedalling of attempts to circumvent the "frozen futility" of the Security Council left no room for surprise when the Canadian government took a prominent part in extending the regional pact system implied by the Brussels Treaty.

In all the intensive build-up to the NATO alliance Canadians were subjected to a one-sided view of developments. And this is the more remarkable since the international picture was sufficiently unnerving without a positive attempt to eliminate the shading. The case then (and it is, at the time of writing, still unqualified by those who are committed to the NATO thesis)[22] was that Russia was obstructing the recovery of western Europe by refusing to participate in the Marshall Plan, that she was intriguing in Greece and Turkey and that she was openly incorporating eastern Europe in her system. The case was dramatically highlighted by the tragic events in Czechoslovakia in February, 1948. It was at this point that the movement for an Atlantic alliance went into high gear. Nearly all of the flood of Canadian speeches on the necessity of a military alliance referred to the irreconcilable opposition of Russian communism and western democracy. They carried the implicit or explicit assumption that any hope of UN-based security must be abandoned. In this way it was hoped that Canadian unity might be preserved while the revolutionary policy was being implemented. As Professor Soward later remarked, "A Soviet Russia, the centre and inspiration of atheistic communism is poles apart from an Italy, the

[21]E.g., speech of Mr. Escott Reid in *Statements and Speeches*, Department of External Affairs, no. 47/12, 1947.
[22]Paul-Henri Spaak, *Why NATO?* Penguin Books, 1959.

home of the Vatican."[23] The other chief aspect of the NATO background in Canada was the openly stated premise of the government (a direct consequence of the abandonment of the Commonwealth and of any hope for the UN) that Canada would make no major policy commitment except in response to an American move.

The point which I am endeavouring to establish is this: that while there were many plausible reasons in 1948–49 for arguing the necessity of military assurances supplemental to the UN system the fervour with which the alliance was launched carried with it a legacy of old-fashioned militarism with which we have been saddled ever since. The alacrity with which the breakdown in the Security Council was exploited, a world-wide American alliance system constructed and the potential internationalism of 1945 jettisoned, has never been held suspect by the orthodox. It is only in the 1960's, when the inevitable fruits of such a monolithic approach have proven bitter, that criticism mounts.

In the origination of NATO, while the advocacy was designed as public education it was constructed with an almost total disregard for historical perspective. Not one speech invited Canadians to consider any part of the explanation of the cold war other than the plausible thesis of insatiable communist imperialism. No one referred to the background of Russia's relations with the "free world" throughout the 1920's and 1930's; to the reception accorded Litvinov's disarmament proposals in the League of Nations; to the diplomatic failure in the summer of 1939 and the consequent Russo-German non-aggression pact; to the mutual suspicions about a second front within the wartime alliance. No one adverted to the increasingly evident intention of the United States (with the supine consent of Ernest Bevin) to subsidize a monopoly capitalist revival in western Europe under demo-Christian placemen; few people (and their number included no Canadian spokesman) made it clear that the frustration of the Security Council by the retention of the veto was not the result alone of Russian insistence and that the veto power was equally dear to the British and American governments. Even fewer proponents of regional pacts suggested that since Russia could not then hope to control a majority in the Assembly or the Council, as did the United States, she had more reason to be jealous of her veto power. But above all, no one referred to the major fact that the ultimate military weapon was at that time possessed by the United States alone.

If the proper approach to the formulation of foreign policy is one of cool and objective appraisal (as we are endlessly advised by everyone from Sir Harold Nicolson to Mr. Pearson) it is entirely remarkable that the debate preceding NATO distorted the history of international relations in the war and inter-war periods, the direction of contemporary American policy and the inevitable Russian sense of insecurity engen-

[23]*Twenty-five Years of Canadian Foreign Policy* (Toronto, 1953), p. 24.

dered by America's unilateral possession of atomic power. It is true that western Europe and even America felt a deep sense of insecurity, but instead of an objective appraisal we got only alarming accounts of the imbalance of conventional armed strength, of Soviet threats of subversion of the French and Italian governments—and, in the wake, of course, the flowering of Senator McCarthy. So impassioned and ubiquitous was the appeal to fear that even yet one hesitates to canvas anything but orthodoxy. Even official Canadian trade unionism is reluctant to oppose the military alliance security myth.

It may be argued that it is all very well, after the crisis is past, to discourse upon the other side of the case; that in fact the real danger was so great that we only saved Europe and ourselves from subordination to Russia by building the NATO "shield." While we may agree, however, that a genuine dilemma existed at the time of NATO's birth we should also be quite clear that a crucial commitment was being made to an increasingly military assessment of the situation—and that this emphasis remained while the justification for it became steadily less credible. What actually happened after 1948?

Building upon the Truman Doctrine,[24] Secretary of State Marshall secured passage of the Economic Co-operation Bill and in April, 1948, $5.3 billion was voted by Congress for the first twelve months of Marshall Plan aid. During the next three years about $12 billion was spent on the economic rehabilitation of western Europe. Few people now question that it was this outstanding piece of statesmanship which was responsible for preventing the further growth of communist strength in the recipient countries. As for the prevention of external communist aggression there is, perhaps, less than universal agreement. The official position, nevertheless is undoubted: NATO provided an advance defence of Europe whose strength deterred Russian resort to force. But is this position valid?

The actual military strength of NATO in Europe never did approach either the original goals or those revised after the Lisbon Conference of 1952.[25] It is equally true that the Canadian ground and air contributions

[24]Between the Congressional appropriation in May, 1947, and 1950, the United States poured $659 million into Greece and Turkey—which sufficiently strengthened the two governments to resist effectively internal communist pressures.

[25]Apart from newspapers (and an article in *Fortune* by C. J. V. Murphy: "A New Strategy for NATO," Jan., 1953) the main sources for the following discussion of NATO strategy (although not the conclusions) are: Department of External Affairs: *Reports, Monthly Bulletins,* and *Reference Papers*; Department of State *Bulletins*; the *NATO Letters*; and the following books: A. C. Turner, *Bulwark of the West* (Toronto, 1953); B. T. Moore, *NATO and the Future of Europe* (New York, 1952); Royal Institute of International Affairs, *Atlantic Alliance: NATO's Role in the Free World* (1952), and *Defence in the Cold War* (1950); Lord Ismay, *NATO: The First Five Years* (Paris, 1955); Klaus Knorr, ed., *NATO and American Security* (Princeton, 1959) (It is interesting that this detailed examination does not once mention Canada.); P. Noel-Baker, *The Arms Race* (London, 1958); C. V. Crabb, *American Foreign Policy in the Nuclear Age* (Evanston, 1960).

have possessed nothing but obsolete or obsolescent equipment. One can only assume from this that the Canadian government never expected those forces to be faced with actual assault—unless, which is most unlikely, it was prepared to face a second Hong Kong. It was because of this situation that the theory of the "shield" underwent so many changes. With scarcely cushioned jolts the theory has shifted from one based upon a major conventional force in Europe sufficient to inflict severe losses upon an aggressor, to the idea of a cheaper "trigger" force capable of setting off massive retaliation, to the current position of a force itself equipped with (American-controlled) nuclear arms. The mixture of theories, indeed, seems never to have been quite straightened away, as is indicated in the review of NATO history by the Secretary-General:

For ten years the 'shield' forces, together with the strategic nuclear arms which form the 'deterrent,' have ensured peace for the West. There is too great a disparity, it is true, between our forces and those of the adversary, and a considerable effort will still be needed to bring our defences up to the required level. Nevertheless, the balance has to a certain extent been corrected. Because it depends primarily on nuclear arms, it has been called the balance of terror.[26]

It now seems abundantly clear that actual military defence never did depend upon the various national contributions to SHAPE's command but, rather, upon the retaliatory power of the United States. It is the widespread realization of this that has led to the growing disaffection of the junior NATO members, and the most recent speculation about increases in the conventional arms component.

The unreality of official arguments for NATO early compelled the Canadian proponents of the alliance to stress an entirely different line of reasoning. It is true, they conceded, that the only force capable of effective retaliation in the event of armed assault was possessed by the United States. But political psychology, they argued, dictated that we should contribute token forces as earnest of our good faith in support of the NATO concept, as evidence of our final commitment to this form of collective security. Even the West German defence ministry began to use this argument about Canada's "token" forces, although, voiced in this quarter, it gave no little offence to some Canadian militia clubs. This argument might be called the "hostage theory" and it never was particularly convincing since no one with an ounce of political realism ever believed that the United States would base a decision to use massive retaliation on whether or not there were a few exposed Canadians in West Germany. To believe this would require a total disregard of the structure of the power balance in the post-war world. It is, of course, possible to pursue the more sophisticated rationalization of the argument, *viz.*, that the peoples of the NATO nations (as distinct from

[26]Spaak, *Why NATO?* p. 21.

their governments) believed that the NATO shield was real and that to secure continuing Congressional commitment to the defence of western Europe it was necessary to keep the American electorate, in particular, from disillusionment. If one follows that argument, one must arrive at one of two conclusions: that it simply is not valid, or, if it is valid the continuing hoax was inexcusable.

In any event, as the refinement and expansion of nuclear power continued, and as Russia acquired similar power (their first atomic bomb was exploded late in 1949) the shield was studded with nuclear weapons and a new phase of ambiguity was entered. On American insistence, and over substantial doubts voiced by France and Belgium, it was decided to admit West Germany to NATO and allow her to rearm (the preliminary decision was arrived at in September, 1950, by the NATO Council).

The negotiation of the Paris Pacts, by which West Germany was restored to grace, revealed momentarily some of the less attractive features of the alliance structure. In Canada, the debate in the House of Commons produced the first serious questioning of the implications.[27] Characteristically, leadership of the opposition fell to Mr. Stanley Knowles. The External Affairs Secretary opened the debate by emphasizing that we must "consolidate our deterrent strength and by removing the greatest temptation of all to aggression which, in the present circumstances, is weakness, strengthen the chances of peace." Mr. Knowles reviewed briefly the history of German militarism, particularly in the Second World War ("we will never forget those six million Jews who were slaughtered during the Hitler regime . . . ") and concluded that a re-armed West Germany would be much more of a danger than an asset since it might well move for forceful reunification and because, its very rearmament, by deepening the gulf between East and West, increased the chances of war. Mr. Knowles was vigorously supported by Mr. Harold Winch and ten other CCF members while the other four, for whom Mr. Coldwell was spokesman, voted with Mr. Pearson.

If the Germans, as well as other reluctant NATO members, were to rearm themselves in earnest, they must be convinced that the United States could get major support to them quickly. But, as General Omar Bradley pointed out (also in September, 1950) to the Armed Services Committee of the House of Representatives, " . . . appraising the power of the atomic bomb, I am wondering whether we shall ever have another large-scale amphibious operation. Frankly, the atomic bomb, properly delivered, almost precludes such a possibility."[28] With the military cards finally on the table, the next step was predictable. It is no more surpris-

[27]Canada, *House of Commons Debates*, 1955, p. 261 ff.
[28]Quoted by Roger Hilsman, "NATO: The Developing Strategic Context" in Knorr, ed., *NATO and American Security*, p. 19.

ing that the step was first considered by Sir Winston Churchill's cabinet (late in 1951) than that the Eisenhower administration eagerly took up the idea early in 1953, urged particularly by Admiral Radford and Secretary of Defence Charles Wilson.

The fresh round of convincing the public was spectacular. Early in 1954 John Foster Dulles decided to reveal that the real defence of the West was, after all, the nuclear bomb and that by relying on "massive retaliation" the United States could cut down drastically the permanent large-scale goals of conventional armament.[29] But this heady gust of realism made nobody happy. While the Secretary of State intimated that he had been misinterpreted, the NATO military pressed hard for the extension of nuclear power to the diminishing forces of the shield. Late in 1954 the NATO Council rubber-stamped the British-American decision and NATO commanders were permitted to plan on the immediate use of nuclear weapons in the case of assault. In order to still a mounting public fear the device of recategorizing atomic weapons was employed. The category of "battlefield" or "conventional" atomic weapon was frequently mentioned and several field exercises with such weapons were carried out. At the same time high-ranking American generals declared that while a full-scale nuclear war would be catastrophic the West could still hope to win it. The British defence White Paper in 1957 was also based openly on this assumption.[30]

Perhaps it was the atomic war games that brought the dawn of realism. Exercises like *Sage Brush* (Louisiana, 1955) and *Carte Blanche* (West Germany, 1956) were prefaced by remarks like that of General Weylan: "These tactical weapons are just as selective as the older weapons. There is no reason to believe any more innocent people would be killed than in any other kind of war."[31] They were followed by comments like that of Mr. Hanson Baldwin: "A nuclear war in western Europe would almost certainly spread into a 'no-holds-barred' conflict, and western Europe, *in any case*, would emerge as a desert—a consummation not likely to win friends or influence people."[32] The now nearly unanimous view that a limited nuclear war is impossible brought NATO to its culminating dilemma. Its ground forces were based upon a power whose use would obliterate the area whose defence was presumably the purpose of the alliance. This dilemma became apparent (and is one of the chief reasons for the sharp increase of tension within NATO since 1958) at about the same time that Russia perfected and began to produce intercontinental ballistic missiles. Possession of nuclear weapons,

[29]"The Evolution of Foreign Policy," Department of State *Bulletin*, XXX, no. 761.

[30]This document (April 4, 1957) also announced sharp reductions in the British armed forces and the decision to rearm with atomic rockets.

[31]Quoted in Noel-Baker, *The Arms Race*, p. 144.

[32]*Ibid.*, p. 147.

together with a considerable choice in the means of delivering them anywhere in the world (long-range bombers, ICBMs, submarines) gave Russia a feeling of security which she had not experienced at any time since 1917. It has led also to the fear that Russian ability to devastate American cities makes less credible American willingness to respond massively to aggression in western Europe.

The conclusion from the preceding discussion is that Canada's traditional approach to the problem of national independence has been almost totally abandoned. We came, in fact, to accept the view that so much of our prosperity and security depended upon the United States that the question of balancing external pressures was of academic interest only. Inside the UN we have occasionally felt sufficiently daring to let it be known that we were not in entire agreement with American stands and even to vote, on lesser matters, outside the American ring. We demurred privately over General MacArthur's plans to cross the Yalu River, we declared that we were not committed to the defence of Quemoy and Matsu, and we voted for Poland over Turkey in 1959 as a candidate for a seat on the Security Council. But none of these actions in any way altered our position before the world as a country which has permitted itself to become an appendage of the United States—economically, militarily and politically. We refuse to vote for the admission of China to UN because the United States does not wish it. Yet China is clearly one of the chief threats to world peace and only through associating her closely with the international community can the threat be abated. United States policy in this respect surely represents the least admirable of American traditions, running back to the Pacific-an-American-lake thesis of McKinley and Theodore Roosevelt.

In NATO and under the NORAD agreement our present position strongly suggests that the history traced in the preceding section is leading inevitably to a further decrease in flexibility. With the smaller members of NATO beginning to complain publicly about the failure of the United States to consult its allies prior to basic policy decisions, Mr. Howard Green declared: "Perhaps we have been at fault. Perhaps we have done a little waffling in the Council ourselves. I think there has been an element in our approach which was against making definite statements. . . . We shall have to work out means of fuller consultation even though we don't always agree."[33] But while this was an intriguing interruption of the normal official silence it coincided with the announcement that Canada was about to join the nuclear club by stockpiling nuclear missiles, under American command, at North Bay and Mont Laurier (as well as by accepting the Lacrosse ground missile for

[33]Toronto *Globe and Mail*, November 5, 1959.

the army). Apart from the fact that the Bomarc's value has been denied by a large number of very competent people, the decision clearly implied the *de facto* establishment of United States bases in Canada and was, therefore, a step backward from the 1947 defence agreements (as was NORAD).[34] The results of our total commitment to United States policy have become clearer every month. Yet we have not fully understood this paradox: we achieved the goal of a treaty-defined North Atlantic relationship at the very time when the revolution in power relationships made it meaningless either as a mainstay of independence or as a security factor. This situation was clarified almost brutally by Professor Melvin Conant of the National War College in Washington when he wrote (*International Journal*, Summer, 1960): "Fifteen years of effort to meet the security requirements of the air age have concluded with the prospect that the Canadian role, from now on, will be marginal and certainly not consequential. . . . As a practical matter, it was understood fully in Ottawa and Washington [in preparing the NORAD agreement] that the control of the continental air defence systems had passed to the United States and the decisions for utilizing assigned forces, wherever located, would not be made in Canada."

Nor do we, apparently, intend to modify the situation by any alternative policy. While we have made contributions to the well-intentioned Colombo Plan these have remained peripheral to the fundamentals of our foreign policy. And despite the obvious potential of the Colombo Plan there is still no evidence that Canada pays more than lip-service to the idea of a countervailing Commonwealth influence at the UN or elsewhere. Up to 1958–59 Canada provided a total of $288.2 million worth of assistance under the Colombo Plan, including the loan of 126 experts on developmental projects. Compared to other items in seven years of Canadian budgets this is hardly a staggering sum. While many of the developmental projects have been of an impressive nature they have still to be set beside the pace of economic growth and community welfare in China. In the Colombo Plan official report for 1957[35] there are some guarded but revealing statements:

The rate of progress was, however, somewhat less than in previous years. Adverse weather conditions which caused a decline in food production, inflationary pressures, heavy imports necessitated by the high tempo of development activities and the slowing down of industrial activity in Europe and America which affected the export trade of the countries of the area, occasioned set-backs . . . India's economy continued to show evidence of considerable strain during the year ending 31 March, 1958. The pressure on India's internal resources, particularly on the balance of payments, which

[34]It is ironic to note that American bases in Africa and Europe are being reduced in number, partly because of fear of annihilation on the part of the allies there and partly because of increasing American reliance upon ICBMs.

[35]*The Seventh Year* (Colombo Plan Bureau, Colombo, 1959).

became evident in 1956–57, was more serious during the year . . . Foreign exchange reserves declined by Rs 2,600 million in spite of a further drawing of Rs 345 million from the International Monetary Fund . . .

It should be emphasized that Colombo Plan Aid, together with some Commonwealth scholarships, two or three vessels for inter-island communications in the West Indies and three million dollars for "African development" are the material measure of our interest in the Commonwealth. The steady Canadian drift away from a position of leadership in the Commonwealth has already been noted. The present position may best be illustrated by reference to the most serious of the post-war crises.

In October, 1956, after long consultation with the French government (and with prior knowledge that Canada would disapprove) the British government advised the Commonwealth High Commissioners in London that Britain and France had issued an ultimatum to Egypt and Israel. Mr. Lester Pearson, reviewing this situation in November, said: "There was no consultation with other members of the Commonwealth . . ." Later he emphasized that the Canadian government had "no advance information that this very important action, for better or for worse, was about to be taken." The importance of the Suez action was still further stressed by Mr. Pearson's declaration that it had nearly resulted in the dissolution of the Commonwealth. The sequel of this affair was the most brilliant success of recent Canadian diplomacy: the creation of the UN Emergency Force and the acceptance of this form of UN intervention by Britain and France. No one would wish to detract from that substantial *détente* (particularly since it could point the way to the future). But it is worth recalling the background.

The reason why Canada was not consulted is to be found not only in the fact that the Eden government was dominated by trigger-happy advocates of gun-boat diplomacy. It was, primarily, the result of forty years of Canadian insistence that prior consultation on Commonwealth foreign policy was unwelcome—because consultation implies responsibility. Why should the British government have consulted Canada when we had made it abundantly clear that we would remain within the Commonwealth only on the condition that any approach to an agreed foreign policy was taboo? One might be nasty about the failure of London to *advise* us of what was going to happen; but to criticize it for not *consulting* us is surely unhistorical. The fact is that having abandoned the substance of the Commonwealth we managed to save it in form by an eleventh hour stop-gap which should never have been necessary.

Before considering a socialist's answer to this complex international situation it is necessary to inject a final factor and thus further complicate the problem. This is, of course, the revolution in military force. Up to this point we have considered nuclear power only in its relation to specific NATO problems. Enough, even so, has been said to indicate that the balancing of that power between Russia and the United States (just as, previously, the unilateral American possession of the bomb) now renders NATO irrelevant. It is now necessary to note the more general relationship of nuclear power and foreign policy.

Despite a continuing official reluctance to admit the impossibility of contemplating strategic nuclear war as an extension of foreign policy the evidence is overwhelming that no major state would use it, in the first instance, either to achieve a goal or to deter attack.[36] It is reasonable to assume that if nuclear war were a conceivable policy such a war would have broken out during one or another of the major crises that have afflicted the world since 1945. It is equally reasonable to assume that the advent of direct conversations between Mr. Khrushchev and Mr. Eisenhower in 1959 was the result of at least temporary public recognition of this prime fact, and thus that those conversations constitute the most important development since 1945 (despite the uneven course of events since the U2 incident and the advent of the Kennedy administration). But while the great nuclear powers cannot base their policies on the assumption that they have nuclear weapons freely at their disposal (that is, they cannot contemplate consciously courting annihilation), they are nevertheless committed to such weapons since they have permitted them to become the basis of defence policy. The main dangers of war may thus be listed categorically: accident, insanity, or an incident in a sensitive area leading to retaliation with "tactical" nuclear weapons which would almost certainly lead to holocaust. It is superfluous to observe that the more widely nuclear arms are spread the greater becomes the danger. It is not superfluous to point out one specific conclusion directly affecting Canada. Because nuclear armament is now an almost meaningless (if exceedingly expensive) status symbol, since it cannot be used effectively in diplomacy or war, its very development has led to a corresponding increase in the value of other tools in the diplomatic chest. Paradoxically, economic influence, moral suasian in the world's councils and political experience have all become more potent instruments of policy as the nature of military power has become more terrifying.

Writing as recently as 1952 it was possible for a right-wing British socialist to observe that, "*Leviathan* is still a better handbook for foreign policy than *Fabian Essays*." An understanding of the power element in politics is the first necessity for a sound foreign policy.[37] It was this sort of starting point that led the right wing of the Labour party to its recent ill-fated refusal to declare decisively against reliance on nuclear weapons

---

[36]The best survey of this problem is Noel-Baker, *The Arms Race.*
[37]Denis Healey, "Power Politics and the Labour Party" in *New Fabian Essays* (London, 1952), p. 161.

—to the position in 1959, also described by Mr. Healey, where the disagreements between Left and Right "are probably due more to the difference between the inhibitions of office and the license of opposition than to genuine conflicts of judgment on the issues themselves."[38]

Canada is caught in a trap just as galling as that in which Britain finds herself. Neither country can be defended against nuclear attack yet each, in the hope of retaining influence and prestige if not security, spends huge sums in the arms race: Britain to maintain an "independent nuclear deterrent," and Canada to "defend" the United States and western Europe with radar and rocket. One cannot help but feel that if Thomas Hobbes were alive today he would opt for the older Fabian belief in seeing things as they are rather than the George III attitudes of our present governments. If the *nature* of military power has changed, and this is undeniable, what virtue is there in operating as if it had not? We must formulate a policy based upon reality, and with an eye more to the future than to the past.

Those conclusions which emerge most clearly from the preceding sections become at once the starting point of any new socialist policy: the defence of our national independence has been abandoned; we have based policy upon considerations that are wholly archaic—especially in the light of American predominance, nuclear power and the rise of Afro-Asia from imperialist control; and we have almost totally ignored the glaringly unequal welfare and opportunities of the world's peoples.

A socialist foreign policy must begin by reasserting the goal of national independence and defining the international purposes for which that independence is to be used. It must emphasize that in a world where the shattering of multilateralism by regional military alliances has intensified bipolarization Canada will deny forthrightly any unlimited attachment to one side in this potential death struggle. This denial must be made not because we cannot distinguish between communism and American democracy, but for a very concrete reason: because we value our historic claim to independence and see it as a creative force in a world given over to mass organization and international inequality. In order to work for an international order in which differences in welfare and opportunity will be steadily minimized, as well as one in which nuclear annihilation will be less likely, a Canadian socialist policy should be firm on several major points.

The essential starting point would be the decision to end Canadian contributions to NATO. By Article 13 of the Treaty we may not formally withdraw from the alliance before 1969; but by the Treaty's other terms, contributions are at all times left to the discretion of the member powers. NATO, as this is being written, is clearly passing through its greatest crisis of confidence. It may or may not disintegrate

[38]"Britain and NATO" in Knorr, ed., *NATO and American Security*, p. 234.

from causes with which Canada has little to do. It is also clear that whatever one may believe about the original necessity of its establishment it is now much worse than obsolete. NATO, as part of the system of military polarization of the world has contributed largely to the tensions of the cold war, particularly after the admission of West Germany. Its existence makes German reunification virtually impossible since in such circumstances the Russians rightly fear a new, militarized Germany linked to NATO. As an alliance which has proven over and over again its inability to become anything more than military it is today a major cause of the ever widening possession of nuclear weapons. In strictly military terms its strategic posture is such that it could never risk being attacked. By virtue of its exposed forward positions it is a standing temptation to our advocates of "pre-emptive attack." It is more than symbolic of our acceptance of "fate" since it involves us inevitably (if it is ever to be used militarily) in the results of decisions taken by a remote power élite upon which we can have no significant influence. Our membership is the proof that we are willing to share the responsibility of destroying civilization in a war which no one can win. Finally, as part of the American alliance system it represents our lack of confidence in the UN and our support of reaction in Europe and Asia. Can all this be the means of "security"?

To the argument that we should exact some specific *quid pro quo* in the case of a general willingness to disband NATO the only logical answer is that since military alliances no longer make sense we will unilaterally abandon them and continue to advocate that others do the same.

It seems unavoidable also that Canada should, without acrimony, take specific steps to restore her independence within North America. She should withdraw from NORAD, withdraw permission for the stationing of American troops for any purpose in Canada, and she should press for revision of the destroyers-for-bases deal and the consequent return of the American bases in Newfoundland to unencumbered Canadian ownership. Since there is general agreement amongst those military leaders who have expressed themselves (and since the known facts speak for themselves) that our huge expenditures in northern defence mean nothing in the light of the most recent missile developments, it is evident that the whole system (except where posts may be useful for civil purposes) should be dismantled.

Two aspects of such a restored independence need particular emphasis. First it would be for no negative purpose but rather an assertion of our disengagement from the spurious military power struggle. It would be non-alignment for the purpose of engaging in international activities with a non-military ethos. Second, such a policy, no matter how conciliatory the tone of its initiation, might provoke some form of American retaliation — most probably a politico-economic pressure involving a slower rate of economic growth in Canada. This possibility should be envisaged and the cost accepted in advance, just as the cost of the National Policy was accepted for basically political reasons.

Defenders of drift and continentalism will at once label such a policy anti-American and isolationist. It is neither. In general, of course, any socialist must be vaguely anti-American, in that the United States represents in the mid-twentieth century a way of life based avowedly on the profit motive and the nearly unlimited influence of privately controlled corporate wealth. That aspect of America cries aloud to be resisted. But there are also many Americans who deplore this aspect and who criticize their government's foreign policy in terms not too different from those which I have employed. Such Americans (if not our own Canadian continentalists) would be quick to welcome a Canadian lead in the direction of egalitarian internationalism and disarmament. Canadian-American relations have never been as simple as the present school of "let's-not-be-nasty-to-Uncle Sam" would have it.

With respect to the second point of isolationism it is perfectly apparent that no one in Canada can return to the "fire-proof house" of the late Senator Dandurand. It is simply a question of what is the most effective method by which we can pursue our traditional and valued independence and also use that independence for the most "unisolationist" purposes. At the end of 1960 there are good grounds to argue that the possibility of American withdrawal from Europe and reliance upon ICBMs, allied to increasingly restrictive trade regulations, threatens Canada with real isolation.

It follows from these premises that our military planning should be based upon a police concept exclusively. This would mean maintaining forces sufficient to police our coasts and to provide a mobile military contribution for any UN-sanctioned purpose — presumably a mixed force in the neighbourhood of 5,000 men.[39] That such a policy of disarmament is in any sense unrealistic is illogical. To argue that it is, one would have to ignore the history of the arms race, our present defencelessness and the diminution of our influence in proportion to the rise in our defence expenditures and our commitment.

The revolution in the nature of military power affects Canada in three precise ways. First, she cannot hope to build her own nuclear weapons system, and therefore, to continue as a committed party in the arms race is to concede unqualified dependence upon American decisions. Second she must face squarely the undeniable fact that no matter how much she spends she cannot procure even minimal defence. Third, to contemplate

---

[39]The problem of survival in a nuclear war is complex and essentially civil, but it would be considerably reduced by a policy of disarmament which would render direct attack purposeless.

even sharing responsibility for use of a force which can destroy civilization within the space of a few hours is immoral by any criterion, utilitarian or religious. How can we avoid the conclusion that this ultimate challenge compels us to treat seriously (and however reluctantly) the basic doctrine of Judao-Christian ethics: that war is no solvent of human relations.[40] The police concept is not perfect, but it has produced a considerable advance within national communities and unless we move rapidly toward it internationally we may well sacrifice even that limited achievement. Canada is not without honour already in the tentative development of the police role internationally; let us advance with determination.

Of very great advantage in refashioning Canadian foreign policy would be a fresh approach to our historic relationship with the Commonwealth of Nations — for both national and international purposes. It follows from the previous discussion in this chapter that we should shift our weight internationally if we hope to regain anything of that balance of external influences which, historically, we have found necessary. It is also clear that the revolution and stalemate in military power have put a premium on the kind of political experience and internationalism represented by the Commonwealth tradition. While it is frequently argued that the Commonwealth has become so loosely connected as to be worthless as an instrument of common policy, and that all previous attempts to create machinery for producing such policy have foundered on the rocks of colonial nationalism, it should also be remembered that the conditions within which the Commonwealth lives have been basically altered. It is no longer conceivable that a common policy should have as its goal an imperial *kriegsverein* based upon colonial tribute; it is no longer in doubt that equality of status and complete independence can be achieved by others than the charter white members and that the new multi-racial Commonwealth is a triumph of political education and experience; and it would not be possible today, in a foreign policy council of the Commonwealth, for London to exercise the predominant role which in the past was so greatly feared, provided that, say, Canada and India both decided to play an active role. The recent severance of South Africa from the Commonwealth strongly suggests the kind of influence that can result from taking decisive positions based upon incontrovertible principles. This was a beginning from which important further advances might well be made. When one considers the present and future importance of Afro-Asia and that the Commonwealth (outside of UN) is the only effective political connection between that area and the West it does not seem simply idealistic to work for its revival.

It is the custom nowadays to declare that the process of disintegra-

[40]One of the best "sermons" on this subject is in C. Wright Mills, *The Causes of World War Three* (New York, 1958).

tion has gone so far that it cannot be reversed. It is argued that the national interests of the Commonwealth members are often divergent and sometimes conflicting. Thus, one must leave well enough alone. Suez should have ended that argument, but it did not. Again, if one reviews the interests of France, West Germany, Portugal, Italy, Turkey and Greece it should be obvious that the Commonwealth could scarcely match NATO for potential and actual clashes between members. Yet we have committed far more to NATO than we ever did in peacetime to the Commonwealth.

Canadian socialists should be particularly conscious of two Commonwealth traditions: first, that Canada has pioneered in the constitutional evolution of the Commonwealth and, second, that in its two most critical periods (the 1840's and 1940's) the Commonwealth idea was both created and saved by the political Left — the Colonial Reformers and the Attlee socialists.[41] Must we, as Canadians on the Left, abandon these traditions in favour of a slick continental prosperity based on the ever more deceptive blandishments of the American brand of democracy and the fallacy of a "North Atlantic community"?

What is required is a revival of leadership and a precise decision to let politics exercise a determining influence upon economics. The possible positive steps are numerous. Canada should propose a regularization of the Commonwealth Prime Ministers' meetings and the establishment of a permanent secretariat. The meetings should be held by rotation in the various Commonwealth capitals (with Ottawa offered as headquarters for the secretariat) and a particular watch should be kept on the tendency to differentiation between the new and old members. A council of foreign ministers should be advocated with the particular purpose of obtaining agreement upon policies to be advanced in the UN. To make such minimum steps as these possible Canada should put certain cards on the table with a view to setting an example and convincing others of the sincerity with which the new policies are put forward: abandonment of military commitment to any regional alliance; revision of our immigration policy to permit the entry of any citizen of a Commonwealth country on the same terms as those available to people of the United Kingdom; ear-marking of at least one billion dollars for a combined programme of direct aid and technical assistance.

Announcement of three major decisions such as these could leave no one in doubt about the seriousness of a Canadian endeavour to provide leadership in the Commonwealth. The ultimate goals of real racial and economic equality and the determination to use national independence for genuinely internationalist purposes would be very clear. Given disarmament and a tax policy which did not ignore such items as capital

[41]In the recent decision on South Africa, there can be no doubt of the political quarter from which emanated the clearest call to act.

gains, the financing of such a programme would not only be feasible, it would provide one necessary area of continuing government spending. If the previous proposals in this policy were implemented Canada and India would find themselves the inheritors of the best social-democratic traditions of the Commonwealth and with identical policies of non-alignment with respect to the alliance structure. Such a development would almost certainly give a preponderance of weight to the advocates of a similar policy in Great Britain. A Commonwealth with this tri-partite leadership, while lacking power in the nineteenth century military sense, would be in an extremely strategic position. It would unques-tionably rally many smaller nations both in western Europe and in Afro-Asia and thus be in a position to exert very considerable pressure upon the Big Two.

Since the goal is egalitarian internationalism one obvious purpose of reviving the Commonwealth would be to obtain an agreed policy of strengthening the UN as a fundamental alternative to regional alliances.

To influence the United Kingdom, Australia and New Zealand to treat the UN as the primary international organization would mean some heavy spade-work if the present Conservative Government of the United Kingdom remains long in power. But are such problems more intractable than those we now face? Indeed, actually facing them would be a stimu-lating departure. To obtain a united Commonwealth vote in UN for the admission of the Chinese government would do more than any access of nuclear power to strengthen both the Commonwealth and the UN. So also would a Commonwealth vote to establish a permanent UN police force along one of the various lines that have been suggested. It is in this field that Canada so far has done her most effective work in UN and the legacy should be exploited. When such a force was proposed by the Secretary-General in 1949, and was promptly turned down, Mr. Lie commented: "Modest as it was, to carry it out would have re-quired a degree of attention and imagination on the part of the men in charge of the foreign policies of the principal member nations . . . but they were too preoccupied with the successive measures in the cold war . . . to give time and thought to what seemed to them to be a less imme-diate issue."[42] The issue is now more immediate than ever. Furthermore, the virtual impossibility of creating a UN force which could engage the nuclear power of any major state reinforces the concept of a para-military police force from which patrol and inspection groups (with, primarily, moral authority) could be sent into areas declared to be dangerous to the world's peace.

Intimately related to this UN goal, and of even more perilous urgency,

---

[42]Quoted in David Ennals, Fabian International Bureau, *Research Series 210*, September 1959. This brochure contains an excellent discussion of the various proposals for a UN police force.

is the advancement of disarmament negotiation. Here it seems clear that Canada has accepted the overblown American insistence on "inspection first" in the continuing disarmament discussions. It is also evident that the long elaboration of the technical difficulties of inspection has been used to mask the reluctance to take the *political* decision to end the arms race. The "sacrifices of sovereignty" implied by a sharp curtailment of military power and the omnipresence of UN inspectors involve politics far more than they involve technicalities. It is here that a third force pressure upon both major nuclear powers (and upon those who wish also to acquire the two-edged bomb) could have its greatest influence. What is needed is the mobilization of a consistent and strong demand within the UN that the most advanced offers made by Russia and the United States (during the ebb and flow of past disarmament talks) be at once seized upon and that a treaty based upon them be signed within the UN framework — a treaty which will provide for simultaneous and drastic disarmament in all fields, and inspection. While the history of the arms race is not such as to encourage ill-considered optimism about its early termination it *is* such as to dictate revolutionary action at this stage. This must be both unilateral, as suggested above, and multilateral in the sense of organized pressure for genuine negotiations. The recent past is, indeed, not without a glimmer of hope for the success of such pressure. If anything, it teaches that the more strictly the possession of nuclear weapons can be confined the greater will be the assurance of the major parties in negotiation. It also suggests that those who advocate the rapid re-building of conventional military power (in the face of nuclear stalemate) serve only to decrease the precarious growth of confidence in any form of negotiation. They exhibit that failure of nerve which is the greatest threat to our civilization.

The most striking facts ignored by the advocates of cautious debate and iron-clad guarantees in a disarmament treaty are that sixteen years of such debate have succeeded only in producing an arms race unequalled in history; the progressive administration of John F. Kennedy began its career by calling for a two billion dollar increase in the American arms budget; and that the only substantial progress towards arms limitation (the moratorium on nuclear weapons testing) was the result of unilateral action which compelled emulation.

To those who cry "visionary," one can only retort that words in this field are no substitute for action and that the nation, or group of nations which will give an unambiguous lead and evidence of good faith will be more realistic by far than the nation that sacrifices the hope of human welfare and equality to secure the most dangerous prestige yet known